D0942753

God's Kingdom
on Earth and in Heaven

GARY CANGELOSI

Copyright © Gary Cangelosi, 2014

Citizens Chapel Press, Inc.
Cornelius, North Carolina

All rights reserved. Printed in the United States of America. No part of this book may be reproduced, stored in a retrieval system, or transmitted, in any form or by any means, electronic, mechanical, photocopying, recording, or otherwise, without the prior written permission of the publisher.

Library of Congress Cataloging-in-Publication Data

Cangelosi, Gary S., 1953-
    God's Kingdom on Earth and in Heaven /
Gary S. Cangelosi
    p.   cm.

    ISBN 978-0-615-53842-6
    ISBN 0-615-53842-6
    1. Millennialism. I. Title
    Library of Congress Control Number: 2011916573

Unless otherwise indicated, all Scripture quotations are from The Holy Bible, English Standard Version™, copyright © 2001 by Crossway Bibles, a division of Good News Publishers. Used by permission. All rights reserved.

Scripture quotations marked NIV are taken from the HOLY BIBLE, NEW INTERNATIONAL VERSION®. Copyright © 1973, 1978, 1984 by International Bible Society. Used by permission of Zondervan Publishing House. All rights reserved.

The "NIV" and "New International Version" trademarks are registered in the United States Patent and Trademark Office by the International Bible Society. Use of either trademark requires the permission of the International Bible Society.

COVER DESIGN
    Creative Director: Gary Cangelosi
    Art Director: Terri Cangelosi
    Millennium illustration: Leonardo da Vinci as modified by John White
    New Heavens and New Earth illustration: Terri Cangelosi

For individual orders of this book: www.CitizensChapelPress.com.

With a little help from my friends,
and a lot of help from my wife, Terri.

Contents

Introduction

Italics in Scripture quotations indicate emphasis added by author.

Conservative evangelical Christians believe that Jesus of Nazareth is the Jewish Messiah, Christ, in fulfillment of Old Testament prophecies. And yet, surprisingly, we cannot agree on the nature of his messianic kingdom. Is it an earthly millennial kingdom, a heavenly kingdom, or both?

When Pilate asked Jesus if he was the King of the Jews, Jesus told him: "My kingdom is not of this world. If my kingdom were of this world, my servants would have been fighting, that I might not be delivered over to the Jews. But my kingdom is not from the world" (John 18:36). Does this mean his kingdom is only a heavenly kingdom that is not of this world and is ushered in when he comes again to take us to his Father's eternal kingdom of heaven, the new heavens and new earth? Does he ever rule over this current Genesis creation as King of kings and Lord of lords?

Based on Old Testament prophecies, the Jewish Messiah was expected by the Jews of the first century to be a descendant of David who would overthrow the tyrannical Roman authorities and become the king and geopolitical ruler of Israel, returning them to a glorious and abundant "Promised Land." His reign would be extended to the whole world, creating a global empire. But instead of establishing his kingdom on this earth, Jesus Christ was crucified by the Romans, was resurrected, and then he ascended to heaven. He left this world without establishing his messianic kingdom.

In the meantime, this evil world continues to operate in a fallen condition. His followers often are persecuted as he was. It is definitely not paradise on earth. Satan continues to be the "god" of this dominion of darkness and, except for the children of God, the "world is under the control of the evil one" (1 John 5:19 NIV). The world continues to be characterized by war, injustice, unrighteousness, and systemic poverty. If Christ were the King of this world, then it would be "under the control of the Holy One" and would be characterized by peace, justice, righteousness, and prosperity.

Where, then, is his earthly messianic kingdom? Can we have a Messiah without a messianic kingdom on earth? When he comes again, does he come back to this earth to finally establish his 1,000-year earthly kingdom, or does he come to destroy this Genesis creation and take us to his Father's heavenly kingdom in the new heavens and new earth, a kingdom not of this world?

The True God of This Genesis Creation

The disciples were expecting the Jewish Messiah to be an extraordinary human being and ruler in the line of David, but they were not expecting him to also be God incarnate. One of the most remarkable things revealed by the New Testament authors is that this Jesus from Nazareth was the eternal Son of God as the second person of the triune God. The first verse of the Bible states that this Genesis creation was created by God: "In the beginning, God created the heavens and the earth" (Gen. 1:1). God merely says the word and speaks this Genesis creation into existence—*ex nihilo*. And in the same chapter, we are first introduced to the triune God: "Then God said, 'Let *us* make man in our image, after *our* likeness'" (Gen. 1:26).

In the first chapter of the gospel of John, the apostle refers to this Genesis account of creation and informs us that the Son of God, who had come into the world through the incarnation, was the very person of the Trinity for whom this Genesis creation was made:

> In the beginning [of the Genesis creation] was the Word, and the Word was with God, and the Word was God. He was in the beginning with God. All things were made through him . . . He was in the world, and the world was made through him . . . And the Word became flesh and dwelt among us . . . No one has ever seen God; the only God, who is at the Father's side, he has made him known. (John 1:1–18)

Paul repeats this remarkable truth about the Son of God: "For by him all things were created, in heaven and on earth, visible and invisible, whether thrones or dominions or rulers or authorities—all things were created through him and for him" (Col. 1:16). Jesus Christ was none other than God incarnate, the eternal Son of God through whom this creation was made. As such, the whole world, not just the nation of Israel, rightfully belongs to him, for it was created by him, through him, and for him.

The Genesis creation was rightfully the Son's kingdom from the very beginning. But through the rebellion of Adam and Eve, Satan was allowed to enter this world, and he usurped Christ's lordship over this world. This powerful demonic intruder now operates as the false god of this world. Could it be that the Son of God's messianic kingdom is a restoration of the Genesis creation to its rightful Lord and King when Satan is completely removed from this world? The earth would once again become God's kingdom on earth with Christ as the true God of this world. It was Christ's world to begin with.

God the Father plays a key role in our being rescued from Satan's dominion and becoming members of the Son's kingdom. Paul informs the Colossians of this fact: "Giving thanks to the Father, who has qualified you to share in the inheritance of the saints in light. He has delivered us from the domain of darkness and transferred us to the kingdom of his beloved Son, in whom we have redemption, the forgiveness of sins" (Col. 1:12–14). And one day, God the Father will restore this Genesis creation to his Son: "For David himself says in the Book of Psalms, 'The Lord [the Father] said to my Lord [the Son], Sit at my right hand, until I make your enemies your footstool'" (Luke 20:42–43).

It seems that the Father told the Son to have a seat at his right hand until he determines it is time for this rebellious world to be taken from Satan and restored to his Son and the members of his kingdom such that the "world would be under the control of the Holy One." Therefore, if there is a 1,000-year messianic kingdom of the Son of God before the Father's heavenly kingdom, we would expect it to extend out from Israel to the entire world, for the whole Genesis creation was made by him and for him.

This is actually what the prophets envisioned: "'As for me, I have set my King on Zion, my holy hill [the kingdom starts in Israel].' I will tell of the decree: The LORD [the Father] said to me, 'You are my Son; today I have begotten you. Ask of me, and I will make *the nations* your heritage, and *the ends of the earth your possession*'" (Ps. 2:6–8). Christ may be destined to be King of Zion, but he is also the Son of God through whom this Genesis creation was made, and, therefore, his Father will give him all the nations to "the ends of the earth." Christ has a divine right to rule this world.

As Mighty God and Prince of Peace, the Messiah, born of a virgin in the town of Bethlehem in Judea, was supposed to rule the world, "the government shall be upon his shoulder," establishing God's kingdom on this earth characterized by peace, justice, righteousness, and prosperity (Isa. 9:6–7). After Jesus Christ was crucified and resurrected, however, he ascended to heaven. As my son likes to say, "He split, leaving us in this rotten world."

But he did not abandon us; in his place he sent the Holy Spirit, who is continuously recruiting repentant sinners into the kingdom. In the meantime, Jesus asks us to be the salt of this world to prevent it from decaying further. Christianity has brought about a great deal of justice and civility, but the world is still under Satan's dark and dangerous regime. Where is the regime change that Jesus and the prophets promised? Where is his messianic kingdom, in which he rules this world as King of kings and Lord of lords?

To further complicate matters, we learn from Jesus and the apostles that Christ comes again on Judgment Day and destroys this Genesis earth, and born again members of his kingdom are then going to be raptured and taken to the new heavens and new earth. In the following verses, Peter links the second coming *and* the resurrection of our immortal bodies, like Christ's resurrected body, to the last day of this Genesis creation and the beginning of our inheritance of the imperishable new heavens and new earth—not to the temporal millennial kingdom on earth:

> [God] has caused us to be born again to a living hope through the resurrection of Jesus Christ from the dead [hope of an immortal body like Christ's], to an inheritance that is imperishable, undefiled, and unfading, kept in heaven for you [destiny of the resurrected saints]. (1 Peter 1:3–4)

> But the day of the Lord [the second coming] will come like a thief, and then the heavens will pass away with a roar, and the heavenly bodies will be burned up and dissolved, and the earth and the works that are done on it will be exposed. . . . But according to his promise [of an immortal body in an eternal kingdom] we are waiting for new heavens and a new earth in which righteousness dwells. (2 Peter 3:10–13)

How then can the raptured saints inherit the earth in the Son's 1,000-year messianic kingdom if the earth is destroyed at his second coming? This makes it exceedingly difficult to understand how the Old Testament prophecies that describe an earthly messianic kingdom and paradise can be fulfilled. How can people marry, have children, build houses, plant vineyards, enjoy the works of their hands, and live long and prosperous lives in an Edenic paradise if the earth no longer exists and the children of God are raptured to a heavenly kingdom where there is no marriage?

Yet the Old Testament and the New Testament—though sparingly—clearly prophesy a Messiah who will usher in an earthly paradise for the whole world before this Genesis creation is destroyed. The Jewish disciples, as students of the Old Testament messianic prophecies, had good reason to believe this, and Jesus never corrected them in this belief. Jesus promised the disciples an earthly messianic kingdom in which they would sit on thrones judging the twelve tribes of Israel (Matt. 19:28). Right before he ascended into heaven, Jesus affirmed there would be a restoration of the kingdom to Israel (Acts 1:7).

In an apparent contradiction, the Bible affirms both—the earthly restoration for one thousand years, as well as the second coming on the last day when the earth is destroyed. From a simple reading of the Scriptures, we can discern that both of these truths are biblical "givens." This presents a tremendous challenge for theologians to develop a coherent eschatology—the study of end times—based on a logical interpretation of the biblical data. How do the saints inherit God's kingdom on earth for a thousand years and then inherit God's kingdom of heaven when Christ comes again on the last day?

Three Proposed Solutions

Theologians over the centuries have come up with three basic solutions to understanding the kingdom of God on earth and in heaven. And each view centers on how and if we inherit the Son's 1,000-year messianic kingdom before we inherit the Father's kingdom of heaven or the new heavens and new earth.

In one camp are amillennialists, who believe there is no literal millennial restoration on this Genesis earth before the eternal kingdom. The world remains under Satan's dominion and could become even more evil before the second coming and the end of the world. Christ comes again on the last day, which includes the rapture of the saints, the renovation (or destruction) of the current heavens and earth, Judgment Day, and then the beginning of the new heavens and new earth. The millennium is just a metaphor of the church today, the departed saints in heaven, or the eternal kingdom itself. The meek only inherit the kingdom of heaven when Christ comes again.

Most important, if amillennialists are correct, then the Son of God as the Messiah never gets to rule over a restored Genesis creation before it is destroyed, even though this creation was made by him, through him, and for him. Satan will have succeeded in robbing this world from its rightful God. Man, as male and female, becoming one flesh, reproducing, and filling the earth, never experiences the joy of this creation as it was originally intended when it was a "good" creation. God's will is never implemented on this Genesis earth as it is in heaven. We only inherit the Father's kingdom to come when Christ comes again to take us to his Father's house.

But Christ has a divine right to rule this world because as the Son of God, this Genesis creation was created for him. And the Son of God, as the Messiah, has yet to create a kingdom on this earth whereby, as King of kings and Lord of lords, he establishes a reign over this earth characterized by peace, justice, righteousness, and prosperity. As a result, there must be a restoration of the Edenic creation to its creator before the eternal kingdom of heaven is ushered in. The Messiah must establish a messianic kingdom.

Postmillennialists agree with amillennialists that Christ comes again on the last day to rapture the saints, destroy this earth, and take us to the Father's kingdom of heaven, but they also believe that before Christ comes again, the world will be Christianized through effective evangelism to usher in a golden era on this earth. They believe that Satan has already been bound and that Christ remains in heaven where he already reigns over this earth as King of kings. But they do not hold to a literal millennium where "the wolf and the lamb shall graze together" and all wars are ended (Isa. 65).

Postmillennialism may offer a marginally better vision of the Son's messianic kingdom on this earth before the kingdom of heaven, but under this view the Old Testament prophecies are never fulfilled. The Genesis creation is never restored to an Edenic paradise. And Satan is certainly not bound, for the world remains his dominion of darkness with habitual evil prevalent in all aspects of man's affairs. Wars are not decreasing but are becoming more lethal as modern technology advances our methods of killing and destruction. Christ continues to be persecuted and suffer, for when we suffer, he suffers, too, because we are his body on earth.

Most important, without some type of resurrection before the millennial kingdom, none of the departed "meek" saints, including the disciples, get to experience the restored Genesis creation before they are raptured and inherit the eternal kingdom of heaven. Only that generation fortunate enough to still be alive when this "golden age" of Christian nations arrives gets to experience Christ's earthly kingdom. The departed saints are out of luck.

Premillennialists believe that there is a restoration of this Genesis creation for a thousand years before we are taken to the Father's kingdom of heaven. They believe that, because Christ did not establish his earthly messianic kingdom at his first coming, Christ must come back to this earth a second time at the beginning of the millennium with the raptured saints to finish this task. Thus, he would finally fulfill all the Old Testament messianic prophecies by establishing the restoration for one thousand years before the children of God inherit the new heavens and new earth.

But, as amillennialists point out, this solution creates a new set of problems, for the New Testament clearly places the second coming of Christ on the last day in conjunction with a resurrection of the immortal body that is taken to heaven—not to the millennial earth: "But our *citizenship is in heaven*, and from it we await a Savior, the Lord Jesus Christ [the second coming], who will *transform our lowly body* to be like his glorious body [the rapture], by the power that enables him even to subject all things to himself" (Phil. 3:20–21). Like Peter, Paul links the second coming and the rapture of the saints directly to the saints inheriting their citizenship in heaven—not their citizenship on this earth. The destiny of the raptured saints at Christ's second coming is our eternal inheritance of the kingdom of heaven—not the inheritance of the restored earth for a thousand years.

Sadly, biblical theologians remain divided on the definition of God's kingdom on earth and in heaven. Even among the early church fathers, the ante-Nicene fathers, there was a difference of opinion concerning a literal millennial reign of Christ on this earth before the kingdom of heaven. Justin (c. 100–165), one of the ante-Nicene fathers, states:

> I admitted to you formerly, that I and many others are of this opinion, and [believe] that such [the millennial reign of Christ] will take place, as you assuredly are aware; but, on the other hand, I signified to you that many who belong to the pure and pious faith, and are true Christians, *think otherwise.* . . . But I and others, who are right-minded Christians on all

points, are assured that there will be a resurrection of the dead, and a thousand years in Jerusalem, which will then be built, adorned, and enlarged, [as] the prophets Ezekiel and Isaiah and others declare.[1]

Justin claims that "right-minded Christians" of his day believed in a literal millennium, but he concedes that other "true Christians" believed otherwise.

Almost two thousand years later, Christians still cannot agree on the nature and existence of a future millennial kingdom of Christ before the heavenly kingdom. In a book appropriately titled *The Millennial Maze*, Stanley J. Grenz makes the following observation concerning sincere Christians, the gospel, and eschatology:

> In the midst of the current climate of uncertainty, however, Christians who have earnestly sought to remain true to the great doctrines of biblical and historic Christianity find themselves unable to articulate with one voice a message of hope for our world. Among the areas dividing the Christian ranks, few have been as explosive as those surrounding the doctrine of "last things," or eschatology. One central point of disagreement involves the meaning of the thousand-year reign of Christ found in the vision of Revelation 20 and hence the expectation of a future millennial kingdom.[2]

Although conservative evangelicals agree that Jesus of Nazareth is the Jewish Messiah, it is truly unfortunate that we have not been able to agree on the nature of his messianic kingdom on this earth before we inherit the Father's heavenly kingdom; nor have we been able to agree on what transpires at Christ's second coming. Yet, as evangelicals, who claim that Jesus of Nazareth is the Messiah, we should, by definition, be able to define the nature of his messianic kingdom. The doctrine of Christ's kingdom should be Christianity 101. Instead, the subject remains confusing, complex, and contentious. People are repenting, believing in the Messiah, having their sins forgiven, and entering into the kingdom of God, but we cannot explain to them what this kingdom represents. Is it an earthly messianic kingdom as envisioned by the Old Testament prophets, or is it a heavenly kingdom as envisioned by the New Testament apostles? Or is it both?

The debate has reached an impasse, with each side unable to convince the others of its respective position by interpreting the relevant biblical data. Kim Riddlebarger, in the book *A Case for Amillennialism*, makes an interesting observation about the prevailing views of eschatology:

---

[1] Justin, *Dialog with Trypho*, 80.2 (Note: Unless otherwise indicated, all quotes of early church fathers from A. Roberts, J. Donaldson, and A. C. Coxe, eds.,1997).

[2] Stanley J. Grenz, *The Millennial Maze: Sorting Out Evangelical Options* (Downers Grove: InterVarsity Press, 1992), 23.

Historically, Protestants have been committed to sola Scripture ("Scripture alone"). . . . In addition, Protestants throughout history have believed that the Scriptures cannot err, since they are God-breathed. If we assume these two points to be true, and if we acknowledge that the three major millennial views contradict one another, we must conclude that at least two of the millennial views and possibly all three are in error. While all of them may be wrong, not all of them can be right.[3]

The three major views do indeed contradict one another in many ways, but the Holy Spirit has been guiding these godly men through the Scriptures for centuries, so they cannot all be completely in error. Maybe we can extract what is correct in each view and come up with a synthesis that can advance the debate over the meaning of the kingdom of God.

For example, premillennialists make a strong biblical case when they assert that there must be a 1,000-year messianic kingdom on this earth when Christ rules his restored Genesis creation before we inherit the eternal new heavens and new earth (he is the Messiah, after all). And postmillennialists make a strong case that Christ is already on his throne in heaven at the right hand of God with all power and authority at his disposal, and he can easily rule this world from heaven when he and the Father decide to do so (he is God, after all). And amillennialists make a strong case that Christ comes again on the last day of this Genesis creation and sits on his Great White Throne to judge all mankind at the general resurrection. The saints will be raptured and inherit the eternal new heavens and new earth, and unbelievers will be raised from Hades and sent to the lake of fire.

Combining these assertions, one could conclude that there is a literal 1,000-year restoration when Christ removes and binds Satan and then rules this world (premillennialists), but he accomplishes this from his throne in heaven without having to return to this earth to establish his reign (postmillennialism). Therefore, his second coming is *after* the millennium on the last day when the raptured, immortal saints are taken to the Father's eternal kingdom of heaven (amillennialism). But if the raptured saints are destined for the eternal kingdom, how then do the saints inherit his messianic kingdom on this earth? In Revelation 20, John informs us that the method by which the saints inherit Christ's millennial kingdom is through the "first resurrection" (Rev. 20:4–5). But what is the nature of this first resurrection?

This is where the teachings of the ante-Nicene millennialists can be very helpful. They believed in a premillennial return of Christ to this earth as do modern premillennialists, but what is not well known about these early millennialists is that they believed the rapture of the saints occurs *after* the millennium at the final or general resurrection when the transformed,

---

[3] Kim Riddlebarger, *A Case for Amillennialism* (Grand Rapids: Baker Books, 2003; 3rd ed., Leicester, England: InterVarsity Press, 2006), 33.

immortal saints (not given in marriage) inherit the eternal new heavens and new earth—an eternal body for an eternal kingdom. Most important, they believed the "first resurrection" at the beginning of the millennial reign of Christ will be of the natural bodies of the departed saints (like Lazarus's resurrection) which can marry and procreate. They understood from the apostle John that the meek shall inherit the Son's restored earth through a resurrection of the natural body and then inherit the Father's kingdom of heaven after the millennium through a resurrection of the immortal body. If they were correct about the "first resurrection" being of the natural bodies of the departed saints with the rapture occurring at the final resurrection, then all that is needed to correct their teachings is to move the second coming from the beginning of the millennium to the last day in conjunction with the rapture. The teachings of these early millennialists will be explored in considerable detail in chapter 12, "The Ante-Nicene Millennialists."

Postrestorationalism

If the millennial reign of Christ is by definition an age of righteous humanity on this earth as portrayed by the prophets, and if the new heavens and new earth are an eternal kingdom for the righteous children of God, then what is God's methodology for establishing his kingdom for his saints on earth and in heaven? As a synthesis of what I believe is correct about these various views (ancient and modern), postrestorationalism proposes that Christ comes again after—*post*—a literal restoration of this Adamic creation for one thousand years. To establish his reign over this world during the millennium, Christ simply binds Satan and rules this world from his throne in heaven at the right hand of God at which time he resurrects all the departed saints in their natural bodies to reinhabit the restored earth. Christ does not need to physically return to this earth to reign as King of kings and Lord of lords. This framework for understanding God's kingdom on earth and in heaven can be outlined as follows:

- After Satan is bound and removed from this world, Christ finally exercises his reign over this world from his throne in heaven.
- All the departed saints are resurrected back into this restored Genesis creation in natural bodies at the "first resurrection."
- The Son's messianic kingdom of peace, justice, righteousness, and prosperity is established on the restored Edenic earth.
- After (post) the 1,000-year restoration of this creation to the true God of this world, Christ comes again on Judgment Day, raptures the saints—asleep or alive—into immortal bodies, destroys this creation, and takes the immortal children of God to the Father's eternal kingdom of heaven, while unbelievers are raised, judged, and sent to the eternal lake of fire.

Eschatology is about the future outcome of God's plan of redemption. If the millennium is an age of righteous humanity on this restored Genesis earth, then it logically follows that God's method of redemption of the departed saints so that they can inherit this kingdom on earth would be through the "first resurrection" of the natural bodies of his departed saints—restored human beings on a restored Edenic earth. And if the new heavens and new earth are the eternal home for the children of God, then the saints would access this heavenly kingdom after the millennium through the final resurrection of an immortal body—an eternal body for an eternal kingdom. Like the refrain in a hymn with many verses, this theme of the two distinct resurrections will be repeated throughout the chapters in this book.

But because of the amount of confusion and strife that continues to surround this debate, many pastors and theologians have grown weary of the subject. Too many books simply rehash the same old debates and make no real progress in breaking the deadlock among theologians over the kingdom of God and our future inheritance. And because the subject remains so contentious with no resolution in sight, many pastors simply avoid the subject altogether. This is unfortunate, for eschatology is not some esoteric subject dedicated solely to deciphering the meaning of the seven seals, trumpets, or bowls of the book of Revelation. Rather, it gets to the very heart of the gospel as it addresses the fundamental questions: What is the kingdom of the triune God? What is our glorious inheritance as children of God? What is the destiny of the raptured saints when Christ comes again?

Theologians are familiar with books on eschatology that often take a point-counterpoint approach to the subject and will find fault with the lack of interaction with the scholarly material on the subject and the relatively few footnotes in this book. The difficulty is that for every verse dealing with the subject, I would have to respond to each of the three respective interpretations of that verse from a postrestorational perspective, resulting in a lengthy book indeed. Instead, I hope that with the presentation of a coherent and convincing biblical case for postrestorationalism, theologians can be persuaded of its truth. The astute reader will recognize that many of my arguments are framed in such a manner that the opposing viewpoint is being refuted. In effect, I do interact with the scholarly material without calling it out with numerous quotes and footnotes.

Conservative evangelicals believe in the authority of the Scriptures, the importance of the historical traditions of the church, and the guiding influence of the Holy Spirit yesterday and today. We also agree that a biblical theology of the past, present, and future should have a high degree of consistency, coherence, congruity, and comprehensiveness. With these principles as a given, let us examine anew the truth about the kingdom of God and his methodology for establishing his kingdom on earth and in heaven.

1

Two Orders of Being

In books on eschatology, theologians often lay out their method of interpreting Scripture, hermeneutics, as a guide to how they understand and organize prophetic literature, particularly as it relates to what is literal and what is figurative. This is not always helpful, however, because theologians then argue incessantly over what is literal and what is metaphorical.

For example, in Revelation 20, the millennial reign of Christ begins when Satan is bound by a great chain and locked up in a pit. The question is not whether Satan, as a fallen angelic being, is literally bound by a steel chain, but whether this symbolically depicts a future supernatural event in the unseen spiritual world whereby this evil, powerful, spiritual being and those evil spirits under his authority are rendered inoperable in this world and are completely removed from influencing and tempting mankind.

The reality is that Satan is an evil spirit, and he influences and tempts both believers and unbelievers. Satan has been operational in this world ever since Adam and Eve rebelled against God, allowing him into this world. He influences every aspect of human activity. If Satan is rendered inoperable in the future and is completely detached from this world, then that would have a profound impact on the world.

Therefore, the question is not whether the binding of Satan with a great chain is metaphorical, but, rather, whether this metaphor describes a real future event in the spiritual realm with immediate ramifications on this earth. A simple analysis of the metaphorical and the literal in these verses does not provide an easy answer.

A more important issue is the theologians' explanation of the *organizing principle* they use to form their biblical theology. For example, many reformed theologians use the different covenants between God and man throughout the Bible to help understand the biblical flow of events—past, present, and future. Likewise, some premillennialists use a variety of dispensations to organize and understand the flow of past and future events described in the Scriptures. Others find that the concept of an inaugurated kingdom that "already is, and is yet to come" helps them understand the kingdom of God today and in the future.

These organizing principles each have merit and in many ways overlap with one another. For example, I think we all agree that after we receive Christ, we are children of God in the kingdom of God in this current covenant or dispensation, but that what we will be like in the future kingdom of heaven or dispensation has not yet been revealed. Or, as John says, "Beloved, we are God's children now [already, in the current covenant, dispensation, or inaugurated kingdom], and what we will be [in the future] has not yet appeared [yet to come in a future age]; but we know that when he appears we will be like him, because we shall see him as he is [in the consummated kingdom]" (1 John 3:2). John is teaching that we are presently God's children and are already in the inaugurated kingdom of God, but there is an eschatological future for God's children when Christ comes again and our bodies are transformed to be like his glorified body.

These organizing principles help us understand the good news that we are now born again as children of God with a real inheritance in God's future consummated kingdom. But, so far, theologians have not come up with an organizing principle and method that helps us understand *what* is yet to come, or how the children of God can inherit the earth for one thousand years and then inherit the kingdom of heaven for eternity.

This chapter explains the *organizing principle* that I use throughout this book and is, in my opinion, the foundation needed to discern and understand the biblical truth about the kingdom of God on earth and in heaven.

The basic organizing principle is that God has created two distinct orders of being for his saints. The first order of being is the Adamic order, which began as described in Genesis. The second order of being is as children of God. The second creation is derived from the first Adamic creation, but it is a distinctly new creation or order of being. The very natures of the two creations are different. As a result, they operate and function differently.

For example, in the Adamic order of being, marriage and reproduction are central operating functions of our nature as human beings. We are male and female given in marriage and reproduce our kind through sexual union, female pregnancy, and the birth of a child. According to Jesus, as children of God, we will not be given in marriage, nor will we reproduce our kind in heaven (Luke 20:34–36). As a result, the family of God in heaven will operate differently than we do today as human families on this earth.

Once we recognize and understand these two distinct orders of being, then the biblical ideology, the kingdom of God, and our future inheritance as God's saints are much easier to understand and organize into a logical system of biblical theology. God's kingdom on earth will be a restoration and redemption of the human experience with a corresponding paradise on this Genesis earth, and God's kingdom in heaven will be for the transformed children of God in an eternal heavenly paradise.

The Adamic Order of Being

When we think of Adam and Eve before the fall, we consider them a man and woman of God. Technically, they were not in the New Testament sense "children of God." For example, Adam would not have addressed God as "Abba, Father" as Jesus did as the Son of God and as we now do as children of God. Adam was created from the dust of the earth, not the dust of heaven (Gen. 2:7). He was not born "of God," nor was he created in heaven as a child of God and then placed onto this planet. This may seem obvious, but the distinction is important. He was made from the dust of the earth as a spiritual-physical being with the breath of life contained within a sexual human anatomy adapted for this Genesis creation. Because both God and mankind (through the breath of life) were spiritual beings, there was true fellowship between the Creator and the biological creature.

What distinguished mankind from the animal world was that man, as male and female, was created in the image of God (Gen. 1:27). For example, as God rules and has dominion over heaven, so, too, man rules and has dominion over the earth as God's vice-regent. God is Lord over heaven and man is lord over the earth—subject to God's Lordship.

Adam and Eve were creatures who would have lived in an earthly paradise in fellowship with their Creator forever if they had not eaten of the tree of the knowledge of good and evil. This did not, however, necessarily make them immortal beings by nature. Even before the fall, they were mortal beings who needed food or outside nourishment to sustain their natural bodies: "And God said, 'Behold, I have given you every plant yielding seed that is on the face of all the earth, and every tree with seed in its fruit. You shall have them for food'" (Gen. 1:29).

In effect, they were living persons, with distinct human spirits, operating within a biological machine or a natural body. A sinless Adam and Eve would have lived continuously, and their descendants would still be alive today. But that does not mean their natural bodies were immortal. Hypothetically, before the fall, if Adam and Eve had decided not to eat food for some reason, they would have eventually starved to death. They were not immortal creatures even in their sinless state.

If they ultimately filled the earth, then all God had to do was say, "It is not good for the earth to be overcrowded; therefore, I will create another planet suitable for mankind." And so on. It is a pretty big solar system.

But after Adam and Eve broke God's commandment not to eat from the tree of the knowledge of good and evil, they became sinful creatures and were cursed by God; they would now experience death. A curse was put on the Genesis earth, as well, causing a change in its ecological system:

> Because you have listened to the voice of your wife and have eaten of the tree of which I commanded you, "You shall not eat of it," cursed is the ground because of you; in pain you shall eat of it all the days of your life; thorns and thistles it shall bring forth for you; and you shall eat the plants of the field. By the sweat of your face you shall eat bread, till you return to the ground, for out of it you were taken; for you are dust, and to dust you shall return. (Gen. 3:17–19)

Not only were they driven out of the Garden of Eden, but now their existence outside the garden would involve a certain level of misery in order to produce sustainable food until they died. Nature was now under a curse by God, just as their mortal or natural bodies were under a curse of death. Yet, when the biological machine that contains the personal spirit breaks down and dies, the spirit or soul of that person continues to exist. The question, at this point in the history of humanity, is what the destiny of the fallen departed spirits would be after they died.

Options of Redemption

At this stage, God had several options. It is helpful to hypothetically explore these options to understand God's plan of redemption through Jesus Christ. The serpent, or Satan, was one of the key characters in the fall of humanity. Satan was a fallen angel, the leader among many fallen angels or demons. These spiritual beings were not created from the dust of the earth, but were originally created in heaven as angels. They do not have bodies, only spirits. That helps define their particular order of being. Now fallen and cursed, many of these unseen evil spirits are operational in this fallen world. At the end of the world, they will be cast into hell or the lake of fire. There is no record of any hope of salvation for Satan and the demons. There is no system of redemption for them. Christ did not die on the cross for their sins.

With this in mind, God's first option toward fallen humanity would be to simply allow us to remain under the curse and die, with our departed spirits destined for hell. We could have all ended up like the demons with no hope of redemption. But in his sovereignty, God decided to institute a means of salvation for humanity. This is evident immediately after the fall of Adam and Eve when it was prophesied to Satan: "I will put enmity between you and the woman, and between your offspring and her offspring; he shall bruise your head, and you shall bruise his heel" (Gen. 3:15). God promised that in the future some person would intervene—with some measure of suffering to the redeemer—and break the connection between fallen man and Satan. Unlike with the demon world, God chose to love humanity and instituted a means of intervention to deliver some of us from Satan's dominion, save us from the curse of death, and restore us to fellowship with our Creator. God, in his own volition and wisdom, decided to institute a means of reconciliation between fallen humanity and himself.

One way of accomplishing this restoration would have been to establish a method of redemption whereby Adam and Eve's descendants would be forgiven of their sins and the curse on man and nature lifted, so that humans could return to a restored Garden of Eden. With this form of redemption, humans would have continued living as husband and wife, reproducing and filling an Edenic earth. In effect, what I call the Adamic order of being would have been restored to the pre-fall condition after some form of redemption, resurrection, and restoration process, and we would have picked up where we left off. We would have become men and women of God again and lived out the original purpose for mankind. We would have been given in marriage becoming one flesh and multiplied, filled, and subdued an Edenic earth.

In fact, the prophets portrayed the messianic kingdom as a restored Genesis paradise for a redeemed humanity. The traditional Jewish understanding of resurrection and restoration of the departed Jewish saints was of a restored human body of flesh and blood that would again marry and have children in God's future restored kingdom on earth.

For example, in Ezekiel's famous vision of the valley of dry bones coming to life, he foresees the departed house of Israel being resurrected into human bodies of flesh and blood with the breath of life breathed into them as they reenter a restored nation on this renewed earth (Ezek. 37). The divided house of Israel and Judah would end, and these resurrected saints of the united house of Israel would then multiply and see their "children and their children's children" (Ezek. 37:25–26). This vision depicts a restoration of the Adamic order returning to an Edenic paradise: "I will make the fruit of the tree and the increase of the field abundant, that you may never again suffer the disgrace of famine among the nations" (Ezek. 36:30). Through a resurrection of the natural bodies of the departed saints, the people of God will enjoy an Edenic paradise on earth with spouses, children, and abundant prosperity.

A New Order of Being as Children of God

However, that is only a part of God's plan of redemption. Instead of merely being saved as human beings and restored to the Garden of Eden, Jesus introduced a salvation and plan of redemption that involves a new order of being as "children of God" who are born "of God" as sons of God, and through a resurrection of bodies like Christ's glorified body, we are ultimately destined, not for the restored earth as restored sexual human beings, but for an eternal kingdom in heaven:

> Blessed be the God and Father of our Lord Jesus Christ! According to his great mercy, he has caused us to be born again to a living hope through the resurrection of Jesus Christ from the dead, to an inheritance that is imperishable, undefiled, and unfading, kept in heaven for you, who by God's power are being guarded through faith for a salvation ready to be revealed in the last time. (1 Peter 1:3–5)

The New Testament writers are revealing something truly extraordinary. And one can sense Peter's utter amazement and excitement from realizing that we, as believers, have become children of God destined to inherit the eternal kingdom of heaven.

Our existence as human beings comes from our natural birth from human parents, but our birth as children of God has a different origin: "But to all who did receive him, who believed in his name, he gave the right to become children of God, who were born, not of blood nor of the will of the flesh nor of the will of man, but of God" (John 1:12–13). Believers are born of God and take their new nature from his being—not from their Adamic parents. We are born of God as his children and become sons of God in a similar way that Christ is the Son of God. In contrast, Adam was not born of God but was *made by* God from the dust of the earth as a man of God destined to live and work on this Genesis earth. He was not born of the Spirit and destined to live with God in heaven as a child of God.

In his famous encounter with the Sadducees, who did not believe in the prophets' vision of a literal resurrection of the natural body, Christ discloses a stunning revelation about a very different kind resurrection for the departed saints. This must have caught the Sadducees, the Pharisees, the disciples, and the Jewish crowd completely off guard. In the new order of being as resurrected sons of God in heaven, we will remain embodied creatures, but our bodies will be immortal, and we will no longer experience human marriage:

> The sons of this age marry and are given in marriage [the Adamic order of being], but those who are considered worthy to attain to that age [believers] and to the resurrection from the dead neither marry nor are given in marriage, for they cannot die anymore, because they are equal to angels and are sons of God [the new order of being], being sons of the resurrection [in the age to come]. (Luke 20:34–36)

In Jesus' day, a son left his parents to marry, and a daughter was given in marriage by her parents. Jesus' said that neither will occur in the eternal resurrection to make it clear that the human experience of marriage will no longer exist when the sons of God are resurrected into immortal bodies that cannot die anymore.

Angels are spirits, not embodied creatures who need food, water, and air to sustain life, but they are immortal creatures, and they do not marry and reproduce. The angels Michael and Gabriel do not have angelic wives that produce little newborn angels. Unlike angels, we will be embodied spirits after being resurrected; but like the angelic order of being, we will be immortal and will not marry and reproduce.

Jesus' description of the eternal resurrection must have dumbfounded his Jewish audience. The traditional Jewish understanding of resurrection was of the natural human body—mortals who experience marriage—that would enter God's restored Edenic kingdom (Ezek. 37). In this Genesis age, humanity is by definition a sexual creation involving persons embodied in male and female natural bodies designed for the union of marriage and reproduction. Yet, in an astonishing revelation, Jesus reveals that in the age to come, the sons of God will no longer experience marriage and will be given a new kind of immortal body adapted for heaven—not for the Genesis earth. In heaven, the resurrected immortal sons of God will live an embodied existence, but will not marry, reproduce, and fill the new heavens and new earth with their offspring.

Most important, Christ is not describing the eternal kingdom of heaven in the age to come as some giant monastery or convent for a restored humanity on a restored earth whereby resurrected male and female human beings will simply abstain from sex and marriage and remain celibate. Rather, he is describing a categorical change in the nature of being for the saints when we are transformed and taken to the heavenly kingdom. The very structure of our human bodies and their function as male and female sexual creatures will be fundamentally changed. We will relate to God the Father as his sons, to each other as brothers in Christ, and even as the bride of Christ when our bodies are transformed to be like his.

Not only will the nature of our immortal bodies be different, but the whole social order in heaven also will be radically different from the current extended human family. For example, none of the following human relationships will exist in the eternal kingdom, for they all derive from marriage between a man and a woman: husband and wife; father and mother; grandfather and grandmother; father-in-law and mother-in-law; uncles and aunts; brothers and sisters; nephews and nieces; grandsons and granddaughters; first, second, and third male and female cousins; and the entire human family of male and female neighbors.

This remarkable truth about the new order of being appears throughout Paul's letters: "You are all sons of God through faith in Christ Jesus, for all of you who were baptized into Christ have clothed yourselves with Christ.

There is neither Jew nor Greek, slave nor free, male nor female, for you are all one in Christ Jesus" (Gal. 3:26–28 NIV). Paul is not simply referring to the basic equality among human beings who can all become members of the body of Christ, although this does have implications in the church today. He is elaborating on Jesus' extraordinary revelation and teaching that the sons of God do not ultimately have ethnic, racial, class, or even sexual distinctions in the eternal kingdom when it is consummated.

Paul teaches that the new order of being as God's children is a distinctly new creation that begins now but is destined for heaven:

> For we know that if the tent [our natural mortal body], which is our earthly home, is destroyed, we have a building from God [an eternal body like Christ's body], a house not made with hands, eternal in the heavens. . . . From now on, therefore, we regard no one according to the flesh [the Adamic order of being]. . . . Therefore, if anyone is in Christ, he is a new creation. (2 Cor. 5:1, 16–17)

Paul is not describing a future renewed humanity in a restored Genesis home, but a new creation as God's children who are destined to indwell a new kind of eternal body in the Father's heavenly kingdom. The current Genesis creation is groaning and waiting for this transition to the eternal kingdom when our current Adamic bodies are redeemed and transformed along with the Genesis creation itself:

> For all who are led by the Spirit of God are sons of God. For you did not receive the spirit of slavery to fall back into fear, but you have received the Spirit of adoption as sons, by whom we cry, "Abba! Father!" The Spirit himself bears witness with our spirit that we are children of God, and if children, then heirs—heirs of God and fellow heirs of Christ, provided we suffer with him in order that we may also be glorified with him. . . . For we know that the whole creation has been groaning together in the pains of childbirth until now. And not only the creation, but we ourselves, who have the firstfruits of the Spirit, groan inwardly as we wait eagerly for adoption as sons, the redemption of our bodies. (Rom. 8:14–23)

The Holy Spirit within us informs us that we are sons of God and causes our inner spirits to long for the day when our bodies will be redeemed and glorified and we are adopted as sons or children of God in God's heavenly home. The Genesis creation itself longs for our change from Adamic creatures to our new order of being as children of God.

A New Kind of Body

Further proof that the new creation is indeed a new order of being, rather than a re-creation of the Adamic order as envisioned by Ezekiel and the other prophets, can be found in Paul's teachings on the final resurrection of the children of God that describe a new kind of spiritual body:

> So is it with the resurrection of the dead. What is sown is perishable; what is raised is imperishable. . . . It is sown a natural body; it is raised a spiritual body. If there is a natural body, there is also a spiritual body. Thus it is written, "The first man Adam became a living being"; the last Adam became a life-giving spirit. But it is not the spiritual that is first but the natural, and then the spiritual. The first man was from the earth, a man of dust; the second man is from heaven. As was the man of dust, so also are those who are of the dust, and as is the man of heaven, so also are those who are of heaven. Just as we have borne the image of the man of dust, we shall also bear the image of the man of heaven. (1 Cor. 15:42–49)

Adam's body was made from the dust of the earth and was a natural body adapted for the Garden of Eden. As children of God, however, we are a new order of being, or a new creation, waiting for our Adamic bodies to be transformed into bodies like Christ's glorified body in order to be taken to the kingdom of heaven—a new kind of body for a new order of being on a new kind of earth. Our spiritual bodies will be real bodies but will be imperishable and in the image of the resurrected Christ from heaven—not in the image of the man of dust. An imperishable body will not need food, water, and air to sustain itself. It will be intrinsically immortal. We will relate to the Father in heaven differently than Adam and Eve did. We will call God the Father "Abba, Father," just as his Son does. This new creation as sons of God requires a new kind of body like his resurrected and glorified Son's; we are transformed into his Son's image.

In the Adamic order of being, we were created in the image of the triune God: "Then God said, 'Let us [the Trinity] make man in our image, after our likeness.' . . . So God created man in his own image, in the image of God he created him; male and female he created them" (Gen. 1:26–27). We currently bear that image. In the new order of being, however, even the image or pattern of creation is different. Instead of being transformed into the image of the Trinity, we are going to be transformed into the image of the Son of God: "For those whom he foreknew he also predestined to be conformed to the image of his Son, so that he might be the firstborn among many brothers" (Rom. 8:29). As a result, we become sons of God the Father as Christ is his Son; we become as brothers to Christ.

Adam was the first human creature made with a natural body, but the resurrected and glorified Christ is the firstborn of the new order of being with a spiritual body who has led the way to the heavenly kingdom—the future home of the succeeding sons of God. Adam was the beginning of the human experience as the first human on this Genesis earth, and the risen and ascended Christ is the firstborn of the new creation as children of God.

Even further evidence that the new creation as sons of God is a truly new order of being and not a restoration of our humanity is that Paul teaches the Adamic body is going to be transformed into a new *unknown* kind of body similar to the way a seed planted in the ground is transformed into a plant. Upon germination, the seed does not come up out of the ground as another seed. Instead, the seed is transformed into a new kind of body as a plant, which is vastly different from the seed that was planted. Likewise, the human body will be transformed into a new kind of body adapted for heaven:

> But someone will ask, "How are the dead raised? With what *kind* of body do they come?" You foolish person! . . . what you sow [the Adamic body] is *not the body that is to be,* but a bare kernel, perhaps of wheat or of some other grain. But God gives it a body as he has chosen, and to each kind of seed its own body. (1 Cor. 15:35–38)

To illustrate what Paul is teaching, consider an acorn and an oak tree. When an acorn is planted, it does not come up out of the ground as another acorn. Rather, upon germination and maturity, the acorn is transformed into an oak tree vastly different in design and structure from the acorn planted in the ground. We cannot determine what the oak tree will be like by examining the acorn's exterior or by cracking it open and analyzing its interior. The acorn itself does not in any way prefigure what the resulting oak tree will be like when germinated. The acorn is one kind of body or entity, and the oak tree is another kind completely different from the original nut. The acorn is transformed into a new entity with a totally different form, structure, and function.

Likewise, the male or female human body that is sown into the ground does not come out of the ground as another resurrected, sexual human body capable of marriage, intercourse, and reproduction. Furthermore, Paul is teaching that we cannot examine or analyze the current Adamic body of flesh and blood and know in advance what kind of body it will become when it is transformed and adapted for heaven. Paul says it is foolish at this time to predict what our raptured bodies will be like by analyzing the Adamic body. The resurrected human bodies of the children of God are going to be transformed into a presently unknown kind of immortal body with a totally different form, structure, and function.

Of course, there is continuity between the acorn and the oak tree. An oak tree does not come from a seashell. And an oak tree does not produce a seashell. But Paul is not stressing continuity. On the contrary, he is emphasizing the discontinuity between the human body of flesh and blood that is sown in the ground when it dies and the bodies that God's children will eventually have when resurrected, transformed, and adapted for heaven. The New Testament authors describe the raptured body as a body that will be perfected, transformed, glorified, and made incorruptible, imperishable, and spiritual—as opposed to one that is mortal.

The apostle John also teaches that the nature of the resurrected body for God's children remains a mystery at this time: "Beloved, we are God's children now, and what we will be has not yet appeared; but we know that when he appears we will be like him, because we shall see him as he is" (1 John 3:2). Like Paul, John freely admits that he does not know what our resurrected bodies as God's children will be like. He does not compare the future resurrected body to the Adamic body. Nor does he compare it to the resurrected body of the pre-ascended Christ. John had seen and touched the pre-ascended Christ and even ate breakfast with him, but he does not reference the pre-ascended resurrected body of Christ as a type or representative example of our resurrected immortal bodies.

Instead, he references the unknown post-ascended glorified body of Christ as the kind of bodies we will have. Our new bodies will be like Christ's, but the exact nature of his ascended glorified body remains a mystery until he comes again and our bodies are transformed to be like his.

If the heavenly kingdom were a restored earth with a resurrected and restored humanity, which we are familiar with, then why would Paul and John teach that the kind of bodies we will have as children of God is such a profound mystery? The answer is that the new heavens and new earth are not designed for a restored sexual human body on a restored Genesis earth. The transformed sons of God are destined to reside in the eternal new heavens and new earth—which have yet to be created! They will not be created until this current Genesis creation passes away (Rev. 20:11—21:1). That is why Paul says it is foolish to speculate as to what kind of bodies we will have at the transformation. The nature of our spiritual bodies, therefore, remains a mystery until Christ comes again and takes us to the new heavens and new earth.

Does this mean we will live a disembodied existence in some boring, ethereal, spiritual world sitting around playing harps all day? Of course not, for the Scriptures plainly teach that our individual spirits will be contained in glorified bodies of some kind and will reside in a real place. Just because the nature of our transformed bodies and the nature of our eternal home remain a mystery at this time does not mean we should imagine it as a boring existence or feel compelled to impose familiar Adamic features onto the eternal existence to make it seem more inviting.

We should simply trust our Creator to use the same infinite creative skills to create the new heavens and new earth that he used to create this current Genesis earth. And we would logically expect the new creation to be even more incredible than the present one.

Parents often have a difficult time explaining to their children what heaven will be like. Directing children to the current Genesis creation with its intricate design will demonstrate that God has a proven track record of awesome creativity. He will use this same infinite creativity to create our new kind of immortal body and its new habitat, the new heavens and new earth.

Today the Two Orders of Being Operate Concurrently

An amazing thing has happened. God could have allowed the Adamic order of being to die off with no plan of redemption. We could have gone the way of the fallen angels with our fallen spirits or souls destined for hell. He could have even created this new order of being from scratch. In his sovereignty, however, God decided to create a new order of being in the image of his Son out of the redeemed Adamic order of being.

But we are born again as children of God now, while we still live in the fallen Adamic order of being. Therefore, we currently live a dual existence. As a believer I am simultaneously a restored man of God in the Adamic order of being and a child of God in the new order of being. I am a citizen of the earth as a descendant of Adam and at the same time a citizen of heaven as a child of God, which is my ultimate eternal destiny.

According to the Adamic order of being, I am one flesh with my wife. Since my wife is a believer, however, she is also a fellow child of God in the new order of being in which there is ultimately no distinction between male and female. She is currently my wife *and* my sister in Christ—two orders of being exist simultaneously with dual citizenship on earth and in heaven.

At the transformation after the final resurrection when we are given a new kind of body, my wife will no longer be my female partner in one flesh, for the Adamic order of being will cease to exist. She will, however, be an eternal fellow child of God. As men or women of God, we are at home as citizens of this Genesis creation. As children of God, we are sojourners on this earth; our real home is in heaven with God.

Today the spirit of a person who is a believer inhabits the Adamic body. But on the last day, that same person or spirit will inhabit a transformed body adapted for heaven. Peter, the husband and man of God, will become Peter, the child of God in heaven. The spirit of Peter, which once inhabited the tent of his Adamic body, will then inhabit the tent of his new spiritual body. We will not lose our individual personhood when we are given a new kind of body to indwell.

In his discussion with the Sadducees, Christ referred to resurrected spirits of the departed saints as real persons such as Abraham, Isaac, and Jacob, who have not yet received their final resurrected bodies (Matt. 22:31–32). Even angels such as Michael or Gabriel, who exist without bodies, maintain their distinctive personhood. In heaven those who walked alongside him will recognize Peter embodied in his immortal spiritual body as the same person who once inhabited a mortal body and fished along the shores of Galilee.

The Virgin Birth in Reverse

Christ was preexistent as the Son of God with the Father before the incarnation. Through the Holy Spirit and the virgin birth, he became a man in the Adamic order of being. He was born of a woman and became a human being. Thus, he became two concurrent orders of being—fully Son of God and fully man. When Christ was on this earth as a human being, he got tired, sleepy, hungry, and thirsty. Theoretically, he could have married and had children. He could even experience mortal death. But after his death and resurrection, he ascended to heaven in a glorified immortal body adapted for heaven; his body is no longer a mortal Adamic body adapted for this Genesis creation.

Our rebirth as children of God is like a virgin birth in reverse. We preexist as a son of man or as a sexual human being, male or female, having been born of human parents. But when we receive Christ, the Holy Spirit comes upon us and causes us to be born of God the Father, and we become sons of God as Christ is a son of God. Then, just as Christ was the Son of God *and* a son of man (human being), so, too, we become children of God at the same time that we are sons of men (human beings). Like Jesus, we are two concurrent orders of being—fully men *and* fully children of God, even though we have not yet received our final immortal bodies. In effect, we are children of God continuing to exist in the tent of this Adamic body temporarily. We are children of God incarnate in our natural Adamic bodies waiting for the return of Christ and the transformation of our bodies to be like his and be taken to the eternal new heavens and new earth.

Our ultimate destiny is as children of God in our new bodies adapted for the new heavens and new earth. The current dual order of existence is only temporary. On the last day of this Adamic creation, God will transform his children's Adamic bodies and take them to heaven. We will no longer live a duality as a natural man or woman of God *and* a child of God but will become exclusively children of God in heaven in a new kind of body, one that is neither male nor female.

This new creation is not a "re-creation" or restoration of the old Adamic order of being; otherwise, there would be marriage in heaven. The Adamic order of being actually comes to an end. The heavenly kingdom is not a restoration of our sexual humanity on a restored Genesis earth in which we marry and fill the earth with our offspring. In heaven, the children of God will not reproduce our own kind. The new creation is a new order of being, and one that is unknown until we experience the final resurrection.

As children of God, what does it mean when the Bible teaches that we should not commit adultery? Ultimately, in the new creation in heaven, it will not mean anything, for in heaven we will not be given in marriage. But because we are living a dual existence on this earth, the commandment telling us how we should function as husbands and wives in the Adamic order of being is still operative. It is important that we function properly as humans and experience a restoration of our humanity while we are on this earth. God has called us to be his children, but he wants us to be men and women of God at the same time. As long as we are on this earth, we should operate according to God's design for the Adamic order of being.

The Corinthian church, with its many problems, appeared to have understood the concept of the new creation in which there is neither male nor female, but they seem to have attempted to implement the new order of being in the present age at the expense of the Adamic order of being. As a result, some within the Corinthian church had begun to forbid sexual relations between husbands and wives. In their opinion, husbands and wives were now brothers and sisters in the new order of being, so human sexual relations were no longer necessary. Paul corrected them by teaching that they were still functioning in the Adamic order of being and, as such, needed to fulfill their marital duties:

> Now concerning the matters about which you wrote: "It is good for a man not to have sexual relations with a woman." But because of the temptation to sexual immorality, each man should have his own wife and each woman her own husband. The husband should give to his wife her conjugal rights, and likewise the wife to her husband. For the wife does not have authority over her own body, but the husband does. Likewise the husband does not have authority over his own body, but the wife does. (1 Cor. 7:1–4)

Husbands and wives should still function as God intended married couples to function even though in the new creation there is ultimately no distinction between male and female as children of God. But as long as we are living a *duality* in both orders of being, we should not commit adultery, and we should fulfill the Adamic mandate to multiply and fill the earth.

The Bible does not belittle the Adamic order of being even though it is temporal. The Bible contains many truths that tell us how we, as men and women of God, should function as human beings. This truth sets us free from false perceptions of what it means to be human and, when acted upon, saves us from malfunctioning as human beings. For example, sexual immorality, whether in the form of adultery or homosexuality, is dysfunctional human behavior. It demonstrates a deep confusion and deception about how we should function as sexual human beings. Biblical truth about man as sexual male and female human beings liberates us from this bondage to self-destructive behavior and restores us to true manhood and womanhood.

Christianity, which restores our Adamic relationship with our Creator, actually restores our humanity. We should be in a loving companionship with God our Creator and behave as humans were designed to function.

It is not natural for man to be alone and autonomous from God. Because of our inherited sinful nature, however, we operate as little human gods subject to no one but ourselves. This alter ego rules our hearts and minds, preventing us from submitting to the true God of our lives. This false "god-self" is self-destructive, for it keeps us in a state of rebellion and alienation from our Creator and leads to ultimate destruction on Judgment Day. Repentance, salvation, and reconciliation to our God liberate us from this god-self, freeing us to be truly human again as we become submissive to God. While we are still on this earth, salvation includes restoration of the human experience—not just salvation from the wrath of God on the last day and being taken to heaven as his children.

Method of Interpreting and Organizing the Scriptures

To understand the kingdom of God on earth and in heaven, it is important to understand and maintain the two distinct orders of being. The Adamic order of being is characterized by humanity with natural, mortal bodies designed for marriage, whereas the new order of being will be characterized by immortality and no marriage. These factors help us determine when a particular Scripture is referring to the Son's messianic kingdom on this restored Genesis earth and when it is referring to the eternal new heavens and new earth in the Father's heavenly kingdom.

For example, when reading about a messianic prophecy in Isaiah or John's vision in Revelation, we simply ask, "Are the authors referring to a restored Adamic creation where God's people live in an Edenic paradise with marriage, children, and amazing longevity, or are they referring to the new order of being in the kingdom of heaven where there is no marriage and immortality?" With this methodology of differentiating between the two orders of being, it is relatively easy to recognize when the prophets are describing God's restored earthly kingdom and when they are referring to God's future heavenly kingdom.

To illustrate this method of interpretation, consider Isaiah's famous prophecy of the restored earth in chapter 65 of Isaiah. He uses the phrase "new heavens and a new earth," but when analyzing his prophecy in context, it becomes readily apparent that he uses this phrase to describe a renewed or renovated Genesis earth; this is different from John's use of the phrase to describe a truly new creation in the eternal kingdom that includes the New Jerusalem. Notice how Isaiah describes the messianic kingdom as an Adamic paradise with a restored earthly Jerusalem on a renewed earth:

For behold, I create new heavens and a new earth, and the former things shall not be remembered or come into mind. But be glad and rejoice forever in that which I create; for behold, I create Jerusalem to be a joy, and her people to be a gladness. I will rejoice in Jerusalem and be glad in my people; no more shall be heard in it the sound of weeping and the cry of distress. No more shall there be in it an infant who lives but a few days [marriage and reproduction], or an old man who does not fill out his days, for the young man shall die a hundred years old [mortality], and the sinner a hundred years old shall be accursed. They shall build houses and inhabit them; they shall plant vineyards and eat their fruit [human habitats and gardens]. They shall not build and another inhabit; they shall not plant and another eat; for like the days of a tree shall the days of my people be, and my chosen shall long enjoy the work of their hands. They shall not labor in vain or bear children for calamity, for they shall be the offspring of the blessed of the LORD, and their descendants with them [extended human families]. Before they call I will answer; while they are yet speaking I will hear. The wolf and the lamb shall graze together; the lion shall eat straw like the ox, and dust shall be the serpent's food [back to the Garden of Eden]. They shall not hurt or destroy in all my holy mountain, says the LORD. (Isa. 65:17–25)

In the restoration in this Adamic age, the people of God will marry, have children, build houses, plant vineyards, and live extremely long lives of peace, prosperity, and happiness in an Edenic paradise. According to the Old Testament prophets, the Son's messianic kingdom is by definition a restoration of the Adamic order of being on this restored Genesis earth in this age.

The heavenly kingdom, on the other hand, is associated with the second coming of Christ and the corresponding rapture and transformation of the children of God who are taken to the Father's heavenly paradise *in the age to come* after this Genesis creation comes to an end. John's visions of a "new heaven and a new earth" apply to the Father's eternal kingdom after the "first heaven and first earth has passed away" (Rev. 21:1). It is characterized by Jesus as a place for the sons of God who after being resurrected "neither marry nor are given in marriage" and become immortal beings. The transformed body is destined for heaven—not for a restored Adamic earth. According to Jesus and his apostles, the kingdom of heaven is, by definition, the future eternal home for the new order of being, the sons of God.

The use of the same terminology—new heavens and new earth—by Isaiah, Peter, and John causes a great deal of confusion among theologians, even though contextually one can easily see that Isaiah is describing an existing earth that is new in the sense that it is restored, renovated, renewed, or made like new; conversely, Peter and John describe a completely new heavens and earth in the Father's eternal kingdom of heaven that replace the current heavens and earth after they are destroyed by God with fire. Isaiah's restored earth may prefigure the heavenly new heavens and new earth, but he is clearly describing an Adamic paradise with mankind building houses, planting crops, and being given in marriage and procreating.

This use of the same figure of speech in different contexts is analogous to the way we use the word *transformed* as having two different meanings. For example, whenever an especially sinful person we know becomes a Christian, we might say, "Bobby has been *transformed* into a *new* person." By this, we simply mean that his character and behavior have dramatically changed, and he is now living a *restored* life of righteousness and holiness in loving fellowship with his Creator and fellow man. We do not mean Bobby's body has literally been transformed into an immortal spiritual body.

However, Bobby, whose life was transformed when he became a Christian, will be truly transformed when his body is changed "in the twinkling of an eye" into a *new* kind of spiritual body—one that is immortal, imperishable, and no longer given in marriage. The *transformation* or renewal of his character is a prelude to the ultimate *transformation* of his body. So, too, Isaiah's prophecy of a "new heavens and new earth," restored to an Edenic paradise with restored human beings, is a prelude to the day God destroys the current earth and creates a *new* heavens and *new* earth that will be the eternal home of the transformed children of God. Isaiah's restored heavens and earth serve as a prototype of the eternal new heavens and new earth.

Confusing the Two Orders of Being

When evaluating biblical references, it is critical to recognize when the Scriptures are referring to the Son's earthly kingdom that involves a restoration of the Adamic order of being and when they are referring to the Father's heavenly kingdom that involves the new order of being as sons of God. Once one understands the two orders of being and their defining characteristics and uses these distinctions as the key organizing principle and method of interpreting the Scriptures, it is easy to understand how many of the mistakes made by theologians in formulating the various systems of eschatology are a result of confusing these two orders of being.

The Premillennialist View

For example, modern premillennialists believe the raptured, immortal, glorified children of God in their spiritual bodies—not given in marriage— will return to this restored Adamic creation to reign with Christ during the millennium. Today's premillennialists may disagree among themselves as to whether the rapture occurs at the beginning, middle, or end of the Great Tribulation, but they all believe that the raptured children of God in their glorified bodies come back to this Genesis earth with Christ to reign with him during his millennial kingdom. But what are the transformed sons of God—no longer given in marriage—doing back on this restored Adamic earth? Will these billions of glorified saints comingle with natural human families? How can this be a fulfillment of the Old Testament vision of a restored Edenic paradise for God's people who, as Isaiah and Ezekiel teach, will marry, have children, build houses, plant vineyards, and live long lives full of peace and happiness? The prophetic vision of the messianic kingdom is definitely portrayed as an Adamic paradise.

Some modern premillennialists recognize this comingling of immortal, glorified saints with mere mortals as a serious problem and attempt to solve it by proposing that the transformed raptured saints do not really come down to the earth to permanently reside during the millennium; rather, they stay in the new heavenly Jerusalem that comes down from heaven but then hovers in the sky above the restored earth. J. Dwight Pentecost, when addressing this thorny issue in his book *Things to Come*, states the following:

> Thus the millennium age will be concerned only with men who have been saved but are living in their natural bodies. This heavenly city [New Jerusalem, which contains the raptured saints in their immortal bodies] will be brought into a relation to the earth at the beginning of the millennium, and perhaps will be made visible above the earth. It is from this heavenly city that David's greater Son exerts His Messianic rule, in which the Bride reigns, and from which the rewarded Old Testament saints exercise their authority in government. If such an interpretation be correct, there would be a solution to the perplexing problem that arises from placing resurrected saints on the earth to mingle freely with the unresurrected during the millennium.[1]

According to Pentecost, Christ and the immortal saints will govern and rule over the mortal creatures on the earth from the New Jerusalem, hovering in the sky. Presumably, the immortal saints go back and forth between the New Jerusalem and the restored earth during this time to assist in ruling over the world. As a result, the resurrected saints do not get to experience the restoration after all as restored human beings on a restored Genesis creation as promised—they essentially only get to watch and help manage it.

Most premillennialists do not wrestle with this dilemma, but to Pentecost's credit, he at least attempts to find a solution. But the sequential outline in Revelation clearly places the New Jerusalem *after* the millennial reign of Christ and after this Genesis creation ceases to exist, when it is described as coming down out of heaven to the "new heaven and new earth"—not on or above the millennial earth:

---

[1] J. Dwight Pentecost, *Things to Come*, 7th ed. (Grand Rapids: Zondervan, 1970), 546.

Then [after the millennium and Great White Throne judgment] I saw a new heaven and new earth, for the first heaven and the first earth had passed away [the end of the Genesis creation], and the sea was no more. And I saw the holy city, a new Jerusalem, coming down out of heaven from God, prepared as a bride adorned for her husband. (Rev. 21:1–2)

Most important, the transformed children of God have no business being on this Genesis earth in their raptured, glorified bodies because, as Paul plainly teaches, they are destined for heaven when they are raptured and caught up to be with the Lord for eternity:

But our citizenship is in heaven [our destiny when raptured]. And we eagerly await a Savior from there, the Lord Jesus Christ [the second coming], who, by the power that enables him to bring everything under his control, will transform our lowly bodies so that they will be like his glorious body [the rapture]. (Phil. 3:20–21 NIV)

Our glorified bodies at Christ's second coming are destined for our citizenship in heaven—not the Son's messianic kingdom on earth.

Premillennialists place the wrong kind of resurrected body in the wrong kingdom of God because they confuse the two orders of being. Placing the children of God in their raptured spiritual bodies on this restored earth is an obvious misfit. According to the Old Testament prophets, the restoration of this Genesis creation in the messianic kingdom is for the restored Adamic order of being; whereas, according to Jesus and the apostles, the raptured and transformed children of God belong in the Father's imperishable kingdom of heaven, or our citizenship in heaven.

The Amillennialist View

Amillennialists also confuse the two orders of being. Because they omit the earthly messianic kingdom, they have no logical place to fulfill the Old Testament prophecies of a restored Genesis creation. As a result, in an attempt to make sense out of these numerous prophetic visions, many amillennialists impose the characteristics of the restored Adamic order of being found in these messianic prophecies onto the eternal new heavens and new earth such that the heavenly kingdom essentially becomes a renovated and restored Genesis earth. For example, Anthony Hoekema, an amillennialist, makes the following observation about heaven as a renovated earth:

There will be a future fulfillment of these prophecies [Old Testament messianic prophecies], not in the millennium, but on the new earth. Whether they are all to be *literally* fulfilled is open to question; surely details about wolves and lambs, and about mountains dropping sweet wine, are to be understood not in a crassly literal way but as figurative descriptions of what the new earth will be like.[2]

According to Hoekema, the children of God inherit a restored Genesis earth as the eternal kingdom. But these messianic visions portray a kingdom of God's people being given in marriage, having children, and living unusually long lives. How can that be a picture of heaven? Jesus informs us that in the kingdom of heaven we will not experience marriage, so it cannot, by definition, be a restoration of the Adamic order of being on an Edenic earth. Marriage and reproduction get to the very core of what it means to be human beings made in the image of God, and, without these essential components of our being, it is difficult to see heaven as a mere extension of the Adamic order of being on a renovated earth.

Randy Alcorn, in his popular book *Heaven*, teaches a similar view of heaven as a restored earth and restored humanity:

> We should expect the New Earth to be like Eden, only better. That's exactly what Scripture promises. Notice the earth's restoration to Edenlike qualities prophesied in these passages: "Indeed, the Lord will comfort Zion; he will comfort all her waste places. And her wilderness He will make like Eden, and her desert like the garden of the Lord; joy and gladness will be found in her, thanksgiving and sound of a melody" (Isaiah 51:3, NASB). "They will say, 'This desolate land has become like the garden of Eden; and the waste, desolate and ruined cities are fortified and inhabited.'" (Ezekiel 36:35, NASB)[3]

Alcorn, like Hoekema, wrongly applies the Old Testament messianic vision of an earthly paradise to the new heavens and new earth.

Premillennialists have the new order of being as the raptured children of God on earth, when it belongs in heaven. And many amillennialists impose the Adamic order of being on heaven, when it belongs on the restored millennial earth. Both systems of understanding God's kingdom on earth and in heaven fail to provide a coherent framework for the biblical data because they confuse and comingle the two orders of being in relation to their respective kingdoms.

The Postrestorational View

With the postrestorational framework, however, the two orders of being are kept distinct, and the distinction between God's kingdom on earth and his kingdom in heaven becomes clear. For example, the 1,000-year messianic kingdom (the Son's kingdom) is a renewal, restoration, or regeneration of the Genesis creation, and through the first resurrection the saints will

---

[2] Anthony A. Hoekema, *The Bible and the Future* (Grand Rapids: Eerdmans, 1979), 276.
[3] Randy Alcorn, *Heaven* (Carol Stream, IL: Tyndale House Publishers, 2004), 244.

repopulate the earth as Adamic creatures in their natural bodies when Christ rules this world from heaven. The regenerated human body will function as male and female in the image of God so that we can fulfill the original Genesis creation mandate—the human experience as originally intended. The messianic kingdom is a human paradise on this restored Genesis earth.

The new heavens and new earth that follow can only be inherited through a process of transformation of the saints—alive or asleep—when Christ returns and takes the Father's children to heaven in glorified bodies. The eternal heavenly kingdom is for the new order of being as God's immortal children.

Because there are two orders of being, there are two facets to the kingdom of God—one, the Son's earthly messianic kingdom for the restored Adamic order of being in this age and two, the Father's heavenly kingdom for the sons of God in the age to come, which is a new creation that occurs after this Genesis creation comes to an end.

By understanding the two distinct orders of being, one can then perform a referential analysis of the Scriptures to determine when the author is referring to the Adamic order of being and its associated restoration in this current Genesis age and when he is referring to the eternal kingdom of heaven in the age to come. Throughout this book I will make the case that the best way to discern whether a particular prophecy or Scripture is a description of the Son's earthly messianic kingdom or the Father's eternal heavenly kingdom is the presence of mortality and marriage, for these are the defining characteristics of the current Adamic order of being. If the prophecy foretells of a world where there is amazing longevity, marriage, and children, then it is describing the Son's messianic kingdom on the restored Genesis earth. But if a particular section of Scripture describes a place where there is no longer death and God's children are immortal and not given in marriage, then it is most definitely speaking of the Father's eternal heavenly kingdom.

To illustrate this methodology, consider the prophet Ezekiel who describes a restoration of the kingdom to Israel with a restored Jerusalem and a rebuilt temple with a stream of water flowing from it that becomes a river with edible fruit trees along its banks:

> As I went back, I saw on the bank of the river very many trees on the one side and on the other. . . . And on the banks, on both sides of the river, there will grow all kinds of trees for food. Their leaves will not wither, nor their fruit fail, but they will bear fresh fruit every month, because the water for them flows from the sanctuary. Their fruit will be for food, and their leaves for healing." (Ezek. 47:7–12)

This is a vision of a river in the earthly city of Jerusalem, restored to a place of peace and abundant prosperity.

In Revelation, John also describes a river in the New Jerusalem on the new earth coming not from a temple, but from the throne of God:

> Then the angel showed me the river of the water of life, bright as crystal, flowing from the throne of God and of the Lamb through the middle of the street of the city; also, on either side of the river, the tree of life with its twelve kinds of fruit, yielding its fruit each month. The leaves of the tree were for the healing of the nations. (Rev. 22:1–2)

Are the two prophets describing the same event or is John using Ezekiel's vision of a restored Jerusalem on a restored earth as a pattern of the New Jerusalem in the eternal new heavens and new earth? The answer is fairly easy to determine as long as one maintains a distinction between the two orders of being. Ezekiel is clearly describing the restored earth because earlier in this same prophecy, he describes human beings experiencing marriage, reproduction, mortality, and even sin, which must be judged:

> They shall dwell in the land that I gave to my servant Jacob, where your fathers lived. They and their children and their children's children . . . And I will set them in their land and multiply them [marriage and reproduction]. (Ezek. 37:25–26)

> They [the priests] shall not marry a widow or a divorced woman, but only virgins of the offspring of the house of Israel . . . In a dispute, they shall act as judges, and they shall judge it according to my judgments [sin still exists]. . . . They shall not defile themselves by going near to a dead person [mortality]. (Ezek. 44:22–25)

This entire prophecy falls within the context of a river flowing from a real temple with real fruit-bearing trees along its banks that will serve as real food for real human beings and their children. Ezekiel is plainly describing a restored Adamic earth with marriage, reproduction, mortality, and even sinful human affairs that require priestly judges.

John, on the other hand, is describing the eternal new heavens and new earth and the New Jerusalem that occur after this Genesis creation and its earthly city of Jerusalem have passed away. The city does not contain a temple, and the children of God are immortal and live in a sinless kingdom:

> From his presence earth and sky fled away, and no place was found for them. . . . Then I saw a new heaven and a new earth, for the first heaven and the first earth had passed away . . . And I saw the holy city, new Jerusalem . . . He will wipe away every tear from their eyes, and death shall be no more [immortality] . . . And I saw no temple in the city, for its temple is the Lord God the Almighty and the Lamb. . . . But nothing unclean will ever enter it, nor anyone who does what is detestable or false [sinless existence], but only those who are written in the Lamb's book of life [the raptured children of

God]. Then the angel showed me the river of the water of life, bright as crystal, flowing from the throne of God and of the Lamb through the middle of the street of the city; also, on either side of the river, the tree of life with it twelve kinds of fruit, yielding its fruit each month. (Rev. 20:11—22:2)

John's vision of the eternal heavenly kingdom may have certain features patterned on the restored earthly kingdom of God, but it is occupied exclusively by the immortal and sinless sons of God who are no longer given in marriage. Therefore, the river with trees bearing fruit along its banks in Ezekiel's prophecy is not the same phenomenon that John describes in the New Jerusalem. Ezekiel's vision of a restored Jerusalem in the earthly kingdom of God may foreshadow or serve as a pattern of the New Jerusalem in the eternal kingdom of heaven as described by John in Revelation. But the two prophets are clearly describing two different kingdoms: one on the restored earth—with marriage, reproduction, and an abundance of food from fruit-bearing trees, where some level of mortality and even sin exists; the other in the eternal new heavens and new earth.

G. K. Beale, a prominent amillennial scholar, makes the same critical mistake as does Hoekema by confusing the two orders of being and messianic prophecies of a restored Genesis creation with the eternal kingdom. In his commentary on Revelation, instead of applying the Old Testament messianic prophecies of Isaiah and Ezekiel to the 1,000-year earthly kingdom of Christ, he consistently applies them to the new heavens and new earth. He writes:

Like Ezek. 40:1-2 [describing the restored Jerusalem and earth], Rev. 21:10 [describing the New Jerusalem] involves the vision of the future temple. What Ezekiel saw was to happen in the future, John also saw as still to happen in the future. The two prophets' visions prophesy the same reality of the final, permanent establishment of God's presence with his people.[4]

Beale takes Ezekiel's prophecies that describe a restoration of the earthly Jerusalem and the restored Genesis creation and applies them to John's vision of the heavenly Jerusalem; he asserts that they are foretelling of the same reality despite the fact that Ezekiel's messianic prophecies describe an Edenic paradise populated by restored Adamic creatures being given in marriage, having children, and enjoying an abundant life on this current earth while John describes the eternal home of the immortal children of God. Beale, as many amillennialists, fails to understand and maintain the distinction between the two orders of being. As a result, he confuses our promised earthly inheritance with our promised heavenly inheritance.

Ezekiel has a vision of the restored earthly Jerusalem on a restored earth, but in Revelation 21, John has a vision of the New Jerusalem on the new

---

[4] G. K. Beale, *The Book of Revelation* (Grand Rapids: Eerdmans, 1999), 1065.

heavens and new earth. These are two very different kingdoms because they are adapted for two different orders of being. The prediction of a restored earth and restored Jerusalem described by Isaiah, Ezekiel, and other prophets may serve as a prototype foreshadowing our heavenly existence, but that only means there needs to be a real restoration of *this earth* for it to be a true prototype of the New Jerusalem in heaven.

The Scriptures contain numerous examples of future events being patterned after a prior event or phenomena. Our exodus from being slaves in Satan's dominion of darkness and being brought into Christ's kingdom is patterned after Israel's exodus from slavery in Egypt and entrance into the Promised Land. It is no surprise that the New Jerusalem on the new earth is patterned after the restored Jerusalem on the restored Genesis earth.

In short, amillennialists are confusing not only the two orders of being but the two kingdoms of the Son and the Father, as well. The Son's messianic kingdom foreseen by the Old Testament prophets is for the restored earthly Jerusalem in the restored nation of Israel on a restored Genesis earth made up of restored humanity operating according to the Adamic order of being; whereas John is describing what takes place after the current Genesis creation has "passed away" and then describes the eternal "new heaven and new earth" and the "New Jerusalem" inhabited by the "sons of God" with a new kind of transformed, immortal body.

According to the Old Testament prophets, the messianic kingdom on this earth is, by definition, a restoration of the Adamic order of being. It is the Son's restored Genesis kingdom. The new heavens and new earth, on the other hand, are, by definition, a new home for the new order of being as immortal children of God in the Father's eternal kingdom.

Renovated or Annihilated?

One issue that needs clarification concerns the nature of the future new heavens and new earth that serve as the eternal home of the children of God (2 Peter 3:13 and Rev. 21:1). Are the current Genesis heavens and earth annihilated by fire and *replaced* with a totally new heavens and earth on the last day, or is Peter describing a fire at Christ's second coming that only burns the surface of the earth whereby this creation is merely *renovated or restored* with the resurrected immortal saints experiencing eternal life on this renewed planet? Scholars differ on the answer. Moreover, one's position on this subject does not necessarily follow a particular eschatology. There are scholars in all three camps that believe either of the above.

For example, Wayne Grudem, a premillennialist, states:

> [E]ven 2 Peter 3:10, which speaks of the elements dissolving and the earth and the works on it being burned up, may not be speaking of the earth as a planet but rather the surface things on the earth (that is, much of the

ground and the things on the ground). . . . God will not completely destroy the physical world . . . but rather he will perfect the entire creation.[5]

In contrast, in his commentary on Revelation, the late John Walvoord, another premillennial scholar, writes that John is describing the annihilation of this current Genesis creation:

> The new heaven and new earth presented here are evidently not simply the old heaven and earth renovated, but an act of new creation. . . . There is remarkably little revealed in the Bible concerning the character of the new heaven and new earth, but it is evidently quite different from their present form of existence.[6]

The answer, however, can have major eschatological implications. For example, having a real earth that is merely renovated or restored allows many amillennialists like Hoekema and Beale to try to fit many of the Old Testament prophecies about an earthly paradise into the context of this renewed earth. We have no further need, therefore, for a 1,000-year earthly messianic kingdom before the heavenly kingdom because heaven is essentially a restored earthly kingdom. Thus, Old Testament prophecies, such as Isaiah 65 and Ezekiel 37, are merely poetic descriptions of this future restored and eternal earth. In effect, the new heavens and new earth become the messianic kingdom on a restored earth.

But this approach fails because even if these prophecies are figurative metaphors, they do not figuratively describe heaven or the eternal life of believers. How can a description of marriage, reproduction, and even mortality in the messianic kingdom describe a renewed earth when none of these human experiences will exist in the supposed renovated earth? These Old Testament prophecies are talking about real Adamic marriages with real children. That is not a figurative picture of heaven. Angels do not marry and reproduce, and neither will we as children of God in the "new heavens and new earth." If what some amillennialists say is true, then these messianic prophecies would be highly inaccurate predictions of what the new heavens and new earth are going to be like.

As to whether we as the children of God are destined for a renovated earth or an entirely new earth, it seems to me that John is describing the utter annihilation of this Genesis creation when he says, "From his presence earth and sky fled away and no place was found for them" (Rev. 20:11). If, on the last day, the existing cosmos has no place in space and time and literally ceases to have a presence, then the children of God must be destined

---

[5] Wayne Grudem, *Systematic Theology* (Grand Rapids: Zondervan, 1994), 1161.
[6] John F. Walvoord, *The Revelation of Jesus Christ* (Chicago: Moody Press, 1966), 311.

for a totally new cosmos of an unknown nature to replace the one completely destroyed.

As Peter says, God created this Genesis creation by his word (*ex nihilo*), and he will simply say the word again and it will cease to exist (2 Peter 3:10–13). Then by his word that can create, destroy, and create anew, he will create a new heavens and new earth (*ex nihilo*) adapted for God's children. A new order of being necessitates a totally new creation.

There will certainly be continuity with this Genesis creation given that the eternal kingdom will be new versions of the current heavens and earth. And it will be a real place for real resurrected beings in real bodies. Paul says that the current Genesis creation is groaning to transcend its current "bondage to decay" for it to somehow become a part of the eternal kingdom (Rom. 8:18–23).

How this all plays out in the end remains a mystery at this time. I am not sure that a verbal or pictorial description of our future home would be helpful at this time anyway, which is why Revelation 21 and 22 relate an almost indescribable New Jerusalem that defies the laws of gravity and physics. The nature of the new heavens and new earth remains a mystery at this time just as the nature of our transformed bodies remains a mystery.

My position on this issue is that the current Genesis creation is entirely destroyed or annihilated and the new heavens and new earth are just that—a totally new creation (*ex nihilo*) that *replaces* the one completely destroyed by fire. It should be noted, however, that one can hold to the renovated view of the new heavens and new earth and still accept the postrestorational view of eschatology and the kingdom of God proposed in this book. Resolving this issue is important, but it is not essential.

Summary

To the apostles and all other believers, Christ revealed something profoundly new. Instead of establishing a method of redemption for humanity that would return fallen mankind to the Garden of Eden where we would pick back up where we started, God is creating a whole new kind of being—a child of God whose ultimate destiny is the eternal kingdom of heaven. In fact, the current Adamic natural body of flesh and blood will have to be transformed into an immortal spiritual body in order to be taken to its home on the new earth.

But because salvation and redemption include a restoration of what it means to be human, it would be truly disappointing if there were not a major restoration of the Adamic order of being and this Genesis creation before this Adamic creation is destroyed and we move on to heaven. Currently, the salvation of the Adamic order of being is very limited because of the curse that remains on the earth, the fallen nature of mankind, and the work and influence of Satan. Many of our human aspirations go unfulfilled.

At times the human experience can be quite miserable. I am currently experiencing a short lifetime of happiness with my wife. But before long, we both will most likely experience old age, sickness, and death. And we continue to live in a dysfunctional and mismanaged world plagued by selfishness and strife. Could it be that God's plan of redemption includes an almost complete reversal of the curse and a restoration of the Adamic order of being before we are taken to the new creation in heaven—a world ruled by its divine Creator who establishes a kingdom on this earth characterized by peace, justice, righteousness, and prosperity?

If amillennialists are right and there is no 1,000-year restoration before the eternal kingdom, then Adam and Eve and their descendants will only be remembered in the annals of eternal history as having lived a largely tragic life. Satan would have triumphed by stealing from the Creator what was rightfully his to delight in and enjoy—a creation that God originally called very good (Gen. 1:31). This creation will never be restored to its intended glory as a tribute to the glory of God.

But wouldn't it be wonderful if God's plan of redemption included the removal of Satan, a suspension of the curse, and a regeneration of his glorious Genesis creation for his resurrected people to enjoy for a thousand years? The Old and New Testament vision of an earthly messianic kingdom would be just the solution for a restoration of the Adamic order of being— the human experience as it was intended to be in all its glory—before this earth is destroyed and the new order of being is ushered in with the new heavens and new earth. It is only fitting that salvation includes a return to the Garden of Eden where we rediscover what humanity—and this creation—could have been like had Adam and Eve not sinned. Our Creator loves his original creation that was "very good" and will once again delight in the glory of the human experience on this restored Genesis earth. The millennial reign of Christ will be an age of righteous humanity. Such a restoration of God's original creation would indeed bring great glory to God.

The Father's heavenly kingdom, on the other hand, is not for a renewed humanity on a renewed Genesis earth—that is the purpose of the 1,000-year restoration. The heavenly kingdom is for a new kind of being with a new kind of body in a new heavens and new earth in which we are immortal sons of God in the image of Christ. Our glorified bodies in this new creation will bring a whole new glory to God.

The key to understanding the kingdom of God and developing a coherent biblical theology is discerning the two orders of being and their defining characteristics and corresponding kingdoms as revealed in the Scriptures. The Son's kingdom is for restored humanity on a restored earth, and the Father's kingdom is for the new order of being as the children of God in his eternal kingdom—the new heavens and new earth. The regenerated *natural* body of the first resurrection is destined for a restored natural earth, and the transformed *spiritual* body at the final resurrection is destined for the new heavens and new earth.

The fact that we, as children of God, are not given in marriage in the eternal age to come is not some mere footnote of our existence in heaven. It is not even a new chapter of our current existence. Rather, it is a whole new book, because being a child of God reflects a fundamental change in the very architecture of our being. The characters—persons or spirits—will not change, but we will inhabit a distinctly new kind of body. As an acorn grows into a mighty oak tree, we will have transformed bodies with a completely different architecture, structure, form, and function. Being children of God constitutes a new order of being, which is why John says that the nature of our glorified bodies remains a complete mystery at this time.

The very architecture of our beings will change because we are no longer going to be male and female in the image of the triune God. Instead, we are going to be in the image of the Son of God as the second person of the Trinity. This will represent a very different relationship with God and with our fellow children of God in heaven. Our family in heaven will be fundamentally different from our family on earth that is composed of male and female siblings, spouses, children, parents, grandparents, grandchildren, and male and female neighbors. None of these relationships will exist in heaven. Once the book is closed on this Genesis creation, the sons of God will inhabit a new heavens and new earth that have yet to be created—a new kind of habitat for a new kind of body.

To understand prophetic Scripture, it is imperative to maintain the two distinct orders of being and their defining characteristics. By doing so one can easily determine that Scriptures are describing two different kingdoms of God—one on the earth and one in heaven.

With this method of interpreting and organizing the Scriptures, let's now begin our journey through the Scriptures to determine the validity of postrestorationalism as the truth about the kingdom of God on earth and in heaven. Premillennialists have everything to gain and nothing to lose by adopting postrestorationalism, for it fully affirms the Old Testament vision of the messianic kingdom on this earth before we inherit the Father's eternal kingdom. Likewise, amillennialists and postmillennialists have nothing to lose, for they already believe Christ comes on the last day to rapture the saints, and everything to gain—such as the Son's messianic kingdom on this earth when this Genesis creation is restored to its rightful Creator and God.

2

On the Road to Emmaus

Based on their reading of numerous Old Testament messianic prophecies, John the Baptist and the disciples believed the restoration, or the messianic kingdom, would begin in their lifetimes, with Jesus the Messiah ushering in the earthly reign:

> But you, O Bethlehem Ephrathah, who are too little to be among the clans of Judah, from you shall come forth for me *one who is to be ruler in Israel, whose origin is from of old, from ancient days*. . . . And he shall stand and shepherd his flock in the strength of the LORD, in the majesty of the name of the LORD his God. And they shall dwell secure, for now he shall be great to the ends of the earth. And he shall be their peace. (Mic. 5:2–5)

They were expecting an earthly ruler who would use God's divine strength to shepherd his people into a kingdom of peace and security that would be extended to the ends of the earth.

Also, the following prophecy in Isaiah declares:

> For to us a child is born, to us a son is given; and the government shall be upon his shoulder, and his name shall be called Wonderful Counselor, Mighty God, Everlasting Father, Prince of Peace. Of the increase of his government and of *peace* there will be no end, on the throne of David and over his kingdom, to establish it and to uphold it with *justice* and with *righteousness* from this time forth and forevermore. The zeal of the LORD of hosts will do this. (Isa. 9:6–7)

These prophecies begin with the birth of Christ who as an adult would sit on the throne of David and then establish the messianic kingdom. The Christ, as Mighty God, would govern this world in such a manner that it would be characterized by peace, justice, and righteousness.

By reading these verses, it is understandable why John the Baptist and the disciples expected this Messiah from Nazareth to overthrow the tyrannical Roman government and establish God's government over this rebellious world in their lifetimes. Instead, the Romans unjustly and violently crucified Christ. Even after he was resurrected, instead of then establishing his messianic kingdom, he ascended back to his Father in heaven, leaving these prophecies unfulfilled.

One of the saddest events in the New Testament occurred when John the Baptist became so confused over the messianic prophecies due to his imprisonment by King Herod that he began to have doubts that Jesus was the Christ. John baptized Christ and had the extraordinary experience of hearing God the Father's voice from heaven saying, "This is my beloved Son, with whom I am well pleased" (Matt. 3:17). As Jesus was coming up out of the water, John saw heaven opened: "And he saw the Spirit of God descending like a dove and coming to rest on him" (Matt. 3:16). This was a fulfillment of the prophecy from Isaiah:

> There shall come forth a shoot from the stump of Jesse, and a branch from his roots shall bear fruit. And *the Spirit of the* LORD *shall rest upon him*, the Spirit of *wisdom and understanding*, the Spirit of counsel and might, the Spirit of knowledge and the fear of the LORD. And his delight shall be in the fear of the LORD. He shall not judge by what his eyes see, or decide disputes by what his ears hear, but with *righteousness* he shall judge the poor, and decide with *equity* for the meek of the earth; and he shall strike the earth with the rod of his mouth, and with the breath of his lips *he shall kill the wicked.* (Isa. 11:1–4)

This prophecy indicated to John the Baptist that the Christ, on whom the Spirit of the Lord had rested, had come to eliminate the wicked and then judge and rule the world with wisdom, understanding, equity, and righteousness. And Herod was surely among the wicked fools who, along with the tyrannical Romans, continued to oppress the poor and the righteous.

At the beginning of his public ministry, in the synagogue in Nazareth, Jesus read from Isaiah: "The Spirit of the Lord is upon me, because he has anointed me to proclaim good news to the poor. He has sent me to *proclaim liberty to the captives* and recovering of sight to the blind, *to set at liberty those who are oppressed*, to proclaim the year of the Lord's favor" (Luke 4:18–19). Yet, while Christ was demonstrating incredible power through amazing miracles such as healing the blind, John the Baptist remained imprisoned by a political tyrant ruling with only earthly powers. Where was the "liberty to the captives" that went along with this miraculous power? Where was the messianic kingdom predicted by the prophets?

Perplexed and despondent as he remained imprisoned, John the Baptist eventually sent his disciples to inquire of Jesus: "Are you the one who is to come, or shall we look for another?" Jesus answered John's disciples by saying, "Go and tell John what you hear and see: the blind receive their sight and the lame walk, lepers are cleansed and the deaf hear, and the dead are raised up, and the poor have good news preached to them" (Matt. 11:3–5).

This was reassuring, but if Jesus was the Messiah, then why didn't he exercise his authority and liberate John from prison? Instead, during Herod's birthday party, John was beheaded and his head presented to Herod's illegitimate wife on a platter. It was this kind of gruesome tyranny that the Messiah was supposed to put an end to.

The Old Testament prophets clearly taught that the messianic rule would have enormous implications on this earth. John the Baptist knew these prophecies well, and he rightfully expected their fulfillment from the Messiah he baptized. Jesus' answer to John was somewhat reassuring, but it did not seem to help John overcome his eschatological confusion. He simply could not connect all the dots and make sense out of these prophecies in relation to the events happening to him. All these prophecies seemed fulfilled in Jesus of Nazareth—except the part where he would "bring forth justice to the nations" starting with "liberty to the captives." Both the Roman rule and King Herod's imprisonment of John for criticizing his immorality were surely unjust. So where was the prophesied messianic reign of justice?

John the Baptist was not the only one confused. The disciples were also familiar with Old Testament prophecies, such as those found in Jeremiah:

> The word that came to Jeremiah from the LORD: . . . "For behold, days are coming, declares the LORD, when I will restore the fortunes of my people, . . . I will bring them back to the land that I gave to their fathers, and they shall take possession of it. . . . I will break his yoke from off your neck, and I will burst your bonds, and *foreigners shall no more make a servant of him.* . . . I will fulfill the promise I made to the house of Israel and the house of Judah. In those days and at that time I will cause a righteous Branch to spring up for David, and *he shall execute justice and righteousness in the land.* In those days Judah will be saved and *Jerusalem will dwell securely.* And this is the name by which it will be called: 'The LORD is our righteousness.'" (Jer. 30:1, 3, 8–9; 33:14–16)

The disciples were so convinced that Jesus, the righteous Branch of David, was going to break the bonds of the foreign Roman yoke, liberate Jerusalem, and establish the messianic kingdom described by the prophets, they made fools of themselves by jockeying for power in the anticipated reign of Christ (cf. Luke 9:46). During the Last Supper, they also disputed "which of them was to be regarded as the greatest" in the impending reign of Christ (Luke 22:24).

Perhaps the most embarrassing episode illustrating their misunderstanding of the timing of Jesus' messianic reign is recorded by Matthew:

Then the mother of the sons of Zebedee came up to him with her sons, and kneeling before him she asked him for something. And he said to her, "What do you want?" She said to him, "Say that these two sons of mine are to sit, one at your right hand and one at your left, in your kingdom." Jesus answered, "You do not know what you are asking. Are you able to drink the cup that I am to drink?" They said to him, "We are able." He said to them, "You will drink my cup, but to sit at my right hand and at my left is not mine to grant, but it is for those for whom it has been prepared by my Father." And when the ten heard it, they were indignant at the two brothers. But Jesus called them to him and said, "You know that the rulers of the Gentiles lord it over them, and their great ones exercise authority over them. It shall not be so among you. But whoever would be great among you must be your servant, and whoever would be first among you must be your slave, even as the Son of Man came not to be served but to serve, and to give his life as a ransom for many." (Matt. 20:20–28)

The mother of James and John was looking forward to her sons ruling with Christ in his kingdom with all the implied power, prestige, and wealth that came with positions of authority in a worldly empire. Ironically, little did she know that for her sons to be on his right and left side in the circumstances at that time would have placed them on the two crosses flanking Christ's in the impending crucifixion! Jesus was focused on the crucifixion and returning to heaven; the disciples were focused on Christ establishing his earthly kingdom and having positions of prominence in his upcoming reign. The crucifixion was not part of their plan.

When these two disciples made fools of themselves by sending their mother to secure high positions of authority in the anticipated messianic reign, Christ gently rebuked them for their lust for power and dominance. But at the same time, he amazingly affirmed the legitimacy of the positions they were requesting. There will indeed be positions of authority and leadership in the restoration, but those positions will be decided by the Father: "To sit at my right hand and at my left is not mine to grant, but it is for those for whom it has been prepared by my Father." In effect, rather than telling the mother that the request itself was wrong or senseless, Christ answered by saying that even though their motives were wrong and their timing was off, they were simply asking the wrong person for positions of authority in the anticipated messianic kingdom.

The disciples believed they had found the true son of David, the Messiah. They had already seen astonishing displays of his supernatural power, beyond anything that even Elijah had done, and they were ready for Jesus to reveal himself in power. Luke says that Jesus had to rebuke them for wanting him to act as Elijah did toward the false priests of Baal:

When the days drew near for him to be taken up, he set his face to go to Jerusalem. And he sent messengers ahead of him, who went and entered a village of the Samaritans, to make preparations for him. But the people did not receive him, because his face was set toward Jerusalem. And when his disciples James and John saw it, they said, "Lord, do you want us to tell fire to come down from heaven and consume them?" But he turned and rebuked them. And they went on to another village. (Luke 9:51–56)

The disciples were even willing to use the sword to prevent Jesus from being arrested:

Jesus said to him, "Friend, do what you came to do." Then they came up and laid hands on Jesus and seized him. And behold, one of those who were with Jesus stretched out his hand and drew his sword and struck the servant of the high priest and cut off his ear. Then Jesus said to him, "Put your sword back into its place. For all who take the sword will perish by the sword. Do you think that I cannot appeal to my Father, and he will at once send me more than twelve legions of angels?" (Matt. 26:50–53)

Jesus claimed to have an almost unbelievable amount of supernatural angelic power at his disposal. In 2 Kings 19:35 we read how a single angel of the Lord struck down 185,000 of the Assyrians who were threatening King Hezekiah of Judah. Twelve legions of angels are twelve thousand in number. If you do the math, that is enough angelic power to kill more than two billion soldiers. But he chose not to ask his Father for protection at his arrest.

The disciples did not understand that Christ must be crucified before he could enter into his glory even though he had repeatedly informed them of this fact: "The Son of Man will be delivered over to the chief priests and scribes, and they will condemn him to death and deliver him over to the Gentiles to be mocked and flogged and crucified, and he will be raised on the third day" (Matt. 20:18–19).

On the road to Emmaus after the resurrection, Jesus rebuked two men who were in the company of the twelve disciples and were completely bewildered by the events that had just transpired concerning this son of David: "And he said to them, 'O foolish ones, and slow of heart to believe all that the prophets have spoken! Was it not necessary that the Christ should suffer these things and enter into his glory?' And beginning with Moses and all the Prophets, he interpreted to them in all the Scriptures the things concerning himself" (Luke 24:25–27).

When these two men returned to Jerusalem and rejoined eleven of the disciples, Jesus appeared to them and said:

"These are my words that I spoke to you while I was still with you, that everything written about me in the Law of Moses and the Prophets and the Psalms must be fulfilled." Then he opened their minds to understand the Scriptures, and said to them, "Thus it is written, that the Christ should suffer and on the third day rise from the dead, and that repentance and forgiveness of sins should be proclaimed in his name to all nations, beginning from Jerusalem." (Luke 24:44–47)

They finally understood that Christ must first be crucified for our sins before he (and his repentant and forgiven followers) could "enter into his glory." But that did not end their expectation for his glorious messianic kingdom on this earth.

Even after Jesus was resurrected, the disciples were still confused about when Christ was going to begin his reign over this world. Maybe they had missed the part about the Messiah being crucified for their sins, but since he had been resurrected in power, why not establish his glorious messianic kingdom now? With his resurrection, he was invincible to the Romans.

It is important to note that they were not anticipating the ascension any more than they had anticipated the crucifixion, even though Jesus had repeatedly forewarned them of his imminent departure back to his Father in heaven: "Jesus said to her [Mary Magdalene], 'Do not cling to me, for I have not yet ascended to the Father; but go to my brothers and say to them, 'I am ascending to my Father and your Father, to my God and your God'" (John 20:17).

Christ had promised the Holy Spirit's coming, and the disciples knew from Old Testament prophecies that there was a direct correlation between the outpouring of the Holy Spirit and the start of the messianic kingdom (Isa. 32:14–16; 44:3; 59:21; Ezek. 36:24–28; 37:14; 39:25–29). Therefore, with the impending outpouring of the Holy Spirit with all its messianic implications, the disciples asked Jesus if he would now begin his reign: "So when they had come together, they asked him, 'Lord, will you at this time restore the kingdom to Israel?' He said to them, 'It is not for you to know times or seasons that the Father has fixed by his own authority'" (Acts 1:6–7). This was the last reported question any human being asked Christ before he returned to heaven.

Notice that Jesus did not rebuke them for misunderstanding the Scriptures or being slow to understand. Instead, Jesus affirmed there would be a restoration, but it was not for them to know the time. He said that the Father has set the time when it will occur, just as the Father will determine who will have positions of authority in his messianic kingdom. It is not a question of *if* the restoration occurs, but *when*.

Some amillennial theologians, like N. T. Wright, assert that the disciples' question was absurd, like asking, "How many hours are there in a mile?"[1] Of course there is no Jewish restoration or earthly messianic kingdom, they declare, for Christ had foretold of the destruction of the temple and the rejection of the unbelieving Jews.

But there is no indication in Jesus' answer that he considered their question about the timing of the messianic kingdom absurd. The disciples knew the multitude of Old Testament prophecies predicting an earthly messianic kingdom emanating from the nation of Israel. They believed he was the long-awaited Messiah, and Jesus had even promised them positions of authority in his earthly kingdom. They had every right to ask when his messianic kingdom would come about. He was the Messiah, after all, and there were many prophecies about his reign that remained unfulfilled.

In the meantime, Christ instructed them to be evangelists, preaching throughout the world that he was the Messiah: "'But you will receive power when the Holy Spirit has come upon you, and you will be my witnesses in Jerusalem and in all Judea and Samaria, and to the end of the earth.' And when he had said these things, as they were looking on, he was lifted up, and a cloud took him out of their sight" (Acts 1:8–9). The Messiah's sudden departure and ascension to heaven must have left the disciples utterly bewildered. The Messiah was supposed to liberate Israel, restore the nation to glory, and even rule the world—and now, he is gone! He left this world without overthrowing the tyrannical Roman Empire and establishing his messianic kingdom!

Christ informed them that there will be a restoration at a time set by his Father, but until then they should try and convince the world that he was indeed the Messiah, who died for their sins, was resurrected, ascended to heaven, and would one day rule the world when the Father says the time is right. But it would take the Holy Spirit to convince anyone of this truth, for a crucified Messiah was a stumbling block to the Jews, who expected the Messiah to rule the world with the "government on his shoulders," and folly to the Gentiles, who thought a true king would not allow himself to be conquered and arrested, much less crucified.

Even after the coming of the Holy Spirit at Pentecost, the disciples still expected a restoration as foretold by the prophets. In one of his earliest sermons to a crowd of Jews, Peter said:

And now, brothers, I know that you acted in ignorance, as did also your rulers. But what God foretold by the mouth of all the prophets, that his Christ would suffer, he thus fulfilled. Repent therefore, and turn again, that your sins may be blotted out, that times of refreshing may come from the

---

[1] N. T. Wright, *Simply Christian* (New York: HarperSanFrancisco, 2006), 122.

presence of the Lord, and that he may send the Christ appointed for you, Jesus, whom heaven must receive until the time for restoring all the things about which God spoke by the mouth of his holy prophets long ago. (Acts 3:17–21)

Peter was associating the restoration with the time when the Jews would finally repent and accept Jesus as their Messiah. They still believed there would be a time for restoring all things as foretold by the holy prophets.

Paul, too, seemed to make this connection. In a long analysis of why the Jews had largely rejected their Messiah and the Gentiles had been grafted in as believers in the Jewish Messiah, Paul said:

Lest you be wise in your own conceits, I want you to understand this mystery, brothers: a partial hardening has come upon Israel, until the fullness of the Gentiles has come in. And in this way all Israel will be saved, as it is written, "The Deliverer will come from Zion, he will banish ungodliness from Jacob; and this will be my covenant with them when I take away their sins." (Rom. 11:25–27)

Volumes have been written speculating what Paul meant in these verses. Did he believe in a future restoration tied to the Jews coming to repentance, as did Peter and the other disciples?

One of the most remarkable prophecies that addresses this issue is found in Micah, foretelling a partial hardening of the Jews before they eventually repent and believe, which then ushers in the messianic kingdom:

But you, O Bethlehem Ephrathah, who are too little to be among the clans of Judah, from you shall come forth for me one who is to be *ruler in Israel*, whose origin is from of old, from ancient days. Therefore he shall give them up [partial hardening] until the time when she who is in labor has given birth; then the rest of his brothers shall return to the people of Israel [the Gentiles come in]. And he [Christ] shall stand [exercise his reign] and shepherd his flock in the strength of the LORD, in the majesty of the name of the LORD his God [the Father, who puts all Christ's enemies under his feet]. And they [Israel and the kingdoms of the world] shall dwell secure, for now he shall be great to the ends of the earth. And he shall be their peace [the worldwide dominion of the Messiah]. (Mic. 5:2–5)

Israel is in a state of pregnancy until the full number of Gentiles comes in. Then she will go into labor and "birth" the believing Jews. According to Micah, this leads to the restoration, when Christ shall stand and exercise his reign to the ends of the earth.

Notice that the prophecy clearly states that he will be ruler in Israel. This is similar to Paul's statement, "The Deliverer will come from Zion, he will banish ungodliness from Jacob." But notice that Micah, as does Romans, says that this will not happen right away: "Therefore *he shall give them up* until the time when she who is in labor has given birth; then the rest of his brothers shall return to the people of Israel" (Mic. 5:3). This corresponds with Paul's long discourse in Romans, describing how Israel is experiencing a hardening "until the fullness of the Gentiles has come in" (Rom. 11:25).

Also notice what Micah says will happen to Israel right after the nation's labor is complete: "And he shall stand and shepherd his flock in the strength of the LORD, in the majesty of the name of the LORD his God. And *they shall dwell secure, for now he shall be great to the ends of the earth. And he shall be their peace*" (Mic. 5:4–5). This is a description of the earthly restoration, where the Christ, born in Bethlehem, will be a "ruler in Israel," and "they shall dwell secure," and his greatness will reach "to the ends of the earth." This is a reference to the Son's messianic kingdom when he restores the entire earth to his dominion. This is in line with Peter's early sermons after Pentecost.

Although Paul did not elaborate in his description of what will happen when the Jews eventually repent and are grafted back in as believers, it is clear from Old Testament prophecies, such as the previous verses in Micah, that this sets in motion the events leading up to the establishment of the messianic kingdom on earth—"They shall dwell secure, for now he shall be great to the ends of the earth. And he shall be their peace." Israel may have been cut off in AD 70 with the destruction of the temple, but Micah, Peter, and Paul foresaw a time when they will repent and become believers in the Messiah, like the Gentiles, resulting in major ramifications on this earth. This great revival among the Jews will mark the time and season when the kingdom of Israel and all other kingdoms of the world are restored to the rightful God of this world, Jesus Christ.

The Messiah has always come from Zion. Salvation is from the Jews. And according to Paul, "The Deliverer will come from Zion" has two parts. The first part required an incarnation and crucifixion (to deliver us from our sins and the wrath of God) and a resurrection (to deliver us from spiritual death). This delivers us from Satan's dominion of darkness and transfers us into the Son's kingdom. But the Deliverer returned to heaven, and we remain in this evil world with Satan as the god of this world.

Paul foresaw a day when the Jews accept their Messiah, which leads to the second part, when the Messiah from Zion delivers this world from Satan and the tyranny of evil; when righteousness will become the order of the day—"He will banish ungodliness from Jacob." The Messiah will then establish his kingdom and finally deliver this world from evil. Until then, the Messiah's mission of deliverance is incomplete. But it is only a matter of time when the restoration will come about. God the Father has staked his reputation on the fact that he will one day restore this Genesis creation to his ascended Son: "Sit at my right hand, until I [the Father] put your enemies under your feet" (Matt. 22:44). Someday the Father, on a day that he has set, will put Christ's enemies under Christ's feet and establish his Son's long-awaited messianic kingdom on this earth.

Finally, we have to consider the difficult book of Revelation, which affirms a Great Tribulation and then Christ's millennial earthly kingdom *before* the eternal new heavens and new earth:

> And they sang a new song, saying, "Worthy are you to take the scroll and to open its seals, for you were slain, and by your blood you ransomed people for God from every tribe and language and people and nation, and *you have made them a kingdom* and priests to our God, and *they shall reign on the earth.*" (Rev. 5:9–10)

Now that the Christ has been crucified and resurrected, and has ascended into heaven, there still will be a future earthly kingdom made up of God's ransomed people from all nations. In line with Micah and other prophets, John is distinctly referencing God's people inheriting a kingdom that is "on the earth" before the saints inherit the new heavens and new earth after this earth disappears (Rev. 20:11).

Consider one of the most famous prophecies of all, in Revelation 20, where John describes what happens after the Great Tribulation, when Satan is bound and imprisoned and the "Deliverer from Zion" completes his mission of establishing his messianic kingdom on this earth. John describes a thousand years of Christ's earthly reign *before* the beginning of the new heavens and new earth:

> They [the martyred saints and the ransomed people of God from all nations] came to life and *reigned with Christ for a thousand years* [on the earth]. The rest of the dead did not come to life until the thousand years were ended. This is the first resurrection. Blessed and holy is the one who shares in the first resurrection! Over such the second death has no power, but they will be priests of God and of Christ, and *they will reign with him for a thousand years.* (vv. 4–6)

Christ will be King of the world. And this earthly kingdom of the Messiah will last for a thousand years. The subjects of the kingdom will be made up of some unbelievers that survive the Tribulation, but, most important, as John previously prophesied, it will include the people of God who have been ransomed from "every tribe and language and people and nation" through the ages. Somehow, through the first resurrection, all God's people, from Abel to the last one martyred in the Great Tribulation, will come to life in order to inherit Christ's earthly 1,000-year messianic kingdom.

This Scripture corresponds to Daniel's prediction of what will happen after the Antichrist's dominion is taken away and the earthly kingdom will be given to the saints, the ransomed people of God from all nations:

> Until the Ancient of Days came [God the Father], and judgment was given for the saints of the Most High, and *the time came when the saints possessed the kingdom.* . . . But the court shall sit in judgment, and his [Satan and the Antichrist's] dominion shall be taken away, to be consumed and destroyed to the end. And the kingdom and the dominion and the greatness of the kingdoms under the whole heaven shall be given to the people of the saints of the Most High. (Daniel 7:22, 26–27)

Daniel also envisioned a worldwide kingdom on this earth, possessed by all God's saints, occurring after the Great Tribulation comes to an end.

The Old Testament contains numerous messianic prophecies that describe the earthly reign of the Messiah. John the Baptist expected it, as did the disciples. Immediately before ascending to heaven, Christ affirmed that the kingdom would be restored to Israel at a time set by the Father. Both Peter and Paul associate the restoration with the unknown time when the Jews repent en masse and accept their Messiah. This follows the sequence of events found in Micah 5:3–5. After the predetermined number of Gentiles are saved and the Jews are grafted back in as believers, then Christ will "stand and shepherd his flock. . . . And they shall dwell secure, for now he shall be great to the ends of the earth." John further wrote that the Messiah's earthly kingdom will last a thousand years. And John's prophecies coincide with those of Daniel that predict a time of great tribulation followed by a time when the saints ransomed from all nations possess the Son's earthly messianic kingdom after Satan's dominion is taken away.

Reading the Old and New Testaments, it becomes apparent that the earthly messianic kingdom is part of the promised inheritance of the saints. The Old Testament contains a large number of messianic prophecies that describe the Messiah's kingdom. Comparatively, the New Testament may not reveal much about the earthly messianic kingdom, but the few references that do appear can easily be linked to the information found in the Old Testament.

For example, in the Beatitudes, Christ says that the meek are blessed and that "they shall inherit the earth" (Matt. 5:5). This is probably a reference to Psalm 37 that states, "For the evildoers shall be cut off, but those who wait for the LORD shall inherit the land. In just a little while, the wicked will be no more; though you look carefully at his place, he will not be there. But the meek shall inherit the land and delight themselves in abundant peace" (Ps. 37:9–11). Christ was apparently alluding to this Old Testament messianic prophecy when he said the meek shall inherit the earth during a time of abundant peace and righteousness. If so, this would be an affirmation by

Jesus that the saints will inherit an earthly kingdom before the heavenly kingdom.

New Testament Emphasis on the Heavenly Kingdom

In the same sermon in which Christ informs us that the meek shall inherit the earth, he tells us that we will also inherit the kingdom of heaven: "Blessed are the poor in spirit, for theirs is the *kingdom of heaven*" (Matt. 5:3). In fact, the New Testament is almost entirely focused on the saints as God's children inheriting the Father's heavenly kingdom. It is truly heaven-centric. For example, Peter preached about the restoration only in his first few outdoor sermons recorded in Acts. In his epistles, he focused exclusively on the children of God inheriting the heavenly kingdom. In his first epistle, Peter said, "He [God] has caused us to be born again to a living hope through the resurrection of Jesus Christ from the dead, to an inheritance that is imperishable, undefiled, and unfading, kept in heaven for you, who by God's power are being guarded through faith for a salvation ready to be revealed in the last time" (1 Peter 1:3–5). Peter no longer was focusing on our inheritance on this earth before our inheritance in heaven. Instead, he only wrote of the hope for God's children of an imperishable inheritance kept in heaven to be revealed on the last day.

Christ and the New Testament authors described the heavenly kingdom as God the Father's kingdom: "In my Father's house are many rooms. If it were not so, would I have told you that I go to prepare a place for you? And if I go and prepare a place for you, I will come again and will take you to myself, that where I am you may be also (John 14:2–3).

Christ informed the disciples that he was about to return to heaven—where he came from before the incarnation—but promised that he "will come again" to take us from this earth *to heaven* in order to join him and his Father in the many rooms in heaven! The second coming is directly associated with our receiving our eternal inheritance of the Father's heavenly kingdom—not the Son's earthly messianic kingdom.

Paul, too, was so focused on heaven that the only time recorded that he directly broached the subject of an earthly kingdom is in Romans 11, and even here, it is implicit and not explicit. Paul is actually being very stealthy about what happens when the Jews are grafted back in. He touches on the subject and quickly moves on to other matters. In chapter 11, "The Stealthy Restoration," we will explore why Paul was purposely obscure about the earthly messianic kingdom and focused almost exclusively on the Father's kingdom of heaven.

Peter even wrote that the current Genesis earth is destroyed at the second coming when the saints inherit the new heavens and new earth:

But the day of the Lord will come like a thief, and then the heavens will pass away with a roar, and the heavenly bodies will be burned up and dissolved, and the earth and the works that are done on it will be exposed. Since all these things are thus to be dissolved, what sort of people ought you to be in lives of holiness and godliness waiting for and hastening the coming of the day of God [the second coming], because of which the heavens will be set on fire and dissolved, and the heavenly bodies will melt as they burn! But according to his promise we are waiting for new heavens and a new earth in which righteousness dwells. (2 Peter 3:10–13)

How then can Christ reign over the earth for another one thousand years if he destroys it when he comes again?

In the disciples' minds, the restoration was supposed to occur during Christ's first coming. Since the restoration did not occur during that time— either before or immediately after the resurrection—the question is, will it happen at his second coming? If so, how does the restoration fit into the New Testament teachings on the second coming?

This is the crux of the debate, for Christ never described his second coming in terms of it coinciding with the beginning of the restoration. There are no New Testament references that tie Christ's second coming and the saints' rapture directly to the beginning of Christ's earthly reign. Rather, as Jesus and the apostles taught, his second coming coincides with the saints' rapture into transformed, glorified bodies and the beginning of our eternal inheritance in the heavenly kingdom.

Christ did not exercise his lordship over Israel and the world during his first coming, much to John the Baptist's and the disciples' surprise. Furthermore, even after his resurrection, he left this world without establishing the messianic kingdom on this earth. He now sits at the right hand of God the Father in heaven waiting for the Father to establish the messianic kingdom. In addition, he said that when he comes again, it will be to take us to his Father's kingdom of heaven, not to his earthly kingdom. Where, then, is his messianic kingdom on this earth? How and when do the meek inherit the earth before inheriting the Father's kingdom of heaven?

In Revelation 20, John teaches that the departed saints, the ransomed people of God from all nations, will indeed experience the first resurrection in order to reign with Christ during the millennium. But what is this first resurrection? Is this when the disciples and the meek people of God inherit the earth and experience the restoration of this Genesis creation, before the last day of this Genesis creation when we inherit the eternal new heavens and new earth? Will the saints experience two resurrections—one to inherit the earth during the Son's messianic kingdom and the other to inherit the Father's kingdom of heaven?

Could it be that the kingdom of the triune God manifests itself as two kingdoms: one being the Son's messianic kingdom on this earth for one thousand years when it is restored to an Edenic paradise, as prophesied by the Old Testament prophets, achieved through the first resurrection of the saints; and the other being the Father's eternal kingdom in heaven achieved through the final resurrection or the rapture of the saints (Rev. 20:4–5, 12)?

But what kind of "first resurrection" would allow the meek to inherit the earth for a thousand years before they are resurrected (raptured) and transformed on the last day to inherit their citizenship in the Father's heavenly kingdom? Maybe the confusion that continues to surround the kingdom of God and our future inheritance is the result of theologians having misunderstood the meanings of the first and the final resurrections of the saints alluded to by John, as well as the manner in which Christ rules over this world.

Another Walk Along the Road to Emmaus

The two men on the walk to Emmaus were hoping and expecting Jesus of Nazareth would be the one to redeem Israel and usher in the promised messianic kingdom (Luke 24:19–21). They could not understand why the Messiah, who was supposed to restore the kingdom to Israel, had to be crucified. The disciples eventually learned that Christ's death on the cross was essential for the forgiveness of our sins, and that there was no other way we could enter the kingdom of a holy God without our sins being paid for and forgiven. But how and when do we inherit God's righteous kingdom on earth and then in heaven?

Some thirty years ago I was on my own similar walk, equally confused, not about Christ's first coming, but struggling to understand his second coming! As a young Christian, I had a cursory knowledge of the various views on Christ's second coming and our future inheritance. But the more I read the Scriptures, the more I kept finding major contradictions between the Scriptures and some of the most basic tenets of the prevailing views. Something was just not right.

I began an extensive study of the scholarly material that underpinned amillennialism, postmillennialism, and premillennialism. I wanted to understand the scriptural basis for these respective views on the second coming and God's kingdom. At first I was taken aback by how much unnatural reorientation of the Scriptures was required to make sense of the different views. Each camp developed a hypothesis and then attempted to fit the Scriptures into their framework. Some verses fit well, but some did not, and the Scriptures often had to be forced to fit their particular eschatology.

For example, amillennialists believe that the second coming and the rapture occur on Judgment Day, but they have to explain away the Messiah's earthly messianic kingdom, which is almost a contradiction in terms— a Messiah without a messianic kingdom. And many of their best scholars have attempted to force the Old Testament messianic prophecies describing an Adamic existence and paradise onto the new heavens and new earth, which is an obvious misfit.

Postmillennialists believe that Christ is already on his throne. We just need to be better evangelists to save this rotten world. But it is self-evident that this world remains Satan's domain, even though we can have a positive influence on it. Satan is definitely not bound and removed from influencing this world. And postmillennialists' vision of the messianic kingdom falls far short of the Old Testament vision. Also, what about the departed meek saints, including the disciples? How do they inherit the earth in this Adamic age before they are raptured and inherit eternal life in the age to come?

Premillennialists believe in a literal millennial reign of Christ in fulfillment of Old Testament messianic prophecies, but they have Christ and the raptured saints coming back to this earth to implement his kingdom, which contradicts the numerous New Testament verses that teach Christ's second coming is on Judgment Day, when this Genesis earth is destroyed and the raptured children of God are taken to the Father's kingdom of heaven, not to the Son's earthly kingdom. Many premillennialists are then forced to devise multiple second comings—one to rapture the saints, another to come to this earth, and still another on the last day to destroy this earth—and a multitude of Judgment Days instead of one. And what in the world are the immortal children of God in their spiritual bodies doing on this restored Genesis earth when they belong in heaven?

If theologians who devise these views on eschatology were compared to architects and builders, one would have to conclude there are major design and structural flaws in their "house of ideas." For example, amillennialism, with its lack of a millennial kingdom before the eternal kingdom, is a pretty barren house with no kitchen, bathrooms, or even roof, for that matter.

Postmillennialism, with its watered-down millennium, is a house with a roof, but the house still has no indoor kitchen or bathrooms. And the house remains in an undesirable neighborhood with Satan still active; thieves sometimes break in and steal what few possessions there are.

Premillennialism adheres to a literal millennium and has many of the right components of the house. But with Christ and the raptured immortal saints returning to this natural world at the beginning of the millennium, many of the key components are in the wrong place. The bathroom is in the middle of the living room, the kitchen is in the attic, and the skylights are in the floor. The house is discombobulated.

None of these systems of eschatology provide a satisfactory solution. The truth about God's kingdom on earth and in heaven seems to have eluded us. Perhaps it is time to go back to the drafting table and come up with a design that puts the biblical components together in such a way that we end up with a beautiful, well-designed house whose form and function meet the Bible's design standards, built "according to code."

After studying the three major views on eschatology, I became deeply disillusioned because not one affirmed what I perceived as two fundamental biblical truths—the existence of a literal messianic kingdom, in fulfillment of all the messianic prophecies, *and then* the second coming and the rapture on the last day or Judgment Day. I did not yet know the solution, but I knew something was terribly wrong with the prevailing views. I realized it was time to take another walk along that road to Emmaus and listen intently while I searched the Scriptures to understand Christ's *second coming* and how we would inherit both his kingdom on this earth *and* his Father's kingdom of heaven as he had promised.

A Redesigned House

I am convinced that Christ saw me agonizing over the inconsistencies of the current eschatological views. Through the Holy Spirit, he came alongside me as I searched the Scriptures for his plan of redemption. One day he took me to Revelation 20, and as I was reading about Christ's millennial reign, I noticed for the first time that none of the thrones that John identified on this earth specifically mentioned Christ as its occupant (Rev. 20:1-5). Rather, John described these as human thrones that were seated on this earth with the authority to judge this world. But if Christ is not on this earth during his 1,000-year reign, then where is he?

It came to me as an epiphany that Christ does not have to physically return to this earth before the millennium to establish a literal reign over this earth. He can bind and remove Satan after the Great Tribulation, rendering him completely inoperative in this world, and then *exercise* his reign, or Lordship, over this earth from his throne in heaven, using the human thrones on earth as his stewards over the restored Genesis creation.

Christ has the authority to reign where he currently resides, at the right hand of the Father in heaven, but he will not exercise this authority until the Father says it is time to do so at the beginning of the restoration when Satan is totally bound. During the millennium, Christ remains on his throne in heaven. The beginning of the millennium, therefore, is *not* the second coming of Christ and the associated rapture of the saints.

This important observation immediately led me to a second crucial question. If the beginning of the millennium is not the second coming of Christ, then what is the nature of the first resurrection described by John? I quickly realized that it could not be the rapture of the saints into their immortal spiritual bodies, because that is inseparably linked with Christ's second coming—which I now understood occurs *after* his millennial reign from heaven, when he comes again to take us to heaven.

Nonetheless, Revelation refers to a first resurrection of the saints at the beginning of the 1,000-year reign. I also knew it could not be a resurrection of just the spirits of the departed saints to heaven as claimed by many amillennialists, because John had already described the martyred saints of the Tribulation as alive in heaven with Christ and as riding on white horses coming out of heaven at the battle of Armageddon.

If the first resurrection was not a resurrection of just the spirits of the departed saints, and if it was not a resurrection of our immortal bodies, I then deduced that the first resurrection John alluded to must be of a body that is adapted for the earthly, millennial kingdom in this age. Then I suddenly realized that the first resurrection could simply be a resurrection of the departed saints back into natural Adamic bodies of flesh and blood as with the resurrection of Lazarus! Lazarus was raised from the dead into a human body, and he may have married and had children after he was brought back to life. Similarly, the saints of the first resurrection can also experience marriage and enjoy the restored Adamic kingdom on this earth.

As I thought about how Christ resurrected Lazarus's body from the dead by simply calling out his name, I realized that Christ surely has the power and the authority to resurrect the saints en masse back into regenerated natural bodies whether they have been dead four days, four years, four hundred years, or four thousand years!

Lazarus was probably buried in an ancient cemetery with thousands of other tombs containing a significant number of believers. If Jesus had directed his shout to all the deceased believers in the graveyard, I am sure they would have come to life as human beings whether they were dry bones or recently buried like Lazarus. What difference does it make if Christ raises a single person back from the dead into a natural body after four days or chooses to raise millions of saints from the dead after any number of years?

John seems to be describing the first resurrection as a similar shout from Christ that is heard around the world, and all deceased believers will come to life to experience the millennial kingdom. If this Genesis creation was created by Christ, then, as the second person of the Trinity and as our Creator, Christ could easily re-create or regenerate the deceased Adamic bodies of his departed saints whose bodies are asleep in the dust of the earth so that they can inherit his 1,000-year messianic kingdom.

Furthermore, I realized that at the beginning of the millennium, Christ could not only resurrect the martyred saints of the Great Tribulation back into natural Adamic bodies to reign with him, but he could also resurrect every saint since Abel, including Peter and the disciples, and the whole "cloud of witnesses" in heaven (Heb. 12:1).

Maybe there is a simple solution to all the confusion that surrounds the second coming and our future inheritance on earth and in heaven. The first resurrection is of the natural, Adamic body, and Christ will establish the

1,000-year restoration by exercising his reign from his throne in heaven at the Father's right hand. He will not need to return to this earth to establish his messianic kingdom. Consequently, his second coming can be after a literal millennium on Judgment Day, when our bodies are transformed and taken to heaven—which is consistent with the New Testament teachings on the second coming and the destiny of the raptured saints being the Father's eternal kingdom. To summarize, the second coming of Christ and the final resurrection take place *after* a 1,000-year messianic kingdom on earth. Thus, the biblical truth about the messianic kingdom and the second coming on the last day are both affirmed.

As my mind raced through the Scriptures, God's plan of redemption suddenly began to make more sense. In Hebrews, we read that Christ does not currently fully *exercise* the authority and power at his disposal. He may be the King of the world, but he is not yet using his divine power to establish his kingdom on the earth as King of kings and Lord of lords:

> "You made him [Christ] for a little while lower than the angels; you have crowned him with glory and honor, putting everything in subjection under his feet." Now in putting everything in subjection to him, he left nothing outside his control. *At present, we do not yet see everything in subjection to him.* (Heb. 2:7–8)

Christ has all the authority necessary to rule the world, but at present we do not see him fully exercising his reign because "we do not see everything in subjection to him." Christ is the King and Lord of this world, but the world currently remains under Satan's influence and dominion—until after the Great Tribulation when Satan will be bound, removed, and no longer operational, and Christ finally uses his great power and exercises his rightful reign over this restored Genesis creation. With Satan removed and the Son of God ruling the world, then the Father's will can be established on earth as it is in heaven, and Christ's long-promised messianic kingdom will be established. The government of this world will finally be on his shoulders.

If Adam and Eve had not sinned, the Son of God would have ruled as King over his Genesis kingdom from his throne in heaven. The world already belonged to him: "For every beast of the forest is mine, the cattle on a thousand hills. I know all the birds of the hills, and all that moves in the field is mine" (Ps. 50:10–11). The world was to be Christ's glorious dominion with humankind in fellowship with him as they multiplied and subdued the earth under his Lordship. But when Satan convinced Adam and Eve to rebel against God, the world came under a curse, Satan entered, and the world became Satan's dominion.

The main reason Christ came to this earth was because he had to die for our sins to rescue us from Satan's dominion of darkness. Once that mission was completed, he departed this world, returning to his Father where he can rule over this creation from his throne in heaven when the time is right.

Since the fall, Satan has been operating as the false god of this fallen world of sinful people. But when this intrusive "god" is bound and removed at the beginning of the millennium, there will be a regime change and the rightful God and ruler of this creation, Jesus Christ, will reign supreme with his resurrected, righteous saints. What better person to properly manage the affairs of mankind than Jesus Christ, who not only knows what it means to be a human on this earth but from his exalted throne in heaven also has the omniscience of God with infinite awareness, understanding, and insight of the affairs of the whole world. This Genesis creation was Christ's to begin with, and the millennial kingdom is simply a restoration of what is rightfully his to manage and enjoy.

When Jesus was arrested and brought before the chief priests and scribes, they asked if he was the Christ. He responded, "But from now on the Son of Man shall be seated at the right hand of the power of God [the Father]" (Luke 22:69). Christ said that his relationship to this world after the crucifixion, resurrection, and ascension would "from now on" be from the "right hand" of God the Father—in heaven. He does not need to come back to this earth to rule the world. As the Son of God, he can simply rule this world from his throne in heaven using his divine power and authority to bring everything on this rebellious earth under his control. In short, the prophets were not exaggerating; there will indeed be a messianic kingdom on this earth when the Messiah will be King of kings and Lord of lords!

Christ has been elected king or president of the world by the Father. But as John the Baptist and the disciples learned, he is currently president-elect and Satan remains the de facto president. Satan's term of office comes to an end when Christ is inaugurated as president and establishes his long-awaited messianic kingdom. At the conclusion of his millennial kingdom on earth, Christ comes again to rapture the saints, judge the world, and take all God's children to his Father's eternal kingdom.

Jesus Affirmed the Restoration Before the Last Day

Let us apply this postrestorational hypothesis to some of Jesus' teachings to see how well the biblical data fits this framework. Let's see if all the right biblical components of this redesigned house have been included and are in the correct places. In Matthew 19, we find an interesting affirmation by Jesus of the two critical components of God's plan of redemption—the disciples' inheritance of the restored earth in this Adamic age and their inheritance of the eternal kingdom of heaven in the age to come. A wealthy man asked Jesus what he must do to obtain eternal life. Jesus tested the man's heart by asking him to sell his possessions and follow him to receive eternal life and his "treasure in heaven." The wealthy man walked away sad because he could not part with his temporal earthly wealth.

Peter asked Jesus: "See, we have left everything and followed you. What then will we have?" (19:27). Jesus' answer was truly amazing—and revealing. He told Peter and the disciples that their reward is not only the privilege of experiencing the restoration on this earth as human beings, but receiving eternal life in heaven in the age to come as well:

> Jesus said to them, "Truly, I say to you, in the new world [the restoration], when the Son of Man will sit on his glorious throne [in heaven], you who have followed me will also sit on twelve thrones [on earth through the resurrection of their natural bodies], judging the twelve tribes of Israel. And everyone who has left houses or brothers or sisters or father or mother or children or lands, for my name's sake, will receive a hundredfold [in the restoration in this age] *and* [in addition] will inherit eternal life [in the heavenly kingdom in the age to come]." (Matt. 19:28–29)

Or, as recorded by Mark:

> "I tell you the truth," Jesus replied, "no one who has left home or brothers or sisters or mother or father or children or fields for me and the gospel will fail to receive a hundred times as much in this present age (homes, brothers, sisters, mothers, children and fields—and with them, persecutions) and in the age to come, eternal life." (Mark 10:29–30 NIV; cf. Luke 18:29–30)

In the new world during this present age, the disciples will receive one hundred times their reward on this earth and even play a key role in its government—something they had been wanting all along. Moreover, *after* experiencing the earthly kingdom in this age, they will inherit eternal life in the age to come as well! Jesus affirms both aspects of God's kingdom—the earthly and heavenly kingdoms—in the same verse.

Notice that Christ characterizes this hundredfold reward in this present age as an Adamic existence with "homes, brothers, sisters, mothers, children and fields." These are human habitats (homes and fields) and human relationships derived from marriage (parents, children, and brothers and sisters). Jesus is probably alluding to Isaiah and the prophets who described the messianic kingdom as one where the people of God will marry, have children, build houses, plant vineyards, and live long lives full of peace and happiness—prophecies the disciples were familiar with.

For example, Isaiah says, "They shall build houses and inhabit them [homes]; they shall plant vineyards and eat their fruit [fields]. . . . They shall not labor in vain or bear children for calamity [extended human families]" (Isa. 65:21–23). When the earth is renewed in the restoration, the disciples will receive a hundredfold in this present Adamic age as restored human beings as they enjoy these houses, fields, vineyards, and extended families.

The disciples surely did not experience an abundant life during their lifetimes. They were filled with great inner joy and peace, but their external lives were miserable at times; their houses and land were confiscated, they were abandoned by family members, persecuted, and finally, martyred. Peter and the rest of the disciples died horrible deaths. How can this prophecy of their receiving a hundredfold in an earthly kingdom come true before they receive the eternal kingdom of heaven on the last day?

By maintaining the distinction between the two orders of being, the solution becomes simple. When Christ binds Satan and begins to exercise his millennial reign from his throne in heaven, he resurrects Peter and the disciples back into natural bodies to live on the restored earth where they will experience their hundredfold reward. Then, to fulfill the second part of his promise, Christ will come again on the last day and resurrect and transform their mortal bodies into immortal bodies, so that they can inherit eternal life in heaven. "In this age" Peter will finally experience the messianic kingdom that he and the other disciples not only longed for but also sacrificed for. And "in the age to come" they will experience eternal life as children of God.

All the departed saints—from Abel to the last one martyred in the Tribulation—will experience the first resurrection of their natural bodies and enter the Son's kingdom. John foresaw: "And they sang a new song, saying, 'Worthy are you to take the scroll and to open its seals, for you were slain, and by your blood you ransomed people for God from every tribe and language and people and nation, and *you have made them a kingdom* and priests to our God, and *they shall reign on the earth*'" (Rev. 5:9–10). Through the first resurrection, all the saints shall physically reign on the earth, while the Son remains in heaven where he rules over this earth from the right hand of God the Father.

After the 1,000-year restoration of this Genesis creation, Christ will come again on the last day of this Genesis creation and rapture and transform our bodies in the final resurrection. We, as sons of God, will then experience eternal life in the new heavens and new earth in the age to come. Heaven will not be characterized by brothers, sisters, and children because we will not be given in marriage. That is because the children of God are a new order of being. Christ is making a clear distinction between the two types of kingdoms the disciples will inherit—one is Adamic and of this Genesis creation ("homes, brothers, sisters, mothers, children and fields"), and the other is of the eternal new creation as God's immortal children.

The meek, no matter how miserable life was or is, shall inherit Christ's kingdom on this earth for one thousand years in a restored Edenic paradise through the first resurrection *and then* inherit eternal life in the Father's heavenly kingdom through the final resurrection of the body. What an extraordinary gospel whereby we inherit the Son's kingdom on earth and then inherit the Father's eternal kingdom in heaven! The wealthy man did not know what he was walking away from. He traded his wealth and life in an unrestored earth for a few short decades for what could have been a hundredfold of prosperity in the renewed earth for a thousand years *and, in addition,* eternal life in heaven as an immortal child of God.

The Greek word for "the new world" (ESV) or "the renewal of all things" (NIV) is more accurately translated "in the regeneration" (ASV). The millennial earthly kingdom is achieved through a process of regeneration of this Genesis creation, which includes the regeneration of the Adamic bodies of the departed saints. But this is not merely a renovation of this earth or the human body. Lazarus was not given a heart transplant when he was brought back to life. After being dead for four days, every cell in his body would have experienced death and degradation. When he was resurrected, his whole body was regenerated.

Likewise, the Genesis creation will not merely be renovated at the beginning of the millennium, but it will be regenerated to its pre-fallen Edenic state. The curse on this earth will be removed, and the entire natural world will go through a radical regeneration, restoring it to its Edenic condition. One could actually describe God's curse on the Genesis earth as a form of *de*generation. Conversely, during the millennial kingdom, God will remove the curse of degeneration and through a process of regeneration will fundamentally restore this creation to its pre-fallen state of paradise.

If we examine the miracles Christ performed while he was on this earth, such as healing the blind and the paralyzed, which require a regeneration of major body parts to their original functions, then we begin to get a sense of what Christ was referring to when he spoke of the future regeneration of this Genesis creation. This regeneration of the earth would also include the regeneration of the bodies of the departed saints, no matter how much they have degenerated over the years.

With this in mind, Matthew 19 and Revelation 20 could be combined, paraphrased, and amplified to read as follows:

> Truly, I say to you, in the regeneration of this Genesis creation, when the Son of Man will sit on his glorious throne in heaven and govern the world, you who have followed me will also sit on twelve thrones on the earth when your Adamic bodies are regenerated through the first resurrection, and you will assist me in judging the twelve tribes of Israel. And everyone who has left houses or brothers or sisters or father or mother or children or lands, for my name's sake, will receive a hundredfold in the regeneration of this creation; and after you experience my earthly kingdom for a thousand years, you will be raptured into an immortal body and join me in heaven and then experience eternal life in my Father's eternal kingdom of heaven.

Another way to understand these events is to describe the original Genesis creation as a *formation* of a creation that was considered "good" by God. After the fall, the Genesis creation experienced a *deformation* when God put it under a curse—similar to a deformed human body. During the millennium, the curse will be almost completely removed, and this Genesis creation will experience a *re-formation* at the same time that our natural Adamic bodies will experience a *re-formation* through the first resurrection. Then, at the final resurrection on the last day, our bodies will experience a *transformation* into a new kind of immortal spiritual body when they are taken to a newly formed heavens and earth.

After the regeneration of this creation and the regeneration of our human bodies, we will experience the magnificence and joy of this Genesis creation for one thousand years. Our restored bodies will come back to life free of any infirmities and defects they may have had before.

When Christ returns, the saints—whether alive or asleep—will then go through a process of transformation, which makes it possible to experience the magnificence and joy of the eternal kingdom of heaven in the "age to come" in the new heavens and new earth. We inherit the earth through the *regeneration* of our natural human bodies, and then we inherit the kingdom of heaven through the *transformation* of our bodies into glorified bodies like Christ's resurrected body—which is why there are two resurrections.

The Son's Kingdom and the Father's Kingdom

The Bible teaches that two distinct kingdoms make up the kingdom of God. The first is the Son's earthly or messianic kingdom, which Jesus promised that we—the disciples and all the saints—will receive before inheriting the Father's eternal kingdom. At the moment of our conversion and rebirth, we enter into the kingdom of God, which entitles us to inherit both the Son's kingdom on earth and the Father's kingdom in heaven.

These two kingdoms can be readily discerned in the Lord's Prayer: "Your kingdom come [the Father's heavenly kingdom], your will be done, on earth [the Son's earthly kingdom] as it is in heaven" (Matt. 6:10). As a first priority, we pray for the return of Christ and the transformation of our bodies, so as children of God the Father, we can inherit the Father's kingdom. Next, we pray for the Son's kingdom when Christ binds Satan and rules the world as King of kings, implementing the Father's will on earth as it is in heaven. Neither prayer has been answered yet, but both will happen on dates and times set by the Father (Acts 1:7 and Matt. 24:36).

In an interesting conversation with the disciples, Jesus said, "You are those who have stayed with me in my trials, and I assign to you, as my Father assigned to me, a kingdom, that you may eat and drink at my table in my kingdom and sit on thrones judging the twelve tribes of Israel" (Luke

22:28–30). The Father assigns the earthly kingdom to his Son. The Son conveys it to his disciples. The disciples, when resurrected, will serve as stewards for the Son over this restored creation through the thrones set up on the earth during the millennium ruling as judges over Israel.

The Father plays a central role in his Son's kingdom, even determining when it begins (Acts 1:7). Jesus, in asking the Pharisees how David could call the son of David "Lord," quoted one of David's psalms: "The Lord [the Father] said to my Lord [the Son], Sit at my right hand, until I [the Father] put your enemies under your feet" (Matt. 22:44). On a day that the Father has set, he will put Christ's enemies under his feet and restore the Genesis creation to his Son. But the Son must first gather those the Father has given him to be in his kingdom—which is where we are today.

The earthly restoration is, in effect, the Son's kingdom restored to him by the Father. This is because "the world was made through him" and "for him" and "he came to his own" (John 1:10, 11; Col. 1:16). Christ was always supposed to be the God of this world, but Satan usurped his Lordship through the fall of Adam and Eve when, by their disobedience to God's commandment, they let Satan into their Edenic paradise. The world has never been the same. Satan is an evil intruder and is characterized as the "ruler of this world." Along with renegade mankind, it is his dominion.

But after Satan is bound and removed from this world at the beginning of the millennium, the Father will restore this world to his Son—the rightful ruler of this Genesis creation! As its Creator he has a divine right to rule over it. This regime change will transform the world. Not only will the true God of this world rule with righteousness, but the Genesis creation itself will be regenerated, along with all the departed saints.

The heavenly kingdom is portrayed in the New Testament as the Father's kingdom. Christ is responsible for ushering it in after he has completed his mission of restoring this Genesis creation to himself through the messianic kingdom. After Christ has completed his reign over this regenerated earth, he will come again and resurrect the Father's children into immortal bodies, thereby overcoming the last enemy, death. He then will take the Father's transformed children to the Father's house for eternity, thus turning over his kingdom to the Father:

> But each in his own order: Christ the firstfruits, then at his coming those who belong to Christ. Then comes the end, when he delivers the kingdom to God the Father after destroying every rule and every authority and power. For he [Christ] must reign [during his messianic kingdom] until he has put all his enemies under his feet. The last enemy to be destroyed is death [through the final resurrection, or rapture, on the last day]. (1 Cor. 15:23–26)

With this framework, we can begin to understand Christ's mission: "But our citizenship is in heaven. And we eagerly await a Savior from there, the Lord Jesus Christ, who, *by the power that enables him to bring everything under his control*, will transform our lowly bodies so that they will be like his glorious body" (Phil. 3:20–21 NIV). After Christ uses his divine power to reestablish his rightful control and dominion over this Adamic creation during his millennial reign, he will then come again and use this same supernatural power to transform our bodies to be adapted for eternity, so that we can inherit our citizenship in the kingdom of heaven. He uses his divine power to establish his millennial kingdom *and* to transform our mortal bodies into immortal bodies like his glorious body.

Once the Son's messianic reign over this earth is complete, he has the task of overcoming death for the Father's children through the final resurrection, when they are given immortal bodies. That is his final mission. He then hands his kingdom of the raptured and transformed children of God over to the Father in heaven.

"Sitting on His Throne"—Three Applications

Christ taught the Jewish leaders that after his crucifixion, resurrection, and ascension, "from now on the Son of Man shall be *seated* at the right hand of power" in heaven (Luke 22:69). In order to correctly understand how and when Christ rules this world from heaven, it is very important to understand the three different ways that the Scriptures portray Christ as *sitting on his throne* in heaven after his ascension. The first type of "sitting" is similar to the way a receptionist in a doctor's office would tell a patient the following: "Have a seat until your name is called." This is equivalent to the manner in which Christ was told to have a seat and wait on the Father to say it is time to exercise his reign (Acts 1:7). Or, as Christ said, "The Lord [the Father] said to my Lord [the Son], Sit at my right hand, until I [the Father] put your enemies under your feet" (Matt. 22:44). Or, as Hebrews says, "But when Christ had offered for all time a single sacrifice for sins, *he sat down* at the right hand of God, *waiting* from that time until his enemies should be made a footstool for his feet" (Heb. 10:12–13). But Christ is not sitting idle while he waits on the Father. Rather, through the Father's sovereign calling and the regenerative power of the Holy Spirit, he is very active redeeming people out of Satan's kingdom from all nations and bringing them into his kingdom, so that when he does eventually rule the world, he will have ransomed subjects from every nation—not just Israel.

The second way in which Christ *sits on his throne* is when he actually takes his seat and governs this world. This is similar to the way an emperor or king in the Roman Empire would enter a government hall and might casually interact with advisors, administrators, or officials until he sat down on his actual throne to begin the process of ruling over the affairs of state. The issue could be a new building project such as a new aqueduct to bring spring water to a city like Antioch, or it could be a matter of arbitration between two provinces or another country. "Sitting" on his throne in this case involves the king actually *governing* the affairs of his kingdom. He is ruling, reigning, or governing over the subjects of his kingdom.

I believe this is what Jesus was alluding to in Matthew 19 when he said, 'Truly, I say to you, in the new world, when the Son of Man will sit on his glorious throne [to rule the world], you who have followed me will also sit on twelve thrones, judging the twelve tribes of Israel" (19:28). Christ will actually govern the world, and the resurrected disciples will assist him in governing the affairs of Israel. Or, as the prophet Isaiah said, "For to us a child is born, to us a son is given; and *the government shall be upon his shoulder*, and his name shall be called Wonderful Counselor, *Mighty God*, Everlasting Father, Prince of Peace" (Isa. 9:6). Or, as John foresaw: "We give thanks to you, *Lord God Almighty*, who is and who was, *for you have taken your great power and begun to reign*'" (Rev. 11:16–17). This is when Christ, as the true God of this creation, will use his great power to become King of kings and Lord of lords and rule this world when he resurrects the departed subjects of his kingdom to receive a hundredfold "in this age."

The third application of Christ *sitting on his throne* is when he judges all mankind on Judgment Day. In our civil and criminal court system, when a judge enters the courtroom and the court officer loudly proclaims "all rise," the courtroom quiets down and the judge takes his seat, strikes his gavel, and the court is in session. From his bench or throne, the judge begins the process of judicial proceedings to determine rewards, fines, or penalties for those on trial. This is similar to Christ sitting on the Great White Throne on Judgment Day when "all rise" and are "judged by what was written in the books, according to what they had done" and either enter the eternal new heavens and new earth with their respective rewards or are sentenced to the eternal lake of fire with their respective punishments (Rev. 20:11–15).

Christ's second coming is always portrayed as occurring on the last day when he comes to sit on his throne to judge the world:

When the Son of Man comes in his glory, and all the angels with him [the second coming], then he will sit on his glorious throne [Great White Throne]. Before him will be gathered all the nations [the final or general resurrection—all rise], and he will separate people one from another as a shepherd separates the sheep from the goats [based on who is in the "book of life"]. And he will place the sheep on his right [those in the book of life], but the goats on the left [those whose "name was not found written in the book of life"]. Then the King will say to those on his right, "Come, you who are blessed by my Father, inherit the kingdom prepared for you from the foundation of the world [the Father's heavenly kingdom in the age to come]." . . . Then he will say to those on his left, "Depart from me, you cursed, into the eternal fire prepared for the devil and his angels [the lake of fire]." . . . And these will go away into eternal punishment, but the righteous into eternal life [in the Father's kingdom]. (Matt. 25:31–46)

When Christ comes again, it will not be before the millennium to establish his reign. Rather, it will be on the last day to judge the world and usher in the eternal kingdom. There is only one incarnation of the Son of God when he actually dwelled on this earth. He does not need to physically return to this earth to rule the world during his millennial reign.

In summary, there are three applications of Christ "sitting on his throne" in heaven: 1) He takes a seat on his throne and waits on the Father to say when it is time for him to rule the regenerated Genesis creation. 2) He takes a seat on his throne when Satan is removed and bound and Christ finally exercises his rule, reign, or government over this world establishing his messianic kingdom on this earth characterized by peace, justice, righteousness, and prosperity. 3) He takes a seat on his throne to judge all human beings and separate the sheep from the goats in order to reward his people with eternal life in the age to come and to punish unbelievers with eternal condemnation in the lake of fire. But all three occur from his throne in heaven where he is seated at the right hand of God the Father. When examining the Scriptures, it is critical to recognize which form of "sitting" the author is referring to.

When attempting to understand the present times and the prophetic future, it is critical to understand the distinction between the ascended Christ sitting on his throne in heaven to wait, rule, and then judge the world. These three important forms of "sitting" can be summarized as follows:

- Sitting and waiting: "But when Christ had offered for all time a single sacrifice for sins, he *sat down* at the right hand of God, *waiting* from that time until his enemies should be made a footstool for his feet" (Heb. 10:12–13).
- Sitting and ruling: "Truly, I say to you, in the new world, when the Son of Man will *sit on his glorious throne* [to rule the world], you who have followed me will also sit on twelve thrones, judging the twelve tribes of Israel" (Matt. 19:28).
- Sitting and judging: "When the Son of Man comes in his glory, and all the angels with him [the second coming], then he will *sit on his glorious throne*. Before him will be gathered all the nations, and he will separate people one from another as a shepherd separates the sheep from the goats" (Matt. 25:31–32).

Reexamining the Ante-Nicene Millennialists

After my initial discovery of postrestorationalism, I began to extensively research the history of millennialism, particularly among the early church fathers who lived and wrote before the First Council of Nicaea in AD 325. I wanted to know if anyone had proposed a similar eschatology. Ante-Nicene millennialists lived at a time not far removed from the apostles, particularly the apostle John, who, according to most scholars, wrote Revelation late in his life, sometime around AD 90. They were in the unique position of having an oral tradition of teachings from people who knew the apostle John. Thus, it is a fair assumption that their views on these subjects would be close to what John believed and taught. Oral traditions in the ancient world were not infallible, but they could be highly reliable.

Because of the inherent credibility of the teachings of the ante-Nicene fathers, it is common for advocates of the various prevailing views of eschatology to reference many of the ante-Nicene fathers' interpretations of the book of Revelation for confirmation of their position. Premillennialists, in particular, often point to the teachings of Papias (c. 60–130), Justin (c. 100–165), Irenaeus (c. 120–202), and other early millennialists to support their eschatology that the second coming of Christ to this earth occurs at the beginning of a literal millennium, and that the saints will be raptured into their transformed, immortal, spiritual bodies—not given in marriage— sometime before the millennium, to reign with Christ.

Renald E. Showers, a premillennial author, exemplifies this claim: "Numerous historians declare that Premillennialism (initially called chiliasm) was the first major millennial view of the Church and that it was the predominant view of orthodox believers from the first to the third centuries. A sampling of historians will be quoted as evidence for this declaration."[2]

Actually, scholars cannot agree on what percentage of the ante-Nicene fathers were millennialists, but they do agree that it was a significant number who were highly respected by the early church and quite influential.

Justin, in the millennial camp, does indeed teach that Christ comes back to this earth to destroy the Antichrist at the beginning of the millennium:

> . . . that two advents of Christ have been announced: the one, in which He is set forth as suffering, inglorious, dishonored, and crucified [the first coming]; but the other, in which He shall come from heaven with glory, when the man of apostasy [the Antichrist], who speaks strange things against the Most High.[3]

---

[2] Renald E. Showers, *There Really Is a Difference!* (Bellmawr, NJ: The Friends of Israel Gospel Ministry, Inc., 2002), 115.

[3] Justin, *Dialog with Trypho*, 110.1.

Upon a careful reading of these early millennialists, however, I discovered that they differed significantly from modern premillennialists in how they understood the nature of the first resurrection. Rather than a resurrection or rapture of the saints into an immortal, spiritual body not given in marriage, they believed, as I do, that the first resurrection alluded to by John (Rev. 20:4–5) at the beginning of the millennial reign of Christ will be a resurrection of the departed saints back into a natural, Adamic body, similar to Lazarus's resurrection, in order to experience Christ's millennial reign.

They also believed that the rapture and transformation of the children of God into their glorified spiritual bodies—not given in marriage—occurs *after* the millennium at the final resurrection or the general resurrection on Judgment Day. They believed that the first resurrection of the saints is of the natural body that can marry and reproduce in a restored 1,000-year Adamic paradise, and that the final resurrection, which occurs at the end of the world, is of the immortal spiritual body adapted for our eternal inheritance in the Father's kingdom. This critically important distinction between these two very different kinds of resurrections by the ante-Nicene millennialists is not well understood by modern scholars.

Justin taught the following about the first resurrection:

> But I and others, who are right-minded Christians on all points, are assured that there will be a resurrection of the dead [the "first resurrection"] and a thousand years in Jerusalem, which will then be built, adorned, and enlarged, [as] the prophets Ezekiel and Isaiah and others declare and we cultivate piety, righteousness, philanthropy, faith, and hope . . . and sitting each under his vine, i.e., each man possessing his own married wife. (*Dial.* 80.2)

Justin believed that the departed and martyred saints would come back to life to reign with Christ on this earth through the first resurrection of a natural body in which the saints would marry, reproduce, and experience the restored Genesis creation as men and women of God for one thousand years as envisioned by the Old Testament prophets Ezekiel and Isaiah. Justin was probably alluding to Ezekiel's graphic vision of the valley of dry bones being resurrected into natural human bodies that will marry, multiply, and see their "children's children" in the glorious promised land or messianic kingdom on earth (Ezek. 37).

Justin taught that after the millennium, during the general resurrection of believers and unbelievers on Judgment Day, the saints will then experience the final resurrection or rapture into eternal bodies adapted for the eternal kingdom of heaven—not given in marriage:

[The saints will] dwell a thousand years in Jerusalem; and that thereafter the general, and, in short, the eternal resurrection [the rapture] and judgment of all men [believers and unbelievers] would likewise take place [at the Great White Throne judgment]. Just as our Lord also said, "They shall neither marry nor be given in marriage, but shall be equal to the angels, the children of the God of the resurrection [an immortal body not given in marriage]." (*Dial.* 81.1)

When Justin referenced Jesus' teaching regarding the final resurrection, he was referring to Christ's answer to the Sadducees:

The sons of this age marry and are given in marriage, but those who are considered worthy to attain to that age and to the resurrection from the dead neither marry nor are given in marriage, for they cannot die anymore [immortal], because they are equal to angels and are sons of God, being sons of the resurrection. (Luke 20:34–36)

According to Justin, only *after* the 1,000-year reign of Christ, at the judgment of all men during the general resurrection, are the children of God raptured into their eternal immortal bodies and taken to the kingdom of heaven, where "they shall neither marry nor be given in marriage." Justin plainly places the resurrection of the transformed, immortal bodies—not given in marriage—on the last day after the millennium.

Irenaeus is another prominent early millennialist who wrote extensively on the nature of the millennial kingdom as being of the restored Adamic creation. He, too, interpreted Christ's answer to the disciples as promising an earthly kingdom through the resurrection of the natural bodies of the saints before the eternal kingdom as a reward for sacrificially following him:

And again He says, "Whosoever shall have left lands, or houses, or parents, or brethren, or children because of Me, he shall receive in this world an hundred-fold, and in that to come he shall inherit eternal life." For what are the hundred-fold [rewards] in this word . . . ? These are [to take place] in the times of the kingdom . . . The predicted blessing therefore, belongs unquestionably to the times of the kingdom, when the righteous shall bear rule upon their rising from the dead [the first resurrection]; when also the creation, having been renovated and set free, shall fructify with an abundance of all kinds of food, from the dew of heaven, and from the fertility of the earth. . . . He promised to drink of the fruit of the vine with His disciples, thus indicating both these points: the inheritance of the earth in which the new fruit of the vine is drunk, and the resurrection of His disciples in the flesh [the natural body]. For the new flesh which rises again is the same which also received the new cup [both are natural Adamic bodies of flesh and blood capable of drinking real wine].[4]

---

[4] Irenaeus, *Against Heresies*, V.33.1–3.

These early millennialists believed that the meek shall inherit the Son's 1,000-year restoration of this Genesis creation through a resurrection of their natural bodies—which could marry and reproduce—and then on the last day, inherit the Father's kingdom of heaven through the resurrection of their immortal bodies—not given in marriage. They believed that those who believe in Christ will first inherit a literal 1,000-year earthly paradise when the earth *and* our human bodies are restored to an Edenic condition (the messianic kingdom), and only after this 1,000-year restoration do we, as children of God, receive our glorious inheritance of heaven through the rapture and transformation of our bodies. The rapture of the saints takes place *after* the millennium at the general resurrection when the children of God are given eternal bodies to be taken to their eternal destiny of heaven.

Even Origen (c. 185–254), one of the early amillennialists and a staunch critic of the millennialists, understood they were teaching that the first resurrection was of a natural body given in marriage. He describes millennialists like Justin and Irenaeus to be "of opinion that the fulfillment of the promises of the [messianic kingdom] are to be looked for in bodily pleasure and luxury . . . that after the resurrection there will be marriages, and the begetting of children, imagining to themselves that the earthly city of Jerusalem is to be rebuilt."[5] Origen correctly understood that the millennialists of his day believed the first resurrection would be of the natural body, and "there will be marriages and the begetting of children" in the restored "earthly city of Jerusalem" during the millennium.

This understanding of the ante-Nicene fathers' teachings concerning the two very different kinds of resurrections mentioned by John is a major difference with modern premillennialism that many scholars have failed to emphasize or even recognize. One could argue that, in regard to the rapture and our going to our eternal inheritance in heaven, the ante-Nicene fathers' eschatology was not premillennial, but postrestorational. Christ may return at the beginning of the millennium to reign over this earth (premillennial return), but the rapture and transformation of the saints and entrance into the eternal kingdom as children of God—not given in marriage—occur *after* the millennial reign of Christ (postmillennial rapture).

The problem with their system of eschatology is that they placed Christ's second coming in conjunction with the first resurrection of the natural bodies of the saints instead of in conjunction with the rapture of the spiritual bodies. Paul plainly teaches that the second coming is associated with the rapture of the immortal spiritual bodies of the saints, not of natural bodies (1 Thess. 4:16–17). This is the flaw that Origen recognized.

---

[5] Origen, *De Principiis* II.11.2.

They had made one critical mistake by placing Christ's second coming at the beginning of the millennium in conjunction with the resurrection of the natural bodies instead of at the end of the millennium in conjunction with the resurrection of the immortal bodies on the last day. But this is easily corrected by realizing that it is not necessary for Christ to return to this world to rule over it. He can simply rule the world from his throne in heaven seated at the right hand of the Father—when the Father says it is time for Satan to be bound and for Christ to use his power to govern this world.

I believe the ante-Nicene millennialists were essentially right, but they had the second coming occurring at the wrong time. This modified millennialism of the early ante-Nicene fathers as presented in this book corrects this inherent flaw and can be referred to as postrestorationalism. Postrestorationalism is, in many ways, a rediscovered and revised understanding of the biblical future as taught by the "right-minded" ante-Nicene fathers.

Typically, theologians do not welcome the introduction of new ideas, for they are usually the harbinger of a new heresy. The traditions of the church under the guidance of the Holy Spirit are given great weight. Theologians look for doctrines that have continuity with the church through the centuries. But postrestorationalism is not new; it is a rediscovery of some of the earliest teachings of the church by Christian leaders who had an oral tradition handed directly from the apostle John who wrote Revelation and is in concert with the core teachings of these early millennialists, more so than modern premillennialism. The teachings of the ante-Nicene millennialists, particularly those related to the two kinds of resurrections, will be explored in greater detail in chapter 12, "The Ante-Nicene Millennialists."

Summary: The Biblical Architecture

There are three fundamental problems with this world: 1) Satan remains the false God of this world with significant influence over the affairs of mankind. 2) It is being mismanaged by unrighteous, sinful men and women. 3) This Genesis creation remains under God's curse.

In the millennial reign of Christ, all three factors are fundamentally altered: 1) When Satan is completely removed from having any influence over mankind, Christ will rule this world from his throne in heaven as the true God of this creation. 2) When the departed righteous saints come to life on this earth through the first resurrection of the natural body, they will properly manage the world with Christ. 3) When the curse is removed, the Genesis creation will be regenerated into its original Edenic condition. As a result of these remarkable changes, we will experience the long-awaited messianic kingdom under Christ and experience an exceptionally abundant life on this earth—a hundredfold reward in this Adamic age.

Postrestorationalism is a real game changer in that it asserts two critical truths that change the whole eschatological discussion. One, in keeping with the Old Testament vision of resurrection (Ezek. 37) and the teachings of the ante-Nicene millennialists, the first resurrection is of the natural bodies of the departed saints. Two, once Satan is removed and bound, Christ exercises his millennial reign over the restored or regenerated earth from his seat or throne in heaven without physically returning to this earth. Therefore, the second coming and the corresponding rapture of the saints occur *after* the millennium on the last day when the transformed and glorified saints are taken to the Father's eternal kingdom of heaven.

There is a regeneration of the Genesis creation "in this age" when Christ will indeed exercise his rightful reign from heaven over this Genesis earth that was created through him, for him, and by him. Then, after this millennial age of righteous humanity, he comes again on the last day to rapture the saints and usher in eternal life for the children of God in "the age to come." In the new heavens and new earth, the Adamic order of being will come to an end, and the transformed immortal "sons of God" will no longer be given in marriage.

The key to figuring out the correct framework for the kingdom of God on earth and in heaven and our glorious inheritance as God's people is to understand and maintain the distinction between the two orders of being. *The Son's messianic kingdom* is always described in the Bible as an Adamic paradise for men and women of God. That is why it is portrayed by the prophets and Jesus as an Edenic paradise with marriage and reproduction. *The new heavens and new earth* are for the resurrected and transformed children of God—a new order of being where there is no distinction between male and female, and we will not be given in marriage. If we apply this simple organizing principle to the Scriptures, the gospel that promises that believers in Christ will inherit the earth *and then* the kingdom of heaven will suddenly start to make more sense.

Because the messianic kingdom on this Genesis earth is by definition a restoration or a regeneration of the Adamic order of being, the "first resurrection" must be of the natural Adamic body. In contrast, the new order of being as God's children is unmistakably destined for the Father's heavenly kingdom. Therefore, the rapture must occur on the last day at the final resurrection because the transformed bodies are destined for the new heavens and new earth—eternal bodies for an eternal kingdom.

I use the terminology *postrestoration* because the word *restoration* is an accurate way to portray the millennium. During Christ's millennial reign, the bodies of living or departed saints are *restored* to ideal Adamic bodies— ones like Adam's and Eve's before the fall; the Genesis creation is *restored* to an Edenic condition; the nation of Israel is *restored* to the land promised to Abraham; and, most important, with Satan removed from this world, Christ is *restored* to his rightful place as the true God and ruler of this world. In effect, the millennial kingdom of Christ is a fundamental restoration of this Genesis creation "in this age" to its Creator.

When a person becomes a Christian, he becomes a child of God and enters into the kingdom of God. Presently we remain in this fallen and cursed world. But in the future, the kingdom of God will manifest itself on the earth as the Son's messianic kingdom when Christ uses his power to rule over his restored Adamic creation. Then, on the last day after this Genesis creation is destroyed by fire, it will manifest itself in heaven as the Father's kingdom with the children of God residing on the *new* earth. Members of the kingdom of God inherit the Son's earthly kingdom and then inherit the Father's kingdom of heaven.

God has devised an ingenious way to fulfill his kingdom promises for his people. The divine power of resurrection is the key to our life today and in the future. Because we are in Christ, today we live resurrected lives of regenerated spirits as born-again believers. But we still experience the death of our human bodies while our resurrected spirits ascend to heaven and wait for the resurrection of our bodies. At the beginning of the millennial reign of Christ, we will experience a resurrected life of our natural bodies in the Son's kingdom. Finally, we will experience an eternal resurrected life of our glorified immortal bodies in the Father's kingdom of heaven.

In summary, postrestorationalism proposes a literal restoration of this Genesis creation for one thousand years, when the departed saints are resurrected back into this restored Adamic creation in natural bodies and Christ exercises his reign over this world from his throne in heaven, thereby establishing the long-awaited messianic kingdom. After this restoration or regeneration of this Adamic creation, the transformation occurs when Christ comes again on the last day, destroys this creation, transforms the saints—asleep or alive—into immortal bodies, and takes the children of God to the Father's heavenly kingdom for eternity. Thus, as Jesus promised, the meek shall inherit the regenerated earth and then the eternal kingdom of heaven. Now that is good news.

3

The Destiny of the
Raptured Saints

In the process of writing this book, I entered into an extensive debate with a premillennial scholar over our respective views. He insisted the Scriptures plainly teach that Christ *and* the raptured saints are destined for the restored earth during the millennial kingdom. The debate was not over the different theories among premillennialists as to when the rapture occurs in relation to the Tribulation (pre-, mid-, or post-tribulational theories). Rather, the debate was whether or not the Scriptures teach that raptured saints in their immortal glorified bodies are destined to come back to this earth along with Christ to experience the earthly millennial kingdom before we inherit the new heavens and new earth.

There are major variations of premillennialism, but they all more or less fall into the same camp—the purpose of the second coming of Christ is not to rapture the saints and usher in the kingdom of heaven on the last day of this earth, but to first come back to the earth with some of the raptured saints to establish a 1,000-year messianic reign, thus fulfilling the Old and New Testament prophecies about the restoration.

The following description by John F. Walvoord, a premillennialist, shows how this view affirms the messianic kingdom:

Premillennialism is founded principally on interpretation of the Old Testament. If interpreted literally, the Old Testament gives a clear picture of the prophetic expectation of Israel. They confidently anticipated the coming of a Savior and Deliverer, a Messiah who would be Prophet, Priest, and King. They expected that He would deliver them from their enemies and usher in a kingdom of righteousness, peace and prosperity upon a redeemed earth. . . . All the major prophets and practically all the minor prophets have

Messianic sections picturing the restoration and glory of Israel in this future kingdom. . . . The Premillennial interpretation offers the only possible literal fulfillment for the hundreds of verses of prophetic testimony.[1]

Premillennialists have a noble objective. They are attempting to affirm the biblical truth of the messianic kingdom. If Jesus is the Messiah, then there must be a messianic kingdom on this earth. But to fulfill this truth, they see the only viable solution as being the physical return of the Messiah back to this earth with the saints in immortal bodies to reign with him and complete what was not accomplished at his first coming.

But Walvoord's assertion that "the premillennial interpretation offers the only possible literal fulfillment for the hundreds of verses of prophetic testimony" is no longer true, for a modified millennialism as presented in this book most definitely affirms Christ's messianic kingdom on earth before the eternal kingdom. But it asserts that the saints come back to this earth at the first resurrection through a resurrection of natural bodies, and only at the *end* of the millennium does Christ come again on the last day at the final or general resurrection to rapture the saints and take them to heaven in their glorified bodies for eternity.

So, what is the destiny of the raptured saints according to the Scriptures? Is it the earth for a thousand years or the kingdom of heaven? In short, when does the rapture occur—sometime before a literal millennium as modern premillennialists assert, or after the millennium on the very last day when the current Genesis earth is destroyed and we are taken to the Father's heavenly kingdom as postrestorationalism proposes?

A Case for Premillennialism

At one point in the debate with the premillennial scholar, I proposed a challenge. I would list the verses that create a direct link between the second coming and the raptured saints being taken to heaven for eternity, and he would list the verses that create a direct link between the second coming and the raptured saints being taken back to this restored earth in the millennial kingdom. Once direct references were noted, then indirect references or inferences could be identified and offered as evidence.

He could not identify any verse that provided a direct link to support his proposition. His references were all indirect and extrapolations. For example, he noted the prophet Zechariah who painted a picture of Christ setting his foot down on this earth: "Then the LORD will go out and fight against those nations as when he fights on a day of battle. On that day his feet shall stand on the Mount of Olives that lies before Jerusalem on the east" (Zech. 14:3–4). Regardless of whether these verses are interpreted literally or metaphorically,

---

[1] John F. Walvoord, *The Millennial Kingdom* (Grand Rapids: Zondervan, 1980), 114.

they offer no direct link between the saints being raptured at this presumed second coming. One can assume that this is when the saints come back to this earth in their glorified bodies, but Zechariah does not link this event directly to a resurrection of the saints into their immortal bodies. One would have to add the rapture to this event described by Zechariah through indirect reference. There is nothing wrong with circumstantial evidence. In fact, it can be very persuasive. But I wanted him to first provide a direct linkage between the second coming, the rapture, and the immortal children of God inheriting the earthly messianic kingdom.

Another favorite section of Scripture that the scholar alluded to was Revelation 19, the battle of Armageddon. Christ is pictured as coming out of heaven on a white horse with the spirits of the saints on white horses following him. But nowhere does John specifically state that Christ lands his white horse on this earth and dismounts it in order to execute his judgment on the Antichrist and his armies. Christ simply calls fire down from heaven to destroy the armies of the Antichrist without physically residing on the earth again.

Further, John does not identify any of the subsequent thrones on the earth as being Christ's (Rev. 20:4). Rather, they are all human thrones. Most important, John does not create a specific link of the rapture of the saints to this event at the end of the Tribulation. Again, premillennialists are forced to make an inference that this is when the raptured saints return to this earth based on their assumption that John is describing the second coming.

Even John Walvoord, a pillar in the premillennial camp, admits in his commentary on Revelation that this section of Revelation 20 describing the millennium does not specifically mention Christ's throne as being physically on the earth: "The interpretation of verse 4 is complicated by a lack of specificity. . . . Who are these sitting on the thrones and what is meant by the judgment given to them? One possibility is that the subject of the verb 'sat' includes Christ."[2] In an extraordinary admission, Walvoord grants there is only a possibility that Christ's throne is included among the thrones on this earth envisioned by John, because nowhere does John specifically identify any of these thrones as being Christ's earthly throne!

Although John does not identify where Christ's throne is located, he does describe these thrones as human thrones set up on this earth to reign with Christ: "Then I saw thrones, and seated on them were those to whom the authority to judge was committed . . . They came to life [in the first resurrection] and reigned with Christ for a thousand years" (Rev. 20:4). The word *they* refers to those who come to life to reign with Christ. Obviously,

---

[2] John F. Walvoord, *The Revelation of Jesus Christ* (Chicago: Moody Bible Institute, 1966; Moody Paperback Edition, 1989), 296.

Christ does not need to come to life in the first resurrection to reign with himself, for he has already been resurrected and has ascended to heaven. John does not refer to any of these thrones as Christ's. They are all described as being occupied by humans who are resurrected to reign with Christ—who has already been resurrected.

Premillennialists base their entire eschatology around this important section of Revelation. And yet they can only speculate as to whether it states that after the Tribulation Christ returns to this earth on his white horse to physically reign on one of these thrones. A plain reading of the text reveals that these are all thrones of humans who "came to life" to reign with Christ.

Since this is such a critical section of Scripture for premillennialists, let's look at these passages more fully and note the incidences where no specific mention is made of Christ's continual descent and actual return to this earth during or after the battle of Armageddon to sit on one of these thrones. This is a long passage, but read it thoroughly, for it is critically important in understanding where Christ is when he reigns over this earth:

> Then I saw heaven opened, and behold, a white horse! The one sitting on it is called Faithful and True, and in righteousness he judges and makes war [Christ leads this celestial battle]. . . . And the armies of heaven [a celestial army composed of the righteous spirits of the departed saints gathered against the earthly army of the Antichrist], arrayed in fine linen, white and pure, were following him on white horses. From his mouth comes a sharp sword with which to strike down the nations [he merely says the word], and he will rule them with a rod of iron [announcing his impending reign]. He will tread the winepress of the fury of the wrath of God the Almighty [his wrath can easily be poured out on the Antichrist and his armies from his celestial position]. On his robe and on his thigh he has a name written, King of kings and Lord of lords [merely identifies who he is, not where he is]. . . . And I saw the beast and the kings of the earth with their armies gathered to make war against him who was sitting on the horse and against his army [no mention that Christ and the celestial armies of heaven have actually landed on the earth in order to engage the Antichrist and his earthly armies—he could simply remain in the celestial realm to fight this battle]. And the beast was captured, and with it the false prophet . . . These two were thrown alive into the lake of fire that burns with sulfur. And the rest were slain by the sword that came from the mouth of him who was sitting on the horse [Christ is pictured as remaining on his horse in the celestial realm when he just says the word and they are destroyed—no mention of the horse being on the plane of the earth], and all the birds were gorged with their flesh [the deceased earthly army on the earth].
>
> Then I saw an angel coming down from heaven, holding in his hand the key to the bottomless pit and a great chain. And he seized the dragon, that ancient serpent, who is the devil and Satan, and bound him for a thousand years, and threw him into the pit, and shut it and sealed it over him, so that

he might not deceive the nations any longer, until the thousand years were ended. After that he must be released for a little while.

Then I saw thrones [human thrones], and seated on them were those to whom the authority to judge was committed. Also I saw the souls of those who had been beheaded for the testimony of Jesus and for the word of God, and who had not worshiped the beast or its image and had not received its mark on their foreheads or their hands. They came to life [on the earth in resurrected bodies] and reigned with Christ [no mention from where Christ reigns—the earth or heaven] for a thousand years. (Rev. 19:11–21; 20:1–4)

The departed spirits of the saints are depicted as coming out of heaven and descending to this earth in resurrected bodies, but as is readily apparent, there is no specific mention of Christ on his white horse actually coming down to the plane of this earth to engage the human armies at the battle of Armageddon. And, as Walvoord candidly admits, there is no specificity in these passages about Christ actually sitting on a throne on this earth to reign as King of kings.

If Christ literally comes back to this earth as premillennialists assert, then one would be able to report that Christ was physically somewhere on this earth after his descent. He could be in Jerusalem one day and Paris the next day. But, in the Olivet Discourse, that is precisely what Christ said one would *not* be able to do when he comes again and would be a surefire way to recognize the Antichrist. He said, "Then if anyone says to you, 'Look, here is the Christ!' or 'There he is!' do not believe it. . . . For as the lightning comes from the east and shines as far as the west, so will be the coming of the Son of Man" (Matt. 24:23–27).

Christ taught that he will not physically return to earth in the second coming. He will not be over here or over there. Therefore, anyone who claims to be Christ operating on this earth is a false Christ, no matter how many signs and wonders he performs. Christ has already come in the flesh. And the next time he comes in the clouds, it will be as a bolt of lightning on the very last day of this Genesis earth, and we will ascend into the clouds to join him in the eternal kingdom (1 Thess. 4:16–18).

The strongest case my premillennial friend made was Paul's connection of the second coming of Christ to the overthrow of the Antichrist at the end of the Tribulation: "And then the lawless one [the Antichrist] will be revealed, whom the Lord Jesus will kill with the breath of his mouth and bring to nothing by the appearance of his [second] coming" (2 Thess. 2:8). Even in this particular verse, however, there is no direct linkage to the rapture or Christ's destiny after his overthrow of the Antichrist. For example, Paul does not say, "Whom the Lord Jesus will kill with the breath of his mouth by the appearance of his coming *down to this earth with the raptured saints.*" Paul does not link the overthrow of the Antichrist with the rapture or with Christ's descent to this earth.

Once again, this is an example where premillennialists must use indirect inferences to make the connection that Christ returns to this earth with the raptured saints when Christ overthrows the Antichrist, for nowhere does Paul link this event to the saints inheriting the earthly messianic kingdom. Because of the lack of direct linkage in this passage, premillennialists themselves are divided as to whether this overthrow of the Antichrist at the end of the Tribulation can be linked to the rapture. Some believe the rapture will have already occurred before the Tribulation or at the middle of the Tribulation. Regardless, Paul does not reference the rapture in this verse, forcing scholars to use indirect references and linkage to other passages.

In a book comparing the pre-, mid-, and post-tribulational theories of when the rapture occurs in relation to the beginning of the earthly millennial kingdom, Gleason L. Archer Jr., who believes in a mid-tribulation rapture, makes the following admission: "As we draw this whole discussion to a close, we must confess that the data of Scripture do not lend themselves to any clear and unambiguous pattern which is completely free of difficulties. . . . a difficult and highly involved matter of controversy."[3] As Archer candidly admits, the rapture cannot easily be placed before the millennium, and all three positions among premillennialists are fraught with inconsistencies. That is because there are no scriptural references that make a direct connection between the second coming, the rapture, and the saints inheriting the earthly kingdom of Christ. One can find references to each of the above, but not together in one complete grouping or linkage, which is one reason premillennialists remain so divided among themselves. Thus, they are all left with ambiguous and difficult inferences and extrapolations.

In his letters to the Thessalonians written sometime around AD 51, Paul makes no mention of the 1,000-year earthly messianic kingdom. At this stage in the growth of the early church, they probably had no knowledge about the millennial kingdom. Revelation was not written until almost forty years later. They had been taught about the Tribulation and the raptured saints inheriting the kingdom of heaven, but there is no evidence in these epistles that they had learned about the saints inheriting the earthly messianic kingdom through a first resurrection. I suggest that you take a moment and read Thessalonians 1 and 2. You will discover that there are no references to the earthly kingdom of Christ, only references to the eternal kingdom.

As a result, one can make the case that Paul goes from the end of the Tribulation directly to the second coming on Judgment Day, bypassing the millennial kingdom altogether, because this young church knew nothing about the messianic kingdom on this earth before the kingdom of heaven.

Paul's formulation could be outlined as follows:

---

[3] Stanley N. Gundry, *Three Views on the Rapture* (Grand Rapids: Zondervan, 1984, 1996), 144–145.

- The end of the Tribulation + the second coming (when the Antichrist is destroyed) + [skips the millennium] + the rapture = Judgment Day and the eternal kingdom of heaven for the saints and eternal hell for unbelievers.

In all his letters, Paul's teachings focus almost exclusively on the saints inheriting the kingdom of heaven, and he rarely broaches the subject of the restoration of the kingdom of Israel. When he does reference the earthly kingdom of Christ in Romans 11, it is a rather obscure and cryptic reference to the messianic prophecies found in Isaiah. Why Paul intentionally avoids teaching the Gentile churches about the Jewish messianic kingdom at this stage of the growth of the early church will be explored in some detail in chapter 11, "The Stealthy Restoration."

Other than the indirect references in these Scriptures, my premillennial friend was not able to provide any direct linkage between the second coming, the rapture, and the glorified saints inheriting the earthly kingdom. This problem seems to plague all premillennialists who have to devise multiple second comings (one to rapture the saints, another to come to the earth, and another to destroy the earth on the last day), multiple raptures, and even multiple judgment days to make sense out of the biblical data.

The Raptured Saints Are Destined for the Kingdom of Heaven

The verses outlined below are part of my answer to this challenge. In this chapter I hope to prove conclusively that when Christ comes again, the destiny of the raptured saints is unmistakably the Father's eternal kingdom of heaven—not the millennial earth. And one does not need circumstantial evidence to make this case. The rapture is not pre-, mid-, or post-tribulation; rather, it is *after* the millennium at the final or general resurrection when the saints are raptured and taken to heaven. I will also attempt to prove that the second coming is inseparably linked to the very last day of this Genesis creation and the Great White Throne judgment. If some of this material seems repetitive, it is because this direct linkage is a recurring theme throughout the New Testament.

When Christ approached his impending crucifixion, resurrection, and ascension, he began to tell his disciples that he was about to return to his Father in heaven. Thomas, confused, said to him: "Lord, we do not know where you are going. How can we know the way?" (John 14:5). Jesus reminded them that he is the only way to the Father and heaven. Christ told them not to be upset about his leaving this world and returning to his Father in heaven, because someday he would return and take them to join him and his Father in heaven for eternity:

Let not your hearts be troubled. Believe in God; believe also in me. In my Father's house are many rooms. If it were not so, would I have told you that I go to prepare a place for you? And if I go and prepare a place for you, *I will come again* and will *take you to myself,* that *where I am you may be also.* (John 14:1–3)

In the first coming, Christ came from his Father in heaven to this world through the incarnation and dwelt among us on this earth (John 1:14). After his crucifixion and resurrection, he ascended and returned to his place in heaven with the Father. At the second coming, Christ will come to take us to join him in his Father's heavenly kingdom—"where I am [heaven] you may be also." Christ ascended to heaven, and when he comes again in the clouds, we will join him and ascend to be with his Father in heaven. These verses can be outlined as follows:

- Christ's second coming ("I will come again") + rapture ("take you to myself") = Father's dwelling in heaven ("Father's house").

Thomas and the other disciples eventually understood what Christ meant by his resurrection and ascension to heaven and our resurrection and ascension to join him. Peter said:

According to his great mercy, he [the Father] has caused us to be born again to a living hope through the resurrection of Jesus Christ from the dead, to an inheritance that is imperishable, undefiled, and unfading, kept in heaven for you, who by God's power are being guarded through faith for a salvation ready to be revealed in the last time. (1 Peter 1:3–5)

Before the children of God can obtain "an inheritance that is imperishable, undefiled, and unfading, kept in heaven," our mortal bodies must first be transformed into eternal, immortal, imperishable bodies like Christ's resurrected body. After we experience a resurrection like Christ's resurrection, we are then destined for heaven; that is what we hope for. This formulation can be diagramed as follows:

- Christ "revealed" + rapture of the children of God (a resurrection like Christ's) = eternal dwelling or "inheritance that is imperishable, undefiled, and unfading, kept in heaven."

No inference, extrapolation, or circumstantial evidence is required here because Peter creates a direct linkage between the second coming, our being raptured, and our inheriting the eternal kingdom of heaven. There is no mention whatsoever that the raptured saints will dwell on or inherit the temporal and perishable earth, as claimed by premillennialists.

In his letter to the Philippians, Paul states the following: "But our citizenship is in heaven. And we eagerly await a Savior from there, the Lord

Jesus Christ, who, by the power that enables him to bring everything under his control, will transform our lowly bodies so that they will be like his glorious body" (Phil. 3:20–21 NIV). Paul is clearly referring to the second coming of Christ from heaven—"we eagerly await a Savior from there." But note that when Christ comes again, the destiny of our transformed "lowly" bodies that will be like "his glorious body" is "our citizenship in heaven." Paul is creating a direct linkage between these events.

This can be diagramed as follows:

- Christ ascended to heaven. He will return from heaven ("we eagerly await a Savior from there") + the rapture of the saints ("transform our lowly bodies") = our citizenship in heaven.

When our Savior comes again and our Adamic bodies are transformed, then we will inherit the eternal kingdom of heaven.

In 1 Corinthians 15, Paul again ties the transformation of our natural bodies—the rapture—directly to the second coming of Christ and to our being taken to the Father's heavenly kingdom:

> But in fact Christ has been raised from the dead, the firstfruits of those who have fallen asleep. For as by a man came death, by a man has come also the resurrection of the dead. For as in Adam all die, so also in Christ shall all be made alive. But each in his own order: Christ the firstfruits, *then at his coming those who belong to Christ. Then comes the end, when he delivers the kingdom to God the Father* after destroying every rule and every authority and power. . . . Behold! I tell you a mystery. We shall not all sleep, but we shall all be changed, in a moment, in the twinkling of an eye, at the last trumpet. For the trumpet will sound, and the dead will be raised imperishable, and we shall be changed." (1 Cor. 15:20–24, 51–52)

Christ was the first to be raised from the dead in an immortal body and to ascend to heaven in a glorified body. Thus, he is the "firstfruits" of the remaining children of God who have departed and whose bodies have "fallen asleep." He was resurrected into an immortal body and ascended to heaven, and we are next to follow. This will occur when he comes again: "Then at his coming those who belong to Christ," which is a reference to believers who will be resurrected from the dead, transformed, and given imperishable bodies like Christ's body. Paul says, "then comes the end, when he delivers the kingdom [of the raptured saints] to God the Father." God the Father is in heaven. Therefore, at his second coming the resurrected saints will be delivered to the Father's kingdom of heaven—or our "citizenship in heaven." There is no mention that the raptured saints will be delivered to an earthly kingdom or to our citizenship on a restored Genesis earth during the millennial kingdom. After the saints are raptured, they will inherit the Father's kingdom of heaven, not the Son's earthly kingdom.

And if Paul means the end of this Genesis creation by the expression "then comes the end," one could logically assume that the second coming and the rapture mark the end of this earth. Christ returns on the last day of this Genesis creation, though not to dwell on this earth and establish the restoration with his glorified saints; rather, he comes again to resurrect and transform our natural bodies into immortal spiritual bodies and then deliver us to the Father in heaven for eternity.

The destiny of the raptured saints after the second coming is heaven—not the restored earth. This formulation would be diagramed as follows:

- "Then at his coming" + the rapture ("those who belong to Christ" are "raised imperishable") + the end of the world ("then comes the end") = the heavenly kingdom ("he delivers the kingdom to God the Father").

Jesus, Peter, and Paul may use slightly different phrases, but they are describing the same event. When Christ comes again, the raptured saints are taken to the Father's kingdom of heaven for eternity. We will ascend to heaven and join Christ to be with his Father. None of these verses describe a *descent* of the raptured saints with Christ to reign on this earth in the messianic kingdom. On the contrary, these verses create a direct link between the second coming and the raptured saints in their eternal bodies inheriting the eternal kingdom of heaven.

This simplified formulation would be diagramed as follows:

- The second coming + the rapture + the last day = the eternal kingdom of heaven for the transformed saints.

So far, none of these verses support the premillennial assertion that the destiny of the raptured saints is the earthly kingdom of Christ for a thousand years before we are taken to heaven for eternity. Rather, the destiny of the raptured saints is plainly the Father's kingdom of heaven—"an inheritance that is imperishable, undefiled, and unfading, kept in heaven." Peter teaches that we will inherit this eternal kingdom when we experience a resurrection and transformation of our Adamic bodies into immortal, imperishable bodies like "the resurrection of Jesus Christ" (1 Peter 1:3–5). The destiny of the raptured saints when Christ comes again is God's kingdom in heaven, not God's kingdom on this earth.

The Second Coming and Judgment Day

The above section should provide ample proof that the raptured saints are destined for the kingdom of heaven for eternity—not the millennial earth. But premillennialists are tenacious in their defense of the return of the raptured saints to this earth to affirm the existence of a literal millennial reign of Christ. There is another important linkage, however, that can be established with Christ's second coming and the rapture of the saints—Judgment Day.

Premillennialists recognize that there is a linkage between the second coming and some form of judgment day. And, because they place Christ's second coming and the rapture at the beginning of the millennial kingdom, they by necessity must place some form of judgment day in association with the end of the Tribulation. Therefore, the "Great White Throne judgment," which occurs after the millennium, must be for unbelievers only. When Judgment Day occurs is a watershed issue for all the views on eschatology, particularly premillennialism.

Premillennialists understand that there is a direct connection between the second coming and Judgment Day. But because they have multiple second comings, multiple "last days," and multiple raptures, Judgment Day becomes very convoluted. Walvoord devised as many as seven separate Judgment Days.[4]

If it can be proven that Christ comes again at the Great White Throne judgment which John teaches occurs after the current heavens and earth are destroyed, then it will be impossible for premillennialists to make the case that the raptured saints come back to this earth for another thousand years. It would be difficult to reign over an earth that has been destroyed.

Let's search the Scriptures to see when Judgment Day occurs in connection to the second coming and the rapture—whether it occurs at the end of the Tribulation or at the end of the world at the Great White Throne judgment when we are taken to the new heavens and new earth.

In his first letter to the Thessalonians, Paul connects Christ's second coming and the rapture of the saints to be with the Lord for eternity to the day when the wrath of God is poured out on unbelievers:

---

[4] "Seven judgments are distinguished in Scriptures as being related in some sense to end-time events. The first of these is the judgment of the church, the body of Christ, at the judgment seat of Christ, usually considered by pretribulationists to have taken place in heaven immediately after the rapture and prior to the return of Christ to the earth. A second divine judgment has to do with the resurrection and reward of tribulation saints as indicated in Revelation 20:4. Closely associated with this is a third judgment of the resurrection and judgment of Old Testament saints as prophesied in the Old Testament in connection with the second advent. The fourth judgment has to do with Gentiles living in the world at the time of the second advent at which time the righteous are separated from the wicked living on the earth. A fifth judgment has to do with living Israel in the world at the time of the second advent who are regathered and judged relative to their place in the millennial reign of Christ. Two final judgments mark the close of the millennium—the judgment of the angels and Satan, and the judgment of the wicked dead at the Great White Throne. Though not mentioned in the Bible, it is apparent that there will be need for a judgment of millennial saints at the close of the millennium in addition to these that are revealed. The time and place of all these judgments, the character of the judgments, and the character of those being judged require that these judgments be distinguished." See John F. Walvoord, *The Millennial Kingdom* (Grand Rapids: Zondervan, 1980), 276–77.

> For they themselves report concerning us the kind of reception we had among you, and how you turned to God from idols to serve the living and true God, and to wait for his Son from heaven, whom he raised from the dead, Jesus who *delivers us from the wrath to come.* (1 Thess. 1:9–10)

Paul links the second coming ("wait for his Son from heaven") to the day when Jesus "delivers us from the wrath to come." But what is this wrath to come and when does this occur according to the Scriptures? Is this a reference to the wrath of God poured out during the Great Tribulation culminating at the battle of Armageddon when the Antichrist is destroyed, as premillennialists claim, or is this a reference to the Great White Throne judgment when unbelievers are judged and sentenced to the lake of fire, which, according to John, occurs after the millennium on the very last day of this Genesis creation (Rev. 20:11–15)?

Because premillennialists have Christ coming again to this earth at the end of the Tribulation, they by necessity connect the "wrath to come" alluded to by Paul to the wrath of God poured out during and at the end of the Great Tribulation. And they find some scriptural evidence for these assertions. For example, in the middle of a discussion of the events of the Great Tribulation, John says, "And he said with a loud voice, 'Fear God and give him glory, because the *hour of his judgment has come,* and worship him who made heaven and earth, the sea and the springs of water.' Another angel, a second, followed, saying, 'Fallen, fallen is Babylon the great'" (Rev. 14:7–8).

John says that when Christ engages the Antichrist in the Battle of Armageddon, "he will tread the winepress of the fury of the wrath of God the Almighty. On his robe and on his thigh he has a name written, King of kings and Lord of lords" (Rev. 19:15–16). Because this judgment is the beginning of the millennial reign of Christ, premillennialists interpret this "fury of the wrath of God" as the judgment seat of Christ when he comes again to separate the sheep from the goats, with the sheep being the raptured saints entering the millennial kingdom and the goats being unbelievers with the mark of the beast being judged and sent to hell.

But John makes no mention whatsoever that at the Battle of Armageddon these kings of the Antichrist and their slain armies are sent to the lake of fire, which only occurs at the Great White Throne judgment after the millennium. They are merely slain, which means they die a mortal death, but not an eternal "second death." They remain in Hades with the rest of deceased unbelievers until a thousand years later when they experience the final resurrection and the Great White Throne judgment; only then do they experience the second death in the lake of fire. The exception is that the beast and the false prophet are sent directly to the lake of fire, bypassing Hades and the Great White Throne judgment altogether (Rev. 19:20).

Unlike the beast and the false prophet, those soldiers who are killed by fire from heaven are not sent directly to the lake of fire, but are held in prison (Hades) until the Great White Throne judgment after the millennium. The slain unbelievers that follow the Antichrist will experience a type of hell on earth during the Tribulation, a form of hell in Hades for a thousand years, and then, finally, hell itself in the lake of fire after the Great White Throne judgment.

Yet, there is still a big difference between this vengeance of God executed at the battle of Armageddon during the Tribulation that can destroy the body, and the *final* wrath of God executed on the last day that can destroy the body and soul—the second death in the lake of fire. The Tribulation wrath is temporal, and some civilian unbelievers not engaged in this battle will even survive it. But the wrath of God on Judgment Day that sends unbelievers to the eternal fire is final, permanent, and eternal.

Sodom and Gomorrah were similarly destroyed by fire in a single day, but this was not the day of judgment for these slain unbelievers. Jesus taught that something much worse was going to happen to anyone who did not believe in him: "And if anyone will not receive you or listen to your words, shake off the dust from your feet when you leave that house or town. Truly, I say to you, it will be more bearable *on the day of judgment* for the land of Sodom and Gomorrah than for that town" (Matt. 10:14–15). The citizens of Sodom and Gomorrah experienced a form of God's judgment when they were destroyed by fire, and they continue to experience God's judgment in Hades where they are currently held. But in the future they will eventually experience God's final wrath *on the day of judgment* on the last day when they experience the second death in the lake of fire. Likewise, those soldiers killed by fire at the battle of Armageddon await the day of judgment at the Great White Throne judgment.

The flood in Noah's day was a devastating form of judgment that wiped out every person on earth except Noah and his family, but this was not the final Day of Judgment either. These historical events, as well as the wrath poured out during the Great Tribulation, represent different kinds of God's judgment, wrath, and vengeance on the unrighteous, but they are merely examples that foreshadow what will happen on the final Day of Judgment, which is why Jesus uses them as merely examples of the wrath to come.

Peter also warns that departed unbelievers and even fallen angels are being kept in darkness and experience some form of punishment (Hades) until the final Day of Judgment:

> For if God did not spare angels when they sinned, but cast them into hell and committed them to chains of gloomy darkness to be kept until the judgment; if he did not spare the ancient world, but preserved Noah, a herald of righteousness, with seven others, when he brought a flood upon

the world of the ungodly; if by turning the cities of Sodom and Gomorrah to ashes he condemned them to extinction, making them an example of what is going to happen to the ungodly; and if he rescued righteous Lot, greatly distressed by the sensual conduct of the wicked (for as that righteous man lived among them day after day, he was tormenting his righteous soul over their lawless deeds that he saw and heard); then the Lord knows how to rescue the godly from trials, and to keep the unrighteous under punishment *until the day of judgment.* (2 Peter 2:4–9)

Even fallen angels have not yet experienced the Day of Judgment when they, too, will be sent to the lake of fire. Likewise, there is a day of judgment that awaits all the unrighteous and ungodly. Currently, unbelievers are all being held under some type of punishment in Hades, but they will not experience the ultimate form of God's wrath until the Day of Judgment.

The final Day of Judgment referenced by Jesus and the apostles determines whether a person is going to be in heaven or in hell for eternity. This is the most important judgment day of all, for it is final and irreversible and the consequences almost unimaginable. Jesus warned, "Do not fear those who kill the body but cannot kill the soul. Rather fear him who can destroy both soul and body in hell" (Matt. 10:28). And where do we find this form of final judgment in Revelation? John teaches that the souls and bodies of unbelievers are sent to hell when they are resurrected from Hades during the final resurrection on the last day of this Genesis earth to face God at the Great White Throne judgment:

Then I saw a great white throne and him who was seated on it. From his presence earth and sky fled away, and no place was found for them. And I saw the dead, great and small, standing before the throne, and books were opened. . . . And the dead were judged by what was written in the books, according to what they had done. . . . Death and Hades gave up the dead who were in them, and they were judged, each one of them, according to what they had done. Then Death and Hades were thrown into the lake of fire. This is the second death, the lake of fire. And if anyone's name was not found written in the book of life, he was thrown into the lake of fire. Then I saw a new heaven and a new earth, for the first heaven and the first earth had passed away, and the sea was no more. (Rev. 20:11—21:1)

There may have been multiple historical occasions when different forms of God's judgment have been poured out on this earth, and even some additional forms of judgment in the future Tribulation, but there are not seven Judgment Days associated with a variety of raptures. There is only one real Day of Judgment, the Great White Throne judgment, and it occurs on the very last day of this Genesis creation.

In summary, when Paul is informing the Thessalonians that they have "turned to God from idols to serve the living and true God, and to wait for his Son from heaven [the second coming and the rapture], whom he raised from the dead, Jesus who delivers us from the *wrath to come*" (1 Thess. 1:9–10), he is referring to the wrath to come at the Great White Throne judgment when Christ comes again and believers are raptured and enter their citizenship in heaven and when unbelievers, who have been held in Hades, are resurrected in body and soul and enter the lake of fire. Simply put, the wrath to come referenced by Paul is the lake of fire, not God's wrath poured out at the end of the Tribulation when "he will tread the winepress of the fury of the wrath of God" at the battle of Armageddon (Rev. 19:15–16).

The Second Coming in Revelation

Revelation can be very complicated because of its symbolic imagery combined with extensive recapitulation, but toward the end of the book, John lays out a fairly simple outline of the prophetic future. After the Tribulation comes to an end, with all its many associated forms of judgment against those with the mark of the beast culminating at the battle of Armageddon, there is the subsequent millennial kingdom when Satan is bound and Christ rules the world for one thousand years with the saints of the "first resurrection." Then, after the millennium, Satan is released one final time. He leads one more failed rebellion against Christ, but is captured and cast into the eternal lake of fire never to be heard from again. Then, John sees the end of the Genesis creation, the final resurrection of all mankind, the Great White Throne judgment of believers and unbelievers, and the beginning of the new heavens and new earth for believers and eternal hell for unbelievers.

But, in this section of Revelation, John does not specifically reference this "day of judgment" at the end of the world as being the second coming of Christ. For example, John does not say, "*And then I saw the Lord return in the clouds to rapture the saints*—and from his presence earth and sky fled away, and then I saw a great white throne and him who was seated on it. . . . And the dead were judged by what was written in the books." If he had included this short description of Christ's second coming with the end of the world and the Great White Throne judgment, it may have saved the church from two thousand years of confusion! Premillennialism would never have been considered as a viable eschatology. Postmillennialism would have been the only viable option, with the debate centering on the nature of the preceding millennial kingdom and the meaning of the "first resurrection."

Maybe it was so obvious to John that Judgment Day was the occasion of Christ's second coming that he did not think it necessary to restate the obvious. Later in the book of Revelation, after his description of the New Jerusalem during his summation, he does, however, make a direct connection between the second coming of Christ *and* Judgment Day when he quotes Christ as explicitly saying that he *comes again* when this Genesis creation *comes to an end* and *all mankind* is judged:

> And he said to me, "These words are trustworthy and true. And the Lord, the God of the spirits of the prophets, has sent his angel to show his servants what must soon take place. 'And behold, I am coming soon. Blessed is the one who keeps the words of the prophecy of this book.' . . . 'Behold, I am coming soon [the second coming], bringing my recompense with me [rewards and punishments], to repay everyone [believers and unbelievers alike] for what he has done [based on what is recorded in the books]. I am the Alpha and the Omega, the first and the last, the beginning [of this Genesis creation] and the end [of this Genesis creation].' Blessed are those who wash their robes, so that they may have the right to the tree of life and that they may enter the city by the gates [the New Jerusalem in the new heavens and new earth]. Outside are the dogs and sorcerers and the sexually immoral and murderers and idolaters, and everyone who loves and practices falsehood [unbelievers in the lake of fire]." (Rev. 22:6–15)

When Christ comes again, it is Judgment Day for all mankind. The books are opened to determine who among mankind are God's children and are resurrected (raptured) to inherit their rewards in the kingdom of heaven and who are resurrected from Hades to inherit their punishments in the lake of fire or hell.

The second coming ("Behold, I am coming soon") described in this section of Revelation can easily be matched up with the formulation of what occurs at the Great White Throne judgment:

- The Omega end of this Genesis creation (Rev. 22:13) = "from his presence earth and sky fled away" (Rev. 20:11).
- "Bringing my recompense with me, to repay everyone for what he has done" (Rev. 22:12) = "And I saw the dead, great and small, standing before the throne, and books were opened. . . . And the dead were judged by what was written in the books, *according to what they had done*" (Rev. 20:12).

Notice, there will be two sets of books opened at this final resurrection: the "book of life" containing the names and deeds of the saints and an unnamed book containing the names and deeds of unbelievers. All the resurrected dead, believers and unbelievers alike, are judged by what is recorded in the two sets of books. Those who are in the "book of life" escape God's final wrath and the lake of fire and enter the new heavens and new earth, whereas resurrected unbelievers experience eternal judgment through the "second death" by being cast into the lake of fire.

This final judgment by Christ when he comes again is unmistakably after the Great Tribulation, after the millennial reign of Christ, and even after the Genesis creation has been destroyed—not at the end of the Tribulation as claimed by premillennialists.

When we say that we as Christians are "saved," we mean we are saved from this final wrath of God and the lake of fire, because we are in Christ and in the book of life and will inherit eternal life in the eternal kingdom of heaven when our bodies are raptured and made immortal.

Another reason John may not have restated the obvious fact that the second coming is at the Great White Throne judgment is because in his gospel he quotes Jesus teaching that his second coming is directly linked to the final day of judgment when the resurrected saints inherit the kingdom of heaven and unbelievers are resurrected, judged, and sent to hell:

> Do not marvel at this, for an hour is coming when all who are in the tombs will hear his voice [at the second coming] and come out [believers and unbelievers], those who have done good to the resurrection of life, [those in the book of life are raptured, judged at the Great White Throne, and inherit eternal life in heaven] and those who have done evil to the resurrection of judgment [unbelievers are raised, judged at the Great White Throne, and inherit the lake of fire]." (John 5:28–29)

The final resurrection involves the resurrection of both believers and unbelievers on Judgment Day, with resurrected believers inheriting eternal life and unbelievers inheriting eternal condemnation.

A blend of John's teachings in his gospel with his teachings in Revelation would read something like the following paraphrase:

> Christ warns us that he is coming soon after his millennial reign. When he does come again, he will destroy this Genesis creation just as easily as he created it. That is why he is the Alpha of this creation and the Omega of this creation. After he destroys this Genesis creation, such that it vanishes from his presence, he will then sit on his Great White Throne to judge all mankind when everyone will be resurrected to face judgment. The saints, who are in the book of life and have done good works, will experience a resurrection of eternal life when they enter the new heavens and new earth. Those who have done evil, because they are not in the book of life, will be raised to be judged according to their evil deeds and will then be sentenced to the eternal lake of fire, where they will experience the second death. Christ will repay everyone for what they have done during their life on this earth when he comes again to resurrect all mankind and judge the world.

Matthew also quotes Jesus as teaching that the second coming coincides with Judgment Day:

When the Son of Man comes in his glory, and all the angels with him [the Omega], then he will sit on his glorious throne [Great White Throne]. Before him will be gathered all the nations [the final resurrection], and he will separate people one from another as a shepherd separates the sheep from the goats [based on who is in the "book of life"]. And he will place the sheep on his right [those in the book of life], but the goats on the left [those whose "name was not found written in the book of life"]. Then the King will say to those on his right, "Come, you who are blessed by my Father, inherit the kingdom prepared for you from the foundation of the world [the Father's heavenly kingdom]." . . . Then he will say to those on his left, "Depart from me, you cursed, into the eternal fire prepared for the devil and his angels [the lake of fire]." . . . And these will go away into eternal punishment [the second death], but the righteous into eternal life [in the Father's heavenly kingdom]. (Matt. 25:31–46)

Premillennialists claim that this "day of judgment" occurs at the end of the Tribulation and at the beginning of the millennial reign of Christ. But Christ creates an unmistakable and inseparable link between his second coming *and* Judgment Day when he will "sit on his throne" to judge between the sheep (believers) who will inherit "eternal life" in his Father's eternal kingdom and the goats (unbelievers) who will be sent to the "eternal fire prepared for the devil and his angels"—that is, the lake of fire or the second death. When Christ comes again on Judgment Day, the resurrected saints are destined for the Father's eternal kingdom of heaven, not the Son's earthly kingdom, and unbelievers are destined for the "eternal fire prepared for the devil and his angels." This can be outlined as follows:

- The second coming + the final resurrection of believers and unbelievers + Judgment Day = Raptured believers inherit the Father's eternal kingdom of heaven, and unbelievers, along with the fallen angels, inherit the lake of fire.

This is precisely what John describes in Revelation at the Great White Throne judgment after the current Genesis creation disappears and Christ opens the books and judges the world, sending those in the book of life (God's children) to the new heavens and new earth and unbelievers to the lake of fire or the second death. When Christ comes again, the raptured saints "escape the wrath to come" on Judgment Day and inherit the kingdom of heaven—not the earthly kingdom.

The parable of sowing good seed among weeds, also in the gospel of Matthew, teaches this same concept:

Then he left the crowds and went into the house. And his disciples came to him, saying, "Explain to us the parable of the weeds of the field." He answered, "The one who sows the good seed is the Son of Man. The field is the world, and the good seed is the children of the kingdom. The weeds are the sons of the evil one, and the enemy who sowed them is the devil. The harvest is the close of the age [the Omega at the end of the Genesis creation, when earth and sky fled from his presence], and the reapers are angels. Just as the weeds are gathered and burned with fire, so will it be at the close of the age [the Genesis age]. The Son of Man will send his angels, and they will gather out of his kingdom all causes of sin and all law-breakers, and throw them into the fiery furnace [the lake of fire]. In that place there will be weeping and gnashing of teeth. Then the righteous will shine like the sun in the kingdom of their Father [in heaven]. He who has ears, let him hear." (13:36–43)

Jesus teaches through this parable that he comes again on the last day of this Genesis creation, Judgment Day, when the saints (the good seed) are resurrected in order to be taken to his Father's heavenly kingdom at the same time that unbelievers (the weeds) are raised to be judged and sent "into the fiery furnace"—the lake of fire.

The New Testament plainly teaches that the destiny of the glorified raptured saints on Judgment Day is the Father's glorious kingdom of heaven—not the Son's earthly kingdom. There is no mention whatsoever of the "raptured" saints inheriting the Son's earthly kingdom "when the Son of Man comes in his glory." The raptured saints are clearly destined for "the kingdom of their Father" prepared for us "from the foundation of the world."

Paul's Epistles

Let's review Paul's teachings to see how well he connects the second coming and the rapture to Judgment Day when the saints inherit the Father's eternal kingdom, not the Son's earthly kingdom. Paul says:

For we know that if the tent [our Adamic body], which is our earthly home, is destroyed, we have a building from God, a house not made with hands, eternal in the heavens. For in this tent we groan, longing to put on our heavenly dwelling [our transformed immortal body in its heavenly setting], if indeed by putting it on we may not be found naked. For while we are still in this tent, we groan, being burdened—not that we would be unclothed, but that we would be further clothed, so that what is mortal may be swallowed up by life. . . . So whether we are at home or away, we make it our aim to please him. For we must all appear before the judgment seat of Christ, so that each one may receive what is due for what he has done in the body, whether good or evil. (2 Cor. 5:1–4, 9–10)

The mortal Adamic body is the earthly dwelling of our regenerated spirits while we are on this earth. To be taken to the eternal kingdom of heaven, however, we need to have immortal bodies like Christ's resurrected body, which will be "our heavenly dwelling" because it is adapted and destined for the kingdom of heaven. Once we as the children of God take on our eternal bodies through the rapture, we will be "eternal in the heavens." That occurs when Christ comes again on Judgment Day when "we must all appear before the judgment seat of Christ" to be rewarded (as believers) with the Father's eternal kingdom or punished (as unbelievers) with eternal destruction.

On Judgment Day, the raptured body—"our heavenly dwelling"—is destined for heaven, not the earth. This can be outlined as follows:

- The rapture (the mortal body transformed into an eternal body) + the judgment seat of Christ = eternal in the heavens or our heavenly dwelling.

Paul's description of the final resurrection of believers and unbelievers on Judgment Day, which is based on what all mankind has done on this earth, is virtually identical to John's phrasing in Revelation:

- "For we must all appear before the judgment seat of Christ, so that each one may receive what is due for what he has done in the body, whether good or evil" (2 Cor. 5:10) = "And the dead were judged by what was written in the books, according to what they had done" (Rev. 20:12), or "Behold, I am coming soon, bringing my recompense with me, to repay everyone for what he has done" (Rev. 22:12).

Paul makes it very clear in his letter to the Colossians that we receive our eternal inheritance in our glorified bodies when Christ comes again on Judgment Day and the wrath of God is poured out on unbelievers:

If then you have been raised with Christ, seek the things that are above [in heaven], where Christ is, seated at the right hand of God [in heaven]. Set your minds on things that are above, not on things that are on earth. For you have died, and your life is hidden with Christ in God [in heaven]. When Christ who is your life *appears* [at the second coming], then you also will *appear with him in glory* [in heaven in an ascended glorified body]. Put to death therefore what is earthly in you: sexual immorality, impurity, passion, evil desire, and covetousness, which is idolatry. On account of these the *wrath of God is coming* [the lake of fire on Judgment Day]. (Col. 3:1–6)

The wrath of God is coming at the very same time that Christ appears again and we are raptured into glorified bodies and taken to the "things that are above," or heaven. These verses can be outlined as follows:

- The second coming ("When Christ who is your life appears") + the rapture ("you also will appear with him in glory") + Judgment Day ("the wrath of God is coming") = heaven ("things that are above, where Christ is, seated at the right hand of God").

Throughout his first letter to the Thessalonians, Paul connects the rapture to the second coming on Judgment Day:

> For they themselves report concerning us the kind of reception we had among you, and how you turned to God from idols to serve the living and true God, and *to wait for his Son from heaven*, whom he raised from the dead, *Jesus who delivers us from the wrath to come* (1:9–10). . . . For what is our hope or joy or crown of boasting before our Lord Jesus *at his coming*? Is it not you? . . . (2:19–20) . . . For the Lord himself will descend from heaven with a cry of command, with the voice of an archangel, and with the sound of the trumpet of God. And the dead in Christ will rise first. Then we who are alive, who are left, will be caught up together with them in the clouds to meet the Lord in the air, and so we will always be with the Lord (4:16–17).

This can be outlined as follows:

- The second coming + the rapture + escape "the wrath to come" on Judgment Day = join Christ in the air to be taken to his Father's eternal kingdom of heaven.

Paul makes this same linkage in his second letter to the Thessalonians:

> This is evidence of the righteous judgment of God, that you may be considered worthy of the kingdom of God [the heavenly kingdom], for which you are also suffering—since indeed God considers it just to repay with affliction those who afflict you [on Judgment Day], and to grant relief to you who are afflicted as well as to us, when the Lord Jesus is revealed from heaven with his mighty angels in flaming fire [the second coming], inflicting vengeance [the wrath of God] on those who do not know God and on those who do not obey the gospel of our Lord Jesus. They will suffer the punishment of eternal destruction [the lake of fire], away from the presence of the Lord and from the glory of his might, when he comes on that day to be glorified in his saints [raptured and transformed into glorified bodies], and to be marveled at among all who have believed, because our testimony to you was believed. (2 Thess. 1:5–10)

There is nothing in these verses that states that Christ is returning with the raptured saints to this earth on Judgment Day. Rather, the second coming occurs at the end of this Genesis creation (the Omega) and the beginning of the eternal kingdom for believers and eternal destruction for unbelievers. This can be outlined as follows:

- The Lord Jesus is revealed from heaven + the rapture of the glorified saints + Judgment Day = The glorified saints inherit the kingdom of heaven + unbelievers face the flaming fire and the punishment of eternal destruction.

This direct linkage between the second coming, the rapture, Judgment Day, and our eternal destiny of the Father's eternal kingdom can be found throughout Paul's epistles. It is the essence of his good news for those who repent and are justified by faith in Jesus Christ.

Since this is so important, let's outline the phrases Paul uses in 1 and 2 Thessalonians. The second coming is referred to as follows:

- "wait for his Son from heaven" (1 Thess. 1:10).
- "the coming of our Lord Jesus" (1 Thess. 3:13).
- "the day of the Lord will come like a thief" (1 Thess. 5:2).
- "at the coming of our Lord Jesus Christ" (1 Thess. 5:23).
- "when the Lord Jesus is revealed from heaven" (2 Thess. 1:7).
- "when he comes on that day" (2 Thess. 1:10).

The second coming of Christ is directly linked to the rapture or the resurrection of the saints into their immortal bodies:

- "when he comes on that day to be glorified in his saints" (2 Thess. 1:10).
- "And the dead in Christ will rise first. Then we who are alive, who are left, will be caught up together with them in the clouds to meet the Lord in the air" (1 Thess. 4:16–17).

The second coming of Christ is directly linked with the saints being delivered from the wrath to come on Judgment Day:

- "Then sudden destruction will come upon them as labor pains come upon a pregnant woman, and they will not escape. . . . For God has not destined us for wrath, but to obtain salvation . . . " (1 Thess. 5:3, 9).
- "inflicting vengeance on those who do not know God" (2 Thess. 1:8).
- "They will suffer the punishment of eternal destruction, away from the presence of the Lord and from the glory of his might, when he comes on that day to be glorified in his saints" (2 Thess. 1:9).

Paul's teachings about the rapture are central to the premillennialists' view that claims the raptured saints are destined for the 1,000-year restoration on this Genesis earth, but all Paul's letters support the proposition that the raptured saints are destined for the eternal kingdom of heaven on Judgment Day, not for the earthly messianic kingdom.

The destiny of the raptured saints being the eternal kingdom of heaven is a recurring theme throughout the New Testament.

Peter's Epistles

Peter describes Christ's second coming in terms of *the end of this earth*, Judgment Day, and the beginning of the new heavens and new earth, when he responds to critics who questioned if there was such a thing as a second coming. I will put into brackets some of John's and Paul's corresponding teachings:

> Scoffers will come in the last days with scoffing, . . . They will say, "Where is the promise of his coming? For ever since the fathers fell asleep, all things are continuing as they were from the beginning of creation." For they deliberately overlook this fact, that the heavens existed long ago, and the earth was formed out of water and through water by the word of God [the Alpha] . . . But by the same word the heavens and earth that now exist are stored up for fire [the Omega], being kept until the day of judgment and destruction of the ungodly [as Paul says, "They will suffer the punishment of eternal destruction"]. . . . But the day of the Lord will come like a thief ["in flaming fire"], and then the heavens will pass away with a roar, and the heavenly bodies will be burned up and dissolved [as John says, "the first heaven and the first earth had passed away"], and the earth and the works that are done on it will be exposed [when the books are opened and the good deeds of believers and the bad deeds of unbelievers will be exposed]. Since all these things are thus to be dissolved, what sort of people ought you to be in lives of holiness and godliness, [storing up good deeds that will be exposed on Judgment Day] waiting for and hastening the coming of the day of God [the second coming], because of which the heavens will be set on fire and dissolved, and the heavenly bodies will melt as they burn [as Paul says, "when the Lord Jesus is revealed from heaven with his mighty angels in flaming fire"]! But according to his promise we [those who "obey the gospel of our Lord Jesus"] are waiting for new heavens and a new earth in which righteousness dwells ["when he comes on that day to be glorified in his saints"]. (2 Peter 3:3–13)

Notice that Peter ties the second coming of Christ not only to the destruction of the current heavens and earth and the beginning of the new heavens and new earth, but also directly to the final day of judgment and the destruction of the unbelievers: "But by the same *word* the heavens and earth that now exist are stored up for fire, being kept until the *day of judgment and destruction of the ungodly*" (2 Peter 3:7). Most important, note how Peter refers to Jesus' promise to come again to take us to the Father's eternal kingdom of heaven—not the millennial kingdom: "But according to his promise [of his second coming and our resurrection], we are waiting for new heavens and a new earth in which righteousness dwells" (2 Peter 3:13).

In his first epistle, Peter makes these same connections:

Blessed be the God and Father of our Lord Jesus Christ! According to his great mercy, he [the Father] has caused us to be born again [as children of God] to a living hope through the resurrection of Jesus Christ from the dead [hope for a similar resurrection of an eternal body], to an inheritance that is imperishable, undefiled, and unfading, kept in heaven for you, who by God's power are being guarded through faith for a salvation ready to be revealed in the last time. In this you rejoice, though now for a little while, if necessary, you have been grieved by various trials, so that the tested genuineness of your faith—more precious than gold that perishes though it is tested by fire [on Judgment Day]—may be found to result in praise and glory and honor at the revelation of Jesus Christ [the second coming on Judgment Day]. (1 Peter 1:3–7)

The phrase "the revelation of Jesus Christ" is referring to the day when Jesus says, "When the Son of Man comes in his glory, and all the angels with him, then he will sit on his glorious throne" (Matt. 25:31). And when Christ comes again, what is the destiny of those the Father has chosen to be his children? Is it the inheritance of this temporal earth for another thousand years? Peter answers this question in the clearest manner possible. When our hope for a resurrection like Christ's resurrection occurs at his second coming, we will receive "an inheritance that is imperishable, undefiled, and unfading, kept in heaven." The destiny of the raptured saints on Judgment Day is unquestionably the eternal kingdom of heaven—not the restored earth.

Peter's teaching on the second coming matches with John's teachings in Revelation as to what occurs at the Great White Throne judgment. Peter says, "The works that are done on it [the earth] will be exposed" when Christ comes again (2 Peter 3:10). This matches precisely what John says will happen when the books, which contain a record of the works or deeds of all mankind, are opened to expose the good and evil done on this earth. *All* the books are opened and all the deeds done on this earth will be exposed and judged. The saints are judged first: "For it is time for judgment to begin at the household of God; and if it begins with us, what will be the outcome for those who do not obey the gospel of God?" (1 Peter 4:17).

The saints are judged differently than unbelievers, however. The saints are judged by burning off their worthless deeds to determine what survives:

For no one can lay a foundation other than that which is laid, which is Jesus Christ. Now if anyone builds on the foundation with gold, silver, precious stones, wood, hay, straw—each one's work will become manifest, for the Day will disclose it, because it will be revealed by fire, and the fire will test what sort of work each one has done. If the work that anyone has built on the foundation survives, he will receive a reward. If anyone's work is burned up, he will suffer loss, though he himself will be saved, but only as through fire. (1 Cor. 3:11–15)

The rewards the believer receives will be based on those good deeds that survive the fire on Judgment Day. The judgment for the unbeliever is radically different because he has no righteousness on his own. The unbeliever is judged to determine the degree of punishment he will experience in the lake of fire based on the extent of his evil deeds done on the earth. In heaven some saints will be given greater rewards, and in hell some unbelievers will be given greater punishment—all depending on what they did in this life, which is recorded in the books.

The basis for judgment of the saints is the information recorded in the book of life. The book that is opened to judge unbelievers is not given a specific name, but, nonetheless, John does describe it as a book used to judge unbelievers (Rev. 20:12). A dual judgment using two sets of books takes place. Believers are judged first and unbelievers are judged last. Notice again that everyone is judged at this time at the Great White Throne: "Then I saw a great white throne . . . Then another book was opened, which is the book of life. And the dead [believers and unbelievers] were *judged by what was* written in the books [plural, for both sets of books], according to what they [believers and unbelievers] had done" (Rev. 20:11–12).

Peter's description of the destruction of the Genesis creation by fire at the second coming of Christ also directly parallels John's description in Revelation: "Earth and sky fled away, and no place was found for them. . . . Then I saw a new heaven and a new earth, for the first heaven and the first earth had passed away, and the sea was no more" (20:11; 21:1). Peter supplies the added detail that these events occur at Christ's second coming.

Perhaps since Peter's epistles had already been written and were well read by the church, John felt it unnecessary to restate the obvious at this point in Revelation. Furthermore, Christ's teachings in the Gospels had already established that his second coming is going to be on Judgment Day, when all mankind would be judged and either brought into heaven or sent to the lake of fire.

Let's compare John's teaching in Revelation to Peter's teaching concerning what transpires at Christ's second coming.

- "Behold, I am coming soon, bringing my recompense with me. . . . the Omega . . . the end" (Rev. 22:12–13) = "Where is the promise of his coming . . . The day of the Lord will come like a thief" (2 Peter 3:4, 10).
- "From his presence earth and sky fled away" (Rev. 20:11) = "Then the heavens will pass away with a roar, and the heavenly bodies will be burned up and dissolved" (2 Peter 3:10).
- "Then I saw a new heaven and a new earth" (Rev. 21:1) = "But according to his promise we are waiting for new heavens and a new earth in which righteousness dwells" (2 Peter 3:13).

- "And I saw the dead, great and small, standing before the throne, and the books were opened. . . . And the dead were judged by what was written in the books, according to what they had done" (Rev. 20:12) = "The earth and the works that are done on it will be exposed" (2 Peter 3:10).
- "Then Death and Hades were thrown into the lake of fire. This is the second death, the lake of fire" (Rev. 20:14) = "The day of judgment and destruction of the ungodly" (2 Peter 3:7).

The similarity between John's description of Christ's second coming on the last day and Peter's description is remarkable. Jesus, John, Paul, and Peter all link the second coming and the resurrection of the saints in their glorified bodies to Judgment Day, when everyone (believers and unbelievers) will be resurrected and judged for what they have done on the earth—the resurrected and/or transformed saints are judged and rewarded in the eternal kingdom of God the Father, and the resurrected unbelievers are judged and sentenced to the eternal lake of fire. This was likely so obvious to John when writing Revelation that he did not bother to restate that the second coming occurs at the Great White Throne judgment. In the apostles' minds this was a given, for Jesus had preached extensively on his second coming on Judgment Day, when we will join him in his Father's kingdom.

Hebrews

The writer of Hebrews also describes the end of this Genesis creation when Christ comes again to usher in the eternal kingdom: "And, 'You, Lord, laid the foundation of the earth in the beginning [the Alpha], and the heavens are the work of your hands; *they will perish,* but you remain; they will all wear out like a garment, like a robe you will roll them up, like a garment they will be changed [the Omega]. . . .'" (Heb. 1:10–12). The garment is the Adamic creation; it will be removed and replaced with a new garment—a new creation:

At that time [the time of Moses] his voice [his word] shook the earth, but now he has promised, "Yet once more I will shake not only the earth but also the heavens ["earth and sky fled away"]." This phrase, "Yet once more," indicates the removal of things that are shaken—that is, *things that have been made*—in order that the *things that cannot be shaken may remain* [heavenly things]. Therefore let us be grateful for receiving a kingdom [a heavenly one] that cannot be shaken, and thus let us offer to God acceptable worship, with reverence and awe, for our God *is a consuming fire* [on Judgment Day]. (Heb. 12:26–29)

God created this Genesis creation by his word, and he will destroy it by his word. He will then create them anew. And a God who is described as "a consuming fire" will have no problem merely saying the word in order that things that can be shaken will be destroyed. Again, this teaching in Hebrews mirrors 2 Peter and Revelation 20 and 21 whereby God wipes out this creation with fire and replaces it with an indestructible, eternal new heavens and new earth—a heavenly kingdom that cannot be shaken.

The writer to the Hebrews teaches that because of Christ's sacrifice for our sins, the saints can look forward to an eternal inheritance in heaven: "the promised *eternal inheritance*, since a death has occurred that redeems them from the transgressions committed under the first covenant" (9:15). And when does the writer say that Christ comes again in order for the faithful saints to receive this eternal inheritance? On the last day, when Christ will appear a second time and the earth is destroyed; it is Judgment Day, when we inherit the eternal, heavenly Jerusalem:

So Christ, having been offered once to bear the sins of many, *will appear a second time*, not to deal with sin but to save those who are eagerly waiting for him (9:28). . . . but encouraging one another, and all the more as you see the Day drawing near [the second coming and Judgment Day]. For if we go on sinning deliberately after receiving the knowledge of the truth, there no longer remains a sacrifice for sins, but a fearful expectation of judgment, and a fury of fire [lake of fire] that will consume the adversaries. . . . "Vengeance is mine; I will repay." And again, "The Lord will judge his people." It is a fearful thing to fall into the hands of the living God. (10:25–31)

The author is teaching that the second coming is on Judgment Day, which will be a day of vengeance for unbelievers and a consuming fire that will remove the things that have been made, or this Genesis creation.

According to Hebrews, the faithful departed saints are waiting for Christ's second coming when this Genesis creation will be removed so that we will inherit the city of the living God, the heavenly Jerusalem:

These all died in faith, not having received the things promised, . . . and having acknowledged that they were strangers and exiles on the earth. . . . If they had been thinking of that land from which they had gone out, they would have had opportunity to return. But as it is, they desire a better country, that is, a heavenly one. Therefore, God is not ashamed to be called their God, for he has prepared for them a city [the heavenly one]. . . . But you have come to Mount Zion and to the city of the living God, the heavenly Jerusalem." (Heb. 11:13–16; 12:22)

Hebrews clearly teaches that Christ comes again when this Genesis creation is destroyed (vanishes) on Judgment Day, and those who have faith in Christ will escape God's vengeance, "judgment, and a fury of fire" and will be taken to the promised eternal inheritance. The Genesis earth will no longer exist because it will have been removed or consumed by fire. Or, as John says, "From his presence earth and sky fled away, and no place was found for them" (Rev. 20:11), which occurs *after* the millennial reign of Christ. As a result, Christ's second coming can only occur after his millennial kingdom on the very last day of this Genesis creation, when the raptured saints are judged and then taken to the new heavens and new earth. The eschatological framework of Hebrews can be outlined as follows:

- Second coming + rapture + end of this Genesis creation + Judgment Day = eternal heavenly inheritance in the New Jerusalem for the faithful saints and a fury of fire for unbelievers.

Summary

Paul sums it up in the following verse: "But our citizenship is in heaven [our destiny when raptured]. And we eagerly await a Savior from there [heaven], the Lord Jesus Christ, who, by the power that enables him to bring everything under his control, will transform our lowly bodies [the rapture] so that they will be like his glorious body" (Phil. 3:20–21 NIV). When Christ comes again, he transforms our Adamic bodies to be like his "glorious body" to take us to our eternal citizenship in heaven—not to our citizenship on this earth during the millennial kingdom.

A close reading of the New Testament reveals that the second coming of Christ is unmistakably linked to the following events:

- The transformation of the saints into immortal bodies in order to dwell with Christ in the eternal kingdom of the Father.
- The destruction of the current Genesis heavens and earth.
- Judgment Day for believers and unbelievers (or the Great White Throne judgment).
- Believers (the children of God) inherit eternal life in the Father's kingdom (the new heavens and new earth) and unbelievers (the children of Satan) face the final wrath of God and are sent to the eternal lake of fire or the second death.

There is overwhelming scriptural evidence that the second coming of Christ takes place on the last day of this Genesis creation on Judgment Day and marks the beginning of the eternal kingdom of heaven for the raptured believers and the eternal lake of fire for unbelievers. Therefore, the destiny of the raptured saints on Judgment Day is the Father's kingdom of heaven— not the restored earth during the millennium as claimed by premillennialists. To establish his millennial kingdom, Christ simply rules the world from his throne in heaven after resurrecting his departed saints into natural bodies at the first resurrection.

4

Daniel and
the Olivet Discourse

When in Jerusalem, much of Christ's ministry and preaching took place at the temple, and he and his disciples would retire at night on the Mount of Olives where the disciples often asked Christ to further explain his teachings of that day. One day, after leaving the temple, Jesus made the following prophecy about the temple itself: "There will not be left here one stone upon another that will not be thrown down" (Matt. 24:2). The disciples were amazed by this prediction of the temple's destruction. The last time the temple had been destroyed was during the Babylonian Empire in 586 BC, when Israel had been persistently unfaithful to their covenant with God despite the repeated warnings by Jeremiah and other prophets. As predicted by Jeremiah and Daniel, however, it was rebuilt and restored by Nehemiah and Ezra during the Medo-Persian Empire around 408 BC and is referred to as the "Second Temple."

During the Greek Empire's domination of Israel, Antiochus IV Epiphanes desecrated the temple in 168 BC. He placed an idol of Zeus in the temple and attempted to force the Jews to worship the Greek gods. After a successful revolt by the Jews led by Mattathias and his sons, the temple practices were restored about six years later.

During the Roman Empire's occupation of Jerusalem, the Romans had wisely let the Jewish temple practices remain in place rather than attempt to impose their pagan forms of worship on the Jewish nation. Herod the Great made significant improvements to the temple in 19 BC. The Second Temple, with its stunning architecture and splendid adornments, had been in existence for more than four hundred years when Jesus shocked the disciples by predicting its destruction once again!

Deeply concerned about Christ's prophecy, the disciples came to him on the Mount of Olives and asked him privately, "Tell us, when will these things be [the temple's destruction], and what will be the sign of your coming and of the close of the age?" (24:3). The disciples are actually asking two questions: 1) How can they recognize when the temple is about to be destroyed? 2) How can they recognize when he is coming again at "the close of the age"? In a prior private conversation, Christ had already defined the phrase "the close of the age" as representing his second coming on Judgment Day when the saints are taken to his Father's heavenly kingdom:

> Then he left the crowds and went into the house. And his disciples came to him, saying, "Explain to us the parable of the weeds of the field." He answered, "The one who sows the good seed is the Son of Man. The field is the world, and the good seed is the sons of the kingdom. The weeds are the sons of the evil one, and the enemy who sowed them is the devil. The harvest is *the close of the age,* and the reapers are angels. Just as the weeds are gathered and burned with fire, so will it be at the *close of the age.* The Son of Man will send his angels, and they will gather out of his kingdom all causes of sin and all lawbreakers, and throw them into the fiery furnace. In that place there will be weeping and gnashing of teeth. Then the righteous will shine like the sun in the kingdom of their Father [the eternal heavenly kingdom]. He who has ears, let him hear." (Matt. 13:36–43)

Thus, Christ's Olivet Discourse covers the whole range of events that will occur on this earth before his second coming. It would have been much easier if the disciples had asked one question about the temple's destruction, received an answer, and then asked the next question about the "sign of your coming and the close of the age." Instead, they asked the two questions concurrently, and Christ's answers cover such a wide range of future events that it makes it difficult for scholars to determine when he is describing events leading up to the temple's destruction and when he is describing events leading up to "the close of the age."

When the Jewish believers in Judea and Jerusalem saw the signs leading up to the temple's destruction during the First Jewish-Roman War (AD 66–73), they heeded Christ's warning to leave Judea and Jerusalem and fled for safety in the hill country around the town of Pella, escaping the terrible tribulation that followed when the Roman soldiers crushed the Jewish revolt by entering Jerusalem to destroy the city and the temple.

Christ references Daniel when he describes the events surrounding the temple's impending destruction (Matt. 24:15). But does Daniel envision another desolation of the temple during a future Great Tribulation that, at its conclusion, leads to the messianic kingdom before the eternal kingdom? Unfortunately, Daniel's visions are complex and have deeply divided scholars over their meaning. The number of scholarly interpretations of

Daniel is remarkable, particularly as scholars attempt to harmonize his visions with the Olivet Discourse based on their own eschatology. There is nothing wrong with investigating whether an individual text or section of Scripture confirms a particular biblical-theological framework as long as we do not force the text to fit a predetermined eschatology. We need to read Daniel through the lens of the New Testament revelation, but we also need to determine from a grammatical-historical analysis of Daniel if his visions actually encompass certain future eschatological events.

By using postrestorationalism as the eschatological framework in this analysis, I will present the case that Daniel's vision *and* the Olivet Discourse do indeed foresee two distinct desolations of the temple, one by the Romans and another by the Antichrist, as well as the subsequent establishment of the messianic kingdom on this earth. Upon completion of these prophetic events, "the close of the age" is at hand—at which time Christ comes again to take us to his Father's heavenly kingdom in "the age to come."

Because of the plethora of opinions on Daniel and the Olivet Discourse, this chapter will not be heavily footnoted as is customary in this kind of analysis. Some of the material in this chapter can be found in commentaries. With postrestorationalism as the framework, I hope to bring a fresh perspective to the interpretation of Daniel and the Olivet Discourse.

The Setting for Daniel's Visions

Daniel's visions occurred when he and the Jewish nation had been exiled during the Babylonian Empire from 587–538 BC, which was later conquered and absorbed by the Medo-Persian Empire. As a young man, Daniel was recognized as a gifted individual and proved to be an administrative genius as he served in key government positions under different rulers throughout his life in exile. He was also a man of great faith and courage whom God used to deliver some of the most important truths about the future Jewish Messiah and his messianic kingdom as they revolve around Israel, Jerusalem, and its temple.

Before being exiled, Israel was given numerous warnings of impending destruction and exile by many prophets, including Jeremiah, because of their continuous and egregious violations of their covenant with God. These violations were not unexpected, however, for Moses had predicted that the Jewish nation would eventually violate their covenant with God, and God would judge the nation by allowing the hostile pagan nations around them to attack and destroy Jerusalem and its temple, sending them into exile as slaves and servants of these pagan enemies (Deut. 28:15–68 and Dan. 9:11–15). Moses and the prophets understood that Israel existed in a satanic and hostile world with many aggressive and dangerous pagan kingdoms constantly at war to conquer and subjugate other nations. It was Israel's fear of these hostile pagan nations and lack of trust in God to protect them that caused them to clamor for a king like Saul (1 Sam. 8–9).

But the only way Israel could count on God's continued protection of their nation and its temple in a world of warring pagan nations was to remain faithful to God's covenant. If they were consistently unfaithful, they would lose this divine protection and even their king could not protect them. And God, in his sovereignty, would use these aggressive pagan nations (more evil than Israel) to judge and discipline Israel.

Jeremiah had the duty of identifying Judea's transgressions of their covenant with God, announcing the impending destruction of Jerusalem and its temple, their exile, and living through these traumatic events. Even after the temple had been destroyed and the people exiled, he still disputed with false prophets left behind in Jerusalem who continued prophesying peace, a return from exile in a couple of years, and the restoration of the temple. Jeremiah responded by saying that Israel existed in an inherently hostile world, and they would continue to be subject to attacks by warring pagan nations as long as they were unfaithful to God's covenant of protection: "The prophets who preceded you and me from ancient times prophesied war, famine, and pestilence against many countries and great kingdoms" (Jer. 28:8). Because Israel has a propensity to violations of the covenant relationship with God (just as Moses foresaw), and it continues to exist in a hostile, satanic world of aggressive warring kingdoms, there could be multiple occasions when Jerusalem and its temple are attacked and desecrated—especially when Israel becomes as pagan as their neighbors.

Wars are extremely damaging to an agrarian society and almost always result in famine and pestilence because the invading armies disrupt the normal agrarian activities of the besieged community and often destroy their crops. The people within the cities under siege become trapped within their protective walls, cutting them off from whatever is left of their crops, leading to starvation and famine when stored supplies within the city run out. The crowding and malnutrition then often leads to pestilence or disease such as cholera, typhus, typhoid, and dysentery.

Mankind has lived with continuous war since Adam and Eve rebelled against God, and Satan entered our world. The armed invasion, domination, exploitation, and thievery of another country represent one of the highest forms of injustice. And even without the scourge of war, God's curse on this Genesis creation remains in place, resulting in plagues, earthquakes, and other natural disasters. Jeremiah is telling the false prophets that Israel still exists in a fallen, demonic world and will continue to experience the consequences when they are unfaithful and God removes his divine protection.

Jeremiah foresees the day, however, when Israel will finally repent and be given a new heart and the Messiah will come and establish Israel as a truly righteous nation: "In those days and at that time I will cause a righteous

Branch to spring up for David, and he shall execute justice and righteousness in the land" (Jer. 33:15). The Messiah will change the fundamental dynamics of Israel and the whole world and will create a kingdom in the land of Israel characterized by "justice and righteousness." And from Revelation we know that the only true exodus from this satanic world of warring nations will take place when Satan is removed and bound and the Messiah rules the world of righteous saints who have been delivered from Satan's dominion of darkness.

Daniel, who was familiar with Jeremiah's prophetic words and the affairs of conquering empires, had multiple visions of "many countries and great kingdoms" or great empires in the future that would directly affect Israel, Jerusalem, and its temple. Jerusalem and its temple will be restored as prophesied by Jeremiah, but Israel will continue to be unfaithful. Jerusalem and its temple will again be desecrated on multiple occasions. These desolations are God-ordained judgments whereby God uses Satan and his warring nations to chastise unfaithful Israel—until the Anointed One comes and establishes a righteous people and puts an end to all wars, ushering in an age of peace and righteousness on this earth; Israel will no longer need to worry about hostile nations attacking their nation, Jerusalem, and their temple.

Ezekiel, who was also in exile, was another prophet with whom Daniel was familiar. Ezekiel foresaw a resurrection and a restoration of Israel in a time of peace, justice, righteousness, and prosperity that will include a restored temple in a future messianic kingdom:

> Therefore prophesy, and say to them, Thus says the Lord GOD: Behold, I will open your graves and raise you from your graves, O my people. And I will bring you into the land of Israel. . . . I will make a covenant of peace with them. It shall be an everlasting covenant with them. And I will set them in their land and multiply them, and will set my sanctuary in their midst forevermore. (Ezek. 37:12, 26)

This everlasting covenant of peace in a world that has known only continuous war and injustice will ensure that Israel and its temple will never be desecrated again. In chapters 40–48, Ezekiel's vision goes into extraordinary detail describing the temple, its grounds, and its administration in the restored city of Jerusalem. New Testament theologians may be uncomfortable with the idea of another temple in the messianic kingdom because of Christ's completed work of atonement, as taught by the writer to the Hebrews, but we need to interpret Daniel in his grammatical-historical context. Daniel's multiple visions center around the temple—with its multiple desolations during future empires or kingdoms and its ultimate restoration as foretold by Ezekiel.

According to Hebrews, Christ's atonement for our sins is far superior to the temple sacrifices, and his sacrifice made many people from all nations righteous. From an eternal perspective, he put an end to the need for sacrifices when he offered his body as the perfect sacrifice. But the letter written to the Hebrews or the Jewish Christians was written before the destruction of the temple in AD 70 at a time when the Second Temple sacrifices were still occurring, and at no time does the Jewish writer condemn these practices. He says they will cease at the same time that the Genesis creation comes to an end (Heb. 8:13; 12:22–28).

Luke tells us that the Jewish Christians in Jerusalem remained "zealous for the law" and continued to meet at the temple and participate in the temple sacrifices (Acts 21:17–26). Hebrews is focused on the New Jerusalem in the eternal kingdom of heaven where Christ is our high priest of heaven; whereas Daniel's vision is focused on the restored Jerusalem in the earthly messianic kingdom. Daniel was a man of this world, and his visions of the messianic kingdom are also of this world—not of the heavenly kingdom. Most important, Daniel and the prophets envisioned another temple in the restored Jerusalem in the messianic kingdom. The complex theological implications of a restored Ezekiel temple in the messianic kingdom in light of Hebrews will be addressed in chapter 14, "Israel and the Church." For now, let's accept the premise that Daniel agrees with Ezekiel that there will be a temple during the restoration.

Daniel, like other prophets of his time, understood that the Jewish Messiah would create a worldwide messianic kingdom of peace and righteousness, with Israel and its temple at the center of his dominion. The restored Ezekiel temple would serve the whole world as a center for worship and prayer, a center for learning and dissemination of truth, and a judicial center for Israel and the world. Wars between "many nations and kingdoms" that put Jerusalem and its temple in constant peril would end, and the world's weapons of war would be pounded into simple agricultural instruments used to create an abundant harvest in a restored Genesis creation.

The restored temple shows up repeatedly in these messianic prophecies. Isaiah references a restored Jerusalem with a restored temple in his famous vision of the messianic kingdom:

> I will rejoice in Jerusalem and be glad in my people; no more shall be heard in it the sound of weeping and the cry of distress. . . . For thus says the LORD: "Behold, I will extend peace to her like a river, and the glory of the nations like an overflowing stream; . . . And they shall bring all your brothers from all the nations as an offering to the LORD, on horses and in chariots and in litters and on mules and on dromedaries, to my holy mountain Jerusalem [restored city], says the LORD, just as the Israelites bring their grain offering in a clean vessel to the house of the LORD [the restored temple]. And some of them also I will take for priests and for Levites, says the LORD" [restored priestly services]. (Isa. 65:19; 66:12–21)

Micah also envisions Israel, Jerusalem, *and its temple* as the center of the Messiah's earthly kingdom:

> It shall come to pass in the latter days that the mountain of the house of the LORD [Jerusalem and its temple] shall be established as the highest of the mountains, and it shall be lifted up above the hills; and peoples [from all nations] shall flow to it, and many nations shall come, and say: "Come, let us go up to the mountain of the LORD, to the house of the God of Jacob [the temple], that he may teach us his ways and that we may walk in his paths." For out of Zion shall go forth the law, and the word of the LORD from Jerusalem. He [Messiah] shall judge between many peoples, and shall decide for strong nations afar off; and they [all nations] shall beat their swords into plowshares, and their spears into pruning hooks; nation shall not lift up sword against nation, neither shall they learn war anymore. (Mic. 4:1–3)

The restored temple is an inseparable component of the messianic kingdom, and, according to the prophets, one day the Messiah and true Lord of this creation will restore Israel, Jerusalem, and its temple in an age of faithfulness, righteousness, peace, justice, and prosperity on this earth.

Daniel would have been familiar with these prophecies. Jerusalem and its temple may experience multiple desolations during future human kingdoms; yet, Israel will ultimately become faithful and righteous, and the Messiah will overcome these warring empires of man, restoring Israel and its temple during his everlasting covenant of peace with Israel and the world. The restoration of Israel becomes a blessing to all mankind.

The failure of scholars to recognize the central role of the temple in Daniel's visions is one reason Daniel and the Olivet Discourse have been so misunderstood. Many theologians believe that after the temple was destroyed in AD 70 as prophesied by Christ, it will never be restored again. As Gentile Christians, we can let our interpretation of Hebrews predispose us against another Jewish temple which can cloud our reading of Daniel.

By simply following what happens to Jerusalem and its temple in Daniel's vision—as well as in Jeremiah, Ezekiel, Isaiah, and Micah—we can understand the events that must occur on this earth before "the close of the age"—when Christ comes again to take us to his Father's eternal kingdom of heaven and the New Jerusalem, which will no longer contain a temple because we will be in the presence of God the Father and Christ in all their glory. But because God in all his glory cannot dwell in the presence of man, he dwells within his saints through the Holy Spirit *and* within the manmade temple, which, when filled with his glory, serves as his abiding presence among mere mortals. When Solomon completed the first temple, it became filled with God's presence: "And when the priests came out of the Holy Place, a cloud filled the house of the LORD, so that the priests could not stand to minister because of the cloud, for the glory of the LORD filled the house of the LORD" (1 Kings 8:10–11). This is a phenomenal event, and the temple, when miraculously filled with God's glory, was no ordinary building.

From beginning to end, the condition of the temple reflects the spiritual condition of Israel, and this is the central theme woven throughout Daniel's visions of five great empires and kingdoms. In his vision Daniel foresees that the Jews will again be unfaithful during the fourth kingdom (the Roman Empire) and the temple will be destroyed again as it had been by the Babylonians. God's covenant with Israel to protect Jerusalem and its temple from hostile nations in this fallen demonic world was contingent upon the Jews remaining faithful to the God of Abraham, Isaac, and Jacob. Rejecting their Messiah when he came into this world was obviously a major violation of their covenant as God's people.

Jesus said:

O Jerusalem, Jerusalem, the city that kills the prophets and stones those who are sent to it [unfaithful Israel]! How often would I have gathered your children together as a hen gathers her brood under her wings, and you would not [unrepentant Israel]! See, your house is left to you desolate [God's judgment]. For I tell you, you will not see me again, until you say, "Blessed is he who comes in the name of the Lord [repentant and faithful Israel]." Jesus left the temple and was going away, when his disciples came to point out to him the buildings of the temple. But he answered them, "You see all these, do you not? Truly, I say to you, there will not be left here one stone upon another that will not be thrown down." (Matt. 23:37—24:2)

During the First Jewish-Roman War (AD 66–73) when Jewish Zealots started a serious revolt against Roman dominance, three Roman legions advanced on Jerusalem, entered the city, ruthlessly put down the revolt, and utterly destroyed the temple. The temple roof contained wooden rafters and support beams, and when it caught fire during the chaos of war, the extensive gold plates on the façade and gold inlays and coverings within the temple melted, seeping into crevices between the stones of the temple walls. After the fire stopped and the molten gold hardened, the Roman soldiers proceeded to overturn every stone to gain access to the solidified gold sandwiched between the stones, thereby fulfilling Jesus' prophecy that not one stone would be left upon another!

The Jewish Zealots who started the revolt against Rome were led by several factions, but the group led by John of Gischala also desecrated the temple. At one point, he and his band of fighters used the temple as a fortress with the Holy Place as the headquarters for their military operations. They plundered the temple's sacred instruments, wine, and oil. All temple sacrifices were halted. These Jewish Zealots desecrated the temple before the Romans did. The Roman armies closed in on Jerusalem and finished the destruction and desolation of Jerusalem and its temple.

But according to Daniel's vision, this is not the last time the temple will be desecrated by unbelievers. There is a short-lived fifth kingdom—lasting seven years—in his vision involving the Antichrist and a final "abomination and desolation" of another temple similar to the desecration by the Greek king Antiochus IV Epiphanes. This is followed by the ultimate restoration of the temple in the messianic kingdom, when, as Jesus says in his lament and prophecy about Jerusalem, the Jews will finally repent and believe in their Messiah: "Blessed is he who comes in the name of the Lord." Their rejection of their Messiah led to the destruction of Jerusalem and the Second Temple, but their acceptance of their Messiah will lead to the restoration of Jerusalem and the Ezekiel temple.

Nebuchadnezzar's Dream

Daniel had one main vision which is an interpretation of a dream of Nebuchadnezzar's and then multiple visions that are amplifications of this original vision. An image of a human figure is divided into five sections representing five great kingdoms and their impact on Israel, its temple, and the world. When the five unrighteous human kingdoms come to an end, then the messianic kingdom becomes a reality and fills the whole world:

> You saw, O king, and behold, a great image. This image, mighty and of exceeding brightness, stood before you, and its appearance was frightening. The head of this image was of fine gold [one], its chest and arms of silver [two], its middle and thighs of bronze [three], its legs of iron [four], its feet partly of iron and partly of clay [five]. As you looked, a stone was cut out by no human hand, and it struck the image on its feet of iron and clay [during the fifth kingdom], and broke them in pieces. Then the iron, the clay, the bronze, the silver, and the gold, all together were broken in pieces, and became like the chaff of the summer threshing floors; and the wind carried them away, so that not a trace of them could be found. But the stone that struck the image became a great mountain and filled the whole earth [the messianic kingdom]. . . . And there shall be a fourth kingdom, strong as iron, because iron breaks to pieces and shatters all things. And like iron that crushes, it shall break and crush all these. And as you saw the feet and toes, partly of potter's clay and partly of iron, it shall be a divided kingdom [the fifth kingdom], but some of the firmness of iron shall be in it, just as you saw iron mixed with the soft clay. And as the toes of the feet were partly iron and partly clay, so the kingdom shall be partly strong and partly brittle. . . . And in the days of those kings the God of heaven will set up a kingdom that shall never be destroyed, nor shall the kingdom be left to another people. It shall break in pieces all these kingdoms and bring them to an end, and it shall stand forever, just as you saw that a stone was cut from a mountain by no human hand, and that it broke in pieces the iron, the bronze, the clay, the silver, and the gold. (Dan. 2:31–45)

The rabbinic teaching in Jesus' day misinterpreted Daniel's vision to represent only four great kingdoms—the Babylonian (head of gold), Medo-Persian (chest and arms of silver), Greek (middle and thighs of bronze), and Roman (legs of iron) with the feet of "iron and clay" belonging to the Roman Empire. They expected the stone—the Messiah—to arrive on the scene at any time and crush the fourth-kingdom Roman Empire. The Messiah would then set up the final great mountain, or kingdom, with Israel and its temple as the center of this worldwide empire that "shall never be destroyed." Consequently, expectations among first-century Jews, including the disciples, for the Messiah to overthrow the fourth-kingdom Roman Empire and set up his own Jewish-led worldwide empire were quite enlivened. The Romans were keenly aware of these messianic rumblings, which explains their sensitivity toward any possible insurrection led by a Jewish messianic figure.

Instead of all roads leading to Rome, under the Jewish Empire all roads would lead to Jerusalem, bringing the wealth of the nations to Jerusalem: "Your gates shall be open continually; day and night they shall not be shut, that people may bring to you the wealth of the nations, with their kings led in procession" (Isa. 60:11). The Romans and all other nations would become subservient to the Jewish Empire centered in Jerusalem. Even the disciples got caught up in the worldly expectations of power and wealth. And with prophecies like this, it is little wonder that the Romans were concerned about a Jewish Messiah leading a revolt against their empire to establish a Jewish one in its place.

But, as the Jews discovered, much to their disappointment, Jesus of Nazareth did not overthrow the Roman Empire and set up his messianic kingdom on this earth. In fact, Christ's refusal to crush the tyrannical Romans and set up his own theocratic earthly kingdom with the wealth of the nations flowing into Jerusalem was one of the main reasons the Jews rejected Jesus of Nazareth as the Messiah. Pontius Pilate mocked this feeble "stone," or powerless Jewish king, when he and his soldiers placed a purple robe on Christ with a crown of thorns and an inscription on the cross itself that read "Jesus of Nazareth, the King of the Jews" (John 19:19). Instead of the "legs of iron" getting crushed by the stone, the stone (rejected by the Jews) was crushed by the "legs of iron."

And when the unbelieving Jews followed false christs among the Jewish Zealots in an attempt to overthrow the Romans, the "legs of iron" crushed their revolt, Jerusalem, and its temple in AD 70. Furthermore, through their efficient war machine, the Romans became even more extensive, powerful, and prosperous throughout the Mediterranean world, reaching as far into Europe as England. Rome's military of iron kept them in power for centuries. The last Roman emperor ruled in the West until AD 476. Since Christ left this earth and ascended to his Father in heaven, wars and rumors of war have continued unabated in these highly fragmented regions of the world, just as he predicted they would.

The first-century Jews failed to take into account an important detail in Daniel's interpretation of the dream. The stone does not crush the "legs of iron," or the fourth-kingdom Roman Empire; rather, it crushes the "feet of iron and clay" that hold up the image, or the four preceding empires. Only when the fifth part of the image is destroyed does the image of satanic warring kingdoms—from head to toe—come to an end and the stone sets up the messianic kingdom: "As you looked, a stone was cut out by no human hand, and it struck the image on its *feet of iron and clay*, and broke them in pieces. Then the iron, the clay, the bronze, the silver, and the gold, all together were broken in pieces" (Dan. 2:34–35). This explains why the "legs of iron" continued to dominate the world for hundreds of years after Christ left this world.

We are still operating within a world made up of "feet of iron and clay"—strong and weak kingdoms—that are the remnant of preceding empires, waiting for further developments to unfold on the world stage during this fifth kingdom. It is during the intrigue surrounding the formation of this short-lived fifth kingdom and another temple associated with it that the stone crushes the "feet of iron and clay," or the image of satanic, sinful human kingdoms, and establishes his kingdom.

Some students of prophecy believe that the feet, comprised of ten toes, represent a future revival of the Roman Empire. But the feet belong to the image as a whole, and their footprints come from all four empires: "Then the iron, the clay, the bronze, the silver, and the gold, *all together* were broken in pieces." The footprints of all four empires can still be seen throughout the Persian Gulf, the Mediterranean world, and large sections of Europe. And, as the vision describes, the remnants of these kingdoms or countries may be strong (iron) or weak (clay), which is what we find in the footprints of these empires today. Daniel had additional visions that pertain to the number ten that occur in the latter days when these feet and their ten toes "partly iron and partly clay"—some strong and some weak—become identified with a terrible beast that has ten horns on his head, including a "little horn" that takes control of all other kingdoms and sets up a fifth kingdom. This particular horn instigates another great tribulation involving the desecration of a rebuilt Jewish temple that will be in existence at that time.

It is important to recognize that the stone does not crush the "legs of iron," or the Roman Empire, which lasted for hundreds of years after Christ left this earth. Rather, the stone's activity comes into play during Satan's final fifth-kingdom empire that revolves around a remnant of nations from the image becoming active at a time when Satan gives the Antichrist, from one of these nations, his power and great authority to rule over all the nations. We are still waiting for the stone to crush the fifth kingdom with "feet of iron and clay," or Satan's final dominion of unrighteous human kingdoms during a time of great deception, powerful demonic activity, and unprecedented tribulation.

The Messiah may have come into the world as the sacrificial lamb during the fourth-kingdom Roman Empire, but he did not crush the warring kingdoms of the world at that time, and he left this world in its fallen condition. It is at the end of the fifth kingdom that the stone crushes the beasts of Satan, binds Satan himself, and sets up an everlasting kingdom of righteousness on this earth; all wars will cease, and Israel and the whole world will be at peace. Or, as Daniel says, "But the stone that struck the image became a great mountain and filled the whole earth. . . . the God of heaven will set up a kingdom that shall never be destroyed" again by any satanic, warring human kingdom.

The Ancient of Days

To understand when the Messiah, or the stone, actually crushes Satan's fifth-kingdom empire and establishes his dominion of righteousness on this restored earth according to Daniel's vision, we need to understand Daniel's description of Christ's relationship to the Ancient of Days, or God the Father. During a discussion of the fourth kingdom and succeeding fifth kingdom in chapter 7, Daniel has an interesting vision that describes Christ's ascension to heaven:

> After this I saw in the night visions, and behold, a fourth beast, terrifying and dreadful and exceedingly strong. It had great iron teeth; it devoured and broke in pieces and stamped what was left with its feet [the fourth-kingdom Roman Empire]. . . . I saw in the night visions, and behold, with the *clouds of heaven* there came one like a son of man, and he came to the Ancient of Days and was presented before him. And to him was given dominion and glory and a kingdom, that all peoples, nations, and languages should serve him; his dominion is an everlasting dominion, which shall not pass away, and his kingdom one that shall not be destroyed. (Dan. 7:7–14)

Christ referred to this part of Daniel's vision and applied it to himself when he was being questioned by the chief priests and scribes to determine if he considered himself the Christ: "Jesus said to him, 'You have said so. But I tell you, from now on you will see the *Son of Man* seated at the right hand of Power and coming on the clouds of heaven'" (Matt. 26:64). After his crucifixion and resurrection, the Son of Man literally ascended into the clouds of heaven into the presence of the Father. Christ entered into the true temple of heaven. The clouds symbolize the glory and presence of God in his heavenly temple, or home, just as they symbolized God's presence in the earthly temple.

The Jews understood the expression "son of man" in Daniel to be a divine being because of his unique relationship to the Ancient of Days. Jesus is not only claiming to be the Christ, but also co-equal to God because he will ascend to the Father's right hand. Jesus was saying that through his resurrection and ascension to heaven to be in the presence of God the Father, he is the fulfillment of this prophecy of Daniel's concerning the "Son of Man." Christ made an incredibly bold claim, and the high priest used his claim to indict him of blasphemy, which warranted the penalty of death: "Then the high priest tore his robes and said, 'He has uttered blasphemy. What further witnesses do we need? You have now heard his blasphemy. What is your judgment?' They answered, 'He deserves death'" (Matt. 26:65–66).

But even though the Son of Man has ascended to the right hand of the Ancient of Days to fulfill Daniel's prophecy, he has yet to remove Satan and establish his dominion over this earth that rightfully belongs to him. He is still waiting on the Father to say it is the season for Satan to initiate his fifth-kingdom empire and the time to crush Satan's last dominion, bind Satan himself, and establish his everlasting dominion over all peoples, nations, and languages on this earth.

Peter continues with the same interpretation of Daniel's vision and the relationship of Christ to the Ancient of Days in his sermon after Pentecost:

> Brothers, I may say to you with confidence about the patriarch David that he both died and was buried, and his tomb is with us to this day. Being therefore a prophet, and knowing that God had sworn with an oath to him that he would set one of his descendants on his throne, he foresaw and spoke about the resurrection of the Christ, that he was not abandoned to Hades, nor did his flesh see corruption. This Jesus God raised up, and of that we all are witnesses. Being therefore exalted at the right hand of God [Ancient of Days], and having received from the Father the promise of the Holy Spirit, he has poured out this that you yourselves are seeing and hearing. For David did not ascend into the heavens, but he himself says, 'The Lord [the Ancient of Days] said to my Lord [Christ], Sit at my right hand, until I make your enemies your footstool.' Let all the house of Israel therefore know for certain that God has made him both Lord and Christ, this Jesus whom you crucified. (Acts 2:29–36)

Instead of the promised son of David sitting on a throne on this earth as human kings would do, this divine Son of David who is now "Lord and Christ" has ascended to the throne of God in heaven at the Father's right hand, where he is *sitting and waiting* until the Father says it is time for Satan to be removed and for the world to experience a regime change and Christ begins his dominion over the restored earth when all his enemies become his footstool. His reign over this world can easily be accomplished from his exalted place in heaven.

In the meantime, Christ continues to rescue and regenerate those whom the Father has chosen from Satan's dominion of darkness. He is building up the members of his kingdom through the evangelism of his disciples and the work of the Holy Spirit. But the regenerated saints remain in this dark, degenerate world with Satan as its ruler, which is why other beasts, or antichrists, continue to appear and sow discord, strife, and war—and persecution against the saints.

Lord-Elect and the Inaugurated Kingdom

Many theologians like to use the term *inaugurated* kingdom of Christ to describe the current position of Christ seated at the Father's right hand, where he has been given an everlasting dominion that has not been fully realized or implemented on this earth. Premillennialists believe the second coming ushers in the consummated 1,000-year messianic kingdom, while amillennialists believe the second coming ushers in the consummated eternal new heavens and new earth.

The second coming ushers in the Father's eternal heavenly kingdom at the close of the age, according to Christ, but the term "inaugurated" kingdom is very misleading because it implies that Christ's reign as King over this world has already been implemented. His reign may have begun over the hearts and minds of the members of his kingdom, who accept him as Christ, but his followers remain in this degenerate creation, and he is definitely not ruling this fallen world. If Christ is the ruling King of this unrighteous world, then he becomes accountable for the atrocities and calamities of this world. When something dreadful happens as the result of evil human actions or natural disasters, people frequently ask, "If Christ is God and he has the power to prevent evil, then why does he allow bad things to happen?" The answer is that, although Christ is indeed God, he is not the current ruler of this world—Satan is!

Christ is the king of his people and the declared king of this world, but that does not mean he is the actual ruling king of those not in his kingdom. John foresaw a future period when Christ as King will use his power to rule the world: "And the twenty-four elders who sit on their thrones before God fell on their faces and worshiped God, saying, 'We give thanks to you, Lord God Almighty, who is and who was, for you have taken your great power and begun to reign [over this earth]'" (Rev. 11:15–17). Christ may be declared King of the world and may be King of those who are in his kingdom, but he surely has not yet begun to use his power to rule the world. John did not envision his actual reign beginning until Satan is bound and the holy saints are resurrected to reign with him in the future millennial kingdom.

Is Christ currently exercising his reign or kingship over the world with the righteous saints? This question can easily be answered by asking some of the following questions: Is Christ currently ruling over righteous leaders of North Korea? Is Christ currently ruling over righteous leaders of Syria? Is Christ the ruling king of Iran? Is Christ the ruling king of Sudan or Somalia? To say that Christ has "taken his great power and begun to reign" as the King of this horribly evil world of unrighteous men and women is almost blasphemy. It is to impugn him with the current actions of Satan and the unrighteous men and women under Satan's control. A hideous insult to Christ, indeed. It is eminently obvious that Christ is not currently ruling this world as King of kings and Lord of lords.

Christ has been given the position of Lord and Christ by the Father upon completion of his work on this earth and his ascension to heaven, but he will not take "office" as King of kings and Lord of lords as long as Satan remains prince of this world. When Christ becomes the King of this world and the Genesis creation is regenerated, we will know it immediately because Satan will be removed, the world will be managed by righteous men and women, the tyranny of evil will no longer be tolerated, and the curse will be removed. A more accurate term to describe Christ's current relationship to this satanic and fallen world would be "Lord-elect." His dominion over this earth with his saints is set to begin on his "inauguration" day—a date determined by the Father—when he rules this world from his throne in heaven. The consummation, or conclusion of his earthly messianic kingdom, would mark "the close of the [Genesis] age" and the beginning of the new creation in the heavenly kingdom in the eternal age to come.

For example, when the president of the United States is elected in November, he is referred to as "president-elect" because he does not begin his term of office until he is inaugurated into office in January of the following year. In the meantime, the sitting president remains in office and continues presiding over the nation. But the president-elect is not idle. During this interim period, he selects the fifteen members of his Cabinet as well as appointing thousands of other people to assist him in his administration when he assumes power on inauguration day.

The Ancient of Days has designated Christ as "Lord-elect" of this world, and Christ is waiting on the Father to say when his inauguration as Lord of this world begins. Meanwhile, in association with the Father, he is selecting the members of his administration who will help him rule when Satan is removed from office. All the deceased members of his kingdom whom he has collected throughout history will experience the "first resurrection" and enter this period of his Lordship and dominion over this world.

We should not confuse Christ being Lord-elect with God's sovereignty. As sovereign, God may allow Satan to operate in this world for a season, even using evil instigated by Satan for his purposes as Jeremiah and the prophets understood. Judas's betrayal of Christ, which Satan inspired, and Christ's crucifixion and atonement for our sins were part of God's sovereign plan. God is sovereign even though he allowed his Son and the members of his body to suffer under Satan's regime. And though we remain in a world under Satan's dominion of darkness, nothing can prevent Christ from gathering the Father's chosen people out of that kingdom and bringing them into his kingdom as his people (Matt. 16:16–19).

The kingdom of God has begun; Christ is Lord-elect, and repentant and regenerated sinners are being brought into his kingdom every day. Christ was given dominion over this world when he became Lord-elect, when after making atonement for our sins, he ascended to the right hand of the Ancient of Days during the fourth kingdom of Daniel. But he does not begin his actual rule and dominion as King over this world until he has finished gathering those into his kingdom the Father has selected, and the Ancient of Days determines it is the time and season for his reign to begin.

Hebrews says, "But when Christ had offered for all time a single sacrifice for sins, he sat down at the right hand of God [the Ancient of Days], *waiting* from that time until his enemies should be made a footstool for his feet. For by a single offering he has perfected for all time those who are being sanctified" (Heb. 10:12–14). His day of inauguration remains in the future.

But before the Messiah can usher in an age of everlasting righteousness on this earth for the saints, there need to be righteous saints—Jew and Gentile—with new hearts under a new covenant who can inherit this righteous kingdom. And before there can be righteous saints, there must be atonement made by the Anointed One for their iniquity. Only then can the Messiah rule over a kingdom made up of righteous saints—which explains why he had to first come into this world to make atonement for our sins. With our sins forgiven, believing Jews and Gentiles are given new hearts under a new covenant, which allows the righteous saints to enter the Messiah's age of righteousness on inauguration day.

During the fourth-kingdom Roman Empire, the Messiah came into this world, but he and Jerusalem and its temple were crushed by the legs of iron; his reign of peace and righteousness over this earth did not begin at that time. Instead, Christ left this world and ascended to the Ancient of Days in heaven, where he remains Lord-elect of this world as he waits on the Father to say it is time for him to crush the Antichrist's fifth kingdom and establish his kingdom. The apostles eventually understood that being given the office of Lord and Messiah over this world and *taking* office and divinely ruling over his messianic kingdom with his righteous saints are two different events.

The Beginning of the Inaugurated Kingdom in Daniel

If Christ became Lord-elect during the fourth-kingdom empire after making atonement for the sins of his people and subsequently ascended to the Ancient of Days, when, according to Daniel, does Christ's inauguration as the Lord of this world begin? This is a critical question to answer in order to fully understand Daniel's visions and Christ's discourse on Daniel. The answer is that Daniel envisions the Ancient of Days *inaugurating* the Anointed One's reign immediately after a particular ruler, who ushers in the Great Tribulation, is destroyed. Daniel repeats this pattern three times in chapter 7 to stress its importance. The Antichrist, who establishes the fifth kingdom of "feet of iron and clay," emerges out of the remnants of the fourth kingdom, or beast, which in turn, emerged out of all prior empires. Daniel's image of the kingdom with feet of ten toes morphs into an image of a kingdom with ten horns. Notice that Christ's reign begins *directly* after this particular horn, or ruler, more terrible than all other ten rulers is destroyed:

> Then I desired to know the truth about the fourth beast, which was different from all the rest, exceedingly terrifying, with its teeth of iron and claws of bronze, and which devoured and broke in pieces and stamped what was left with its feet [the fourth-kingdom Roman Empire], and about the ten horns that were on its head [the fifth kingdom], and the other horn that came up and before which three of them fell, the horn that had eyes and a mouth that spoke great things, and that seemed greater than its companions [the Antichrist that emerges out of the ten-horn kingdom]. As I looked, this horn made war with the saints and prevailed over them [the Great Tribulation], until the Ancient of Days [God the Father] came, and judgment was given for the saints of the Most High, and the time came when the saints possessed the kingdom [inauguration day]. (Dan. 7:19–22)

When Christ was crucified by the "legs of iron," he ascended to the Ancient of Days where he was told to have a seat and wait for his term of office to begin. Now, Daniel is informing us that his term of office begins at a specific point in the future when a particular horn, or ruler, makes war against the saints during a Great Tribulation. It is at the conclusion of this final fifth kingdom that the Ancient of Days comes and establishes his Son's kingdom such that the "time came when the saints possessed the kingdom." Daniel is establishing a definite sequence of events: the inauguration of the Messiah's reign begins directly after this period of Great Tribulation caused by the Antichrist when the Son of Man finally uses his great power to rule the world with the members of his kingdom.

Most of the saints living at that time would be killed because the horn prevailed over them. So how can the following prophecy come true: "the time came when the saints possessed the kingdom"? The answer, of course, is through the power of resurrection. Daniel knew from Ezekiel 37 that the method whereby the departed or martyred saints come to possess the messianic kingdom on the restored earth would be through a resurrection of their natural bodies.

None of the four great kingdoms described by Daniel lasted forever. The subjects of those kingdoms all died. Or, another kingdom through weapons of war killed and conquered them, taking their place. Christ's kingdom over this earth is an entirely different kind of kingdom. If one of the members of his kingdom dies before his inauguration day, Christ has the divine power of resurrection at his disposal so that the saints can inherit and possess his earthly kingdom when the Ancient of Days decides it is time to give the Son his dominion! This resurrection of the departed saints is an essential component to the implementation of the Son's kingdom on this earth. It is the only way that all the saints from Abel onward can possess his earthly kingdom.

Daniel repeats the sequence of Christ's inauguration occurring directly after the Great Tribulation, providing further details in chapter 7:

> As for the ten horns, out of this kingdom ten kings shall arise, and another shall arise after them; he shall be different from the former ones, and shall put down three kings. He shall speak words against the Most High, and shall wear out the saints of the Most High, and shall think to change the times and the law; and they shall be given into his hand for a time, times, and half a time. But the court shall sit in judgment, and his dominion shall be taken away, to be consumed and destroyed to the end. And the kingdom and the dominion and the greatness of the kingdoms under the whole heaven shall be given to the people of the saints of the Most High; their kingdom shall be an everlasting kingdom, and all dominions shall serve and obey them. (Dan. 7:24–27)

This last evil king considers himself the sovereign God and Creator when he attempts to "change the times and the law." And he turns against the true saints with a vengeance, wearing them out. After this Antichrist is destroyed, Satan's dominion over the world's fallen kingdoms is taken away and given to the Son of Man and "the people of the saints of the Most High." His dominion over every nation under the whole heaven is finally inaugurated. Because it is an everlasting kingdom, never again will these demonic forces of evil over the kingdoms of fallen mankind prevail over the saints of the Most High. But the pattern is the same: it is after Satan's and his Antichrist's fifth-kingdom dominion is taken away and destroyed that the messianic kingdom is implemented on this earth by the Ancient of Days.

At the beginning of this vision, Daniel describes a form of court and judgment taking place in heaven by the Ancient of Days, where the evil deeds of this Antichrist and his followers have been recorded with the resultant judgments dispensed on them:

I considered the horns, and behold, there came up among them another horn, a little one, before which three of the first horns were plucked up by the roots. And behold, in this horn were eyes like the eyes of a man, and a mouth speaking great things. As I looked, thrones were placed, and the Ancient of Days took his seat [in the court of heaven]; his clothing was white as snow, and the hair of his head like pure wool; his throne was fiery flames; its wheels were burning fire [he is angry and ready to dispense judgment]. A stream of fire issued and came out from before him; a thousand thousands served him, and ten thousand times ten thousand stood before him; the court sat in judgment, and the books were opened. I looked then because of the sound of the great words that the horn was speaking. And as I looked, the beast was killed, and its body destroyed and given over to be burned with fire. As for the rest of the beasts, their dominion was taken away, but their lives were prolonged for a season and a time. (Dan. 7:8–12)

This vision of God on his throne in judgment should not be confused with the Great White Throne judgment after the millennium when the books are opened, even though there are some similarities (Rev. 20:11–12). Daniel's vision of God's judgment takes place during the Great Tribulation when the little "horn" comes onto the scene. The books kept in heaven will record the ever-increasing evil deeds perpetrated against the saints when he makes war against them. When the court sits in judgment, God will begin to parcel out judgments on the world led by the beast, or the little horn.

This is exactly what we find in Revelation: "Then I heard a loud voice from the temple [in the court of heaven] telling the seven angels, 'Go and pour out on the earth the seven bowls of the wrath of God'" (Rev. 16:1). Out of the temple of heaven also come seven plagues along with the seven golden bowls full of the God's wrath that are unleashed on the world of the "little horn" or the Antichrist (Rev. 15:5–8). These judgments come to a culmination when Daniel says the "beast was killed, and its body destroyed and given over to be burned with fire," which coincides with what Revelation describes as occurring at the battle of Armageddon at the end of the Great Tribulation:

And the beast was captured, and with it the false prophet who in its presence had done the signs by which he deceived those who had received the mark of the beast and those who worshiped its image. These two were thrown alive into the lake of fire that burns with sulfur. And the rest were slain by the sword that came from the mouth of him who was sitting on the horse, and all the birds were gorged with their flesh. (Rev. 19:20–21)

In Revelation, as in Daniel, this is directly followed by the inauguration of Christ's millennial reign over this earth with his resurrected saints.

In subsequent visions described in chapters 11 and 12, Daniel repeats the description of the messianic kingdom being established directly after the Great Tribulation. Satan is described in the Scriptures as the ruler of this dominion of darkness, but he is restrained by the amount of deception and evil he can inflict on this world; otherwise, the Great Tribulation would be an everyday event for Israel and the saints. Daniel reveals that the main power and angelic being that God uses to restrict Satan is Michael the archangel who protects Israel and the saints from Satan and his Antichrist. The removal of Michael's restraint of Satan marks the emergence of the Great Tribulation by the Antichrist against the saints:

> And the king shall do as he wills. He shall exalt himself and magnify himself above every god, and shall speak astonishing things against the God of gods [the Antichrist]. . . . At that time shall arise Michael, the great prince who has charge of your people [Michael, who restrains Satan and protects Israel, is removed, which leads to Satan's incarnation into the Antichrist]. And there shall be a time of trouble, such as never has been since there was a nation till that time" [the unprecedented Great Tribulation and desecrations brought on by Satan and the Antichrist]. But at that time [at the conclusion of this Great Tribulation] your people shall be delivered [the restoration], everyone whose name shall be found written in the book [only the saints inherit the kingdom]. . . . "How long shall it be till the end of these wonders?" And I heard the man clothed in linen, . . . that it would be for a time, times, and half a time, and that when the shattering of the power of the holy people comes to an end all these things would be finished [at the end of the Great Tribulation]. . . . And from the time that the regular burnt offering is taken away and the abomination that makes desolate is set up, there shall be 1,290 days [three years and seven months]. Blessed is he who waits and arrives at the 1,335 days. But go your way till the end. And you shall rest and shall stand in your allotted place at the end of the days [in the kingdom]. (Dan. 11:36; 12:1–13)

Paul also writes that the removal of the one who restrains Satan marks the beginning of the Great Tribulation: "And you know what is restraining him now so that he may be revealed in his time. For the mystery of lawlessness is already at work. Only he who now restrains it will do so until he is out of the way. And then the lawless one will be revealed" (2 Thess. 2:6–8). Paul assumes his readers are familiar with Daniel and already know who the restrainer is, so he does not identify him as Michael. The Thessalonians were aware that Satan was already at work in this world because they were experiencing significant persecution (2 Thess. 1:4). Yet, Michael limits him, preventing him from having full reign over this world through the Antichrist. When Michael "arises," or is removed from restraining Satan, then the Antichrist or "the lawless one will be revealed," and a time of trouble that is unparalleled in the history of the world will begin.

Michael as the agent who prevents Satan from having unlimited access to this world also corresponds with John's teaching in Revelation:

Now war arose in heaven, *Michael* and his angels fighting against the dragon. And the dragon and his angels fought back, but he was defeated and there was no longer any place for them in heaven. And the great dragon was thrown down, that ancient serpent, who is called the devil and Satan, the deceiver of the whole world—he was thrown down to the earth, and his angels were thrown down with him. . . . for the accuser of our brothers has been thrown down, who accuses them day and night before our God. And they have conquered him by the blood of the Lamb and by the word of their testimony, for they loved not their lives even unto death. Therefore, rejoice, O heavens and you who dwell in them! *But woe to you, O earth and sea, for the devil has come down to you in great wrath, because he knows that his time is short!* (Rev. 12:7–12)

Michael is involved in a celestial battle that results in Satan being unleashed on the world. Satan comes down in great wrath because he knows that he will only be here for three-and-one-half years. Daniel, Paul, and John all describe the severity of evil that will take place on earth after the restrainer is removed. This short period of human history has no rival.

Although we live in a fallen world and see a great deal of the activity of Satan all around us, he is still limited in his ability to persecute the saints and wreak havoc on this earth. The book of Job contains a good example of the evil that Satan can inflict upon saints when he is unrestrained. When Satan appeared before the throne of God and accused Job of being faithful to God only because of his prosperous life, God took the challenge and allowed Satan unrestrained access to Job with one exception—he could not kill Job. Satan then turned Job's once healthy and prosperous life into a life of absolute misery (Job 1:8–12).

In Revelation, Satan appears before God as he did with Job, as the accuser of the brethren: "for the accuser of our brothers has been thrown down, who accuses them day and night before our God" (Rev. 12:10). But during the Great Tribulation, Michael will no longer restrain him. Satan is subsequently thrown down to the earth to attack all believers in much the way he left the throne of God and attacked Job—with the difference being that he will be able to kill the saints.

Daniel teaches that the "time of trouble, such as never has been" will be followed by a time that "your people shall be delivered" (12:1). Daniel is further told that he "shall rest [sleep] and shall stand [be resurrected]" in his "allotted place [of position and authority] at the end of the days [in the messianic kingdom]" (12:13). Daniel knew from Ezekiel 37 that the Son of Man will deliver his departed saints from the grave into the messianic kingdom by the resurrection of their natural bodies. Daniel probably did not fully understand that there will be two distinct resurrections as further revealed by John, but he goes on to describe the final resurrection when the saints will inherit the eternal kingdom on Judgment Day: "And many of those who sleep in the dust of the earth shall awake, some to everlasting life, and some to shame and everlasting contempt. . . . and shall stand in your allotted place at the end of the days" (Dan. 12:2, 13). The phrase "everlasting life" means eternal life; this is the first time this terminology is used in the Scriptures because it is in reference to the eternal kingdom. With the benefit of Revelation, we can know that when these visions come to fruition "at the end of the days," Daniel and the saints shall receive their "allotted place" in the messianic kingdom through the "first resurrection" of the natural body, and then in the eternal new heavens and new earth through the final resurrection of the immortal body.

Most important, Daniel teaches that it is after this period of Great Tribulation that the saints will be delivered and the inauguration of the messianic kingdom on this earth takes place. This pattern is so prevalent in Daniel's visions that it becomes an *axiom*, or self-evident truth. This simple axiom can be outlined as follows:

- Unrestrained Satan + Antichrist + Great Tribulation + three-and-one-half years + death and destruction of Antichrist = inauguration of messianic age of righteousness.

This sequence matches the same pattern established in Revelation in which the inauguration of Christ's millennial reign begins when the Antichrist is destroyed and Satan is removed.

The Seventy Weeks

Daniel's famous vision of the seventy weeks provides an excellent summary and outline of the events surrounding the temple that lead up to the messianic kingdom and the restoration of Israel, Jerusalem, and its temple. Christ refers to this vision when he mentions Daniel in the Olivet Discourse: "So when you see the abomination of desolation spoken of by the prophet Daniel, standing in the holy place (let the reader understand)" (Matt. 24:15). The phrase "let the reader understand" is a direct link to Daniel's vision of the seventy weeks when Gabriel came to Daniel in response to his prayer for the restoration of Jerusalem and its temple: "while I was speaking in prayer, the man Gabriel, . . . came to me . . . He made me understand, speaking with me and saying, 'Oh Daniel, I have come out to give you insight and understanding'" (Dan. 9:21–22). Christ is telling us to read and understand Daniel's vision of the seventy weeks in conjunction with his discourse in order to understand what must take place on this earth before he comes again at the close of the age.

Deciphering and understanding Daniel's vision of the seventy weeks is something like the work of a CIA analyst working on a terrorist plot—taking the raw intelligence data collected from a variety of sources and connecting the dots in such a way that the plot can be deciphered, hopefully before it is executed. Some of the raw data needed to understand Daniel's vision of the seventy weeks comes from his prior visions and some comes from other prophets of his day.

A careful analysis reveals that the vision of the seventy weeks includes two future desolations of the temple—one being the destruction in AD 70 during the fourth kingdom and the second occurring during the Great Tribulation of the fifth kingdom—followed by the restoration of the Ezekiel temple in the messianic kingdom. Once these two separate desolations of the temple are identified, we then examine the Gospel accounts of the Olivet Discourse to determine how they relate to Daniel's seventy weeks.

Daniel was doing some intelligence gathering and analysis of his own and was aware of the data from Jeremiah that the desolations of Jerusalem and its temple by the Babylonians would last about seventy years (Jer. 25:11):

> In the first year of Darius the son of Ahasuerus, by descent a Mede, who was made king over the realm of the Chaldeans—in the first year of his reign, I, Daniel, perceived in the books the number of years that, according to the word of the LORD to Jeremiah the prophet, must pass before the end of the desolations of Jerusalem, namely, seventy years. (Dan. 9:1–2)

Daniel would have been aware that Jeremiah had also foreseen the day when the transgressions of Israel under the old covenant would be forgiven, and they would be given a new covenant and new hearts, and Jerusalem and its temple would be restored and rebuilt:

> Behold, the days are coming, declares the LORD, when I will make a new covenant with the house of Israel and the house of Judah, not like the covenant that I made with their fathers on the day when I took them by the hand to bring them out of the land of Egypt, my covenant that they broke, . . . But this is the covenant that I will make with the house of Israel after those days, declares the LORD: I will put my law within them, and I will write it on their hearts. And I will be their God, and they shall be my people. . . . For I will forgive their iniquity, and I will remember their sin no more. . . . Behold, the days are coming, declares the LORD, when the city [and its temple] shall be rebuilt for the LORD from the Tower of Hananel to the Corner Gate. (Jer. 31:31–38)

Reading Jeremiah, Daniel probably thought that his prophecy about the restoration of the temple in seventy years and the above prophecy about the restoration of the hearts of Israel were tied together. Daniel then begins to pour out his heart in prayer confessing Israel's transgressions and asking for God's mercy and forgiveness in the fulfillment of these prophecies (9:1–19). Daniel's prayer is for the restoration of Israel, Jerusalem, and its temple according to these promises: "Now therefore, O our God, listen to the prayer of your servant and to his pleas for mercy, and for your own sake, O Lord, make your face to shine upon your *sanctuary*, which is desolate" (9:17).

Then the angel Gabriel appears to Daniel to answer his prayer with yet another extended vision of the prophetic future related to Israel, Jerusalem, and its temple. Unfortunately for Daniel and Israel, Gabriel informs Daniel that it will take much longer than seventy years for Israel to truly repent and be given a new heart in order to fully restore Israel and its temple. In fact, it will take seventy times seven years to usher in a righteous kingdom of Israel, and there will be even more occasions when Israel is unfaithful and punished for their transgressions and the temple desecrated.

Ezekiel, a contemporary of Daniel, also provides important data needed to understand this vision. He, along with Isaiah and Micah, foretold the restoration of Israel that included a restored Jerusalem with a restored temple in the messianic kingdom (Ezek. 40—48). Ezekiel's highly detailed vision of the restored temple in an age of righteousness occurred in 573 BC, and this section of Daniel's vision occurred only thirty-four years later in 539 BC, so Daniel would have been familiar with Ezekiel's vision of the restored temple.

Daniel's vision begins with an introductory overview that culminates with the anointing of the "most holy place" (the Ezekiel temple) during Israel's age of righteousness, which is followed by an amplification of this vision that includes a sequential breakdown of the seventy weeks and the events that will lead up to this final phase of the restoration of Israel and its temple:

> Seventy weeks are decreed about your people [Israel or the Jews] and your holy city [Jerusalem], to finish the transgression, to put an end to sin, and to atone for iniquity, to bring in everlasting righteousness [the messianic kingdom], to seal both vision and prophet, and to anoint a most holy place [restore the temple]. [End of overview.] Know therefore and understand that from the going out of the word to restore and build Jerusalem to the coming of an anointed one, a prince, there shall be seven weeks. Then for sixty-two weeks it shall be built again with squares and moat, but in a troubled time. And after the sixty-two weeks, an anointed one shall be cut off and shall have nothing. And the people of the prince who is to come shall destroy the city and the sanctuary [Jerusalem and the temple]. Its end shall come with a flood, and to the end there shall be war. Desolations are decreed. And he shall make a strong covenant with many for one week, and for half of the week he shall put an end to sacrifice and offering [in another temple]. And on the wing of abominations shall come one who makes desolate, until the decreed end is poured out on the desolator. (Dan. 9:24–27)

In the overview, the seventy weeks are complete when the most holy place is anointed. The word *anoint* means "to consecrate for religious service," and the "most holy place" is a reference to the holy of holies or the manmade temple. The words *everlasting righteousness* mean "to bring in righteousness of ages" or an "age of righteousness." Daniel knows the prophecies of Jeremiah, Ezekiel, Isaiah, and Micah in regard to the restoration of Israel and its temple in the messianic kingdom. Within this grammatical-historical context, there are sound reasons to conclude that the phrase "to anoint a most holy place" during an age of continuous righteousness refers to the reestablishment of religious services at the restored Ezekiel temple in the messianic kingdom after the renewal and restoration of Israel.

In the amplified section, the seventieth week is interrupted midway by the desolator with an end to sacrifice and offering at a temple, and this final week comes to an end three-and-one-half years later when the "decreed end is poured out on the desolator." This brings us full circle to the time when Israel's transgressions are finished, the temple is restored, and the most holy place is anointed for sacrifice and offering in the age of everlasting righteousness. But instead of this complete restoration of Israel and its temple being accomplished in seventy years, the angel Gabriel tells Daniel it will take as many as seventy weeks for Israel to accomplish a true restoration of their hearts and minds in order to finally "anoint a most holy place" in a restored Jerusalem.

Paul, along with the prophets, foresees the day that Israel will repent in mass (Rom. 11:17–27). That does not mean, however, that all Jews at that time will become believers. The Gentiles are now repenting, but even they remain a minority within their nation. As such, there will remain a significant number of unbelieving Jews who will not turn from transgression, and they will get caught up in the false worship of the Antichrist, accepting him as their Messiah. This will be the ultimate transgression of unbelieving Jews. The majority of first-century Jews rejected their Messiah and in collusion with the Romans had him crucified. Likewise, a significant number of unbelieving Jews in the future will accept Satan's false christ as their Messiah. Terrible tribulation followed Israel's rejection of Christ in AD 70, and great tribulation will follow Israel's acceptance and worship of the Antichrist. This final act of rebellion by unbelieving Jews with its corresponding desolation of the temple will finish the transgression of unbelieving Israel.

The concept of weeks can be understood as sabbatical years—seven years—based on the way jubilees were computed. A sabbath week would be seven years with the year of jubilee occurring after ten sabbath weeks, or every seventy years (10 x 7 years = 70 years). One week would represent seven years instead of seven days, and we would multiply the particular number of "sevens" times the number "seven" to compute the number of years in Daniel's vision. Thus, we have 7 + 62 + 1 = 70 weeks of years until Christ's inauguration by the Ancient of Days.

Let's do the math. The first seven weeks would be seven times seven or forty-nine years (7 x 7 = 49). Many scholars date the call to restore the temple to its full priestly services to the decree of Artaxerxes I in 457 BC based on Ezra 7:11–16. Readers of Daniel's vision would then know that forty-nine years from the decree of Artaxerxes, the temple functions of sacrifice and offering would be restored in 408 BC (457 - 49 = 408), which is historically accurate. We also know from Nehemiah and Ezra that the returning Jews faced significant opposition when they rebuilt the temple (Neh. 4—6 and Ezra 4); Daniel refers to it as "a troubled time" (9:25).

It is another sixty-two weeks (62 x 7 = 434 years) until the Anointed One arrives on the scene (408 BC - 434 = AD 27). This places Christ around AD 27—or the approximate time of Christ's public ministry and crucifixion, when he is "cut off," which means his age of everlasting righteousness was not inaugurated at that time. Instead, after atoning for our sins, he ascends to heaven where, as Lord-elect, he waits until the end of the seventy weeks for the inauguration of his dominion over this earth. Gabriel tells Daniel that after the Anointed One is cut off, yet another destruction of the city and its temple, similar to the Babylonian destruction, will follow: "the city and the sanctuary" will be destroyed, which occurred in AD 70.

At this point, we have sixty-nine (7 + 62) out of seventy sevens accounted for, with only one seven-year period remaining before the inauguration of the Messiah's kingdom of everlasting righteousness on this earth. But because the "anointed one" is cut off and ascends to the Ancient of Days where he waits until the Father determines it is time for the Son of Man to exercise his reign over this world, we do not know how many years go by until the last seven-year period occurs and Christ's inauguration day arrives. Only the Father knows the times and seasons when the last week will unfold and the kingdom will be restored to Israel and his Son (Acts 1:6–7).

And because the majority of the Jews rejected their Messiah, they have been cut off as fruit-bearing believers as well. In the meantime, repentant Gentiles have been grafted in as believers in the Jewish Messiah, with new hearts under the new covenant. But we do not know how long it will be until all the predetermined number of believing Gentiles are brought in and the Jews are grafted back in as believers. It could be two thousand years, or it could be four thousand years, before the Jews finally repent and are given new hearts under the new covenant and the last seven-year period begins. Only the Father knows how many saints will possess his kingdom. As a result, the counting of years by sabbatical weeks halts after the Son of Man is cut off and ascends to heaven, where he waits on the Father to finish gathering those he has chosen from all nations to enter his kingdom.

During this interim period leading up to the final seven years and Christ's inauguration, Daniel says the world will go on as usual: "to the end there shall be war. Desolations are decreed." Wars between unrighteous nations will continue, as well as famines and earthquakes (as the world remains under God's curse), until the end of the final seventieth week.

Daniel tells us the final seven-year period starts when the desolator makes "a strong covenant with many for one week, and for half of the week he shall put an end to sacrifice and offering." The phrase "a strong covenant with many" means to put in force an injunction or make a strong agreement between many parties. Scholars have different opinions about what the word *many* refers to. Some think it is a reference from Isaiah: "Out of the anguish of his soul he shall see and be satisfied; by his knowledge shall the righteous one, my servant, make *many* to be accounted righteous, and he shall bear their iniquities" (Isa. 53:11). It is true that Christ's atonement when he was cut off made many people from all nations righteous, and, from an eternal perspective, he put an end to sacrifice when he offered his body as the perfect sacrifice.

But in the grammatical context of Daniel's vision, the Anointed One was cut off and atoned for our sins after sixty-two weeks from the restoration of the Second Temple—not during the seventieth week: "And after the sixty-two weeks, an anointed one shall be cut off." Therefore, since the phrase "a strong covenant with *many* for one week" occurs during the seventieth week, the word *many* probably has another referent.

Based on the fact that Daniel has recently been gathering data directly from Jeremiah about the desolation and restoration of Jerusalem and its temple, it is much more likely that Jeremiah is also the source of the references "strong covenant with *many* for one week" involving the "end to sacrifice and offering" in a temple when Jeremiah discusses the reasons that Jerusalem and its temple are so susceptible to being desolated: "The prophets who preceded you and me from ancient times prophesied war, famine, and pestilence against *many* countries and great kingdoms" (Jer. 28:8). In this grammatical-historical context, the word *many* likely refers to the "*many* countries and kingdoms" at continuous war that kept attacking Israel and its temple. Therefore, a "strong covenant with *many* for one week" would mean a strong covenant of peace between these "many" warring countries and kingdoms *and* Israel, which would initially protect Jerusalem and its temple.

Further evidence that the word *many* refers to kingdoms that enter into a strong covenant is bolstered by its reference to the Antichrist's dealings with nations in Daniel 11:39: "He shall deal with the strongest fortresses with the help of a foreign god. Those who acknowledge him he shall load with honor [those who enter into a strong covenant with him]. He shall make them rulers over many [peoples or nations] and shall divide the land [under his control] for a price." Through his effective war machine, he consolidates control so that he can parcel out positions of power and authority to these *many* allied nations under his covenant.

At the beginning of this seven-year period, Israel will have a false sense of security because this strong covenant of peace to protect Jerusalem and its temple only lasts for three-and-one-half years, at which time the temple is desecrated in a manner reminiscent of the desecrations of Antiochus: "and for half of the week he shall put an end to sacrifice and offering. And on the wing of abominations shall come one who makes desolate." The desolator then inflicts abominations on Israel, its temple, and the world during a period of great tribulation for the next three-and-one-half years until he is killed, "until the decreed end is poured out on the desolator." The "decreed end" for the desolator is probably the lake of fire. This brings the last seven-year week to a conclusion and completes the seventy weeks.

The vision pertaining to the seventy weeks ends when the desolator is destroyed because it is at that time that the Anointed One, previously cut off after he atoned for iniquity and ascended to the Ancient of Days, brings in everlasting righteousness, or his inaugurated dominion, to this earth; the "most holy place" (the Ezekiel temple) is finally restored and anointed for priestly services. This follows the same pattern, or axiom, established in other visions of Daniel: the end of this period of great tribulation caused by the desolator in this final week marks the time when the Anointed One's reign begins and the saints experience his everlasting righteousness.

Any departed saints, however, will need to be resurrected in order to participate in his messianic kingdom. That, of course, is what Ezekiel 37 envisions with the resurrection of the Jewish saints, and Revelation 20 envisions with the first resurrection of saints from all nations. Saints from all nations will join Jewish saints when Israel, Jerusalem, and its temple are fully restored—which will "seal both vision and prophet" according to Daniel, Jeremiah, Ezekiel, Isaiah, and Micah.

The following phrase "anointed one, a prince" is another section of Daniel that has caused much debate among scholars:

> Know therefore and understand that from the going out of the word to restore and build Jerusalem to the coming of an *anointed one, a prince,* there shall be seven weeks. . . . And after the sixty-two weeks, an anointed one shall be cut off and shall have nothing. And the people of the *prince* who is to come shall destroy the city and the sanctuary. . . . And he [the prince] shall make a strong covenant with many for one week, . . . And on the wing of abominations shall come one who makes desolate, . . . (9:25–27)

The word *prince* simply means "ruler." The prince, or ruler, is somehow involved in the destruction of the city and the sanctuary, and since he is to come again, he will be involved in the succeeding final week of abominations. But who is the prince, and who are the people that belong to the prince? Is this a reference to Christ the *anointed one, the prince* that was cut off, or is this a reference to the succeeding prince that brings abominations and desolations on Israel and the world?

Some scholars insist that from a grammatical standpoint, the prince must be the same reference to the prior anointed one, a *prince*, and therefore the people of the prince are *unbelieving Jews of the Jewish "anointed one, a prince"* who brought destruction onto the temple by their rejection of their Messiah and their revolt against Rome. They interpret the succeeding verses pertaining to his putting an end to sacrifice and offering with abominations as a recapitulation of the prior destruction of the temple, or the city and the sanctuary, so that these verses are referring to the same event. Prophetic Hebrew writings often incorporate this form of repetition and parallelism. Based on this interpretation, the seventy weeks and the Olivet Discourse contain references to a single desolation of the temple. And since this desolation has already taken place in AD 70, Daniel and Christ do not envision another Great Tribulation involving another temple. Thus, all seventy weeks were fulfilled within the generation of the unbelieving Jews of Jesus' day, and the inauguration of Christ's kingdom on this earth has already begun. But it is evident that Satan remains in office, as indicated by the continuation of warring nations and systemic injustice, and that Christ's reign of righteousness over this world has emphatically not been inaugurated. Obviously, the interpretation of "the people of the prince who is to come shall destroy the city and the sanctuary" is pivotal to correctly understanding this vision.

Unbelieving Jews and zealots were no doubt involved in the revolt against Rome that inevitably led to the destruction of the city and the sanctuary, but let's not forget the role the pagan Romans played in the city's demise. From a historical perspective, a more accurate interpretation would be that the people involved in this destruction in AD 70 were both unbelieving Jews who started the revolt *and* pagan Romans who ruthlessly put down the revolt.

Christ may have pronounced judgment on Jerusalem and the temple and prophesied its destruction, but he did not lead the unbelieving Jews and the tyrannical Romans in their brutal destruction of Jerusalem and the temple. The Romans were not benevolent dictators of Israel. Led by Satan, they were illegitimate conquerors and oppressors who were covetous, murderous thieves of the nation of Israel. So it simply does not make sense to say that the "unbelieving Jews and pagan Romans of the prince [Christ]" caused the destruction of the city and the temple. These evildoers were definitely not *his* people. God, in his own sovereignty, may have used the pagan nation of Babylon to destroy the Jewish temple in Jeremiah's day and the pagan nation of Rome to once again discipline Israel by destroying the temple, but the pagans and evildoers are never referred to as "his people."

Even Daniel was aware of the fact that a demonic or Satanic prince can be behind the actions of evil human rulers and their kingdoms that require the help of an angelic prince to resist and contain him: "The prince of the kingdom of Persia withstood me twenty-one days, but Michael, one of the chief princes, came to help me" (Dan. 10:13). Christ also makes it clear in his discussions with the Pharisees that unbelievers belong to Satan, who is their spiritual father, and they are his people. Thus, Satan is the prince of evil rulers who led his people (unbelievers) to go to war and commit atrocities in this dominion of darkness—not Christ.

Therefore, the "people of the prince [Satan] who is to come shall destroy the city and the sanctuary" would surely refer to unbelieving Jews and pagan Romans, and to the evil, satanic rulers who led them to war and the brutal destruction of Jerusalem and the Second Temple in AD 70. And it is Satan "who is to come" that leads the *succeeding* evil desolator and unbelievers in that day, bringing even greater abominations and desolations upon Israel and another temple—and the world—during the final week, when "he shall put an end to sacrifice and offering."

The Messiah, by definition, is supposed to put an end to all wars and establish a kingdom of peace on this earth. Satan and his incarnation into the human Antichrist will come to this world masquerading as the true Christ. The Antichrist will deceive the whole world into thinking he is the true "prince" by establishing a covenant of peace between many warring nations and Israel ("covenant with many").

Christ's temptation in the wilderness is very revealing: "And the devil took him up and showed him all the kingdoms of the world in a moment of time, and said to him, 'To you I will give all this authority and their glory, for it has been delivered to me, and I give it to whom I will. If you, then, will worship me, it will all be yours'" (Luke 4:5–7). Satan is the father of lies, but there is some truth in his boastful claim. The worldly, warring nations of this earth bent on aggression and greed are indeed part of his authority and dominion. As a result, it is not surprising that all four of the kingdoms, or empires, that Daniel envisioned had "princes"—kings, emperors, or rulers—whom Satan deluded into believing they were gods incarnate, and they demanded to be worshiped as such. These "princes" were Satan's men.

The future desolator, or Antichrist, is no exception, as Paul makes clear. When Michael is removed and Satan is given unrestrained access to the Antichrist, he will enter the temple and make himself out to be God:

> Let no one deceive you in any way. For that day will not come, unless the rebellion comes first, and the man of lawlessness is revealed, the son of destruction, who opposes and exalts himself against *every* so-called god or object of worship, so that he takes his seat in the temple of God, proclaiming himself to be God, . . . The coming of the lawless one is by the activity of *Satan* with all power and false signs and wonders, and with all wicked deception for those who are perishing, because they refused to love the truth and so be saved. (2 Thess. 2:3–10)

Satan is directly connected with the human Antichrist who thinks he is God incarnate and enters the temple to make this bold claim. Since God has supposedly arrived within the temple itself, sacrifices to God are no longer necessary, which is why he puts an end to sacrifices and offering.

In Revelation, John makes this same connection:

> And to it [the beast] the dragon [Satan] gave his power and his throne and great authority. . . . And they worshiped the dragon [Satan], for he had given his authority to the beast [Antichrist], and they worshiped the beast, saying, "Who is like the beast, and who can fight against it?" And the beast was given a mouth uttering haughty and blasphemous words [claims to be God], and it was allowed to exercise authority for forty-two months [three-and-one-half years, or the second half of the seventieth week]. (Rev. 13:2–5)

Because of the unrestrained influence of Satan, this is no ordinary kingdom. Therefore, in the context of what *succeeds* the "people of the prince who is to come" which leads to "abominations" by "one [Satan and his deluded Antichrist] who makes desolate, until the decreed end is poured out on the desolator," one can conclude that the "prince" is synonymous with Satan or the Antichrist who, like other prior deluded rulers in the four kingdoms, thinks he is God. Christ was God incarnate, and the Antichrist will, in effect, be Satan incarnate during the final week.

In the Olivet Discourse, Jesus also makes this same connection of this "prince" to a "false christ." Jesus is referencing the final seventieth week of Daniel when he says:

> So when you see the abomination of desolation spoken of by the prophet Daniel, standing in the holy place [when the desolator puts "an end to sacrifice and offering"] . . . Then if anyone says to you, 'Look, here is the Christ!' or 'There he is!' do not believe it. For false christs and false prophets will arise and perform great signs and wonders, so as to lead astray, if possible, even the elect." (Matt. 24:15, 23–24)

One of the great signs of the Antichrist will be that he brings peace to the warring nations of this world and Israel. After accomplishing the remarkable feat of bringing peace to a section of the world that has never known peace and receiving the world's adoration, he will likely become deluded by Satan and his own pride into thinking he is the Messiah and savior of the world. And Israel's temple would logically be the focus of his ministry, as he claims to be God and demands to be worshiped, thereby eliminating the need for further sacrifices, as he has "put an end to sacrifice and offering." John also places the temple at the center of attention during the Tribulation: "Then I was given a measuring rod like a staff, and I was told, 'Rise and measure the temple of God and the altar and those who worship there, but do not measure the court outside the temple; leave that out, for it is given over to the nations, and they will trample the holy city for forty-two months [three-and-one-half years]'" (Rev. 11:1-2).

With these interpretations in mind, let's revisit this vision of the seventy weeks and see how well it harmonizes with the Olivet Discourse. Daniel prays for the restoration of Jerusalem and its temple after seventy years, only to be told by the angel Gabriel that it will take seventy weeks of years to complete this restoration and usher in the messianic kingdom:

- **Seventy weeks are decreed about your people and your holy city** [before Israel, Jerusalem, and its temple will be truly restored],
- **to finish the transgression, to put an end to sin,** [for the punishment of repeatedly breaking their covenant with God],
- **and to atone for iniquity** [through the Messiah's atoning sacrifice],
- **to bring in everlasting righteousness** [the inauguration of the Messiah's dominion over this earth with his saints],
- **to seal both vision and prophet** [to fulfill this vision and all the other messianic prophecies pertaining to Israel, Jerusalem, and its temple],
- **and to anoint a most holy place** [establish the Ezekiel temple in the messianic kingdom]. [End of introduction and overview]
- **Know therefore and understand that from the going out of the word to restore and build Jerusalem** [as foretold by Jeremiah] **to the coming of an anointed one, a prince** [the coming of the Messiah into this world],
- **there shall be seven weeks. Then for sixty-two weeks it** [Jerusalem and the temple] **shall be built again with squares and moat** [After 49 years, Jerusalem and the temple are rebuilt by Nehemiah and Ezra, with priestly functions restored in 408 BC],
- **but in a troubled time** [Nehemiah and Ezra experienced great opposition during the rebuilding of Jerusalem and the temple].
- **And after the sixty-two weeks, an anointed one shall be cut off** [After 434 years in AD 27, the Messiah will come, but he will be rejected and crucified in order to "atone for iniquity." During this fourth-kingdom of "legs of iron," he will ascend to heaven: "with the clouds of heaven there came one like a son of man, and he came to the Ancient of Days" (Dan. 7:13)].
- **and shall have nothing** [He did not receive the messianic kingdom of righteousness at that time—the world remains Satan's unrighteous regime. The Son of Man is Lord-elect and sits and waits on the Ancient of Days to determine when it is time for the inauguration of his kingdom].

- **And the people** [unbelieving Jews and pagan Romans] **of the prince** [Satan] **who is to come** [in the future desolation and tribulation] **shall destroy the city and the sanctuary. Its end shall come with a flood** [Roman troops poured into the city in AD 70, bringing utter desolation to the city and the temple],
- **and to the end** [of Satan's reign over this world of wicked, warring kingdoms] **there shall be war** ["For nation will rise against nation, and kingdom against kingdom" (Matt. 24:7 and Jer. 28:7–8)].
- **Desolations are decreed** ["there will be famines and earthquakes in various places" (Matt. 24:7 and Jer. 28:7–8)].
- **And he** [the prince and "false christs and false prophets" that "will arise and perform great signs and wonders, so as to lead astray" (Matt. 24:24)] **shall make a strong covenant with many** [a peace agreement between Israel and the many warring countries hostile to Jerusalem] **for one week** [seven years],
- **and for half of the week he shall put an end to sacrifice and offering** [After three-and-one-half years, the Antichrist puts an end to the temple sacrifice and offerings because he enters the temple and declares himself to be God: "So when you see the abomination of desolation spoken of by the prophet Daniel, *standing in the holy place*" (Matt. 24:15)].
- **And on the wing of abominations shall come one** [the Antichrist] **who makes desolate** [As Daniel says, "At that time shall arise Michael, the great prince who has charge of your people. And there shall be a time of trouble, such as never has been since there was a nation till that time. . . . And from the time that the regular burnt offering is taken away and the abomination that makes desolate is set up, there shall be 1,290 days" (12:1, 11). Or, as Jesus says, "So when you see the abomination of desolation spoken of by the prophet Daniel, standing in the holy place, . . . For then there will be great tribulation, such as has not been from the beginning of the world until now, no, and never will be" (Matt. 24:15, 21)],
- **until the decreed end is poured out on the desolator** [As Daniel says, "And as I looked, the beast was killed, and its body destroyed and given over to be burned with fire. . . . But the court shall sit in judgment, and his dominion shall be taken away, to be consumed and destroyed to the end (7:11, 26). Or, as John says, "And the beast was captured, and with it the false prophet . . . These two were thrown alive into the lake of fire that burns with sulfur (Rev. 19:20)].

With the destruction of the desolator, or the Antichrist, the seventy weeks are now complete. It is time for the Messiah to be inaugurated as Lord of this world in order to bring in an everlasting righteousness that includes the "most holy place," or the Ezekiel temple, which will never be desecrated again. Or, as based on Daniel's axiom outlined in other visions:

- "As you looked, a stone was cut out by no human hand, and it struck the image on its feet of iron and clay, and broke them in pieces. . . . the stone that struck the image became a great mountain and filled the whole earth. . . . the God of heaven will set up a kingdom that shall never be destroyed" (Dan. 2:34–35, 44).
- "Until the Ancient of Days came, and judgment was given for the saints of the Most High, and the time came when the saints possessed the kingdom" (Dan. 7:22).
- "And the kingdom and the dominion and the greatness of the kingdoms under the whole heaven shall be given to the people of the saints of the Most High; their kingdom shall be an everlasting kingdom, and all dominions shall serve and obey them" (Dan. 7:27).
- "But at that time your people shall be delivered, everyone whose name shall be found written in the book" (Dan. 12:1).

Because the Anointed One has made atonement for the sins of the saints under the new covenant, the righteous saints, which include Jewish and Gentile believers, now have God's laws written on their hearts when they enter into the messianic kingdom, an age of righteousness or righteous living on this restored Genesis earth. If they have departed before the Great Tribulation or are martyred during that time of great trial, "the people of the saints of the Most High" whose names are written in the book of life shall be delivered through the resurrection of their natural bodies to inherit Christ's inaugurated messianic kingdom on this earth: "the time came when the saints possessed the kingdom." These things take place to "seal both vision and prophet" or to fulfill Daniel's multiple visions and the words of the prophets Jeremiah, Isaiah, and Ezekiel pertaining to the restoration of Israel, Jerusalem, and its temple.

In Daniel's vision, the condition of the temple is indicative of God's relationship with Israel. With unfaithful Israel operating in a satanic age of warring kingdoms on this earth, the temple will continue to experience desolations, culminating in the worst desecration by Satan during the Great Tribulation. But at that time the Ancient of Days will take action and restore Jerusalem and its temple one final time, ushering in an age of righteousness. Under the new covenant, with Christ ruling the world, Israel and all the saints, Jew and Gentile, will remain faithful. As a result, God's covenant with his people will no longer be broken, and the temple will never again be destroyed due to the transgressions of unbelieving Jews. This is what Daniel was hoping and praying for.

As Jesus says in his exposition of Daniel in the Olivet Discourse, once these visions and prophecies pertaining to the Genesis heavens and earth have been fulfilled, the Adamic age will end, and "the Son of Man comes in his glory" to rapture the saints into the clouds to the Father's heavenly kingdom, where, in the very presence of the Ancient of Days, there will no longer be a temple. Or, according to John, the everlasting kingdom of the saints of the Most High transitions from the restored Genesis earth to the eternal new heavens and new earth.

The Two Desolations in the Gospels

As the preceding analysis demonstrates, Daniel's vision of the seventy weeks contains two separate occasions when the temple will be desecrated: the first desecration occurred during the fourth-kingdom "legs of iron" in AD 70 when the temple building itself was destroyed, and the second occurs during the fifth-kingdom "feet of iron of clay" in the seventieth week and short reign of Satan and the desolator when the temple sacrifices are suspended for a season. Yet, in the Olivet Discourse as recorded by Matthew, Mark, and Luke, Jesus references the desecration of the temple only once. Does this single reference pertain to the first desolation of Daniel that occurred in AD 70 after the Anointed One was cut off, or does it pertain to the second desolation that will occur during the seventieth week of the short reign of the desolator? This question has caused considerable debate and confusion among scholars.

Since the events surrounding the two desolations of the temple in Daniel's vision have some striking similarities, Christ's single reference in the Olivet Discourse could refer to both. Christ comingles the two desolations in Daniel's vision of the seventy weeks and leaves it to the Gospel writers to emphasize one or the other. Luke emphasizes the first desolation and destruction of the temple in AD 70 after "the anointed one shall be cut off" when he records Christ warning the disciples to be on the lookout for the time "when you see Jerusalem surrounded by armies, then know that its desolation [destruction] has come near" (21:20). But Luke never uses the phrase the "abomination of desolation" that refers to the seventieth week. In contrast, Matthew and Mark emphasize the second desolation and specifically reference the "abomination of desolation spoken of by the prophet Daniel" (Matt. 24:15; cf. Mark 13:14).

Luke may have had strategic reasons not to emphasize the second desolation that leads to the inauguration of the messianic kingdom. His Gospel focuses on the eternal kingdom and is tailored more toward the Greco-Roman world while Matthew's Gospel is directed more toward a

Jewish audience. Evangelists like Luke had to be careful referring to a stone that would crush the Roman Empire and set up a Jewish messianic empire. To avoid any geopolitical threat to the Romans, Luke emphasizes the Romans' destruction of the temple and Christ's second coming on the last day of this Genesis creation when the saints will experience the final resurrection and inherit the heavenly kingdom. This may have seemed strange to the Romans, but it would not have presented a challenge or threat to their government. The Messiah's earthly kingdom is quite stealthy in the New Testament. This topic is addressed in detail in chapter 11, "The Stealthy Restoration."

Before analyzing the two approaches in the Gospels, it helps to identify in Daniel the two different ways that Jerusalem and its temple can be desecrated, which in turn serve as two precedents for its future desolation during the seventy weeks. One way is demonstrated by the invasion of the Babylonian armies that surrounded the city and, when Jerusalem fell, brought utter destruction to the city and complete destruction of the temple building itself. Sacrifices ceased because the temple building no longer existed. When the Jews were sent away in exile, the Babylonians brought in other pagan ethnic people who trampled on the holy city and the temple grounds. This form of desolation is similar to the first desolation described by Daniel when he says they "shall *destroy* the city and the sanctuary" (9:26), which occurred in AD 70 when the Roman armies surrounded Jerusalem and then destroyed the city and the temple building.

The second form of desecration occurred during the Greek Empire under the reign of Antiochus IV Epiphanes when the temple was desecrated for a season, but the building itself was not destroyed. Daniel 11:1–35 refers to him as a "little horn" whose rule began insignificantly, but in his brilliant and cunning ways, he becomes a great and powerful king over the region around Israel. He attempted to impose pagan worship on the Jews by force, even desecrating the temple by erecting an altar to Zeus in the temple precincts and offering swine as sacrifices. Daniel describes this event as a form of abomination that desolates the temple: "Forces from him shall appear and profane the temple and fortress, and shall take away the regular burnt offering. And they shall set up the *abomination that makes desolate*" (Dan. 11:31).

Antiochus may have shown up with armed forces to put an end to the priestly sacrifices and impose pagan idol worship in the temple, but he did not make war against Israel at that time because the region was already one of his provinces, and the Jews had not started a revolt against his rule. He began the desecration of the temple during a time of peace when Israel was firmly under his control. He subsequently slaughtered tens of thousands of Jews who refused to worship the Greek pagan idols set up in the Jewish temple. Antiochus was so proud of his exploits that he became delusional and began to think of himself as "Epiphanes" meaning the "illustrious one" or "God manifest." Antiochus represents a type of antichrist with his delusions of deity and his extreme persecution of God's people. Eventually, this desecration instigated a successful revolt by Mattathias and his sons. Most important, the temple building itself was not destroyed, and after a little more than six years (2,300 days), the sanctuary was restored to its regular functions and the persecution of the Jews came to an end (Dan. 8:9–14). Hanukkah, also known as the Festival of Lights, is an eight-day Jewish holiday commemorating the rededication of the temple in Jerusalem at that time.

This form of desecration of the temple can be outlined as follows:

- Occurs during a time of relative peace and stability.
- The priestly sacrifices in the temple are halted.
- A pagan idol of a pagan god is set up within the temple, creating an abomination in God's temple.
- The Jews are forced to worship this pagan god or face severe persecution and death.
- Severe persecution follows for years until the forces of evil are removed from power and the temple is restored.

Antiochus's "abomination that makes desolate" (11:31) lasts for 2,300 days which serves as a prototype of the future Antichrist. And it is no coincidence that the vision suddenly transitions to the future Antichrist in verse 36: "He [the future Antichrist] shall exalt himself and magnify himself above every god, and shall speak astonishing things against the God of gods." This leads to the Great Tribulation when Michael is removed as the restrainer of Satan and another even greater desolation follows: "And from the time that the regular burnt offering is taken away and the *abomination that makes desolate* is set up, there shall be 1,290 days" (12:11). The abomination of the temple caused by Antiochus that lasted for 2,300 days is clearly a forerunner of the future abomination of the temple caused by the Antichrist that lasts for 1,290 days.

Antiochus's form of desecration is very similar to the second desolation in the seventieth week; the temple building itself is not destroyed by soldiers, but it is desecrated when the desolator "shall put an end to sacrifice and offering," he demands to be worshiped, and great tribulation follows. And, similar to the desecration by Antiochus, after several years, the priestly temple functions are restored—with the major difference being that after this final restoration of the Ezekiel temple, the messianic age of righteousness is ushered in. And instead of celebrating Hanukkah, believing Jews and their Gentile brothers will be celebrating the messianic kingdom itself!

Thus, we have two forms of desolation of the temple: The Roman desolation as exemplified by the Babylonian armed invasion and destruction of the temple, and the desolation by the Antichrist as exemplified by Antiochus with the forced imposition of pagan idol worship within a standing temple. And these subtle but substantial differences between the two types of desolations described by Daniel appear in the Gospel accounts of the Olivet Discourse with Luke emphasizing the first desolation after Christ is "cut off" and Matthew and Mark emphasizing the second desolation in the seventieth week. Let's examine Luke's account, then Matthew's account, and then analyze their differences:

> *Daniel's first desolation*: "And after the sixty-two weeks, an anointed one shall be cut off and shall have nothing. And the people of the prince who is to come shall destroy the city and the sanctuary. Its end shall come with a flood, and to the end there shall be war. Desolations are decreed." (9:26) =

> *Luke's reference to the first desolation*: "And they asked him, 'Teacher, when will these things be, and what will be the sign when these things are about to take place?' . . . 'when you see Jerusalem surrounded by armies, then know that its desolation has come near. Then let those who are in Judea flee to the mountains, and let those who are inside the city depart, and let not those who are out in the country enter it, for these are days of vengeance, to fulfill all that is written [in reference to the destruction of the "city and the sanctuary"]. Alas for women who are pregnant and for those who are nursing infants in those days! For there will be great distress upon the earth and wrath against this people. They will fall by the edge of the sword and be led captive among all nations, and Jerusalem will be trampled underfoot by the Gentiles, until the times of the Gentiles are fulfilled.'" (21:7–24)

The first significant difference in Luke's account is that he only records the first part of the disciples' question about how to recognize when the Second Temple is about to be destroyed, and, unlike Matthew and Mark, he does not include their second question about the signs and events that would lead to the close of the age. Luke records, "And they asked him, 'Teacher, when will these things be, and what will be the sign when these things [the destruction of the temple] are about to take place?'" (21:7). Luke's version of the Olivet Discourse emphasizes the warning signs that will lead to the destruction of the first-century temple.

When analyzing the two accounts, it is important to remember Daniel's axiom that the conclusion of the second desolation leads directly to the restoration of Jerusalem and the "anointing of the most holy place," or the reestablishment of the Ezekiel temple in the age of righteousness. Another key indication that Luke's account is describing the first desolation of the temple and not the second desolation is that Luke records Christ describing Jerusalem in the aftermath of its destruction as existing as a Gentile city without a temple: "But when you see Jerusalem surrounded by armies, then know that its desolation has come near. . . . and Jerusalem will be trampled underfoot by the Gentiles, until the times of the Gentiles are fulfilled" (Luke 21:20–24). Until 1948, Jerusalem has been "trampled" on by a succession of invading Gentile nations and people. Even today, much of East Jerusalem, although annexed by Israel after the 1967 Six-Day War, remains occupied by Gentile Palestinians, and the temple mount itself contains a mosque. Jerusalem and its temple are clearly still being trampled on by Gentiles, and the region exists in an almost perpetual state of war, or as Daniel says, "to the end there shall be war."

Luke describes this desolation of Jerusalem and its temple as occurring when the city is "surrounded by armies," similar to the Babylonian desolation: "But when you see Jerusalem surrounded by armies, then know that its desolation has come near." During the First Jewish-Roman War, the Romans amassed several legions of soldiers to lay siege to Jerusalem. The Roman armies surrounded the city and built a trench and a wall encircling the city, and everyone trapped within the city could no longer escape. Those who tried were caught, killed, and their bodies strewn over the Roman wall for all to see. Many died of starvation or from internal factions fighting each other. When the city fell, both the city and the temple were destroyed.

Luke also emphasizes the fact that when the saints see an army amassing around Jerusalem, they can easily escape the tribulation that will fall on the occupants of the city by fleeing from Judea and the city to the mountains. The Jewish saints of the first century heeded Christ's warning, fled the region, and escaped the tribulation that fell on those who remained in Jerusalem. Unbelieving Jews did not follow Christ's advice; they experienced horrible tribulation during the siege and were either killed by the soldiers or captured and sold as slaves to other regions of the empire. Notice, too, that Luke says that this tribulation is not directed against the saints, but is specifically directed against the unbelieving Jews: "for these are days of vengeance [against the generation of Jews who rejected Christ], to fulfill all that is written. . . . For there will be great distress upon the earth and wrath against this people [unbelieving Jews]." Again, the saints did not experience this tribulation because it was not directed against them.

In contrast, both Matthew's and Mark's accounts of the Olivet Discourse match the final week of Daniel's second desolation. Unlike Luke, Matthew records Christ as making specific reference to the "abomination of desolation spoken of by the prophet Daniel." Also notice that Jesus does not warn the saints to be on the lookout for armies surrounding the city; rather, he says to be on the lookout for the time when the desolator actually appears *within* the temple itself "standing in the holy place," when, as Daniel says, he puts "an end to sacrifice and offering." Moreover, in Daniel's vision, there is no evidence that the Antichrist brings an army against Jerusalem when he enters the temple and makes himself out to be God and discontinues the sacrificial rituals (cf. 2 Thess. 2:3–12; Rev. 5—19). Daniel describes this second desolation as occurring during a period of peace after a strong covenant is made between warring nations and Israel. He makes no mention of armies because this desolation does not take place during a time of war or siege against Jerusalem, but in a time of peace. We get the impression that the Antichrist and his entourage of false prophets will be operating freely in Jerusalem at this time because he will be accepted by the deceived people; he will simply walk into the temple to desecrate it during the middle of the seventieth week:

Daniel's second desolation: "And he shall make a strong covenant with many for one week, and for half of the week he shall put an end to sacrifice and offering [when he enters the temple]. And on the wing of abominations shall come one who makes desolate, until the decreed end is poured out on the desolator." (9:27) =

Matthew's reference to the second desolation: "So when you see the abomination of desolation spoken of by the prophet Daniel, standing in the holy place (let the reader understand), then let those who are in Judea flee to the mountains. . . . For then there will be great tribulation, such as has not been from the beginning of the world until now, no, and never will be. . . . Then if anyone says to you, 'Look, here is the Christ!' or 'There he is!' do not believe it. For false christs and false prophets will arise and perform great signs and wonders, so as to lead astray, if possible, even the elect." (24:15–24; cf. Mark 13:1–23)

In Daniel's amplified descriptions of the Great Tribulation of those days, he teaches that the saints will be targeted and unable to escape this time of great trial: "As I looked, this horn *made war with the saints and prevailed over them*, . . . He shall speak words against the Most High, and *shall wear out the saints* of the Most High, and shall think to change the times and the law; and *they shall be given into his hand* for a time, times, and half a time" (Dan. 7:21–25). According to Matthew's account, Jesus still warns the saints in Judea to flee to the mountains when this second desolation unfolds, but he seems to indicate that the saints will get caught up in this unprecedented "great tribulation" and not be able to escape it as easily as they did during the Roman desolation: "For then there will be great tribulation [against the saints], such as has not been from the beginning of the world until now, no, never will be." The first desolation is directly against the unbelieving Jews, and the second desolation is directly against the saints.

In Revelation, John makes this same observation:

And the beast was given a mouth uttering haughty and blasphemous words, and it was allowed to exercise authority for forty-two months [three-and-one-half years]. It opened its mouth to utter blasphemies against God, . . . it was allowed to *make war on the saints and to conquer them*. . . . If anyone is to be taken captive, to captivity he goes; if anyone is to be slain with the sword, with the sword must he be slain. Here is a call for the endurance and faith of the saints. (Rev. 13:5–10)

During the first desolation in AD 70 when the Roman armies attacked the city, the saints were able to effectively escape the tribulation that followed by simply fleeing the city and the region beforehand. Thus, the Roman armies directed their war against the unbelieving Jews who revolted against Rome and remained in Jerusalem. But Daniel, Christ, and later, John, describe the second desolation of the temple as a time when the saints will experience persecution, much like the persecutions of Antiochus. Christ warns to be on the lookout, not for armies, but for the "false christ" (the desolator or the beast) that will enter the temple and blaspheme God by pretending to be God. The desolator and his deluded followers will "make war" specifically on the saints. As John says, this period of unprecedented "great tribulation" *against the saints* will require an unusual amount of endurance and faith on their part.

Although similarities do exist in Daniel's vision between the two desecrations of Jerusalem and its temple, there are significant differences as well, which the Gospel writers recognize. Luke uses Jesus' reference to the temple's destruction to emphasize the first desolation, which is similar to the destruction by the armies of Babylon. Jerusalem and the temple will be surrounded by armies and the temple utterly destroyed, and the saints will easily be able to escape this tribulation by being on the lookout for these gathering armies and simply getting out of Judea and hiding in remote mountainous regions. The Roman armies directed their vengeance against the unbelieving Jewish Zealots, not the saints. And the world continues in its current fallen condition—the Gentiles continue to trample on Jerusalem and the temple mount, and wars continue to be waged.

Even during the Babylonian destruction of Jerusalem and its temple, Jeremiah told the Jews they could escape persecution and death if they followed his advice and peacefully went into exile accepting God's certain judgment against Jerusalem:

And to this people you shall say: "Thus says the LORD: Behold, I set before you the way of life and the way of death. He who stays in this city shall die by the sword, by famine, and by pestilence, but he who goes out and surrenders to the Chaldeans who are besieging you shall live and shall have his life as a prize of war. For I have set my face against this city for harm and not for good, declares the LORD: it shall be given into the hand of the king of Babylon, and he shall burn it with fire." (Jer. 21:8–10)

Those who remained in the city faced the wrath of the Babylonian army. But Jeremiah was considered a traitor for advising surrender: "Then the priests and the prophets said to the officials and to all the people, 'This man deserves the sentence of death, because he has prophesied against this city, as you have heard with your own ears'" (Jer. 26:11). Christ was accused of a similar crime when he spoke of the temple's impending destruction and reconstruction, or resurrection, in three days (Matt. 26:60–62).

Matthew and Mark, on the other hand, take other clues from Christ's discourse on Daniel and emphasize the second desolation in Daniel's vision that is similar to the desecration by Antiochus. The temple building itself is not destroyed by armies. Instead, during a deceptive time of peace, the desolator desecrates it when the "false christ" performs "great signs and wonders" to delude unbelievers into thinking he is the Christ. He enters the temple "standing in the holy place" and puts an end to sacrifice and offering. The Antichrist and his followers subsequently make war against the saints with a vengeance unmatched in the history of the world. He will prevail over the saints even if they attempt to hide in remote areas. It will take great faith to endure this Great Tribulation.

But the most important feature of this last desolation is that after three-and-one-half years when the desolator is destroyed, and the Tribulation comes to an end, the seventy weeks will be complete, and the Son of Man's kingdom of everlasting righteousness will be established by the Ancient of Days: "the time came when the saints possessed the kingdom." All nations will experience peace on earth when Israel and Jerusalem are restored and its temple is anointed as the "most holy place"—never to be desecrated by Satan and fallen man again.

The Restoration in the Olivet Discourse

At first glance, it appears that Christ does not explicitly reference the restoration that follows the Great Tribulation of the seventieth week as Daniel outlines. He does, but these are stealthy references. Once properly understood, they are a clear affirmation of the messianic kingdom being established *after* the Great Tribulation and *before* "the close of the age" and the beginning of the heavenly kingdom.

In Matthew's account of Daniel's second desolation that occurs during the seventieth week, after warning the disciples about the Great Tribulation, Christ makes an interesting statement about the "gospel of the kingdom" that succeeds this period of tribulation: "And because lawlessness will be increased, the love of many will grow cold. But the one who endures to the end will be saved. And this gospel of the kingdom will be proclaimed throughout the whole world as a testimony to all nations, and *then* the end will come" (Matt. 24:12–14).

Could the "gospel of the kingdom" that serves as a "testimony to all nations" be a reference to the age of "everlasting righteousness" that occurs upon completion of the seventy weeks, as Daniel and the prophets describe must take place on this earth before "the end will come"?

Today many evangelists teach that the preaching of the gospel throughout the world must be accomplished before the Tribulation can begin. However, there is biblical support for the assertion that Christ's reference to the "gospel of the kingdom" is equivalent to the inauguration of his kingdom after the seventieth week. The gospel, or good news, includes the fact that Christ is rightfully Lord and Savior of this world and that there will be an earthly kingdom of righteousness realized on this earth when he exercises his divine Lordship over this world. He may be Lord-elect, but the world has not yet experienced his inaugurated reign over this earth. Since he is the true Creator of this world, he has a divine right to reestablish his kingdom, or dominion over this earth, before it comes to an end. Thus, the inauguration of "this gospel of the kingdom" on this Genesis earth would indeed be a tremendous testimony to all nations that he is the true Christ and prince, or ruler, of this world.

Christ is likely quoting from Isaiah because the prophet equates the "good news" not only with the preaching of the gospel, but also with the full realization and implementation of Christ's future reign, when the whole world actually hears, sees, and *experiences* his messianic kingdom:

> How beautiful upon the mountains are the feet of him who brings good news, who publishes peace, who brings good news of happiness, who publishes salvation, who says to Zion, "Your God reigns" [the gospel realized when Christ exercises his reign as Lord]. The voice of your watchmen—they lift up their voice; together they sing for joy; for eye to eye they see the return of the LORD to Zion. Break forth together into singing, you waste places of Jerusalem, for the LORD has comforted his people; he has redeemed Jerusalem. The LORD has bared his holy arm before the eyes of all the nations, and all the ends of the earth shall see the salvation of our God [as a "testimony to all nations"]. (Isa. 52:7–10)

This is a remarkable prophecy because it teaches that the "gospel of the kingdom" is both a proclamation that Christ is God and Savior and that someday he will redeem this world when he exercises his worldwide reign that "all the ends of the earth shall see the salvation of our God." If part of the good news is the fully implemented reign of Christ before the eyes of all the nations, then the 1,000-year messianic kingdom that the prophets describe is indeed the "gospel of the kingdom" that Jesus talked about; it will be realized on this earth after the Great Tribulation when the Son finally sits on his throne in heaven at the right hand of the Ancient of Days and establishes his earthly kingdom—which is what Daniel teaches will occur after the desolator is destroyed and the seventy weeks are complete.

Following is a summary of this section of the Olivet Discourse:

1. The destruction of the temple: "there will not be left here one stone upon another that will not be thrown down" (Matt. 24:2).
2. Then "the beginning of birth pains" as the current world experiences wars, rumors of wars, famines, and earthquakes (Matt. 24:6–8).
3. Next, the full labor of the Great Tribulation: "the abomination of desolation spoken of by the prophet Daniel" (Matt. 24:15).
4. Then the worldwide restoration is given birth, or realized: "And this gospel of the kingdom will be proclaimed throughout the whole world as a testimony to all nations" (Matt. 24:14).
5. Upon completion of all these prophecies, "the end will come" when the Son of Man comes again on Judgment Day at the close of the Genesis age when heaven and earth pass away (Matt. 24:14).

According to Jesus, after this gospel is "proclaimed [preached and realized] throughout the whole world as a testimony to all nations," *then* "the end will come," when Christ comes again and we inherit the eternal age to come. This answers the disciples' question concerning "the sign of your coming and of the close of the age." The close of the Genesis age is after the Second Temple is destroyed, after a future Great Tribulation and desecration of another temple involving the Antichrist, and after the "gospel of the kingdom" or the messianic kingdom is inaugurated and realized on this earth. Christ does include the restoration as a part of the major events leading up to his return on the last day. Upon completion of these major eschatological events, all the signs leading up to his second coming and the end of this age will be complete—then the Son of Man will come again and usher in the Father's eternal kingdom "in the age to come."

Satan and the Millennium

It is important to read and understand Daniel within his grammatical-historical context and not read too much into his visions from later revelation. Yet Christ wants us to synthesize all his Word. The Olivet Discourse is a synthesis of Daniel's visions *and* the prophets combined with the events of Christ's day, as well as additional revelation of future events. Furthermore, Revelation is the "Olivet Discourse Part Two," for as Jesus says to John, "The revelation of Jesus Christ, which God gave him to show to his servants *the things that must soon take place.* He made it known by sending his angel to his servant John" (Rev. 1:1). Through Revelation, Jesus is still informing us about what must take place before he comes again at the close of the age. Revelation is a continuation of Daniel's vision *and* the Olivet Discourse, providing substantial additional data that Daniel did not have access to.

Revelation sheds considerable light on the meaning of one fascinating section of Daniel's obscure visions. Daniel is describing the Great Tribulation and the messianic kingdom when he says:

> I looked then because of the sound of the great words that the horn was speaking. And as I looked, the beast was killed, and its body destroyed and given over to be burned with fire [the human Antichrist is killed]. As for the rest of the beasts [Satan and his demons], their dominion was taken away, but their lives were prolonged for a season and a time [they continue to exist for a period of time before being destroyed]. . . . As I looked, this horn [the Antichrist] made war with the saints and prevailed over them, until the Ancient of Days came, and judgment was given for the saints of the Most High, and the time came when the saints possessed the kingdom. (Dan. 7:11–12, 21–22)

When this teaching is compared to John's vision of the millennial reign of Christ, it begins to make more sense. The "beast" (singular) in Daniel's vision represents the human Antichrist or the horn; and "the rest of the beasts" represent Satan and his demons. The beast is killed and his body is destroyed by fire, but the lives of the beasts, or demons, are prolonged to live on for another day. In regards to the beast and his false prophet, John says that toward the climatic end of the Great Tribulation, "the beast [human Antichrist] was captured, and with it the false prophet who in its presence had done the signs by which he deceived those who had received the mark of the beast and those who worshiped its image. These two were thrown alive into the lake of fire that burns with sulfur" (Rev. 19:20). This matches Daniel's account: "the beast was killed, and its body destroyed and given over to be burned with fire." John adds the detail that the beast and his false prophet are thrown body and soul into the "lake of fire."

But notice what happens to Satan in John's vision and how this matches Daniel's vision:

> Then I saw an angel coming down from heaven, holding in his hand the key to the bottomless pit and a great chain. And he seized the dragon, that ancient serpent, who is the devil and Satan, and bound him for a thousand years, and threw him into the pit, and shut it and sealed it over him, so that he might not deceive the nations any longer, until the thousand years were ended. After that he must be released for a little while (Rev. 20:1–3) = "As for the rest of the beasts, their dominion was taken away [the regime change from Satan to Christ as Lord of this world], but their lives were prolonged for a season and a time [a thousand years]." (Dan. 7:12)

Unlike the human Antichrist, Satan and his demons are not destroyed at the beginning of Christ's millennial reign. It is after Satan's final release and deception that they are destroyed and sent to the lake of fire:

> And when the thousand years are ended, Satan will be released from his prison and will come out to deceive the nations that are at the four corners of the earth, Gog and Magog, to gather them for battle; their number is like the sand of the sea. And they marched up over the broad plain of the earth and surrounded the camp of the saints and the beloved city, but fire came down from heaven and consumed them, and the devil who had deceived them was thrown into the lake of fire and sulfur where the beast and the false prophet were, and they will be tormented day and night forever and ever. (Rev. 20:7–10)

Satan's dominion is taken away during Christ's millennial reign, but he is released one final time to instigate one last rebellion and war of aggression against God and his saints. But his attempt to reestablish his dominion over the kingdoms of this world fails because the armies he gathers from Gog and Magog are destroyed by fire before they can harm Jerusalem, and Satan and his demons are subsequently thrown into the lake of fire for eternity, never to be heard from again.

Isaiah provides some of the same subtle hints about Satan's activity during the messianic kingdom, further explained by Revelation 19. Notice Isaiah's reference to the cosmic changes in the heavens that precede the removal of Satan and the beginning of Christ's reign:

> For the windows of heaven are opened, and the foundations of the earth tremble. The earth is utterly broken, the earth is split apart, the earth is violently shaken. The earth staggers like a drunken man; it sways like a hut; its transgression lies heavy upon it, and it falls, and will not rise again. On that day the LORD will punish the host of heaven [Satan and his demons], in heaven, and the kings of the earth [the Antichrist, false prophet, and kings that follow him into battle], on the earth. They [the host of heaven] will be gathered together as prisoners in a pit; they will be shut up in a prison [Satan and the demons are seized, bound, and thrown into a pit which is sealed], and after many days [one thousand years] they will be punished [thrown into the lake of fire]. Then the moon will be confounded and the sun ashamed, for the LORD of hosts reigns on Mount Zion and in Jerusalem, and his glory will be before his elders [Christ's millennial reign with his resurrected saints, including those who sit on thrones as ruling elders]. (Isa. 24:18–23)

In a later vision, Isaiah still foresees the final cosmic destruction of the Genesis creation and the transition to the eternal age to come: "Lift up your eyes to the heavens, and look at the earth beneath; for the heavens vanish like smoke, the earth will wear out like a garment, and they who dwell in it will die in like manner; but my salvation will be forever, and my righteousness will never be dismayed" (Isa. 51:6). This correlates with what John says occurs after the millennium when earth and sky fled from his presence; the saints inherit the new heavens and new earth and the New Jerusalem (Rev. 20:11; 21:1–2).

Prophetic Summations

Daniel's visions usually start with an overview or summary and then are followed by an expanded version. Sometimes the short overview will omit major components of the overall framework of the future. For example, one could take the five major events listed as a summary of this section of the Olivet Discourse and omit event number four, the "gospel of the kingdom," and proceed directly from the end of the Tribulation to the second coming on the last day. The remaining events are true, but they do not provide a complete picture. Theologians refer to this phenomenon as "telescoping," for when you focus on a distant object in space, closer objects become blurred and get passed over.

Prophetic summations are known for these types of omissions. Consider Isaiah's prophecy of the Messiah's birth and his subsequent reign:

> For to us a child is born, to us a son is given; and the government shall be upon his shoulder, and his name shall be called Wonderful Counselor, Mighty God, Everlasting Father, Prince of Peace. Of the increase of his government and of peace there will be no end, on the throne of David and over his kingdom, to establish it and to uphold it with justice and with righteousness from this time forth and forevermore. (Isa. 9:6–7)

From reading this summation, we could easily come to the false conclusion that as soon as the Messiah is born and comes into this world, the inauguration of his messianic kingdom immediately follows. The disciples made this mistake, as had the two men on the road to Emmaus. But from reading other expanded prophecies in Isaiah 52, we know that before the Messiah governs this world with peace and justice, he will be despised, rejected, oppressed, a man of sorrows, grief stricken, smitten by God for our transgressions, crushed for our iniquities, cut off and killed, buried in a rich man's tomb, and then resurrected when his days are prolonged so that he will see his children when they inherit his kingdom of righteousness on this earth. Isaiah further reveals that since most of his children will have died before he finally establishes his administration over this world, there must be a resurrection of these departed saints in order for them to be a part of his kingdom: "Your dead shall live; their bodies shall rise. You who dwell in the dust, awake and sing for joy" (Isa. 26:19).

Centuries later, John's vision in Revelation also reveals that the saints will experience two resurrections in order to access God's kingdom. In keeping with Ezekiel's vision, the first resurrection will be of the natural bodies of the departed saints, which will enable them to inherit the Son's messianic kingdom for one thousand years. And in keeping with Paul's understanding of the transformed body, the final resurrection will be of the immortal bodies, which will enable the saints to inherit the Father's eternal new heaven and new earth.

When looking at any prophetic overview, it is extremely important that we take into consideration all other expanded details that have been revealed by that prophet and other prophets, as well as any expanded revelation found in the New Testament. With this in mind, let's examine a notoriously difficult summation that Daniel makes, which Christ references in the Olivet Discourse. In these summations, it appears that the "gospel of the kingdom" is omitted entirely, so that the second coming at the "close of the age" occurs immediately at the end of the Great Tribulation. Let's read Daniel's summation and then compare it to Christ's:

> At that time shall arise Michael, the great prince who has charge of your people. And there shall be a time of trouble, such as never has been since there was a nation till that time. But at that time your people shall be delivered, everyone whose name shall be found written in the book. And many of those who sleep in the dust of the earth shall awake, some to everlasting life, and some to shame and everlasting contempt [final resurrection]. And those who are wise shall shine like the brightness of the sky above; and those who turn many to righteousness, like the stars forever and ever. (Dan. 12:1–3)

> For then there will be great tribulation, such as has not been from the beginning of the world until now, no, and never will be. . . . Immediately after the tribulation of those days the sun will be darkened, and the moon will not give its light, and the stars will fall from heaven, and the powers of the heavens will be shaken. *Then* will appear in heaven the sign of the Son of Man, and then all the tribes of the earth will mourn, and they will see the Son of Man coming on the clouds of heaven with power and great glory. And he will send out his angels with a loud trumpet call, and they will gather his elect from the four winds, from one end of heaven to the other [the final resurrection at Christ's second coming]. (Matt. 24:21–31)

The main difference between Daniel's summation and Christ's summation is that Christ adds the description of the cosmic changes that take place in the heavens immediately after the Great Tribulation, which are followed by the final resurrection of the saints. This coincides with the writer to the Hebrews' description of what happens to the Genesis creation when it is completely shattered and utterly destroyed:

> At that time his voice shook the earth, but now he has promised, "Yet once more I will shake not only the earth but also the heavens." This phrase, "Yet once more," indicates the removal of things that are shaken—that is, things that have been made [the Genesis cosmos]—in order that the things that

cannot be shaken may remain. Therefore let us be grateful for receiving a kingdom that cannot be shaken [the eternal New Jerusalem], and thus let us offer to God acceptable worship, with reverence and awe, for our God is a consuming fire [the burning up of this Genesis creation and the subsequent lake of fire]. (Heb. 12:26–29)

At first reading, it appears that Christ is teaching that immediately after the Tribulation, the heavens and earth are destroyed, and he comes again on Judgment Day at the final resurrection, bypassing the restoration altogether. Amillennialists may use this summation to make the case that there is no 1,000-year messianic kingdom and that Christ returns immediately after a Great Tribulation to destroy this Genesis creation and take us to heaven. But from other expanded sections of Daniel's vision, we already know that an inauguration of the messianic kingdom will take place after the Tribulation and before the earth comes to an end, when "the kingdom and the dominion and the greatness of the kingdoms under the whole heaven shall be given to the people of the saints of the Most High."

Earlier in the Discourse, Christ said that after the Great Tribulation, the "gospel of the kingdom" would be realized on this earth before the close of the age. And, of course, Revelation also teaches that the 1,000-year messianic kingdom will follow the Great Tribulation—before we experience the final resurrection on Judgment Day and inherit the eternal new heavens and new earth.

Just as Isaiah's summation starts with the birth of the Messiah and leads immediately to the Messiah's inaugurated reign—omitting the crucifixion and many other major events—so, too, Daniel and Christ are abbreviating the future in their summations by leaving out the messianic kingdom.

There is another way to interpret Daniel's and Christ's summations that would include a subtle reference to the restoration. As the letter to the Hebrews reveals, the cosmic changes in the heavens and on the earth can refer to the complete destruction of the Genesis creation on Judgment Day. There is plenty of scriptural evidence, however, that the partial and temporary changes in the cosmos represent a form of God's judgment on the affairs of man and signal a major transition of events on this earth that lead up to the messianic kingdom—not to the end of the world. And Christ's reference to the cosmic changes in the heavens and on the earth after the Great Tribulation could be a reference to the transition to the messianic kingdom as well as the transition to the eternal heavenly kingdom.

This was demonstrated by the prophecy in Isaiah:

For the windows of heaven are opened, and the foundations of the earth tremble. The earth is utterly broken, the earth is split apart, the earth is violently shaken. . . . On that day the LORD will punish the host of heaven [Satan and his demons], in heaven, and the kings of the earth [the

Antichrist and his deluded followers], on the earth. . . . Then the moon will be confounded and the sun ashamed, for the LORD of hosts reigns on Mount Zion and in Jerusalem, and his glory will be before his elders [Christ's reign]. (Isa. 24:18–23)

According to this sequence, the cosmic changes in the heavens and the earth—physical and spiritual judgments—signal the inauguration of Christ's reign over Israel and Jerusalem, not the end of the world.

The prophet Haggai uses similar language to describe God's judgments on this world as the transition to the inauguration of the Messiah's reign over this earth: "For thus says the LORD of hosts: Yet once more, in a little while, I will shake the heavens and the earth and the sea and the dry land. And I will shake all nations, so that the treasures of all nations shall come in, and I will fill this house with glory, says the LORD of hosts" (Hag. 2:6–7). Unlike Hebrews, Haggai is not describing the end of the world and the subsequent New Jerusalem; instead, he is describing the treasures of the nations being brought into the restored earthly Jerusalem and its temple.

Joel, too, uses analogous language to describe God's judgment on the world at the end of the Tribulation before he ushers in the messianic kingdom:

The earth quakes before them; the heavens tremble. The sun and the moon are darkened, and the stars withdraw their shining. The LORD utters his voice before his army, for his camp is exceedingly great; he who executes his word is powerful. For the day of the LORD is great and very awesome; who can endure it? . . . Then the LORD became jealous for his land and had pity on his people. The LORD answered and said to his people, "Behold, I am sending to you grain, wine, and oil, and you will be satisfied; and I will no more make you a reproach among the nations." (Joel 2:10–19)

Joel references cosmic changes on the earth and in the heavens to demonstrate God's judgment on this earth and the transition to the restoration and regeneration of this earth during the messianic kingdom.

God's cosmic judgments on this creation could reflect real events in the physical world (e.g., earthquakes), but they could also have a metaphorical meaning to describe the changes in the spiritual world or heavens. They could reflect the cosmic regime change of Satan as the ruler of this dominion of darkness characterized by war, injustice, and unrighteousness to Christ becoming the King of kings and Lord of lords of this world when he removes the demonic host of heaven and creates a dominion of light, peace, justice, and righteousness as envisioned by the prophets. Daniel describes this cosmic shift in dominion when the resurrected saints inherit the kingdom:

But the court shall sit in judgment, and his [the Antichrist's] dominion shall be taken away, to be consumed and destroyed to the end. And the kingdom and the dominion and the greatness of the kingdoms under the whole heaven [the cosmic change in dominion] shall be given to the people of the saints of the Most High [during Christ's reign]. (Dan. 7:26–27)

Daniel, Isaiah, Haggai, and Joel all use similar language to describe God's judgments and the cosmic changes in the heavens at the end of the Great Tribulation that reflect the incredible regime change associated with the destruction of the Antichrist, the removal of Satan, and the establishment of Christ as the true King and Lord of this restored Genesis earth. When Christ refers to the cosmic changes in the heavens and the earth that take place immediately after the Great Tribulation, he could be referring to these prophecies. Christ is describing an earth-shattering change of governance from Satan as the god of this world to the Son of God as the true God of this world.

But there could be real impacts on the physical world as well, as indicated in Revelation. Toward the end of the Great Tribulation, leading up to the battle of Armageddon, John vividly describes God's cosmic judgments poured out on the world of the Antichrist and his followers because of their war against his saints:

Then I heard a loud voice from the temple telling the seven angels, "Go and pour out on the earth the seven bowls of the wrath of God [his judgments]." . . . The third angel poured out his bowl into the rivers and the springs of water, and they became blood. . . . The fourth angel poured out his bowl on the sun, and it was allowed to scorch people with fire. They were scorched by the fierce heat, . . . And I saw, coming out of the mouth of the dragon and out of the mouth of the beast . . . And they assembled them at the place that in Hebrew is called Armageddon. The seventh angel poured out his bowl into the air, . . . And there were flashes of lightning, rumblings, peals of thunder, and a great earthquake such as there had never been since man was on the earth, so great was that earthquake. (Rev. 16:1–18)

Further proof that John could be describing real physical changes in the cosmos is found in the crucifixion of Christ. When Christ was dying on the cross, the sun was darkened, and when he died, the earth shook:

Now from the sixth hour there was darkness over all the land until the ninth hour. . . . And Jesus cried out again with a loud voice and yielded up his spirit. And behold, the curtain of the temple was torn in two, from top to bottom. And the earth shook, and the rocks were split. The tombs also were opened. And many bodies of the saints who had fallen asleep were raised, and coming out of the tombs after his resurrection they went into the holy city and appeared to many. (Matt. 27:45–53)

There is an interesting pattern established by this event. God's cosmic judgments against the world for crucifying his Son—the darkened sun and the earthquake—are followed by a resurrection of many of his saints.

This distinctive pattern of Christ's crucifixion followed by God's cosmic judgment followed by Christ's resurrection may be the key to understanding Daniel's and Christ's summations. The messianic kingdom of Christ is bracketed by God's cosmic judgments. Cosmic judgments occur at the beginning of the millennium and at the end of the millennium on the last day of this Genesis creation. Here is a simple diagram of the series of events immediately following the Great Tribulation:

- [cosmic changes] + millennial age of righteousness + [cosmic changes] = eternal age.

And we know from Revelation 20 that there are two resurrections of the saints associated with each form of cosmic judgment—one at the beginning of Christ's millennial reign and another at the end of his millennial reign. The Scriptures teach that each type of cosmic change is associated with a corresponding resurrection, which enables the saints to inherit two forms of God's kingdom, one on the earth and one in heaven.

The cosmic judgments described by the prophets that occur toward the end of the Great Tribulation lead directly to the first resurrection during the Son's messianic kingdom, and the cosmic judgments at the end of the millennium on the last day (when the Genesis creation is completely destroyed by fire) lead directly to the final resurrection of the saints and the Father's eternal heavenly kingdom. Thus, the cosmic changes Christ referred to that take place immediately after the Great Tribulation bracket the beginning of the 1,000-year messianic kingdom with its corresponding resurrection and the end of his millennial kingdom with its corresponding resurrection. These events can be outlined as follows:

- God's cosmic judgments on the world during the Great Tribulation reflected by real physical changes in the heavens and earth, and the cosmic regime change in the spiritual realm + first resurrection = millennial reign of Christ.
- After the millennial reign of Christ, the final resurrection + God's cosmic judgment on the Genesis creation when it is burned up and destroyed = eternal new heavens and new earth.

The events surrounding Christ's crucifixion set the pattern. After God's cosmic judgments (physical and spiritual), there is a major eschatological transition that includes a corresponding resurrection. With this interpretation in mind, let's reread Christ's summation along with these amplifications:

Immediately after the tribulation of those days the sun will be darkened, and the moon will not give its light, and the stars will fall from heaven, and the powers of the heavens will be shaken [representing real physical events in the heavens and on the earth and a cosmic shift in power and rule in the spiritual realm from Satan and the Antichrist to the Messiah's reign when the saints experience the "first resurrection"]. *Then* [during Christ's kingdom] will appear in heaven the sign of the Son of Man, and then all the tribes of the earth will mourn, and they will see the Son of Man coming on the clouds of heaven with power and great glory [the second coming on Judgment Day when the Genesis cosmos is destroyed]. And he will send out his angels with a loud trumpet call, and they will gather his elect from the four winds, from one end of heaven to the other [the final resurrection and entrance into the Father's eternal kingdom]. (Matt. 24:29–31)

What happens immediately after the Tribulation is the cosmic change in rule over this world, or the restoration, when the gospel of the kingdom of the Messiah is realized on the earth. And then, during the time of this restoration, the Son of Man comes again. After the Tribulation and after the reign of Christ over this earthly dominion is complete, the Son of Man comes again to destroy this Genesis cosmos, judge the world when the books are opened, gather his elect at the rapture, and take them to his Father's eternal kingdom of heaven.

In the final analysis, because this section of the Olivet Discourse is a summation and is by definition incomplete, it is difficult to determine which of the two resurrections Christ is referring to when he tells of the changes in the cosmos. From Daniel, Isaiah, Ezekiel, Micah, Haggai, Joel, and the prophets, one can easily make the case that he is referring to the physical and spiritual changes in the cosmos at the end of the Great Tribulation, which lead to a real resurrection when the saints inherit the messianic kingdom. And from the New Testament writers and prophets, one can make the case that Christ is referring to the final Judgment Day when the Genesis cosmos is destroyed and we experience the final resurrection of the immortal body that is then taken to the Father's eternal kingdom. Or, if we view the cosmic changes caused by God's judgments as a form of bracketing of the beginning of his earthly kingdom and the end of it, then Christ could be referring to both resurrections.

Daniel's axiom establishes that the Most High's everlasting kingdom begins immediately after the Great Tribulation. Without access to Revelation, what Daniel probably did not fully understand is that during this everlasting kingdom of God, there would be two resurrections of the saints with each preceded by cosmic signs in the heavens—one at the beginning of his kingdom and another at the end, in order to inherit the Father's eternal kingdom. An amplification of his summation follows:

At that time shall arise Michael, the great prince who has charge of your people [Satan is released to incarnate the Antichrist and deceive unbelievers]. And there shall be a time of trouble [the Great Tribulation], such as never has been since there was a nation till that time. But at that time [during the "everlasting kingdom"] your people [the saints] shall be delivered [at the beginning of the Messiah's reign, believers will be delivered from the grave and from this deadly persecution through the "first resurrection"], everyone whose name shall be found written in the book [only believers are delivered]. And many of those who sleep in the dust of the earth shall awake [the final resurrection on Judgment Day at the end of "that time" of the messianic kingdom], some to everlasting life [those in the book of life will then inherit the new heavens and new earth], and some to shame and everlasting contempt [those not found in the book of life will inherit the lake of fire]. And those who are wise shall shine like the brightness of the sky above; and those who turn many to righteousness, like the stars forever and ever [the rewards given to the saints on the last day at the Great White Throne judgment]. (Dan. 12:1–3)

By using biblical data or intelligence from other Scriptures, we can see that after the Great Tribulation, the phrase "at that time" would encompass both forms of the cosmic judgments of God *and* both forms of resurrections that occur during God's everlasting kingdom. Granted, this interpretation requires reading a great deal into this summation, but this process of bracketing information is no different than reading into Isaiah's summation about the birth and reign of the Messiah the information about his crucifixion and atonement for our sins, as Christ makes clear to the two men on the road to Emmaus: "And he said to them, 'O foolish ones, and slow of heart to believe *all* that the prophets have spoken! Was it not necessary that the Christ should suffer these things and enter into his glory?' And beginning with Moses and all the Prophets, he interpreted to them in *all* the Scriptures the things concerning himself" (Luke 24:25–27). When it comes to the existence of Christ's 1,000-year messianic kingdom before the eternal kingdom of heaven, those theologians who deny a literal millennial kingdom would be wise to follow Christ's advice and methodology and take into consideration *all* the Scriptures that pertain to God's messianic kingdom on this earth before he comes again to take us to the eternal new heavens and new earth.

This Generation

After Jesus describes all the events that must occur on this Genesis earth according to the prophets before he comes again at the close of this Adamic age, he makes the following statement:

From the fig tree learn its lesson: as soon as its branch becomes tender and puts out its leaves, you know that summer is near. So also, when you see all these things, you know that he is near, at the very gates. Truly, I say to you, *this generation will not pass away until all these things take place.* Heaven and earth will pass away, but my words will not pass away. But concerning that day and hour no one knows, not even the angels of heaven, nor the Son, but the Father only. (Matt. 24:32–36)

Students of eschatology have hotly debated the meaning of the phrase "this generation will not pass away" until *all* these prophecies are fulfilled and Christ comes again on Judgment Day to take us to heaven. What does "this generation" mean? Does it refer to the generation of Jewish people to whom Christ was speaking? Christ is clearly addressing Jews in the discourse as indicated by his lament and pronouncement of judgment on the Jews and their temple: "Truly, I say to you, all these things will come upon this generation. Oh Jerusalem, Jerusalem, the city that kills the prophets . . . See, your house [the temple] is left to you desolate" (Matt. 23:36–38). The temple was indeed destroyed about forty years later, which would have been in the lifetime of the generation of unfaithful Jews who heard Christ's lament and judgment. But as has been shown, Daniel's vision and the Olivet Discourse cover a much broader range of events than the destruction of the Second Temple. Daniel's vision of the seventy weeks includes the first desolation, the second desolation, and the ultimate restoration of Jerusalem and the Ezekiel temple in the messianic age of righteousness, or the fulfillment of the "gospel of the kingdom" on this earth.

Scholars known as *full* preterists, who do not believe in a future Great Tribulation or a future millennium, believe that "*all these things*" Christ predicted in the Olivet Discourse (and in Daniel) occurred in the lifetime of the generation of Jews who heard Christ; otherwise, Christ would have been a false prophet. But the destruction of the temple in AD 70 certainly did not usher in an age of "everlasting righteousness" on this earth. The Romans' greed and lust for the worldly resources and goods of other nations under their militant subjugation continued unabated for hundreds of years. And the world continues to experience wars, famines, earthquakes, and all the other ill effects of a cursed creation under the influence of Satan. Most important, the second coming of Christ on Judgment Day at the close of the age has not occurred.

Partial preterists believe that most of these prophecies were fulfilled by AD 70 during "this generation" of first century Jews who heard Christ's words, but not all, so that the second coming and a few other events are still in the future. Obviously, Christ's reference to all prophecy pertaining to this Genesis age being fulfilled in "this generation" must have a wider range of meaning than merely the lifetime of Jews of his day.

When analyzing the Olivet Discourse, Christ expects us to synthesize his teachings with those of the Old Testament prophets. For instance, Christ references Daniel, who, in turn, references Jeremiah. Therefore, when performing a referential analysis of the meaning of "this generation," one should not omit Jeremiah's citation. In fact, Christ is probably referring to Jeremiah's understanding of the Jews when he used the phrase "this generation." Jeremiah describes two generations of Israel, or the Jews. One generation is hardhearted and unfaithful to their covenant with God; they even refuse to listen to the prophets sent by God. Their transgressions lead to the destruction of Jerusalem and its temple and to their exile. In Jesus' day a similar generation of unbelieving Jews refused to listen to the Messiah himself and they, too, would see Jerusalem and its temple destroyed.

But Jeremiah describes another generation of Israel whose "offspring" will one day be given a new heart under a new covenant and, as faithful believers, will prosper in a restored Jerusalem in the messianic kingdom. In the following passage, Jeremiah describes these two different kinds of generations of Jews:

> And it shall come to pass that as I have watched over them to pluck up and break down, to overthrow, destroy, and bring harm [unfaithful generation sent into exile], . . . "Behold, the days are coming, declares the LORD, when I will make a new covenant with the house of Israel and the house of Judah, not like the covenant that I made with their fathers on the day when I took them by the hand to bring them out of the land of Egypt, my covenant that they broke, though I was their husband, declares the LORD. But this is the covenant that I will make with the house of Israel after those days, declares the LORD: I will put my law within them, and I will write it on their hearts. And I will be their God, and they shall be my people. . . . For I will forgive their iniquity, and I will remember their sin no more." Thus says the LORD, who gives the sun for light by day and the fixed order of the moon and the stars for light by night, who stirs up the sea so that its waves roar—the LORD of hosts is his name: "If this fixed order departs from before me, declares the LORD, then shall the *offspring of Israel* cease from being a nation before me forever." Thus says the LORD: "If the heavens above can be measured, and the foundations of the earth below can be explored, then I will cast off all the offspring of Israel for all that they have done, declares the LORD. Behold, the days are coming, declares the LORD, when the city shall be rebuilt for the LORD [Jerusalem restored]." (Jer. 31:28–38)

Despite God having brought them out of bondage in Egypt into the Promised Land, the Jews proved to be unfaithful under the old covenant, and God sent them into exile for their transgressions. But someday "the offspring of Israel," or another generation of Jews, will experience a new covenant of forgiveness and righteousness springing from a new heart, which leads to the nation's restoration in the messianic kingdom—and

Jerusalem and its temple will be rebuilt for the LORD. These prophecies concerning this future generation of the righteous "offspring of Israel" are as certain to occur as the fixed operation of the sun, moon, and stars of the heavens and even the foundations of the earth.

To demonstrate that Christ is most likely quoting from Jeremiah, notice the striking parallels to Jeremiah's references to the fixed operations of the heavens and the earth when Christ refers to "this generation":

> So also, when you see all these things [all visions and prophetic events described by Daniel, Jeremiah, and the prophets], you know that he is near, at the very gates. Truly, I say to you, this generation will not pass away until all these things take place. Heaven and earth will pass away, but my words will not pass away." (Matt. 24:33–35)

All the prophecies related to unfaithful *and* faithful generations of Israel are as certain to be fulfilled as the continued existence and operation of the heavens and earth! Based on Jeremiah, Christ is saying that there are two generations of Israel related to Jerusalem, its temple, and the future. The generation of his day, like the one in Jeremiah's day, kills the prophets sent to them and remains unfaithful; it will see the destruction of their temple in their lifetime as Daniel foretold. Another generation, their offspring, will experience the "new covenant" and as faithful believers will experience the restoration of Israel, Jerusalem, and its temple in the messianic kingdom as Daniel also foretold. Christ is quoting from Daniel *and* Jeremiah relative to the temple's destruction (during an unfaithful generation) and the ultimate restoration of Israel and its temple (during a faithful generation), when the "most holy place" is anointed in the messianic kingdom and the "gospel of the kingdom," according to Isaiah, is realized on this Genesis earth before the "close of the age."

There was a remnant of faithful Jews in Jesus' day, but as a whole that generation of Jews was hardhearted, blind, and unregenerate despite Christ having shown them many great signs, wonders, and displays of love, compassion, and forgiveness. As a result, that generation of unfaithful Israel would experience the desecration of the temple in their lifetime as foretold by Daniel—"And the people of the prince who is to come shall destroy the city and the sanctuary. Its end shall come with a flood." This would be for the transgression of having rejected their Messiah. In the meantime, the baton has passed to believing Gentiles who are experiencing the new covenant. But someday, as Jeremiah foresees, a generation of Jews will repent and believe in their Messiah, which leads to the messianic kingdom.

The prophet Zechariah also rails against the unfaithful generation of Jews in his day and pronounces God's judgment against them: "Behold, I am about to make Jerusalem a cup of staggering to all the surrounding peoples.

. . . For I will gather all the nations against Jerusalem to battle, and the city shall be taken and the houses plundered and the women raped" (Zech. 12:2; 14:2). But he also foresees the day when a generation of Jews will repent and believe in their crucified Messiah, which leads to the day when the LORD will be the King of the world and the city of Jerusalem, restored:

> And I will pour out on the house of David and the inhabitants of Jerusalem a spirit of grace and pleas for mercy, so that, when they look on me, on him whom they have pierced, they shall mourn for him, as one mourns for an only child, and weep bitterly over him, as one weeps over a firstborn. . . . On that day there shall be a fountain opened for the house of David and the inhabitants of Jerusalem, to cleanse them from sin and uncleanness. . . . On that day living waters shall flow out from Jerusalem, half of them to the eastern sea and half of them to the western sea. It shall continue in summer as in winter. And the LORD will be king over all the earth. On that day the LORD will be one and his name one. . . . Then everyone who survives of all the nations that have come against Jerusalem shall go up year after year to worship the King, the LORD of hosts, and to keep the Feast of Booths. (Zech. 12:10; 13:1; 14:8–9, 16)

Isaiah also refers to a generation of the offspring of Israel that will be given new hearts, which leads to the restoration:

> "And a Redeemer will come to Zion, to those in Jacob who turn from transgression," declares the LORD. "And as for me, this is my covenant with them," says the LORD: "My Spirit that is upon you, and my words that I have put in your mouth, shall not depart out of your mouth, or out of the mouth of your offspring, or out of the mouth of your children's offspring," says the LORD, "from this time forth and forevermore." (Isa. 59:20–21)

Isaiah foresees a faithful generation of Jews who will repent and "turn from transgression" to become believers filled with the Holy Spirit, which leads to the redemption of Zion, or Israel, in the messianic kingdom.

Paul also writes that the Jews in his day were an unbelieving generation. But based on Isaiah, Paul also foresees the day when the "offspring of Israel" will experience the new covenant and will be given new hearts and minds:

> For if you [Gentiles] were cut from what is by nature a wild olive tree, and grafted, contrary to nature, into a cultivated olive tree, how much more will these, the natural branches [Jews], be grafted back into their own olive tree. Lest you be wise in your own conceits, I want you to understand this mystery, brothers: a partial hardening has come upon Israel, until the fullness of the Gentiles has come in. And in this way all Israel will be saved, as it is written, "The Deliverer will come from Zion, he will banish ungodliness from Jacob; and this will be my covenant with them when I take away their sins." (Rom. 11:24–27)

Just as believing Gentiles have experienced the new covenant and the filling of the Holy Spirit, so, too, the descendants of Israel will one day believe; Israel will finally "turn from transgression," which will lead to the Messiah's long-promised redemption of Israel.

Interestingly, this "offspring of Israel" that will be grafted back into the new covenant coincides with the final abomination of desolation caused by the desolator in the seventieth week of Daniel's vision. This believing generation of Jews will therefore see the Antichrist desecrate their temple. Some may flee and successfully hide from the Antichrist, while others may be martyred during this period of severe persecution. A short three-and-one-half years later, however, they will enter into the messianic age of righteousness. And, according to Isaiah and Ezekiel, they will enter into the age of restoration and righteousness through a resurrection of their natural bodies, or through the first resurrection, as John later reveals. Or, these believing Jews may be supernaturally protected from the Antichrist during the 1,260 days of his reign of terror (cf. Rev. 12) and enter the millennial age of restoration unharmed.

Therefore, Christ's reference to all prophecies being fulfilled during "this generation" covers the whole spectrum of the prophetic future—not just the temple's destruction in AD 70. The generation of unfaithful Jews in Jesus' day experienced the desolation of their temple in their lifetime (AD 70), and the repentant generation of their offspring—of faithful Israel with a new heart—will experience another desolation of the temple during the Great Tribulation. But this completes the seventy weeks and leads directly to the Messiah's kingdom of everlasting righteousness, when "the kingdom and the dominion and the greatness of the kingdoms under the whole heaven [Israel and all nations] shall be given to the people of the saints [Jew and Gentile] of the Most High."

In a world ruled by the Messiah, Israel will never again have to worry about hostile, warring nations desecrating Jerusalem and its temple. Even when Satan is released at the end of the millennium and inspires Gog and Magog to come against Jerusalem, Jerusalem and its temple will not be harmed because the armies of Gog and Magog will be destroyed by fire from heaven before they enter Jerusalem, and Satan will be forever banished to the lake of fire (Rev. 20:10).

According to Jesus, the fulfillment of these prophecies relative to Israel and their offspring is as certain as the fixed operation of the heavens and earth. After the fulfillment of all these things pertaining to Israel and this age, the close of the age is at hand and the second coming "is near, at the very gates"—when this Genesis creation of heaven and earth will actually disappear (the Omega) and be replaced with the Father's eternal kingdom.

Summary

During his first coming, Christ—the supernatural stone—did not smash the fourth-kingdom Roman Empire, or the "legs of iron." Instead, he was crushed by the legs of iron, crucified, and cut off without having establishing his worldwide empire. He subsequently ascended to the Ancient of Days where he became Lord-elect of this world, waiting on the Father to determine when Satan's term of office will end and his inauguration as true Lord of this creation begins. He even allowed the temple to be desecrated and destroyed by the unbelieving Jews and the pagan Roman armies. The world continues to experience a cursed creation ("famines and earthquakes") and the consequences of rebellious mankind (under the influence of Satan) mismanaging this world ("wars and rumors of wars").

In the meantime, because he has made atonement for the sins of mankind under a new covenant, he is gathering repentant sinners that the Father has chosen from all nations or ethnic groups into his righteous kingdom. At the moment of conversion and the regeneration of our spirits, we are redeemed from Satan's dominion of darkness and become eternal members of God's kingdom, and Christ becomes the Lord of our lives. The members of his kingdom enjoy the spiritual benefits of being fully reconciled with Christ and his Father and being filled with the Holy Spirit, but the saints remain in a hostile, satanic world and continue to experience the regular depravations of this degenerate creation and, for some Christians, even persecutions from Satan and his followers. And our regenerated spirits remain embodied within a degenerate human body in the process of rapidly aging and dying. It is definitely not paradise on earth. We have experienced an exodus from Satan's dominion, but we have yet to experience an exodus from this fallen world and entrance into the regenerated earth.

Currently, Gentile believers make up a disproportionate number of the members of Christ's kingdom. But as Jeremiah, Isaiah, and Paul make clear, a future generation of Jews will be grafted back in as believers in the new covenant and join the Messiah's kingdom. This, in turn, soon leads to the season when the Ancient of Days takes action against Satan and his kingdoms of this world on behalf of his Son, and the time arrives for his Son to sit on his throne in heaven and exercise his dominion over the regenerated Genesis earth with his regenerated saints.

We know that one day Christ will return and give us immortal bodies and take us to his Father's eternal kingdom of heaven, but this does not mean he has abandoned the promise that his people will experience an age of righteousness on a regenerated earth as the prophets proclaimed. The meek will inherit the restored earth through the first resurrection of natural bodies before they inherit heaven through the final resurrection of immortal bodies. The gospel of the kingdom has always included the messianic kingdom when Christ, as the true God and Creator of this world, sits on his throne in heaven and establishes an earthly kingdom characterized by peace, justice, righteousness, and abundant prosperity. As Jesus says, this messianic kingdom must be realized "throughout the whole world as a testimony to all nations, and then the end will come" when "the Son of Man comes in his glory" and "will sit on his glorious throne" to judge the world on the last day of this creation, taking the transformed saints to his Father's eternal kingdom of heaven and sending unbelievers to eternal judgment.

To make sense of the Olivet Discourse, we have to do the hard work of intelligence analysts and gather and synthesize data from a variety of prophetic sources. From Daniel we discover Daniel's axiom. From Jeremiah we discover the meaning of "this generation." From Ezekiel and Isaiah we learn about the resurrection and restoration of Israel and its temple in a worldwide messianic kingdom of peace and righteousness. From Revelation, we discover that the Messiah's inaugurated reign over this earth will last a thousand years before his kingdom transitions to the eternal new heavens and new earth. From the Olivet Discourse, parts one and two, in combination with Daniel, Jeremiah, and the prophets, we can make a strong case for a Great Tribulation followed by the messianic kingdom before we inherit the Father's kingdom. And Christ expects us to synthesize these Scriptures.

The following outline, based on Daniel's vision of the seventy weeks as expounded upon by Jesus, summarizes the flow of major biblical events:

1. As foretold by Jeremiah, after the Babylonian and Persian exile, Jerusalem and the temple was rebuilt and restored by Nehemiah and Ezra: "to restore and build Jerusalem" (Dan. 9:25).

2. But there was significant opposition to this restoration: "it shall be built again with squares and moat, but in a troubled time" (9:25).

3. In AD 27, 408 years later, the "anointed one" enters this world (9:26).

4. But he was rejected as Messiah by the unbelieving Jews and crucified by the pagan Romans: "shall be cut off and shall have nothing" (9:26). Yet, in the process, he makes atonement for our sins (Isa. 53).

5. As a result of this terrible transgression by the Jews, the Roman armies destroyed the city of Jerusalem and its temple in AD 70: "And the people of the prince who is to come [again] shall destroy the city and the sanctuary" (Dan. 9:26).

6. The destruction by the armies pouring into the city is thorough and brutal: "Its end shall come with a flood" (9:26). The temple building itself is utterly destroyed without a single stacked stone remaining.

7. Jerusalem and its temple mount will continue to be trampled on by the Gentiles. Wars, famines, and earthquakes will continue to occur for an unknown period of time: "and to the end there shall be war. Desolations are decreed" (9:26).

8. When the Father determines it is the season for the Great Tribulation, the seven-year Tribulation begins when the Antichrist establishes a peace treaty between Israel and the warring nations that threaten it: "And he shall make a strong covenant with many for one week" (9:27). Through the signs and wonders performed by the Antichrist and his false prophets, a great delusion falls upon unbelievers who believe the Messiah has come to the earth.

9. The treaty is broken by the Antichrist after three-and-one-half years. The Great Tribulation begins when the Antichrist enters another rebuilt temple and makes himself out to be God: "and for half of the week he shall put an end to sacrifice and offering" (9:27).

10. Through the Antichrist and false prophets, Satan creates an unprecedented worldwide reign of false worship and terror against the saints, who refuse to worship the false Christ, for three-and-one-half years: "And on the wing of abominations shall come one who makes desolate" (9:27). "He shall speak words against the Most High, and shall wear out the saints of the Most High, and shall think to change the times and the law; and they shall be given into his hand for a time, times, and half a time" (7:25). "For then there will be great tribulation, such as has not been from the beginning of the world until now, no, and never will be" (Matt. 24:21).

11. The Tribulation ends when the Antichrist and his false prophets are thrown into the lake of fire: "until the decreed end is poured out on the desolator" (Dan. 9:27). Satan and his demonic hosts are removed from this world for a season (Dan. 7:12 and Rev. 20:1-3).

12. This completes the seventy weeks and the time has come for the age of "everlasting righteousness." The Anointed One is inaugurated into office by the Father and his reign from heaven begins: "until the Ancient of Days came, and judgment was given for the saints of the Most High, and the time came when the saints possessed the kingdom" (Dan. 7:22). Based on Ezekiel 37 and Revelation 20, the departed saints inherit the Son of Man's 1,000-year age of righteousness through the "first resurrection" of the natural body.

13. Now that the Jews are grafted back in as believers and are given new hearts and a new covenant, Israel, Jerusalem, and its temple are restored during the Messiah's reign: "Seventy weeks are decreed about your people and your holy city, . . . to bring in everlasting righteousness, . . . and to anoint a most holy place" (9:24). Or, as Christ says, "this gospel of the kingdom will be proclaimed throughout the whole world as a testimony to all nations, and *then the end will come*" (Matt. 24:14 based on Isa. 52:7–10).

14. According to Daniel, Ezekiel, Isaiah, and John, Satan makes one more attempt to inspire unbelievers and warring nations to attack and destroy Jerusalem and its temple. But his armies of Gog and Magog are destroyed by fire before they reach Jerusalem, and he is subsequently sent to the lake of fire forever: "As for the rest of the beasts [Satan and his demons], their dominion was taken away [removed for a thousand years], but their lives were prolonged for a season and a time [for a thousand years]" (Dan. 7:12). As John further tells us: "And when the thousand years are ended, Satan will be released from his prison and will come out to deceive the nations that are at the four corners of the earth, Gog and Magog, . . . And they marched up over the broad plain of the earth and surrounded the camp of the saints and the beloved city [Jerusalem], but fire came down from heaven and consumed them, and the devil who had deceived them was thrown into the lake of fire and sulfur where the beast and the false prophet were" (Rev. 20:7–10; cf. Ezek. 38—39). This fulfills both "vision and prophet" pertaining to Israel, Jerusalem, and its temple, and the nations of the world.

15. After all of the prophetic words of Christ and the Scriptures pertaining to this Genesis creation have been fulfilled, it is time for "heaven and earth" to pass away at the close of the Genesis age. It is time for the second coming of Christ on Judgment Day: "And many of those who sleep in the dust of the earth shall awake, some to everlasting life, and some to shame and everlasting contempt" (Dan. 12:2). Or, as Jesus says, "When the Son of Man comes in his glory, . . . he will sit on his glorious throne [Great White Throne]. Before him will be gathered all the nations [the final resurrection], . . . Then the King will say to those on his right, 'Come, you who are blessed by my Father, inherit the kingdom [heavenly kingdom] prepared for you from the foundation of the world.' . . . Then he will say to those on his left, 'Depart from me, you cursed, into the eternal fire prepared for the devil and his angels.' . . . And these will go away into eternal punishment [lake of fire], but the righteous into eternal life [new heavens and new earth]" (Matt. 25:31–46).

Admittedly, because the disciples asked Christ a twofold question pertaining to the signs leading to the destruction of the first-century temple as well as the signs leading to Christ's second coming at the close of the age, the Olivet Discourse as an exposition of Daniel and the prophets is difficult to navigate. In addition, Luke's nuanced emphasis on the first desolation and destruction of the temple described by Daniel, and Matthew's and Mark's emphasis on the second desolation described by Daniel compound the complexity of the Olivet Discourse.

We can still build a strong grammatical-historical case for the existence of a future Great Tribulation and a subsequent messianic kingdom on this Genesis earth from Daniel and the Old Testament prophets. Using postrestorationalism as the framework for interpreting the Scriptures is the key to unraveling the complexity of Daniel, the Olivet Discourse, and Revelation. And once we harmonize the Olivet Discourse and Revelation with Daniel's vision of the future, along with Jeremiah, Isaiah, Ezekiel, and the prophets, a logical flow of prophetic events can be determined.

It would be very difficult to create a logical sequence of the future based solely on this outdoor sermon. However, there is plenty of other biblical data that can be synchronized with this sermon to make sense out of all of the events Christ references that must occur before he comes again at "the close of the age" to usher in the eternal "age to come." The book of Revelation, serving as Christ's Olivet Discourse Part Two, fills in many of the blanks.

The shear breadth of Daniel's vision as expounded upon by Christ is remarkable as it flows from the time of Babylonian captivity all the way to the end of the world and the final resurrection on Judgment Day at the "close of the age," when wise and righteous men and women of faith like Daniel will be rewarded with eternal life and escape the final wrath of God: "And many of those who sleep in the dust of the earth shall awake, some to everlasting life, and some to shame and everlasting contempt. And those who are wise shall shine like the brightness of the sky above; and those who turn many to righteousness, like the stars forever and ever" (Dan. 12:2–3).

5

Satan's Kingdom

Currently, Satan continues to be operational in this world, instigating all sorts of evil schemes to destroy mankind and keep fallen men alienated from their Creator. Because of their sinful nature, unbelievers are naturally responsive to Satan. As John says, "We know that we are children of God, and the whole world is under the control of the evil one" (1 John 5:19 NIV). This control over fallen mankind, however, is limited by God through the restraining work of Michael. Satan is even pictured as having to approach the throne of God as he interacts with God and man.

Satan can be compared to a vicious, rabid dog. This dog, however, is on a leash; God restrains just how much evil Satan can accomplish. But one day, Michael will be removed, and this rabid dog will be unleashed. Then we will find out what this world is like under the unrestrained rule of Satan in cooperation with unregenerate, rebellious, fallen humanity. Things will get much worse in the future Great Tribulation before Satan is fully bound and the restoration begins.

But why would God allow an unrestrained Satan to have so much influence and power over the world? Perhaps God wants heaven and earth to witness what would have happened to humanity under Satan's rule and influence if God had not intervened with a plan of redemption. What would the world be like if fallen Satan and fallen man, his spiritual children, were given free rein to act out a godless existence? In the Great Tribulation, we will find out.

The Antichrist and the Rebuilt Temple

For the Tribulation to begin, a Jewish temple must be in place for the Antichrist to enter and make himself out to be God (Matt. 24:15–16 and 2 Thess. 2:3–4). An Islamic mosque, the Dome of the Rock, however, currently occupies the temple mount. It was built in 691 when Muslims controlled Jerusalem. Israel must also exist as a nation, which occurred in 1948. The Jews had been without a nation since 135 when they were driven from their homeland in the Second Jewish-Roman War (132–135).

As long as the rebuilt temple is not in place for the Antichrist to enter, we know that the Tribulation is not at hand. Someday, however, according to Daniel's prophecy, there must be another temple for the abomination of desolation to enter, which means the current mosque will be destroyed, either by natural causes, such as an earthquake, or by manmade causes, and replaced with another temple. It could be blown up by Zionist radicals or perhaps even demolished by the government of Israel in retaliation for a terrorist act by Islamic radicals. Or, Islamic terrorists could destroy it to instigate a war. It may even be inadvertently destroyed by stray rockets launched by terrorists, such as Hezbollah or Iran.

Regardless of how it is destroyed, a Jewish organization in Israel presently has blueprints and is ready to begin construction of a new temple once the Dome of the Rock no longer occupies the ancient temple mount. The future destruction of the mosque and Israel's determination to build a temple in its place will undoubtedly cause another major conflict in the region. This war over the temple construction could be the event that leads up to the beginning of the seven-year period of the Tribulation, which begins with a war followed by a period of peace that will be established when the Antichrist makes a covenant of peace between Israel and her many enemies. The Antichrist will have to be a gifted and effective leader if he is to bring Israel and her many surrounding enemies to peace, particularly if this is a war over the rebuilding of the temple in place of the Dome of the Rock.

Once the construction of a new temple has begun, it will require extraordinary diplomatic skills to persuade Israel's enemies to agree to a covenant of peace with the temple still standing. The Antichrist will have to convince the many Palestinians and Islamic nations to not only abandon their hopes of seeing a rebuilt mosque, but also that it would be to their advantage to establish peace with Israel. And he will have to convince Israel that he can be trusted to broker and maintain this peace agreement.

How the Antichrist will accomplish this stunning act of diplomacy, we do not know. But one thing is certain—he will be universally admired for the accomplishment. Perhaps he allows this success and admiration to go to his head and begins to delude himself into believing that he is the savior of the world. Then, with God allowing Satan to begin using his powers to create a powerful delusion among unbelievers, the world rapidly will begin to believe this lie as well.

These events should be easily recognizable to an observant Christian. According to Daniel, once the peace treaty is established, the Tribulation officially begins and the church will have three-and-one-half years to prepare for the second half of the Tribulation when Satan is no longer restrained, the Antichrist becomes deluded and enters the temple claiming to be God, and the persecution phase begins.

In Revelation, John describes his vision:

> And the beast [the human Antichrist] that I saw was like a leopard; its feet were like a bear's, and its mouth was like a lion's mouth. And to it the dragon [Satan] gave his power and his throne and great authority. One of its heads seemed to have a mortal wound, but its mortal wound was healed, and the whole earth marveled as they followed the beast. And they worshiped the dragon, for he had given his authority to the beast, and they worshiped the beast, saying, "Who is like the beast, and who can fight against it?" (Rev. 13:2–4)

Here is a beast who imitates Christ—he receives a mortal wound but is somehow resurrected. People will worship the dragon, Satan, who had given his authority to the beast, the human Antichrist. We worship God the Father who gave the Son authority. In effect, Satan acts like God the Father, and the beast acts like God the Son. The human Antichrist presents himself to the world as the true Messiah and enters the temple to be worshiped as God.

There has been much discussion among scholars concerning the beast that is mortally wounded, healed, and comes back to life. Apparently, this resurrection resembles the one Lazarus experienced, except the one that returns to life is an unbeliever. It is unclear as to whether it is Satan or God who brings the beast back to life. Regardless, like all unbelievers, while he is living, the beast has no real understanding of hell. Upon death, however, this person will understand hell, for he will get a taste of the wrath of God: "And just as it is appointed for man to die once, and after that comes judgment" (Heb. 9:27).

When he is mortally wounded, he will find himself in Hades where he will be immediately judged—confronted with the finality of his ultimate destiny of hell. When his human spirit comes back to life from Hades after getting a taste of hell and re-inhabits his former mortal body, he will know with absolute certainty that he is like a demon—with no hope of redemption, destined for hell and the lake of fire in only three-and-one-half years. He will realize that he has a very limited amount of time to experience any carnal pleasures on this earth before being sent to the lake of fire, and he will direct his rage against God and his saints.

He might even be possessed by Satan. This will not be some ordinary demonic possession by one or more demons. Rather, it will be unrestrained Satan himself. The human Antichrist will be an incredibly powerful and evil human being. He will have legions of other demons at his disposal. When Satan is thrown down to earth from heaven, John warns, "Woe to you, O earth and sea, for the devil has come down to you in great wrath, because he knows that his time is short!" (Rev. 12:12).

Satan and the human Antichrist will know that their time on this earth is limited, and both will be full of demonic wrath that will be directed against Christians. Their rule over this world will be one of madness, vengeance, and rage. According to Jesus, this outpouring of demonic wrath on the earth is unprecedented in the history of the world: "For then there will be great tribulation, such as has not been from the beginning of the world until now, no, and never will be" (Matt. 24:21).

Is the Antichrist a Jew or a Gentile?

Among theologians who believe in a future Great Tribulation, there is considerable disagreement as to whether the Antichrist or the desolator will be a Jew or a Gentile. The answer, surprisingly, depends on how various scholars translate a key Hebrew text found in Daniel 11:36 that can be translated "gods of his fathers" (ESV) or "God of his fathers" (NKJV). The Hebrew word for God is *elohim,* which is a plural form of God, probably out of respect. If the correct translation is "gods of his fathers" then it would probably indicate that the Antichrist will be pagan and will not respect his own pagan religious heritage. But if it is translated "God of his father," it is probably referring to the God of Abraham, Isaac, and Jacob—a common phrase used in the Old Testament to describe Jews. In this case, the reference would be to a Jew who does not respect his fathers' Jewish religious heritage and will create a form of deity around himself as he becomes the deluded Antichrist. Here is the key text that is at the center of this controversy:

> And the king shall do as he wills. He shall exalt himself and magnify himself above every god, and shall speak astonishing things against the God of gods. He shall prosper till the indignation is accomplished; for what is decreed shall be done. He shall pay no attention to the *gods of his fathers,* or to the one beloved by women. He shall not pay attention to any other god, for he shall magnify himself above all. (Dan. 11:36–37 ESV)

The translation of "god(s) of his fathers" depends on how the translators interpret the verse. If they assume that the king being described is not a Hebrew, then they translate the word *elohim* as "gods" to refer to polytheistic religions. If they assume that Daniel is referring to a Jew, they translate it as "God." Thus, one can legitimately translate this phrase either way, depending on one's prior assumptions about the ethnic nature of the Antichrist. I lean toward "God of his fathers," such that the Antichrist will be a deceived Jewish leader. When Christ warns us to be on the lookout for false messiahs, he would surely be referring to false Jewish messiahs because there were really no equivalent Gentile "messiahs" in the pagan world at the that time. It would not have made any sense to the disciples for Christ to warn them to be on guard against some pagan Roman impostor.

In Christ's interpretation of the "abomination of desolation spoken of by the prophet Daniel," he says: "Then if anyone says to you, 'Look, here is the Christ!' or 'There he is!' do not believe it. For false christs and false prophets will arise and perform great signs and wonders, so as to lead astray, if possible, even the elect" (Matt. 24:23–24). Christ is clearly speaking to his Jewish audience, and it would have been very strange indeed if he was warning his disciples to be on the lookout for some unknown pagan Gentile "christ." That is not to say that the Jewish Antichrist will not create a blend of Jewish beliefs with neo-pagan beliefs centered on his own deity and demands to be worshiped.

Daniel also says that the Antichrist will be an aggressive militaristic leader with the help of a foreign god, which is probably a reference to Satan:

> He shall honor the god of fortresses instead of these. A god whom his fathers did not know he shall honor with gold and silver, with precious stones and costly gifts. He shall deal with the strongest fortresses with the help of a foreign god [probably Satan]. Those who acknowledge him he shall load with honor. He shall make them rulers over many and shall divide the land for a price. (Dan. 11:38–39)

Apparently, a future militarist Jewish leader will emerge in modern day Israel and with the help of Satan embark on a military campaign to conquer many of the nations around Israel. He will meet significant resistance from several countries (Dan. 11:40–45), but, with Satan's help, he will be able consolidate power and reward those loyal to him.

The False Elijah

In a showdown with the prophets of Baal, Elijah called fire down from heaven (1 Kings 18:37–39). Later in Israel's history, Elijah is prophesied to come before the coming of the Lord (Mal. 4:5–6). Jesus taught that, in effect, Elijah has already come in the form of John the Baptist (Matt. 11:14; 17:12). During the Tribulation there will be a false Elijah on the earth who will use miraculous signs involving fire to convince people that the Antichrist is the Messiah:

> Then I saw another beast rising out of the earth [the false Elijah]. It had two horns like a lamb and it spoke like a dragon. It exercises all the authority of the first beast in its presence, and makes the earth and its inhabitants worship the first beast, whose mortal wound was healed. It performs great signs, even making fire come down from heaven to earth in front of people, and by the signs that it is allowed to work in the presence of the beast it deceives those who dwell on earth. (Rev. 13:11–14)

By impersonating a great prophet like Elijah, the beast paves the way for the false Christ. People will believe he is Elijah who was prophesied to return to earth as a forerunner to the Christ. The beast will also perform many convincing miraculous signs and wonders. During the Tribulation there will be a great deception and distortion of many other Old Testament prophecies like the one in Malachi involving Elijah.

The apostle John warns us about false Antichrists:

> Beloved, do not believe every spirit, but test the spirits to see whether they are from God, for many false prophets have gone out into the world. By this you know the Spirit of God: every spirit that confesses that Jesus Christ has come in the flesh is from God, and every spirit that does not confess Jesus is not from God. This is the spirit of the antichrist, which you heard was coming and now is in the world already. (1 John 4:1–3)

There are indeed already false prophets and teachers in the world today who deny that Christ already came in the flesh. During the Tribulation, however, John informs us in the book of Revelation that there will be massive deception—multitudes will deny Christ is God incarnate and instead worship the beast as the true incarnate God.

Believers in the Tribulation

What happens to Christ's followers who do not believe the deceptions of Satan and the Antichrist? Most premillennialists are also pretribulationalists or midtribulationalists, meaning that they believe the church is raptured or removed from this earth before the persecution phase of the Great Tribulation begins. But the case has already been made that the rapture, or the transformation, occurs on the last day—after the Tribulation and after the restoration. Therefore, believers will surely experience the Tribulation.

Revelation is quite clear. Once Michael the archangel stops restraining Satan, he attacks believers with a vengeance:

> And the beast was given a mouth uttering haughty and blasphemous words, and it was allowed to exercise authority for forty-two months [three-and-one-half years]. It opened its mouth to utter blasphemies against God, blaspheming his name and his dwelling, that is, those who dwell in heaven. Also it was allowed to make war on the saints and to conquer them. And authority was given it over every tribe and people and language and nation, and all who dwell on earth will worship it, everyone whose name has not been written before the foundation of the world in the book of life of the Lamb that was slain. If anyone has an ear, let him hear: If anyone is to be taken captive, to captivity he goes; if anyone is to be slain with the sword, with the sword must he be slain. Here is a call for the endurance and faith of the saints. (Rev. 13:5–10)

If we have an ear to listen to what John is teaching, we should know that Satan and the Antichrist will be able to exercise authority over this world during the second half of the Tribulation such that the saints will experience captivity—imprisonment and torture—and/or be slain. That is, unless some can successfully remain in hiding during this three-and-one-half-year period. As John says, this will necessitate an enduring faith by God's saints.

Some scholars in the premillennial camp argue that the word *church* is used only in the beginning of the book of Revelation, in the letters to the various congregations. Then, after John begins describing the persecution phase of the Tribulation, he refers to believers as *saints*; the word *church* is no longer used. They interpret this as proof that the church is no longer on earth, but is somehow raptured from this world before the Tribulation begins; therefore, the persecuted "saints" John refers to must be people who become believers after the rapture and thus endure the terrors of the Great Tribulation.

I believe there is another, much simpler explanation for this change in terminology. The term *church* is used to describe a physical assembly of saints as well as the spiritual body of Christ. Once the Tribulation begins, Christians will no longer be gathering together. Without the mark of the beast, they will be scattering to remote wilderness areas to avoid capture, torture, and execution.

When the saints "see the abomination of desolation spoken of by the prophet Daniel, standing in the holy place" (Matt. 24:15), they will not be gathering at First Baptist Church, First Presbyterian Church, or First Assembly of God. Instead, they will be heading for the mountains in wilderness areas as Jesus advised: "For then there will be great tribulation, such as has not been from the beginning of the world until now, no, and never will be" (Matt. 24:21).

I cannot imagine any functioning churches or assemblies from this point on—only saints hiding, running for their lives. No wonder John refers to believers as saints during this period and not the church as an assembly of the saints.

The Letter to the Church at Philadelphia

Another section of the Bible many premillennial scholars use to assert that the church does not go through the Tribulation is the letter to the church at Philadelphia found in the early chapters of Revelation. This particular assembly of believers had been faithful in enduring much persecution from the unbelieving Jews in their community. As a reward, Jesus made the following promise: "Because you have kept my word about patient endurance, I will keep you from the hour of trial that is coming on the whole world, to try those who dwell on the earth" (Rev. 3:10).

Much ink has been spilled on this one verse. Some scholars argue that this verse proves the church does not go through the Tribulation but is raptured beforehand—kept "from the hour of trial." Some amillennialists argue that this verse somehow proves there is no future literal Tribulation at all! Neither position, however, makes logical sense out of the text. First, these were real congregations in real cities in the Roman Empire with real problems, real successes, and real failures. We can learn much from the advice they received, particularly if our church is similar to theirs. But the letters were specifically written to them to address their particular situation.

Most important, if the reward to the church at Philadelphia is taken at face value, then this church and any other church must be capable of experiencing the Tribulation! Let me provide an illustration. My children are now grown, but imagine if my son at age five did something he was not supposed to do. I could tell him to go sit in the corner and think about what he did for ten minutes. But if I told you that I took his driving privileges away for two weeks, you would reply, "Wait a minute, he does not have a driver's license, much less know how to drive. How can that be a punishment?" Of course, you would be right. If he is too young to drive, how could I punish him by taking away his driving privileges? He has to be driving for me to take away his driving privileges as a form of punishment.

Assume the theory that the church is raptured before the Tribulation is true. Jesus tells the church at Philadelphia that he will reward them for being faithful in their circumstances by keeping them from the Tribulation. But the church replies, "Wait a minute, I do not have to go through the Tribulation—I am raptured to heaven before it begins. How can I be rewarded with not having to go through the Tribulation?" The church would be right. The church, therefore, must be able to experience the Tribulation for a reward to *not* go through the Tribulation to have any meaning.

How did God fulfill his promise to reward this particular church? Because he sets the "times and seasons" when all this will take place, he simply chose not to let it happen in the lifetime of this particular church. There did, though, have to be a logistical possibility of it happening to that specific church; otherwise, Jesus would have been promising a false reward.

Many metaphors are used in the book of Revelation to describe the future, but the church at Philadelphia was not a metaphor. It was a first-century church that was faithful to God. God, in turn, rewarded it. This church could rest assured that the horrific events described in the remainder of Revelation would not happen in its lifetime. It would be spared from having to endure the Great Tribulation because it had patiently endured hardship and remained faithful to God.

Jesus even tells us to pray that, when the Antichrist enters the temple pretending to be God, our attempts to flee not occur in the winter: "Pray that your flight may not be in winter or on a Sabbath" (Matt. 24:20). Why pray for good weather to escape something that will never happen to us?

There is nothing wrong with praying to not experience the Tribulation. Some scholars even interpret part of the Lord's Prayer as a prayer to escape the future Tribulation. Garry Wills makes the following observations: "What the King James Version renders as 'Lead us not into temptation' (Matt. 6:13) is more properly 'Do not carry us into Trial,' where the word *Trial* (*Peirasmos*) means the apocalyptic ending of time."[1]

If Wills is correct, then the Lord's Prayer could be outlined as follows:

Pray like this:
"Our Father in heaven, hallowed be your name [a prayer of worship].
Your kingdom come [the heavenly kingdom], your will be done, on earth as it is in heaven [the restoration].
Give us this day our daily bread, and forgive us our debts, as we also have forgiven our debtors.
And lead us not into temptation, but deliver us from evil [today, and also from the future Great Tribulation]." (Matt. 6:9–13)

The Lord's Prayer, in effect, covers the three major eschatological events, as well as our daily physical and spiritual needs for life. We should pray to be delivered from Satan's unbridled evil perpetrated on the saints during the Great Tribulation—but that means we are indeed capable of experiencing it.

144,000 Protected

There is one highly symbolic section of Revelation that could be interpreted to mean that a select group of Jewish saints will be completely protected from Satan and the Antichrist during the Tribulation. They are not protected by being raptured out of this world; rather, they remain on this earth and are supernaturally protected by God:

She [Jews] gave birth to a male child [Jesus], one who is to rule all the nations with a rod of iron [the future restoration], but her child [Jesus] was caught up to God and to his throne [Christ ascended to heaven], and the woman [believing Jews] fled into the wilderness, where she has a place prepared by God, in which she is to be nourished for 1,260 days [during the persecution phase of the Tribulation]. (Rev. 12:5–6)

John further says:

---

[1] Garry Wills, *Head and Heart* (New York: The Penguin Press, 2007), 366.

And when the dragon [Satan] saw that he had been thrown down to the earth [after Michael the archangel is removed], he pursued the woman who had given birth to the male child [Satan goes after these believing Jews]. But the woman was given the two wings of the great eagle so that she might fly from the serpent into the wilderness [on this earth], to the place where she is to be nourished for a time, and times, and half a time [the three-and-one-half years]. . . . Then the dragon became furious with the woman and went off to make war on the rest of her offspring [Gentile believers], on those who keep the commandments of God and hold to the testimony of Jesus. (Rev. 12:13–17)

John refers to these as 144,000 Jewish believers from every tribe of Israel (Rev. 7:4). Whether this refers to all Jewish believers at that time or just a certain number is unclear. But this protection is similar to that of the two witnesses in front of the temple (Rev. 11:3–5). Some may object to God supernaturally protecting Jewish and not Gentile believers from Satan's persecution. But it is God's prerogative to do what he wants. God has his own reasons for protecting these Jewish believers during the Tribulation. We will find out later what those reasons are. It should be noted, however, that this protection only applies to Jewish believers, not to Jewish unbelievers living at that time.

Jewish believers will have to decide for themselves whether my interpretation of this obscure prophecy is correct—that they will be supernaturally protected from the Antichrist. Otherwise, they should head for the mountains along with Gentile believers.

God's Wrath During the Tribulation

Revelation describes the Tribulation as a period when God will pour out his great wrath on the earth as a result of widespread idolatry and extreme evil perpetrated against his saints. Much of Revelation is devoted to describing God's wrath on this world during the Tribulation. This wrath is similar to the wrath of God poured out on Egypt, though many times greater. But it is not the final wrath of God experienced by unbelievers on the last day when the world is destroyed and unbelievers experience the second death when they are sent to the eternal lake of fire.

This is another area where many premillennialists offer evidence that the church does not experience the Great Tribulation, but is raptured before this wrath occurs. They base this on the fact that, as Christians, we are promised elsewhere in the New Testament to be saved from the wrath of God: "Since, therefore, we have now been justified by his blood, much more shall we be *saved by him from the wrath of God*" (Rom. 5:9). Or, "and to wait for his Son from heaven, whom he raised from the dead, Jesus who *delivers us from the wrath to come*" (1 Thess. 1:10).

But these premillennialists acknowledge that Revelation identifies saints who do endure the Tribulation. These are allegedly people who become believers after the rapture of the church saints before the Tribulation begins. But if New Testament promises about escaping God's wrath of the Great Tribulation apply to the church saints, then why would not the same promises apply to the non-church saints during the Tribulation? The pretribulational logic in this area is fundamentally flawed. If believers, those justified by Jesus' blood, escape God's wrath *by right*, then it should make no difference if they are believers before or after the Tribulation begins. In fact, becoming a believer after the Tribulation begins will take tremendous courage. Why should they be singled out as having to endure the Great Tribulation, and those who were believers before the Tribulation get a pass?

The biggest flaw in these assertions, however, is the failure to distinguish between God's wrath poured out during the Tribulation *and* the final wrath of God on Judgment Day. Verses in Romans, 1 Thessalonians, and elsewhere that speak of saints being saved by Christ "from the wrath of God" are not referring to the wrath of the Tribulation but rather to the final wrath of God on the last day at the Great White Throne judgment, which is the second death and the lake of fire (Rev. 20:11–15). Now, *that* is the wrath of God.

Paul teaches that the saints "wait for his Son from heaven . . . Jesus who delivers us from the wrath to come [the second death and the lake of fire]" (1 Thess. 1:10). Jesus teaches this same thing: "When the Son of Man comes in his glory, and all the angels with him, then he will sit on his glorious throne. . . . Then he will say to those on his left, 'Depart from me, you cursed, into the *eternal fire prepared for the devil and his angels*'" (Matt. 25:31, 41). And this is exactly what John says occurs at the Great White Throne judgment—not at the end of the Tribulation. All believers are delivered from the wrath of the eternal fire of hell on the last day, not from the wrath of God poured out on the world during the Tribulation.

Moreover, during the Tribulation, the saints are exempt from many of God's acts of vengeance on those with the mark of the beast in much the same way that the Jews in Egypt were passed over, because his wrath was not directed at them. The angels of wrath described in Revelation will only direct their vengeful anger at those with the mark of the beast; they will pass over the saints who do not bear this mark:

> So the first angel went and poured out his bowl on the earth, and harmful and painful sores came upon the people who bore the mark of the beast and worshiped its image [unbelievers]. . . . The fourth angel poured out his bowl on the sun, and it was allowed to scorch people with fire. They were scorched by the fierce heat, and they cursed the name of God who had power over these plagues. They [unbelievers] did not repent and give him glory. (Rev. 16:2, 8–9)

184 GOD'S KINGDOM ON EARTH AND IN HEAVEN

Also, believers living during the Tribulation will be given a special seal
of God on their foreheads that will allow the angels of wrath to identify and
pass over them:

> And the fifth angel blew his trumpet, and I saw a star fallen from heaven to
> earth, and he was given the key to the shaft of the bottomless pit. He opened
> the shaft of the bottomless pit, and from the shaft rose smoke like the smoke
> of a great furnace, and the sun and the air were darkened with the smoke
> from the shaft. Then from the smoke came locusts on the earth, and they
> were given power like the power of scorpions of the earth. They were told
> not to harm the grass of the earth or any green plant or any tree, but only
> *those people who do not have the seal of God on their foreheads*. They were
> allowed to torment them for five months, but not to kill them, and their
> torment was like the torment of a scorpion when it stings someone. And in
> those days people will seek death and will not find it. They will long to die,
> but death will flee from them. (Rev. 9:1–6)

With this seal of God on their foreheads, during the Tribulation believers
will be exempt from forms of God's wrath poured out on unredeemed
mankind.

The saints will not be able to escape all God's judgments on the world
because some judgments will affect the entire planet. Believers in hiding or
in prison will simply get caught in the cross fire:

> And there were flashes of lightning, rumblings, peals of thunder, and a great
> earthquake such as there had never been since man was on the earth, so
> great was the earthquake. The great city was split into three parts, and the
> cities of the nations fell, and God remembered Babylon the great, to make
> her drain the cup of the wine of the fury of his wrath. And every island fled
> away, and no mountains were to be found. And great hailstones, about one
> hundred pounds each, fell from heaven on people; and they cursed God for
> the plague of the hail, because the plague was so severe. (Rev. 16:18–21)

This appears to happen near the end of the Tribulation. It is doubtful
many Christians will still be alive; most will have been martyred and will be
watching these events from heaven. There will be a few, though, who will
either still be in prison or have succeeded in hiding in remote mountainous
locations, perhaps in a cave, who have escaped the beast's capture. In my
opinion, death resulting from a collapsing cave due to an earthquake would
be a welcome event after trying to survive in a cold, dark, damp cave for
three-and-one-half years in constant fear of being found. Or if a Christian
was imprisoned and being tortured, and one-hundred-pound hailstones
began falling from heaven causing massive destruction, he would likely
shout, "Hallelujah!"

Christians should not fear physical death. Like Paul, we look forward to our spirits joining the Lord in heaven. Christians who get caught in this cross fire will be able to rejoice at the calamity befalling the world, for they will know that the end of the Tribulation is near. They will know that in a short time they will be part of the first resurrection and the glorious 1,000-year restoration that follows.

Faithful Saints in the Tribulation

During the Tribulation, the days for nominal Christianity will be over. As the Tribulation unfolds, the tares in the church will receive the mark of the beast, whereas the wheat, or God's elect, will not. The tares will no longer believe it beneficial to be part of a persecuted group of believers. As Satan deludes them, they will even turn against former church members:

> Then they will deliver you up to tribulation and put you to death, and you will be hated by all nations for my name's sake. And then many will fall away and betray one another and hate one another. And many false prophets will arise and lead many astray. And because lawlessness will be increased, the love of many will grow cold. But the one who endures to the end will be saved. (Matt. 24:9–13)

The Tribulation will separate the wheat from the tares.

As the Tribulation progresses, conditions for Christians become so intolerable that John teaches they are better off dead than alive, as they suffer extreme torture and persecution:

> Here is a call for the endurance of the saints, those who keep the commandments of God and their faith in Jesus. And I heard a voice from heaven saying, "Write this: Blessed are the dead who die in the Lord from now on." "Blessed indeed," says the Spirit, "that they may rest from their labors [enduring persecution], for their deeds follow them!" (Rev. 14:12–13)

John says that it is actually a blessing to be killed rather than continue to endure satanic torture.

So many Christians are slain during this time that Revelation reports a great multitude of them singing from heaven, where their spirits go after death. This is similar to the departed saints who are described in Hebrews as a crowd of witnesses in heaven watching the world (Heb. 12:1). Revelation describes these martyred saints of the Tribulation:

> After this I heard what seemed to be the loud voice of a *great multitude in heaven*, crying out, "Hallelujah! Salvation and glory and power belong to our God, for his judgments are true and just; for he has judged the great prostitute who corrupted the earth with her immorality, and has avenged on her *the blood of his servants.*" (Rev. 19:1–2)

Because this demonic tyranny is worldwide, it will be difficult for Christians to escape capture or death. Satan's universal system of personal identification will make survival almost impossible without allegiance to the false Christ: "Also it [the second beast] causes all, both small and great, both rich and poor, both free and slave, to be marked on the right hand or the forehead, so that no one can buy or sell unless he has the mark, that is, the name of the beast or the number of its name" (Rev. 13:16–17).

During Adolf Hitler's Nazi reign of terror in the 1940s, many Jews were given shelter and hidden by Gentiles opposed to Hitler. Osama Bin Laden was able to safely hide in remote areas of Afghanistan and even in a densely populated area of Pakistan for more than ten years because those with similar religious ideologies were willing to help him. During the Tribulation, however, Christians will likely receive no help from deluded unbelievers bearing the mark. The saints will surely stand out without this mark, and unbelievers will report any Christian they find, considering it an act of service to their god, the Antichrist.

Today there is a significant underground church in China despite persecution from the communist government. When these Chinese believers are "above" ground, they look like every other citizen. As long as they are careful with whom they share their faith, they can carry on normally. In contrast, the unmarked believers during the Tribulation will be easily identifiable in any public setting as the unfaithful enemies of the Antichrist. As a result, believers will have to remain in complete seclusion, hiding from everyone except fellow believers. And this is why public worship services and evangelism as we know it will cease.

For fear of being captured, Christians will no longer preach from the pulpits, the street corners, or the airwaves. Attempting to evangelize during this time would be comparable to a Jew giving a political speech in the streets of Berlin during the height of Jewish persecution in the Nazi era. He would immediately be arrested and, no doubt, tortured and killed. Besides, preaching to unbelievers in hopes that they would be converted would likely be futile, for God says he will send a powerful delusion on the world of unbelievers such that they really believe the lies of Satan (2 Thess. 2:11).

Revelation informs us of one exception. There will be two Christian witnesses preaching directly in front of the Jewish temple who will be supernaturally protected (Rev. 11). They are brave and powerful and have the prophetic voices of Old Testament prophets like Elijah, Elisha, and Jeremiah. They remain in the temple area during the Tribulation for 1,260 days, preaching the truth and assailing the beast and those who worship him. Their message will be one of impending judgment, such as Jeremiah's, rather than of repentance and salvation. But there is no indication in Revelation that anyone with the mark of the beast is converted as a result of their fiery exhortations.

When their testimony ends, God allows the beast to kill them, and the entire world rejoices at their death. Out of disrespect, no one will bury them, leaving them to rot in the street. Then, after three-and-one-half days, God breathes into them the breath of life and they are resurrected. God calls from heaven, and, like Elijah, they ascend to heaven in a cloud.

The Revival of Babylon

Hitler's slaughter of approximately six million Jews and others in occupied parts of Europe took place in a few short years. By comparison, hundreds of millions of Christians will be killed in the three-and-one-half years of the Tribulation! John foresees the great multitude of the spirits of these martyred Christians at the throne of God in heaven:

> After this I looked, and behold, a great multitude that no one could number, from every nation, from all tribes and peoples and languages, standing before the throne and before the Lamb, clothed in white robes, with palm branches in their hands, and crying out with a loud voice, "Salvation belongs to our God who sits on the throne, and to the Lamb!" . . . Then one of the elders addressed me, saying, "Who are these, clothed in white robes, and from where have they come?" I said to him, "Sir, you know." And he said to me, "These are the ones coming out of the great tribulation. They have washed their robes and made them white in the blood of the Lamb." (Rev. 7:9–14)

There are so many saints slain during this reign of Satan that John says they are too numerous to count. How can unbelievers become so deceived and depraved that they kill so many fellow human beings? The answer has a lot to do with the renewed ancient pagan religion of Babylon that Satan inspires during this time, which included human sacrifice among its rituals. The great prostitute in Revelation 19:2 is actually a city described as Babylon from which the Antichrist reigns. During the millennium, Jerusalem will become a prosperous city. During the Tribulation, Satan sets up a counterfeit Jerusalem—Babylon. Not only will Babylon flourish, but it will also become incredibly immoral and godless.

The reign of Satan is a counterfeit version of the reign of Christ during the millennium. Not only are signs and wonders performed during the Tribulation, but earthly prosperity is also realized. An unbeliever could easily be fooled into thinking that a golden messianic age has finally arrived as prophesied in the Old Testament. A prophecy about the ultimate destruction of Babylon describes this great wealth, as well as the incredible depravity inspired by demonic pagan worship:

And he [an angel from heaven] called out with a mighty voice, "Fallen, fallen is Babylon the great! She has become a dwelling place for demons, a haunt for every unclean spirit, a haunt for every unclean bird, a haunt for every unclean and detestable beast. For all nations have drunk the wine of the passion of her sexual immorality, and the kings of the earth have committed immorality with her, and the merchants of the earth have grown rich from the power of her luxurious living." (Rev. 18:2–3)

The great, ancient Babylonian Empire, with Babylon as its capital, was the source of numerous forms of pagan worship. Human sacrifice took place during many of these pagan rituals. Pyramid-like structures, similar to a ziggurat, played an integral part in these pagan ceremonies; human sacrifices were made to the gods atop these structures.

Even some Jews, unfaithful to the Mosaic covenant, practiced these pagan religions and sacrificed their firstborn who were burned alive:

And they [Israel and Judah] abandoned all the commandments of the LORD their God, . . . and they made an Asherah and worshiped all the host of heaven and served Baal. And *they burned their sons and their daughters as offerings* and used divination and omens and sold themselves to do evil in the sight of the LORD, provoking him to anger. (2 Kings 17:16–17)

With Satan unrestrained during the Great Tribulation, the world will experience a renewed, Babylonian-style pagan worship, incorporating some of the most ungodly practices of those ancient pagan ceremonies. As a result, the blood of the captured saints flows in a form of pagan sacrifice: "And on her forehead was written a name of mystery: 'Babylon the great, mother of prostitutes and of earth's abominations.' And I saw the woman, drunk with the blood of the saints, the blood of the martyrs of Jesus" (Rev. 17:5–6). The pagan sacrifice of the saints is so extensive that John depicts the city of Babylon as drunk with their blood.

It is difficult to understand how those with the mark of the beast can be deceived into believing that sacrificing Christians is a form of worshiping God. But the study of history teaches that humans, as a group, can be thoroughly deluded into believing the most incredible false ideologies. Ancient Egyptians, during the Old Kingdom period (2575–2150 BC), buried their rulers in massive pyramids that they believed would carry the dead pharaohs into the afterlife. When a pharaoh died, his closest servants were killed and buried with him, so that they could continue serving him in the afterlife.

Perhaps one of the most bizarre pagan religions was practiced by the Aztec civilization, which reached its height during the fifteenth century. Aztecs worshiped the sun god, Huitzilopochtli, and believed that humans must be sacrificed regularly to appease him; otherwise, the sun would not rise and their crops would fail. One of the most notable architectural structures of the Aztec civilization is the ziggurat. Resembling a stepped pyramid, it functioned as a temple. The priest would have a human captive dragged to the top. There, on an altar, the priest would slash open the victim's chest and pull out the still-pumping heart to feed the blood to the sun god. The Aztecs created an army whose sole purpose was to collect captives for these regular sacrifices. Historians estimate that more than fifty thousand people were captured and sacrificed to the sun god in this manner every year. Yet, these industrious, bright people built one of the most complex and sophisticated empires of its day with prosperous, magnificent cities—much like the false Babylon.

In the modern era, we have witnessed examples of massive delusion and atrocity. During Hitler's Nazi regime, many Germans believed their race to be superior, according to Darwinian evolution, and all other races subordinate. They considered Jews to be defective humans capable of contaminating the master race, so they eliminated an estimated six million Jews to advance the evolution of man.

The Babylonians, Egyptians, Aztecs, and Nazis were terribly deluded about God and truth. These are but a few examples throughout history of people who committed unthinkable acts in the name of their gods and false ideologies. In Romans, Paul speaks of mankind's innate propensity for evil and deception and of God sometimes giving them over to delusion: "And since they did not see fit to acknowledge God, God gave them up to a debased mind to do what ought not to be done" (Rom. 1:28). During the Tribulation, the minds and hearts of unbelievers will be similarly given over to deception and depravity:

> The coming of the lawless one is by the activity of Satan with all power and false signs and wonders, and with all wicked deception for those who are perishing, because they refused to love the truth and so be saved. Therefore God sends them a strong delusion, so that they may believe what is false. (2 Thess. 2:9–11)

Satan will further deceive the world with false prophets who will make inanimate idols miraculously speak:

> Then I saw another beast rising out of the earth. . . . It performs great signs, even making fire come down from heaven to earth in front of people, and by the signs that it is allowed to work in the presence of the beast it deceives those who dwell on earth, telling them to make an image for the beast that was wounded by the sword and yet lived. And it was allowed to give breath to the image of the beast [an idol], so that the image of the beast might even speak and might cause those who would not worship the image of the beast to be slain. (Rev. 13:11–15)

The saints will not worship this idol, no matter how convincing it is; they will be slain for their refusal to worship the world's "god." In the Olivet Discourse, Christ informs us that these signs and miracles will be powerfully convincing, but will not deceive the elect: "For false christs and false prophets will arise and perform great signs and wonders, so as to lead astray, if possible, even the elect" (Matt. 24:24).

In today's secular world, it is difficult to imagine Satan reviving the ancient Babylonian religion involving human sacrifice. Many people seem to care little about spiritual matters and pay even less attention to anything religious, much less pagan. At some point, however, modern man will again crave the spiritual dimension of life. The world will transition from this secular view of reality, becoming more receptive to the spiritual dimension and thus susceptible to Satan's delusions.

Satan will distort Old Testament prophecies to convince unbelievers that the Antichrist is the promised Messiah and that Christians who reject this Antichrist should be slaughtered. Satan could easily distort the following prophecy in Malachi to justify purging the world of saints, eliminating those who do not believe in him:

> Behold, I send my messenger and he will prepare the way before me. And the Lord whom you seek will suddenly come to his temple [the beast enters the temple proclaiming he is God]; and the messenger of the covenant in whom you delight, behold, he is coming, says the LORD of hosts. But who can endure the day of his coming, and who can stand when he appears? For he is like a refiner's fire and like fullers' soap. He will sit as a refiner and purifier of silver, and he will purify the sons of Levi and refine them like gold and silver, and they will bring offerings in righteousness to the LORD. (Mal. 3:1–3)

Those with the mark of the beast will be deceived into thinking they are serving the Lord when they are "purifying" the world by eliminating false believers (those who believe in Jesus Christ).

Satan will have the power to create many clever delusions. Perhaps he will convince unbelievers that since the first Christ had to come as a living sacrifice, then his followers (the saints), who are his body, must also be sacrificed to complete the atonement of humanity's sins to God. Satan might deceive people into believing that by sacrificing Christians, they are offering a service to God in a necessary act of worship. During the Tribulation, the body of Christ (the saints) could be sacrificed in some type of bizarre pagan religious worship emulating the Lord's Supper. Maybe that is why Babylon is characterized as being "drunk with the blood of the saints."

Interestingly, Satan does not attack only the saints; his nature to kill and destroy extends to unbelievers as well. In Revelation 9, it appears that a previously unknown class of demons, unlike any mentioned in the Bible, is released from the bottomless pit. Apparently, these demons are not operational today because of their extreme evil power. They are compared to locusts and scorpions. They do not attack saints but unbelievers, and their torment is so great that "in those days people will seek death and will not find it. They will long to die, but death will flee from them" (9:6). After these demons appear, four more fallen angels arrive who seem to gather an army so destructive that "a third of mankind [is] killed, by the fire and smoke and sulfur coming out of their mouths" (9:18).

The Complexity of Revelation

Revelation is often difficult to follow because it describes various stages of the Tribulation, but not necessarily in the order they occur. There are seven plagues, seven bowls of wrath, and seven trumpets describing God's wrath on the world as the Tribulation unfolds. It is difficult to create a simple timeline in which all these prophecies occur. To further complicate matters, Revelation will describe one future event, then abruptly skip ahead and portray another future event, and then return to a description of the prior future event. Theologians refer to this as "recapitulation."

For instance, the declarations of Christ's ultimate victory and reign appear sporadically throughout the book, sometimes occurring in the midst of the plagues that occur during the Tribulation. In Revelation 11, several of the woes of God are described as he executes his wrath on the earth: "And at that hour there was a great earthquake, and a tenth of the city fell. . . . The second woe has passed; behold, the third woe is soon to come" (vv. 13–14). At this point, one expects a discussion of the "third woe"; however, the description of events is interrupted by a seventh angel blowing a trumpet: "And there were loud voices in heaven, saying, 'The kingdom of the world has become the kingdom of our Lord and of his Christ, and he shall reign forever and ever'" (v. 15). Then, immediately after this interruption to announce ultimate victory, the third woe of the Tribulation is described.

This juxtaposition of time and events would be like the Allies celebrating Germany's surrender and the end of World War II on D-Day, that infamous day the Allies stormed the beaches of Normandy, France—one year before Germany actually surrendered. In a way, the Allies could celebrate the invasion of D-Day as the end of the war, for it was the beginning of the end, though Allied troops would not reach Berlin until a year later, bringing an end to Hitler's regime.

Likewise, in Revelation, the beginning of the Great Tribulation is also celebrated as the beginning of the end with the impending restoration only three-and-one-half years away. That is why references to the forthcoming restoration are scattered throughout the Tribulation prophecies. The Tribulation may be a horrific period for believers, and even unbelievers, but it marks the short countdown (1,260 days) to the day Satan is bound and Christ finally exercises his messianic reign over this world, establishing a true holy and godly kingdom of righteous humanity.

The Plagues of Revelation

As the blood of hundreds of millions of innocent Christians flows, it is little wonder that God begins to visit his wrath on the world. As the world becomes unbearably evil in his sight, God displays his anger by creating a variety of plagues.

Revelation 16 describes some of the forms of God's wrath: "harmful and painful sores came upon the people who bore the mark of the beast and worshiped its image"; another bowl made the sea "like the blood of a corpse, and every living thing died that was in the sea"; another bowl changed "the rivers and the springs of water, and they became blood"; another bowl caused the sun "to scorch people with fire. They were scorched by the fierce heat, and they cursed the name of God who had power over these plagues"; another angel sent from heaven "poured out his bowl on the throne of the beast, and its kingdom was plunged into darkness. People gnawed their tongues in anguish and cursed the God of heaven for their pain and sores. They did not repent of their deeds" (16:2–11). And more plagues follow.

Because Babylon is the world center of the satanic worship and sacrifice of the saints, it is destroyed by fire in a single day, like Sodom and Gomorrah: "For this reason her plagues will come in a single day, death and mourning and famine, and she will be burned up with fire; for mighty is the Lord God who has judged her" (Rev. 18:8).

Understandably, when this false Jerusalem is finally destroyed, there is great celebration in heaven by millions of martyred saints:

> After this I heard what seemed to be the loud voice of a great multitude in heaven, crying out, "Hallelujah! Salvation and glory and power belong to our God, for his judgments are true and just; for he has judged the great prostitute who corrupted the earth with her immorality, and has avenged on her the blood of his servants." (Rev. 19:1–2)

It is a hallelujah chorus indeed, for they are about to march into battle with Christ to destroy the Antichrist and the false prophet and take control of the world.

The Battle of Armageddon

At this point, the world will be a wreck. Virtually all the saints will have been slain during the Antichrist's reign of terror. Only a small number of saints will have successfully hidden in wilderness areas. Many unbelievers also will have been killed. Earthquakes and plagues will have devastated the planet. But a significant number of unbelievers will have survived.

Yet one final, great battle will remain before the Tribulation comes to an end: Armageddon. It is during this battle that Christ will demonstrate the full measure of his anger over the idolatry and the evil perpetrated against his people, the saints, during this terrible period of human history: "He will tread the winepress of the fury of the wrath of God the Almighty" (Rev. 19:15). In Revelation 19, Christ is depicted as coming out of heaven riding on a white horse. He is called "Faithful and True, and in righteousness he judges and makes war" (19:11). John also describes Christ as wearing a robe dipped in blood. These descriptions are symbolic, yet they depict a concrete reality of the unseen world of spiritual forces in real warfare.

To understand this section of Revelation, it is helpful to look at similar precedents from biblical history. Two specific episodes involving Elijah and Elisha are very revealing. Elijah never experienced death; he literally ascended into heaven. Immediately before Elijah's departure, he and Elisha are conversing: "And as they still went on and talked, behold, chariots of fire and horses of fire separated the two of them. And Elijah went up by a whirlwind into heaven. And Elisha saw it and he cried, 'My father, my father! The chariots of Israel and its horsemen!' And he saw him no more" (2 Kings 2:11–12).

What exactly did Elisha see? He got a glimpse of the unseen angelic spiritual world that protected Israel. Were these actual chariots and horsemen? Probably not, but they obviously appeared in some fashion for Elisha to see them. Angels appear in bodily form to be seen, but they do not have human bodies for they are only spirits.

On another occasion, Elisha is with a servant. An earthly army, with horses and chariots, surrounded their city. Elisha's servant became very concerned:

> And the servant said, "Alas, my master! What shall we do?" He said, "Do not be afraid, for those who are with us are more than those who are with them." Then Elisha prayed and said, "O LORD, please open his eyes that he may see." So the LORD opened the eyes of the young man, and he saw, and behold, the mountain was full of horses and chariots of fire all around Elisha. (2 Kings 6:15–17)

The unseen celestial world of heaven is never far away. Mark reports how at the baptism of Jesus the "heavens" were opened and the voice of God the Father could be heard: "And when he came up out of the water, immediately he saw the heavens opening and the Spirit descending on him like a dove. And a voice came from heaven, 'You are my beloved Son; with you I am well pleased'" (Mark 1:10–11). When the celestial heavens were opened, the Father did not have to physically descend to this earth to speak to those on the earth. Rather, he could speak from the celestial heavens, and those on the earth could audibly hear him.

On yet another occasion, as Jesus was being arrested, one of his disciples took a sword and cut off an ear of one of the high priest's servants who had come to arrest him. Jesus then told his disciples: "Do you think that I cannot appeal to my Father, and he will at once send me more than twelve legions of angels?" (Matt. 26:53). Jesus, like Elijah and Elisha, knew what powers existed around him in the angelic or celestial world of heaven, which surround us at all times.

The spirits of the departed saints slain during the Tribulation seem to be involved in this celestial yet earthly battle, for they are described as "the armies of heaven, arrayed in fine linen, white and pure, . . . following him on white horses" (Rev. 19:14). In Hebrews, the dead saints are described as witnesses in heaven. In Revelation 19, they are no longer only watching what is happening on earth, but are engaged with Christ in this important battle. There is no evidence, though, that they fight in the battle. Satan's army is swiftly destroyed with just the sword from the mouth of Christ. After Christ and his celestial army of angels and saints win the decisive victory, the Great Tribulation comes to an end; the false prophet and the Antichrist are captured and sent to the lake of fire, and Satan is subsequently bound. The millennial reign of Christ then follows.

Premillennialists claim this section of Revelation 19 is a picture of the "second coming" of Christ when Christ comes out of the celestial heaven on his white horse, literally lands on this earth, destroys the Antichrist and his armies, and dismounts his horse to reside on the earth on one of the "thrones" depicted by John. One could see him, touch him, and eat with him. There are many problems with this interpretation, but the main one is that nowhere does John describe Christ continuing his downward descent to this earth and dismounting his white horse to reside here with his saints (Rev. 19:19–21; 20:1–4). That John "saw heaven opened" and had a vision of Christ on a white horse does not mean John was seeing the second coming of Christ in the clouds. This vision of the unseen world of heaven is not too different from Stephen's vision of Christ when he was about to be stoned to death:

> Now when they heard these things they were enraged, and they ground their teeth at him. But he, full of the Holy Spirit, gazed into heaven and saw the glory of God, and Jesus standing at the right hand of God. And he said, "Behold, I see the heavens opened, and the Son of Man standing at the right hand of God." (Acts 7:54–56)

In a similar fashion, John sees "heaven opened," but now he sees the celestial armies of the saints led by Christ interacting with the spiritual and physical forces in this world in a victorious battle at Armageddon. But John does not describe Christ on his white horse leaving the celestial realm and descending to the plane of the earth, dismounting, and walking on this earth.

Furthermore, although the large armies gathered at Armageddon are destroyed by the "sword" or spoken word of Christ from his celestial white horse, many civilians not engaged in this battle will survive and be living when Christ's millennial reign begins. This is borne out by a prophecy in Zechariah which clearly states that there will be "survivors" of this battle who will be required to go to Jerusalem and worship Christ:

> And this shall be the plague with which the LORD will strike all the peoples that wage war against Jerusalem: their flesh will rot while they are still standing on their feet, their eyes will rot in their sockets, and their tongues will rot in their mouths. . . . Then *everyone who survives* of all the nations that have come against Jerusalem shall go up year after year to worship the King, the LORD of hosts, and to keep the Feast of Booths. And if any of the families of the earth do not go up to Jerusalem to worship the King, the LORD of hosts, there will be no rain on them. (Zech. 14:12–17)

Among the unbelievers will be "survivors of all the nations" who will enter into the messianic kingdom and be grateful for Christ's subsequent reign of peace, justice, and righteousness. Those who are ungrateful will suffer the consequences.

Isaiah also teaches that there will be a small number of unbelievers who survive the Tribulation: "Therefore a curse devours the earth, and its inhabitants suffer for their guilt; therefore the inhabitants of the earth are scorched, and few men are left [survivors]" (Isa. 24:6). During the millennium, unbelievers will continue to populate the earth, which is why Christ will have to rule with a "rod of iron" to prevent evil and establish peace on this earth. Further proof that some unbelievers will still be in the world during the millennium is that at the end of that period, when Satan is released one final time, he is able to deceive these unbelievers and lead them into one final rebellion against God (Rev. 20:7–9).

Yet, with the majority of Christians martyred during the Tribulation, there must be some kind of resurrection of the departed spirits of these saints for the world to be repopulated with the saints; otherwise, Christ will be ruling over mainly unbelievers who have survived the Tribulation. According to John, this repopulation of the world with the deceased saints will be achieved through the "first resurrection."

Summary

Why does God allow Satan to instigate the Great Tribulation? Maybe God allows this unparalleled Tribulation to reveal the full extent of the fallen nature of mankind and what a truly godless humanity under the direct influence of Satan is capable of. It will also reveal the righteous indignation of a Holy God who will vent the "fury of the wrath of God the Almighty" against the evil perpetrated against his saints by Satan and his followers.

In contrast, the messianic kingdom that follows will demonstrate what the human experience would have been like had Adam and Eve not rebelled, allowing Satan into our world. Imagine a world without Satan; a world ruled by its divine Creator populated by a restored humanity who love and worship the true God of this world. The subsequent millennial reign of Christ will be a world of righteous humanity where humans love God and love and serve one another.

6

The Son's Kingdom

The apostle John records in his Gospel that when Christ was arrested, the soldiers mocked what they thought was the powerless Jewish king by placing a royal purple robe on him and twisting together a crown of thorns to set on his head. Pilate also mocked Christ when he wrote an inscription to put on the cross: "Jesus of Nazareth, the King of the Jews" (John 19:19). To the Romans, the concept of a Messiah who did not fight to establish his reign and allowed himself to be arrested and even crucified was an absurdity and deserving of ridicule.

During the battle of Armageddon, John sees Christ wearing another robe and bearing another inscription: "From his mouth comes a sharp sword with which to strike down the nations, and he will rule them with a rod of iron. . . . On his robe and on his thigh he has a name written, King of kings and Lord of lords" (Rev. 19:15–16). The mockery is over! It is time for the Messiah to destroy the pagan armies of man, render Satan inoperative, and reveal the reigning Messiah to the world. It is time for the Jewish Messiah to "come from Zion" and deliver Israel and rule the whole world from sea to sea. It is Christ's inauguration day as King of this world.

It is time for Christ to take all the people of God (Jew and Gentile alike), whom he has ransomed by his blood, and make them into a kingdom that will reign on the earth during the restoration:

> Worthy are you to take the scroll and to open its seals, for you were slain, and by your blood you ransomed people for God from every tribe and language and people and nation, and you have made them a kingdom and priests to our God, and *they shall reign on the earth.*" (Rev. 5:9–10)

Or as Daniel predicts, after the dominion of the Antichrist and Satan is taken away, the kingdom of the world will be given to the saints:

> But the court shall sit in judgment, and his [the Antichrist's] dominion shall be taken away, to be consumed and destroyed to the end. And the kingdom and the dominion and the greatness of the kingdoms under the whole heaven shall be given to the people of the saints of the Most High; their kingdom shall be an everlasting kingdom, and all dominions shall serve and obey them. (Dan. 7:26–27)

It is time for God the Son to establish his kingdom on this earth and for the meek to inherit the earth for one thousand years. Immediately after Armageddon, John says:

> Then I saw an angel coming down from heaven, holding in his hand the key to the bottomless pit and a great chain. And he seized the dragon, that ancient serpent, who is the devil and Satan, and bound him for a thousand years, and threw him into the pit, and shut it and sealed it over him, so that he might not deceive the nations any longer, until the thousand years were ended. After that he must be released for a little while. (Rev. 20:1–3)

John uses several metaphors to describe what will occur in the supernatural realm of angels and demons. In the ancient world, dangerous criminals were often chained and put into a dungeon or pit to prevent them from doing any further harm. In this supernatural scene, we learn that an angel uses a key to open a bottomless pit and with a great chain binds and imprisons Satan in this pit. The angel even seals it to prevent any possibility of his escape. Satan's complete removal from this world represents a pivotal event in the history of the world.

Paul teaches that in the current world Satan and his demonic influences are very active: "Put on the whole armor of God, that you may be able to stand against the schemes of the devil. For we do not wrestle against flesh and blood, but against the rulers, against the authorities, against the cosmic powers over this present darkness, against the spiritual forces of evil in the heavenly places" (Eph. 6:11–12). During the Great Tribulation, Satan and his evil forces will have unrestrained influence over this world with devastating results. But in the millennium, all these spiritual forces of evil and cosmic powers of darkness will be totally removed from this world.

Today it is impossible to understand the magnitude of this event. Since the fall of Adam and Eve, Satan has been operational in this world. For generation after generation Satan has corrupted humanity. But John foresees a period when Satan and his demons will have no control or influence over this world whatsoever. At no time since the fall of Adam and Eve has this occurred. Even before the fall, Satan was in the Garden of Eden as a tempter. Now, he will not be around to even tempt mankind, much less influence the affairs of man.

Consider the extent of evil that Satan has instigated through sinful mankind throughout history—ancient and modern. Remember the ancient empires and their pagan religions. Think about current affairs. Read the daily news. As a result of Satan's removal, there will be monumental changes in every conceivable aspect of life on this earth. To understand God's kingdom on this earth, it is imperative that one fully grasp the significance of Satan being bound and no longer operational in this world for one thousand years. The righteous world during the millennium will be categorically different from the current one Paul describes.

After Satan is bound, Revelation resumes in a chronological progression. John says:

> *Then* I saw thrones, and seated on them were those to whom the authority to judge was committed. Also I saw the souls of those who had been beheaded for the testimony of Jesus and for the word of God, and who had not worshiped the beast or its image and had not received its mark on their foreheads or their hands. *They came to life and reigned with Christ for a thousand years.* The rest of the dead did not come to life until the thousand years were ended. This is the first resurrection. Blessed and holy is the one who shares in the first resurrection! Over such the second death has no power, but they will be priests of God and of Christ, and they will reign with him for a thousand years. (Rev. 20:4–6)

For the earth to be repopulated with the saints "from every tribe and language and people and nation" so that they can experience the messianic kingdom, they must be resurrected back into natural bodies. But before we examine the scriptural basis for a resurrection of the natural body of the departed saints, let us first examine how Christ establishes his reign during the millennium.

Christ Exercises His Reign from Heaven

The Scriptures teach that Christ already has full authority but does not currently fully exercise that authority to reign over this world. Paul states that Christ is now seated at the right hand of God the Father and has all authority:

> and what is the immeasurable greatness of his power toward us who believe, according to the working of his great might that he worked in Christ when he raised him from the dead and *seated him at his right hand in the heavenly places,* far above all rule and authority and power and dominion, and above every name that is named, not only in this age but also in the one to come. (Eph. 1:19–21)

After Jesus was arrested and brought before the chief priest and scribes, they asked him if he was the Christ. He responded, "But from now on the Son of Man shall be seated at the right hand of the power of God [the Father]" (Luke 22:69). Now ascended and seated on the throne of David in heaven at the right hand of God the Father, Christ has all the power and authority necessary to rule the world.

But in the letter to the Hebrews, we learn that Christ does not currently fully *exercise* the authority and power at this disposal:

> You made him [Christ] for a little while lower than the angels; you have crowned him with glory and honor, putting everything in subjection under his feet." Now in putting everything in subjection to him, he left nothing outside his control. *At present, we do not yet see everything in subjection to him.* (Heb. 2:7–8)

Though he reigns supreme by his position of authority at the right hand of the power of God, he at present does not fully exercise that reign, because we do not see everything in subjection to him. This is quite obvious, for we daily see the results of both Satan and depraved humanity. The world remains Satan's imperial dominion with the vast majority of sinful men hostile to God. And just as Christ did not use his power and authority to prevent his arrest and crucifixion, so, too, he does not prevent Satan from persecuting his followers today and even more so in the future Great Tribulation. That is why we continue to pray to the Father that he deliver us from evil.

It is only after the Battle of Armageddon, followed by the destruction of the beast and the false prophet and the binding of Satan at the end of the Tribulation, that Christ will begin to *fully exercise* his authority and power and *reign* supremely. Then God's righteous will is finally implemented on earth as it is in heaven, and the Deliverer from Zion delivers this world from Satan's tyranny of evil.

How will Christ exercise his messianic reign after the Tribulation ends? Will he exercise it from his current throne in heaven, or will he return to this earth to rule? The answer is simple. He reigns from his current throne in heaven. He does not need to come back to the earth to do what he already has full authority to do. Once Satan is bound, Christ can easily achieve everything he wants to accomplish on this earth from his throne in heaven.

This is the only way he can exercise his reign, for when he does return on the last day, it is to destroy this world, rapture the saints, and usher in the Father's heavenly kingdom—not the Son's earthly kingdom. Notice when John describes the first resurrection (when the saints come back to life on this earth and reign with Christ), there is no mention of Christ physically coming to the earth to reign with them. "They came to life and reigned with

Christ for a thousand years" (Rev. 20:4). These resurrected saints can easily reign with Christ without him being here on this earth. They are on this earth, and he is in heaven. John simply says they "reigned with Christ." There is not a single reference in Revelation 20 to the throne of Christ being on this earth. That is because Christ remains on his throne in heaven; thus, these are the thrones of men on earth who have been resurrected to reign with Christ as he rules from heaven. Just as we walk with him today without his physical presence, so, too, we will reign with him in the millennium without his actual presence.

A major theme of the Old Testament is that Christ could have been the Israelites' king "from on high" had they remained faithful and submissive. When Israel was brought out of Egypt, God was supposed to be their king. But they were afraid of the hostile, satanic, pagan countries surrounding them. Not trusting God to lead and protect them, they succumbed to fear and demanded a human king to protect them. God gave them Saul:

> And the LORD said to Samuel, "Obey the voice of the people in all that they say to you, for they have not rejected you, but they have rejected me from being king over them. According to all the deeds that they have done, from the day I brought them up out of Egypt even to this day, forsaking me and serving other gods, so they are also doing to you." (1 Sam. 8:7–8)

God could have been their king, though he was in heaven. It was their fear and lack of faith that led to their demand for an earthly human king.

But after Satan is removed from this world, he will be powerless to influence the nations. That changes everything! During his messianic reign, Christ will not only be king of Israel, but King of kings and Lord of lords of the whole world. No longer will Israel have to fear any hostile nation—or will any other nation have to fear aggression—which is why all wars will come to an end during this time.

It is not necessary for Christ to come back to this earth to fulfill all the messianic prophecies. Note one example from the Old Testament. David knew the Lord was fully capable of ruling this world from heaven:

> Arise, O LORD, in your anger;
>> rise up against the rage of my enemies.
>> Awake, my God; decree justice.
> Let the assembled peoples gather around you.
>> *Rule over them from on high* [rule from heaven];
>> let the LORD judge the peoples.
>> Judge me, O LORD, according to my righteousness,
>> according to my integrity, O Most High.

O righteous God,
>who searches minds and hearts,
>*bring to an end the violence of the wicked*
>and make the righteous secure. (Ps. 7:6–9 NIV)

David's prayer comes true in the restoration. Christ brings an end to the violence of the wicked by destroying the Antichrist, binding Satan, and establishing righteousness by ruling from on high over his assembled peoples gathered on the earth through the first resurrection.

As previously noted, Christ can be compared to the world's president who has been elected or designated but has not yet been inaugurated to fully exercise his term in office. During the interim, Satan reigns as de facto president. That is not to say that Christ is inactive. Just as a president-elect is selecting his cabinet, staff, and members of his administration, so, too, Christ is busy building his church through the centuries and gathering his cabinet officials who will one day rule (on thrones) with him when the time comes for his inauguration. Satan's term of office will end when he is bound. At that time Christ will begin his rule as the world's president.

Christ has all power and authority available to him, and he continues to use this authority to build his church by rescuing his people from Satan's dominion of darkness. But he does not yet use his power to eliminate his enemies. As a result, the church (his body) continues to suffer hardship, persecution, and demonic opposition, just as Christ did when he was on this earth. Christ himself continues to suffer to this day, for when we suffer, he suffers too.

It is not because Christ lacks the power to control Satan, overcome his enemies, prevent persecution, rule this world, and restore this creation to an Edenic state. While on the earth, his miracles demonstrated a complete mastery over demons, nature, and even physical death. But Christ did not use his authority and power to intervene and free John the Baptist from Herod's unjust imprisonment and ultimate execution. When Christ was arrested, he told his disciples that he could ask the Father and, immediately, more than twelve legions of powerful angels could be at his disposal to prevent his arrest (Matt. 26:53). He had the power to be the ruler of this world, but it was not yet time for him to fully exercise his reign.

Read Hebrews again with this analogy in mind:

"You [the Father] have crowned him with glory and honor, putting everything in subjection under his feet" [he is designated president by the Father]. Now in putting everything in subjection to him, he left nothing outside his control [as president he will have complete control over the affairs of this world]. At present, we do not yet see everything in subjection to him [he has not yet begun to fully exercise his reign]. (Heb. 2:7–8)

Currently, Christ is not using his powers to rule the world, restore nature, and heal our bodies. Instead, he is using his power to build his church. Through his disciples and the Holy Spirit he is continually gathering new members to add to his kingdom. Though Satan and his demonic army are continually opposing Christ during this process, he cannot prevent Christ from collecting those the Father has given to him (Matt. 16:17–18). Christ is gathering the elect and building his church despite demonic opposition. But the redeemed members of his kingdom remain in this fallen world. As children of the light in this dominion of darkness, we will continue to experience trials and tribulations until the day Christ subjects all things unto himself and takes office as the true God of this world.

That is not to say that our sovereign God is not currently involved in the affairs of this world. Sometimes God does, in fact, send an angel to free his imprisoned saints, as he did with Peter (Acts 12:7). Sometimes he does heal people. But often he does not intervene, as in the case of Peter's crucifixion, John the Baptist's beheading, as well as Paul's extended imprisonment and ultimate execution. Again, God is sovereign. He can orchestrate the affairs of his people in such a way that Satan's attacks work out for the good of those who love him. James says that we should count it all joy when we encounter trials of any kind, for this testing of our faith produces character and maturity (James 1:2–4).

As king, Christ wore a crown of thorns and was crucified. The members of his kingdom also carry a cross today. That is, until his reign begins when he rules from his throne in heaven and we will no longer carry a cross but will reign with him as he triumphs over evil. Neither Christ nor his body of believers will ever be persecuted again.

Daniel also pictures Christ as the Son of Man remaining in heaven with the Father as he is given dominion over this world:

> I saw in the night visions, and behold, with the clouds of heaven [a symbol of divine authority] there came one like a son of man [a divine being in heaven] and he came to the Ancient of Days [God the Father—in heaven] and was presented before him [in heaven]. And to him [Christ the son of man] was given dominion [over the earth from his position in heaven with the Father] and glory and a kingdom, that all peoples, nations, and languages [on the earth] should serve him; his dominion is an everlasting dominion, which shall not pass away, and his kingdom one that shall not be destroyed. (Dan. 7:13–14)

The designation "son of man" was one of Christ's favorite ways of describing himself when he was on this earth. It is used twenty-eight times in the gospel of Matthew alone. In Daniel, the "son of man" is a reference to a divine being remaining in heaven with God the Father (the Ancient of Days) when his reign over this earth begins. Nowhere in Daniel does the prophet portray the Son of Man coming to this earth with his Father to exercise his reign. Instead, the Father gives the Son his earthly kingdom while both of them remain in heaven.

This interaction between the Father and the Son takes place in heaven when it is determined by the Father that it is time for the Son of Man to rule the world—which is why Christ teaches that after the incarnation and ascension "from now on the Son of Man shall be seated at the right hand of the power of God [the Father in heaven]" (Luke 22:69).

John also foresees the day when Christ will use his immeasurable power to rule this world: "And the twenty-four elders who sit on their thrones before God fell on their faces and worshiped God, saying, 'We give thanks to you, Lord God Almighty, who is and who was, [a divine, eternal being] for *you have taken your great power and begun to reign*'" (Rev. 11:16–17). Christ may have the divine power to rule this world, but it is only when Christ takes his power and finally uses it that the Son's kingdom is established on earth. And with Satan the false god of this world removed and Christ using his great power to rule, then, and only then, "the kingdom of the world has become the kingdom of our Lord and of his Christ" (Rev. 11:15). This matches beautifully with Daniel's vision of the day when the Son of Man is given dominion and glory and a kingdom by the Father (the Ancient of Days) "that all peoples, nations, and languages should serve him."

Christ could easily put an end to the persecution of his saints and the misery and sickness in this world. But he is waiting on the Father to finish gathering into his kingdom his elect from all "peoples, nations, and languages."

Waiting on the Father

Understanding how the triune God operates in relation to the kingdom of God is rarely discussed, yet it is essential to understanding the prophetic future. The Son has been waiting on the Father who has established the times when the Son will take over as King of this world and reestablish his complete authority over his Genesis creation.

Before Christ ascended to his throne in heaven to rejoin the Father, the disciples asked Jesus: "'Lord, will you at this time restore the kingdom to Israel?' He said to them, 'It is not for you to know times or seasons that *the Father has fixed by his own authority*'" (Acts 1:6–7). Within the Trinity, the Father has the authority to determine *when* the Son's reign will begin. It is only a matter of time before the Father says the seven-year Tribulation will begin, and at its end, Christ will begin to fully exercise his office as Lord of Israel and this world.

Quoting from a psalm of David, Jesus told his listeners: "The Lord [the Father] said to my Lord [Christ], Sit at my right hand [the Father's right hand], until I [the Father] put your [Christ's] enemies under your feet" (Matt. 22:44). This important relationship between the Father and the Son, as it relates to the Son's messianic kingdom, can be found throughout the New Testament. Hebrews says, "But when Christ had offered for all time a single sacrifice for sins, he sat down at the right hand of God, *waiting* [on the Father] from that time until his enemies should be made a footstool for his feet" (Heb. 10:12–13). After his ascension, Christ sat down at the Father's right hand in heaven and is waiting on the Father to decide the time for him to *exercise* his reign as King of the world when the Father will put all his enemies under his feet. It is only a matter of time, which the Father controls, for the Tribulation to begin and end and then for Christ to reign in the restoration. Christ is currently waiting until the Father says it is time for him to be inaugurated as Lord and King of this world.

The story of King Saul and David is a good illustration of this concept. When King Saul disobeyed God, the kingdom of Israel was given to David, a man after God's own heart (1 Sam. 13:8–14). Subsequently, Samuel found young David as a shepherd in Bethlehem and anointed him as the king of Israel (1 Sam. 16:13). There was one problem—Saul was still ruling as king at the same time David was anointed king. As a result, although David was the anointed king, he did not rule as king at that time. He had to *wait* until God removed Saul as king of Israel.

In the meantime, Saul persecuted, hounded, and harassed David for years. One day as Saul was pursuing him, David and his small army caught Saul and his men off guard and asleep. One of David's men wanted to take the opportunity to kill Saul, so David could begin his reign. But David said, "'Do not destroy him, for who can put out his hand against the LORD's anointed and be guiltless?' And David said, 'As the LORD lives, the LORD will strike him, or his day will come to die, or he will go down into battle and perish'" (1 Sam. 26:9–10).

Even though David knew God had anointed him to rule over Israel, he waited on the Lord to set the time when Saul would be removed, and only then would it be his time to rule. David refused to set the time of his reign by killing Saul when he had the opportunity. Eventually, the Lord decided it was time for Saul's reign to come to an end, and he was killed in battle. David, the anointed one, then began his reign as king.

The prophets foretold a day when out of Bethlehem will come a son of David, whose origins are from eternity, who will sit on the throne of David and establish a kingdom in Israel and rule the whole world with justice and righteousness (Mic. 5:2–5; Isa. 9:6–7). The word *Messiah* actually means the "anointed one." But there is one problem. Satan remains the current ruler of this world and continues to persecute and harass Christ and his followers, even though Christ has been anointed king. The world remains Satan's dominion.

The day will come, however, when the Father will determine it is time for Satan to be removed, and then the anointed Christ, the son of David, will *stand* and use his great power to begin his rightful reign over this world. Just as David, the anointed king of Israel, waited on God to remove Saul so his reign could begin, so, too, Christ, the anointed king of Israel and the world, is waiting on God the Father to remove Satan so his reign can begin.

The "Coming" of His Reign

The beginning of the restoration is not the second coming of Christ to this earth, but it is the coming of the full exercise of his reign over this earth from his throne in heaven. The figurative use of the word *coming* to describe Christ's future reign over this world has confused many theologians, particularly premillennialists who often take the word literally in that Christ does come to this earth a second time to reign over it. But the biblical use of the word *coming* to describe the exercise of his kingship over Israel without his physical presence is well established in the Scriptures.

This manner of coming can be found in Exodus where the Jewish captivity in Egypt represents our captivity in Satan's evil dominion. After centuries of slavery and oppression, God comes down and rules with authority and power through Moses as he leads the Israelites out of Egypt into the Promised Land: "Then the LORD said, 'I have surely seen the affliction of my people who are in Egypt and have heard their cry because of their taskmasters. I know their sufferings, and *I have come down* to deliver them out of the hand of the Egyptians and to bring them up out of that land to a good and broad land . . .'" (Exod. 3:7–8). But the expression "I have come down" does not mean God literally descended to this earth and operated through an incarnation of a human body to liberate his people in Egypt and take them into the Promised Land. Rather, the Lord stayed in heaven and used Moses as his means to exercise his rule and liberate his people.

In the millennium Christ will use resurrected men to sit on human thrones in his coming reign. Thus, the expression "they reigned with Christ for a thousand years" can easily be understood as a time when the Lord from on high comes down in supernatural power to implement his will on this earth through his people and delivers us from Satan's dominion and places us on the renewed earth.

Moses and the Israelites experienced firsthand this power of the right hand of the Almighty Lord in heaven as God delivered his people out of Egyptian bondage and took them to the Promised Land. In the song of Moses, the Israelites recognized what could be accomplished from God's right hand in heaven:

Then Moses and the people of Israel sang this song to the LORD, saying, "I will sing to the LORD, for he has triumphed gloriously; . . . Pharaoh's chariots and his host he cast into the sea, and his chosen officers were sunk in the Red Sea. The floods covered them; they went down into the depths like a stone. Your right hand, O LORD, glorious in power, your right hand, O LORD, shatters the enemy [supernatural power from heaven]. In the greatness of your majesty you overthrow your adversaries; you send out your fury; it consumes them like stubble. At the blast of your nostrils the waters piled up [figure of speech to describe the LORD in battle]; . . . You stretched out your right hand; the earth swallowed them. . . . You will bring them in and plant them on your own mountain, the place, O LORD, which you have made for your abode, the sanctuary, O Lord, which your hands have established. The LORD will reign forever and ever. (Exod. 15:1–18)

The Lord did not have to physically come down to this earth to fight alongside Moses to rescue his people and plant them in the Promised Land. Rather, he accomplished their deliverance through his supernatural glorious power from his right hand in heaven. Similarly, the 1,000-year restoration is the coming of his reign over this earth. The redeemer "comes to Zion," just as he came to Moses and the Israelites, delivering them from Pharaoh's oppressive dominion into the Promised Land. But during the restoration or regeneration of this Genesis creation, the Promised Land will be the long-awaited messianic kingdom that extends from Israel throughout the world.

God is more than capable of ruling this world through his use of supernatural power while he remains on his throne in heaven. The Old Testament pattern of God *dwelling* with his people through the temple demonstrates how God can come to his people without coming in a physical body. The land of Palestine was, in effect, a divine sanctuary for God with his people, but that does not mean the Lord God was physically present on this earth in order to be with them and rule over them. God is even described as walking among his people: "I will make my dwelling among you, and my soul shall not abhor you. And I will walk among you and will be your God, and you shall be my people" (Lev. 26:11–12). God did not literally walk among them and dwell with them as he did during the incarnation.

When the prophets do speak of a literal coming, such as Christ's first coming and incarnation, they are very explicit in describing a real human being on this earth: "Rejoice greatly, O daughter of Zion! Shout aloud, O daughter of Jerusalem! behold, your king is coming to you; righteous and having salvation is he, humble and mounted on a donkey" (Zech. 9:9). This coming of the king of Israel is a description of a real person riding on a real donkey into the real city of Jerusalem.

Isaiah also gives us a graphic portrayal of an actual person on this earth during his first coming:

For he grew up before him like a young plant, and like a root out of dry ground; he had no form or majesty that we should look at him, and no beauty that we should desire him [had a real appearance as a man that was neither majestic nor particularly handsome] (53:2). As many were astonished at you—his appearance was so marred, beyond human semblance, and his form beyond that of the children of mankind (52:14). And they made his grave with the wicked and with a rich man in his death, although he had done no violence, and there was no deceit in his mouth (53:9).

This prophetic vision of the Messiah's first coming and crucifixion is one of a real human being on this earth—one who is severely beaten, experiences death, and is buried in a rich man's grave. But the coming of his messianic *reign*, on the other hand, is phrased in language and figures of speech identical with those used by Moses and the prophets to speak of his coming rule over Israel when they were delivered into the Promised Land. He ruled them from his throne in heaven with the temple functioning as his dwelling place on earth. This explains why Ezekiel sees yet another temple and royal dwelling place in the future messianic kingdom (Ezek. 40—43).

The Old Testament uses many figures of speech common to the ancient world to describe God's use of supernatural power and authority over this world from his throne in heaven. The prophet Zechariah, for example, uses many figures of speech, such as, "On that day there shall be a fountain opened for the house of David and the inhabitants of Jerusalem, to cleanse them from sin and uncleanness" (Zech. 13:1). Does this mean that a real water fountain will be created to cleanse them from sin and uncleanness? There is no reason to interpret these verses in a hyper-literal manner for them to convey real eschatological changes in the world.

Below is a quote from an e-mail I received from Dr. Larry Walker (one of the translators of the NIV Bible), who describes the nature of how language was used by many of the biblical authors:

After working on Bible translation (NIV) since 1968 I became much more informed on how language works and how non-literal does not mean less accurate! For example, the unusual language of "cloud riding," which is not necessarily literal, was used in the ancient Near East for depicting victory and triumph. The Canaanite deity Baal is depicted this way not only because he is a storm god but also because he "prevails," an expression used in typical Hebrew parallelism with his cloud riding. The Hebrew psalmist makes use of this non-literal cloud-riding imagery when he applies to Jehovah what had earlier been used in Canaanite of Baal (cf. Ps 68:4). When the LORD came to Egypt in judgment riding on a cloud (Isa 19:1), no one saw him; and when the Lord Christ came upon Jerusalem in judgment in 70 AD no one saw him physically. The attempt to make such language always literal has obscured the meaning behind the texts. The same is true of the collapsing cosmos language (sun, moon, stars; cf. Gen 1:16) which has not been understood because of attempts to make it literal when it often refers to the collapse of other "ruling" or "governing" bodies. . . . In Gen 1:16 we are told that God made the sun and moon to "govern" or rule over. Then in Gen 37:5 we read about Joseph's strange dream and in vss. 9-10 his brothers seem to understand the ruling properties of the heavenly bodies. Later in the Bible, we can understand that the darkening and falling of these heavenly bodies signals the collapse of government.[1]

The Old Testament is full of this type of imagery in which the Lord comes in power to rule and govern this earth without physically coming to this earth. Zechariah uses some of the same phrasing that Moses used to describe the coming of the Lord to establish his kingdom:

> Then the LORD will go out and fight against those nations as when he fights on a day of battle [as he did with Moses and Joshua]. On that day his feet shall stand on the Mount of Olives that lies before Jerusalem on the east, and the Mount of Olives shall be split in two from east to west by a very wide valley, so that one half of the Mount shall move northward, and the other half southward. . . . Then the LORD my God will come, and all the holy ones with him. . . . On that day living waters shall flow out from Jerusalem, half of them to the eastern sea and half of them to the western sea. . . . *And the LORD will be king over all the earth.* . . . Jerusalem shall dwell in security. (Zech. 14:3–11)

The Lord will come and be king over all the earth during the messianic kingdom, but this does not mean that he and his angels will physically reside on this earth any more than they physically resided with Moses when the Lord came down to deliver the Israelites into the Promised Land. As the song of Moses proclaims, the Lord can rule from heaven:

> This is the blessing with which Moses the man of God blessed the people of Israel before his death. He said, "The LORD came from Sinai and dawned from Seir upon us; he shone forth from Mount Paran; he came from the ten thousands of holy ones, with flaming fire at his right hand. Yes, he loved his people, all his holy ones were in his hand; so they followed in your steps, receiving direction from you, when Moses commanded us a law, as a possession for the assembly of Jacob. Thus the LORD became king in Jeshurun, when the heads of the people were gathered, all the tribes of Israel together. (Deut. 33:1–5)

This is yet another example of the Old Testament use of figures of speech to describe the Lord's supernatural intervention. This does not mean that the

---

[1] Larry L. Walker, retired seminary professor of Semitic languages (e-mail message to author, March 12, 2009).

Lord and his ten thousands of holy ones literally came and physically appeared to them in the Sinai and resided on the earth.

Furthermore, the expression "he came with ten thousand of holy ones" to liberate his people and become their king in the Promised Land is almost identical to the language Zechariah uses when he says, "The LORD my God will come, and *all the holy ones with him*" in order to establish the messianic kingdom. Premillennialists construe Zechariah's words to mean that the Messiah literally comes down to this earth. But in the historical record in Deuteronomy, the Lord did not literally come to this earth to rule as king.

Zechariah is simply speaking of the coming of his reign through the implementation of his supernatural power, much like Moses spoke of the Lord coming from Sinai to save his people through the use of supernatural power. The Lord was able to manage this victory and redemption of his people from his throne in heaven and become their king without physically appearing to the Israelites.

These verses in Zechariah picture Christ setting his foot down on the Mount of Olives. Premillennialists interpret this verse in a hyper-literal fashion to mean Christ physically returns to this earth to exercise his reign with the Mount of Olives being his initial landing spot. But, as has been previously established concerning the Exodus of the Jews from Egypt, the expression "I have come down" can also figuratively describe the exercise of God's power, authority, and reign from heaven over the affairs of man.

A more logical interpretation, in light of how this expression is used in the Old Testament, as well as what the rest of the New Testament teaches about Christ's second coming on the last day when the earth is destroyed, is that this is a figurative expression of Christ taking a stand to destroy the armies that come against Jerusalem and overthrow the reign of Satan.

Even today, we use the expression "put your foot down" figuratively to mean that you have had enough of unruly conduct and are using your authority to establish order. Zechariah is using a similar metaphor to describe Christ putting his foot down on the Mount of Olives when he has had enough of ungodly conduct and destroys the Antichrist, the false prophet, and the armies surrounding Jerusalem in order to establish a government of peace and justice in this world.

In Revelation, John uses other metaphors to describe how Satan is bound with a great chain when, as the prophets predict, Christ begins to make his enemies a "footstool for his feet" from his throne in heaven at his Father's right hand. Satan is not literally bound by a steel chain, and the Father does not literally have a "right hand." Nor do Christ's enemies literally become a footstool for Christ's feet. Likewise, the expression "standing on the Mount of Olives" does not have to be interpreted in a hyper-literal manner for a literal restoration to take place. John speaks of a day when Satan is bound and the Lord will use his great power to rule over his kingdom from his supernatural throne in heaven.

The expression "putting all things under one's feet" (Ps. 8:6) is a similar figure of speech of the ancient Near East for the exercise of kingly authority (cf. Josh. 10:24; 1 Kings 5:3). Likewise, Zechariah's statements "his feet will stand on the Mount of Olives" when a "fountain" is opened for the inhabitants of Jerusalem can similarly be interpreted as when the Lord fights Israel's enemies with supernatural power and then exercises his divine Kingship over Zion and the rest of the world when the world becomes a "footstool for his feet."

The expression in Zechariah 14:3 "as he fights on a day of battle" is similar to the numerous times he fought alongside Israel during their battles against the Pharaoh's armies and the Promised Land's inhabitants. Moses, Joshua, David, and Solomon knew all too well the importance of the Lord fighting with them in battle. But this does not mean the Lord appeared on the earth, in their presence, with weapons of war, and engaged in field combat alongside them. Zechariah's use of figurative language is a common Old Testament practice of using anthropomorphisms to describe the interaction of God's supernatural world with this natural world. This is standard Old Testament motif.

Because the New Testament never mentions the physical return of Christ to this earth, premillennialists are forced to look for figures of speech in the Old Testament to which they can apply a hyper-literal interpretation to support their assertion that the Messiah physically comes to this earth again as he did through the virgin birth. During the incarnation, Christ rode a donkey when he entered Jerusalem to be crucified. But when he begins his kingship over this world, he will be riding a white horse in the celestial sphere as he makes war against the armies of the Antichrist. Out of his mouth will come a "sharp sword with which to strike down the nations." Does anyone believe a sword will literally come out of his mouth? Hopefully not. Likewise, the vision of Christ riding on a white horse is a figurative description of Christ engaging the forces of evil at the same time that he calls down fire from heaven to destroy the Antichrist and his armies at the end of the Tribulation. He can simply rule over this world from the right hand of God when the world's earthly powers are made a "footstool for his feet."

Having said this, there are examples of Christ who has ascended to heaven briefly touching the natural world in a supernatural manner. The resurrected and ascended Christ appeared to Paul at his conversion, but Paul only got a glimpse of his glory, and it was not a "second coming" appearance of Christ. Paul was blinded by the glory of the risen Lord and had to be miraculously healed.

Zechariah may be describing a similar momentary supernatural touching of the Mount of Olives by the risen and glorified Lord to instantly regenerate the earth. It would not surprise me if the risen Christ touches the Mount of Olives in a manner similar to the way he appeared to Paul to cause the immediate and instantaneous regeneration of this Genesis creation to begin the restoration. This could explain some of the miraculous physical changes described by Zechariah when Christ sets his foot down on the Mount of Olives (cf. Zech. 14).

But the glorified Christ does not have to be on this earth to accomplish miraculous things. He can easily act from any distance or from his throne in heaven to implement God's will on this earth. Consider the faith and experience of the centurion who had a paralyzed servant at home and went to Jesus and said, "Lord, I am not worthy to have you come under my roof, but *only say the word*, and my servant will be healed" (Matt. 8:8). The centurion understood that Jesus did not have to physically go to his home for the servant to be healed. During the millennium, Christ can simply say the word from heaven, and the earth will be regenerated and healed. Christ can easily impose his Father's will on this earth as it is in heaven from his throne in heaven.

Consider the power Jesus displayed when he and the disciples were in a boat during a storm and Christ calmed the sea: "He said to them, 'Where is your faith?' And they were afraid, and they marveled, saying to one another, 'Who then is this, that he commands even winds and water, and they obey him?'" (Luke 8:25). The "who" is God incarnate, the Son of God, who now sits at the Father's side in heaven. The "who" is the Creator of the world. As John says, "He was in the beginning with God. All things were made through him, and without him was not any thing made that was made" (John 1:2–3). If Christ, as God the Creator, could miraculously calm a terrible storm while he was on this earth, then surely we should have the faith to know that he can miraculously change and cure this world from his position in heaven during his millennial reign.

One can believe in a *literal* 1,000-year reign of Christ by realizing that Christ can establish his millennial kingdom from his throne in heaven. One only needs a faith like the centurion's. The Messiah has already come into this world. He then ascended to the right hand of the Father in heaven with all authority and power given to him. The Father has promised to give the Son the dominion of the world at a time and date that he has set. When the Father says it is time, then Satan will be bound and Christ will exercise his reign over this world from heaven at the right hand of the Father.

Another text from Zechariah used by premillennialists as further proof of a physical return of Christ to this earth is: "And I will pour out on the house of David and the inhabitants of Jerusalem a spirit of grace and pleas for mercy, so that, when they look on me, on him whom they have pierced, they shall mourn for him, as one mourns for an only child, and weep bitterly over him, as one weeps over a firstborn" (Zech. 12:10). Premillennialists interpret this to mean that the Jews will repent when they see Christ on this earth when he comes again, and that they will be able to see the marks on his body from the crucifixion, much as Thomas saw him.

But this is not too different from what Jesus taught the disciples about the "vision" of faith without actually seeing him:

> Then he said to Thomas, "Put your finger here, and see my hands; and put out your hand, and place it in my side. Do not disbelieve, but believe." Thomas answered him, "My Lord and my God!" Jesus said to him, "Have you believed because you have seen me? *Blessed are those who have not seen and yet have believed.*" (John 20:27–29)

I have not physically seen the marks of Christ's risen body as Thomas did, but by faith I have indeed seen him and believe in him. One does not have to physically see the risen Lord and his marks of crucifixion to repent and mourn over his death and resurrection for us.

One day "the house of David and the residents of Jerusalem" will also have faith and will see the risen Lord, and there will be a great revival among the Jews. But Christ does not have to physically appear to them as he did to Thomas. Christ's pierced body can be seen through the eyes of faith: "Blessed are those who have not seen and yet have believed." Christ was referring to believers who could see the truth with their spiritual eyes and to unbelievers who could not see because their spiritual eyes were blind.

Christ told the disciples that by seeing him, they had seen the Father even though they did not physically "see" the Father. Jesus told Philip and the disciples: "I am the way, and the truth, and the life. No one comes to the Father except through me. If you had known me, you would have known my Father also. From now on you do know him and have seen him" (John 14:6–7). Did Philip actually see the Father? No, Christ readily admits that these were figures of speech: "I have said these things to you in figures of speech" (John 16:25).

Zechariah foresaw a day when the household of Israel will experience a "spirit of grace and pleas for mercy, so that, when they look on me, on him whom they have pierced, they shall mourn for him." He was speaking of a future day of nationwide repentance when the Jewish people finally open their spiritual eyes to see that their Messiah has indeed already come and has died for them. This does not have to mean that Christ must physically appear before them for them to believe and repent anymore than he does for believers today. This is not a proof text for Christ's physical return to this earth whereby the repentant Jews will visibly see and touch the marks of his crucifixion as Thomas did. Nor am I "spiritualizing" these verses any more than Christ was "spiritualizing" words when he told Philip he had "seen" the Father. We *can* see Christ and his Father through the eyes of faith.

Of course, there will be a day at the end of the world when Christ will come again, appear in the sky, and everyone who has ever lived will see him. Those who are alive at the time will see him, and unbelievers in Hades will be resurrected at the general resurrection of all men to see him and then face the Great White Throne judgment. John says, "Behold, he is coming with the clouds, and every eye will see him, even those who pierced him, and all tribes of the earth will wail on account of him. Even so. Amen. 'I am the Alpha and the Omega,' says the Lord God, 'who is and who was and who is to come, the Almighty'" (Rev.1:7–8). This is describing the Omega or end of the world and Judgment Day at the Great White Throne judgment. And on this day even unbelievers of the first century who witnessed his crucifixion will see him when they are raised up from Hades to face Christ in judgment.

To better understand how the Old Testament prophets could speak of the "coming" of the Messiah to reign over this world without Christ physically returning to the world, consider the following analogy. Assume a group of al-Qaeda terrorists kidnapped the U.S. ambassador to Afghanistan and took him to one of their hidden training camps. Suppose that the ambassador was able to quickly and secretly use his cellphone to contact and inform the president of the United States, and the president told him: "Rest assured, I will come and rescue you, and the terrorists will have hell to pay." Does this mean that the president will literally suit up in commando gear and carry out the mission himself? Probably not. Instead, when the hideout is discovered and the time is right, he will order an elite commando unit to go in under the cover of darkness and rescue the ambassador. Then, I imagine he will order the U.S. Air Force to rain down a firestorm of destruction on the training camp. But the president orchestrates the mission of "his coming" to rescue the ambassador and destroy his enemies without leaving the Oval Office at the White House. Likewise, Christ, as the all-powerful president of this world, can execute his will on this earth from his throne in heaven without physically coming to this earth. The Deliverer can rescue his people from his divine office in heaven.

Let's take this illustration one step further. Assume that the ambassador is a close friend of the president. After the rescue, the president calls the ambassador and informs him that after his term in office as president is over, he will come and pick him up in his private jet, and they will celebrate his safe return at a resort in Bermuda, far from all the cares of the world. In this case, the president does plan on physically "coming to pick him up" to take him to be with himself on the island paradise. This is similar to Christ's second coming. Christ physically "comes" and take us to be with him in his Father's heavenly paradise.

But to administer justice in Afghanistan, all the president had to do was say the word from the Oval Office as commander-in-chief; his army commandos would accomplish the mission for him. In similar fashion,

Christ from his throne in heaven at the right hand of the Father (his divine Oval Office) can easily destroy his enemies on this earth and accomplish his mission of justice and peace in this world without physically coming back to this earth. Then, once that 1,000-year mission is accomplished, he will indeed come back to take those who really know him to his Father's heavenly paradise for an eternal celebration.

This analogy between a human leader and the Son of God breaks down, however. What if the terrorists had killed the U.S. ambassador before the president was able to send his commandos to rescue him? There would be nothing the president could do to right the situation. His friend would be dead. But a supernatural "president" and Creator with the power of resurrection at his disposal could easily rectify the situation and deliver his dead friend into his earthly paradise. The power of resurrection changes everything. We enter into the kingdom of God the moment of our conversion, and we become ambassadors of Christ. But if we die before Christ begins his earthly reign, we can rest assured that we will still inherit the regenerated earth because of the first resurrection.

The First Resurrection

This brings us to the crucial question: What is the first resurrection, and who came to life to reign with Christ on this earth for a thousand years? The Bible defines several types of resurrections, so let's start by eliminating certain types of resurrections as possibilities. The rapture of the saints is always associated with Christ's second coming on Judgment Day when the current heavens and earth are destroyed, and our bodies are transformed into immortal bodies and taken to the eternal kingdom of heaven. Since the beginning of the millennium is not the actual second coming of Christ on the last day and its associated rapture of the saints, the first resurrection cannot be the resurrection of the immortal bodies of the saints. It must be another kind of resurrection.

The Bible speaks of a resurrection of the spirits of believers, both at conversion when we are raised from the dead spiritually (Rom. 6:3–4), as well as when our bodies die and our spirits are raised up to heaven while our bodies sleep in the dust of the earth (Matt. 22:31–32; Heb. 12:1, 23). These are resurrections of the spirits of the saints but not of their bodies. John was already well aware that the departed saints have risen to be with the Lord and refers to them singing and worshiping in heaven: "After this I heard what seemed to be the loud voice of a great *multitude in heaven*, crying out, 'Hallelujah! Salvation and glory and power belong to our God'" (Rev. 19:1). He portrays these departed spirits of the saints as riding out of heaven on white horses with Christ at the end of the Tribulation (Rev. 19:14). Since the first resurrection is not a resurrection of just the spirits of the saints or the rapture of the bodies of the saints, that leaves one alternative. The first resurrection mentioned by John must be a resurrection of a natural Adamic body adapted to this regenerated Genesis creation.

When trying to understand John's vision, it is critical to remember the following prophecy in Isaiah 65 in which the Son's messianic kingdom on this earth is characterized by marriage and reproduction:

> I will rejoice in Jerusalem and be glad in my people; no more shall be heard in it the sound of weeping and the cry of distress. No more shall there be in it *an infant* who lives but a few days, or an old man who does not fill out his days, for the young man shall die a hundred years old, and the sinner a hundred years old shall be accursed. They shall build houses and inhabit them; they shall plant vineyards and eat their fruit. They shall not build and another inhabit; they shall not plant and another eat; for like the days of a tree shall the days of my people be, and my chosen shall long enjoy the work of their hands. They shall not labor in vain *or bear children* for calamity, for they shall be the offspring of the blessed of the LORD, and *their descendants* with them. Before they call I will answer; while they are yet speaking I will hear. (Isa. 65:19–24)

Isaiah describes the people of God in the messianic kingdom as experiencing marriage and reproduction in an Adamic paradise.

Therefore, the first resurrection described by John in Revelation 20 must be a resurrection of a natural body that is in the Adamic order of being—as in the case of Lazarus, who could have married and had children after his resurrection. The messianic kingdom is by definition a restoration of the Adamic order of being when this Genesis creation is regenerated into a restored Edenic creation by its Creator.

Lazarus was brought back to life in an unregenerate world still under God's curse and still under Satan's dominion. The Pharisees were conspiring to have him killed because of the attention his resurrection was bringing to Christ (John 12:10). He likely did not live many more years in this fallen world, and his second opportunity at life was probably not much more pleasant than the first. But the circumstances for Lazarus and all the departed saints will be vastly different after the "first resurrection" at the beginning of the millennium because Satan will be bound, Christ will be governing the world, and the Adamic creation will be regenerated to an Edenic condition.

The lesson Jesus was trying to teach Martha, Lazarus's grieving sister, was that not only does he have the power and authority to resurrect Lazarus on the last day to take him to heaven, but he also has the power to resurrect the saints into restored natural bodies at his will and command, which serves as further proof that he will rapture him on the last day:

Jesus said to her [Martha], "Your brother will rise again." Martha said to him, "I know that he will rise again in the resurrection on the last day" [into an immortal body]. Jesus said to her, "I am the resurrection and the life. Whoever believes in me, though he die, yet shall he live, and everyone who lives and believes in me shall never die [believers only go to sleep]. Do you believe this?" She said to him, "Yes, Lord; I believe that you are the Christ, the Son of God, who is coming into the world." (John 11:23–27)

After being dead for four days, Lazarus would have experienced significant decay. Yet, with a shout and command, Christ resurrected his natural body, restoring him to life and health. If Christ could raise a believer like Lazarus from the dead while he was on this earth, he can easily do so on a much greater scale when he reigns from heaven.

Christ refers to the final resurrection on Judgment Day:

For as the Father raises the dead and gives them life, so also the Son gives life to whom he will. . . . Do not marvel at this, for an hour is coming when all who are in the tombs will hear his voice and come out, those who have done good to the resurrection of life, and those who have done evil to the resurrection of judgment [the general resurrection at the Great White Throne judgment]." (John 5:21–29)

In referencing "an hour is coming," Christ is alluding to the final resurrection on the last day when the righteous, "those who have done good," will be resurrected, transformed, and taken to heaven at the same time that the bodies of unbelievers, "those who have done evil," are resurrected to face judgment (Rev. 20:11–15).

That does not, however, preclude a resurrection of the natural bodies of believers before the last day as the resurrection of Lazarus demonstrates. Everyone who dies as a believer in Christ is merely asleep in the Lord and can therefore hear his voice now, as well as on the last day, Judgment Day. Jesus called out Lazarus's name and, as a believer, Lazarus could hear Jesus' voice and came back to life in a natural body. Christ can raise anyone who can hear his voice from the dead whenever he wishes. And he can also resurrect his people en masse if he so chooses.

Lazarus was not the only one to experience a resurrection of the mortal body during Christ's first coming. There was the ruler's twelve-year-old daughter (Mark 5:39–41), a widower's only son (Luke 7:12–15), and possibly several others. Matthew records that after Jesus died on the cross and was raised from the dead, many saints were resurrected back into mortal bodies:

And Jesus cried out again with a loud voice and yielded up his spirit. And behold, the curtain of the temple was torn in two, from top to bottom. And the earth shook, and the rocks were split. The *tombs also were opened. And many bodies of the saints who had fallen asleep were raised, and coming out of the tombs* after his resurrection they went into the holy city and appeared to many. (Matt. 27:50–53)

The question is not whether God is *capable* of resurrecting saints into mortal bodies, but whether it is his expressed *will* to do so on a massive scale in the future.

The apostle John, who witnessed Lazarus's resurrection, envisioned just such a day (Rev. 20:1–4) when believers like Lazarus will hear Christ calling them to life again in the first resurrection, in an hour that "is now here," into natural bodies. When Christ begins his reign from heaven at the right hand of the Father, he will bring back to life those whom he calls out to live by simply waking them up from their sleep:

> Also I saw the souls of those who had been beheaded for the testimony of Jesus and for the word of God, and who had not worshiped the beast or its image and had not received its mark on their foreheads or their hands. They came to life and reigned with Christ for a thousand years. The rest of the dead [unbelievers] did not come to life until the thousand years were ended. This is the first resurrection. Blessed and holy is the one who shares in the first resurrection! Over such the second death [hell] has no power, but they will be priests of God and of Christ, and they will reign with him for a thousand years. (Rev. 20:4–6)

John makes it clear that only the blessed and holy believers are resurrected in order to experience the restored earth during Christ's reign. Unbelievers, on the other hand, remain in Hades and will experience the final resurrection on Judgment Day when they experience the "second death."

The phrase "the second death has no power" over these resurrected believers does not mean these saints are in their immortal bodies. Rather, the second death is a reference to the eternal lake of fire or hell, which occurs for unbelievers on the last day after the earth and sky disappear and after the final judgment, the Great White Throne judgment: "Then Death and Hades were thrown into the lake of fire. This is the *second death*, the lake of fire. And if anyone's name was not found written in the book of life, he was thrown into the lake of fire" (Rev. 20:14–15).

John is simply saying that the joy of experiencing the first resurrection is for believers only and, as the eternal children of God, they will never experience the second death. There is no point in rewarding the departed proud with the inheritance of the earth. Only the meek shall inherit the earth through the first resurrection.

In contrast to those blessed and holy saints who are resurrected and experience the restoration are the unbelievers: "The rest of the dead did not come to life until the thousand years were ended" (Rev. 20:5). As unrepentant unbelievers, they are not blessed and holy; they experience one mortal death and are then held in Hades until they experience the final resurrection after the thousand years to face the Great White Throne judgment and, subsequently, the second death. During the restoration, their departed spirits remain waiting in Hades. John is saying that those who experience the first resurrection are saints, not unbelievers and, as such, they will never face hell or the second death because their names are written in the book of life.

The First Resurrection Includes All the Saints

John explicitly states that the saints who get to experience the first resurrection are those who had not worshiped the beast and were martyred during the Tribulation: "Also I saw the souls of those who had been beheaded for the testimony of Jesus . . . who had not worshiped the beast or its image . . . They *came to life* and reigned with Christ for a thousand years" (Rev. 20:4). There is no mention of other saints from other time periods. John may have emphasized this specific group to give those who have to experience the terrible Tribulation confidence that they will experience the joy of the restoration as compensation for the suffering and martyrdom they will endure. It is because of the certainty of this joy set before them that they will be able to endure the Antichrist's reign of terror.

But what about believers who lived and died before the Tribulation, including Old Testament saints? What about the departed disciples who left everything to follow Christ? John may specify a particular group of martyrs, but this does not preclude others. For instance, he does not say, "And *only* those martyred in the great tribulation will experience the first resurrection."

It is a fair extrapolation to assume that all deceased saints—from the time of Abel to Abraham to Peter and up to and through the Tribulation—will be resurrected into restored, natural Adamic bodies to inherit the earth during the 1,000-year restoration. There is biblical evidence to support this interpretation. Earlier in Revelation, before describing the Tribulation, John teaches that *all the saints* Christ has ransomed from all time will experience the restoration:

> Worthy are you to take the scroll and to open its seals, for you were slain, and by your blood you ransomed people for God from every tribe and language and people and nation, and you have made them a kingdom and priests to our God, and they shall reign on the earth. (Rev. 5:9-10)

In this vision, Christ unseals the scroll before the Tribulation begins. Christ has already ransomed many people for God, and these people from all nations will be a part of the Son's kingdom and shall reign on the earth. The only way these departed saints can experience his earthly kingdom is for them to participate in the first resurrection. If this interpretation is correct, then John is teaching that all people ransomed by God—from Abel to those martyred during the Great Tribulation—will inherit Christ's millennial kingdom and shall reign with Christ through the first resurrection.

Daniel, like John, also specifically notes that the martyred saints of the Tribulation will experience the restoration when Christ overcomes the Antichrist: "As I looked, this horn *made war with the saints and prevailed over them*, until the Ancient of Days came, and judgment was given for the saints of the Most High, and *the time came when the saints possessed the kingdom*" (Dan. 7:21–22). Daniel foresaw that during the reign of the Antichrist, the saints will be martyred. But he also wrote that there will come a time when God will restore these martyred saints so that they will inherit the messianic kingdom on earth.

Later in his prophecy, however, Daniel, like John, seems to imply that *all saints* will take part in the messianic kingdom:

> But the court shall sit in judgment, and his dominion shall be taken away, to be consumed and destroyed to the end [the Tribulation comes to an end]. And the kingdom and the dominion and the greatness of the kingdoms under the whole heaven shall be given to the people of the *saints of the Most High*; their kingdom shall be an everlasting kingdom, and all dominions shall serve and obey them. (Dan. 7:26–27)

The expression "the people of the saints of the Most High" could easily refer to all saints of all time and not just those martyred during the Tribulation.

There is even more evidence in the Gospels. For example, Christ says to those in the first century: "Blessed are the meek [believers], for they shall inherit the earth" (Matt. 5:5). How can the departed meek of the first century who heard Christ's words "inherit the earth"? This promise can only be fulfilled if the meek who heard Christ are resurrected into natural bodies in order to inherit the earth in the restoration. If the meek die and are only resurrected on the last day to inherit heaven, they will not have inherited the earth as promised.

It also seems reasonable to assume that the meek from other time periods would be included in this promise. This seems to be a general truth and principle: "The meek [believers of all time] shall inherit the earth" just as all believers will inherit heaven. The meek shall inherit the earth through the first resurrection of their natural bodies, and then inherit the kingdom of heaven through the final resurrection of their immortal bodies.

The Resurrection of the Old Testament Saints

The Old Testament messianic prophecies were revealed primarily to a Jewish audience and believers who, like the disciples, were looking forward to the messianic kingdom on this earth. The prophecies were made specifically to them, and yet they were not fulfilled in their lifetimes. What about this Old Testament remnant who were faithful to the God of Abraham, Isaac, Jacob, and Moses? Will they also be a part of the first resurrection and experience the restoration? There is considerable biblical evidence that Abraham and other Jewish believers, the remnant, whose spirits are alive with God in heaven, will also enter into the earthly 1,000-year reign of Christ through the first resurrection. They, too, will be resurrected back into the Adamic flesh and will be able to marry and have children.

In the important prophecy of the valley of dry bones, Ezekiel graphically portrays this Adamic resurrection of the Jewish remnant where there is a regeneration of human bodies with bones, ligaments, muscles, and skin coming together to form natural bodies that go on to experience marriage and reproduction. At the time of Ezekiel's writing, the Jewish believers listening to the prophet were caught up in the brutal destruction of their nation by the Babylonians and had been carried away into exile with no hope of seeing their homeland again. They knew that most of their fellow believers and family members were dead, and that they, too, were going to die in captivity. Yet, here is Ezekiel promising them a return to a glorious Promised Land! But such a return was inconceivable in their lifetimes. What good is a promise of a restored Promised Land if they are all going to die in captivity? As a result, they felt hopeless and probably let Ezekiel know it: "Behold, they say, 'Our bones are dried up, and our hope is lost; we are clean cut off'" (Ezek. 37:11).

So how does God propose to bring the believing remnant into the promised messianic kingdom, those who have no chance of being alive when the restoration takes place? Through a resurrection of their natural bodies! The power of resurrection allows all these promises to come true for God's people. This important prophecy is lengthy, but note that the destiny of these Jewish believers after the resurrection of their human bodies is not heaven, but the land of Israel—an earthly kingdom:

> The hand of the LORD was upon me, and he brought me out in the Spirit of the LORD and set me down in the middle of the valley; it was full of bones. . . . Then he said to me, "Prophesy over these bones, and say to them, O dry bones, hear the word of the LORD. Thus, says the Lord GOD to these bones: Behold, I will cause breath to enter you, and you shall live. And I will lay sinews upon you, and will cause flesh to come upon you, and cover you with skin, and put breath in you, and you shall live, and you shall know that I am the LORD."
>
> So I prophesied as I was commanded. And as I prophesied, there was a sound, and behold, a rattling, and the bones came together, bone to its bone. And I looked, and behold, there were sinews on them, and flesh had come upon them, and skin had covered them. But there was no breath in them. Then he said to me, "Prophesy to the breath; prophesy, son of man, and say to the breath, Thus says the Lord GOD: Come from the four winds,

O breath, and breathe on these slain, that they may live." So I prophesied as he commanded me, and the breath came into them, and they lived and stood on their feet, an exceedingly great army.

Then he said to me, "Son of man, *these bones are the whole house of Israel.* Behold, they say, 'Our bones are dried up, and our hope is lost; we are clean cut off.' Therefore prophesy, and say to them, Thus says the Lord GOD: Behold, I will *open your graves and raise you from your graves,* O my people [the remnant]. And *I will bring you into the land of Israel* [an earthly kingdom]. And you shall know that I am the LORD, when I open your graves, and raise you from your graves, O my people. And I will put my Spirit within you, and you shall live, and *I will place you in your own land.* Then you shall know that I am the LORD; I have spoken, and I will do it, declares the LORD." (Ezek. 37:1–14)

The problem for those with no hope of living to see the promises of a restoration to the Promised Land fulfilled is solved by the supernatural power of resurrection of the natural bodies of the departed Jewish saints. Note the Genesis parallel of God breathing life into these reconstituted human bodies. God took dust and breathed life into Adam and he became a living being. He made Eve from one of his bones, a rib. In Ezekiel's vision, God takes bones from the deceased people of God, the "whole house of Israel," and re-creates Adamic bodies and breathes life into them so they can experience the messianic kingdom.

Ezekiel later describes these resurrected saints as being reproductive human beings who will see "their children and their children's children" (37:25). And the destiny of these resurrected saints is the restored earth, not heaven: "I will take the people of Israel from the nations among which they have gone, and will gather them from all around, and bring them to their own land" (37:21). These resurrected people are not in immortal bodies destined for heaven; rather, they are resurrected into human bodies destined for the earth, as a real nation in their own land. Ezekiel gave his people a graphic picture of an actual resurrection of their natural bodies, which would inhabit the natural world of the restored Promised Land.

Next, Ezekiel describes how the divided nation of Israel will be rejoined in this process with the resurrected King David as their ruler:

And I will make them one nation in the land, on the mountains of Israel. And one king shall be king over them all, and they shall be no longer two nations, and no longer divided into two kingdoms. . . . My servant David shall be king over them, and they shall all have one shepherd. . . . They shall dwell in the land that I gave to my servant Jacob, where your fathers lived. They and their children and their children's children shall dwell there forever, and David my servant shall be their prince forever. (Ezek. 37:22–25)

Since Christ is reigning over this world from heaven, the "servant David" may be King David who will be resurrected back into the mortal flesh in the Adamic order of being to serve as king over a reunited Israel.

Ezekiel describes this prince as being mortal, given in marriage, and having children, which excludes the possibility of the prince being Christ: "Thus says the Lord GOD: If the prince makes a gift *to any of his sons* as his inheritance, it shall belong to his sons. It is their property by inheritance" (Ezek. 46:16). King David is also given a specific piece of property: "What remains on both sides of the holy portion and of the property of the city shall belong to the prince. Extending from the 25,000 cubits of the holy portion to the east border, and westward from the 25,000 cubits to the west border, parallel to the tribal portions" (Ezek. 48:21).

Jeremiah, too, predicts a resurrected King David: "And it shall come to pass in that day, declares the LORD of hosts, that I will break his yoke from off your neck, and I will burst your bonds, and foreigners shall no more make a servant of him. But they shall serve the LORD their God and *David their king, whom I will raise up for them*" (Jer. 30:8-9; cf. Hos. 1:10-11; 3:4-5). The resurrected King David will probably sit on one of the thrones described by John and rule over Israel along with the resurrected disciples who will serve as twelve judges over the nation of Israel (Matt. 19:28-29).

These prophecies concerning the Jewish saints—some of whom endured captivity, exile, heartache, as well as death—can literally be fulfilled when God resurrects them to live in Christ's promised, earthly kingdom. These visions of an earthly paradise were not merely grandiose visions that some future generation would attain. Nor were they merely exaggerated visions of the eventual return to the land of Israel after their captivity in Babylon. Rather, through resurrection, these visions of a "Promised Land" likened to an Edenic paradise will actually come true for the saints who heard these prophecies from Ezekiel. Now, that is poetic justice.

Premillennialists do not interpret Ezekiel's prophecy literally, which is difficult to reconcile with their strong adherence to a literal interpretation of the Scriptures. They claim that Ezekiel's vision represents a figurative description of the future reunification of Israel and does not describe a future resurrection of the Jewish remnant from all the tribes of Israel. But this is wholly inconsistent with their hermeneutics.

The following quote by Douglas Kennard, a premillennial theologian, aptly represents this interpretation: "Additionally, Ezekiel's vision of the valley of dry bones is better seen as a metaphor describing Israel's national resurrection and reunion, rather than a personal resurrection of individuals (Ezek. 37)."[2] Perhaps the reason modern premillennialists interpret these

---

[2] Douglas Kennard, *Messiah Jesus: Christology in His Day and Ours* (New York: Peter Lang, 2008), 334.

verses metaphorically is that Ezekiel describes a resurrection of natural bodies given in marriage, which flatly contradicts their view of the raptured saints coming back to this earth in the millennial messianic kingdom. They claim to believe in a literal understanding of the messianic kingdom as envisioned by Ezekiel and the prophets, but they do not accept what the prophets teach about the nature of the resurrected bodies of the saints.

When the remnant of Old Testament saints from the various tribes of Israel come back to life, they will surely be reunited into one nation. Their dividing of the nation after Solomon's reign was an act of sin and rebellion. But Ezekiel is not just making a spiritual point about the future reunification of the nation during the messianic kingdom. He is describing the only way the promises of a messianic kingdom could be fulfilled for these people who were destined to die in captivity. They will be resurrected and will enter into the renewed Promised Land so that they will know that the Lord is indeed the Lord and is faithful to his promises.

Premillennialists claim to be advocates of the literal fulfillment of Old Testament messianic prophecies, but they do not believe in some of the most important prophecies that explain how the remnant of believing Israelites come to possess the messianic kingdom through a resurrection of their natural bodies. Because Ezekiel is describing a resurrection of departed Jewish saints into their natural bodies, premillennialists do not know what to make of Ezekiel's vision.

Arnold G. Fruchtenbaum, a prominent premillennial scholar, when writing about the resurrected King David, said the following:

> But directly under the Messianic King, having all authority over all Israel, will be the resurrected David, who is given both titles of king and prince. . . . Just as all the Gentile nations will have kings, so will Israel. The difference is that the Gentile kings will all have their natural bodies [survivors of the Tribulation], while David will have his resurrected body [raptured body]. There are several passages that speak of David as being king over Israel . . . Jeremiah 30:9 . . . Ezekiel 34:23–24 . . . Hosea 3:5 . . . In keeping with literal interpretation, it is best to take the text as it reads, meaning the literal David, who in his resurrected form [transformed immortal body], will function as king over Israel.[3]

The problem with Fruchtenbaum's literal interpretation is that he completely ignores the fact that Ezekiel describes this resurrected David as having a natural body, which is why he is depicted as having sons: "If the prince makes a gift to any of his sons as his inheritance, it shall belong to his sons. It is their property by inheritance" (Ezek. 46:16). How can David have

---

[3] Arnold G. Fruchtenbaum, *The Footsteps of the Messiah* (San Antonio: Ariel Press, 2004), 396-397.

children if he is in his raptured and glorified body? When it comes to Ezekiel's vision of the valley of dry bones, premillennialists are at a loss as to how to interpret it because they believe that the first resurrection is of the immortal bodies, not the natural bodies, of the risen saints.

Premillennialists often refer to the ante-Nicene millennialists to lend credence to their belief that the raptured saints return to this earth at the beginning of the millennium. But these early millennialists taught that Ezekiel and the prophets were describing a resurrection of the Adamic human body that would marry and reproduce—not the raptured body, which they believed occurred at the general resurrection on Judgment Day when the saints inherit the kingdom of heaven. Justin ties these prophecies in Ezekiel depicting an Adamic restoration with John's revelation:

> But I and others, who are right-minded Christians on all points, are assured that there will be a resurrection of the dead [the "first resurrection"] and a thousand years in Jerusalem, which will then be built, adorned, and enlarged, [as] the prophets Ezekiel and Isaiah and others declare and we cultivate piety, righteousness, philanthropy, faith, and hope, . . . and sitting each under his vine, i.e., each man possessing his own married wife."[4]

The millennialists of the early church fathers saw the first resurrection of Revelation 20 as a conduit for the fulfillment of the messianic prophecies found in Ezekiel and Isaiah that foretold an Edenic paradise on earth when the resurrected people of God will inherit the messianic kingdom in their natural human bodies and experience marriage and reproduction.

N. T. Wright, an amillennial theologian, also asserts that Ezekiel's vision is metaphorical:

> Ezekiel 37 is perhaps the most famous of all 'resurrection' passages in the Old Testament; it is most obviously allegorical or metaphorical; . . . For the Temple-centered Ezekiel, one of Israel's main problems was impurity; cleansing from impurity formed a key part of his promise of restoration (36:16–32). . . . Of all the unclean objects an observant Jew might encounter, unburied corpses or bones would come near the top of the list. That is the state, metaphorically, to which Israel has been reduced.[5]

The exposed bones may represent the depravity of Israel at the time, but God has always been in the business of saving sinful people and making them his people once more. Wright recognizes that the purpose of Ezekiel's prophetic vision is restoration: "The overall aim of the prophecy at this stage of the book was to point to a renewal of Israel's national life in which the

[4] Justin, *Dialogue with Trypho*, 80.2.
[5] N. T. Wright, *The Resurrection of the Son of God*. Vol. 3 of *Christian Origins and the Question of God* (Minneapolis: Fortress Press, 2003), 119.

Davidic monarchy would be restored, the nation would be reconstituted, and (ultimately) a new Temple would be built. But uncleanness remains at the heart of the problem."[6] But isn't cleansing the unclean and promising them resurrection what salvation is all about?

What Wright fails to explain is how this promised restoration could become a reality for those believing Jews who heard Ezekiel's prophecy, for they were doomed to die in Babylonian captivity. Without a resurrection, they would never experience the restoration as promised. According to Wright, instead of giving these people true hope for a resurrection in a future restoration, Ezekiel is adding insult to injury by feeding these hopeless people useless grandiose visions. Some future generation of Jewish saints may be fortunate enough to experience the promised reunification and restoration, but his listeners and all other departed Jewish believers will remain dry bones or in their graves because the promise of resurrection in these passages is merely metaphorical. But there is no internal biblical evidence that Ezekiel meant his prophecies to be interpreted metaphorically, which is why he goes into considerable detail describing the resurrected natural bodies and the restored kingdom.

Ezekiel, in the most graphic manner possible, is distinctly foretelling the day that the Lord will resurrect the Jewish remnant into Adamic bodies so that they can inherit the Promised Land in the future restoration. God even stakes his very reputation on a literal fulfillment:

> And you shall know that I am the LORD, when I open your graves, and raise you from your graves, O my people. And I will put my Spirit within you, and you shall live, and I will place you in your own land. Then you shall know that I am the LORD; I have spoken, and I will do it, declares the LORD." (Ezek. 37:13–14)

The resurrection of the Jewish saints into natural bodies, so that they can return to the Promised Land, is the proof that the initiator of these promises is indeed the LORD. The power of resurrection sets the biblical God apart from all other pagan gods, and someday he will do it and prove that he is the only true God and creator of this Genesis creation.

Isaiah also describes a bodily resurrection for the departed Jewish saints who will usher in the messianic kingdom: "Your dead shall live; their bodies shall rise. You who dwell in the dust, awake and sing for joy!" (Isa. 26:19). Wright concedes that this passage in Isaiah describes a literal resurrection of the human body and that there is the *possibility* of a real restoration after this resurrection:

---

[6] Ibid., 119.

The original Hebrew refers literally to bodily resurrection, and this is certainly how the verse is taken in the LXX and at Qumran. It is still possible, of course, that here resurrection is, as we shall see in Ezekiel, a metaphor for national restoration; but the wider passage, in which God's renewal of the whole cosmos is in hand, opens the way for us to propose that the reference to resurrection is intended to denote actual concrete events.[7]

Wright is uncertain as to whether Isaiah intended his prophecy to be a metaphor for a future national restoration, or whether Isaiah intended to describe a literal resurrection of the human bodies of the departed Jewish saints for them to inherit concrete events such as a literal restoration. But how will the departed Jewish saints inherit the promised messianic kingdom without a literal resurrection?

Isaac's Imperative

The Old Testament remnant had received numerous promises from the prophets of a return to the Promised Land during the reign of the Messiah. But how were the Jewish believers to inherit the messianic kingdom if they died before Christ's reign began? Abraham faced a similar dilemma when God told him to sacrifice Isaac as a young man through whom the prophetic promises had been made. How could God then fulfill his promises about Isaac's descendants if Isaac was killed? Resurrection is the answer:

> By faith Abraham, when he was tested, offered up Isaac, and he who had received the promises was in the act of offering up his only son, of whom it was said, "Through Isaac shall your offspring be named." He considered that God was able even to raise him from the dead, from which, figuratively speaking, he did receive him back. (Heb. 11:17–19)

Abraham reasoned that if he obeyed God and sacrificed Isaac, it was imperative that God raise Isaac from the dead in his natural body for the promises made by God pertaining to Isaac and his descendants to come true. Likewise, for the Old Testament prophecies of an earthly messianic kingdom for God's remnant to come true, it is imperative that there be a resurrection of the Adamic bodies of these departed saints. This is the only way the departed remnant can inherit the promised messianic kingdom before they inherit the kingdom of heaven.

With the promises made to the disciples, as well as promises made to the Old Testament saints, it is fair to conclude that the Lord will resurrect all the saints—from Abel to the Jewish remnant in Ezekiel's day to the last saint martyred during the Tribulation—into natural bodies for them to experience the restoration. John teaches the following:

---

[7] Ibid., 117.

Then the seventh angel blew his trumpet, and there were loud voices in heaven, saying, "The kingdom of the world has become the kingdom of our Lord and of his Christ, and he shall reign forever and ever." And the twenty-four elders who sit on their thrones before God fell on their faces and worshiped God, saying, "We give thanks to you, Lord God Almighty, who is and who was, for you have taken your great power and begun to reign. The nations raged, but your wrath came, and the time for the dead to be judged, and *for rewarding your servants, the prophets and saints, and those who fear your name*, both small and great, and for destroying the destroyers of the earth." (Rev. 11:15–18)

Someday all the God-fearing people of this world—the prophets and all the saints—will be rewarded by experiencing the messianic reign when Christ exercises his reign from heaven: "you have taken your great power and begun to reign," and the kingdom of the world becomes his kingdom when all the blessed and holy saints experience the first resurrection at the beginning of his millennial reign.

That this messianic kingdom is made up of a ransomed people from "every tribe and language and people and nation" (Rev: 5:9) correlates with the Great Commission given to the disciples:

All authority in heaven and on earth has been given to me. Go therefore and make disciples of all nations, baptizing them in the name of the Father and of the Son and of the Holy Spirit, teaching them to observe all that I have commanded you. And behold, I am with you always, to the end of the age. (Matt. 28:18–20)

As a result of our fulfillment of the Great Commission, all nations will experience the restoration in fulfillment of all Christ's teachings and promises.

The Disciples Finally Reign with Christ

Revelation states, "Then I saw thrones, and seated on them were those to whom the authority to judge was committed" (Rev. 20:4). This matches what Christ promised the disciples who were willing to sacrificially follow him: "Truly, I say to you, in the new world, when the Son of Man will sit on his glorious throne [in heaven as he reigns over the regenerated earth], you who have followed me will also *sit on twelve thrones* [in the Son's kingdom on earth], judging the twelve tribes of Israel" (Matt. 19:28). When Christ begins to fully exercise his reign as he sits on his throne in heaven, then the disciples will be rewarded in the new world, or the restored earth, by being resurrected into natural bodies so they can sit on twelve thrones and judge the twelve tribes of Israel. These twelve thrones are probably among the thrones John describes in Revelation.

There could certainly be more thrones involved here than those of the disciples, for the entire world will be ruled by Christ. I am sure Christ will establish thrones of resurrected saints in all parts of the world. Note again what John foresees: "Then I saw thrones [from all over the world], and seated on them were those to whom the authority to judge [the whole world] was committed" (20:4). This is in keeping with Daniel's vision of a world-wide kingdom on this earth from every tribe and language and people and nation.

During the regeneration, the resurrected Jewish disciples will serve as judges over the twelve tribes of Israel, while some of the other Gentile saints who are resurrected will likely be selected to judge over their respective nations. Because the disciples have made disciples out of all nations, Christ will designate resurrected saints from Israel to Greece to Australia to Papua New Guinea to Brazil to rule over their respective people. That is how he will be King of kings and Lord of lords over all the nations of the world.

The disciples—and their disciples—were promised an abundant inheritance *in this Adamic age* before we inherit eternal life in the age to come: "And everyone who has left houses or brothers or sisters or father or mother or children or lands, for my name's sake, will receive a hundredfold [in the restoration in this age] *and* [in addition] will inherit eternal life [in the age to come through the transformation]" (Matt. 19:29; cf. Mark 10:29-30). This prophecy that everyone who is willing to sacrificially follow Christ will experience a hundredfold of houses or brothers or sisters or father or mother or children or lands can only be fulfilled if there is a resurrection of all the saints into natural Adamic bodies that can marry, reproduce, and live in human habitats on the renewed earth.

Isaiah confirms this promise to God's chosen people of a richly rewarding human experience in the restoration: "They shall build houses and inhabit them; they shall plant vineyards and eat their fruit. . . . my chosen shall long enjoy the work of their hands. They shall not labor in vain or bear children for calamity" (65:21-23). Christ is probably alluding to this prophecy in his answer to the disciples. God's chosen people, or everyone who is a believer, will indeed receive a hundredfold in this Adamic age when they experience the first resurrection and enjoy living with their large extended families and working on land that is abundantly fruitful.

Remarriage in the Restoration

This brings up an interesting question about the first resurrection and remarriage reminiscent of the question the Sadducees asked Jesus (Matt. 22:23-32). The conservative Jewish or rabbinic understanding of the Old Testament promise of a resurrection was one of a natural body. But the Sadducees, as the liberals of their day, doubted the rationality of any bodily resurrection and had devised what they thought was a clever reason not to believe in a resurrection of the human body. If a female believer died having had multiple husbands during her lifetime, who would be her husband in the next life? They thought this presented an insolvable dilemma for those who believed in a resurrection of the natural body.

Jesus' answer dealt with the final resurrection of the immortal body at the transformation, in which the resurrected saints will be like the angels and no longer be given in marriage, which surely caught all his Jewish listeners off guard, including those who believed in a resurrection of the natural body. This revelation of another kind of resurrection of the sons of God as immortals not given in marriage was unheard of before Jesus' answer. It was not a part of the Old Testament vision. But his answer does not preclude a prior "first resurrection" of a natural body in keeping with the Jewish understanding of a resurrection of the human body before this final resurrection, as the resurrection of Lazarus and others proves.

And just as Lazarus could have remarried and become a father after his resurrection, so, too, those who participate in the first resurrection can marry and have children. But what if a believer who has been married, possibly several times, to a believing wife (or wives) dies and is resurrected along with his previous wife (or wives) into a mortal body at the first resurrection? Who will be his wife in the restoration?

This is an interesting question and is one of the most frequently asked questions I am asked when speaking about postrestorational eschatology. Some people want to be sure that in the restoration they will have the same spouse as they are deeply in love with today. Others may want to know if they will have the opportunity to start over with a new, more suitable helpmate.

This perceived problem is not that difficult to solve. A man is one flesh with his wife until one or both dies: "A wife is bound to her husband as long as he lives. But if her husband dies, she is free to be married to whom she wishes, only in the Lord" (1 Cor. 7:39). The marriage bond is broken at death. A widow can remarry without committing adultery. Therefore, the departed saints who experience the first resurrection of natural Adamic bodies will be free to marry whomever they wish. Some may want to marry the person they married before, while others may welcome this second chance to find a more suitable helpmate. Jacob may have been married to Leah and Rachel, but he loved Rachel and will probably want to be one flesh with her after the first resurrection—assuming Rachel will have him!

Spirits of the Righteous Made Perfect

As saints die, our spirits go to heaven to be with the Lord. The mortal body returns to dust, where Christ describes it as in a state of sleep. The saints who have died and are in heaven with Christ are also described as an assembly of "spirits of the righteous made *perfect*" (Heb. 12:23). Their perfected spirits remain in heaven until they come back to re-inhabit their resurrected or regenerated mortal bodies at the beginning of the 1,000-year reign of Christ.

Does this mean that these perfected spirits of the departed saints will no longer have a sinful nature and will no longer sin when they are resurrected to live again on the earth during the restoration? And if they are sinless, will they die again? If the curse of sin is death, and they no longer have a sinful nature and do not sin, will they no longer be subject to the penalty of death?

These are questions that greatly troubled some of the early church millennialists. Many of these millennialists had a difficult time reconciling the idea of the spirits of the deceased saints going to heaven and being made perfect coming back to a restored, yet imperfect, world because there will still be some unbelievers who sin. They also believed that after the saints have tasted the heavenly paradise, it would be a form of retrogression for their spirits to come back to an earthly paradise and comingle with sinners.

To address this perceived problem, the early millennialists developed a teaching that the spirits of the deceased saints go to a subterranean world that is neither heaven nor hell. This temporary abode of the spirits of the departed saints was the forerunner of the concept of purgatory. In this subterranean place of the dead, their spirits are not made perfect, and they do not get a taste of the heavenly paradise. It is then acceptable for them to come back to life as mortals in the earthly millennium without being retrogressive. These church fathers thought they were solving a problem, but they actually created a huge credibility problem for millennial beliefs. As a result, this false teaching was a major factor in millennial beliefs being discredited by critics.[8]

There is a better solution to this dilemma of the spirits of saints who have tasted of heaven coming back to live as mortals again in a world that is restored but not perfect. During the incarnation, Christ was a mortal man who was tempted by Satan, yet he did not sin. He had the advantage of being God, but he was still tempted in every way we are. We also know that Adam and Eve lived in the Garden of Eden without sinning for some time before succumbing to Satan's temptation.

Furthermore, there is going to be a major difference between the world we know today and the world during the restoration. Satan will be bound and no longer operative. This has never been the case in the history of the world. Even Adam and Eve lived in a world with satanic temptation. But in

---

[8] For an excellent review of these teachings and their consequences, see Charles E. Hill, *Regnum Caelorum: Patterns of Millennial Thought in Early Christianity* (Grand Rapids: Eerdmans, 2001), esp. 19-20.

the restoration, no demonic forces will be present to tempt us. It is difficult to imagine a world without temptation or the influence of demons, yet that is what the 1,000-year reign of Christ will be.

Most important, when we come back to this earth in the first resurrection, our spirits, as the Scriptures teach, will have already been made perfect. As a result, we will no longer have a sinful nature. With Satan no longer around to tempt us, and Christ ruling the world with absolute control over the affairs of man, we will live in total submission to the Father. God's will is finally accomplished in our lives "on earth as it is in heaven." Having been in heaven perfectly submissive to God, we will be on earth perfectly submissive to God. There is no reason a saint whose spirit has been made perfect in heaven cannot return to this earth in an Adamic mortal body without a sinful nature and no longer sin in a restored earth that is not absolutely perfect. These resurrected saints, with perfected spirits, will be restored to a pre-fall condition as human beings able to live without sin for a thousand years, before they enter the new heavens and new earth.

Thus, if the saints who have been made perfect in heaven return to an environment with no temptation, it is very conceivable that they can and will live sinless mortal lives during the restoration. This may seem difficult to imagine because all we know is a daily life of temptation, sin, conviction, confession, and cleansing. Even though we have had a bath that cleanses us from all sin, Christ has to regularly wash our feet. At this time, sin and confession are all we know: "If we say we have no sin, we deceive ourselves, and the truth is not in us" (1 John 1:8).

We can imagine a heavenly life without sin, but sin is so much a part of our daily experience that it is hard to imagine coming back to this earth and living a sinless life. This may seem strange to us now, but it probably makes sense to our brothers and sisters in heaven who already know what it is like to have their spirits made perfect.

Mortality in the Restoration

Will the multitude of the spirits of the righteous who are made perfect and come back to life at the first resurrection be capable of experiencing mortal death? The Scriptures teach, "For the wages of sin is death, but the free gift of God is eternal life in Christ Jesus our Lord" (Rom. 6:23). If they do not have a sinful nature and do not sin, then there is no reason for them to experience death. They will be alive when Christ comes again on the last day. Revelation says, "They came to life and reigned with Christ for a thousand years" (20:4). This seems to imply that those who experience the first resurrection will live for the entire thousand years. Just because we will have mortal bodies does not mean we have to experience death. Adam and Eve had mortal bodies before the fall, and they would have continued to live had they not rebelled against God. They and their descendants would be alive today if they had not succumbed to Satan's temptation. That does not mean they were *immortal* creatures before the fall.

There will also be unbelievers who survive the Tribulation and enter into the millennium. The curse on this creation is evidently not completely removed during the restoration, for the prophets envisioned humans who will experience death, even if they live for hundreds of years. Isaiah described how sinners in the messianic kingdom will still experience death: "No more shall there be in it an infant who lives but a few days, or an old man who does not fill out his days, for the young man shall die a hundred years old, and the sinner a hundred years old shall be accursed" (Isa. 65:20). There will still be sinners in the messianic kingdom, and some forms of sin will be of such magnitude that they will be cursed with premature death.

Some surviving unbelievers will undoubtedly become believers when they witness the miraculous regeneration of this Genesis creation, but that does not mean they automatically lose their sinful natures and are no longer capable of sinning. Those who survive the Tribulation will still have a sinful nature and can, therefore, experience mortal death.

But what about the small number of Christians who succeed in hiding from the Antichrist during the Tribulation and enter into the millennial kingdom in the same spiritual condition they were in before? With Satan bound, will they continue to sin? Since they have not died and had their spirits made perfect in heaven, they, in all likelihood, will still have their sinful natures and be capable of sinful thoughts and behavior and possibly even experience mortal death when their bodies fall asleep. The same would be true of children born of sinners during the restoration that become Christians. They, too, will not be made perfect and will inherit sinful natures, thus being capable of experiencing death.

The restoration may reverse most aspects of the fall, but it is not a complete return to the sinless Garden of Eden as evidenced by the presence of sinful unbelievers and the fact that Christ must rule this world with a rod of iron to shepherd sinful people into peaceful living. The final rebellion at the end of the millennium when Satan is released one last time is conclusive proof of the presence of sinful unbelievers during the millennial reign (cf. Rev. 20:7–9). It also speaks volumes about the deep sinful nature of fallen man that they will respond to Satan's final temptation and rebel against Christ even after experiencing the regenerated Genesis creation and Christ's reign of righteousness.

We should make a distinction between perfected "holy" saints who are resurrected into natural bodies without sinful natures and will not experience death during the thousand-year reign of Christ and unbelievers, or even living converts, who will still have sinful natures and can therefore experience sin and mortal death. The millennial kingdom will be a mixture of unbelievers, converts, and believers who survive the Tribulation who will still have sinful natures and thus be capable of death, as well as perfected saints of the first resurrection who, I believe, will not have sinful natures and will live the entire one thousand years to see Christ come again on the last day. They will be alive when the rapture occurs.

Return to Paradise

Let's address another issue that bothered early millennialists. They believed that the saints who had gone to heaven and tasted of the heavenly paradise would not want to regress to living in an earthly paradise. This is the reason they conceived the idea of a subterranean holding place for the departed saints. I believe that our brothers in heaven will indeed want to return to an earth that is restored and ruled by Christ even though their spirits have tasted heaven.

To understand this, one must remember that the deceased saints are not in the final eternal state of heaven. They are only spirits made perfect in heaven. They have tasted of heaven, but they have not yet entered the new heavens and new earth and the New Jerusalem. Also, they have not yet received their transformed, immortal bodies, nor have they received their final inheritance and rewards. They are not eating from the "tree of life" in the New Jerusalem. According to Revelation, these events do not take place until after the 1,000-year restoration—at the transformation. They are in heaven as perfected spirits and experience the joy and peace of God's presence, but they have not yet received the final inheritance of their heavenly dwelling in glorified bodies.

In addition, the following verses in Revelation indicate that they still feel a major connection to the human experience on earth:

> When he opened the fifth seal, I saw under the altar [in heaven] the souls of those who had been slain for the word of God and for the witness they had borne. They cried out with a loud voice, "O Sovereign Lord, holy and true, how long before you will judge and avenge our blood on those who dwell on the earth?" Then they were each given a white robe [a symbol of holiness and perfection] and told to rest a little longer, until the number of their fellow servants and their brothers should be complete, who were to be killed as they themselves had been. (Rev. 6:9–11)

As the martyred saints eagerly watch the events of the Tribulation unfold, they remain intensely focused on its conclusion when the Antichrist and his armies will be destroyed. They are looking forward to inheriting the Son's forthcoming kingdom on earth. God's kingdom on earth must occur before they inherit the eternal new heavens and new earth.

Furthermore, John emphatically says it is a real blessing for the perfected spirits of the holy saints who have tasted of heaven to come back to the restored earth through the first resurrection: "Blessed and holy is the one who shares in the first resurrection!" (Rev. 20:6). If John teaches that it is a blessing for the holy or perfected saints to return to this earth through the first resurrection to inherit the Son's kingdom, then it would *not* be retrogressive. The departed saints may have tasted the paradise in heaven, but they will be returning to a paradise on the Son's restored Genesis earth.

There must be a fundamental need for God's people to live out the human experience in a restored Genesis creation before we, as sons of God, move on to the new heavens and new earth—a new creation for a new order of being. And just because we will be leaving God's presence in heaven when we come back to the earth does not mean we have left his presence. Through the Holy Spirit interacting with our perfected human spirits in restored bodies, we will remain in intimate fellowship with God just as Jesus remained in intimate fellowship with his Father during his incarnation.

Most important, the 1,000-year restoration will obviously bring great glory and pleasure to God as he once again delights in his magnificent Genesis creation before he finally destroys it and ushers in the age to come. What better way to accomplish this than by sending all the perfected spirits of his beloved Adamic creatures—from Abel to the last one martyred in the Tribulation—back to this earth through the first resurrection to be his people on the very earth he created. The saints will come back as humans in the image of God and fulfill their original creation mandate.

Since the departed saints have not yet experienced the new heavens and new earth, there is no reason to assume it would be retrogressive for them to come back to this earth as physical human beings to finally experience what it means to be men and women of God in the Genesis human experience. After we have fulfilled the Adamic order of being in an Edenic paradise and this creation comes to an end, then we will be ready to move on to a heavenly paradise in the new creation as children of God in the new heavens and new earth.

Grief in the Restoration

A number of theologians are puzzled by Isaiah's description of the restoration as a time when some people will continue to experience death, yet at the same time, "no more shall be heard in it the sound of weeping and the cry of distress" (Isa. 65:19). They would ask Isaiah the rhetorical question, "If people still experience death in the restoration, then would not people still weep when their loved ones die?"

Isaiah's description of the lack of grief during the future messianic kingdom must be understood in the context of the time he was writing.

The Jewish people were experiencing tremendous hardship as God was beginning to send them into exile. Surely, there was much weeping and great distress as many were being killed or taken into slavery to a foreign, pagan land. The loss of the Promised Land was a heart-wrenching experience. In this context, Isaiah's prophecy of a restoration with the Messiah ruling over a restored Israel with absolute justice would surely be a time when the sounds of such weeping and distress no longer existed.

I doubt that people will be wailing in anguish when a believer who did not experience the first resurrection falls asleep during the restoration. Once the restoration begins, the surviving saints who have witnessed the first resurrection, as well as the deceased saints who have experienced it, will know with certainty that the final resurrection will take place in a thousand years. As a result, they will not weep as people do today because the hope and assurance of the final resurrection to come will be very comforting.

Consider the case of Lazarus. The first time Lazarus died, Martha, Mary, and their friends wept deeply (John 11:33). Jesus also wept. When Lazarus died the second time, however, I doubt that Martha and Mary mourned as profoundly, if at all. They had already experienced firsthand the power of resurrection, and most important, they knew with even greater certainty that Lazarus would be resurrected on the last day.

Consequently, when Isaiah foresees a day when "no more shall be heard in it the sound of weeping and the cry of distress," this can indeed be an accurate portrayal of the messianic kingdom. The restoration prefigures the time in heaven when there will be no weeping because death will be eliminated when our bodies are made immortal: "He will wipe away every tear from their eyes, and death shall be no more, neither shall there be mourning nor crying nor pain anymore, for the former things have passed away" (Rev. 21:4). Only in the heavenly kingdom will there be complete immortality and thus no tears, mourning, or pain.

Old Testament Prophecies

While Revelation contains only a few verses devoted to the millennium, with a few early announcements scattered throughout the book, the Old Testament contains a vast number of prophecies of the earthly messianic kingdom. To use a modern term, the millennial reign of Christ depicted in Revelation 20 serves as a type of hyperlink to the considerable information that already exists in the Old Testament. Many of these Old Testament messianic prophecies are in the context of Israel's impending exile for unfaithfulness, their existing captivity, or their eventual return from exile when God promises to restore them to the Promised Land. Living as captives in a foreign land ruled by pagan kings and tyrants serves as a pattern for mankind living in a fallen world under the dominion of Satan.

And the prophecies foretelling their deliverance from these pagan dominions and return to the Promised Land become an opportunity for God, through the prophets, to describe a future time when they and the rest of the world will be completely delivered from Satan's regime and brought into the ultimate Promised Land of the messianic kingdom. This pattern of bondage and then deliverance into a future golden era is the context for most of the messianic prophecies. And these messianic prophecies can easily be recognized as descriptions of the future restoration of the whole world, for the visions go far beyond the simple return of the Israelites to their own homeland. The prophets were not exaggerating when they foretold a Genesis creation restored to an Edenic condition.

Most of these prophecies are Israel-centric, with the messianic kingdom revolving around a restored Israel. But these prophecies also picture this restoration extending far beyond Israel, encompassing the entire world with Israel as the center of this messianic kingdom. In the restoration Christ is not only the King of the Jews but King of the whole world. All believers, Jew and Gentile, from all nations will be part of the restoration.

This makes sense, because the Gentile believers have joined Jewish believers, the true spiritual descendants of Abraham, as brothers in the Jewish Messiah. And the Jewish Messiah is the Son of God through whom the world was created. As a result, one would expect his rule to include the whole world and all his people from all nations. The kingdom is restored to Israel, yet this yields blessings for the world. Peace and prosperity will flow from Israel to the world, resulting in an outpouring of gratitude from all nations. Christ's reign extends from Zion to the ends of the earth. All nations will become his rightful possession:

> "As for me, I have set my King on Zion, my holy hill." I will tell of the decree: The LORD said to me, "You are my Son; today I have begotten you. Ask of me, and I will *make the nations your heritage, and the ends of the earth your possession.* You shall break them with a rod of iron and dash them in pieces like a potter's vessel." (Ps. 2:6–9)

As Almighty God, the Jewish King will rule the entire world establishing a government that will create worldwide peace, justice, and righteousness: "He shall speak peace to the nations; his rule shall be from sea to sea, and from the River to the ends of the earth (Zech. 9:10).

In the Bible, the word *mountain* is often used as a metaphor referring to a nation or kingdom. Christ will rule the world, and he will establish Israel as the chief mountain or the center of his reign:

> It shall come to pass in the latter days that the mountain of the house of the LORD shall be established as the highest of the mountains, and it shall be lifted up above the hills; and peoples shall flow to it, and many nations shall

come, and say: "Come, let us go up to the mountain of the LORD, to the house of the God of Jacob, that he may teach us his ways and that we may walk in his paths." *For out of Zion shall go forth the law, and the word of the LORD from Jerusalem. He shall judge between many peoples, and shall decide for strong nations afar off*; and they shall beat their swords into plowshares, and their spears into pruning hooks; nation shall not lift up sword against nation, neither shall they learn war anymore; but they shall sit every man under his vine and under his fig tree, and no one shall make them afraid, for the mouth of the LORD of hosts has spoken. (Mic. 4:1–4)

Christ's rule will be centralized in Zion, or Israel, but his kingdom of peace will extend from sea to sea to the ends of the earth. Israel will also serve as an international high court. But instead of being at The Hague in the Netherlands, it will be in Jerusalem with Christ as judge.

A contemporary example of mountains as symbolic of a hierarchy of powerful nations is found in the following from an article about China: "Chinese look out their windows and see one great mountain, the United States, plus several big hills (Japan, the EU, Russia). Most Americans look out their windows and see multiple hills, one of which is China."[9]

In gratitude for the peace and blessings that Christ will bring to the world through Israel's governance, people from everywhere will flood Israel with gifts of appreciation. It is not the Israel of today, however, that will earn such respect. It will be Christ's reign through a nation of resurrected Jewish believers, the remnant, that will capture the world's appreciation. Isaiah foresees this day:

And nations shall come to your light, and kings to the brightness of your rising. Lift up your eyes all around, and see; they all gather together, they come to you; your sons shall come from afar, and your daughters shall be carried on the hip. Then you shall see and be radiant; your heart shall thrill and exult, because the abundance of the sea shall be turned to you, the *wealth of the nations shall come to you*. . . . Your gates shall be open continually; day and night they shall not be shut, that people may bring to you the wealth of the nations, with their kings led in procession. (Isa. 60:3–11)

Most of us would chafe at the idea of showing this kind of gratitude to Israel, or to any other nation in the current world. But Isaiah is speaking of an Israel made up of the true Jewish saints, including the disciples, who will be humbly reigning with Christ over a world of peace and absolute justice. Today, Christians are often deeply moved by visiting Israel. Imagine our response during the restoration.

---

[9] Ross Terrill, "What if China Fails? The Case for Selective Failure," *Wilson Quarterly*, Autumn 2010, 73.

Most important, Christ's global empire through Israel will not resemble the ancient empires or even modern forms of imperialism where nations are subjugated so that the ruling nation reaps unjust material benefit from the oppressed nations. The gifts we bring to Israel will not be tribute; they will be gifts of gratitude for the peace and prosperity that the Messiah will bring to the whole world. Furthermore, I imagine the nations, with their respective Gentile thrones or ruler-servants, will be fairly autonomous.

God used Israel to bring the Messiah into this world, bringing great spiritual blessings to all nations. And when the messianic kingdom is finally realized on this earth, it will bring unmatched spiritual *and* material blessings to the world. As a result, it will be no surprise that the nations of the world will defer to Israel's governance and eagerly bring material gifts of appreciation. Paul reports how even the churches in the Roman Empire wanted to show the church in Jerusalem their appreciation for the spiritual blessings their nation had brought to them:

> At present, however, I am going to Jerusalem bringing aid to the saints. For Macedonia and Achaia have been pleased to make some contribution for the poor among the saints at Jerusalem. For they were pleased to do it, and indeed they owe it to them. For if the Gentiles have come to share in their spiritual blessings, they ought also to be of service to them in material blessings. (Rom. 15:25–27)

When the Gentile nations experience the incredible spiritual and material blessings of the messianic kingdom, we will, out of overwhelming joy and abundance, send gifts of appreciation to Jerusalem.

Ruling with a Rod of Iron

Shepherds used a rod as a staff to control sheep and to keep predators away. John describes Christ ruling with a rod of iron: "From his mouth comes a sharp sword with which to strike down the nations, and he will rule them with a rod of iron" (Rev. 19:15). To rule with a rod of iron refers to the destruction of the armies (or enemies) who attack Christ and his celestial army at the end of the Tribulation. It may also refer to ruling with complete authority and power to protect the world from the tyranny of evil.

There will still be unbelievers in the restoration with sinful natures. And even without Satan in the world to tempt them, they will have evil thoughts that left unchecked may lead to sinful actions. Although unbelievers may have evil thoughts and desires, I do not believe that Christ will allow any resulting evil actions to occur, but will use his supernatural powers or his rod of iron to prevent evil thoughts from turning into evil actions.

Christ will not only macromanage this world by preventing wars between nations, but he will also micromanage it to prevent evil actions at all levels of human activity. He will prevent violence between nations as well as violence within households. No longer will a greedy and petty dictator terrorize a nation, or an ill-tempered or drunken husband abuse his family.

How Christ will prevent evil actions from occurring, we do not know. But we do know from biblical precedents that he can be creative when he wants to avert evil. For example, when two angels, as men, went to rescue Lot before Sodom was destroyed by fire, the men of the city who surrounded Lot's house to molest the angels were struck with blindness, rendering them incapable of committing the crime (Gen. 19:11).

The Old Testament contains other examples of the Lord intervening in creative and miraculous ways to prevent evil. King Jeroboam's hand is shriveled up when he raises it against a prophet of God. Later, when he repents, it is instantly restored (1 Kings 13:4, 6). A servant of Elisha's fraudulently collects payment from Naaman for a miraculous healing (2 Kings 5:25–27). This servant commits a white-collar crime, and God administers justice by striking him with leprosy.

God does not often intervene in the affairs of men in such miraculous ways to establish justice, but these historical precedents indicate his ability to do so when he chooses. When Christ is ruling the world from his throne in heaven, his intervention will be immediate and his justice will be fair and comprehensive. If the person is repentant, as King Jeroboam was, then the punishment can be reversed and Christ can restore him or her. If Christ determines that some people are simply incorrigible and not worthy of this world, he can remove them, as he did Ananias and Sapphira when they committed fraud and lied to the Holy Spirit (Acts 5:1–11).

God knows the location of evil perpetrators, and he knows what they are thinking and doing this very moment. He could instantly snatch them from this world. We searched for ten years for Osama Bin Laden. But Christ knows exactly where terrorists are and can remove them from this world in an instant while they are still in the planning stages of an act of terror. In the restoration, evildoers will be removed before they can act on their evil intentions:

> The LORD is in his holy temple; *the LORD's throne is in heaven; his eyes see,* his eyelids test the children of man. The LORD tests the righteous, but *his soul hates the wicked and the one who loves violence.* Let him rain coals on the wicked; fire and sulfur and a scorching wind shall be the portion of their cup." (Ps. 11:4–6)

From his throne in heaven, God sees exactly what evildoers are thinking and planning to do on this earth. He is in a unique position to prevent injustice and administer justice.

Our justice system, by comparison, is seriously flawed. We cannot always prevent people from committing crimes and hurting others. An abused wife, for example, can report her dangerous husband, but it is very difficult for police to provide constant protection. Then, assuming we can find the criminal, arrest them, and convict them, we can only guess at the retribution it will take to punish and rehabilitate them. They may spend decades in prison when the first month of their incarceration would have been enough to convince them to live decent and civil lives. If we knew their hearts, we could release them and allow them to perform community service to make amends for their crimes.

We are not omniscient, nor can we read hearts and minds. But Christ does know hearts and minds and is in the perfect position to determine the right proportion and duration of whatever punishment he chooses. With Christ's perfect administration of justice, we will no longer need prisons or instruments of war.

Christ will not be a tyrannical ruler as he rules with a rod of iron. He will be a just ruler as he puts an end to the tyranny of evil this world has known since the fall. No longer will a Cain be able to slay an Abel. No longer will corporate executives or employees embezzle money. No longer will law enforcement officers have to search for fugitives. No longer will nations have to search for terrorists. During the restoration, the day of terrorists, evil dictators, warlords, drug gangs, organized crime, and corrupt politicians will be over. The world will finally experience comprehensive justice at all levels of life. Evil will not be tolerated.

Through his omniscience, Christ will orchestrate a worldwide reign of peace, justice, and righteousness at all levels of society. He will settle disputes throughout the world, working through his resurrected judges as arbiters and peacemakers. Through the Holy Spirit, he will give them the wisdom they will need to settle any conflict and create a final and just peace between nations and people.

In contrast, today we are experiencing the evil injustices of Satan's dominion of darkness. A 2005 article reported the worldwide estimate for bribery, embezzlement, and other forms of corruption to be more than $1 trillion a year: "In Angola, where most people live on less than $1 a day, nearly $1 billion in oil revenues vanished from state coffers in 2001—three times the amount of all the humanitarian aid the country received from abroad during that year."

The article also states that in Uganda "between 1991 and 1995, local officials siphoned off eighty-seven percent of the grant money primary schools were supposed to receive from the central government."[10] The news media regularly contains these kinds of stories.

I look forward to a world of justice where this kind of corruption is not tolerated; a world where children will be wanted and adored, and women will be treated with dignity and respect. Schools will be a safe haven thriving with vitality and learning. Neither corruption nor the criminal court system will even exist. In the restoration, the world will finally be peaceful and civilized. The millennium will truly be an age of righteous humanity.

The Regeneration of Nature and an Abundant Life

Since the fall, the earth has displayed the results of sin and God's curse. And after the Tribulation and the plagues God inflicts upon the world, the earth will be in a deplorable condition. But when Christ begins his reign from heaven, he will restore this creation to an Edenic state through a process of regeneration. This will affect nature, agriculture, and animal life:

> I will make with them a covenant of peace and banish wild beasts from the land, so that they may dwell securely in the wilderness and sleep in the woods. And I will make them and the places all around my hill a blessing, and I will send down the showers in their season; they shall be showers of blessing. And the trees of the field shall yield their fruit, and the earth shall yield its increase, and they shall be secure in their land. . . . And I will provide for them renowned plantations so that they shall no more be consumed with hunger in the land . . . And you are my sheep, human sheep of my pasture, and I am your God, declares the Lord GOD. . . . And they will say, "*This land that was desolate has become like the garden of Eden.*" (Ezek. 34:25–31; 36:35)

Nature itself is fundamentally restored, so much so, that desolate places will become like the Garden of Eden. Notice, too, that the Lord will shepherd his sheep to an abundant life on this restored earth.

As their Good Shepherd, Jesus, alluding to this prophecy, promises his followers that he will one day lead them to an abundant life: "The thief comes only to steal and kill and destroy. I came that they may have life and have it abundantly. . . . I am the good shepherd. I know my own and my own know me" (John 10:10, 14). Currently we may experience an abundant internal life of the Spirit that is full of love, joy, and peace. But we do not always experience an abundant external life on this earth. Often, even our inner lives experience a form of suffering due to the struggles against this fallen world. Paul experienced both inner and external suffering because of his following Christ, his Good Shepherd:

[10] Jakob Svensson, "Eight Questions about Corruption," *Journal of Economic Perspectives*, Summer 2005; quoted in *Wilson Quarterly*, Winter 2006, 73.

Are they servants of Christ? I am a better one—I am talking like a madman—with far greater labors, far more imprisonments, with countless beatings, and often near death. Five times I received at the hands of the Jews the forty lashes less one. Three times I was beaten with rods. Once I was stoned. Three times I was shipwrecked; a night and a day I was adrift at sea; on frequent journeys, in danger from rivers, danger from robbers, danger from my own people, danger from Gentiles, danger in the city, danger in the wilderness, danger at sea, danger from false brothers; in toil and hardship, through many a sleepless night, in hunger and thirst, often without food, in cold and exposure. And, apart from other things, there is the daily pressure on me of my anxiety for all the churches. Who is weak, and I am not weak? Who is made to fall, and I am not indignant? . . . For the sake of Christ, then, I am content with weaknesses, insults, hardships, persecutions, and calamities. For when I am weak, then I am strong. (2 Cor. 11:23–29; 12:10)

For someone who experienced an abundant internal life of the Spirit, Paul lived a pretty miserable life. With the Holy Spirit in his heart, he still experienced inner anguish over his fellow Jews who had not yet received Christ: "I am speaking the truth in Christ—I am not lying; my conscience bears me witness in the Holy Spirit—that I have great sorrow and unceasing anguish in my heart" (Rom. 9:1–2).

Even Christ, who was filled with the Holy Spirit without measure (John 3:34), experienced considerable anguish while he was on this earth. He agonized over the physical condition of the multitudes that came to him to be healed. He was often exasperated by the disciples' slowness of understanding. He was deeply disturbed by the hardness of heart of the people. He was infuriated by the irrational opposition he received from the Pharisees and other religious leaders. He lamented the failure of Jerusalem to recognize the coming of their own Messiah: "O Jerusalem, Jerusalem, the city that kills the prophets and stones those who are sent to it! How often would I have gathered your children together as a hen gathers her brood under her wings, and you would not!" (Luke 13:34). His intense public ministry was often exhausting, and he thought foxes and birds had better homes and places of rest than he did: "And Jesus said, "Foxes have holes, and birds of the air have nests, but the Son of Man has nowhere to lay his head" (Luke 9:58). On a human level, he did not live what we would call a happy or abundant life.

But Christ was not exaggerating when he promised his followers an abundant life on this earth. And this promise is not simply a metaphorical description of our current inner spiritual condition or our future heavenly existence. The abundant life on this earth will take place during the Son's kingdom when through the first resurrection the saints inherit an earthly paradise. Christ as the Good Shepherd will bind Satan, reverse the curse on this world, and then, through the first resurrection, bring his sheep—

including Paul and the disciples—back to this earth to experience an abundant life without any internal or external suffering or anguish in a creation that has been restored to its Edenic state. It will be the kind of life Adam and Eve's descendants would have experienced under the Lordship of Christ had Adam and Eve not succumbed to Satan's temptation.

Those who advocate a prosperity gospel apparently do not understand the current world. Presently, we experience deprivation and all the other ill effects of living in a world under God's curse and under Satan's dominion. Christ promises that at times we will experience hardship. Christians often feel entitled or privileged and expect to be exempt from the things that plague mankind. But we should expect misery in this fallen world. And being a child of God can even intensify Satan's attacks.

Jesus did not "promise us a rose garden" in this life. Paul knew this all too well. The prosperity gospel is misplaced. Only in the restoration will there be true prosperity and material well-being for those who believe in Christ's gospel. At that time he indeed does promise us a rose garden, because the curse will be removed and, with Satan out of the way, the world will be ruled by Christ and righteous saints.

Please do not misunderstand. There is nothing wrong with hard work, resourcefulness, and taking advantage of opportunities to experience material success and comfort during this current age. And we should be very much engaged in efforts to counter the effects of this fallen creation and correct the poverty and injustice in this world. But we should be willing to sacrifice everything to follow Christ. We should take comfort in any hardship we experience by looking forward to Christ's coming reign when we will experience an abundant life beyond anything we can experience today.

Consider Job's story. God allowed Satan to decimate Job's economic prosperity, his family, and his health. The only thing Satan could not do was take Job's life. Job patiently endured, remaining faithful to God. And then God restored Job:

> And the LORD restored the fortunes of Job. . . . And the LORD blessed the latter days of Job more than his beginning. And he had 14,000 sheep, 6,000 camels, 1,000 yoke of oxen, and 1,000 female donkeys. He had also seven sons and three daughters. . . . And in all the land there were no women so beautiful as Job's daughters. . . . And after this Job lived 140 years, and saw his sons, and his sons' sons, four generations. And Job died, an old man, and full of days. (Job 42:10–17)

Saints who suffer physical, social, and material deprivation during this current era will receive a hundredfold in the restoration. And instead of living for 140 years like Job, the saints will get to enjoy these blessings for a thousand years!

The foreknowledge and certainty that we will someday experience an abundant life in the future restoration should give us an innate immunity against any hardship and protect us from bitterness and resentment toward God. We can rest assured that God will make it up to us in the restoration.

Human health will be restored, as well. Many saints throughout the ages have suffered terrible illnesses and handicaps, but not so in the restoration. Just as Christ forgave sins and healed while he was on this earth, he will heal people on a massive scale as he resurrects them to be in the restoration:

> And no inhabitant will say, "I am sick"; the people who dwell there will be forgiven their iniquity. Say to those who have an anxious heart, "Be strong; fear not! Behold, your God will come with vengeance, with the recompense of God. He will come and save you." Then the eyes of the blind shall be opened, and the ears of the deaf unstopped; then shall the lame man leap like a deer, and the tongue of the mute sing for joy. (Isa. 33:24; 35:4–6)

The healings Christ performed while he was on this earth are only a foretaste of what he will do when he takes his great power and begins to reign as the Messiah and restores his departed saints to healthy and whole bodies free of any previous affliction, ailment, or defect.

Just as the vegetation of the earth will be restored, animal life, too, will be profoundly affected as God re-creates conditions on the earth that existed before the fall, when the abundant vegetation of the Garden of Eden provided food for man and the animal kingdom:

> And God said, "Behold, I have given you every plant yielding seed that is on the face of all the earth, and every tree with seed in its fruit. You shall have them for food. And to every beast of the earth and to every bird of the heavens and to everything that creeps on the earth, everything that has the breath of life, I have given every green plant for food." And it was so. And God saw everything that he had made, and behold, it was very good. And there was evening and there was morning, the sixth day. (Gen. 1:29–31)

Before the fall, all the trees and plants produced vegetation that was good for food for humans and the other living creatures. Apparently, all the earth's vegetation was edible. There were no poisonous plants, berries, fruit, or mushrooms. The account suggests that humans and other living creatures were vegetarians. After the fall, the curse, and the flood, the eating habits of man and the other creatures changed. It was after the catastrophic flood that God introduced the eating of meat: "Every moving thing that lives shall be food for you" (Gen. 9:3).

The earth's ecological system was fundamentally altered by the fall and the flood. The biblical record of the changes in plant and animal life after the curse is not altogether clear. Is poison ivy a plant that existed before the fall and was altered after the curse to become inedible and a true nuisance, or did God introduce it as a new kind of plant after the fall? We really do not know how this change came about, but one thing is for sure—poison ivy in its current form did not exist before the fall, for it is surely not edible.

The vegetation of the earth contains numerous inedible weeds and plants, many of which are a nuisance. Poisonous plants can be found all over the world. No doubt the flood had a negative impact on the vegetation in the world. Humans and animals now required additional nutrients from other living creatures to maintain a healthy diet. Even with this addition to their diet, the expected life spans of humans fell significantly. Needless to say, we are a long way from the Garden of Eden.

Many questions raised by the Genesis accounts of creation remain unanswered. For example, many animals, such as bears, eat both plants and other animals for nutrition. Carnivores, such as lions and alligators, eat mainly meat from the muscle of other creatures. How did these meat-eating animals come about if before the fall they, like man, were to eat only plants? The biblical record provides little information about the changes God made to the animal kingdom after the fall. It does indicate a fundamental change to plant biology whereby many plants function as weeds and are no longer edible. One can logically assume that God also made fundamental changes to many aspects of animal life, as well. Just as he introduced plants that were a nuisance, inedible, and even poisonous, he likely introduced poisonous creatures, such as some snakes, spiders, and insects.

We know that the initial creation was designed to be vegetarian, and that all the plants were edible. At some point after the fall, a fundamental change occurred in plant and animal life as a result of God's curse on this creation. The Genesis accounts simply do not tell how and when all these changes took place. Yet, Isaiah foresaw the day when the original "good" creation will be restored, affecting the whole animal kingdom:

> The wolf shall dwell with the lamb, and the leopard shall lie down with the young goat, and the calf and the lion and the fattened calf together; and a little child shall lead them. The cow and the bear shall graze; their young shall lie down together; and the lion shall eat straw like the ox. The nursing child shall play over the hole of the cobra, and the weaned child shall put his hand on the adder's den. They shall not hurt or destroy in all my holy mountain; for the earth shall be full of the knowledge of the LORD as the waters cover the sea. (Isa. 11:6–9)

Animals in the wild are fearful, and rightfully so. Lions, leopards, wolves, and bears feed on sheep, goats, and various cattle. Their newborns are particularly vulnerable. This predator-based ecological system is a tragic one.

Outlining Isaiah's remarkable prophecy reveals the magnitude of this change during the coming restoration:

- The wolf will live with the lamb.
- The leopard will lie down with the goat.
- The lion and the calf will feed together.
- A little child shall be able to lead the lion and the calf.
- The bear and the cow (and their young) will graze together.
- The lion will eat straw like the ox.
- A nursing child will be able to play over the hole of the cobra.
- A weaned child will be able to put his hand on the adder's den.

Isaiah is describing an extraordinary change in the ecological system of this creation as the Genesis creation is restored to an Edenic condition. All animals will live peacefully together with mankind as they are restored to the vegetarian-based ecology that existed before the fall. The lion will be able to lie down beside a lamb as they both relax after eating a meal of lush plant food. The animal kingdom will no longer be fearful, but friendly and happy; we can truly enjoy each other's company. It will be fun to play with a raccoon and a fox without fear of being bitten and contracting rabies.

The Holy Spirit in the Restoration

The Holy Spirit will play a major role in establishing righteousness in this world during the restoration. The following prophecies seem to fore-shadow yet another type of Pentecost (Phase 2) during the restoration. While Christ remains in heaven with the Father, he in effect comes to the world through the person of the Holy Spirit, just as he came back to the disciples and to us through the Holy Spirit, beginning at Pentecost. It is through the Holy Spirit that we shall see the face of Christ in the restoration:

I will give you a new heart, and a new spirit I will put within you. And I will remove the heart of stone from your flesh and give you a heart of flesh. And I will put *my Spirit* within you, and cause you to walk in my statutes and be careful to obey my rules. You shall dwell in the land that I gave to your fathers, and you shall be my people, and I will be your God. . . . Then they shall know that I am the LORD their God, because I sent them into exile among the nations and then assembled them into their own land. I will leave none of them remaining among the nations anymore. And *I will not hide my face anymore from them, when I pour out my Spirit upon the house of Israel*, declares the Lord GOD. (Ezek. 36:26–28; 39:28–29)

"And a Redeemer will come to Zion, to those in Jacob who turn from transgression," declares the LORD. "And as for me, this is my covenant with them," says the LORD: "*My Spirit that is upon you*, and my words that I have put in your mouth, shall not depart out of your mouth, or out of the mouth of your offspring, or out of the mouth of your children's offspring," says the LORD, "from this time forth and forevermore." (Isa. 59:20–21)

Currently, we continue to sin and grieve the Holy Spirit despite the fact that the Holy Spirit indwells us. In the restoration, we will not only be free from temptation because Satan will be bound, but, according to the prophets, we will also be uniquely filled with another outpouring of the Holy Spirit. Just as we now see Christ through the Holy Spirit, so, too, Israel and the saints of the restoration will see him. The "Redeemer *will come* to Zion" when the Holy Spirit is poured out upon the believers during the restoration, and he will dwell in our midst. Christ's presence will be so intensely felt that it will be as if he were in our very presence. Christ the Redeemer does not have to physically return to Zion to establish his kingdom so that we can actually see his face. All he has to do is *pour out his Spirit upon the house of Israel* and all believers.

As a result of the outpouring of the Holy Spirit and the regeneration of this Genesis creation, the restoration will be a time of tremendous joy and thanksgiving for what Christ will accomplish on this earth during his reign. We read and use the psalms today in worship and song. But the restoration gives them a much deeper meaning as they beautifully and poetically describe the earth bursting into songs of praise for the reign of Christ:

> Oh sing to the LORD a new song,
>> for he has done marvelous things!
> His right hand and his holy arm
>> have worked salvation for him.
> The LORD has made known his salvation;
>> he has revealed his righteousness in the sight of the nations.
> He has remembered his steadfast love and faithfulness
>> to the house of Israel.
> All the ends of the earth have seen
>> the salvation of our God.
> Make a joyful noise to the LORD, all the earth;
>> break forth into joyous song and sing praises!
> Sing praises to the LORD with the lyre,
>> with the lyre and the sound of melody!
> With trumpets and the sound of the horn
>> make a joyful noise before the King, the LORD!
> Let the sea roar, and all that fills it;
>> the world and those who dwell in it!
> Let the rivers clap their hands;
>> let the hills sing for joy together
> before the LORD, for he comes
>> to judge the earth.
> He will judge the world with righteousness,
>> and the peoples with equity. (Ps. 98:1–9)

We finally get to experience God's will being done on earth as it is in heaven. And the Son of God will rejoice and delight in his people and creation, and we and the whole creation will reciprocate in joyful thankfulness.

The Old Testament is full of praise for the forthcoming regeneration of this Genesis creation. Isaiah says, "For the LORD comforts Zion; he comforts all her waste places and makes her wilderness like Eden, her desert like the garden of the LORD; *joy and gladness* will be found in her, *thanksgiving and the voice of song*" (51:3).

Human Aspirations Fulfilled in the Restoration

We all experience the joys and miseries of this life with an astonishing degree of variation. Some are successful, prosperous, and healthy, as well as members of a wonderful family and social network of friends. Some are relatively content and fulfilled in their human experience. Others are impoverished, plagued by disease, without family or friends, and deeply unhappy with life on this earth. This has been true throughout history. But none of us should be pleased with this current fallen world.

Peter makes an interesting observation about Lot when he was living in Sodom: "And if he rescued righteous Lot, greatly distressed by the sensual conduct of the wicked (for as that righteous man lived among them day after day, he was tormenting his righteous soul over their lawless deeds that he saw and heard)" (2 Peter 2:7–8). Granted, Sodom was an especially wicked place, but there are many things in this current world that should bring distress and torment to the righteous person's soul. We should all be greatly disturbed by the evil around us and the current fallen creation. If we are not, it says something about our inability to discern evil and the fallen nature of this world and our insensitivity to the world's suffering.

We are so far removed from the Garden of Eden that we have lost any sense of the ideal condition of both nature and mankind. We have become so acclimated to this fallen sinful world that we fail to realize how abnormal it really is. But we can still discern the beauty that remains in fallen nature and mankind despite God's curse on this creation. This residual beauty should only make our aspirations for an ideal world even greater. We should long for the unspoiled beauty of a world like the Garden of Eden without the effects of sin. In the restoration, we will finally get to experience such an existence and our deepest human aspirations will be fulfilled. Under the Lordship of Christ, nature will be restored and mankind will operate in a world once again fitting to be called "good."

Today, we are fortunate if we live to be seventy and experience seventy seasons of spring. But God desires for us to enjoy a thousand spring seasons in his restored creation in this Genesis age and then eternal life in the age to come. Remember, Jesus told the disciples and his followers to anticipate receiving a "hundredfold" in the coming messianic kingdom. A "hundred-fold" indicates we should have both deep and broad aspirations for a far superior human experience than the current one. No matter where we are in life, no matter what level of suffering we are experiencing, and no matter how distressed we are by the evil around us, we should always joyfully look forward to the restoration and then the transformation.

Barren wives can look forward to the first resurrection and having all the children and grandchildren they desire. Imagine being able to raise children without fear of their being influenced by drugs, gangs, or rampant sexual immorality. Imagine being able to travel anywhere in the world and not having to worry about contaminated drinking water or malaria-carrying mosquitoes. Imagine being able to visit any area in any city in any country without fear of being mugged, molested, or murdered. Imagine cities without slums or urban blight.

Many of the Old Testament prophecies are cast in a setting of misery, and the prophets were deeply disturbed by the evil and distress around them. But at the same time, they could see what God had in store for those who loved him. They had a vision of God as the Good Shepherd resurrecting and rewarding his faithful followers with healthy human bodies and an overflowing abundance in his future earthly kingdom.

Throughout history, some saints may have lived pleasant, though short, lives. But all have lived with some level of misery, sickness, and death. Some, as Hebrews teaches, lived miserably as a result of their faith:

> Some were tortured, refusing to accept release, so that they might rise again to a better life. Others suffered mocking and flogging, and even chains and imprisonment. They were stoned, they were sawn in two, they were killed with the sword. They went about in skins of sheep and goats, destitute, afflicted, mistreated—of whom the world was not worthy—wandering about in deserts and mountains, and in dens and caves of the earth. (11:35–38)

Not all of us have experienced such misery, but we have all lived in a fallen world with satanic evil and the effects of sinful mankind all around us.

Hebrews says that those who lived by faith when they died were looking forward primarily to the kingdom of heaven, not necessarily the restoration: "But as it is, they desire a better country, that is, a heavenly one. Therefore God is not ashamed to be called their God, for he has prepared for them a city. . . . the city of the living God, the heavenly Jerusalem" (Heb. 11:16; 12:22). This is as it should be, for they did not look to the world for security and well-being, which the world in its current condition cannot give. They looked beyond their current circumstances and placed their faith in God and his character: "And without faith it is impossible to please him, for whoever would draw near to God must believe that he exists and that he rewards those who seek him" (Heb. 11:6). They knew that in seeking God first and trusting in his character no matter what they had to endure in this life, God would reward them with his presence in heaven.

But notice what happens when we, like the saints of old, get our priorities right by seeking first God's kingdom of heaven: "For the Gentiles seek after all these things, and your heavenly Father knows that you need them all. But seek *first* the kingdom of God and his righteousness, and *all these things will be added to you*" (Matt. 6:32–33). As Hebrews attests, "these things" may not be added to us in our current lifetime. Nonetheless, God does promise that when we have our hearts set first on him and joining him in his heavenly kingdom, then "all these things [peace and material well-being] will be added" to us as well.

How is this accomplished? Those saints who are faithful and willing to sacrifice physical and material well-being in this current fallen world, to be with God in heaven for eternity, also get to experience this world in its ideal, restored condition when this creation is regenerated in the restoration. God does indeed reward those who seek him with a hundredfold in this age and then eternal life in the age to come. Now, that is biblical justice.

Jesus said something interesting that now makes sense: "You will be delivered up even by parents and brothers and relatives and friends, and some of you they will put to death. You will be hated by all for my name's sake. But *not a hair of your head will perish*. By your endurance you will *gain your lives*" (Luke 21:16–19). If we are betrayed by our family or friends and are put to death because of our faith, our bodies rot and return to dust. But in the restoration, we regain our lives when our natural human bodies are resurrected and raised with full heads of hair. Thus, not a single hair will perish in the process!

What an amazing gospel. As members of the kingdom of God, the saints are promised a glorious inheritance on this earth in the Son's kingdom *and* an eternal inheritance in the Father's kingdom. The meek saints will inherit this world in a restored Edenic paradise for a thousand years through a resurrection of the mortal body *and then* inherit eternal life in the new heavens and new earth through a resurrection of their immortal bodies. No wonder Paul said, "What no eye has seen, nor ear heard, nor the heart of man imagined, what God has prepared for those who love him" (1 Cor. 2:9).

Creativity and Stewardship in the Restoration

One of the most important characteristics that demonstrates how man is made in the image of God is mankind's creativity. In the Genesis creation accounts, we see God first *conceiving* this creation, then *designing* it, and finally *building* it. Furthermore, he continues to sustain and *operate* this creation: "And he is before all things, and in him all things hold together" (Col. 1:17). Like God, mankind also has these creative abilities as we rule over this earth. We can conceive, design, build, and then operate what we have built. In the restoration, we will experience an explosion of creativity in all areas of life.

One area that will have a significant effect on the quality of life in the restoration will be the way mankind conceives, designs, builds, and operates urban and rural habitats. Cities and towns will be intelligently designed with well-planned streets, great architecture, beautiful landscaping, and great places for people to gather in community. Imagine these cities and towns surrounded by pristine rural countrysides with picturesque agricultural communities. Our deepest human aspirations for a well-designed and beautiful environment will be fulfilled during the restoration.

John envisioned thrones set up to reign with Christ over this world. Christ, as our master, did not come to be served, but to serve. Likewise, those saints set up on thrones to rule and judge with him will be chief servants among men as we use our innate creativity to develop an advanced human civilization on the regenerated earth. And I imagine there will be hierarchical positions of authority and responsibility (servanthood) at all levels of human government, society, and culture. For example, the assigned stewards of Christ's kingdom may be in charge of something as simple as managing the well-designed, beautiful landscaping of the streets and pedestrian ways. These streets and paths will be lined with magnificent shade and fruit-bearing trees and well-kept, beautiful shrubs and flowers—along with creative fountains, outdoor art, and sculpture.

We are so used to civil authorities and law enforcement officers using penalties and force to prevent irresponsible or criminal behavior, it is difficult for us to imagine a completely different kind of stewardship wherein creative people conceive, design, build, and manage an Edenic human paradise and civilization. But once Christ regenerates this Genesis creation and resurrects the many stewards to oversee it, this creation will be managed under Christ with righteous saints as his stewards as it was originally intended to be managed by Adam and Eve and their descendants.

The Everlasting Kingdom

The description of the messianic reign of Christ as an *everlasting* kingdom that *only* lasts for one thousand years is another area of confusion among scholars: "Your kingdom is an everlasting kingdom, and your dominion endures throughout all generations" (Ps. 145:13). Or as Daniel says, "And the kingdom and the dominion and the greatness of the kingdoms under the whole heaven shall be given to the people of the saints of the Most High; *their kingdom shall be an everlasting kingdom*, and all dominions shall serve and obey them" (7:27). Some claim that because the 1,000-year restoration comes to an end, it cannot be an everlasting kingdom. Therefore, these visions must be a metaphorical reference to the kingdom of heaven, which *is* everlasting.

Some premillennial scholars, however, translate the Hebrew word for *everlasting* in this context to mean the temporal messianic kingdom:

> The fourth purpose of the Seventy Sevens is: to bring in everlasting right-eousness or more literally, "to bring in an age of righteousness," which is what the Hebrew word for everlasting really means. This age of righteous-ness is called the Messianic kingdom and the Millennium. This is the same point made by Isaiah 1:26; 11:2-5; 32:17; Jeremiah 23:5-6; and 33:15-18.[11]

This interpretation may be correct, but let's assume that Christ's reign of righteousness that begins on this earth is everlasting in that it continues for eternity. Daniel seems to imply that once the Tribulation ends, the everlast-ing reign of Christ's kingdom of the saints begins. Or as John says in the book of Revelation: "'The kingdom of the world has become the kingdom of our Lord and of his Christ, and he shall reign forever and ever.' . . . 'for you have taken your great power and begun to reign'" (11:15–17). Christ's reign is everlasting because once Christ begins to use his great power and has begun to reign in the restoration, his reign will continue forever; Satan's final rebellion and attack on Jerusalem after the millennium does not succeed!

Christ destroys Satan's army of Gog and Magog with fire before it can conquer Jerusalem (Rev. 20:7–9). Subsequently, Satan is thrown into the lake of fire for eternity. Therefore, the reign of Christ continues uninterrupted. The world ends shortly after this, but the everlasting kingdom, or reign, continues, because Christ merely transfers the subjects of his kingdom, his people, from this earth, which is destroyed, to the new heavens and new earth through the transformation, the rapture. What Daniel says is true. Once Christ exercises his 1,000-year messianic reign on this earth, his everlasting kingdom begins and never ends—whether it is on this earth or in heaven. Once Christ's kingdom begins, his reign lasts forever—even though the world is destroyed and God's people transition from God's kingdom on earth to his kingdom in heaven.

Isaiah also describes the restoration as a period when God's salvation is first demonstrated on earth, and then *after* the earth is destroyed, his salvation continues for eternity:

> For the LORD comforts Zion; he comforts all her waste places and makes her wilderness like Eden, her desert like the garden of the LORD; joy and glad-ness will be found in her, thanksgiving and the voice of song. . . . My righteousness draws near, *my salvation has gone out*, and my arms will

---

[11] Fruchtenbaum, *The Footsteps of the Messiah*, 191.

judge the peoples; the coastlands hope for me, and for my arm they wait [the restoration]. Lift up your eyes to the heavens, and look at the earth beneath; for the heavens vanish like smoke, the earth will wear out like a garment, and they who dwell in it will die in like manner [the end of the world]; but *my salvation will be forever*, and my righteousness will never be dismayed [the eternal kingdom at the transformation]. (Isa. 51:3–6)

According to Isaiah, salvation not only includes the restoration of this earth to an Edenic condition, but it also includes an eternal kingdom that will be established after this current heavens and earth "vanish like smoke" and "wear out like a garment." The 1,000-year restoration in this age comes to an end, but this does not mean his reign ends. His kingdom, or reign, over restored Adamic creatures merely transfers from this earth to heaven and continues for eternity when the saints are raptured and transformed into glorified bodies adapted for heaven as the children of God the Father. Christ turns his everlasting kingdom of redeemed saints over to the Father in such a way that he and his kingdom of saints are made subject to the Father forever. Christ continues to reign over his subjects while he is subject to the Father. That is because he remains the head of his bride, his body of trans-formed believers.

At the end of the Tribulation when Satan is bound, Christ's everlasting reign does begin and continues for eternity. Satan's attempt to interrupt it after the millennium fails. That is why Daniel characterizes the overthrow of the Antichrist and the beginning of the messianic kingdom as the beginning of the everlasting kingdom. After the Tribulation, Christ establishes a kingdom that never ends, whether it is located on earth or is transferred to the new heavens and new earth. The earth and the heavens may vanish, but his salvation will be forever.

Summary

Today, Satan orchestrates the affairs of sinful man. The result is many sour and discordant sounds in a world that is full of selfishness, greed, and strife—even war. The world is badly out of tune. But when the Mighty God, who orchestrated the creation of this world, removes this alien conductor and reclaims his creation, the Prince of Peace will then orchestrate the affairs of man, and the sounds in this world will be harmonious and joyful once more. The regenerated earth will be in tune again. The world will be so thrilled by Christ's conducting such magnificent works that even the "rivers clap their hands" and the "hills sing for joy" when he comes to "judge the world with righteousness, and the peoples with equity" (Ps. 98:1–9). In the restoration, when our deepest human aspirations will be fulfilled, we will sing and rejoice every day—for hundreds of years—until Christ comes again on the last day to take us to heaven.

Christ healed many people in the short time of his earthly ministry in a very small part of the world. But the rest of world history has not experienced such healing. Most saints through the ages have lived short lives with varying degrees of misery. In the restoration, however, all God's saints—from Abel to the last one martyred in the Tribulation—will, through the first resurrection, experience humanity as it was intended before the fall. God will almost completely remove the curse that causes the fallen state of this creation and restore it to its original glory. What better way for God to reward his people of all ages than for them to come back to this world when it has been restored to an Edenic paradise? No matter what deprivation or misery the people of God may have experienced in their first life on this earth, it will all be wonderfully made up to them when they inherit the earth when Christ is ruling over it. Only *after* the completion of this restored dominion of Christ *over* restored mankind *over* his restored Genesis creation will this Adamic creation come to an end.

The regeneration of the Genesis creation is a part of the gospel *and* a part of the salvation message—a salvation of this order of being, even if it is temporary. As Christians, because we have received him, we have both the right to become children of God now and for eternity *and* the right to experience what it means to be men and women of God in a restored Genesis creation. That is good news! Salvation *of* this world during the restoration and, ultimately, salvation *from* this world, when it is destroyed by fire, unbelievers are sent to hell, and we enter into the eternal kingdom of heaven as children of God—this is the message of salvation and the kingdom of God we should be bringing to the world.

In the Olivet Discourse, Jesus insists that the gospel of the kingdom be preached and realized on this earth *before* the end of the world and the beginning of heaven: "But the one who endures to the end will be saved. And this gospel of the kingdom will be proclaimed throughout the whole world as a testimony to all nations, and then the end will come" (Matt. 24:13–14).

The "gospel of the kingdom" is that Jesus Christ is the Lord of this Genesis creation, which was created through him, by him, and for him. The earthly kingdom rightfully belongs to him. He is Lord of this creation even if we do not see it now and the world does not receive him. In the restoration, however, his creation will be restored to him when he begins his reign as Lord and King of this earth. During the millennium, the triune God will once again get to delight in mankind—his people, created in his own image, ruling over his creation as men and women of God.

The Creator, together with the saints from all history, will experience this Adamic creation as it was originally intended when God called this creation "good." He will restore it to its original glory before he destroys it and takes his people to a totally new glorious creation in his heavenly kingdom. For one thousand years the world will see the gospel of the kingdom fulfilled when he exercises his reign over the whole world from his throne in heaven. Several Old Testament prophecies, especially the following psalm, support the proposition that the restoration is the gospel being proclaimed to all nations before the end of the world:

> Oh sing to the LORD a new song,
>> for he has done marvelous things!
> His right hand and his holy arm
>> have worked salvation for him.
> The LORD has made known his salvation;
>> he has revealed his righteousness in the sight of the nations.
> He has remembered his steadfast love and faithfulness
>> to the house of Israel.
> All the ends of the earth have seen
>> the salvation of our God.
> . . . He will judge the world with righteousness,
>> and the peoples with equity. (Ps. 98:1–9)

The gospel includes the fact that he is Lord of this earth, his creation, which will be demonstrated during the restoration as a testimony to all nations when "all the ends of the earth have seen the salvation of our God." As Christ told the disciples, these extraordinary prophecies of the messianic kingdom being seen and experienced all over the world (the gospel of the kingdom) must be fulfilled on this Genesis earth; then, and only then, *the end will come* when he comes again on Judgment Day to take the children of God to his Father's kingdom of heaven for eternity.

Many missionary movements are built upon the premise that the gospel must be preached throughout the world *before* the Son's millennial kingdom can begin. These Old Testament prophecies coupled with what Jesus taught the disciples at the Olivet Discourse, however, make it clear that it is the proclamation *and the fulfillment* of the gospel *through* the 1,000-year restoration that completes the mission of proclaiming that Jesus is Lord of this Genesis creation. The end of this age will only come *after* the restoration of the Adamic order of being.

7

The Last Day

Before the second coming of Christ and our being taken to the Father's kingdom of heaven on the last day, there is one final major eschatological event that must take place on this Genesis earth before the end of this world.

Satan's Last Stand: Gog and Magog

At the end of the Tribulation, only the beast and the false prophet are permanently sent to hell. Satan is seized by an angel and bound "so that he might not deceive the nations any longer, until the thousand years were ended" (Rev. 20:3). He is not destroyed but rendered inoperative. At the end of the millennium, when he is unbound from his imprisonment, he will instigate one last rebellion of fallen mankind against God and his people. Satan demonstrates an uncanny ability to deceive unbelievers by marshaling a large army "like the sand of the sea":

> And when the thousand years are ended, Satan will be released from his prison and will come out to deceive the nations that are at the four corners of the earth, Gog and Magog, to gather them for battle; their number is like the sand of the sea. And they marched up over the broad plain of the earth and surrounded the camp of the saints and the beloved city, but fire came down from heaven and consumed them. (Rev. 20:7–9)

The beloved city is probably Jerusalem, and the camp of the saints is likely a settlement of believers.

Many unbelievers who survive the Tribulation and enter the restoration will likely become believers as a result of witnessing the miraculous restoration unfold. But not all survivors of the Tribulation will become believers. These people will reproduce and multiply during the restoration. Some of their children may become believers, but some will not. The vast majority of people on earth, however, will likely be believers. Nonetheless, at the end of the one thousand years, there will be a significant number of unbelievers for Satan to deceive, recruit, and form an army for his final battle against God and his people. Satan's power of deception is remarkable, for the world will have just experienced an earthly paradise under the reign of Christ for a thousand years. Yet, for one last time, Satan exposes fallen mankind's susceptibility to deception and greed.

A more detailed description of the battle involving Gog and Magog can be found in Ezekiel. Differences in the Revelation and Ezekiel accounts surrounding this battle have been a flash point among scholars. Some believe these verses in Revelation 20 contain a recapitulation of the battle of Armageddon, which occurs *before* the millennial reign of Christ. But John clearly placed this event after the millennium when he wrote, "And when the thousand years are ended, Satan will be released." And the similarities between Ezekiel's account of Gog and Magog and John's are too numerous for this not to be the same event.

Ezekiel also places Gog and Magog after the restoration as does Revelation. Ezekiel first tells of the dry bones of Israel coming to life as the people of the Lord in the Promised Land during the restoration (Ezek. 37). Then, in the next chapter, the events of Gog and Magog take place *after* this restoration:

> After many days [the restoration] you will be mustered. In the latter years ["when the thousand years are ended"] you will go against the land that is restored from war [they will live securely without war], the land whose people were gathered from many peoples upon the mountains of Israel, which had been a continual waste. Its people were brought out from the peoples and now dwell securely, all of them [during the restoration]. You will advance, *coming on like a storm*. You will be like a cloud covering the land, you and all your hordes, and *many peoples with you*. (Ezek. 38:8–9)

This corresponds to Revelation, which also describes this approaching army after the millennium: "Their number is like the sand of the sea. And they marched up over the broad plain of the earth and surrounded the camp of the saints and the beloved city" (Rev. 20:8–9).

John could not have made it any plainer. Ezekiel's vision of Gog and Magog comes directly after the restoration: "And when the thousand years are ended, Satan will be released from his prison and will come out to deceive the nations that are at the four corners of the earth, Gog and Magog, to gather them for battle" (Rev. 20:7–8). This is not a discussion of the battle of Armageddon before the millennium, but a discussion of events concerning Gog and Magog *after* the millennium.

During the restoration, wars will not take place because Satan will be bound, and Christ, the Prince of Peace, will rule the world. Villages and cities will have no need for walls or gates to defend themselves against hostile invasions. "He shall judge between many peoples, and shall decide for strong nations afar off; and they shall beat their swords into plowshares, and their spears into pruning hooks; nation shall not lift up sword against nation, neither shall they learn war anymore" (Mic. 4:3).

Returning to Ezekiel, we find the people of Gog and Magog inspired by Satan attacking a land of "unwalled" villages that have recovered from war:

> Thus says the Lord GOD: On that day, *thoughts will come into your mind*, and you will *devise an evil scheme* and say, "I will go up against the land of *unwalled* villages. I will fall upon the *quiet people who dwell securely*, all of them *dwelling without walls, and having no bars or gates*, to *seize spoil and carry off plunder*, . . . You will come from your place out of the uttermost parts of the north, you and many peoples with you, all of them riding on horses, *a great host, a mighty army*. You will come up against my people Israel, like a cloud covering the land." (Ezek. 38:10–16)

After one thousand years of peace and prosperity, Israel will have accumulated great wealth. A portion of this wealth is from gifts from other nations in gratitude for the joy and blessings brought about by the reign of the Jewish Messiah. Satan will form a mighty army from those he has tempted with resentment and greed, deceiving them into believing they can easily overtake this city that has no military defenses. But with Christ continuing his reign from heaven, they will not succeed:

> But on that day, the day that Gog shall come against the land of Israel, declares the Lord GOD, my wrath will be roused in my anger. For in my jealousy and in my blazing wrath I declare . . . I will summon a sword against Gog on all my mountains, declares the Lord GOD. Every man's sword will be against his brother. With pestilence and bloodshed I will enter into judgment with him, and *I will rain upon him and his hordes and the many peoples who are with him torrential rains and hailstones, fire and sulfur.* (Ezek. 38:18–22)

This destruction by supernatural fire coincides with Revelation 20:9: "And they marched up over the broad plain of the earth and surrounded the camp of the saints and the beloved city, *but fire came down from heaven and consumed them.*" Ezekiel 39:12 reveals that the death toll is high: "For seven months the house of Israel will be burying them, in order to cleanse the land." This is followed by a period of seven years, when Israel will return to the battle scene and make fuel from weapons that remain (Ezek. 39:9–10).

Revelation 20:9–10 records that Satan then meets his ultimate destiny in the lake of fire, never to be heard from again: "But fire came down from heaven and consumed them, *and the devil who had deceived them was thrown into the lake of fire and sulfur* where the beast and the false prophet were, and they will be tormented day and night forever and ever." After Gog and Magog are destroyed and Satan is permanently sent to hell, the earth remains in its restored state with Christ continuing his reign over this world from heaven.

The Fig Tree Is Ripe

We know from Ezekiel 39:9–10 that the earth will exist for at least seven more years in order to clean up the massive destruction in this battlefield. After the seven-year cleansing of the land, every prophecy dealing with this earth will have been fulfilled, except for those pertaining to the last day. The Great Tribulation, as prophesied by Daniel, Christ, Paul, and John, will have taken place. The restoration, as prophesied in the Old and New Testaments, will have occurred. And Satan's final deception of mankind at Gog and Magog—and his eternal banishment to hell—will have taken place, as prophesied by Ezekiel and John. Every prophecy about this Genesis earth is fulfilled except for those pertaining to Christ's second coming on the last day when the earth itself is destroyed.

The world at that time still does not know *when* the second coming will occur. But we know his return will be at a time established exclusively by the Father: "But concerning that day and hour no one knows, not even the angels of heaven, nor the Son, but the Father only" (Matt. 24:36). After Satan is sent to the lake of fire and the events surrounding Gog and Magog are complete, we will know, however, that the fig tree will be ripe and his second coming could happen at any moment:

> From the fig tree learn its lesson: as soon as its branch becomes tender and puts out its leaves, you know that summer is near. So also, when you see *all these things*, you know that he is near, *at the very gates*. Truly, I say to you, this generation will not pass away *until all these things take place*. Heaven and earth will pass away, but my words will not pass away. (Matt. 24:32–35)

With every prophetic word pertaining to this Genesis creation fulfilled, the second coming will be imminent—he is "at the very gates."

On the Mount of Olives, the disciples came to Christ and asked him, "Tell us, when will these things be, and what will be the sign of your coming and the close of the age?" (Matt. 24:3). Jesus, preaching from Daniel, then gave the disciples a broad outline of future events that must occur before he comes again at the close of the age. After all these prophetic events have occurred, it will be time for the human experience to come to an end. It will be time to bring an end to the Adamic order of being and this Genesis creation. It will be time for heaven and earth to pass away. It will be time for the meek to inherit the Father's kingdom of heaven and the proud to inherit the lake of fire. It will be *the last day* or *the Omega*.

With the Son's messianic kingdom fulfilled on earth in this age, it will be time for the second coming when the children of God will be raptured and become immortal beings and inherit the Father's eternal kingdom of heaven in the new heavens and new earth in "the age to come." The purpose of the second coming on the last day is to usher in the Father's kingdom of heaven—not the Son's messianic kingdom.

It will also be time for our dual existence on this earth (as men and women of God and as children of God) to come to an end and for the new creation as the children of God to be fully revealed in its eternal home with God the Father. First John 3:2 says, "Beloved, we are God's children now, and what we will be has not yet appeared; but we know that when he appears we will be like him, because we shall see him as he is." As Jesus is the Son of God, so, too, we will be made into his image as sons of God the Father.

The Second Coming

The second coming occurs on the last day and is a combination of several events. It is the second coming of Christ in the clouds to retrieve the saints and take them to heaven. The saints are resurrected (if asleep) and, along with the saints who are still alive, are transformed into immortal bodies and taken to heaven. The current heavens and earth are then destroyed by fire, and the new heavens and new earth are created as the permanent home for the raptured children of God.

The last day is also Judgment Day for all mankind at the Great White Throne judgment ("to repay everyone for what he has done") when the books are opened. The saints will be tested with fire to burn off unrighteous deeds and to determine what good deeds will survive and be rewarded in heaven. Unbelievers will rise from Hades and be judged to determine their corresponding punishment in the eternal lake of fire.

The teachings on the last day are scattered throughout the Scriptures and do not always include a discussion of all these events. But as one reads the New Testament, in particular, one finds that these events are linked, in one fashion or another, to Christ's second coming on the last day (the Omega of this Genesis age). And the purpose of the last day is to usher in the Father's eternal kingdom of heaven for his children in "the age to come."

To properly organize much of the prophetic literature of the Bible, it is important to understand the events linked to Christ's second coming. The premise of this book is that Christ's second coming can be logically linked by the biblical data to the following major events that occur on the last day:

- The resurrection of the saints as children of God in the new creation, when our bodies are glorified and transformed into immortal, imperishable bodies and taken to heaven.

- The last day of this Genesis creation when it is annihilated by God with fire and subsequently replaced with the new heavens and new earth in the age to come.
- Judgment Day, or the Great White Throne judgment, when all people (believers and unbelievers) are judged and sent to their eternal destinies in heaven or hell.

Using this brief outline, let us examine the biblical data and see how well these events contextually link to the second coming of Christ. John describes the next major eschatological event after the armies of Gog and Magog are destroyed and Satan is thrown into the lake of fire (Rev. 20:10):

Then I saw a great white throne and him who was seated on it. From his presence earth and sky fled away, and no place was found for them. And I saw the dead, great and small, standing before the throne, and books were opened. Then another book was opened, which is the book of life. And the dead were judged by what was written in the books, according to what they had done. And the sea gave up the dead who were in it, Death and Hades gave up the dead who were in them, and they were judged, each one of them, according to what they had done. Then Death and Hades were thrown into the lake of fire. This is the second death, the lake of fire. And if anyone's name was not found written in the book of life, he was thrown into the lake of fire. Then I saw a new heaven and a new earth, for the first heaven and the first earth had passed away, and the sea was no more. And I saw the holy city, new Jerusalem, coming down out of heaven from God, prepared as a bride adorned for her husband. (Rev. 20:11—21:2)

This is the end of the current heavens and earth, for "earth and sky fled away." This is also the final resurrection and Judgment Day and the beginning of the new heavens and new earth for believers whose names are written in the book of life. This, too, is the beginning of hell for unbelievers whose names are not found in the book of life.

Christ himself describes his second coming as occurring on Judgment Day:

"Behold, I am coming soon, bringing my recompense with me, to repay everyone for what he has done [Judgment Day]. I am the Alpha and the Omega, the first and the last, the beginning [of this Genesis creation] and the end [of this Genesis creation]." Blessed are those who wash their robes, so that they may have the right to the tree of life and that they may enter the city by the gates [the New Jerusalem in the new heavens and new earth]. (Rev. 22:12–14)

The second coming ("I am coming soon") is directly linked to Christ's judging all mankind, the end of this Genesis creation, and the saints entering the eternal city of God—which matches what John teaches will occur at the Great White Throne judgment.

Glorification

Because of mankind's sinfulness, the entire human experience falls short of the glory of God's original Genesis creation. The 1,000-year restoration will essentially restore this glory of the Adamic order of being, and God will once again delight in his creation. But there is a new kind of glory that awaits the children of God in the age to come. Glory is directly associated with the second coming, our raptured bodies, and heaven itself. Our new bodies are even referred to as transformed bodies that will be like Christ's glorified body: "who will transform our lowly body to be like his glorious body, by the power that enables him even to subject all things to himself" (Phil. 3:21). Immediately after describing the final judgment, Revelation proceeds with a description of the glory of heaven:

> Then I saw a new heaven and a new earth, for the first heaven and the first earth had passed away, and the sea was no more. And I saw the holy city, new Jerusalem, coming down out of heaven from God, prepared as a bride adorned for her husband. And I heard a loud voice from the throne saying, "Behold, the dwelling place of God is with man. He will dwell with them, and they will be his people . . . and death shall be no more [immortality], neither shall there be mourning nor crying nor pain anymore, for the former things have passed away" [the mortal Adamic order of being ceases to exist]. And he who was seated on the throne said, "Behold, I am making all things new" [the new order of being]. . . . And he said to me, "It is done! I am the Alpha and the Omega, the beginning and the end [from the beginning of the Genesis creation to the end of the Genesis creation]. . . . The one who conquers will have this heritage, and I will be his God and he will be my son" [we are children of God]. . . . "Come, I will show you the Bride, the wife of the Lamb" [the body of Christ]. And he carried me away in the Spirit to a great, high mountain, and showed me the holy city Jerusalem coming down out of heaven from God, having the glory of God, its radiance like a most rare jewel, like a jasper, clear as crystal. (Rev. 21:1–11)

The "Bride, the wife of the Lamb" is equated to the New Jerusalem and depicted as having the glory of God. Whereas Old Testament prophets described the restoration as an earthly paradise with mortal human beings, the kingdom of heaven is described as glorious with the sons of God now in immortal, glorified bodies ("death shall be no more"). The second coming and Judgment Day are described as a glorious event: "When the Son of Man *comes in his glory*, and all the angels with him, then he will sit on his *glorious* throne" (Matt. 25:31).

Christ, knowing that his mission on this earth was about to be completed, looked forward to the time when his followers given to him by his Father would be with him in heaven to see his glory:

> I glorified you on earth, having accomplished the work that you gave me to do. And now, Father, *glorify me* in your own presence *with the glory* that I had with you before the world existed. . . . Father, I desire that *they also*, whom you have given me, may be with me where I am [in heaven], to *see my glory* that you have given me because you loved me before the foundation of the world. (John 17:4–5, 24)

Colossians teaches this same concept:

> If then you have been raised with Christ, seek the things that are above [in heaven], where Christ is, seated at the right hand of God. Set your minds on things that are above, not on things that are on earth. For you have died, and your life is hidden with Christ in God [in heaven]. When Christ who is your life *appears* [the second time], then you also will *appear with him in glory* [in heaven]. (Col. 3:1–4)

When Christ appears again at his second coming, we will appear with him in glory in heaven.

Peter also referred to the glory we will experience at Christ's second coming on Judgment Day when our good deeds will be exposed:

> Blessed be the God and Father of our Lord Jesus Christ! According to his [the Father's] great mercy, he has caused us to be born again to a living hope through the resurrection of Jesus Christ from the dead [we hope for the same resurrection], to an inheritance that is imperishable, undefiled, and unfading, kept in heaven for you, who by God's power are being guarded through faith for a salvation ready to be revealed in the last time. In this you rejoice, though now for a little while, if necessary, you have been grieved by various trials, so that the tested genuineness of your faith— more precious than gold that perishes [when this earth is burned up and destroyed] though it is tested by fire—may be found to result in praise and *glory* [at the final judgment] and honor at the revelation of Jesus Christ [the second coming]. (1 Peter 1:3–7)

All this takes place at the revelation of Jesus Christ on the last day, not before the millennium. The restoration is mentioned in numerous teachings throughout the Bible; nowhere is it described as a place of immortality or as an imperishable kingdom. Only in Revelation 21:4, after earth and sky have fled away and the saints enter the eternal kingdom, is immortality of the saints mentioned: "and death shall be no more."

The second coming of Christ in the clouds and the resurrection and rapture of believers into immortal bodies clearly signal the beginning of the

THE LAST DAY 265

glorious kingdom of heaven for believers and hell for unbelievers on the last day; in no way do they indicate the beginning of the earthly restoration where there is mortality and marriage in an earthly paradise.

Comes Like a Thief

The familiar metaphor of Christ coming like a thief in reference to his second coming in the clouds to take us to his Father's kingdom has caused a great deal of confusion among theologians. Paul wrote, "For you yourselves are fully aware that the day of the Lord will *come like a thief in the night*. While people are saying, 'There is peace and security,' then *sudden destruction* will come upon them as labor pains come upon a pregnant woman, and *they will not escape*" (1 Thess. 5:2–3).

Some scholars interpret this to mean that Christ can return at any moment to rapture the saints and judge the world and construct entire systems of eschatology around this metaphor of coming "like a thief" (e.g., pretribulational premillennialists). The idea that this metaphor teaches that Christ could come at any moment was never true, even at the time Paul wrote this letter to the Thessalonians, because certain prophetic events still had to take place before Christ could come again.

The first letter to the Thessalonians was written in AD 51, when it was obvious several prophecies had not been fulfilled. For example, Christ could not have come again before Peter died, for Christ predicted that Peter would be martyred before he came again (John 21:18–19). But Peter was still alive in AD 51. Also, Christ could not have come before the temple was destroyed, for he predicted the temple's destruction. The temple was not destroyed until AD 70.

Therefore, the assertion that Paul was teaching the church at Thessalonica that Christ could come at any moment, "like a thief," to rapture them is unfounded. If he had come in AD 51 to rapture the believers at Thessalonica, then Peter would have been alive at his second coming, the temple would have still been in existence, and Jesus would have been a false prophet. If Christ could not have come at any moment for the Thessalonians to whom the letter was written, then it certainly cannot be true for us; otherwise, the grammatical-historical method of interpretation has no meaning. For the "any moment" rapture to be true for us, it would have had to have been possible for those to whom the letter was first written.

Even today, other prophecies must be fulfilled before Christ can come again. For the Antichrist to come, Israel must exist again as a nation (which did not occur until 1948), and for the Antichrist to begin his reign of terror, the temple must exist for him to enter and make himself out to be God. This temple does not exist today. A mosque, the Dome of the Rock, sits on the temple mount.

Dispensational pretribulationalists put great emphasis on this verse, but Paul's metaphor of Christ coming "like a thief" cannot be construed to mean "at any moment." The Tribulation cannot even begin until there is a rebuilt temple for the Antichrist to enter.

To resolve this confusion, we must observe that Paul's use of the metaphor of Christ coming "like a thief in the night" applies to *unbelievers,* not to faithful believers. Christ is only coming like a thief in the night to those who are in darkness and say there is peace and security with nothing to worry about. A sudden destruction like labor pains will come upon unbelievers. He does not come like a thief in the night to believers: "But you are not in darkness, brothers, for that day to surprise you like a thief. For you are all children of light, children of the day. We are not of the night or of the darkness" (1 Thess. 5:4–5). Believers will not be surprised when Christ comes again!

There is a fundamental difference between not knowing *when* Christ is coming again and knowingly expecting him. If I know Christ is coming, but do not know when, then when he does arrive, I might say: "I did not know *when* you were coming, but I knew you *were* coming and have been eagerly *waiting* for you, *expecting* your arrival." To me, he will be like an expected guest—not like an unexpected thief.

The unbeliever, on the other hand, will say: "You caught me completely off guard. I did not believe you were God. What a surprise, for I certainly did not expect to see you come as the judge of the world!" Many will not be expecting this Jesus of Nazareth—who lived in the first century in the small country of Israel under Roman rule who was crucified and then disappeared—to be the God of the universe who created the world, who will destroy the world, who will judge the world, and who will cast unbelievers into hell. Because they do not know him, they will not be expecting his return, much less be waiting for him. They certainly will not be prepared for Judgment Day and the sudden destruction that is going to come upon them. They will not be clothed in the righteousness of Christ, and their self-righteousness will not save them.

When an unbeliever dies, I do not think he is immediately made aware that Jesus Christ is Lord God, the Creator, and Judge of the universe. Rather, I believe he or she remains in Hades in a state of darkness and confusion, not knowing the truth about Christ until the last day and only at the second coming does the unbeliever realize why he or she has been in Hades.

I often think about how shocked Islamic suicide bombers will be when they find themselves in Hades the moment after death, instead of paradise. They will be even more surprised when Christ comes again on Judgment Day to resurrect them to appear before the Great White Throne judgment. Instead of Allah rewarding them with a dozen virgins, they will be sent to the lake of fire. All unbelievers are in for a difficult awakening. They are deluded and ignorant, or perhaps simply dismissive, of the fact that Christ is Lord and is coming again like a thief in the night to judge the world.

In contrast, when a believer dies, I believe his or her spirit is immediately raised to heaven where he or she joins Christ (whom the believer already knows) and becomes a witness to the events unfolding in the world. Whether a believer is alive on this earth at his second coming or the believer's spirit is with the Lord in heaven, the believer will not be surprised on the last day for he or she already knows that Jesus is Lord. A believer already has a relationship with him whether he or she is alive or asleep.

It makes no difference whether a person is dead or alive in regard to whether or not he or she is expecting Christ. Hebrews 9:26–28 includes the Old Testament saints who are asleep among those who are characterized as "eagerly waiting for him": "But as it is, he has appeared once for all at the end of the ages to put away sin by the sacrifice of himself. . . . so Christ, having been offered once to bear the sins of many, will *appear a second time*, not to deal with sin but to save those who are *eagerly waiting* for him." Saints who are alive at the time of his coming, as well as those who have died, are eager for him to come and transform their bodies to be like his and take them to the New Jerusalem in the Father's kingdom of heaven.

Conversely, Christ will come like a thief to unbelievers, whether they are dead in Hades or alive on the earth when he appears a second time, for they will not be eagerly waiting for him. Second Peter 3:10 uses the same figure of speech to describe the second coming in reference to Judgment Day and the end of the world: "But the day of the Lord will *come like a thief*, and then the heavens will pass away with a roar, and the heavenly bodies will be burned up and dissolved, and the earth and the works that are done on it will be exposed."

This figure of speech is often used in the Scriptures to describe the sudden occurrence of an event or act of judgment. For example, one could say that the wrath of God against Pharaoh and his army at the Red Sea was an unexpected coming of judgment by God like a thief in the night. If Pharaoh and his army had been expecting such a judgment, they would not have marched into the parted Red Sea in pursuit of Moses and the Israelites. They were foolish but not stupid. Likewise, the armies that follow Satan at Gog and Magog will be foolish to attack God's people, but Christ's wrath poured out on them will be sudden and unexpected.

The Scriptures also have a unique way of approaching time. Numerous examples throughout the Bible express the idea of long periods of time condensed into but a brief moment. In Psalms, King David says that "in just a little while" the meek shall inherit the land in the restoration (he wrote this psalm over three thousand years ago):

Be still before the LORD and *wait patiently for him*;
> fret not yourself over the one who prospers in his way,
> over the man who carries out evil devices!

Refrain from anger, and forsake wrath!
> Fret not yourself; it tends only to evil.

For the evildoers shall be cut off,
> but those who wait for the LORD shall inherit the land.

In just a little while, the wicked will be no more;
> though you look carefully at his place, he will not be there.

But the meek shall inherit the land
> and delight themselves in abundant peace. (Ps. 37:7–11)

The restoration might not occur for another two thousand years, but from David's perspective, time collapses for the righteous while they "sleep," and the meek will inherit the land soon. David died thousands of years ago, and I might die a hundred years before the restoration begins. But time will collapse for both of us, and as "meek" believers, we will inherit the earth through the first resurrection "in just a little while." In effect, David only had to wait for the end of his lifetime to be ready for the restoration to take place. Everything David and his righteous contemporaries longed for will indeed come true "in just a little while."

The prophet Isaiah offered another example of condensing many years into a brief moment. Like Paul, he prophesied that the Jews will be hardened but someday be grafted back in: "'For a brief moment I deserted you, but with great compassion I will gather you. In overflowing anger for a moment I hid my face from you, but with everlasting love I will have compassion on you,' says the LORD, your Redeemer" (Isa. 54:7–8). This "brief moment" has lasted more than two thousand years; the Jews have yet to be grafted back in.

This collapsing of time is mentioned throughout the Bible in relation to believers who wait for Christ's earthly kingdom as well as his heavenly kingdom. I often think about believers who lived many years before me, and whatever time period I consider, it is as if they lived yesterday. From my perspective, the history of the world has collapsed up to my lifetime. Because of the way time collapses for believers when they die, the Bible can speak of events happening to believers "in just a little while" or in "a brief moment."

In the Days of Noah and Sodom

Another area of confusion among theologians over Christ's second coming on the last day results from mistakenly believing the earth will be characterized by evil at the time of Christ's second coming. Many arrive at this conclusion because Christ references the days of Noah and Sodom, a time of evil, in relation to his second coming (Luke 17). This is important to address, because the postrestorational position has Christ continuing his messianic reign of peace, righteousness, and justice even after Satan is released one final time and then is destroyed forever. If Satan is destroyed at the battle of Gog and Magog and Christ continues his reign over this earth, then one would expect to find a world of peace and righteousness at the time of his return—not a time of evil such as in the days of Noah and Sodom.

We should be careful not to read too much into this analogy. In reading Christ's words, notice that he never states that people are engaged in evil activity when he comes again on the last day. Rather, unbelievers will be doing normal daily activities. Because of the apparent tranquility of everyday life, Christ's coming will be an unexpected event for unbelievers; but for believers, as it was for Noah and Lot, his coming on Judgment Day will be anticipated because they know him and believed his forewarnings:

> And he said to the disciples, "The days are coming when you will desire to see one of the days of the Son of Man, and you will not see it. And they will say to you, 'Look, there!' or 'Look, here!' Do not go out or follow them. For as the lightning flashes and lights up the sky from one side to the other, so will the Son of Man be in his day. But first he must suffer many things and be rejected by this generation. Just as it was in the days of Noah, so will it be in the days of the Son of Man. They were *eating and drinking and marrying and being given in marriage*, until the day when Noah entered the ark, and the flood came and destroyed them all. Likewise, just as it was in the days of Lot—*they were eating and drinking, buying and selling, planting and building*, but on the day when Lot went out from Sodom, fire and sulfur rained from heaven and destroyed them all—so will it be on the day when the Son of Man is revealed. On that day, let the one who is on the housetop, with his goods in the house, not come down to take them away, and likewise let the one who is in the field not turn back. Remember Lot's wife. Whoever seeks to preserve his life will lose it, but whoever loses his life will keep it. I tell you, in that night there will be two in one bed. *One will be taken* and the other left. There will be *two women grinding together. One will be taken* and the other left." (Luke 17:22–36)

Christ is not even comparing the conditions of evil in the days of Noah to the condition of the world at his second coming. In fact, the reverse is true. Christ is merely describing the goings on of ordinary life. People are "eating and drinking and marrying and being given in marriage" and "buying and selling, planting and building," and women are "grinding together." Christ makes no mention of a grossly immoral people such as those at the time of Noah when "the wickedness of man was great in the earth, and that every intention of the thoughts of his heart was only evil continually. . . . Now the earth was corrupt in God's sight, and the earth was filled with violence" (Gen. 6:5, 11).

The purpose of this analogy to the judgments poured out during Noah's day and on Sodom and is to teach that Christ's second coming on Judgment

Day will be unexpected by unbelievers and expected by believers—just as the flood was a surprise to unbelievers, but expected by Noah and his family; and just as the fire and sulfur were a surprise to the citizens of Sodom, yet expected by Lot. Both Noah and Lot believed the Lord's forewarning and were prepared and escaped God's judgment. Likewise, believers know and expect that Christ will one day come back to rapture them, destroy the world with fire, and sit on a throne of judgment. When this happens, believers will not be surprised. In Luke 17, Christ teaches the important lesson that his second coming will happen suddenly: the unbeliever will not expect it nor be able to escape it; whereas the believer will not only expect it but will welcome it and escape the wrath of God, as did Noah and Lot.

Therefore, if this analogy by Christ is not an attempt to communicate the depravity of the world at the time of his coming, but rather to reveal how ordinary life will be at his sudden appearance on Judgment Day, then it coincides well with the postrestorational view of the world after the one thousand years, after Gog and Magog, and after Satan is thrown into the lake of fire—the time when Christ continues to exercise his reign over this earth. This will be a time of ordinary, peaceful, human experiences with people "eating and drinking and marrying and being given in marriage" and "buying and selling, planting and building."

The Last Days

Scholars also wrestle with the belief of the New Testament writers that they were living in the last days: "*The end of all things is at hand*; therefore be self-controlled and sober-minded for the sake of your prayers" (1 Peter 4:7). This belief can be found throughout the New Testament.

John also quotes Jesus as using this type of language: "Behold, *I am coming soon*, bringing my recompense with me, to repay everyone for what he has done" (Rev. 22:12). This concept of Christ coming soon is similar to David's use of the phrase "in just a little while" or Isaiah's use of "for a brief moment." Here we are almost two thousand years later and the Tribulation, the restoration, and the second coming have not yet occurred.

Even in Peter's day, however, some people were already beginning to mock Christ's return because it had not happened yet:

This is now the second letter that I am writing to you, beloved. In both of them I am stirring up your sincere mind by way of reminder, that you should remember the predictions of the holy prophets and the command-ment of the Lord and Savior through your apostles, knowing this first of all, that scoffers will come in the last days with scoffing, following their own sinful desires. They will say, "Where is the promise of his coming? For ever since the fathers fell asleep, all things are continuing as they were from the beginning of creation." (2 Peter 3:1–4)

The world was marching on, as usual, with no sign of his supposed coming in judgment. Peter answered: "But do not overlook this one fact, beloved, that with the Lord one day is as a thousand years, and a thousand years as one day. *The Lord is not slow to fulfill his promise as some count slowness*, but is patient toward you, not wishing that any should perish, but that all should reach repentance" (2 Peter 3:8-9).

The Lord's experience of time is different from ours. From the Lord's perspective, the passing of ten years, one hundred years, one thousand years, and even ten thousand years is not evidence that his coming is slow to happen. We are still in the last days, though it is almost two thousand years later. From the Lord's perspective, it is as if only two days have passed. And God has his reasons for extending the time, one being that he is waiting for more humans to repent and come into his fold before Christ does come on Judgment Day to bring an end to this human experience. In the meantime, he wants us to anticipate his coming so that we take his words seriously and respond accordingly.

John Could Be Alive When Christ Returns

Jesus had an interesting conversation with Peter and the disciples in which he informed Peter that he (Peter) was going to be martyred before he returned: "'When you are old, you will stretch out your hands, and another will dress you and carry you where you do not want to go.' (This he said to show by what kind of death he was to glorify God.) And after saying this he said to him, 'Follow me'" (John 21:18-19). He would not return in Peter's lifetime because Peter would be martyred before he returned. The conversation that follows is even more remarkable:

> When Peter saw him [the apostle John], he said to Jesus, "Lord, what about this man?" Jesus said to him, "*If it is my will that he remain until I come, what is that to you*? You follow me!" So the saying spread abroad among the brothers that this disciple was not to die; yet Jesus did not say to him that he was not to die, but, "If it is my will that he remain until I come, what is that to you?" (John 21:21-23)

Christ left them with the impression that all prophetic events yet to take place—such as the destruction of the temple, the Tribulation, and the restoration—*could* take place in John's lifetime and that John could still be alive when Christ returned! But Jesus only taught the disciples that John *could* be alive when he returned—not that he *would* be alive. Yet, in what scenario could John have possibly been alive at his second coming? On one hand, Christ prophesied that the temple of his day would be completely destroyed. This occurred in AD 70. But a temple must be rebuilt for the Tribulation to begin. Both Christ and Paul predicted that the "abomination of desolation spoken of by the prophet Daniel" would enter the temple and proclaim he is God, and then the three-and-one-half years of the Great Tribulation would break out.

Revelation says that the restoration will last at least one thousand years. After that time, Christ could return—and the apostle John could possibly still be living! How could all these predicted events happen in such a way that John *could* (for Jesus did not say "would") still be alive when Christ returns? First of all, Jesus only said it was a possibility that John would be alive when he returned. He also freely admitted that only the Father knew the times and seasons of the restoration and his second coming. Even so, there must be a logical sequence of all prophetic events that *could* transpire for John to potentially still be alive when Christ returns. Following is a hypothetical scenario that could have occurred to allow for the fulfillment of the major prophetic events and for the possibility of John still being alive at Christ's second coming.

John was still a young man during this conversation between Christ and Peter, perhaps still a teenager. Let us assume that he was eighteen years old when Christ ascended into heaven and John began waiting for his return. Forty years later, the Jews initiated a rebellion, causing the Roman emperor to declare war against them, destroying their temple in the process. The temple was destroyed in AD 70, so John would have been about fifty-eight years old at the time. Having been forewarned by Jesus of the temple's destruction, John would have headed for the mountains to escape the destruction of Jerusalem.

Then, assume ten years go by and an influential Jewish person, perhaps the famous Jewish historian Josephus, was able to meet with the emperor in Rome and convince him that restoring both Jerusalem and the temple would be beneficial for the empire. The Jews had learned their lesson. The empire would not be at risk for another revolt. This is not that farfetched, for Josephus did actually have connections to the emperor and served as an advisor on Jewish affairs. Assume the emperor heeded Josephus's council and advice. The Romans were exceptional builders and could have rebuilt the temple in perhaps ten years. John would now be seventy-eight years old.

Assume another ten years go by and Paul's prayers for the Jews are answered—their hearts are no longer hardened, and they are grafted back into the natural olive tree. A major revival takes place among the Jews. John is now eighty-eight years old.

Next, the gears of the Great Tribulation start to turn. Another war breaks out with the Jews, but this time the Antichrist makes a peace treaty, or covenant, between Israel and her enemies. Then, three-and-one-half years later, the Antichrist enters the rebuilt temple proclaiming to be God, and the second half of the Great Tribulation begins. John would be about ninety-one years old. But when John sees the abomination of desolation enter the temple, he would heed Christ's advice again and head for the mountains to hide from the Antichrist.

Having safely hidden in some remote cave in the wilderness, John would be ninety-five years old when the Tribulation ends and Satan is bound and Christ begins his 1,000-year reign from his throne in heaven. Nature is then regenerated to an Edenic state. In this restored habitat, people can live for hundreds of years; if someone dies at one hundred years old, he is still considered a youth.

John survives the Tribulation and enters the restoration in which any infirmity he may have had is healed. As a result, he could possibly live for one thousand more years. At the end of the millennium, John would be one thousand and ninety-five years old. Next, Satan is released one final time to deceive the world. But before he can harm anyone, he and his army are destroyed.

Ezekiel informs us that it takes more than seven years to clean up after the destruction of Gog and Magog. After seven years, all the prophetic events have been fulfilled and Christ can come at any moment. John is a healthy 1,102 years old. He lives longer than Adam (930 years), Seth (912 years), and even Noah (950 years). Perhaps ten more years go by, and Christ suddenly returns and finds John still living at the ripe old age of 1,112!

What Christ said to the disciples was true. He only said that John "could" have been alive when he returned, not that he "would" be. The early church operated upon the premise that all the prophetic events could take place within their lifetimes, so they could still be alive when Christ returned. Theoretically, as illustrated above, all those events could have taken place in the disciples' lifetimes, with Christ returning while they were still alive.

All these events could unfold in our lifetime, just as they could have unfolded in John's. At this time, however, even though Israel has become a nation again, the Jewish temple has yet to be rebuilt. Apparently, God is still patiently gathering more of his children into his kingdom. He obviously wants a large family. But according to Peter, from God's perspective, only two days may have passed. God may even wait another couple of "days" for the restoration to begin, meaning that he might not send his Son back until after the year 5000.

The world—including the church—has entered a period of earth's history characterized as the "last days." Together, the incarnation, crucifixion, resurrection, and ascension represent the pivot point in human history. All history that follows these events, including the restoration, is part of the last days, until Christ returns a second time on the very last day, when the earth is destroyed and the saints inherit the kingdom of heaven.

The Sequence of Events on the Last Day

Many events take place at the second coming of Christ on the last day. Determining the exact chronological order of these events is not an easy task. For example, on the last day, Christ comes in the clouds, the saints are resurrected for eternal life, the unbelievers are resurrected for destruction, the earth is destroyed, and everyone is judged at the Great White Throne judgment. But which comes first, the transformation of believers, asleep or alive, or the resurrection of unbelievers to face judgment? The answer is more complex than one might expect, because Christ used numerous parables to describe these events and each parable has a slightly different sequence. The point of the parable might not be to teach the exact sequence of the events that take place, but simply to teach that all these events take place on the last day. Consider the parable of the weeds in Matthew 13. The weeds represent unbelievers who are destined for hell, and the wheat represents believers destined for heaven:

> And the servants of the master of the house came and said to him, "Master, did you not sow good seed in your field? How then does it have weeds?" He said to them, "An enemy has done this." So the servants said to him, "Then do you want us to go and gather them?" But he said, "No, lest in gathering the weeds you root up the wheat along with them. Let both grow together until the harvest [the last day], and at harvest time I will tell the reapers, Gather the weeds first [unbelievers are removed] and bind them in bundles to be burned [in the lake of fire], but gather the wheat [believers] into my barn [heaven]." (Matt. 13:27–30)

Christ tells the angels to first gather and remove the unbelievers and then to gather or rapture the believers to be taken to heaven.

In contrast, when the second coming is compared to the days of Noah and Lot, one could conclude that the righteous are removed first and the unrighteous are left behind to be destroyed along with the earth. On the other hand, when Christ describes two women grinding grain together, he says that one is taken to where the "vultures will gather," which would represent unbelievers. Thus, the unbelievers are taken away to be destroyed, and believers are left behind (Luke 17:24–37). Even within the same analogy to the times of Noah and Lot, one can come up with two seemingly opposite scenarios: believers are removed first, and then unbelievers are destroyed; or, unbelievers are removed first to be destroyed, and believers are left behind for the angels to take to meet Christ in the clouds at his second coming.

The parable of the ten virgins in Matthew 25 provides yet another version of the sequence of events of the final resurrection and judgment on the last day. Those prepared for Christ's return enter into heaven to meet the coming bridegroom, Christ, *leaving behind* those who are unprepared and shut out of the kingdom of heaven (Matt. 25:1–13).

In the final analysis, it is difficult to determine the exact sequence of the events on the last day. I am not sure that determining their exact sequence is even an important issue, for they all happen "in the twinkling of an eye." I will take the position that unbelievers are removed first and then believers are resurrected and transformed. *Then*, the current heavens and earth are destroyed by fire, and the books are opened with everyone being judged at the Great White Throne judgment.

Summary of the Last Day

When Christ comes again after the restoration, he will take us to be with him to see and experience the glory of his Father's kingdom in heaven for eternity. The last day can be outlined as follows:

1. People will be leading normal lives; they will be eating, drinking, marrying, buying, selling, planting, building, and grinding grain when Christ comes again (Luke 17:22–36).
2. Christ returns on a day and at an hour determined exclusively by God the Father. No one else knows that time—not the Son, nor any of the angels (Matt. 24:36).
3. Christ descends from heaven with angels and with the spirits of the departed saints who are asleep (1 Thess. 4:14–18); he suddenly appears in the clouds like a bolt of lightning in the sky that is seen all over the world. "For as the lightning flashes and lights up the sky from one side to the other, so will the Son of Man be in his day" (Luke 17:24).
4. Christ cries out a command "with the voice of an archangel, and with the sound of the trumpet of God" (1 Thess. 4:16).
5. Angels are sent out by Christ to gather all unbelievers, alive and dead, for judgment and destruction (Matt. 13:30). All deceased unbelievers are resurrected into bodily form from Hades where their fallen spirits have been held until the day of judgment (Rev. 20:13).
6. Angels are then sent out to gather all the saints (Matt. 24:31). Those who are asleep are resurrected first and those who are still alive on this earth will be "caught up together with them in the clouds to meet the Lord in the air" (1 Thess. 4:15–17). Their natural bodies are transformed into glorified bodies that are immortal, incorruptible, imperishable, and adapted for heaven (1 Cor. 15:52–53).
7. The Genesis heavens and earth are completely destroyed by fire— they flee from his presence (2 Peter 3:10–13 and Rev. 20:11; 21:1).
8. Christ then sits on the Great White Throne in heaven, because all judgment has been given to him (John 5:25–29).

9. All the saints who are in the book of life are judged first and given their rewards (1 Peter 4:17). They are judged by fire to test the quality of their works. The good works that survive affect our eternal existence in heaven (1 Cor. 3:11–15).

10. Unbelievers are judged next, according to their deeds (Rev. 20:12–13). The saints will testify against them.

11. All unbelievers are sent to the lake of fire, or hell, and experience the second death (Rev. 20:14–15).

12. The saints—the children of God whose names are in the book of life—enter the new heavens and new earth to be with God in heaven for eternity (Rev. 21:1 and 2 Peter 3:13).

14. The dualism of our existence ends. We are no longer male and female nor given in marriage; we are now solely children of God. What we will be like as children of God remains a mystery, but we know that when he appears, we will be like him (1 John 3:2).

15. The New Jerusalem, the bride of Christ, is now prepared as a bride adorned for her husband. The wedding between Christ and his bride is consummated (Rev. 21:2).

16. Now that Christ has destroyed every rule and every authority and power including the last enemy, death, he delivers the kingdom over to the Father and is subject to the Father (1 Cor. 15:24–28).

17. Christ exclaims, "It is done! I am the Alpha and the Omega, the beginning and the end." He has finished the work the Father has given him (Rev. 21:6). In the Father's eternal kingdom of heaven we will see God's face. There will be neither night nor sun, for the Lord God will be our light. And we shall reign in his heavenly kingdom forever and ever (Rev. 22:4–5).

8

The Transformed Body

After the 1,000-year messianic kingdom, all the saints experience the final resurrection or transformation of the natural body into an immortal spiritual body when we are taken to the Father's kingdom of heaven. Christ was referencing this resurrection of God's children in his answer to the Sadducees:

> And Jesus said to them, "The sons of this age [those in the Adamic order of being with a natural body] marry and are given in marriage, but those who are considered worthy to attain to that age and to the resurrection from the dead [believers] neither marry nor are given in marriage, for they *cannot die anymore*, because they are equal to angels and are *sons of God*, being sons of the resurrection." (Luke 20:34–36)

In this final resurrection of the sons of God, the transformed body is made immortal and is no longer given in marriage. The Genesis Adamic order of being with marriage and reproduction comes to an end, and the new heavenly creation begins for God's immortal children in the eternal age.

Paul also describes the transformed body:

> So is it with the resurrection of the dead. . . . It is sown a natural body; it is raised a spiritual body. If there is a natural body, there is also a spiritual body. . . . I tell you a mystery. We shall not all sleep, but we shall be changed, in a moment, in the twinkling of an eye, at the last trumpet. For the trumpet will sound, and the dead will be raised imperishable, and we shall be changed. For this perishable body must put on the imperishable, and this mortal body must put on immortality. (1 Cor. 15:42–44, 51–53)

Paul further teaches that the Adamic body will be transformed into a body like the ascended, glorified, and resurrected body of Christ:

The first man [Adam] was from the earth, a man of dust; the second man is from heaven. As was the man of dust, so also are those who are of the dust, and as is the man of heaven, so also are those who are of heaven. *Just as we have borne the image of the man of dust, we shall also bear the image of the man of heaven.* I tell you this, brothers: flesh and blood cannot inherit the kingdom of God, nor does the perishable inherit the imperishable. (1 Cor. 15:47–50)

Paul teaches that we shall "bear the image of the man of heaven" when he returns. Currently, our natural bodies are like the man from the earth—a mortal body of flesh and blood made from the dust of the earth. Our spiritual bodies, however, will not be like our current mortal Adamic bodies. They will be in the image of Christ's glorified body. In a sense, our bodies will be made from the "dust of heaven."

The New Testament says very little about the nature of the transformed bodies that the children of God will possess in the age to come. The apostle John admitted that he, too, did not know what this future body for God's children would be like:

See what kind of love the Father has given us, that we should be called children of God; and so we are. The reason why the world does not know us is that it did not know him. Beloved, we are God's children now, and *what we will be has not yet appeared*; but we know that when he appears *we will be like him*, because we shall see him as he is. (1 John 3:1–2)

Even though we are already the eternal children of God, having experienced the regeneration of our spirits, John teaches that the nature of our future transformed bodies as God's children will remain a mystery until the last day when Christ appears in the sky to redeem his saints and transform our bodies to be like his resurrected body. Being a child of God destined for a new creation necessitates a new kind of body adapted to the new heavens and new earth.

But what will this heavenly spiritual body be like? How similar will it be to the natural Adamic body? Again, the Bible teaches that it is truly a mystery. None of us has gone to heaven and seen the glorified, resurrected Christ. Even the departed saints in heaven are only "spirits made perfect" for they have not yet received their glorified bodies.

The Traditional View of the Spiritual Body

Is the spiritual body composed of "spirit" like that of an angel, or does it still have a material component? Through the centuries, various unorthodox teachings have proposed that Paul taught that the resurrected body will be exclusively spiritual in form with no material substance. But if this were the case, why would Christ go to the trouble of resurrecting the body *from this earth* to transform it? It makes no sense to return to a material world to resurrect and transform a material body if the ultimate nature of that body is to be purely spiritual.

It would be far simpler to transform existing spirits in heaven into supposedly spirit-only entities. We know, however, that the Lord ascended to heaven in bodily form and that he comes back to this earth in the clouds in his glorified body. We also know that the final resurrection is a transformation of a real body. As a result, one would expect there to be some continuity with the material body. The redeemed spirits of individual persons will not be disembodied spirits in some ethereal world. The new heavens and new earth will be a real place inhabited by real resurrected beings in real bodies.

Angels are beings who do not have bodies to contain their spirits. Jesus taught that we will be like angels in that we will not be given in marriage; however, unlike angels, we each will indeed be a spirit contained within a glorified body. The final resurrection is a resurrection and transformation of a body, not just of the spirit.

Christ experienced a resurrection of his body, and the disciples visibly witnessed his ascension into heaven in bodily form. Angels even testified that he would return in the clouds in bodily form:

> And while they were gazing into heaven as he went, behold, two men stood by them in white robes, and said, "Men of Galilee, why do you stand looking into heaven? This Jesus, who was taken up from you into heaven [in bodily form], will come in the same way as you saw him go into heaven [in bodily form in the clouds]." (Acts 1:10–11)

Most scholars through the centuries have taken a more traditional position and consider the statement "we shall be like him" as a clue to what our resurrected bodies will be like. To determine the nature of our final resurrected bodies, they refer to the characteristics of the *pre-ascended* resurrected body of Christ while he was still on this earth.

This approach is highly problematic, however, because we do not know if Christ's resurrected body experienced some type of transformation and glorification *after* he ascended to heaven and returned to his Father. If it did, then our future bodies will not be like the *pre-ascended* body of Christ before it was glorified; rather, they will be like the *post-ascended* glorified body of Christ.

Many scholars have made the assumption that Christ's ascended body remains essentially the same as his pre-ascended body. Thus, our transformed bodies will be modeled after what we know about the *pre-ascended* body of Christ. Before the ascension, Christ was indeed in a material resurrected body with flesh and bones, for he could be seen and touched.

Christ even ate with the disciples. He was neither a ghost nor like an angel in spirit form. Thomas could see and touch the marks of the cross on his body:

> And he said to them, "Why are you troubled, and why do doubts arise in your hearts? See my hands and my feet, that it is I myself. Touch me, and see. For a spirit does not have flesh and bones as you see that I have." And when he had said this, he showed them his hands and his feet. And while they still disbelieved for joy and were marveling, he said to them, "Have you anything here to eat?" They gave him a piece of broiled fish, and he took it and ate before them. (Luke 24:38–43)

Christ taught that a spirit does not have flesh and blood. But he stood before them with a body of flesh and blood that could be touched and could consume food. He was a male in bodily form before his crucifixion, and he still looked like and walked like a man after his resurrection. His body, though, was not like Lazarus's resurrected natural body. Lazarus had to eat and sleep to live because he was still mortal. Christ could eat, but he did not have to because his body had become immortal.

One of the key passages in this debate is Paul's statement: "I tell you this, brothers: flesh and blood cannot inherit the kingdom of God, nor does the perishable inherit the imperishable" (1 Cor. 15:50). The unorthodox interpret this to mean the body that will inherit heaven will not be a material body of flesh and blood like Christ's after the resurrection. Rather, it will be an unknown spiritual entity devoid of a real body. The more orthodox position, on the other hand, interprets this verse to mean the current Adamic body of flesh and blood in its *mortal* state cannot inherit heaven; however, flesh and blood that is somehow made immortal and imperishable, can. *Immortal* "flesh and blood," like Christ's pre-ascended body, can inherit the kingdom of heaven.

The resurrection is of the flesh, but the flesh is made immortal. Once immortal, we may take nourishment, but it will not be necessary because our bodies will be imperishable. Therefore, according to this view, we will be in immortal bodies of flesh and blood and even remain identifiable as male and female in heaven, but we will not function on a sexual level in heaven and will not marry. Some say we will have sexual organs but they will be dormant. Scholars have different opinions about which Adamic features of the current body of flesh and blood will transfer to the heavenly kingdom.

The over-spiritualized interpretation of Paul's teachings on the final resurrection is highly problematic and has consistently been considered heretical by the church. But the more traditional position is also problematic for a variety of reasons. The difficultly comes in trying to understand the nature of an immortal Adamic body. Before the fall, Adam and Eve were by nature mortal because they needed food for nourishment and air to breathe to sustain their bodies. They were dependent upon their external environment for sustenance—air, water, and food to sustain their natural bodies.

In the Adamic order of being, perishable food and air are necessary to support a human anatomy of flesh and blood. The digestive and circulatory systems are only two of the many complex biological systems that maintain the human body. However, it is difficult to imagine the anatomy of an immortal and imperishable body of flesh and blood that requires no outside sustenance to survive. What is an imperishable digestive tract that does not need food or water? If we do not need to digest food and breathe air to live, why even have a digestive tract and respiratory system?

It is even more difficult to imagine an order of being as children of God that has no sexual identity or function. At present, our sexual anatomy as male and female has a profound impact on our spiritual, mental, and biological makeup. The male and female sexual organs and reproductive systems are integral to how our bodies were designed and created, as well as how they function. The biomechanics of the Adamic body are specifically adapted for marriage, reproduction, and life on this earth.

Being male and female gets to the very core of the human experience, whether it is as husband or wife, father or mother, son or daughter, brother or sister, grandfather or grandmother, nephew or niece, or uncle or aunt. None of these kinds of relationships will exist in heaven, for they are all a derivative of marriage and, subsequently, reproduction.

That we are not given in marriage in heaven after the final resurrection will not be a mere sidebar of our existence in the new creation. Heaven will not be like a monastery or convent with resurrected males and females simply abstaining from sex and marriage. Our immortal bodies will be categorically different from the sexual ones we are familiar with.

In a correspondence on this subject, one theologian, who chooses to remain anonymous, concluded the following in reference to the final resurrection: "The whole hope of humanity is not some kind of spiritual bliss in heaven, but the resurrected life—both physical and material, soul and body, full humanity . . . And a human being [in heaven] is not a complete human being apart from the material and spiritual components fashioned in Eden."

I agree that heaven is not some "spiritual bliss" devoid of real bodies. But how can we experience full humanity in heaven as fashioned in Eden if we do not experience marriage and reproduction and the many relationships derived from the union of marriage? According to Genesis, full humanity means being in the image of God as male and female, being given in marriage and becoming one flesh, and filling the world as we reproduce. Being male and female as sexual beings who can become one flesh and reproduce our kind in order to fill the earth is the defining characteristic of what it means to be human or man-"kind." Yet neither gender distinctions nor marriage nor reproduction nor extended human relationships will exist in heaven after the transformation of our bodies. So, how does one define "full humanity" in the heavenly kingdom without these most fundamental aspects of our humanity? How can heaven be a continuation of mankind or sexual humanity without its most basic architecture?

These categorical changes in bodily form and function are ample proof that the new transformed immortal body is a very different kind of body than the current Adamic one designed and structured around marriage and reproduction. This change in essence of being is of such magnitude that Paul taught that as God's children we will have a new kind of body adapted for the new heavens and new earth. Paul seems to be going out of his way to say that the transformed body is not going to be like the human male or female body of flesh and blood that can cleave to one's spouse and become one flesh (1 Cor. 15:44–50).

If the premise of this book is correct about the nature of the first resurrection being that of a natural body, then the 1,000-year messianic kingdom is indeed a resurrection and restoration of our full humanity on this earth as fashioned in Eden. According to the prophets Isaiah and Ezekiel, the messianic kingdom on earth is by definition a restoration of the Adamic order of being on a regenerated earth.

But the final resurrection is not a restoration of humankind into an Edenic setting with a few minor alterations. Nor is it a continuation of the human experience as we know it. For those in Christ, where there is neither male nor female, who have become children of God, the final resurrected body must be transformed into a new kind of body adapted for the new heavens and new earth—not for a regenerated Edenic earth.

Not only is the biological makeup of our future bodies a mystery, but so are the physics of the new heavens and new earth where these transformed bodies will reside. For example, the biological structure of the human body is adapted to the gravitational physics of our earthly home. Will there be gravity on the new earth? When Christ ascended to heaven, he defied gravity as he entered into the clouds. Is he no longer subject to the physics of mass and gravity? We do not know, yet this could have a profound effect on our future bodies.

We know as much about the physics of heaven as we do about how angels talk to God or to one another, for that matter. How can they speak and communicate when they do not have bodies with vocal cords and eardrums? The biomechanics and the physics of the current Adamic existence are not necessarily transferable to heaven. Nothing in the Scriptures tells us to impose these aspects of our earthly experience onto the heavenly experience. Indeed, the current Adamic creation will be redeemed from destruction and brought into the new creation, but that does not mean our future eternal existence will be an extension of the Adamic order of being and a return to the Garden of Eden. New Testament ideology reveals the mystery that on the last day, the Adamic order of being ends, and an entirely new order of being is created for the children of God to experience an entirely new creation in the new heavens and new earth.

The purpose of the final resurrection is not to return us to a restored earth. That is the purpose of the first resurrection when the saints are brought back to life in natural bodies to experience a restored Genesis creation—full humanity as it was intended to be. The purpose of the final resurrection is to transform the bodies of the children of God for his children to live with him in the new heavens and new earth for eternity. The heavenly kingdom is not a restoration of the Adamic order of being, but the beginning of a new creation for God's children. A new order of being requires a new kind of body.

Our Resurrected Body
Shall Be Like the *Ascended* Body of Christ

Much of the confusion among theologians in the more traditional camp apparently comes from their unsubstantiated assertion that our final resurrected bodies will be like the *pre-ascended* resurrected body of Christ. It could very well be similar in some ways to the pre-ascended body that the disciples ate with on the shores of the Sea of Galilee. On the other hand, it could be in a glorified and transformed state very different from the one the disciples experienced that morning.

Now that Christ has ascended to heaven, no one really knows what the *post-ascended,* glorified, resurrected body of Christ is like. No biblical reference specifically states that Christ's *post-ascended* body is the same as his *pre-ascended* resurrected body. When Christ ascended into heaven, his glorified body could have experienced a remarkable transformation that would have adapted his body for the glorious state of his Father's heavenly kingdom.

Let us take another look at the Scriptures. When Jesus was on this earth in his pre-ascended resurrected body, he was clearly functioning in a physical, Adamic body. His disciples attested to this, for the risen Lord had appeared to the disciples and even ate with them. Since he has ascended to his glory in heaven, however, no one has seen him, and thus no one knows what his post-ascended glorified body is like. If our resurrected spiritual bodies will be like the pre-ascended body of Christ, the disciples could have easily referenced this kind of body as a type of our future bodies. But John freely admitted he *does not know* what Christ's ascended body and our resurrected bodies will be like: "What we will be *has not yet appeared*" (1 John 3:2). But the pre-ascended, resurrected Christ *had appeared* to John and the disciples!

If our future bodies are going to be like the pre-ascended body of Christ, John could have simply said they were going to be like the resurrected body he saw, touched, and ate with. But instead of referencing the known pre-ascended body of Christ, John referenced the *unknown* glorified body of Christ that will be revealed from heaven on the last day—that is, the post-ascended body of Christ. As a result, John said *he does not know what we shall be like*—it is a mystery to him. Consequently, when John said, "We shall be like him," he could not be referencing the resurrected Christ who appeared on the earth before the ascension; rather, he was referencing *the Christ from heaven* who has *not yet appeared*. In addition, not a single New Testament writer referenced the *pre-ascended* body of Christ as being representative of our final resurrected bodies!

Many theologians presume to know more than the apostles when they reference the pre-ascended body of Christ as representative of our final resurrected bodies. In doing so, however, they are extrapolating, for there is no apostolic teaching in the Scriptures that confirms this. Their extrapolation might be correct, but it is not an exegesis of a New Testament text. If the apostles did not know the nature of the glorified body of Christ after he ascended to heaven, then surely none of us can know.

The Glorified Body of Christ

Significant biblical evidence supports the proposition that the *post-ascended* resurrected body of Christ in its glorified state in heaven is very different from the *pre-ascended* resurrected body that appeared to the disciples. *After the ascension*, Christ's body experienced a process of glorification and transformation and is in a state that no one in an Adamic body has yet seen or can see at this time.

Consider the apostle Paul, who claimed that he, too, saw the resurrected Christ, just as the other disciples claimed after they touched him and watched him eat. Paul, however, did not become a believer until Christ had already returned to the glory of heaven. As a result, Paul saw the resurrected Christ *after the ascension* and after he was in his glorified body in heaven. This is a critical distinction. Paul saw a very different resurrected Christ than the other disciples saw. Paul's conversion did not involve someone witnessing to him; he was converted when he actually saw and heard the *ascended and resurrected* Christ:

He [Christ] was raised on the third day in accordance with the Scriptures, and that he appeared to Cephas, then to the twelve. Then he appeared to more than five hundred brothers at one time, most of whom are still alive, though some have fallen asleep. Then he appeared to James, then to all the apostles. Last of all, as to one untimely born, he appeared also to me [after the ascension]. (1 Cor. 15:4–8)

His appearance was untimely to Paul because, again, he did not become a believer while Christ was still on this earth in his resurrected body. Paul saw him after he had already ascended to heaven. Christ had to reappear in some fashion for Paul to see that he had indeed been resurrected.

But how did the post-ascended resurrected Christ appear to Paul? Was he in a bodily form that Paul could see and touch? Could Paul have sat down with the resurrected Christ and eaten breakfast with him along the road to Damascus? No, for Christ's *glorified* body in its transformed state was so bright that it blinded Paul! His sight was later restored through a miraculous healing (Acts 9:17–18). Paul only caught a glimpse of the glorified resurrected Christ from heaven and it was enough to blind him.

In contrast, none of the other disciples were blinded when they saw the resurrected Christ. Then again, they saw him *before* he had ascended to his glory in heaven and *before* his body had been transformed and glorified. Had they seen his glorified body, they, too, would have been blinded. While witnessing to King Agrippa, Paul revealed more of what he saw:

> At midday, O king, I saw on the way a light from heaven, *brighter than the sun*, that shone around me and those who journeyed with me. And when we had all fallen to the ground, I heard a voice saying to me in the Hebrew language, "Saul, Saul, why are you persecuting me? It is hard for you to kick against the goads." And I said, "Who are you, Lord?" And the Lord said, "I am Jesus whom you are persecuting." (Acts 26:13–15)

From what we learn about Paul's vision of the post-ascended risen Lord, one could argue that it would have been impossible for Christ to appear to Peter and the other disciples in his glorified, transformed body because the very sight of him would have blinded all who saw him. Again, the key difference is that Peter and the other disciples saw the resurrected Christ *before* he had ascended to heaven while he was still in an Adamic body of flesh and blood, whereas Paul got a glimpse of the glorified, resurrected Christ *after* he had ascended to heaven. The difference is astounding.

In his letter to Timothy, Paul teaches that since Christ ascended to heaven and is in his glorified immortal body, no one in a natural body has seen or can see the ascended risen Lord:

> To keep the commandment unstained and free from reproach until the *appearing of our Lord Jesus Christ*, which he will display at the proper time—he who is the blessed and only Sovereign, the King of kings and Lord of lords, who alone has immortality, *who dwells in unapproachable light*, whom *no one has ever seen or can see*. To him be honor and eternal dominion. Amen. (1 Tim. 6:14–16)

Paul knew from firsthand experience that the ascended, resurrected Christ was an unapproachable light. According to Paul, the ascended, resurrected Christ is in a transformed bodily form that no one in the natural Adamic state has seen or even can see until we, too, are transformed to be like him when he comes again. Until then, the ascended Christ remains unapproachable to human beings. None of the other disciples saw or had the ability to see the glorified immortal Christ. In contrast, the *pre-ascended* Christ could not only be seen, but he could be approached and touched by human beings.

The transfiguration, witnessed by Peter, James, and John, prefigures what the transformed body of Christ will be like at his second coming. This event reveals more about what Christ will be like when he comes again in glory than the pre-ascended resurrected body that the disciples saw in the Upper Room. Like Paul, these three apostles got a glimpse of what Christ's glorified body will be like at his second coming:

> "For the Son of Man is going to come with his angels *in the glory of his Father*, and then he will repay each person according to what he has done. Truly, I say to you, there are some standing here who will not taste death *until they see* the Son of Man *coming in his kingdom*." And after six days Jesus took with him Peter and James, and John his brother, and led them up a high mountain by themselves. And he was *transfigured* before them, and *his face shone like the sun, and his clothes became white as light*. (Matt. 16:27—17:2)

Normal human bodies do not shine with the glory and brilliance of the sun. Christ was attempting to give Peter, James, and John some idea of what the nature of his glorified body will be like when he returns in the clouds on the last day. His transfigured appearance, although not quite the blinding light Paul witnessed, was still extraordinary. His "face shone like the sun, and his clothes became white as light," which parallels Paul's description of Christ's glorified resurrected body as appearing brighter than the sun. We can look at the sun for only a minute before being blinded, but Paul was instantly blinded when he saw the risen Lord, because Christ's glorified body was even brighter.

It is no wonder that John, who witnessed this remarkable transfiguration, later writes in his epistle that the nature of our future transformed bodies remains a mystery until he appears on the last day. Again, for this is a critical distinction, John does not reference the pre-ascended resurrected body of Christ as an example of the nature of our future glorified bodies. The transfiguration, which was but a foretaste of the future, glorified, risen Christ, obviously had a profound and lasting impact on John: "We know that when he appears [from heaven] *we will be like him*, because we shall see him as he is" [in his fully transfigured, glorified state] (1 John 3:2).

The second coming of the glorified resurrected Christ is also described in the New Testament as an event so bright that it will literally light up the sky from east to west: "For as the lightning comes from the east and shines as far as the west, so will be the coming of the Son of Man" (Matt. 24:27). One gets the impression that the light from his glorified body will be seen all over the world. What an incredibly bright light!

Therefore, the pre-ascended resurrected body of Christ that the disciples could see, approach, and touch without being blinded cannot represent the nature of his glorified body that will be revealed when he comes again. Consequently, the pre-ascended non-glorified resurrected body of Christ does not represent what our bodies will be like when they are transformed to be like his post-ascended glorified body.

When Christ comes again, our bodies will be transformed and glorified to be like his ascended glorified body, and only then will we finally be able to see the glorified body of Christ and dwell in the very presence of the triune God in all his glory in the heavenly kingdom. I believe Jesus and the apostles are trying to teach us that our bodies are going to be like the *ascended glorified Christ* from heaven—not like the pre-ascended risen Christ. Therefore, we should not look to the risen Adamic body of Christ while he was still on this earth as a model for our future bodies.

Why, then, did Christ appear after his resurrection and before his ascension as a man of flesh and blood who could be seen and touched? For the simple reason that had he appeared in his glorified state, as he did with Paul, he would have blinded all who saw him. It would not have been possible for them to see and touch the transformed, glorified, risen Lord as long as they were in their Adamic bodies. And had he not shown himself in the form of a resurrected man, they would have thought they had merely seen a ghost. They needed to witness the resurrected Christ to know that he was truly alive: "As they were talking about these things, Jesus himself stood among them, and said to them, 'Peace to you!' But they were startled and frightened and *thought they saw a spirit*" (Luke 24:36–37).

The best way to authenticate his bodily resurrection and convince them that he was not a ghost was for him to return as a man, as Lazarus did, in his non-glorified state. Christ did not say that the body of flesh and blood the disciples saw was his final glorified body. No New Testament writer referred to this pre-ascended body as representative of Christ's glorified body or our future glorified bodies. On the contrary, they taught that our bodies will be transformed to be in the likeness of the glorified Christ, which no one has seen or can see at this time. Jesus taught us that his body at the transfiguration represents a foretaste of his glorified body at his second coming, rather than his body in the Upper Room that Thomas touched and examined.

Immediately before he was crucified, Christ prayed to his Father, saying, "And now, Father, *glorify me in your own presence* with the *glory* that I had with you before the world existed" (John 17:5). One day we will be able to join Christ and be in the very presence of the glory of God the Father in heaven. But the only way mere mortals can be in the presence of such unsearchable glory is after our Adamic bodies have been transformed and glorified to be like Christ's post-ascended glorified body.

The purpose of the final resurrection, or transformation, is to change us into embodied beings who can enter into the very presence of God the Father and see Christ in all his glory—the glory he had with the Father before the world was created. Our transformed bodies are destined for the Father's house in heaven: "In my Father's house are many rooms. If it were not so, would I have told you that I go to prepare a place for you? And if I go and prepare a place for you, *I will come again* and will take you to myself, *that where I am* you may be also" (John 14:2–3). Christ prayed, "Father, I desire that they also, whom you have given me, may be with me where I am, to see my glory that you have given me because you loved me before the foundation of the world" (John 17:24).

An Adamic body of flesh and blood cannot be in the glorious presence of God the Father. Paul wrote, "I tell you this, brothers: flesh and blood cannot inherit the kingdom of God, nor does the perishable inherit the imperishable. Behold! I tell you a mystery. We shall not all sleep, but *we shall all be changed*" (1 Cor. 15:50–51). Only after our Adamic bodies have been transformed and changed into a new kind of glorified body will we be able to enter into the very presence of God the Father in all his glory in heaven. We do not know what the nature of our transformed bodies will be like any better than Paul or John knew. We *do* know, however, that we will be transformed into the image of the *glorified* Christ from heaven—not into the image of the Adamic man from the dust of this earth.

Christ the God-Man

It has been a matter of orthodox teaching since the time of the early church that once Christ—the second person of the Trinity—became incarnate, he is forever a God-man, even after his resurrection and ascension. I concur with this position. Christ clearly ascended to heaven in bodily form. He did not leave his body behind and become only a spiritual being in heaven. He remains incarnate in a glorified body of some kind. But many also believe that the ascended Christ remains in an Adamic kind of body. This position maintains that the Son of God, having become human in the Adamic order of being through the virgin birth, will remain so for all eternity, even after his ascension to heaven, and that Christ will always have two natures—God and man. A more accurate description would be that Christ remains a God-man with an unknown kind of glorified body.

Before the incarnation, Christ did not have a human body. During the incarnation, Christ became the God-man with an Adamic body. After his resurrection and ascension to heaven, in some extraordinary way, he retains his body as the God-man for eternity. He continues as the God-man with a body, but his Adamic body has been transformed into a glorified body of an unknown kind. His body is a type of body that is unlike the current Adamic body of flesh and blood capable of marriage and reproduction.

Theologian Gary W. Derickson asserts the more traditional belief that Christ remains an Adamic kind of man:

He will remain a human eternally, as affirmed in Psalm 110 (per Heb. 5:6), by his eternal designation as a priest according to the order of Melchizedek. And since he will never cease being a human, he will never cease having certain responsibilities that come from being a human.[1]

In a book on Christology, Donald Macleod says the same thing:

The one who is with us is the one seated at the right hand of the Majesty on High. But that very one is also the dust of the earth; transfigured dust, but still dust. It is as such, as the God-man, that he gives us the privilege of eating and drinking not merely in remembrance of him, but with him, at his table. Neither the divine nor the human is now excluded from anything he does.[2]

According to these scholars, Christ is both the second person of the Trinity *and* a human being with an Adamic body, even after his ascension. Consequently, when we join him in heaven after our resurrection, we will be able to literally eat and drink with him as humans in heaven. The primary scriptural basis for these assertions of Derickson's and Macleod's seems to be from the epistle to the Hebrews. Christ is said to be our permanent high priest and thus, in their thinking, an Adamic kind of man forever:

So also Christ did not exalt himself to be made a high priest, but was appointed by him who said to him, "You are my Son, today I have begotten you"; as he says also in another place, "You are a priest forever, after the order of Melchizedek." In the days of his flesh, Jesus offered up prayers and supplications, with loud cries and tears, to him who was able to save him from death, and he was heard because of his reverence. Although he was a son, he learned obedience through what he suffered. And being made perfect, he became the source of eternal salvation to all who obey him, being designated by God a high priest after the order of Melchizedek. (Heb.5:5–10)

---

[1] Gary W. Derickson, "Incarnational Explanation for Jesus' Subjection in the Eschaton," in *Looking into the Future - Evangelical Studies in Eschatology*, ed. David W. Baker (Grand Rapids: Baker Book House, 2001), 229–230.

[2] Donald Macleod, *The Person of Christ* (Downers Grove: InterVarsity Press, 1998), 199.

This particular teaching in Hebrews, however, is a typology. Christ is indeed a "high priest" after the order of Melchizedek. His priesthood for the saints is very real, but so is his atonement for our sins as the sacrificial Lamb of God. That atonement does not make him to be, literally, a lamb. Saying that Christ is our high priest in heaven forever does not mean that he is a literal Adamic man of flesh and blood who serves as our high priest and operates in a temple of stone and mortar in heaven.

When the angels appeared after Christ's bodily ascension in the clouds and said he would return in like manner, they did not mean that he would come back in the same kind of body he departed with. For example, when Christ departed this earth, he did not light up the sky as lightning does, allowing him to be seen from as far as east is to the west (Matt. 24:27). But, when he returns in the clouds on the last day in bodily form to redeem and transform his saints, he will return in his glorified body, which will be brighter than the sun and will light up the whole world, from the east to the west. His return in the clouds in his glorified body will be categorically different from his departure in the clouds in his non-glorified body.

The *nature* of Christ's ascended glorified body remains as much of a mystery as the nature of our transformed bodies. Christ remains the God-man with a real body. But we do not know what kind of body he now has in his glorified state in heaven. We do know, however, that when he returns, we shall be transformed into his image. At that time we will know what it is like to be in the image of the God-man from heaven.

We are familiar with the Adamic body, and as a result, we have a tendency to impose the characteristics of this body onto the resurrected body. But Paul taught that the body of the glorified Christ is not a body with which we are in any way familiar. Neither Derickson nor Macleod has seen the post-ascended Lord as Paul saw him, nor have they been to heaven and seen Christ in his glorified body. To claim that Christ is presently in a body that is essentially like the current human body is claiming far more than the Scriptures warrant.

Some of the confusion stems from Jesus telling his disciples that they would eat and drink with him in his kingdom: "You are those who have stayed with me in my trials, and I assign to you, as my Father assigned to me, a kingdom, that you may eat and drink at my table in my kingdom and sit on thrones judging the twelve tribes of Israel" (Luke 22:28–30). This is probably a reference to Christ's earthly messianic kingdom where the disciples in their regenerated bodies will reign with Christ for one thousand years judging the twelve tribes of Israel. After experiencing the first resurrection, they will be able to eat and drink at the Lord's table because they will be in human bodies in a restored Genesis creation. And Christ does not have to be present on the earth for the disciples to experience his presence at that time, any more than he does now when we share in the Lord's Supper today.

What Kind of Bodies Will We Have?

The Greco-Roman world in which Paul preached did not believe in a resurrection of the human body. They thought of resurrection as a form of resuscitation of a corpse, which they found repugnant. If there was such a thing as an afterlife, only the soul went into eternity. But Paul preached a gospel in which the resurrected Christ would return on the last day, and the resurrected departed spirit and soul of a believer would be rejoined with the resurrected body of that person, which would simultaneously be transformed into an immortal body and taken to heaven to be with God for eternity. The Greco-Roman Corinthian church, which believed in this incredible gospel, wanted to know what kind of resurrected bodies we would have after our transformation and entrance into heaven. Would it be a resuscitation of our current kind of human bodies?

Paul's response was a strong rebuke for their asking about something fundamentally unknowable at this time. Paul called people foolish who think they can know what kind of resurrected bodies we will have:

> But someone will ask, "How are the dead raised? With what *kind* of body do they come?" *You foolish person!* . . . what you sow [the Adamic body] is *not the body that is to be*, but a bare kernel, perhaps of wheat or of some other grain. But God gives it a body as he has chosen, and to each kind of seed its own body. (1 Cor. 15:35–38)

God determined what kind of body humans would have when he created Adam and Eve. But that does not represent the kind of body that we will have in the final resurrection. The same God who created the Adamic body will determine what kind of body his children will have when they are resurrected and taken to his heavenly kingdom. Until that time, Paul admonishes us not to foolishly speculate as to the kind of body God will provide us for our future heavenly dwelling. The Adamic body was created and adapted for the Genesis home, but the future body for God's children will be created and adapted for our eternal home in heaven. The future body will not be recognized as Adamic; it will be a new kind of body that God will choose to give us at that time.

Paul compares this transformation process of the Adamic body that dies and returns to the dust of the earth to a variety of kernels or seeds that are sown into the ground, die, and experience germination. This may seem quite obvious, but when a seed is planted and germinates, the result is not another seed exactly like the one planted. Rather, the seed is transformed into an entity that is very different from the original seed. It is sown as a seed, but it comes up out of the ground as a plant!

A seed, in effect, dies when it germinates, for it ceases to have a hard shell or encasing; it is transformed into a plant as the outer casing fall away.

The resulting mature plant is incredibly different from the seed that was planted. The seed usually has a hard outer coating or shell and is relatively small. In contrast, the mature plant that grows from this germinated seed or nut can be a blade of grass, a bush, or even an enormous tree. Paul is saying that when a seed is planted, the result is something amazingly different!

The plant has a connection to the original seed, but the plant's body or design is completely different from that of the original seed sown in the ground. Paul is not stressing continuity of form and function in this analogy; rather, he is stressing the incredible discontinuity between the two *kinds* of entities—the seed versus the resulting plant. Likewise, the new kind of spiritual body we will inherit will be vastly different from the Adamic kind of body that is sown into the ground when it dies. Not once does Paul reference the pre-ascended resurrected Christ as a pattern for the kind of body we will have when our bodies are transformed to be like his.

Imagine that you lived in an area of the world with a climate that was not conducive to growing pecan trees and that you had never seen a mature pecan tree before. I show you a small pecan and ask, "What do you think this nut would look like if it was planted, germinated, and grew?" By examining the pecan itself, you would have no idea what the resulting plant would look like. You could not look at the pecan, examine its outer shell, or crack it open and analyze its internal structure and imagine that it would grow into an enormous 100-foot-tall pecan tree with an extensive root system, large trunk, and magnificent system of branches and leaves.

The small pecan itself does not in any way *prefigure* what the pecan tree will be like. If I showed you a pecan in one hand and pointed to a full-grown pecan tree, the differences would astound you. The mature tree represents a profound transformation of a small pecan after it was planted in the ground. The pecan and the resulting tree do not even remotely look alike.

Paul is trying to teach us that the Adamic body sown in the ground when we die does not prefigure the body we will have when it is raised, transformed, and adapted for heaven. One cannot discern what this new body will be like by analyzing the Adamic body, any more than one can discern what a pecan tree will look like by analyzing the pecan. The nut takes on a new *form* after it is *transformed* through the process of germination. Similarly, at the final resurrection, the current Adamic body will take on a new *form* of existence when it is *transformed* into a new kind of body adapted for the Father's kingdom of heaven.

Because Paul's analogy helps us understand this important subject, let us take it one step further. Imagine you had been born and raised on the International Space Station and had never been to the earth nor seen pictures of it. You knew nothing about the earth's plants and trees. Suppose a visitor from earth arrived on the space station and showed you a handful of nuts and seeds that he had brought with him and asked you to describe what the earth's vegetation looked like based on analyzing them. There is no way you could predict the kind of plants that would emerge from these nuts and seeds, not to mention what the earth itself would look like as a result.

As children of God contained in a natural body, we are like nuts and seeds awaiting our transformation into a new kind of body to be taken to a new heavens and new earth, which have yet to be created. Not only will our bodies be different, but the place where he takes us will be also. At this time we are unable to predict what kind of body God will give these human "seeds" at the transformation. Both the nature of the transformed body and the nature of the new heavens and new earth are mysteries to us now.

Because the Corinthians' question about the kind of body we will have was so important, Paul continued with his analogy to demonstrate God's immense creative ability to design and form different kinds of living creatures, even different kinds of heavenly bodies, in this current Genesis creation:

> For not all flesh is the same, but there is one kind for humans, another for animals, another for birds, and another for fish. There are heavenly bodies and earthly bodies, but the glory of the heavenly is of one kind, and the glory of the earthly is of another. There is one glory of the sun, and another glory of the moon, and another glory of the stars; for star differs from star in glory. (1 Cor. 15:39–41)

Paul is making a simple, yet profound, point about God's proven ability to create unique kinds of bodies—animals, birds, and fish—for different settings. Some bodies are designed to function on the ground, while some are designed to operate in the air or in water. The body of an elephant is vastly different from that of an eagle, which is different from that of a dolphin, yet God created them all. Each kind of body is adapted to its environment. The elephant would have difficulty navigating the clouds, the eagle would not survive for long in the depths of the ocean, and the dolphin could not function on the ground or in the air. Even the planets and stars are very different. The illumination of the sun is different from that of the moon, which is different from that of the various stars.

Paul's point is that our Creator has already demonstrated remarkable creativity when he formed all kinds of creatures and heavenly bodies adapted for different habitats and settings. As a result, we can trust this Creator to use his boundless creativity again when he transforms the current Adamic bodies of his children into a new kind of body adapted for a new heavens and new earth. This new kind of spiritual body will be very different from the current natural Adamic body, yet just as unique and even more glorious than the current body.

Paul establishes a principle of *discontinuity* between our current sexual kind of human body of flesh and blood and the unknown kind of body that will result from the transformation of our current human bodies into glorified bodies like Christ's resurrected body. The mystery of what kind of body we will have in the heavenly kingdom should not concern us; we should simply trust in God's proven creativity demonstrated by this complex and interesting Genesis creation as we look forward to a very different kind of body in heaven.

There is, however, some continuity between a seed and the plant it produces. A pecan produces a pecan tree, not a blade of grass. The Adamic body is of material substance. It seems fair to assume that the new kind of body that sprouts from this seed will also be of material substance. Because Paul calls it a spiritual body does not mean it is nonmaterial or just spirit, like that of angels. We will be like angels in that we will have no sexual identity nor be given in marriage, but we will always differ from them because our spirits will be contained within bodies. That Paul describes the resurrected body as a spiritual body actually indicates it is a physical or material containment vessel for the spirit of a person. But the exact nature of the material aspects of our eternal bodies and the eternal kingdom remain unknown.

Further evidence of the continuity between the Adamic creation and the new creation can be found in Paul's letter to the Romans:

> For I consider that the sufferings of this present time are not worth comparing with the glory that is to be revealed to us. For the creation waits with eager longing for the revealing of the sons of God. For the creation was subjected to futility, not willingly, but because of him who subjected it, in hope that the creation itself will be set free from its bondage to decay and obtain the freedom of the glory of the children of God. For we know that the whole creation has been groaning together in the pains of childbirth until now. And not only the creation, but we ourselves, who have the firstfruits of the Spirit, groan inwardly as we wait eagerly for adoption as sons, the redemption of our bodies. (Rom. 8:18–23)

In ways we cannot comprehend, the Adamic creation longs for the transformation of our bodies as sons of God. We do not know how the entire Adamic creation is going to be destroyed on the last day, and yet, somehow be brought into the new heavens and new earth for the children of God in the new order of being. Paul does not tell us how this will take place, probably because he did not know himself. It remains a fascinating mystery until the last day. Only then will we understand the continuity between our current Adamic bodies and Genesis creation and our new spiritual bodies in the new heavens and new earth. But it is important that we not impose the nature of this current Genesis creation onto the new creation, just as we should not impose known characteristics of the sexual Adamic body onto the glorified body.

Christ does not describe the new heavens and new earth as a renewed or restored Genesis earth with restored sexual human beings. As the creator of this Adamic order of being, he says that this Genesis creation will come to its Omega, and he describes the eternal kingdom as a new creation for the transformed children of God: "And he who was seated on the throne said, 'Behold, I am making all things new.' Also he said, 'Write this down, for these words are trustworthy and true'" (Rev. 21:5).

Summary

We know that the spiritual body will be like the body of Christ in all its glory; however, we do not know the nature of his glorified body, now that he has ascended to heaven. The ascended Christ is in a body that is currently an "unapproachable light" that no one has seen or can see until we, too, are transformed when he comes again to take us to heaven. Paul got a mere glimpse of that body, and it blinded him. Because the nature of Christ's glorified body remains a mystery, so does the nature of our transformed spiritual bodies. We simply do not know what kind of bodies we will have until they are transformed on the last day.

There is a tendency among many theologians to pattern the transformed body the saints will inherit on the *pre-ascended* resurrected Christ—one that is immortal, yet of Adamic "flesh and blood." But the New Testament teaches that when Christ appears a second time, we will be like the *post-ascended,* glorified, resurrected Christ—the "man from heaven." I believe that when Paul says, "I tell you this, brothers: flesh and blood cannot inherit the kingdom of God" (1 Cor. 15:50), he means just that. The Adamic kind of body that is flesh and blood, male and female, as fashioned in Eden, even if immortal, is not the kind of body we will have in heaven. It is a mistake to impose the current Adamic order of biology and physics onto an existence that the Bible clearly says is unknowable until that existence is created. The new heavens and new earth will be a new environment for the sons of God, which requires a new kind of body adapted for this new creation.

According to Paul, it is foolish for believers on this side of heaven to try to predict what kind of body we will have at the final resurrection. Paul's admonition should cause us to be more cautious when making claims about the design, function, and characteristics of our transformed bodies, as well as speculating about the nature of our eternal home in the new heavens and new earth.

We can rest assured that the same amazing creativity demonstrated by our Creator in the original Genesis creation will be exemplified once more when Christ comes and transforms our current Adamic bodies into glorious bodies like his. Most important, the divine Architect will give us new transformed bodies whose form and function will enable us to dwell in the new heavens and new earth in the very presence of the triune God for all eternity—a new kind of body for a new kind of dwelling place for the eternal children of God.

The Front Book Cover Symbols

At this point, the reader should have a good idea of what the illustrations on the cover of this book symbolize. The symbol of the man and woman in a perfect square and circle depicts the Adamic order of being with man as male and female in the image of God. In the millennium, when God the Son rules from heaven, the saints from all time will experience a regeneration of their Adamic bodies on a restored Edenic earth. During the restoration, man—as male and female, created in the image of God—will be given in marriage and will reproduce and form communities as we subdue the earth. Thus, the symbol represents a restoration to what it means to be men and women in the image of God in an ideal environment on this earth. The human experience will reach its ultimate fulfillment during this time.[3]

The second symbol illustrates our future raptured and transformed body at Christ's second coming in the clouds. The body is not depicted because the exact nature of this future body is unknown at this time. The square and circle signify that we will have a real body or containment vessel in the heavenly kingdom. And the geometric shapes transcending into an infinite center of pure light represents the eternal aspects of the glorified body in heaven as it is made immortal and imperishable and brought into the presence of God in all his glory. The use of the Star of David within the square and circle represents the way in which the Son's messianic kingdom is brought into the Father's eternal kingdom on the last day.

---

[3] The restoration illustration is based upon a drawing by the Renaissance artist Leonardo da Vinci. Drawn in 1487, it is known as the Vitruvian Man. Marcus Vitruvius was a Roman architect in first century BC and authored the famous treatise on architecture entitled *De Architectura*, which covers such subjects as architecture, engineering, urban planning, and machinery. In it, Vitruvius describes the ideal proportions of the human body, which were considered a vital component of good design. Intellectuals of the Renaissance were typically chauvinists. So, I further developed the drawing by superimposing a female figure in place of one of the male figures. As a result, the symbol now represents man, as male and female, in the image of God.

9

The New Jerusalem

After the 1,000-year reign of Christ and the current heavens and earth are destroyed, John says, "Then I saw a new heaven and a new earth, for the first heaven and the first earth had passed away, and the sea was no more. And I saw the holy city, *new Jerusalem*, coming down out of heaven from God, prepared as a bride adorned for her husband" (Rev. 21:1–2). John then describes a vision of a cubed city, which he equates to the bride of Christ, with streets of gold and with foundations, walls, and gates made of a vast array of precious stones and minerals. It is, in effect, a jeweled city.

The nature of this New Jerusalem is another subject that has puzzled biblical scholars over the years. Is it a physical city with real streets of gold or is John's vision a figurative description of a celestial city that is essentially indescribable at this time without the use of metaphors?

Some scholars believe John is depicting a literal cubed city with actual streets of gold and gates of pearls. But some indications in John's description tend toward a more figurative presentation of this future heavenly city. For example, the unbelievers outside the city gates are described as dogs: "Blessed are those who wash their robes, so that they may have the right to the tree of life and that they may enter the city by the gates. Outside are the *dogs* and sorcerers and the sexually immoral and murderers and idolaters, and everyone who loves and practices falsehood" (Rev. 22:14–15). If the streets and gates are to be interpreted literally, will there also be actual dogs outside the gates of heaven? I do not think so.

The dogs are a metaphorical representation of evil people, in general, who are excluded from entering the city of God. At this point in Revelation, the unrighteous will be in the lake of fire—not outside the gates of the eternal city. If the dogs are a metaphor for unrighteous unbelievers kept outside the gates of heaven, then would not the gates themselves, as well as the cube-shaped city with streets of gold, also be metaphors? Probably so, but that does not mean the city described is not an actual place.

What makes this analysis so difficult is that John also refers to objects in the New Jerusalem, such as the "tree of life," which we know from Genesis is indeed real in some fashion:

> I warn everyone who hears the words of the prophecy of this book: if anyone adds to them, God will add to him the plagues described in this book, and if anyone takes away from the words of the book of this prophecy, God will take away *his share in the tree of life and in the holy city,* which are described in this book. (Rev. 22:18–19)

Genesis describes the existence of a tree of life from which Adam and Eve could have eaten. God banished them from the Garden of Eden so that, presumably, they could not eat of this tree and live in a permanent fallen state (Gen. 3:22–23). John seems to be saying that both the tree of life and the holy city are real in some sense.

I do not propose to know when John is being literal or metaphorical. It is far too complicated for anyone to resolve this side of heaven. If some want to believe there are streets of gold, fine. But they had better enjoy urban living, for this cubed city will have to accommodate billions of saints who have lived over the centuries.

In many ways, the nature of the New Jerusalem in heaven described by John in Revelation is as much of a mystery as the nature of the future spiritual body. Just as we do not know what kind of eternal bodies we will have after the rapture, we really do not know what kind of city this will be until we get to heaven in our new bodies and experience it. This, however, does not mean the New Jerusalem and the new heavens and new earth are not real places. Just as our spiritual bodies are going to be real bodies or containment vessels of some unknown kind, our eternal home will also be a real dwelling place. Perhaps metaphor is the best method for God to use to communicate what this city will be like to earthlings whose only frame of reference is the human experience.

Just as we can trust God to use his proven creativity to create a new kind of body for his saints, so, too, we can trust God to use his infinite creativity to create a new eternal dwelling place for his glorified children. In the meantime, in an attempt to give us some idea of the glory and magnificence of the new earth, Christ gave John a vision of a city from our Adamic frame of reference but imbued it with an almost unimaginable magnificence. It is God's way of letting us know that we are destined for a new creation that is beyond anything we can imagine at this time.

Through the use of metaphors describing objects known to his readers, John provides points of reference in the Roman world—such as weddings, cities, walls, gates, streets, rivers, trees—that gave his contemporary readers, and us, some comprehension of the sheer beauty and splendor of this future abode for God's people. John's vision is grounded in its grammatical-historical context where the typical city in the ancient world was surrounded by walls with secure gates for protection against murderous invaders. Even though our modern cities may be surrounded by interstate highways, outer loops, greenways, or suburban sprawl instead of fortified walls, we can still relate to his Greco-Roman vision of a walled city of God.

John also uses metaphorical language to describe the "river of the water of life" in Revelation:

> Then the angel showed me the river of the water of life, bright as crystal, flowing from the throne of God and of the Lamb through the middle of the street of the city; also, on either side of the river, the tree of life with its twelve kinds of fruit, yielding its fruits each month. The leaves of the tree were for the healing of the nations. (Rev. 22:1–2)

We know from other biblical precedents that Christ used the language of "rivers of living water" metaphorically to describe the flow of spiritual life through our hearts by the Holy Spirit. This "living water" is not real H_2O. But the flow of spiritual life coming from the Holy Spirit is very real. Jesus used this same metaphor when speaking to the crowds:

> On the last day of the feast, the great day, Jesus stood up and cried out, "If anyone thirsts, let him come to me and drink. Whoever believes in me, as the Scripture has said, 'Out of his heart *will flow rivers of living water.*'" Now this he said about the Spirit, whom those who believed in him were to receive, for as yet the Spirit had not been given, because Jesus was not yet glorified. (John 7:37–39)

The rivers of living water are not real streams but represent the life coming from the Holy Spirit that flows in our hearts. Jesus said to the Samaritan woman at the well: "Everyone who drinks of this water will be thirsty again, but whoever drinks of the water that I will give him will never be thirsty forever. The water that I will give him will become in him a spring of water welling up to eternal life" (John 4:13–14).

In Revelation, John records Jesus using this same metaphor again for those residing in the eternal New Jerusalem: "It is done! I am the Alpha and the Omega, the beginning and the end. *To the thirsty I will give from the spring of the water of life* without payment" (Rev. 21:6). Is the river described in the New Jerusalem a metaphor for the river of life from the Spirit, or does it represent an actual river instead? We do not know. If we interpret it as an actual river with real trees along its bank, we could be seriously *underestimating* its meaning as a symbol of the flow of life from the Spirit in the kingdom of heaven. On the other hand, perhaps the river is real in some unknown celestial manner, and in over-spiritualizing its characteristics we could be underestimating its meaning. Perhaps John is describing a real river that merges with the flow of the Spirit's life into a new, previously unknown, heavenly phenomenon. One thing is certain, though: living in God's city will entail a flow of life from the Holy Spirit beyond anything we have ever experienced on this earth as Spirit-filled human beings.

The New Testament may use metaphorical language to describe the New Jerusalem, but it is a real place with unknown transcendent spiritual qualities. And just as the transformed body will be a real body, but remains a mystery at this time, so, too, the exact nature of the New Jerusalem remains unknown until it is revealed on the last day.

The Bride and the New Jerusalem

To further complicate matters, John combines what may be metaphorical descriptions of this magnificent city with the New Testament concept of the body of Christ as the bride of Christ:

> And I saw the holy city, new Jerusalem, coming down out of heaven from God, prepared as a *bride adorned for her husband.* . . . "Come, *I will show you the Bride, the wife of the Lamb.*" And he carried me away in the Spirit to a great, high mountain, and showed me the *holy city Jerusalem* coming down out of heaven from God, having the glory of God, its radiance like a most rare jewel, like a jasper, clear as crystal. (Rev. 21:2, 9–11)

John says that the city is actually a representation of the bride of Christ, which is the body of Christ composed of all the saints.

The marriage metaphor of Christ and his body is a fascinating New Testament theme. To gain some understanding of what John is describing when he paints a picture of the New Jerusalem adorned as the bride of Christ, it helps to understand some aspects of a Roman city and of a Roman bride in the historical setting from which John was writing. The Roman Empire was revered throughout the ancient world for its incredible cities with advanced engineering and architectural wonders. The Romans were marvelous city builders, probably the greatest of the ancient world. They built walled cities with triumphal arches, grand public buildings, large amphitheaters, beautiful marketplaces, public squares, and tree-lined streets. Many of these trees were laden with fruit. And many Roman streets were not dirt roads but were paved with stones. A section of the famous Appian Way, a stone-paved road begun in 312 BC that extended from Rome, still exists to this day.

The Romans also developed a highly advanced system of waterways known as aqueducts, which are among one of the greatest achievements of the ancient world. Spanning for almost five hundred miles, these above- and belowground structures took spring water from the mountains to the cities where municipal fountains gushed with clean spring water. Though slums and poor sanitation could be found in urban areas of the empire, when compared to other empires, the Greco-Roman civilization was renowned for its engineering, architecture, urban planning, and great cities.

The following is a description of the city of Antioch in Mark Antony's (83–30 BC) and Cleopatra's (69–30 BC) day: "A scenic, well-provisioned river city at the foot of a majestic mountain, with a colonnaded downtown grid and an ample supply of stadiums and gardens, monumental fountains and natural springs. . . . with delightful baths and a lively market."[1]

Alexandria, Egypt, founded by Alexander the Great in 331 BC, was also a magnificent city. Its main street, the Canopic Way, was stunning:

> Alexandria's ninety-foot-wide main avenue left visitors speechless, its scale unmatched in the ancient world. You could lose a day exploring it from end to end. Lined with delicately carved columns, silk awnings, and richly painted facades, the Canopic Way could accommodate eight chariots driving abreast. The city's primary side streets too were nearly twenty feet wide, paved with stones, expertly drained, and partially lit at night. From its central crossroads—a ten minute walk from the palace—a forest of sparkling limestone colonnades extended as far as the eye could see. . . . Industry divided the neighborhoods as well: one quarter was devoted to the manufacture of perfumes and to the fabrication of their alabaster pots, another to glassworkers. . . . Altogether it was a mood-altering city of extreme sensuality and high intellectualism, the Paris of the ancient world.[2]

John's readers were also exposed to the elaborate clothing and jewelry of the women of the Roman world. They were noted for their elaborate attire and jewelry, particularly on their wedding day. When these women became Christians, their obsession with extravagant clothing and jewelry presented a problem for the early church. Paul addressed this issue: "Women should adorn themselves in respectable apparel, with modesty and self-control, not with braided hair and gold or pearls or costly attire" (1 Tim. 2:9).

In the ruins of Pompeii, an ancient Roman city buried under volcanic ash in AD 79, archeologists have found an unusually large amount of gold jewelry, which helps us understand the problems Paul was confronting. The women of Pompeii frequently adorned themselves in gold from head to toe. Excavated jewelry includes gold hair braids, earrings, necklaces, upper armbands, forearm bands, wristbands, rings, belts, anklets, and even gold toe rings. Many of these gold adornments were encrusted with pearls, emeralds, and other precious stones. One can only imagine what a Roman woman

[1] Stacy Schiff, *Cleopatra* (New York: Little, Brown and Company, 2010), 191.
[2] Ibid., 67-68.

might have looked like on her wedding day, dressed in her finest clothing and wearing the finest jewels in her possession. Pompeii may have been more extravagant than other Roman cities, but not by much. Its patron deity was Venus, the Roman goddess of love (eros) and beauty. In Pompeii, a wealthy Roman bride would have been beautifully adorned for her husband.

John merges these two images, a beautiful Roman city and the lavishly adorned bride of the Roman world, in his description of the New Jerusalem. Like a Roman woman adorned on her wedding day, John describes the bride of Christ as a magnificent city with its foundations, walls, gates, and streets made out of the purest gold and every kind of precious stone one can think of. This remarkable city, or "bride," is described further:

> The foundations of the wall of the city were adorned with every kind of jewel. The first was jasper, the second sapphire, the third agate, the fourth emerald, the fifth onyx, the sixth carnelian, the seventh chrysolite, the eighth beryl, the ninth topaz, the tenth chrysoprase, the eleventh jacinth, the twelfth amethyst. And the twelve gates were twelve pearls, each of the gates made of a single pearl, and the street of the city was pure gold, transparent as glass. (Rev. 21:19–21)

This jeweled city, like a Roman bride, is decked out from head to toe—or from its foundations to its walls, gates, and streets. Understanding the Roman setting from which John was writing is the key to understanding this vision of the New Jerusalem as a bride on her wedding day.

The Bride of Christ

Numerous typologies can be found throughout the Bible. These biblical patterns serve the purpose of describing a spiritual reality, whether present or future. The lamb without blemish, sacrificed by the high priest, becomes a type of the sinless Christ, sacrificed for us on the cross. The breaking of bread and drinking of wine is a type, or pattern, of the shed blood of Christ and his broken body. Human marriage is a typology of the church as the bride of Christ and is one of the most interesting in the Scriptures. Obviously, our oneness with Christ is of the spirit, not of the flesh: "Do you not know that your bodies are members of Christ? . . . But he who is joined to the Lord becomes one spirit with him" (1 Cor. 6:15–17). It is this typology that John uses to describe the New Jerusalem as the bride coming down out of heaven. This is a wedding procession between Christ and his body.

Let us look more closely at the concept of the church as the bride of Christ. In the Jewish culture of the time, parents often chose their son's bride. We know that God the Father chooses us as the bride for his Son and then draws us to Christ. This wedding arrangement was made by the Father before the foundation of the world: "Blessed be the God and Father of our

Lord Jesus Christ, who has blessed us in Christ with every spiritual blessing in the heavenly places, even as he chose us in him before the foundation of the world, that we should be holy and blameless before him" (Eph. 1:3–4). Our marriage to his Son has been prearranged.

There is another important distinctive of the Jewish wedding that is critical to understand in order to grasp the concept of the marriage between Christ and the church. In modern Western marriages, a couple becomes engaged and then gets married on their wedding day, coming together in one flesh. In the Jewish tradition at the time of Christ, however, when a couple became engaged, they were considered married from that point on, even though the marriage would not be consummated until the wedding feast. That is the reason Joseph wanted to divorce Mary when she became pregnant through the Holy Spirit, even though from a modern perspective, they were only engaged. The Jewish wedding feast marked the day when the married couple consummated the marriage, and they became one flesh.

With this in mind, we can understand that presently the body of Christ, made up of all believers, is in a state of engagement—or marriage, in the Jewish tradition—with Christ. But in Revelation, we find the marriage is actually consummated at the transformation. We are currently the engaged bride of Christ. When we are taken to heaven, we will receive our spiritual bodies for the marriage with Christ to be consummated.

To better understand how the marriage of Christ and his bride, the church, is similar to our Adamic marriage, it is important to note some of the essential elements of the Adamic marriage. The three basic principles or components of a loving marriage companionship are: (1) oneness of the two persons, (2) equality of nature between the persons, and (3) hierarchy between the persons. Consider the equality of being of the persons. For the union of male and female to take place in the Adamic marriage, the husband and wife must be equal in nature. A female chimpanzee, for example, was not a suitable helpmate for Adam because it was of a lesser order of being of an inferior nature. Eve was a suitable helpmate because she was of the same order of being and nature as Adam. She was of man-"kind," for she was created from Adam's rib and fashioned as a female form of man.

How is this relevant to our marriage to Christ? Currently, as creatures in the Adamic order of being, we are not suitable to become the bride of Christ because we are of an inferior order of being. Christ cannot become one with a being that is made from the dust of the earth. There must be a *type* of equality of being with Christ, just as Eve had to be of the same nature as Adam for them to become one flesh.

Christ's nature is as the Son of God. Therefore, for us as Adamic creatures to be considered suitable to become the bride of Christ, we must first become a child or son of God. We must obtain a type of equality in nature of being with Christ for us to be considered as his bride. The equality we will have after this transformation is only a type of equality of being. We will not be equal to God in nature. We will not become God. Nonetheless, this new kind of nature will have a type of equality with Christ such that we are made a suitable marriage partner and can become his bride in heaven. This is essentially what takes place when we are born again: "But to all who did receive him, who believed in his name, he gave the right to become children of God, who were born, not of blood nor of the will of the flesh nor of the will of man, but of God" (John 1:12–13). When we are born of a man and woman, we receive an Adamic nature. But when we are born of God, we gain an additional nature as children or sons of God.

As Adamic human beings, we cannot be considered as a potential bride for the Son of God, which is why we must first be born "of God" and become sons of God as Christ is the Son of God. And for the marriage to be consummated in heaven, we must become like him when he appears again and transforms our bodies to be like his (1 John 3:2). We must be made like him to be made a suitable marriage partner—just as Eve was fashioned from Adam. When Christ returns to consummate the marriage, he will transform our lowly bodies to be like his glorious body, just as Adam's rib was transformed into Eve. Because Adam and Eve were of the same nature, they could be joined as one flesh. Likewise, Christ can become one with his body of believers once our bodies are transformed to be like his glorified body.

But the Scriptures also teach that there is hierarchy in the marriage relationship between a man and a woman, which mirrors the hierarchy in our marriage relationship with Christ. Christ is the head of the church as the husband is the head of his wife. The wife is to be submissive to her husband as the church is to be submissive to Christ.

In Ephesians, Paul makes a comparison between human marriage and Christ's marriage to the church. The essential components of oneness, equality, and hierarchy can be found in both marriages:

> Wives, submit to your own husbands, as to the Lord. For the husband is the head of the wife *even as Christ is the head of the church, his body*, and is himself its Savior. Now as *the church submits to Christ*, so also wives should submit in everything to their husbands. Husbands, love your wives, as Christ loved the church and gave himself up for her, that he might sanctify her, having cleansed her by the washing of water with the word, so that he might present the church to himself in splendor, without spot or wrinkle or any such thing, that she might be holy and without blemish. In the same way husbands should love their wives as their own bodies. He who loves his wife loves himself. For no one ever hated his own flesh, but nourishes and cherishes it, *just as Christ does the church, because we are members of his body*. "Therefore a man shall leave his father and mother and hold fast to his wife, and the two shall become one flesh." This mystery is profound, and I am saying that *it refers to Christ and the church*. (Eph. 5:22–32)

We, the church, have become a new order of being in a marriage-type relationship with Christ that is patterned after Adamic marriage where the partners are of the same nature or equality of being, there is hierarchy among the partners, and there is oneness in marriage.

Paul describes this truth of Christ and the church as his bride as a profound mystery. It is easy to misinterpret this mystery because when comparing these two kinds of marriage relationships, Paul goes back and forth between discussing a husband and his wife and Christ and his church. Notice that immediately before the Genesis quote describing a man leaving his father and mother to cleave to his wife, Paul says, "just as Christ does the church, because we are members of his body." At this point, Paul has shifted the discussion and is speaking of Christ and the church when he quotes from Genesis—not the husband and wife as one would expect when reading this verse. After quoting from Genesis, Paul again reminds his readers that he is referencing Christ and the church: "This mystery is profound, and I am saying that it [the Genesis quote] refers to Christ and the church."

The profound mystery to which Paul alludes is that through the incarnation Christ leaves his Father in heaven, comes to this earth, and marries those the Father has given him; in doing so, they become one flesh or one body with Christ, his Son. With this in mind, let us read this intriguing Scripture again and see how our marriage to Christ is patterned after Adamic marriage:

> In the same way husbands should love their wives as their own bodies. He who loves his wife loves himself. For no one ever hated his own flesh, but nourishes and cherishes it, [at this point Paul is talking about the Adamic marriage] just as Christ does the church, because we are members of his body [Paul has now shifted the discussion to the marriage between Christ and the church]. "Therefore a man [Christ] shall leave his father and mother [Christ left his Father in heaven during the incarnation] and hold fast to his wife, and the two [Christ and the church] shall become one flesh" [Christ and the church are joined in marriage as one body]. This mystery is profound, and I am saying that it [the Genesis verse] refers to Christ and the church. (Eph. 5:28-32)

The marriage between Christ and the church, his body, has yet to be consummated, for we are still in Adamic bodies. Yet, as children of God, we are engaged—or married, in the Jewish sense. For the wedding to be completed, we must receive our final spiritual bodies of the same nature as Christ's resurrected body: "Just as we have borne the image of the man of dust, we shall also bear the image of the man of heaven" (1 Cor. 15:49). Just as Adam's rib was transformed into a female form of the human body, so, too, our human bodies will be transformed into a body like Christ's, allowing for the consummation of the marriage in heaven between companions of

306 GOD'S KINGDOM ON EARTH AND IN HEAVEN

the same nature. Adam said, "This at last is bone of my bones and flesh of my flesh; she shall be called Woman, because she was taken out of Man" (Gen. 2:23). On the last day Christ will be able to say that, at last, the transformed saints have glorious spiritual bodies of the same nature as his. Then the marriage will be consummated at the marriage feast: "And the angel said to me, 'Write this: Blessed are those who are invited to the marriage supper of the Lamb.' And he said to me, 'These are the true words of God'" (Rev. 19:9).

Moreover, before we can become the body of Christ in heaven, we must first be made pure:

> Husbands, love your wives, as Christ loved the church and gave himself up for her, that he might sanctify her, having cleansed her by the washing of water with the word, *so that he might present the church to himself in splendor, without spot or wrinkle or any such thing, that she might be holy and without blemish.* (Eph. 5:25–27)

In Revelation, as heaven approaches, John sees the church, or Christ's bride, purified and made holy and ready for the wedding:

> Then I heard what seemed to be the voice of a great multitude, like the roar of many waters and like the sound of mighty peals of thunder, crying out, "Hallelujah! For the Lord our God the Almighty reigns. Let us rejoice and exult and give him the glory, for *the marriage of the Lamb has come, and his Bride has made herself ready*; it was granted her to clothe herself with fine linen, bright and pure"—for the fine linen is the righteous deeds of the saints. . . . Then I saw a new heaven and a new earth, for the first heaven and the first earth had passed away, and the sea was no more. And I saw *the holy city, new Jerusalem*, coming down out of heaven from God, *prepared as a bride adorned for her husband.*" (Rev. 19:6-8; 21:1–2)

This is the final wedding procession as the holy and pure bride made suitable for Christ comes from God, the Father, who gives the bride away, and is now ready for Christ, her husband. The bride has now made herself ready and is adorned for her husband with fine linen, bright and pure and arrayed with the splendor of precious jewels befitting any bride.

John continues, as he describes the remarkable splendor of the New Jerusalem as the bride of Christ adorned with gold and precious stones:

> "Come, I will show you the Bride, the wife of the Lamb." And he carried me away in the Spirit to a great, high mountain, and showed me the holy city Jerusalem coming down out of heaven from God, having the glory of God, its radiance like a most rare jewel, like a jasper, clear as crystal. (Rev. 21:9–11)

In Ephesians, Paul says Christ sacrificially loved his body, "so that he might present the church to himself *in splendor*" (Eph. 5:27). Now John sees the bride presented in all her splendor. The bride is finally ready to be presented to her husband and is magnificently adorned with every kind of precious stone one can imagine—jasper, sapphire, agate, emerald, onyx, carnelian, chrysolite, beryl, topaz, chrysoprase, jacinth, and amethyst.

This concept of the body of Christ being the bride of Christ is profound. It may be used as a metaphor of our current relationship to Christ, but it also represents a future transcendent reality. The Adamic typology of marriage becomes a pattern for the spiritual reality of a new eternal relationship between Christ and the church that is very real indeed. Something truly amazing is taking place. Our relationship to Christ is best described by the New Testament writers as a type of marriage.

The full extent of this new order of being and new relationship to God's Son was unforeseen by the Old Testament writers. The gospel that Paul and the disciples preached was a mystery that is now beginning to unfold:

> Of this gospel I was made a minister according to the gift of God's grace . . . to preach to the Gentiles *the unsearchable riches of Christ,* and to bring to light for everyone what is *the plan of the mystery hidden for ages in God* who created all things, so that *through the church* the manifold wisdom of God might now be made known to the rulers and authorities in the heavenly places. (Eph. 3:7–10)

God has a plan, one that involves the church, which is made up of redeemed Adamic creatures who become children of God. As such, they are suitable to become the bride of his Son when on the last day they are transformed into immortal, imperishable, and incorruptible—holy and pure—bodies like Christ's body.

Believers who become children of God and the bride of Christ are promised unsearchable riches in Christ: "But, as it is written, 'What no eye has seen, nor ear heard, nor the heart of man imagined, what God has prepared for those who love him'—these things God has revealed to us through the Spirit" (1 Cor. 2:9–10). As Paul says, only God through the Holy Spirit could have revealed such a profound mystery. No one could have preconceived what will happen to the children of God on the day the marriage to Christ is consummated.

This is a major New Testament theme that John reinforces in the final chapters of Revelation: "for the marriage of the Lamb has come, and his Bride has made herself ready." We go from the Adamic marriage in Genesis between a man and a woman to the mystery of the marriage of the Lamb between Christ and the children of God in Revelation.

When one ponders that the Father devised this wedding plan before the foundation of the world—that we were to be in Christ, as members of his body, and destined to become his bride in the new heavens and new earth—it makes one wonder if this Adamic world could have been created to serve as a model or pattern of the future and not merely as an end unto itself. God did not intend for this Adamic creation to exist for the sole purpose of living out a human existence on the Genesis earth. The Adamic marriage that we experience on earth prepares us for the marriage of the Lamb in heaven.

As children of God in the new order of being, we are currently betrothed to Christ. When Christ comes again for his bride, the Adamic order of being will come to an end, and we will be raptured to heaven and will finally experience the glory of the new creation as the bride of Christ and as the children of God the Father for eternity.

Many aspects of the restoration will prefigure the new heavens and new earth and the New Jerusalem. I think that after we experience the 1,000-year restoration, we will have a much better idea of what heaven is going to be like. For example, the abundance of the restored earthly Jerusalem serves as a pattern of the future New Jerusalem that John describes as having streets paved with gold and city walls made of precious stones. Isaiah describes the exceeding abundance of the earthly Jerusalem during the restoration: "Your gates shall be open continually; day and night they shall not be shut, that people may bring to you the wealth of the nations, with their kings led in procession. . . . they shall call you the City of the LORD, the Zion of the Holy One of Israel (Isa. 60:11–14). During the restoration, the kings of the earth will bring the wealth of the nations into the earthly Jerusalem in gratitude for a world of peace and prosperity. Its physical beauty will be remarkable. By experiencing this magnificent city for one thousand years, we will have a much better understanding of John's vision of the New Jerusalem, which comes down out of heaven after the earthly Jerusalem is destroyed.

In his description of the New Jerusalem, notice John uses the same pattern of kings bringing their glory into the city as Isaiah used in describing the Jerusalem of the restoration. We can take no material wealth with us to heaven, but believers can take the glory of our wealth of good deeds and rewards that we receive at the Great White Throne judgment into the New Jerusalem. The restored earthly Jerusalem of the restoration prefigures the New Jerusalem of the new heavens and new earth:

> Its lamp is the Lamb. By its light will the nations walk, and the kings of the earth will bring their glory into it, and its gates will never be shut by day—and there will be no night there. They will bring into it the glory and the honor of the nations. But nothing unclean will ever enter it, nor anyone who does what is detestable or false, but only those who are written in the Lamb's book of life. (Rev. 21:23–27)

Summary

In Revelation, Christ gives John a vision of the New Jerusalem. John's vision draws upon some of the magnificent Roman architecture and city planning of his day as well as the beauty of a Roman bride adorned in splendor for marriage on her wedding day. The New Jerusalem is arrayed like a beautiful bride, representing the consummation of the wedding of Christ and his bride, the church.

Adamic marriage serves as a type of the consummation of the wedding that will take place in heaven between Christ and his bride. As a man leaves his parents and cleaves to his wife, so, too, Christ left his Father in heaven to come to this earth to die for his people and to cleave to his wife, the church. As in the Jewish wedding tradition, we are now engaged to Christ, but still considered married, with the wedding taking place on the last day in heaven.

God the Father has been planning this wedding in heaven since before the foundation of the world. The 1,000-year restoration will be the rehearsal dinner. Our experience of the restoration and the magnificent city of the earthly Jerusalem will enable us to better foresee the incomparable beauty and joy of the future New Jerusalem in the new heavens and new earth.

10

Eschatology and the Trinity

I have read many books on eschatology, and one of the most neglected subjects as it relates to the biblical future is a study of the triune God in relation to God's kingdom on earth and in heaven. Understanding how the triune God functions internally and how the Son relates to the Father is essential to understanding both the Son's messianic kingdom, as well as the Father's eternal kingdom.

For example, there is implied hierarchy within the Trinity when the Father tells the Son to sit at his right hand until he (the Father) makes his Son's enemies a footstool for his feet (Heb. 1:13). Even today, the Son, who has returned to heaven, continues to wait on the Father to determine the seasons and time for his messianic reign to begin (Acts 1:7). The Father seems to have authority over the Son as pertaining to when Christ will receive his messianic kingdom.

The hierarchy within the Trinity has become a controversial subject among contemporary evangelicals. Historically, many of the important church councils were formed to combat heresies that, in one form or another, demeaned the deity of Christ or viewed him as inferior to God the Father. Many of their findings and declarations were designed to counter these views of an inferior or subordinate Son and defend the truth that the Son is fully equal to God the Father. These councils, however, do not really grapple with the modern observation of the Son being equal in nature with the Father and at the same time subordinate to the Father.

Today, theologians are divided into two camps concerning the Trinity. The egalitarian camp believes that the Godhead is a partnership among persons of the Trinity who are equals with no hierarchy. They conclude that Christ was submissive to the Father on this earth only as the *man* portion of his dual nature; once he returned to heaven, he resumed his original equal partnership with the Father and is no longer submissive to him.

The traditional camp, also referred to as the complementarian position, believes that the Father, Son, and Holy Spirit are all equal in nature as God and all three form one God—but there is a form of hierarchy within the Godhead: the Holy Spirit is submissive to the Son, and the Son is submissive to the Father. Traditionalists maintain that this hierarchy existed *before* the incarnation, *during* the incarnation, and continues to exist *after* the incarnation. It is eternal and unchanging and is not merely the result of Christ becoming a man.

Interestingly, much of this controversy was precipitated by the debate over whether wives should be submissive to their husbands, a debate that began with feminists in the 1970s. How you understand the marriage relationship can affect how one understands the Trinity and vice versa. If man as male and female is in the image of God, then the marriage relationship of male and female as one flesh would be a reflection of the Godhead. God said, "Let us [the triune God] make man in our image, after our likeness. . . . So God created man in his own image, in the image of God he created him; male and female he created them" (Gen. 1:26–27).

The Old Testament does not clearly portray the Trinity, but we know from the New Testament that three persons make up the "us" of the God of Genesis. God is one being but three persons. In our human marriage as one flesh, there are two persons—male and female. For something to be in the image of another, however, it does not have to be an exact replica of that image. For example, I am a three-dimensional person with height, width, and depth, but when I look into a mirror and see an image of myself, I see a two-dimensional image with height and width, but not depth. Similarly, a marriage of two persons can still be in the image of a triune God.

From an egalitarian perspective of marriage, if the Godhead is a loving companionship of three equal persons without hierarchy, then our two-person marriage should reflect this egalitarian relationship, and the wife should not be submissive to her husband. That Eve was told that Adam would now "rule over" her (Gen. 3:16) is a result of the fall and should be reversed through redemption and salvation. We should be restored to the pre-fall egalitarian marriage in the image of an egalitarian God.

From the complementarian perspective, the apostles Paul and Peter teach that a wife should be submissive to her husband, not as a result of the fall, but by design (Eph. 5:22–24; 1 Peter 3:1–7). The marriage couple is in the image of a Godhead that is a loving companionship of three persons of equal nature who are hierarchically related and form one God. Likewise, the husband and wife are a loving companionship of two persons of equal nature who are hierarchically related—the husband being the loving head of a submissive wife—and form one flesh.

Understanding the structure of the internal relationship of the triune God can have major implications on how the Adamic marriage should function. The Godhead has a type of architecture, and our human marriage should be modeled on that design and structure because man, as male and female given in marriage, is in the image of the triune God.

Consequently, the debate over headship and submission in marriage as taught by Paul and Peter has precipitated a debate over the internal structure of the Godhead. This controversy over submission has become a major point of contention among conservative evangelicals, not only over how marriage should be structured, but how the Godhead itself is structured. The church is currently experiencing a serious doctrinal debate over the Trinity, as it has several times in the past—with, as we shall see, major implications on the nature of the kingdom of God.

Confusing the Two Orders of Being

Apart from one's view of the Trinity, I believe much of the confusion over submission within marriage stems from a lack of understanding and differentiation between the two orders of being—the Adamic order of being as male and female given in marriage and the new order of being as children of God where there is no distinction between male and female, because we are not given in marriage. As children of God in the new creation, there is complete equality with no hierarchy. In heaven, the husband will not be the head of a submissive wife because she will no longer be his wife. If there is a hierarchy in heaven among the children of God, it will not be based on male or female designation, for these gender designations will no longer exist.

But as long as we are on this earth, we continue to live a duality. My wife, a fellow child of God in Christ, remains my wife in the Adamic order of being until we are transformed and taken to heaven on the last day. Only then will there be no male or female distinctions, because there will be no marriage, and thus, no headship and submission. While we remain on this earth, the two orders of being operate concurrently; the new creation does not cancel out or replace the Adamic order of being. If the Bible teaches that there is headship and submission in the Adamic marriage, then we should continue to function accordingly even though we have already become children of God and a new creation.

Paul, like Christ, did indeed teach a revolutionary concept when he introduced the idea of becoming a child of God in which there would be no sexual distinctions and no marriage in this new order of being. But this new creation does not usurp the existing Adamic order of being until the last day. Until then, we should seek to live out the Adamic order of being, even if that involves hierarchy and submission in marriage.

Paul seems to go out of his way to point out that submission is still operable in the Adamic marriage though we are now in Christ in the new order of being: "Wives, submit to your husbands, *as is fitting in the Lord*" (Col. 3:18). Even though we are now in the Lord as a new creation in Christ, it is still fitting and appropriate that a wife should submit to her husband.

Paul was not confused by the two orders of being; rather, he understood that they operated concurrently as long as this creation continued to exist. In the new order of being, the wife *ultimately* would not be submissive, because in heaven there would no longer be marriage. In the meantime, as long as we are living in this Genesis creation, we should continue to function in the Adamic order of being—husbands and wives should fulfill their marital duties, and wives should continue to be submissive to loving husbands. According to Paul, submission in marriage is a part of the design of the original Adamic marriage and is not a result of the fall when the rule over the woman became harsh. The harshness is remedied when the husband loves the wife sacrificially as Christ loves and serves the church.

Mutual Submission?

Proponents of egalitarianism have developed another interpretation of Paul's letter to the Ephesians that is often used to circumvent the teaching of female submission in marriage. They specifically target Paul's phrase: "submitting to one another out of reverence for Christ" (Eph. 5:21), and interpret it to mean mutual submission between husbands and wives. This concept of reciprocal submission has become pervasive in the modern evangelical mind and regularly appears in sermons, marriage materials, Christian magazines, and numerous books on the subject.

Despite its broad acceptance in evangelical circles, a more accurate examination of Ephesians reveals that Paul never taught that there should be mutual submission between a husband and a wife. Paul's phrase "submitting to one another" is an introductory statement to the following three groups of "one to another": wives (one) are to submit to their husbands (another), children (one) are to obey their parents (another), and slaves (one) are to obey their masters (another).

Paul is not describing some sort of reversible submission in which the wife and husband should submit to each other. If that were the case, then the parent should submit to and obey the child as much as the child should submit to and obey the parent. To apply the concept of mutual submission in this context is linguistic nonsense. We should all serve one another, but submission and servanthood are two related, but very different, concepts. Christ, as Lord and Master, may serve us, but that does not mean he is ever submissive to us. On the other hand, we are always submissive to Christ as we are commanded to serve him.

Anyone in a position of authority should be a true servant of those in a subordinate position, but that does not mean the authority figure is being submissive to his or her subordinates. Christ served Peter by washing his feet, but in doing so, he was not being submissive to Peter. Christ told Peter that he had to submit to his serving him in this fashion in order to maintain his cleansed relationship with him (John 13:5–10). In the process, Christ served Peter but never submitted to Peter. We, on the other hand, submit to and serve Christ.

As human beings we encounter many different kinds of hierarchical relationships that involve authority and submission. The husband-wife relationship, the parent-child relationship, the employer-employee relationship, and the military sergeant-private relationship are just a few of these hierarchical relationships. Each is different. And we should never confuse these relationships with another: a husband should never treat his wife as if she were his child or his employee, and a sergeant should never treat his spouse or children as if they were military personnel under his command.

Another misconception about submission in marriage or other relationships is that the subordinate person should be docile. On the contrary, wives, employees, or children should be free to speak their minds and, when necessary, be respectfully confrontational. They should be permitted to offer their insights and opinions. They have just as much right to be proactive and take initiative as the person whose headship they are under. They should be creative and assertive with their ideas.

And there are legitimate grounds for insubordination. A wife should not submit to a husband who insists that she break the law by filing a fraudulent income tax return or selling illegal drugs. Nor should a wife or child submit to physical abuse. An employee should not submit to an employer who tells him to perform an illegal activity. Even in the military, with its very strict hierarchical structure, a soldier should not submit to his commanding officer when he commands him to commit a war crime.

The Structure of the Trinity

Our marriages being in the image of God works both ways. We can project the architecture of the Godhead onto our marriage relationship, or we can project the architecture of our marriage relationship onto the Godhead. If we can determine that our marriage is an egalitarian relationship, then the Godhead would be an egalitarian relationship. Conversely, if there is hierarchy in our human marriage, then one would logically expect hierarchy in the Godhead.

Let's return to the subject of the Trinity itself and see what the Scriptures teach about the architecture of the Godhead and what implications this has on the kingdom of God. Egalitarians believe that the Son is submissive to the

Father, but they attribute this submission to his incarnation as a man. They claim that Christ as the Son of God was not submissive to the Father, but Christ as the Son of Man in his human nature was submissive to God the Father just as all humans should be. As the second Adam, Jesus was submissive to the Father in his human nature. The God portion of his dual nature, however, remained in equal partnership.

Egalitarians go so far as to assert that, as the Son of God, Christ was not submissive to the Father *before* the incarnation, and now that he has returned to the Father in heaven, he has resumed a relationship of equal partnership with the Father. The Father is no longer the head of Christ. Thus, the eternal Godhead—before, during, and after the incarnation—is a partnership among equals without any form of hierarchy.

Let's examine the Scriptures to determine if this is true. If it can be shown that the Son of God is eternally submissive to the Father, then there is hierarchy in the Godhead with many eschatological implications. We will begin with an analysis of Christ's relationship to the Father *during* the incarnation. However, this can be somewhat difficult. For example, how do we distinguish Christ's relationship to the Father as *Son of God* from his relationship to the Father as a *man of God*? As an incarnate man, he is submissive to the Father, as all men should be. Hebrews says:

> Since therefore the children share in flesh and blood, he himself likewise partook of the same things . . . In the days of his flesh, Jesus offered up prayers and supplications, with loud cries and tears, to him who was able to save him from death, and he was heard because of his reverence. Although he was a son, he learned obedience through what he suffered. And being made perfect, he became the source of eternal salvation to all who obey him. (Heb. 2:14; 5:7–9)

From these verses, one senses that although Christ was the Son of God who did not need to learn obedience in order to be perfect, he learned obedience as a man and proved that he was a perfect man because of his perfect obedience. As the Son of God, he was perfect before the incarnation, so the writer of Hebrews must be referring to his proving his perfection as a man in the flesh. Christ, as a human being, was truly submissive and obedient to the Father—even to the point of death on the cross—"not my will, but yours, be done" (Luke 22:42).

Perhaps this refers to Jesus as the second Adam who was perfectly submissive to God the Father through all trials and temptations. But this does not prove that Christ, as the second person of the Trinity, was not also being submissive to the Father at the same time. When Jesus said, "not my will, but yours, be done," he could have been speaking as both the Son of Man *and* the Son of God. Nothing in these verses supports the egalitarian claim that Christ as a man was submissive to God the Father, but that Christ as the Son of God was not also being submissive to him. Both—Christ the man and Christ the Son of God—could have been submissive to the Father simultaneously.

Therefore, the best way to resolve this dispute about whether Christ is submissive to the Father as the Son of God is to look at verses that indicate what their relationship was like *before* the incarnation and what it is now like *after* the ascension—after Christ returned to the glory he had with the Father before the world began. If the Scriptures indicate that Christ was in a subordinate role to the Father before the incarnation and after his return to heaven, then the egalitarian assertion can be refuted.

The Structure of the Trinity Before the Incarnation

Let us search for scriptural evidence that reveals Christ's relationship to the Father in heaven *before* the incarnation. If the egalitarian position is correct—that God the Father and God the Son are equal and were in an egalitarian and nonhierarchical partnership before the incarnation—then how did the Father and the Son decide who was going to come to this earth to die for mankind's sins?

Egalitarian logic would infer that the Son could as easily have sent the Father to the earth to die for our sins as the Father sending the Son. In this scenario, the incarnate Father would have been obedient to the point of death and reconciled us to the Son, in heaven. And who in this partnership would decide which one would become incarnate and die on the cross for our sins? Did the Father volunteer or did the Son volunteer? How did they decide? Did they flip some type of celestial coin?

These questions may appear silly; however, from an egalitarian view of the Trinity, they are valid. From an egalitarian perspective, John 3:16 could read as follows: "For the Son of God so loved the world, that he gave his only Father, that whoever believes in him should not perish but have eternal life. For the Son of God did not send his Father into the world to condemn the world, but in order that the world might be saved through him [the Father]."

If reading these verses in this manner deeply disturbs you as much as it does me, then you will begin to understand the importance of this issue. This rewording of these verses supports the egalitarian position that the Father and Son are equal in partnership and mutually submissive to each other, and that the Son could have sent the Father to this world to die on the cross. But from a biblical perspective, this concept of equal partnership between God the Father and God the Son seems absurd. The entirety of the New Testament teaching on the way in which the Son relates to the Father directly opposes it.

Egalitarians could possibly argue that when Jesus of Nazareth reached maturity as a man, the Father sent the *man*, Jesus, to begin his public ministry. The man, Jesus, was then submissive to the Father. However, Jesus informs us that the sending of the Son of God began *in heaven*, not in Nazareth, and that he came down from heaven to the earth to do the predetermined will of the Father who sent him from heaven: "For I have *come down* from heaven, *not to do my own will* but the *will of him who sent me*" (John 6:38). The Father had a purpose in mind before he sent his Son into this world. The Father initiated and willed this purpose—the Son did not. The Father *sent* the Son from heaven to the earth to accomplish what the Father had willed. This sending began in heaven—not in Nazareth.

The gospel of John, in particular, emphasizes this theme of the Father sending the Son from heaven according to the Father's will and command. Note specifically that *the Father* sent the Son to this world to die on the cross for us. Jesus himself said:

> "All that the Father gives me will come to me, and whoever comes to me I will never cast out. *For I have come down from heaven*, not to do my own will but the will of him who sent me. And this is the will of him who sent me, that I should lose nothing of all that he has given me, but raise it up on the last day. . . . " (John 6:37-39). So Jesus proclaimed, as he taught in the temple, "You know me, and you know where I come from? *But I have not come of my own accord.* He [the Father] who sent me [from heaven] is true, and him you do not know. I know him, for I come from him [in heaven], and *he sent me* [from heaven]" (John 7:28-29). . . . "For I have not spoken on my own authority, *but the Father who sent me has himself given me a commandment—what to say and what to speak.* And I know that his commandment is eternal life. What I say, therefore, I say as the Father has told me." (John 12:49-50)

Before the Father sent Christ into this world, he had devised a plan that we should be in Christ and have eternal life. To accomplish this plan, he sent his Son into the world to become a man and die on the cross. And the Father commanded the Son to say and do the things necessary to bring salvation and eternal life to those chosen by the Father. But the whole process of sending takes place from heaven before the Son became incarnate.

The Father's act of election before the creation of the world also strongly affirms that hierarchy existed within the Godhead before the incarnation. Paul teaches the following:

> Blessed be *the God and Father* of our Lord Jesus Christ, who has blessed us *in Christ* with every spiritual blessing in the heavenly places, even as he [the Father] chose us in him [Christ] *before the foundation of the world*, that we should be holy and blameless before him. In love he [the Father] predestined us for adoption through Jesus Christ, according to the purpose

of his will [the Father's will], to the praise of his glorious grace, with which he [the Father] has blessed us in the Beloved. In him [Christ] we have redemption through his blood, the forgiveness of our trespasses, according to the riches of his [the Father's] grace, which he lavished upon us, in all wisdom and insight making known to us the mystery of his [the Father's] will, according to his purpose, which he set forth in Christ as a plan for the fullness of time, to unite all things in him, things in heaven and on earth. (Eph. 1:3–10)

The Father's decision and plan for us to be adopted as children of God took place even before the world was created and *before* Christ became a man.

Peter also confirms that it is the *Father's* great mercy that has caused us to be born again: "Blessed be the God and *Father* of our Lord Jesus Christ! According to his [the Father's] great mercy, he has caused us to be *born again* to a living hope through the resurrection of Jesus Christ from the dead" (1 Peter 1:3).

Where did Paul and Peter learn that it is the Father who causes people to accept Christ and be born again? From Jesus:

Now when Jesus came into the district of Caesarea Philippi, he asked his disciples, "Who do people say that the Son of Man is?" And they said, "Some say John the Baptist, others say Elijah, and others Jeremiah or one of the prophets." He said to them, "But who do you say that I am?" Simon Peter replied, "You are the Christ, the Son of the living God." And Jesus answered him, "Blessed are you, Simon Bar-Jonah! For flesh and blood has not revealed this to you, *but my Father* who is in heaven. And I tell you, you are Peter, and on this rock [the revealing work of the Father] I will build my church, and the gates of hell shall not prevail against it [Nothing can prevent the Father from revealing Christ to those he has chosen]." (Matt. 16:13–18)

In his reply to Peter, Jesus used a metaphor that is often misunderstood. The rock—the solid foundation from which Christ was to build his church made up of the Father's children—was not Peter or his profession of faith; rather, it was *the Father* who revealed to Peter that Jesus was the Christ! Nothing—neither Satan nor the gates of hell—can stop *the Father* from revealing Christ to those *he* has chosen to become his children and the bride of his Son. Christ is going to build his church on the sovereign election of *the Father* who draws people to himself.

These verses provide strong biblical evidence that there was hierarchy within the triune God before the incarnation. No celestial coin was flipped. The Father is the developer and architect behind the plan of redemption, which he conceived and planned before the foundation of the world. And the Son is the builder who has been given the task of implementing and executing the Father's preconceived set of plans.

The Structure of the Trinity After the Ascension

Let's examine the relationship within the Trinity after Christ returned to heaven. There is significant New Testament evidence that Christ is presently in a subordinate role now that he has ascended to heaven; and further, that he will remain in a subordinate role even after this world comes to an end. In his first letter to the Corinthians, Paul writes:

> But in fact Christ has been raised from the dead, the firstfruits [the first to be raised in an immortal body] of those who have fallen asleep [believers]. For as by a man [Adam] came death, by a man [Jesus] has come also the resurrection of the dead. . . . But each in his own order: Christ the firstfruits [his resurrection into an immortal body and his ascension to heaven], then at *his coming* [his second coming] those who belong to Christ [the rapture of the saints]. Then comes the end [of the world], when he delivers the kingdom [established during the millennium] to God the Father after destroying every rule and every authority and power [Armageddon, the beast, the false prophet, Gog and Magog, Satan, etc.]. For he must reign [as Messiah] until he [the Father] has put all his enemies under his feet [which he does during the restoration]. The last enemy to be destroyed is death [which occurs at the final resurrection]. For "God [the Father] has put all things in subjection under his feet." But when it says, "all things are put in subjection," it is plain that he [the Father] is excepted who put all things in subjection under him [the Father was never in subjection to Christ]. When *all things* are subjected to him [the restoration, the demise of Satan, and finally death itself], then the Son himself will also be *subjected to him* [the Father] who put all things in subjection under him, that God may be all in all. (1 Cor. 15:20–28)

Paul is teaching about the resurrected and ascended Christ—not the earthly ministry of the man from Nazareth. And he seems to go out of his way to make it clear that the Father, in particular, is never a part of the things that are made subject to Christ during his messianic reign. When the last enemy, death, is destroyed at Christ's second coming, Christ will then turn his entire kingdom of believers over to the Father. He will continue to be the head of his body, but he and his kingdom of believers will be *subject* to the Father.

It seems that the Father has given Christ authority temporarily, so that Christ might bring everything back into submission to the Father. After Christ finishes the last assignment of resurrecting the Father's children into immortal bodies and takes us to heaven, then "the Son himself will also be subjected to him" for all eternity. Hierarchy can be discerned throughout this entire eschatological drama.

When the Father says it is time for Christ to reign at the beginning of the millennium, the restoration will begin. We will then experience God's kingdom on earth. This hierarchy can be illustrated as follows:

The Father *subjects the world*
to the Son of Man *who has dominion over*
mankind *who has dominion over*
a regenerated Genesis creation.

Using Revelation as a guide, this sequence of events that Paul describes can be outlined as follows:

1. Adam brings sin and death into the world.
2. The Father sends Christ into the world through the incarnation as the second perfect Adam. After the sinless Christ is crucified for our sins, he is resurrected by the Father into an immortal body as the firstfruits of those who belong to Christ and are the children of God the Father.
3. The Father put everything in subjection to Christ. Yet, Christ is still waiting for the Father to say it is time for him to exercise his reign over this world so the Father can put his enemies under his feet.
4. The messianic kingdom will be established when the Father says that it is time for everything to be subject to Christ.
5. Christ exercises his reign during the restoration when he destroys every rule, authority, and power that is against God. The Father's will is done on earth as it is in heaven.
6. After one thousand years, when Satan is released, Christ destroys the armies of Gog and Magog and finally Satan himself.
7. At this point, only one enemy remains to be conquered—death.
8. Then at his coming, Christ destroys the final enemy, death, through the resurrection of believers—who belong to Christ and have been chosen by the Father—into immortal bodies.
9. Christ will have finished the work of the Father and then turns his kingdom of transformed children of God over to the Father in the eternal kingdom of heaven.
10. Christ will then, as always, be subject to the Father.

After Christ has fulfilled all the Father's plans for this Genesis age in the restoration, he will then proceed with the final mission of the Father—to destroy death for the Father's children by transforming the believers' bodies into immortal ones like his. When all Christ's enemies have been destroyed, including death itself, everything will have been made subject to the Father. Christ then delivers the kingdom of transformed believers over to the Father. Yet he himself will remain submissive to the Father in heaven.

After Christ rose from the dead and ascended into heaven, the Father told him to sit at his right hand in heaven until *he decided* that it was time for his Son to reign in the restoration. The Father is not subject to this reign of Christ during the restoration. Rather, Christ will exercise his reign from the Father's right hand during this time. After the restoration, when *the Father decides* that it is time for the world to end and the new order of being to begin in heaven, *he will send* his Son back in the clouds to retrieve us, transform us, and take us to heaven. At that time all enemies will have been destroyed, and Christ will turn his kingdom over to the Father. Christ will have finished the work that the Father preplanned and commissioned him to do regarding the restoration of this Genesis creation.

This is powerful scriptural evidence that the Son is eternally submissive to the Father, and that this submissive relationship plays an essential and strategic role in the eschatological future. These Scriptures offer convincing evidence that a form of hierarchy exists in the Godhead between the Father and his Son—before, during, and after the incarnation.

The Holy Spirit, too, is fully God. But note that after Christ's ascension, the Holy Spirit was sent by Christ and is submissive to Christ, just as Christ was sent by the Father and is submissive to the Father. Just as Christ did not come from heaven on his own authority to speak his own words, the Holy Spirit was sent by Christ, is under the authority of Christ, and will speak only what he hears. Just as Christ came to glorify the Father, the Holy Spirit came to glorify the Son:

> But when the Helper comes, whom *I will send to you* from the Father, the Spirit of truth, who proceeds from the Father, he will bear witness about me. . . . When the Spirit of truth comes, he will guide you into all the truth, for *he will not speak on his own authority*, but *whatever he hears he will speak*, and he will declare to you the things that are to come. *He will glorify me*, for he will take what is mine and declare it to you. All that the Father has is mine; therefore I said that he will take what is mine and declare it to you." (John 15:26; 16:13–15)

The Holy Spirit is fully God and yet is submissive to Christ just as Christ is fully God and is submissive to the Father and his plans.

Summary

The eternal relationship within the Trinity plays a profound role in how the drama of God's plan of redemption began, unfolds, and ends. The Father conceived of his plan of redemption before the foundation of the world. Then he sent his Son into this world as a human being to accomplish his plan of the cross as the central means of reconciliation with fallen mankind. But the plan does not stop there. The Father has a plan to restore this

Genesis creation to his Son, for this creation was made through the Son, by the Son, and for the Son. Once Christ's enemies have been made a footstool for his feet by the Father through the Son's messianic kingdom, then the Father will complete his plan of redemption by sending his Son to rapture the saints, destroy this Genesis creation, and take the transformed children of God to the Father's eternal kingdom of heaven. As Paul teaches, the Father plays a key role in this plan of redemption:

> In him [Christ] we have redemption through his blood, the forgiveness of our trespasses, according to the riches of his grace [the Father's], which he lavished upon us, in all wisdom and insight making known to us the mystery of his will [the Father's], according to his purpose, which he set forth in Christ as a plan for the fullness of time, to unite all things in him [Christ], things in heaven and on earth. (Eph. 1:7–10)

The Father has a plan for the fullness of time to unite all things in Christ, things in heaven and on the earth. This is why Christ is now sitting at the Father's right hand *waiting* on the Father, for only the Father knows the times or seasons that both the restoration in this age and the transformation in the age to come will take place.

After the restoration is accomplished, the Father gives Christ the very important task of resurrecting the Father's children into immortal bodies, so that his children can dwell with him in heaven. Note that this occurs when Jesus comes again at the last trumpet when the transformed saints inherit the Father's heavenly kingdom: "then at *his coming* those who belong to Christ. Then comes the end [of the world], when he delivers the kingdom [established during the restoration] to God the Father after destroying every rule and every authority and power" (1 Cor. 15:23–24).

Paul informs us that after Christ has finished his work of *reigning* as Messiah over this restored Adamic world of mortals during the restoration and destroys all his enemies including Satan, he will proceed to finish the work that the Father has given him, which is to destroy death itself, the last enemy of the Father's children. Christ uses the same power that enabled him to subject all things to himself during the restoration to then transform our mortal bodies to be like his glorious, immortal, resurrected body.

When Christ finished his work on earth given to him by his Father, he then ascended to heaven in the clouds. When Christ finishes his work of restoring this Genesis creation and the Father says it is time, he will return on the last day in the clouds to transform our lowly bodies and take us to our eternal citizenship in heaven as children of the Father and as his bride.

The Father so loved the world that he sent his Son to this world to become incarnate as a man and die on the cross for our sins so that we who receive Christ and become children of God may be reconciled to the Father. The Father is the originator of this great plan of redemption. He has a plan for the fullness of time, to unite all things in Christ—things in heaven and on earth. As Paul says, it was the Father "who has blessed us in Christ with every spiritual blessing in the heavenly places, even as he [the Father] chose us in him before the foundation of the world, that we should be holy and blameless before him. In love he [the Father] predestined us for adoption [as children of God] through Jesus Christ" (Eph. 1:3–5).

The New Testament has a substantial amount of revealed truth about how the Trinity functions in relation to the kingdom of God on earth and in heaven. This study of the loving relationship between the Father, the Son, and the Holy Spirit—persons of the triune God who are of equal nature, but hierarchically related and form one God—is a major biblical theme that has long been neglected by theologians who have written about the kingdom of God. Understanding this relationship within the triune God is critical to understanding the gospel, our salvation, our regeneration, and our future inheritance on earth and in heaven.

The love of the Father, Son, and Holy Spirit among themselves and toward us permeates all biblical doctrine on the subject of the kingdom of God. The central motivation behind God's plan of redemption is his love for fallen man. The Father's love, in particular, seems to be a driving force behind this whole plan of redemption. The Father must have truly loved us to devise such a remarkable plan of salvation. As John teaches, "For God [the Father] so loved the world, that he gave his only Son, that whoever believes in him should not perish but have eternal life" (John 3:16). We have all read and heard this verse so many times that we sometimes miss the central motivation behind this revealed doctrine. It is all about the *love* of the Father—for his Son and for us.

Paul strives for us to grasp the love within the Trinity that is behind this incredible gospel of the kingdom of God: "Giving thanks to the Father, who has qualified you to share in the inheritance of the saints in light. He has delivered us from the domain of darkness and transferred us to the kingdom of his *beloved* Son, in whom we have redemption, the forgiveness of sins" (Col. 1:12–13). The Father loves his Son and extends that love to us by saving us from Satan's dominion of darkness and bringing us into his beloved Son's kingdom—which will manifest itself on earth during the millennium and in heaven when the kingdom composed of transformed believers is taken to the Father's home.

Books on the kingdom of God tend to be very analytical and academic as they perform a referential analysis of the Scriptures to develop a coherent biblical theology. But let's not forget that behind all this doctrine about the kingdom of God is a Supreme Being who must love us more than we can ever imagine. The kingdom of God is all about the love of God within the Trinity and the love of God toward us. God's plan of redemption is all about the love of the triune God.

11

The Stealthy Restoration

If the postrestorational framework for understanding God's kingdom on earth and in heaven is correct, and it has taken us almost two thousand years to discover this system of eschatology, it makes one wonder why Jesus and all the biblical writers were not clearer in their teachings on the Son's earthly kingdom and then the Father's heavenly kingdom. In many ways, the biblical teaching of the Son's messianic kingdom on this earth has a "stealthy" quality. In both the Old and New Testaments, numerous writers give us fragments of data about the restoration, but no one writer gives us a complete explanation. No one book or letter of the Bible offers a detailed description of how the restoration unfolds and fits into the overall flow of future events. Some of the prophetic literature is straightforward, but much of it contains highly symbolic language.

The book of Revelation comes closest to providing a general outline, but the book of Revelation is difficult to understand. It seems God has given us a giant, complex puzzle to solve with pieces of critical information scattered throughout the Bible, with the best outline found in the book of Revelation!

Why would God want the truth about the Son's kingdom on this earth before the kingdom of heaven to be difficult to discern? I have developed a theory as to why the restoration, in particular, is not more clearly explained in the Bible. I believe God intentionally inspired the authors of Scripture to be vague when writing about Christ's earthly kingdom. The information about the messianic kingdom on this earth is stealthy by design.

Certain aspects of the first coming of Christ as the suffering servant were intentionally obscure. If we had lived in the first century, with only the Old Testament as a resource, few of us would have figured out that the Messiah first had to suffer and be sacrificed for our sins before entering into his glory in heaven. Even the Old Testament prophets wondered how their own prophecies would play out: "Concerning this salvation, the prophets who prophesied about the grace that was to be yours searched and inquired carefully, inquiring what person or time the Spirit of Christ in them was indicating when he predicted the sufferings of Christ and the subsequent glories" (1 Peter 1:10–11).

If the prophets themselves had difficulty understanding the Messiah's crucifixion and the subsequent events, it is no wonder that the disciples also had trouble understanding it. The idea that the Messiah, who was supposed to overthrow Israel's enemies and reign over Israel establishing a kingdom with peace, justice, and righteousness, had to be crucified before he could begin his messianic reign completely befuddled them, even though Christ had repeatedly told them in advance that his crucifixion was necessary before he would enter into his glory.

With only the Old Testament to draw upon, the disciples would have been hard-pressed to know that the Messiah was going to be God incarnate, the second person of the Trinity. Perhaps he would be a powerful ruler like King David, who would have supernatural help from God in fighting his enemies, but surely not the Son of God incarnate with unlimited power and authority over this creation.

When Christ calmed the furious storm on the Sea of Galilee, the disciples wondered, "Who then is this, that he commands even winds and water, and they obey him?" (Luke 8:25). As King David's descendant, they expected a powerful *man* as an earthly king anointed by God to set up a theocratic kingdom. But they did not expect him to be the Son of God incarnate who took part in the creation of the world itself. The creator of the world was visible before their eyes, in the form of a man. This explains their utter astonishment as he demonstrated complete mastery over nature.

It may make more sense to us today, because like Monday morning quarterbacks, we know how the game ended. But if we had been in their place, we, too, would have been just as surprised to see how these prophecies about the Messiah unfolded. Jesus of Nazareth turns out to be God incarnate, is crucified, and then resurrected; but instead of then establishing his messianic kingdom on earth, he ascends to heaven returning to his Father! And he promises that when he comes again, he will then take them to heaven to be with him and the Father for eternity. Even then, they understandably asked, "So, where is the promised messianic kingdom?" Theologians are still asking that question, but the answer evades us, just as the first coming and the crucifixion initially befuddled the disciples.

The Use of Parables

Jesus' use of parables demonstrates how God often wanted certain aspects of the kingdom to remain less obvious, even obscure. His parables often had dual objectives. They taught the disciples important truths or lessons but remained intentionally ambiguous to unbelievers: "And when his disciples asked him what this parable meant, he said, 'To you it has been given to know the secrets of the kingdom of God, but for others they are in parables, *so that seeing they may not see, and hearing they may not understand.* Now the parable is this . . .'" (Luke 8:9–11).

Is the restoration itself similar to a parable in that God wanted it to be obscure to unbelievers yet discernible by believers? If so, believers still have to thoroughly research the difficult teachings on the restoration in order to "know the secrets of the kingdom of God" on earth and then in heaven.

Consider the book of Revelation, which serves as the best guideline for the Son's kingdom on earth for a thousand years after the first resurrection, and then the Father's eternal kingdom of heaven after the final resurrection. To the unbelieving Roman authorities, Revelation would have been an enormous and complicated parable. Imagine Roman authorities trying to make sense of it. They could read Revelation all day long and still end up exasperated at the incomprehensibility of the book. It is difficult enough for believers to navigate and decipher; for unbelievers it would have been an impossible task.

There is an interesting encounter recorded in the book of Acts that demonstrates how difficult it was for the Roman authorities to understand Christianity in general, much less the book of Revelation. Paul is under arrest and being interrogated by Governor Festus and King Agrippa. Paul begins his defense by acknowledging that King Agrippa was "familiar with all the customs and controversies of the Jews" (Acts 26:3). But after listening to Paul explain even the basics of the gospel, Governor Festus interrupts Paul and says in total exasperation: "Paul, you are out of your mind; your great learning is driving you out of your mind" (Acts 26:24). Imagine his reaction if Paul had attempted to explain the prophetic book of Daniel!

Why would God intentionally make the messianic kingdom difficult to understand by Roman unbelievers in positions of authority by putting a majority of the information in books such as Daniel and Revelation? If the Roman authorities had understood these teachings about the messianic kingdom on this earth, they would have perceived the future reign of Christ with his Christian followers as a serious threat to their empire. Christ's millennial kingdom on this earth is a worldwide empire with all nations made subservient to Christ, the King of the world. Prophetic books such as Daniel and Revelation provide an effective way for God to deliver his message about the future reign of Christ to his discerning followers, and, at the same time, disguise it from hostile unbelievers of that time who would have undoubtedly felt threatened by the books' contents and predictions had they understood them.

Rome Was a Pagan State

It is important to remember that the Roman Empire was not a secular democracy with religious liberty. Rather, it was a pagan state with a pantheon of established pagan gods and made up of numerous city-states with their own pagan deities. Because the Romans had conquered hundreds of nations and people groups, there was some level of pluralism and tolerance as long as the central gods of the empire were honored and the emperors were worshiped. The Romans were generally tolerant of the pagan nations they had conquered, making it easier for these nations to be assimilated.

The reason they conquered nations was not to spread their religion, per se, but to enrich themselves with the resources of the regions they controlled and with taxes or tribute from the people they conquered. Their civilization became one of the greatest civilizations in the ancient world, one marked by a great deal of good government and even civility—unless a person, group, or nation was perceived as forming an insurrection or revolt. The Romans were utterly ruthless in their repression of threats to their empire and civilization—and source of great wealth.

The conquered Jews, who worshiped a monotheistic God and refused to worship pagan idols or the emperors, were particularly difficult to assimilate and govern. If the Jews were forced to worship the pagan Roman gods or worship the Roman emperor, they would immediately revolt and it would cost the Romans time and resources to put down the rebellion. The Romans wanted the tribute and taxes that came from the region of Israel, not their religious loyalty. Being pragmatic, they allowed Israel to have some measure of autonomy and self-government through the Sanhedrin. And the Romans were smart enough to leave the Jewish temple intact and not construct pagan temples in Israel. The dispersed Jews living in Roman cities were allowed to worship their one God and were not required to worship the emperor or the pagan Roman gods.

At first the Gentile Christians were considered a subgroup of the Jewish faith and were granted the same exemption as the Jews. But the Jews hostile to Paul and the early church made a determined and ultimately successful effort to convince the Roman authorities that these Christ-followers were not a part of Judaism and the exemption should not be extended to them. The Romans then attempted to force the Gentile Christians to worship pagan deities. In the letters to the seven churches in Revelation 2 and 3, it is quite evident that with this exemption lifted, these churches were often severely persecuted by local authorities loyal to their pagan religions.

Paul's Ministry to the Gentiles

Understanding Paul and his ministry to the Gentiles of the pagan Roman world helps us understand why God kept the truth about the earthly messianic kingdom disguised in books such as Daniel and Revelation. Paul was an exceptionally well-educated Jewish scholar, trained as a Pharisee under the great Jewish teacher Gamaliel (Acts 22:3). At the same time, he was a Roman citizen, having grown up in Tarsus, the capital city of the Roman province Cilicia and home of a famous Roman university. Paul understood how both the Jewish and Roman world operated.

After his dramatic conversion, Paul got off to a rather difficult start as an evangelist and was almost killed by the Jews (Acts 9:28–29). Paul then went into seclusion for ten years in Tarsus to prepare for his ministry to the Roman Gentiles (Gal. 2:1). During these years, he continued to evangelize among the Hellenized Jews and Gentiles of Tarsus. This allowed him time to formulate his gospel message and consider the strategic implications of preaching it to the Jews and Gentiles throughout the Roman Empire. After this ten-year period, Paul's ministry to the Gentiles began in earnest when he responded to Barnabas's request for help in the Roman city of Antioch.

In Paul's outdoor sermons and his letters to the predominantly Gentile churches there is almost no mention of the restoration of the kingdom to Israel or of Christ's future messianic empire. The only direct reference is in Romans, and it is intentionally ambiguous and obscure: "And in this way all Israel will be saved, as it is written, 'The Deliverer will come from Zion, he will banish ungodliness from Jacob; and this will be my covenant with them when I take away their sins'" (Rom. 11:26–27). His reference to the prophecy in Isaiah is pregnant with meaning, but he does not expound on it.

Paul, as a Jewish scholar, could have certainly provided more details about the Jewish restoration as described in Isaiah and the Prophets, but chose not to. I think Paul knew more about the restoration than he reveals, but he had good reason not to put it in writing. He leaves his Roman audience with a cryptic explanation. Paul focused his teachings almost exclusively on the kingdom of heaven.

It is important to remember that Paul was a "Jewish" missionary who preached and addressed his letters primarily to Gentiles and Roman churches scattered throughout the Roman Empire:

> On the contrary, when they saw that I had been entrusted with the gospel to the uncircumcised, just as Peter had been entrusted with the gospel to the circumcised . . . and when James and Cephas and John, who seemed to be pillars, perceived the grace that was given to me, they gave the right hand of fellowship to Barnabas and me, that we should go to the Gentiles and they to the circumcised. (Gal. 2:7–9)

Paul knew that he would be operating primarily in the imperial Roman world, which he understood well. He seems to have intentionally avoided the subject of the earthly kingdom and reign of Christ over this world during the formative years of the church.

When Paul first entered a new Roman city, he customarily sought out any local synagogue where the dispersed Jews normally gathered. He preached that Jesus of Nazareth was indeed the Messiah and invited people to join the kingdom of God—an amazing assertion given that Rome and the Roman emperors still ruled their world. Some of the Jews believed his teaching, but most soon became hostile and used whatever means they could to provoke the Roman authorities to arrest Paul by falsely accusing him of leading an insurrection:

> Now when they had passed through Amphipolis and Apollonia, they came to Thessalonica, where there was a synagogue of the Jews. And Paul went in, as was his custom, and on three Sabbath days he reasoned with them from the Scriptures, explaining and proving that it was necessary for the Christ to suffer and to rise from the dead, and saying, "This Jesus, whom I proclaim to you, is the Christ." And some of them were persuaded and joined Paul and Silas, as did a great many of the devout Greeks and not a few of the leading women. But the Jews were jealous, and taking some wicked men of the rabble, they formed a mob, set the city in an uproar, and attacked the house of Jason, seeking to bring them out to the crowd. And when they could not find them, they dragged Jason and some of the brothers before the city authorities, shouting, "These men who have turned the world upside down have come here also, and Jason has received them, and *they are all acting against the decrees of Caesar,* saying that *there is another king, Jesus."* And the people and the city authorities were disturbed when they heard these things. (Acts 17:1–8)

This reveals what Paul was up against as he attempted to spread the gospel that Jesus of Nazareth was the Messiah throughout the Roman world. His message made no mention of Christ in the future restoration reigning from heaven over the earth as King of kings and Lord of lords. Nonetheless, many of the dispersed Jews accused Paul of leading an insurrection against Caesar by advocating "another king, Jesus" despite the fact that his gospel message focused almost exclusively on Christ crucified and the kingdom of heaven—not Christ's earthly kingdom.

Paul preached and wrote about Christ crucified, resurrected, and ascended to heaven, and whose followers one day would be resurrected into immortal bodies to join him in heaven. This may have seemed absurd to the Romans, but surely not grounds to accuse him of leading a revolt against Caesar. The Roman authorities may have thought Paul was out of his mind, but they could not accuse him of promoting an insurrection by teaching his followers that Jesus Christ would someday establish a worldwide kingdom on earth.

From the Romans' perspective, Paul was teaching people to follow a dead Messiah who had been crucified and had supposedly been raised from the dead and had ascended to heaven and who would someday return to take his followers to be with him in his Father's heavenly kingdom—strange, but surely not a geopolitical threat. Besides, how could a dead Jew from Nazareth become the ruler of the world? The very assertion was ludicrous to begin with.

None of Paul's letters emphasize the earthly reign of Christ in the restoration. If they had, his foes would surely have turned them over to the Roman authorities as evidence of his disloyalty. Paul's letters to the churches were not kept private but were circulated freely among the churches. I can well imagine that they were regularly turned over to the Roman authorities and checked for seditious material. Paul had to be very careful what he preached and what he put into writing. He seems to have deliberately avoided discussion of the messianic kingdom and for good reason.

For strategic reasons, Paul decided to focus his gospel message on repentance and the kingdom of heaven. His objective was to bring as many Gentiles into the kingdom of heaven as possible. Paul's message was heaven-centric, not earth-centric. He may have figured that if he could get the pagan Gentiles to believe in Christ and make it to heaven, that the restoration would come with the territory, whether they knew about it or not. Jesus himself had taught that if we seek first the kingdom of heaven, all these things—including the restoration—would be added to us.

To further understand Paul's strategy, it is important to remember that the Old Testament vision of the messianic kingdom involves more than the geopolitical entity of the nation of Israel. It is a vision of a worldwide empire in which Christ uses Israel to rule over all other nations. The Jewish Messiah will rule the world as a global empire with Jerusalem as its capital.

The Romans were infamous as conquerors who paraded the kings, soldiers, and spoils from their conquests in triumphal processions through the gates and streets of Rome. They built triumphal arches at the gates as monuments to celebrate significant victories. Many of these still stand today.

Instead of all roads leading to Rome with the wealth of the nations being brought to the Roman Empire, the Old Testament vision of the Jewish messianic kingdom reverses this parade. All roads lead to Jerusalem with all the nations bringing their wealth into Israel through the gates of Jerusalem: "Your gates shall be open continually; day and night they shall not be shut, that people may bring to you the wealth of the nations, with their kings led in procession" (Isa. 60:11). This vision of the messianic kingdom made the Romans subservient to the Jewish empire centered in Jerusalem. This is why Romans were hypersensitive toward any person or group teaching about the promised Jewish Messiah with his associated earthly kingdom.

What if Paul's sermons and writings had included a clear message about the future messianic kingdom on this earth and he had spoken freely of the day when Christ would *rule this world through Israel?* Imagine how the Roman authorities would have reacted to Paul had he entered a city such as Thessalonica and begun preaching from the following messianic psalm:

> May he have dominion from sea to sea, and from the River to the ends of the earth! May desert tribes bow down before him and his enemies lick the dust! May the kings of Tarshish and of the coastlines render him tribute; may the kings of Sheba and Seba bring gifts! May all kings fall down before him, all nations serve him! (72:8–11)

The concept of a Jewish Messiah having worldwide dominion would not have been well received by the Roman authorities. Neither Caesar nor his governors or magistrates would have embraced the idea that they would one day be ruled by a Jewish messianic king who would require them to "bow down before him," to "lick the dust" under his feet, and to "serve him" and "render him tribute" in order to enrich Jerusalem. The Old Testament contains numerous prophecies of this kind.

When it came to teaching about Christ's earthly kingdom, the apostles had to use caution. They had to steer clear of many of the Old Testament messianic prophecies that focused on the earthly kingdom of Christ. This explains the book of Revelation—it delivers the message about the 1,000-year restoration, but the message is cleverly hidden in apocalyptic language that would have been difficult for the Romans to decipher.

Paul did not elaborate on the coming messianic reign of Christ described by the prophets because it would have infuriated the Romans, who would have prosecuted Paul and the early church with a vengeance. The prophets, such as Isaiah, focused on the earthly kingdom of Christ, while Paul distanced himself from it and, instead, focused his gospel message almost exclusively on the kingdom of heaven that is not of this world and is attained by a resurrection of the dead through the transformation of the body. He would say and write such things as the following: "God . . . raised us up with him and seated us with him in the heavenly places in Christ Jesus" (Eph. 2:4–6). Or, "But *our citizenship is in heaven.* And we eagerly await a Savior from there, the Lord Jesus Christ, who, by the power that enables him to bring everything under his control, will transform our lowly bodies so that they will be like his glorious body" (Phil. 3:20–21 NIV).

The Romans would have considered the ideas of Christians joining their king in a heavenly kingdom reached by a resurrection of an immortal body bizarre, even nonsensical, but essentially harmless and not a real geopolitical threat to their great empire. When the Jews falsely accused Paul of "acting against the decrees of Caesar, saying that there is another king" of this world, the Roman authorities investigated the matter and, upon learning of Paul's "otherworld" religious ideology, concluded that the charges were groundless. Paul at times invoked his rights as a Roman citizen so that the Roman authorities would perform proper investigations, which would expose the false charges. But, if Paul had articulated a clear vision of the future earthly messianic kingdom, the Jews hostile to him would have had the ammunition they needed to accuse him before the Roman authorities of preaching a message of sedition. As a result, Paul, as an apostle to the Gentiles, was limited in what he could reveal about the future earthly messianic kingdom preceding the eternal heavenly kingdom. Paul was often imprisoned for his opposition to pagan idol worship and emperor worship, but this was simply unavoidable.

The Jews Were Already Considered a Threat

Because of their monotheism and their messianic expectations the dispersed Jews, as well as the nation of Israel, were difficult for the Romans to govern. There were also Zionist Jews, a small sect who eagerly awaited the Messiah to appear and lead a violent overthrow of the Roman government. The Romans were hypersensitive to any Jewish talk about a Messiah and his coming kingdom. Jews hostile to Paul knew that if they accused him of "acting against the decrees of Caesar, saying that there is another king," the Roman authorities would immediately attempt to arrest him.

Paul and the other apostles evangelizing during the Roman Empire had to be careful what they said about Jesus as the Messiah and the nature of his future earthly reign, especially during this stage in the growth of the early church. If Roman authorities felt threatened by a Jewish Messiah, they could be utterly brutal in their response. For example, Herod, appointed "king of the Jews" by the Roman Senate, slaughtered hundreds of children in Bethlehem because he felt threatened by the wise men's report of the mere birth of the Messiah.

Rome's apprehension toward the messianic expectations of the Zionist Jews was well founded. During the First Jewish-Roman War (AD 66–73), the result of a Zionist-led rebellion against Rome, the Romans responded with great force, slaughtering more than a million Jews in Jerusalem and destroying the temple itself as foretold by Jesus. The Jewish believers in Jerusalem refused to participate in this rebellion and took Christ's advice and headed to the mountains to escape this tribulation.

In the Second Jewish-Roman War (AD 132–135), Simon bar Kokhba, regarded by many Jews to be the Messiah, led another major revolt against Rome. In response, the Roman authorities amassed a vast army to squelch the rebels, and within three years the revolt was brutally crushed. The majority of the Jewish population were killed, exiled, or sold into slavery.

Rome's tolerance had run out. The Jewish nation of Israel was dissolved as a nation. Israel was not restored as a sovereign nation until 1948, when it was reestablished by the United Nations.

Paul and other believers got into enough trouble for their opposition to pagan idols, pagan temple worship, and emperor worship; they did not need the additional persecution for advocating a competing earthly kingdom. Despite Paul's great care to avoid being a geopolitical threat to the Romans, he was *still* persecuted: "more imprisonments, with countless beatings, and often near death. Five times I received at the hands of the Jews the forty lashes less one. Three times I was beaten with rods. Once I was stoned" (2 Cor. 11:23–25).

Many unbelieving Jews were determined to rid themselves of Paul, just as some were determined to rid themselves of Christ himself. I can envision Paul in the public square being asked questions designed by these Jews to entrap him—questions of how the Messiah will rule over the nations, for instance. Paul preached almost exclusively on the transformation and the kingdom of heaven; he gave the opposition no grounds to accuse him of being a Zionist or an insurrectionist. He heeded Christ's advice and was as shrewd as a serpent and as innocent as a dove (Matt. 10:16). It would be safer for Gentile converts to discuss the coming messianic kingdom after Christianity had obtained some legitimacy, even liberty, than it would have been for a Jewish evangelist like himself.

One can get a sense of the apprehension of the Roman emperors toward a *Jewish* messianic kingdom from the following incident recorded by the church historian Eusebius (c. 263–339) in which the Christian grandchildren of James, the brother of Christ, were interrogated by the Emperor Domitian (emperor from AD 81–96) about their beliefs on the earthly reign of the Messiah:

> They were brought to the Emperor Domitian by the Evocatus [a re-enlisted veteran soldier]. For Domitian feared the coming of Christ as Herod also had feared it. And he asked them if they were descendants of David, and they confessed that they were. . . . And when they were asked concerning Christ and his kingdom, of what sort it was and where and when it was to appear, they answered that it was not a temporal nor an earthly kingdom, but a heavenly and angelic one, which would appear at the end of the world, when he should come in glory to judge the quick and the dead, and to give unto every one according to his works. Upon hearing this, Domitian did not pass judgment against them, but, despising them as of no account, he let them go, and by a decree put a stop to the persecution of the Church.[1]

---

[1] Eusebius, *Church History*, III.20.1-7.

We do not know if they answered honestly and only believed in the heavenly kingdom, or if they actually believed in a future earthy messianic kingdom but kept the truth about Christ's earthly kingdom to themselves so as to not pose a threat to the Roman Empire.

It is important to recognize the nationalistic aspect of the Old Testament vision of a messianic kingdom—God's worldwide empire with religious and political authority centralized in regenerated Israel. Paul, in particular, as an evangelist to the Gentiles, had to be wise in what he preached and wrote during this critically important time of the church formation.

Paul's conservative approach to social issues is another example of avoiding unnecessarily offending the Roman authorities: "All who are under the yoke of slavery should consider their masters worthy of full respect, *so that God's name and our teaching may not be slandered*" (1 Tim. 6:1 NIV). Paul's message focused on the crucifixion and the kingdom of heaven. Teachings dealing with social justice issues could come later, as a result of converts living out the ethical teachings of Christianity.

Paul knew how to accommodate his teachings to his particular historical setting, so that the core truths about the kingdom of God would continue to spread with as little hindrance as possible:

> For though I am free from all, I have made myself a servant to all, that I might win more of them. To the Jews I became as a Jew, in order to win Jews.... To those outside the law I became as one outside the law ... that I might win those outside the law. . . I have become all things to all people, that by all means I might save some. I do it all for the sake of the gospel, that I may share with them in its blessings. (1 Cor. 9:9–23)

As any missionary should, Paul understood the world he was operating in.

A comparable example today would be Christian missionaries operating in communist China. Their primary objective is spiritual formation and church-building, not nation-building or spreading democracy. Building churches, both spiritually and physically, is challenging enough without the political persecution due to agitating for democratic or representative governments. In due time, there is a good chance China will become a republic with civil and religious liberty. But missionaries, like Paul, are wise not to be in the vanguard of such efforts.

An Already Complicated Situation

Paul faced many challenging issues, such as helping recently converted Gentile Christians from pagan backgrounds escape a world filled with idol worship. For example, some Gentile converts wanted to continue attending pagan banquets and feasts with old friends, where the food they would eat had been sacrificed to idols. Also, there were Gentile converts who came from a hedonistic lifestyle that included visiting temple prostitutes. Some believed that once their sins were forgiven by Christ's crucifixion, they could continue to live immorally with impunity.

Paul also had to deal with legalistic Jewish church members who wanted Gentile converts to be circumcised and follow Jewish customs. Since the Gentiles were now following the "Jewish" Messiah, the legalists wanted them to, in effect, become Jewish proselytes and a part of Judaism. Paul's ministry to the Gentiles was challenging. One can only imagine the difficulty he would have faced presenting the news of a future Jewish restoration in which the Jewish Messiah would rule the world through Israel.

Instead, Paul focused on the eternal kingdom of heaven, teaching pagan converts that they did not have to become circumcised Jews to enter into the kingdom of God, but they did have to escape the corruption of the pagan world, begin worshiping the true God, and learn how to live holy and righteously as children of God. They were destined for heaven to live for eternity with a holy God, and Paul wanted them to act accordingly.

The Stealthy Book of Revelation

The key teaching about the millennium occurs in the stealthy book of Revelation, or the Apocalypse of John, which was not written until AD 95, almost forty-five years after Paul penned his letters to the Thessalonians. Roman authorities could read the Gospels and the letters of the apostles without finding incriminating evidence against the apostles and the early church for "acting against the decrees of Caesar" by saying "there is another king" who intends to overthrow the Romans and rule this world. And they would have found Revelation particularly baffling. Revelation speaks of an earthly kingdom, as does Daniel, but it is buried deeply in apocalyptic language. Even if they read as far as chapter 20, which describes Christ's millennial reign, they would probably consider the teaching of the first resurrection complete nonsense and thus, the book as a whole, preposterous and ultimately, harmless.

The Romans found the idea of a resurrection or resuscitation of a dead body repugnant. This concept was not a part of their pagan ideologies. The Greek philosophers, too, considered the idea of a resurrection of the body absurd. Plato taught that only the immortal spirit or soul continued to exist after death. None of the early Greek or Roman philosophical schools of thought included the idea of a resurrection of the body.

Followers of the Greek philosopher Epicurus (341–270 BC) and his Roman disciple Lucretius (99–55 BC) doubted there was a soul and taught that there was no afterlife whatsoever. Hedonism was an offshoot of this philosophy. If people are neither rewarded nor punished in the afterlife based upon how people lived their earthly lives, then why not experience wanton pleasures in this life?

The idea of a resurrection of the material body was very difficult for the pagan Romans to comprehend and accept. To the Romans, "Christ crucified" was a contradiction in terms. And the idea that his martyred followers would someday be resuscitated through a "first resurrection" into mortal bodies to rule with this crucified Messiah for a thousand years, would have been considered especially ridiculous and meaningless.

The Old Testament prophets presented a more extensive vision of a messianic kingdom led by the Messiah, but the Romans believed this Jewish "king" from Nazareth was dead. The Romans were far more concerned about living people who claimed to be the Messiah and incited the Jews to revolt, which is exactly what happened in the First and Second Jewish-Roman Wars.

The brightest Christian minds have struggled to understand the book of Revelation. It would have been a futile effort for the pagan Romans to try to comprehend it. Chapter 20 conveys the truth about the future reign of Christ to the discerning believer, but would not have made sense to the pagan Roman mind. Thus, without alerting and alarming Roman authorities of a competing world empire, God cleverly used the prophetic writing of Revelation to communicate the truth about the restoration, which is so elaborately described in the Old Testament. Just as a stealth bomber delivers its payload without being detected by radar, so, too, God delivers the truth about the future messianic kingdom without detection by the Roman government.

For some Christian theologians, the book of Revelation may be a little too "under the radar." For example, amillennialists fail to detect the 1,000-year restoration on their radar screens. They have completely missed the biblical teaching about the messianic kingdom on this earth before the saints inherit the kingdom of heaven on the last day. Their radar is truly defective.

Although premillennialists have detected the restoration on their radar, they have misunderstood how and when the "stealth bomber" is going to deliver its payload. They claim that Christ must physically come back to this earth to establish the restoration—despite the numerous New Testament teachings that when Christ comes again, the earth is destroyed and believers are taken to heaven in their transformed bodies for eternity.

Postrestorationalism, however, not only detects the restoration in the Old and New Testaments, but also correctly interprets how God delivers and implements it. After the Tribulation, when Satan is given unrestrained power over this world for a short period of time, Christ binds Satan and rules over this world from his throne in heaven; he resurrects all the deceased saints into natural bodies to enjoy the messianic kingdom for one thousand years. Through the regeneration of both this earth and our sleeping bodies, he finally delivers the restoration as envisioned by the prophets.

After this restoration, the transformation occurs when Christ comes again, destroys this world, and takes us in our transformed bodies to his Father's eternal heavenly kingdom in the "age to come." The truth about the restoration and then the transformation on the last day is in the Scriptures, including Revelation. But our radars have failed, until now, to properly detect these truths.

The Letters to the Thessalonians

In his letters to the Thessalonians, Paul deals with several important eschatological events, such as the coming of the Antichrist and the Great Tribulation, the rapture, and the second coming of Christ on Judgment Day. But he makes no mention of the earthly messianic kingdom. This is quite understandable given Paul's strategic approach of spreading the gospel in the hostile Roman world without offending the Roman authorities any more than necessary. It was in Thessalonica that Paul was falsely accused of leading an insurrection to set up the Jewish messianic kingdom—"they are all acting against the decrees of Caesar, saying that there is another king, Jesus" (Acts 17:7). Yet, the church in Thessalonica experienced significant persecution from the Roman religious establishment unrelated to the idea of a Jewish insurrection or earthly messianic kingdom.

These two letters are among Paul's first epistles and were written some-time around AD 51. The believers at Thessalonica had only become Christians a few years earlier. The letters contain information about the Antichrist and the Tribulation but no information about the restoration. Revelation, on the other hand, which contains important information on the millennial reign of Christ, was not written until almost forty-five years later. Revelation is the only section of the New Testament that lays out the vision of a 1,000-year reign of Christ when Satan is bound *after* the Tribulation. Most of the Thessalonians Paul addressed in his epistles were likely dead when Revelation began circulating among the churches.

Many theologians, when reading these letters, fail to read them in their historical context. They seem to read them as if the Thessalonians had access to the entire New Testament, including the book of Revelation. In reality, the Thessalonians probably had no knowledge of the earthly messianic kingdom before the heavenly kingdom. The Thessalonians did not have the complete New Testament as a resource.

The Thessalonians were obviously already familiar with the teachings of the future Tribulation as described by Daniel, for Jesus had elaborated on this subject in the Olivet Discourse and Paul further elaborates on the subject in his letters to them. They were beginning to experience significant persecution and were trying to discern whether or not it related to the predicted Great Tribulation. Apparently, some were spreading the false teaching that the Great Tribulation had already begun and that Christ had somehow come again to rapture the saints, leaving them behind. But nowhere in these letters does Paul directly reference the messianic kingdom.

For example, in his second letter to the Thessalonians, Paul discusses the Tribulation and proceeds directly to the second coming, omitting the restoration altogether:

> Now concerning *the coming of our Lord Jesus Christ and our being gathered together to him*, [the second coming and the transformation of believers] we ask you, brothers, not to be quickly shaken in mind or alarmed, either by a spirit or a spoken word, or a letter seeming to be from us, to the effect that the day of the Lord has come. Let no one deceive you in any way. For that day [the second coming] will not come, *unless the rebellion comes first*, and the man of lawlessness is revealed, the son of destruction, who opposes and exalts himself against every so-called god or object of worship, so that he takes his seat in the temple of God, proclaiming himself to be God [the Tribulation]. Do you not remember that when I was still with you I told you these things? And you know what is restraining him now [Michael the archangel] so that he may be revealed in his time. For the mystery of lawlessness is already at work. Only he [Michael] who now restrains it [Satan] will do so until he is out of the way. And then the lawless one [the Antichrist] will be revealed, whom the Lord Jesus will kill with the breath of his mouth and bring to nothing by the appearance of his coming [second coming]. (2 Thess. 2:1–8)

These omissions of the restoration in Paul's letters to the Thessalonians have confused amillennialists and premillennialists alike. If these specific sections of Scriptures are used as the basic framework for a comprehensive sequence of future events, and all those events must fit into these condensed versions of the future, then it would be easy to arrive at false conclusions.

Amillennialists do not believe in a future millennial reign of Christ, but some amillennialists do believe there will be a Tribulation before the end of the world. They would incorrectly formulate the above version of the future as follows:

- The end of the Tribulation + the second coming (when the Antichrist is destroyed) + the rapture + Judgment Day = kingdom of heaven for the raptured saints.

Premillennialists, on the other hand, believe in a millennial reign of Christ after his second coming. They assert Paul is teaching that Christ comes again after the Tribulation when the Antichrist is destroyed and then establishes the millennial kingdom. Premillennialists might incorrectly render the paraphrase: "And then the lawless one will be revealed, whom the Lord Jesus will kill with the breath of his mouth and bring to nothing by the appearance of his coming—when, after first appearing in the clouds, he continues his downward descent to this earth to engage the Antichrist face to face on this earth and then establish his messianic kingdom on this earth."

The premillennial extrapolation would be as follows:

- The end of the Tribulation + the second coming (when the Antichrist is destroyed) + the rapture + Judgment Day = the millennial reign of Christ on this earth.

Premillennialists are filling in the blanks with the above formulation, for there is no biblical evidence that the Thessalonians had any understanding of the earthly reign of Christ before the kingdom of heaven.

As demonstrated in chapter 3, "The Destiny of the Raptured Saints," Paul and other New Testament writers create a direct link between the second coming and the raptured saints being taken to their eternal dwelling place in heaven at the same time that unbelievers are sent to hell for eternity on Judgment Day. This biblical formulation would be as follows:

- The second coming + the rapture + the end of the world + Judgment Day = the eternal kingdom of heaven for believers and hell for unbelievers.

How, then, do we explain Paul's connection of Christ's second coming with the overthrow of the Antichrist at the end of the Tribulation and the end of the world on Judgment Day?

Upon closer examination of Paul's writings, it becomes apparent that when addressing the Thessalonians, Paul proceeds from the overthrow of the Antichrist at the end of the Tribulation directly to the second coming and the rapture of the saints on Judgment Day on the last day of this Genesis creation—omitting the millennial kingdom altogether.

Paul never associates the second coming with the beginning of the messianic reign in any of his epistles. Only in Romans 11 does Paul directly reference the restoration. Even there, it is an obscure and veiled reference and not connected to the second coming of Christ; rather, it is connected to the time when the Jews finally repent and are grafted back in as believers, and then the messianic kingdom begins to unfold.

Paul consistently teaches in all his letters that when Christ comes again to gather us, it will be to resurrect us at the transformation to take us to our citizenship in heaven (Phil. 3:20–21). In 2 Thessalonians, Paul teaches that the steadfastness, faithfulness, and endurance the church has shown during persecution were evidence they were worthy of the kingdom of heaven—not the messianic kingdom on this earth. Paul describes the second coming of Christ when he is revealed from heaven on Judgment Day:

This is evidence of the righteous judgment of God, that you may be considered worthy of the kingdom of God, for which you are suffering— since indeed God considers it just to repay with affliction those who afflict you, and to grant relief to you who are afflicted as well as to us, *when the Lord Jesus is revealed from heaven* with his mighty angels in flaming fire [the second coming], inflicting vengeance on those who do not know God and on those who do not obey the gospel of our Lord Jesus. *They will suffer the punishment of eternal destruction* [lake of fire], away from the presence of the Lord and from the glory of his might, *when he comes on that day to be glorified in his saints* [raptured and transformed]. (2 Thess. 1:5–10)

Paul teaches that the second coming is directly linked to when the saints are transformed and taken to heaven, and unbelievers, such as those who persecuted the church at Thessalonica, are punished with "eternal destruction" on Judgment Day—which occurs after the millennium at the Great White Throne judgment.

In his second letter to the Thessalonians, Paul in no way supports the premillennial position that at Christ's second coming he comes with the saints to this earth to establish his messianic kingdom. The messianic kingdom on this earth is nowhere to be found in these two letters. In none of Paul's writings can we contextually link the second coming with the earthly messianic kingdom. In 2 Thessalonians, Paul skips the restoration altogether and proceeds from the end of the Tribulation when the Antichrist is destroyed directly to Christ's second coming on the last day.

Why does Paul completely skip the 1,000-year restoration? The most logical explanation is that the Thessalonians probably had no understanding of the restoration at that time. They had only learned about their inheritance of the kingdom of heaven. They were a very young, mostly Gentile church early in Paul's ministry. Paul kept them focused on living righteously, enduring persecution, being prepared for even greater persecution in the future Tribulation, and looking forward to heaven when Christ comes again. Paul had multiple strategic reasons not to teach on the earthly messianic kingdom, especially during this time in the church's formation. Paul may have intentionally avoided teaching the Thessalonians about the restoration, even if it meant giving them an incomplete picture of the prophetic future.

Paul's second letter to the church at Thessalonica addressed a matter that was causing much confusion. A false teaching was being spread in that particular church that Christ had already come: "Now concerning the coming of our Lord Jesus Christ and our being gathered together to him, we ask you, brothers, not to be quickly shaken in mind or alarmed, either by a spirit or a spoken word, or letter seeming to be from us, *to the effect that the day of the Lord has come*" (2 Thess. 2:1–2).

They were already experiencing persecution for their refusal to engage in pagan worship and emperor worship and were afraid that maybe the

Great Tribulation had already begun; maybe Christ had come and gone back to heaven without taking them with him. To refute this false teaching, Paul had to remind them that the Great Tribulation must first take place before the Lord comes again. And for the Great Tribulation to begin, the Antichrist must first come and enter the temple making himself out to be God (2 Thess. 2:4). Since no one had entered the temple in this fashion, the Antichrist had not yet come and the Tribulation had not yet taken place. This meant that Christ had not yet come again, and they had not been left behind. They could rest assured that these rumors were false. Paul's objective in writing the letter was to quickly refute a false teaching and move on to other important matters—such as teaching these young believers how to endure persecution and live godly lives in a pagan culture as they looked forward to Christ's coming to take them to heaven.

With the benefit of Revelation, however, we are in the fortunate position of being able to understand a great deal more about what occurs when the Antichrist is destroyed. Let's take what we know about the prophetic future from Revelation and combine it with Paul's abbreviated version of the second coming. The following bulleted points demonstrate how Paul's teaching would sequence using Revelation to fill in the events Paul omits:

> Now concerning the coming of our Lord Jesus Christ and our being gathered together to him, we ask you, brothers, not to be quickly shaken in mind or alarmed, either by a spirit or a spoken word, or a letter seeming to be from us, to the effect that the day of the Lord has come. Let no one deceive you in any way. For that day will not come, unless the rebellion comes first, and the man of lawlessness is revealed, the son of destruction, who opposes and exalts himself against every so-called god or object of worship, . . . And then the lawless one will be revealed, whom the Lord Jesus will kill with the breath of his mouth and bring to nothing . . .
>
> - At the end of the Tribulation the Antichrist and the false prophet "were thrown alive into the lake of fire" (Rev. 19:20).
> - An angel from heaven seizes Satan and binds him "for a thousand years" to prevent him from deceiving the nations (Rev. 20:2).
> - The millennial reign of Christ begins as Christ exercises his reign from heaven. Through the "first resurrection," the departed saints come to life to reign with Christ (Rev. 20:4–6).
> - At the end of the millennium, Satan is released "to deceive the nations" in one last rebellion, Gog and Magog. Fire comes down from heaven and consumes the attacking army. Satan himself is thrown into the lake of fire forever (Rev. 20:7–10).
>
> . . . by the appearance of his coming (2 Thess. 2:1–8).
>
> - Then the final resurrection occurs, earth and sky are destroyed, Judgment Day begins, the raptured saints are taken to the new heavens and new earth and unbelievers experience the second death (Rev. 20:11—21:1).

Paul condensed all the above bulleted events and proceeded directly from the end of the Tribulation when the Antichrist is destroyed to the second coming of Christ when the saints are raptured and taken to heaven. Since the Thessalonians probably knew nothing about the millennial kingdom, it would have made no sense for Paul to provide details and then have to explain them.

Paul's statement that the Antichrist will be destroyed at Christ's second coming is correct given the Thessalonians' lack of knowledge about the restoration, but it is not technically correct with the millennium factored into the flow of the prophetic future. Paul was limited in the ways he could refute the false teaching spreading among the young Christians at Thessalonica because of their limited understanding of the future. An abbreviated explanation of any event will always be incomplete and technically incorrect to some degree.

A Jewish evangelist like Paul did not need recently converted pagans in the Roman city of Thessalonica (where the Jews had already falsely accused him of leading an insurrection) getting excited about and then spreading the news of an impending earthly messianic kingdom led by a Jewish Messiah who would overthrow the tyrannical Roman Empire. Like building a campfire in a dry forest on a windy day, broadcasting the news of a coming Jewish-led messianic kingdom would have resulted in a highly combustible situation.

For those who play cards, the following analogy may help clarify the situation. The infant church at Thessalonica did not have a full deck of cards to draw upon because Paul had not dealt them any of the face cards. All he had to do to trump their pair of sixes (dealing with the false rumors of the second coming in relation to the Antichrist) was to show them a pair of aces. He did not need a royal flush to overcome their pair of sixes. If, today, we want to build a royal flush that includes the "king of hearts" ruling the world, then we need the rest of the face cards that come from the whole New Testament, particularly Revelation. We would be making a terrible mistake if we tried to create a royal flush from the incomplete set of cards dealt to the Thessalonians.

This is an important section of Paul's teachings that has confused premillennialists and amillennialists alike. An illustration from World War II may help explain why Paul omitted the teaching on Christ's 1,000-year earthly kingdom. The Allies stormed the beaches of Normandy on June 6, 1944. About eleven months later, on May 8, 1945, Nazi Germany surrendered unconditionally to the Allies—Victory over Europe Day (VE Day). Based on these dates, on what date was Europe liberated? If you answered May 8, 1945 (VE Day), that would be an incomplete answer to the question as to when "Europe" was liberated.

Only Western Europe was liberated on that date, for East Germany and Eastern Europe then fell under the tyranny of the Soviet Union. Those regions of Europe went from suffering under the tyranny of Hitler and the Nazi Fascists to suffering under the tyranny of Stalin and the Soviet communists. The Cold War between the Soviet Union and the United States and its Cold War allies began and continued for the next forty-six years, until December 25, 1991, with the dissolution of the Soviet Union. All Europe was not liberated at the end of World War II in 1945. It could be argued that World War II did not end until the Cold War ended.

Let's assume that I am teaching a class of seventh graders about World War II in their first Western History class. Imagine I am halfway through the course, and I have only educated them on the basics of the German occupation and the invasion of Normandy and march to Berlin, but I have not yet taught them about the subsequent Soviet Union occupation of much of Germany and Europe and the ensuing Cold War. Then, as class is about to end, I tell them that Europe was liberated when Germany surrendered to the Allies in the spring of 1945. This statement is true based on their lack of knowledge of the succeeding Cold War, but it is not technically correct.

If, on the other hand, had I wanted to be more technically precise, I could have concluded the class by telling them that all Europe was finally liberated on December 25, 1991, when the Soviet Union ceased to exist during President George H. W. Bush's administration. But since they were uneducated about the Cold War and had probably not yet learned about President Bush, they would have been utterly baffled and confused by this more technically complete statement.

Paul faced a similar situation when instructing the church at Thessalonica who, as new Gentile converts, probably had no knowledge of a 1,000-year restoration taking place before the last day and the eternal inheritance in heaven. Like my seventh graders who had not yet learned about the Cold War, these Thessalonians did not yet know about the millennial kingdom. If Paul had ended his letter with a reference to Christ's second coming after a future literal millennial kingdom, he would have confused them even more. Since they already knew about the future Tribulation, Paul taught them that the Antichrist would be destroyed at the second coming of Christ even though the answer is a great deal more involved than this.

I taught the seventh graders that World War II ended in 1945, but I left out the forty-six-year Cold War because they had not yet learned about these events. Likewise, Paul taught these early believers that the second coming came at the end of the Tribulation, but he left out the 1,000-year messianic kingdom and Satan's final release because they had not yet learned about these events.

The second letter to the Thessalonians is very short and written to young converts, so Paul gave them the condensed version of the prophetic future of the world, leaving out the many bulleted items I presented previously, including the millennial reign of Christ. History lessons are always abbreviated in some way. When teaching prophetic history, there also will be abbreviated versions with even major events sometimes omitted.

That Paul gave the Thessalonians an abridged version of the second coming of Christ at the end of the Tribulation by leaving out the 1,000-year messianic reign does not surprise me—particularly in light of Paul's possible strategic reasons for not wanting them to know about the Messiah ruling the world at this stage in the church's development.

And most important, as a Jewish evangelist operating within the hostile Roman world, Paul would have realized that if he had articulated a clear vision of a Jewish Messiah someday ruling the world with Rome being subservient to him, there would have been a severe backlash against him *and* the Thessalonican Christians, stunting the advancement of the kingdom at this critical stage of its development and intensifying the persecution they were experiencing.

And if today's theologians only use Paul's "CliffsNotes" version of the prophetic future given to the Thessalonians and ignore the broad outline of future events laid out in Revelation and elsewhere, then they will arrive at a false understanding of the events surrounding the second coming of Christ.

Revelation, although stealthy, provides the most comprehensive outline of the prophetic future. Using Revelation as our guide to supplement Paul's abbreviated version, we can create the following formulation of his teachings to resolve this apparent contradiction:

- The end of the Tribulation when the Antichrist is overthrown + Satan is bound + first resurrection + millennial reign of Christ + Satan released and Gog and Magog + Satan's final destiny in hell + second coming + final resurrection and the rapture + the end of the world + Judgment Day = the eternal kingdom of heaven for believers and hell for unbelievers.

As an Old Testament scholar, no doubt Paul could have inundated the Thessalonians with information on the earthly messianic kingdom. The Old Testament is full of information on the earthly kingdom of Christ, when he will be King of the world. Instead, apparently for a variety of spiritual, tactical, and strategic reasons, Paul distanced himself from Christ's earthly reign and focused on the new creation, the new order of being, and a believer's eternal inheritance in heaven.

Using some idiomatic expressions, Paul's avoidance of the earthly messianic kingdom and its nationalistic ramifications for Israel could be described as not wanting to "open a can of worms" or touch the subject "with a ten-foot pole." He wanted to "keep it under wraps," while he went about the difficult task of evangelizing the Roman world by teaching them that Jesus of Nazareth is the Jewish Messiah. Roman authorities would then naturally want to know, "Where then is his messianic kingdom? Is Paul laying the groundwork for an insurrection by trying to convince our people to follow this Jewish Messiah, or King?" By focusing on the saints inheriting the kingdom of *heaven*, Paul avoided having to answer these obvious questions.

Paul did, however, leave us with some subtle hyperlinks to the Old Testament prophecies. In his letter to the Romans, Paul created an elusive link to Isaiah where many of the "face" cards concerning the messianic kingdom can be found ("And a Redeemer will come to Zion," Isa. 59:20).

To use another analogy from World War II, he used a code name or phrase for a major future event to disguise it—similar to using code names during World War II for major impending offensive attacks. As General Dwight D. Eisenhower and the Allies were preparing for D-Day and the eventual overthrow of the Nazi regime, they used the code name "Operation Overlord" to describe the impending battle in order to hide the planned invasion from German intelligence. This code name predicted an historical event with monumental consequences—the overthrow of the Nazi regime and the liberation of most of Europe. Paul wrote, "The Deliverer will come from Zion," but when reading Isaiah, the discerning reader will note that this phrase is a code name that predicts an historical event with monumental consequences for Israel and the world, when Christ will overthrow Satan's regime and restore the nations of the world to an age of righteousness.

Paul could preach freely about citizenship in heaven, an essentially harmless message. But preaching about citizenship on this earth, when Christ as King of kings and Lord of lords will be the geopolitical ruler of the world through Israel as the chief ruling state, required caution. The subject was reserved for a later day, after the church was firmly established and a measure of religious liberty allowed for a fuller discussion. The early church fathers, including Justin and Irenaeus in the 100s, began to examine John's teachings on the millennial kingdom in the book of Revelation alongside what Isaiah and the prophets taught about the messianic kingdom on this earth. Revelation reintroduced the truth that the ransomed people of God would indeed inherit the earth during Christ's reign before inheriting the new heavens and new earth.

Christ's Stealthy Approach to His Messianic Kingdom

During the years of his public ministry, Christ himself carefully navigated the subject of his messianic reign on earth. His message, like Paul's, focused almost exclusively on the kingdom of heaven; and he, too, never led an insurrection. Yet, Jews hostile to Jesus vehemently insisted he was attempting to overthrow the Roman government and establish his messianic kingdom. They pleaded their case before Pontius Pilate:

> And they began to accuse him, saying, "We found this man misleading our nation and forbidding us to give tribute to Caesar, and saying that he himself is Christ, a king." And Pilate asked him, "Are you the King of the Jews?" And he answered him, "You have said so." Then Pilate said to the chief priests and the crowds, "I find no guilt in this man." But they were urgent, saying, "He stirs up the people, teaching throughout all Judea, from Galilee even to this place." (Luke 23:2–5)

Roman governors of Judea had one of the most difficult assignments in the Roman world, for the Jews were easily agitated into riots and revolts because of their deep aversion to idol worship and their longing to be liberated by their long-awaited Messiah. Jesus deeply disappointed the religious leaders because he refused to exercise his power and overthrow the tyrannical Roman occupation during his first coming. Even Pilate recognized Jesus was not a threat to Roman authorities and concluded that the charges against him were unfounded. But the unbelieving Jews persisted and at the first sign of a brewing riot, Pilate succumbed to the manipulation of the religious leaders and crucified an innocent man.

Jesus often spoke about the earthly kingdom *and* the heavenly kingdom without causing the Roman authorities to think the messianic reign was imminent. Consider his answer to Pilate after the Jews accused him of leading an insurrection and turned him over to Pilate for trial and execution:

> So Pilate entered his headquarters again and called Jesus and said to him, "Are you the King of the Jews?" Jesus answered, "Do you say this of your own accord, or did others say it to you about me?" Pilate answered, "Am I a Jew? Your own nation and the chief priests have delivered you over to me. What have you done?" Jesus answered, "*My kingdom is not of this world. If my kingdom were of this world, my servants would have been fighting*, that I might not be delivered over to the Jews. *But my kingdom is not from the world.*" Then Pilate said to him, "So you are a king?" Jesus answered, "You say that I am a king. For this purpose I was born and for this purpose I have come into the world—to bear witness to the truth. Everyone who is of the truth listens to my voice." Pilate said to him, "What is truth?" After he had said this, he went back outside to the Jews and told them, "I find no guilt in him." (John 18:33–38)

Christ admitted he is the King of the Jews. He also said his kingdom is not of this world, and therefore his servants will not fight for him, at least not at this time. Therefore Pilate had nothing to worry about. Jesus' answer that his kingdom was "not of this world" presented no threat to the Roman Empire that Pilate represented. Pilate recognized his innocence and tried to free him. This strange man only talked of a celestial kingdom—not of this world.

What did he mean by the statement that his kingdom is "not of this world"? This might imply that there is no earthly kingdom. Amillennialists are fond of quoting these verses to support their claim that there is no earthly kingdom, only the heavenly kingdom on the last day. When properly interpreted, Christ's answers do indeed affirm the earthly kingdom that is not of this world *as well as* the heavenly kingdom that is also not of this world.

We know from Revelation and other Scriptures that Christ's kingdom *does include* an earthly reign as King of kings during the restoration—before the eternal heavenly kingdom begins. Revelation says that during the battle of Armageddon, at the end of the Tribulation, Christ will use his servants to fight and overthrow the kingdoms of this world and will indeed rule this world as King of kings and Lord of lords:

> [A]nd in righteousness he judges and *makes war.* . . . And the armies of heaven [his servants], arrayed in fine linen, white and pure, were following him on white horses. From his mouth comes a sharp sword with which to strike down the nations, and he will rule them with a rod of iron [earthly kingdom]. He will tread the winepress of the fury of the wrath of God the Almighty. On his robe and on his thigh he has a name written, King of kings and Lord of lords [over *this* world]. (Rev. 19:11–16)

This is a vision of Christ with the armies of heaven in a victorious battle to overthrow the Antichrist and establish his earthly kingdom. How could Jesus be telling Pilate the truth about his kingdom? There must be a dual meaning in the phrase "my kingdom is not of *this* world" that Pilate did not understand, and that, apparently, many theologians have not understood.

Rightly understood, Christ's answer contains a veiled reference to his earthly kingdom in the restoration. In his clever use of the phrase "not of *this* world," Christ was also saying his earthly kingdom is not of this current satanic world, where selfish and greedy rulers enlist armies of men to fight, murder, and conquer other nations to gain power, glory, and material wealth. Christ's earthly kingdom will not be led by satanic rulers who use the weapons of Pilate's world to lord it over their subjects.

Christ's kingdom *of this world* will not begin until Satan is bound and no longer able to influence and control rulers like Pilate. Jesus' kingdom will be a very different kind of worldly kingdom than Pilate knew. Christ's earthly kingdom will be one of peace, justice, and righteousness, and the rulers under his authority will be true servants, like their master:

> But Jesus called them [his disciples, who were jockeying for positions of authority in his messianic kingdom] to him and said, "You know that

the rulers of the Gentiles *lord it over them*, and their great ones exercise authority over them. It shall not be so among you. *But whoever would be great among you must be your servant*, and whoever would be first among you must be your slave, even as the *Son of Man came not to be served but to serve*, and to give his life as a ransom for many." (Matt. 20:25–28)

Pilate and his Roman overlords were enriched as they exploited the people under them. When the disciples are resurrected to sit on the twelve thrones to rule over Israel during the restoration, they will be chief servants of their subjects, as was their master. This will not be a kingdom of Pilate's world, where rulers abused and exploited their subjects, selfishly demanding unjust tribute to enrich their own lives and kingdoms. Christ was skillful with his words. In his answer to Pilate, Christ refuted his accusers and spoke the truth about his future kingdoms—the one in heaven *and* the one on this earth—neither of which is of "this world"!

Pilate had no understanding of these kinds of kingdoms—an earthly one ruled by God and characterized by absolute justice with human rulers who are true servants, or a heavenly one characterized by God's presence with his people made perfect in immortal, glorified bodies. This truth about Christ's kingship and kingdom on earth and in heaven totally escaped Pilate, who was unsure whether or not truth existed.

Pilate tried to wash his hands of the affair; he knew Jesus was innocent of leading an insurrection. But in the end he unjustly and unknowingly crucified the Lord God of the universe—and the future ruler of this world. The truth is that this same Lord will one day lead an insurrection against this world ruled by Satan, but he will do it from heaven, using the armies of heaven. Christ, the King, will overthrow Satan and banish him from this world for one thousand years. Then he will rule this world from heaven, using his saints whom he will resurrect to rule with him. Christ will truly be King over this earth before he takes his kingdom of believers to his Father's eternal home in heaven.

Peter and the Restoration

Peter also made few references to the restoration when the meek shall inherit the earth. But, like Paul, he probably knew a great deal more about it than his writings reveal. Peter mentioned the restoration when he first began preaching to the Jews after Pentecost, but he never mentions the subject in his later epistles. In Acts, we read:

Repent therefore, and turn again, that your sins may be blotted out, that times of refreshing may come from the presence of the Lord, and that he may send the Christ appointed for you, Jesus, whom heaven must receive *until the time for restoring all the things* about which God spoke by the mouth of *his holy prophets long ago.* (3:19–21)

Peter was preaching to a distinctly Jewish audience, and he clearly affirms that there will be a future restoration in fulfillment of the words of the prophets. This early sermon gives the impression that Peter taught the restoration would take place when Christ comes again. This seems to support the premillennial position.

Peter did not specifically state, however, that Christ will come back to this earth to accomplish the restoration. Peter did not say how Christ will accomplish this restoration. He could do it from heaven with the "coming" exercise of his reign. But let's assume that premillennialists are right and that Peter means Christ literally comes to this earth to establish his messianic kingdom as described by the holy prophets.

This would contradict what Peter taught in his later writings, when the more mature Peter revealed that the second coming coincides, not with the beginning of the restoration, but with Judgment Day when this earth is destroyed and we inherit the new heavens and new earth. When those who scoffed at the idea of Jesus coming again asked Peter where was "the promise of his coming [his second coming]," Peter answered:

> But the day of the Lord will come like a thief, and then the heavens will pass away with a roar, and the heavenly bodies will be burned up and dissolved, and the earth and the works that are done on it will be exposed. . . . the heavens will be set on fire and dissolved, and the heavenly bodies will melt as they burn! But *according to his promise we are waiting for new heavens and a new earth* in which righteousness dwells. (2 Peter 3:10–13)

Second Peter connects the promise of Jesus' second coming to our eternal inheritance of heaven, not to the earthly messianic kingdom described by the Old Testament holy prophets.

And in Peter's first epistle he makes it clear that when we are raptured or resurrected into our immortal bodies, we are taken to the eternal kingdom of heaven:

> Blessed be the God and Father of our Lord Jesus Christ! According to his great mercy, he has caused us to be born again to a living hope through the resurrection of Jesus Christ from the dead [the rapture], to an *inheritance that is imperishable, undefiled, and unfading, kept in heaven for you,* who by God's power are being guarded through faith for a salvation ready to be revealed in the last time. (1 Peter 1:3–5)

Peter desired believers to be resurrected into immortal bodies as Christ was; he also said that this resurrection will occur when Christ comes again on the last day when the current earth is destroyed by fire at which time Christ will take us to our imperishable inheritance in heaven.

Peter did not mention his hope for the restoration of the nation of Israel that he preached about in his early sermons after Pentecost. At that time, Peter wanted the Jews to repent so that God could send the Christ to begin the restoration, but he was not clear about what kind of "sending" this represents. In his mature epistles, however, Peter wanted his readers to repent so they would not perish on the day the Lord returns and destroys the earth; he wanted them to receive an inheritance that is "imperishable, undefiled, and unfading, kept in heaven" for them.

Peter's formulation would be as follows:

- The promise of his second coming + rapture of the saints + destruction of the current Genesis earth = inheritance of the eternal new heavens and new earth.

If Christ destroys the earth by fire when he comes again and ushers in the eternal "new heavens and a new earth," it will no longer be possible for him to restore "all the things about which God spoke by the mouth of his holy prophets long ago" during an earthy messianic kingdom because the Genesis earth will no longer exist! What is the explanation for the apparent contradiction between Peter's early teaching during his outdoor sermon when he affirms the restoration and his written teaching in his two epistles?

The book of Acts describes the apostles as they came to grips with the gospel and the kingdom of God. Peter's impromptu sermon occurred shortly after Pentecost. That does not mean, however, that Peter and the other apostles had received all the revelation needed to understand all future events. It would take time for the Holy Spirit to remind them of Christ's words and bring them to a fuller understanding of the prophetic future. Apparently they did not understand everything Jesus said in the Olivet Discourse, for there were many things that would occur before his messianic reign began.

The book of Acts records many things Peter said and did that were not always correct. For example, it took some time for Peter, as a Jew, to overcome his aversion to associating with Gentiles, much less evangelizing them whereby they, too, would be baptized by the Holy Spirit, as he and the Jewish disciples had been at Pentecost. The account of Peter preaching to Cornelius and his Gentile household illustrates Peter's growing understanding of the truth about the inclusion of the Gentiles in Christ's kingdom. And it took a supernatural vision commanding Peter to eat unclean food for him to consider defying his Jewish instincts: "And there came a voice to him: 'Rise, Peter; kill and eat.' But Peter said, 'By no means, Lord; for I have never eaten anything that is common or unclean.' And the voice came to him again a second time, 'What God has made clean, do not call common'" (Acts 10:13–15). Notice Peter's growth:

Now while Peter was inwardly perplexed as to what the vision that he had seen might mean, behold, the men who were sent by Cornelius, having made inquiry for Simon's house, stood at the gate and called out to ask whether Simon who was called Peter was lodging there. . . . The next day he rose and went away with them, . . . And on the following day they entered Caesarea. Cornelius was expecting them and had called together his relatives and close friends. . . . And he said to them, "You yourselves know how unlawful it is for a Jew to associate with or to visit anyone of another nation, but God has shown me that I should not call any person common or unclean. So when I was sent for, I came without objection. I ask then why you sent for me [he still did not yet understand]." . . . So Peter opened his mouth and said: "Truly I understand that God shows no partiality, but in every nation anyone who fears him and does what is right is acceptable to him. . . . While Peter was still saying these things, the Holy Spirit fell on all who heard the word. And the believers from among the circumcised who had come with Peter were amazed, because the gift of the Holy Spirit was poured out even on the Gentiles. For they were hearing them speaking in tongues and extolling God. Then Peter declared, "Can anyone withhold water for baptizing these people, who have received the Holy Spirit just as we have?" And he commanded them to be baptized in the name of Jesus Christ. (Acts 10:17–48)

Peter grew in knowledge as he came to terms with the shocking reality that these Gentiles had not only believed in Christ but had also received the Holy Spirit. When he reported the episode to the Jewish believers in Jerusalem, he initially came under harsh criticism and had to explain and justify to them the events that took place:

Now the apostles and the brothers who were throughout Judea heard that the Gentiles also had received the word of God. So when Peter went up to Jerusalem, the circumcision party criticized him, saying, "You went to uncircumcised men and ate with them." But Peter began and explained it to them in order: "I was in the city of Joppa praying . . . As I began to speak, the Holy Spirit fell on them just as on us at the beginning. And I remembered the word of the Lord, how he said, 'John baptized with water, but you will be baptized with the Holy Spirit.' If then God gave the same gift to them as he gave to us when we believed in the Lord Jesus Christ, who was I that I could stand in God's way?" When they heard these things they fell silent. And they glorified God, saying, "Then to the Gentiles also God has granted repentance that leads to life." (Acts 11:1–18)

Peter continued to discern the truth by remembering the "word of the Lord." He may also have remembered other sayings of Jesus as well: "And I have other sheep that are not of this fold. I must bring them also, and they will listen to my voice. So there will be one flock, one shepherd" (John 10:16). As he searched for the truth and remembered Jesus' words under the

Holy Spirit's guidance, Peter concluded that repentant Gentiles would be included in Christ's kingdom.

Likewise, it would take some time for the Holy Spirit to remind Peter and the apostles of Jesus' words and lead them into a fuller understanding of the future. They did not receive instantaneous and exhaustive knowledge at Pentecost about how the messianic kingdom would unfold. Jesus promised, "When the Spirit of truth comes, he will guide you into all the truth, for he will not speak on his own authority, but whatever he hears he will speak, and he will declare to you *the things that are to come*" (John 16:13). Peter gave his first sermon on the restoration after a few weeks of thought and reflection following Christ's ascension; whereas he wrote his second epistle sometime around AD 64–67, after thirty years of reflection under the Holy Spirit's guidance on Jesus' words about "the things that are to come."

Luke records a short sermon that occurred a few weeks after Pentecost in which Peter apparently associated the future Jewish restoration with some type of coming of Christ (Acts 3:20–21). But at that time Peter did not know how or if the pagan Gentiles would be included in the Jewish restoration. And just as he was able to resolve this issue by remembering Jesus' words concerning John's baptism being replaced with a baptism of the Holy Spirit, I believe that over time, as Jesus promised, the Holy Spirit led him to connect the dots from Jesus' words concerning what really occurs when he comes again. Jesus repeatedly taught the disciples that he would come again on Judgment Day when the sheep and the goats would be separated, with the sheep being taken to heaven for eternity and the goats being sent to hell. In Peter's epistles written thirty years later under the inspiration of the Holy Spirit, Peter remembered Jesus' words and clearly taught, as Jesus did, that upon his second coming the following events would occur:

> [T]he heavens will pass away with a roar, and the heavenly bodies will be burned up and dissolved [the earth is destroyed], and the earth and the works that are done on it will be exposed [on Judgment Day when the books are opened]. . . . But according to his promise we are waiting for new heavens and a new earth in which righteousness dwells. (2 Peter 3:10–13)

Peter eventually concluded that Christ will come again at the end of the world to destroy it, rather than to re-inhabit it. But that does not mean he no longer believed in a future restoration. He simply shifted his focus to our eternal inheritance, probably for many of the same reasons Paul did.

Peter and Paul had their differences, but they met together in Jerusalem along with other Jewish elders to discuss policy and strategy. And I imagine they had discussions about how they would spread the good news that Jesus was indeed the Messiah among Jews and Gentiles without unduly alarming and provoking the Roman authorities and giving the unbelieving Jews grounds of accusing them of leading an insurrection. It is imperative we remember that Peter and Paul lived when Israel and the Jews were under the Roman Empire's dominion.

After Pentecost, Peter never mentioned the restoration again in his recorded epistles. He apparently came to the same conclusion as Paul—that the messianic kingdom should be kept under wraps until the church had become firmly established. Once established, then others could continue to connect the dots and begin openly discussing the future messianic kingdom on this earth before our eternal inheritance.

Tendency Toward Materialism

The Old Testament prophets described the restoration as an earthly paradise. Another reason Christ and the New Testament writers may have downplayed the restoration was because they were aware of mankind's tendency to be worldly and materialistic. Because of the natural lust for the things of this world, if the apostles had emphasized the earthly paradise, many people would have been attracted to the gospel and joined the church for the wrong motives.

The situation Christ faced after he had made bread and fish for the five thousand serves as a good example. As a result of this miracle, the crowd wanted to make him king by force (John 6:14–15). They thought Christ would continue to miraculously provide them an abundance of food, and they would never have to work the ground again. Sadly, they looked to the Messiah to provide only material things to sustain the physical body. They were searching for life in both the pleasures of the flesh and of this world—and not in Christ himself as the source of true spiritual life. Humans miss the Garden of Eden, but not its Creator. Christ taught them that the Spirit, and not the flesh, offered life.

The following day, Jesus preached an intentionally disturbing sermon that would put an end to their eagerness to make him king by force in order to reap worldly rewards. It also taught the disciples an important lesson about the true source of life:

> Truly, truly, I say to you, you are seeking me, not because you saw signs, but because you ate your fill of the loaves. Do not labor for the food that perishes, but for the food that endures to eternal life, which the Son of Man will give to you. . . . I am the living bread that came down from heaven. If anyone eats of this bread, he will live forever. And the bread that I will give for the life of the world is my flesh. . . . unless you eat the flesh of the Son of Man and drink his blood, you have no life in you. Whoever feeds on my flesh and drinks my blood has eternal life, and I will raise him up on the last day. For my flesh is true food, and my blood is true drink. (John 6:26–55)

After Jesus preached about eating his flesh and drinking his blood to obtain the true source of life, he no longer had to worry about the crowd's desire to make him king: "After this many of his disciples turned back and no longer walked with him" (John 6:66). The sermon deeply disturbed his disciples, and he had to further explain: "It is the Spirit who gives life; the flesh is of no avail. The words that I have spoken to you are spirit and life" (John 6:63).

Jesus told them not to labor in vain for the food that perishes, but for the food that endures to eternal life. He wanted them to get their priorities in order and to stop focusing on the earthly aspects of the kingdom. But as the reaction to Jesus' feeding of the five thousand reveals, humans have a tendency to focus on the worldly aspects of the messianic kingdom and ignore the most important thing missing in our lives—spiritual life derived from having a restored relationship with our Creator.

Many people came to Jesus to be healed, not because they wanted to be reconciled with a holy God and spend eternity with him, but so that they could be healed of their infirmity in order to return to living a sinful and materialistic life separate from God. Luke's Gospel records such an occasion: Ten lepers asked Jesus to heal them. But when he healed them, only one turned and thanked Jesus. The rest, presumably, went off to live a worldly life with no thought of God or true spiritual life (Luke 17:11–19). If Jesus were walking the earth today, I am sure many people would go to him for healing and then turn around and continue lives of rebellion against God.

Jesus' presence generated large crowds of people wanting to be healed, many with the wrong motives. Imagine the crowds if he had presented a clear vision of the coming messianic kingdom when the earth is restored to an Edenic paradise.

In reading Irenaeus (c. 120–202), an early millennialist, one can detect how some of the worldly pleasures of the restoration were already getting exaggerated in his day. Irenaeus envisioned the millennial kingdom as a time when the saints will not even have to work for food:

> For what are the hundred-fold [rewards] in this word . . . ? These are [to take place] in the times of the kingdom, . . . which they shall not be engaged in any earthly occupation; but shall have a table at hand prepared for them by God, supplying them with all sorts of dishes.[2]

Irenaeus distorted the messianic kingdom as a time when the saints will not be engaged in agricultural work or other gainful employment; instead, like the manna from heaven, God will prepare a feast for them! Irenaeus failed to realize that Adam and Eve had to work even in the Garden of Eden.

---

[2] Irenaeus, *Against Heresies*, V.33.2.

Irenaeus also envisioned the messianic kingdom as a time of an incredible abundance of wine:

> The predicted blessing, therefore, belongs unquestionably to the times of the kingdom, when the righteous shall bear rule upon their rising from the dead; when also the creation, having been renovated and set free, shall fructify with an abundance of all kinds of food, from the dew of heaven, and from the fertility of the earth: as the elders who saw John, the disciple of the Lord, related that they had heard from him how the Lord used to teach in regard to these times, and say: The days will come, in which vines shall grow, each having ten thousand branches, and in each branch ten thousand twigs, and in each true twig ten thousand shoots, and in each one of the shoots ten thousand clusters, and on every one of the clusters ten thousand grapes, and every grape when pressed will give five and twenty metretes of wine.[3]

Whether this oral tradition comes from Christ, or not, we do not know. Christ could have said something similar that was exaggerated through the oral tradition. A messianic prophecy in Amos has some similarity: "'Behold, the days are coming,' declares the LORD, 'when the plowman shall overtake the reaper and the treader of grapes him who sows the seed; mountains shall drip sweet wine, and all the hills shall flow with it'" (9:13). Irenaeus may have combined Christ's promise to the disciples that they would "receive a hundredfold" in the restoration (Matt. 19:29) with this prophecy in Amos whereby it was embellished into an ever-expanding grapevine that produces ten-thousandfold of branches, grape clusters, and grapes with which to make an excessive quantity of wine—the hills literally dripping with wine.

According to John, Jesus taught many things that were not recorded in the Gospels (John 21:25). If Irenaeus's account is correct, except for the exaggerations, then Christ probably made many references to the restoration that were not included in the Gospels. Knowing mankind's propensity to approach Christ with worldly motives, it is conceivable that the Holy Spirit had the Gospel writers omit some of Christ's teachings pertaining to the Edenic restoration.

Another reason the New Testament writers did not emphasize the restoration may be that believers will receive the earthly kingdom whether or not they know about it. The New Testament focuses on eternal life with the Father in heaven, whereas the restoration is a temporal kingdom lasting only one thousand years. We could gain the whole world—even one thousand years of earthly paradise—but if we forfeit our souls because we do not have true spiritual life, it is meaningless in the end.

---

[3] Ibid., *AH*, V.33.3.

God desires for us to *first* seek fellowship with him in his eternal kingdom of heaven, and all these earthly things, that is, the restoration, will be added to us: "But seek first the kingdom of God and his righteousness, and all these things [the hundredfold rewards in this age] will be added to you" (Matt. 6:33). Christ, first and foremost, wanted people to be drawn to *him*, not to an earthly paradise. Heaven is about a person and a place. When Christ comes again, we will experience a life of companionship with the Father, the Son, and the Holy Spirit in heaven for eternity. That is eternal life. Christ said, "Father, the hour has come; glorify your Son that the Son may glorify you, since you have given him authority over all flesh, to give eternal life to all whom you have given him. And this is eternal life, that they know you the only true God, and Jesus Christ whom you have sent" (John 17:1–3). Knowing the person of heaven and being with him in heaven for eternity is what we should set our hearts on.

The Nature of Prophecy to Condense Time

Another reason it has been so difficult for Christian theologians to discern the eschatology of the Scriptures is that prophetic literature of the Bible has a tendency to condense time, skip over major future events, and predict events in no logical order. Old Testament prophets will be addressing Jews about to go into exile, or already in exile, and then, when speaking of their eventual return to the Promised Land, suddenly begin talking about the future restoration. In some instances, Old Testament prophecies about the coming Messiah go from his arrival in this world directly to his reign— neglecting to mention the Messiah's rejection and crucifixion at his first coming. Sometimes the writer is simply trying to be brief and wants to convey one aspect of the prophetic future. If the writers included everything in sequential order each time they wrote about the future, their writings would be very cumbersome.

The well-known prophecy in Isaiah of Christ's birth provides a good example of how easily prophecy can be misinterpreted if God's entire revelation is not taken into account:

> For to us a child is born, to us a son is given; and the government shall be upon his shoulder, . . . Of the increase of his government and of peace there will be no end, on the throne of David and over his kingdom, to establish it and to uphold it with justice and with righteousness from this time forth and forevermore. The zeal of the LORD of hosts will do this. (Isa. 9:6–7)

Isaiah prophesies the birth of Jesus and then immediately describes Jesus' Davidic throne and government in the restoration—a reign of peace, justice, and righteousness. This prophecy bypasses the crucifixion, the current period of time, and the future Tribulation. Prophecies such as these caused John the Baptist to experience doubt and confusion when Herod imprisoned him. The Messiah had arrived, so where is the kingdom of justice against the tyranny of evil, and where is the liberty for the captives?

Because biblical prophecy often skips or condenses major events, it is always important to develop a comprehensive framework of prophecy based on the entire Bible. Chapters 51–54 of Isaiah, for example, contain references to major components of biblical history from the beginning of this Genesis creation to its end but not necessarily in any logical sequence. Using the New Testament, particularly Revelation, as a guide, it is amazing how many of these jumbled events can be put into an order. Some of the major past and future events described in Isaiah are listed below:

The Creation of the World
"[A]nd have forgotten the LORD, your Maker, who stretched out the heavens and laid the foundations of the earth" (51:13).

The Call of Abraham
"Look to Abraham your father and to Sarah who bore you; for he was but one when I called him, that I might bless him and multiply him" (51:2).

The Exodus
"Was it not you who dried up the sea, the waters of the great deep, who made the depths of the sea a way for the redeemed to pass over?" (51:10).

Into Exile
"Wake yourself, wake yourself, stand up, O Jerusalem, you who have drunk from the hand of the LORD the cup of his wrath, who have drunk to the dregs the bowl, the cup of staggering. . . . devastation and destruction, famine and sword; who will comfort you?" (51:17–19).

Return from Exile
"Therefore hear this, you who are afflicted, who are drunk, but not with wine: Thus says your Lord, the LORD, your God who pleads the cause of his people: 'Behold, I have taken from your hand the cup of staggering; the bowl of my wrath you shall drink no more'" (51:21–22).

The Crucifixion
"But he was wounded for our transgressions; he was crushed for our iniquities; upon him was the chastisement that brought us peace, and with his stripes we are healed. All we like sheep have gone astray; we have turned every one to his own way; and the LORD has laid on him the iniquity of us all. . . . And they made his grave with the wicked and with a rich man in his death, although he had done no violence, and there was no deceit in his mouth" (53:5–9).

Christ's Resurrection

"Yet it was the will of the LORD to crush him; he has put him to grief; when his soul makes an offering for sin, he shall see his offspring [the children of God]; he shall prolong his days [resurrection]; the will of the LORD shall prosper in his hand" (53:10).

The Temporary Rejection of the Jews

"For a brief moment I deserted you, but with great compassion I will gather you. In overflowing anger for a moment I hid my face from you, but with everlasting love I will have compassion on you," says the LORD, your Redeemer" (54:7–8).

The Restoration

"How beautiful upon the mountains are the feet of him who brings good news, . . . 'Your God reigns.' . . . Break forth together into singing, you waste places of Jerusalem, for the LORD has comforted his people; he has redeemed Jerusalem. The LORD has bared his holy arm before the eyes of all the nations, and all the ends of the earth shall see the salvation of our God" (52:7–10).

The Last Day

"Lift up your eyes to the heavens, and look at the earth beneath; for the heavens vanish like smoke, the earth will wear out like a garment, and they who dwell in it will die in like manner; but my salvation will be forever, and my righteousness will never be dismayed" (51:6).

Isaiah goes from the Genesis creation in the beginning to the end of the world when the Genesis heavens and earth "vanish like smoke." But we have to "cut and paste" his writings to create a logical flow out of these events.

Summary

As an Old Testament scholar, Paul probably knew much more about the future messianic reign of Christ than he revealed. But it is likely that during the church's formative stage, he intentionally let the message of the earthly messianic kingdom go dormant. As a Jewish evangelist in a pagan Roman Empire, Paul was in enemy territory. And many people, particularly the dispersed Jews, were determined to find incriminating evidence against him that would lead to his imprisonment.

Paul, who suffered greatly as a Jewish missionary, probably knew that revealing the details of the future Jewish messianic kingdom would provide his enemies with ammunition to accuse him before the Roman authorities of leading an insurrection. His one direct reference to the restoration is in Romans 11, which is obscure. As a result, his writings are not the best resource for learning about the restoration. Paul, like Jesus, focused on our being rescued from Satan's dark dominion and receiving our future inheritance in the Father's heavenly kingdom. The book of Revelation with its links to the Old Testament prophets is our best guide to understanding Christ's earthly kingdom.

The restoration is a somewhat vague teaching in the Bible. The most definitive statement about the 1,000-year reign of Christ occurs in the apocalyptic book of Revelation, which speaks volumes about God's intention to make it difficult to discern and hidden from those hostile to the church. I think Christ intentionally downplayed the restoration in the New Testament and focused instead on the transformation and the kingdom of heaven.

Christ promised the disciples they would receive a hundredfold reward during the regeneration of this earth, which is a reference to his kingdom on this earth when he rules the world from his throne in heaven (Matt. 19:28–29; cf. Mark 10:29–30 and Luke 18:29–30). He probably taught the disciples many other similar teachings, but the Holy Spirit may have led the Gospel writers to suppress these teachings when they formulated their Gospels.

One can see the strategic plan of God in such a scenario. The gospel that Jesus was the Messiah had to be spread initially by Jewish missionaries, like Paul, to a Gentile world under Roman domination. In this setting, the nation of Israel, which rejected Jesus as the Messiah, was still looking for a Messiah to liberate them from the Romans. As such, the Romans were understandably hypersensitive to any talk of a Jewish Messiah. These were dangerous times to be speaking and writing about an earthly messianic kingdom in which Jesus of Nazareth would someday rule as King of kings and Lord of lords. The apostles and the early churches were already facing persecution by their refusal to worship the emperor and the many pagan idols throughout the Roman Empire.

But God does not leave later generations in the dark. With the clever apocalyptic book of Revelation, particularly chapter 20, God gives us a window into the Old Testament, which contains an extensive description of the future messianic kingdom on this earth. In Revelation, like a stealth bomber delivering its payload, God reintroduces the messianic kingdom, so elaborately described in the Old Testament, without exposing this truth to the Roman authorities.

12

The Ante-Nicene Millennialists

The apostles' strategy paid off. During the next few hundred years, despite periodic episodes of severe persecution, the church grew rapidly, making significant inroads in all strata of Roman society. The church leadership also shifted to Gentile believers who were in a better position to openly discuss the existence and the nature of the stealthy "Jewish" restoration. Many of the ante-Nicene fathers began to interpret Revelation 20 literally. They were known as millennialists, millenarians (Latin), or chiliasts (derived from the Greek word for one thousand years).

One can see a similar strategic caution as that of the apostles being exercised by the early millennialist, Justin (c. 100–165), a Gentile evangelist. Even after the First Jewish-Roman War (66–73) when Jerusalem was sacked and the Second Jewish-Roman War (132–135) when the entire nation of Israel was dissolved, there remained an inherent hostility by the Roman authorities to the "Jewish" concept of a messianic kingdom on this earth. When writing his two *Apologies* (155), intended as evangelistic treatises for his non-Christian Roman audience, Justin made no mention whatsoever of the millennial kingdom or the restored city of Jerusalem and nation of Israel. Instead, these books focus on the last day and the eternal kingdom of heaven as a reward for believers and warn about eternal damnation for unbelievers. But when writing a book intended exclusively for the church titled *Dialogue with Trypho*, Justin wrote freely about the millennial kingdom when Christ will "appear in Jerusalem" and destroy his enemies.

Even if this book were discovered by Roman authorities and Justin was interrogated because of its contents, this type of material was more easily defended by a Gentile evangelist than a Jewish evangelist like Paul. The Romans would be hard-pressed to make a case against Justin, with no ethnic connection to the dispersed Jews, for instigating a Jewish insurrection, especially when the nation of Israel no longer existed!

Since the apostles had for the most part avoided the subject of the earthly kingdom in their written Gospels and Epistles, many early Gentile church fathers, despite threats from the Roman authorities, began to collect and piece together the oral traditions of the words of Jesus and the disciples concerning the future restoration. Soon, Gentile Christian philosophers and budding theologians were discerning the stealthy information on the earthly messianic kingdom from the Old Testament prophets, Jesus' words, the Epistles, the book of Revelation, and oral history. They began to connect the dots from Christ's allusion to a hundredfold reward "in this age" when the disciples would sit on "twelve thrones" judging Israel to the "thrones" of the "first resurrection" mentioned in John's vision of a millennial kingdom on this earth. They also began to link these key New Testament teachings to the visions of Isaiah, Ezekiel, and other prophets where they found a treasure trove of information on the earthly kingdom before the eternal kingdom.

As a result, a significant number of well-respected ante-Nicene fathers became millennialists, and the early church historians indicate that those closest to the apostle John, who had access to oral history from the apostle, developed a robust form of millennialism. Papias (c. 60–130) was reputed to have been a disciple of the John. He determined to gather information on the millennial kingdom from the oral history of people who had known Jesus and the apostles. This is similar to Luke gathering the oral history from the eyewitnesses of Christ in order to "write an orderly account" of the life of Christ (Luke 1:2–3).

Brian E. Daley describes this oral tradition in *The Hope of the Early Church*:

> Papias, bishop of Hierapolis in Phrygia in the early second century, apparently also had had close contact with the community in which the Johannine writings were produced. He is known to have collected material about Jesus and his disciples from oral sources, and to have arranged it in five books entitled Explanations of the Words of the Lord. According to Irenaeus (*AH* 5.33.3-4), book 4 of Papias' collection contained, among teachings attributed to Jesus, a vivid description of a coming millennial kingdom, in which the fruitfulness of the earth will be increased to staggering proportions for the sake of the risen saints. Papias' authority became the basis of Irenaeus' own millennial expectations at the end of the second century.[1]

---

[1] Brian E. Daley, *The Hope of the Early Church* (Peabody, MA: Hendrickson Publishers, 2003), 18.

Papias, writing soon after John wrote Revelation, was able to gather enough oral history to devote an entire book to the subject of the millennial kingdom based on the Scriptures, combined with the oral history of the teachings of Christ and the apostles, particularly John. In contrast, the New Testament references to the restoration could fit on two pages. Unfortunately, Papias's books were lost, although we have fragments and quotes of his writings from other authors of the period.

In the ancient Roman world, handwritten books were costly, so the people relied heavily on oral history for the transfer of news and knowledge. Oral traditions in the ancient world were not infallible, but they could be highly reliable. Because these early disciples, such as Papias, reputedly had firsthand interpretations from John himself about the meaning of some of his teachings, particularly those relating to the first resurrection and the millennium, it is a fair assumption that their views on these subjects would be close to what John actually believed and taught, and it makes their teachings that much more important.

Patristic scholars debate whether or not millennialism became the predominant view of the ante-Nicene fathers. Orthodox millennialism never made it into the early creeds, but neither was it affirmed or condemned by the early church councils. The evidence suggests that amillennialists and millennialists respected each other as orthodox Christians, a situation similar to our position today. And belief in a millennial kingdom never became a litmus test for orthodoxy or heresy. In my opinion, it is doubtful that chiliasm became the majority view because of the stealthy nature of the 1,000-year messianic kingdom in the New Testament. Amillennialism, with its New Testament focus on the heavenly kingdom, probably remained the dominant view. The default teaching of the New Testament is the kingdom of heaven. To develop a millennial view required a great deal of orchestration of some obscure teachings found in books like Revelation and Daniel.

In this chapter, I hope to prove that postrestorationalism is, in reality, a rediscovery of the teachings of these early millennialists with a few important modifications. Whereas they had the second advent in the wrong place—occurring at the beginning of the 1,000-year reign of Christ instead of at the end of it—they correctly understood that the first resurrection described by John in Revelation 20 was a resurrection "in this age" of all the saints into *natural* bodies who can experience marriage during the millennium. I will also demonstrate that they understood that the rapture of the saints into *spiritual* bodies not given in marriage will occur *after* this 1,000-year restoration at the final and general resurrection at the end of the world on Judgment Day, when the saints asleep or alive will be transformed into immortal, "celestial" bodies and taken to heaven. The ideas presented in this book are not new but are a rediscovered and modified version of the teachings of early millennialists.

Until now, modern premillennialists have been able to claim that their views accurately represent the beliefs of early chiliasts. There are two key components to modern premillennialism. The first is that Christ physically returns to this earth in a second coming to destroy the Antichrist and establish his millennial kingdom. In this regard, their views are similar to those of the ante-Nicene millennialists.

The second major component of modern premillennialism is that the saints who have died before this second coming are raptured into their transformed immortal and glorified bodies sometime before the millennium and return to reign with Christ on this earth. Regardless of when the rapture occurs—pre-, mid-, or post-tribulation—all three modern premillennial positions maintain that these resurrected or "raptured" saints represented by the first resurrection are transformed and given their final spiritual bodies and, as such, are not given in marriage during the millennium. Only human survivors of the Tribulation remain in their natural bodies and therefore experience marriage and reproduction.

Regarding the "first resurrection" described by John, however, the ante-Nicene millennialists taught that the departed saints will be raised into natural, Adamic bodies, as Lazarus was raised, in order to experience the millennial kingdom with Christ when he returns to this earth. Because the resurrected saints are in their restored or regenerated human bodies, they, along with human survivors of the Tribulation, can thus marry, reproduce, and see their children's children. Only *after* the 1,000-year reign of Christ at the final judgment during the general resurrection of believers and unbelievers are the saints raptured and receive their transformed, immortal bodies not given in marriage and are taken to the new heavens and new earth as God's eternal children. Their teachings relative to the nature of the first and the final resurrections are categorically different from all modern versions of premillennialism.

It may seem strange or absurd to modern readers that they associated the second coming of Christ with the resurrection of *natural* bodies when the New Testament plainly teaches that when Christ returns in the clouds, the saints will be raptured into *spiritual* bodies. Nonetheless, that is what they taught.

This understanding of their views regarding the two different kinds of resurrection was originally presented as a paper at a regional conference of the Evangelical Theological Society.[2] Theologians in the audience were very surprised by this thesis. One prominent theologian, upon reading the paper, e-mailed me the following response: "I have never encountered this odd view of patristic eschatology."

---

[2] Gary S. Cangelosi, "The Ante-Nicene Fathers Were Not Premillennialists" (paper, Southwest Regional Meeting, Dallas, TX, March 27-28, 2009).

Some premillennial patristic scholars strongly oppose my thesis and insist that it was *heretical* versions of "carnal chiliasm" that taught that the "first resurrection" was of the natural body, not the early Christian millennialists. These theologians insist that the early millennialists taught that the "first resurrection" will be of the raptured body and only those human survivors of the Tribulation will experience a life of the natural body.

Some of the early chiliastic heretics such as Cerinthus (c. 100) did teach that the first resurrection was of the natural body that would eat, drink, and marry. But they also taught that during the millennium these resurrected humans in their natural bodies would engage in hedonistic behavior such as gluttony, drunkenness, and licentiousness when the restored earth produces an overabundance of food and wine. These heretical versions of chiliasm were roundly condemned by all the church fathers.

The Greco-Roman world was indeed a stew of Greek philosophies, pagan religions, and heathenism when Christianity entered into their world. And, as one would expect in a satanic world of deception, there were numerous heretical distortions of Christ's millennial reign that began almost simultaneously with John's writing of the book of Revelation. The ante-Nicene fathers had to contend with Gnostic and heathen counterfeit versions of the millennial kingdom.

Moreover, all the orthodox ante-Nicene fathers—amillennialists and millennialists alike—held beliefs that would be considered false teachings by today's standards. But there is a categorical difference between the more orthodox teachings of the early Christian millennialists, which may have had some carnal characteristics, and the false teachings of the heretical chiliasts that turned the millennium into a hedonistic paradise.

For example, Augustine (354–430), who had a fling with hedonism before his conversion, was initially a millennialist but was later repulsed by the worldly aspects of a 1,000-year Edenic paradise and, for a variety of other reasons, became an amillennialist. In his book *The City of God*, Augustine does not describe or condemn the heretical versions of carnal chiliasm; rather, he describes the early "Christian" versions of millennialism with their tendency toward carnality:

And this opinion would not be objectionable, if it were believed that the joys of the saints in that Sabbath shall be spiritual, and consequent on the presence of God; for I myself, too, once held this opinion. But, as they assert that those who then rise again shall enjoy the leisure of immoderate carnal banquets, furnished with an amount of meat and drink such as not only to shock the feeling of the temperate, but even to surpass the measure of credulity itself, such assertions can be believed only by the carnal. They who do believe them are called by the spiritual Chiliasts, which we may literally reproduce by the name Millenarians.[3]

Augustine is definitely not describing Gnostic heretical versions of "carnal chiliasm" like those of Cerinthus because he was never a Gnostic heretic and admits that he was once a "Millenarian" himself. He was inclined to accept millennialism had it not been for its tendency to interpret the millennial kingdom as a carnal and unspiritual paradise. Augustine, who spent a lifetime combating the latent effects of carnal lusts from his own pre-Christian experimentation with hedonism, was predisposed to oppose carnal pleasures of the natural body in an Edenic paradise.

Origen (c. 185–254), another earlier amillennialist, was even more Neoplatonic than Augustine. He, too, was critical of his fellow Christian millennialists for the worldly aspects of their beliefs:

> Certain persons . . . are of opinion that the fulfillment of the promises of the future [millennium] are to be looked for in bodily pleasure and luxury. After the resurrection [the "first resurrection"], such bodily structures as may never be without the power of eating, and drinking, and performing all the functions of flesh and blood, . . . that after the resurrection there will be marriages, and the begetting of children [natural human body] . . . Such are the views of those who, while believing in Christ [true Christians], understand the divine Scriptures in a sort of Jewish sense.[4]

Origen describes these early millennialists as Christians (not heretics) who held the view that the first resurrection will be of the natural body and will eat, drink, marry, and reproduce in the millennial kingdom of Christ. If Origen's description is accurate, then it provides good collaborating evidence that these early Christian chiliasts believed the saints of the first resurrection will be raised in natural Adamic bodies and will experience "marriage, and the begetting of children."

Modern premillennialists often infer that ante-Nicene millennialists represent their views to legitimize their eschatology. The credibility and historic authenticity of modern premillennialism depends on what early millennialists really believed, which may explain the significant opposition to my thesis that they believed the "first resurrection" will be of the natural body. I have even been accused of reintroducing a carnal chiliastic heresy.

In this chapter I present the case for my reading and understanding of these early millennialists, and the reader can decide if I have rediscovered their teachings or if I am reviving a chiliastic heresy. If my analysis is correct, then modern premillennialists will no longer be able to claim that their view

---

[3] Augustine, *The City of God*, trans. Marcus Dods (New York: Random House, 1950), 20.7.

[4] Origen, *De Principiis* II.11.2.

accurately represents those of early Christian millennialists. Please patiently read these patristic writings; they are important. It takes a great deal of work and concentration to understand their teachings, for they were not the most lucid writers, especially by modern standards.

We all bring presuppositions or certain biases to our studies. Modern premillennialists believe the first resurrection represents the raptured body and look for confirmation for this assertion when reading the early millennialists. I believe the first resurrection is of the natural body and the rapture is at the final resurrection, so I am inclined to look for confirmation of this belief among the early millennialist writings. It is difficult to be objective and unbiased, particularly with so much depending on the outcome of the analysis. We must try to be objective, however, and approach these writings in their grammatical-historical context.

The Nature of the First and Final Resurrection

There are two defining characteristics of the raptured body that can help determine where early millennialists placed the rapture: the raptured body will be similar to the angels in that it will be immortal and will no longer experience marriage. Jesus alluded to these two characteristics in his answer to the Sadducees:

> The sons of this age marry and are given in marriage [the Adamic order of being], but those who are considered worthy to attain to that age and to the resurrection from the dead neither marry nor are given in marriage, for they cannot die anymore [are immortal], because they are equal to angels and are sons of God, being sons of the resurrection. (Luke 20:34–36)

Paul wrote:

> So is it with the resurrection of the dead. . . . It is sown a natural body; it is raised a spiritual body. If there is a natural body, there is also a spiritual body. . . . I tell you a mystery. We shall not all sleep, but we shall be changed, in a moment, in the twinkling of an eye, at the last trumpet. For the trumpet will sound, and the dead will be raised imperishable, and we shall be changed. For this perishable body must put on the imperishable, and this mortal body must put on immortality. (1 Cor. 15:42–44, 51–53)

The question of when immortality actually begins—at the first resurrection or at the final resurrection—is ambiguous in some early millennialists' writings. Perhaps this is because they believed the saints who experience the first resurrection will live for the entire one thousand years—possessing immortal natural bodies. However, in regard to the second characteristic of Jesus' description of the raptured body that we will "neither marry nor are given in marriage," they consistently describe the final resurrection as of the kind of body that is *not given in marriage* because it is destined for the Father's kingdom of heaven.

Since the beginning of immortality is ambiguous in their writings, let's examine their teachings by using the description of marriage (natural body) or non-marriage (raptured body) to determine how they defined the first and final resurrections.

Justin (c. AD 100–165)

Justin is one of the earliest millennialists. In *Dialogue with Trypho*, he describes Christ's millennial kingdom and the events leading up to the eternal new heavens and new earth. Justin lays out a clear sequence of events by describing the millennial kingdom accessed by the first resurrection and then describing the final resurrection of the saints—*after* this millennium—at the general resurrection on Judgment Day as the raptured body that is *not given in marriage*:

> And further, there was a certain man with us, whose name was John, one of the apostles of Christ, who prophesied, by a revelation that was made to him, that those who believed in our Christ would dwell a thousand years in Jerusalem [through the "first resurrection"]; and that thereafter [after the millennium] the general, and, in short, the eternal resurrection and judgment of all men [Great White Throne judgment] would likewise take place. Just as our Lord also said, "They shall neither marry nor be given in marriage, but shall be equal to the angels, the children of the God of the resurrection" [the final resurrection of the raptured body].[5]

When Justin refers to an "eternal resurrection" that occurs "just as our Lord also said," he is referring to Christ's description of the resurrection in his answer to the Sadducees. Justin taught that the rapture of the "eternal" body not given in marriage is *after* the millennial reign of Christ at the final resurrection!

Justin further taught that before we are taken to the New Jerusalem in our raptured bodies at the final resurrection, we experience the first resurrection that will allow us to inherit the restored earthly city of Jerusalem in the messianic kingdom as foretold by the prophets:

> But I and others, who are right-minded Christians on all points, are assured that there will be a resurrection of the dead [the first resurrection], and a thousand years in Jerusalem, which will then be built, adorned, and enlarged, [as] the prophets Ezekiel and Isaiah and others declare. (*Dial.* 80.2)

---

[5] Justin, *Dialogue with Trypho*, 81.1.

In a later chapter, Justin describes two particular groups of Christians who will experience the "first resurrection." One group is those of his day who were experiencing persecution and martyrdom. Another group is those who will be slaughtered by the Antichrist during the future Tribulation. For Justin, however, it does not matter if and when a Christian is unjustly killed by evil people, for all deceased saints are effectively invincible because they are destined to experience a literal first resurrection in order to experience Christ's future millennial kingdom.

Justin provides a broad overview of the prophetic future that covers the first coming of Christ, the events of his day, the future Tribulation, the second coming, and the ensuing millennial reign of Christ when all wars will end. Most important, notice how he describes the first resurrection of departed or martyred saints at Christ's second coming at the beginning of the millennium as of the natural body that will experience marriage. Justin often uses multiple forms of abbreviation and recapitulation. To assist in navigating his teachings, some of the events I believe he is describing are placed in brackets:

O unreasoning men! understanding not what has been proved by all these passages, that two advents of Christ have been announced: the one, in which He is set forth as suffering, inglorious, dishonored, and crucified [the first coming]; but the other, in which He shall come from heaven with glory [the second advent to this earth to destroy the Antichrist and establish his kingdom], when the man of apostasy [the Antichrist], who speaks strange things against the Most High, shall venture to do unlawful deeds on the earth against us the Christians [during the Great Tribulation], who, having learned the true worship of God from the law [became Christians], and the word which went forth from Jerusalem by means of the apostles of Jesus [warnings about the future man of apostasy or "abomination of desolation"], have fled for safety to the God of Jacob and God of Israel ["let those who are in Judea flee to the mountains"]; and we who were filled with war, and mutual slaughter, and every wickedness [large numbers of Christians are killed during the Tribulation], have [he now transitions to the messianic kingdom] each through the whole earth changed our warlike weapons,— our swords into ploughshares, and our spears into implements of tillage [as depicted by Isaiah and Micah],—and we [martyred or departed saints that experience the first resurrection] cultivate piety, righteousness, philanthropy, faith, and hope [during Christ's kingdom of righteousness], which we have from the Father Himself through Him who was crucified [the Father's promise to subject all things to his Son who died for our sins]; and sitting each under his vine, i.e., each man possessing his own married wife [the resurrected saints experience marriage]. For you are aware that the prophetic word says, "And his wife shall be like a fruitful vine." Now [shifting back to his day] it is evident that no one can terrify or subdue us who have believed in Jesus over all the world [Christianity is spreading and believers are being persecuted]. For it is plain that, though beheaded, and crucified, and thrown to wild beasts, and chains, and fire, and all other kinds of torture, we do not give up our confession [because of the hope for the first resurrection]; but the more such things happen, the more do others and in larger numbers become faithful, and worshippers of God through the name of Jesus [persecution and martyrdom only cause the church to grow even more]. (*Dial.* 110)

Justin teaches that the deceased saints—those being martyred in his day as well as those who will be slaughtered in the future Tribulation—are resurrected back into natural, Adamic flesh and blood that can marry in order to experience the Adamic paradise as foretold by the Old Testament prophets. He believed that the meek shall inherit the earth, the messianic kingdom, through a resurrection of a natural body that will experience marriage. Then, on the last day after the millennium, the children of God will inherit the kingdom of heaven through an eternal resurrection or rapture of an immortal body that, as Jesus taught, will not be given in marriage.

Justin believed the first resurrection is of the natural body in keeping with Ezekiel's and Isaiah's vision of the restored Adamic paradise, and the final resurrection is of the raptured body of the sons of God in keeping with Christ's teaching on the resurrection, as described to the Sadducees, when the saints are taken to the Father's eternal kingdom.

Old and New Testament Versions of Resurrection

One of the best ways to resolve how Justin and other early millennialists understood the first and the final resurrections is to identify Scriptures they reference when describing each resurrection and then read those Scriptures to determine what kind of resurrected body they are describing. For example, we saw how Justin places the final "eternal resurrection" of the saints *after* the millennium in direct reference to Jesus' answer to the Sadducees, which describes the raptured body not given in marriage. When describing the "first resurrection," however, he does not reference Jesus' answer to the Sadducees; instead, he references the prophetic visions of Ezekiel and Isaiah: "there will be a resurrection of the dead, and a thousand years in Jerusalem, which will then be built, adorned, and enlarged, [as] the prophets Ezekiel and Isaiah and others declare" (*Dial.* 80.2).

Justin creates a direct correspondence between the "resurrection of the dead" at the beginning of the millennium and the teachings of "Ezekiel and Isaiah" to how the saints will inherit the restored millennial Jerusalem. The first resurrection is equivalent to what the prophets Ezekiel and Isaiah believed concerning the future resurrection of the saints that ushers in the messianic kingdom. Thus, if in doubt as to how Justin understood the nature of the first resurrection, simply read what these Old Testament prophets taught on the subject.

For example, in Ezekiel's famous vision of the valley of dry bones coming to life, he foresees the departed house of Israel being resurrected into human bodies of flesh and blood with the breath of life breathed into them as they reenter a restored nation on this renewed earth (Ezek. 37). The divided house of Israel and Judah end, and these resurrected saints of the united house of Israel experience marriage and see their "children and their children's children" (37:25-26).

Ezekiel describes a graphic picture of the resurrection of the natural body reconstituted with bones, flesh, tendons, skin, and given the breath of life in the manner of the creation of Adam and Eve. This massive resurrection of natural bodies continues the creation mandate to reproduce, fill, and subdue the earth. This future resurrection of the Adamic order of being in a restored Genesis creation enables the resurrected saints to enjoy an Edenic paradise on earth with spouses, children, and abundant prosperity.

Ezekiel is *not* describing the raptured, immortal spiritual body of the sons of God not given in marriage, as described by Jesus and Paul, that is destined for the Father's kingdom of heaven. He is unmistakably describing a resurrection of the natural bodies of the departed saints who will dwell on the restored Genesis earth. These are two very different visions of the resurrected body. One is of the *natural* body given in marriage destined for the earthly messianic kingdom, and the other is of the raptured *spiritual* body not given in marriage destined for the heavenly kingdom.

It should be noted that modern premillennialists do not read Ezekiel's prophecy of the resurrection of natural bodies literally. They claim that Ezekiel's vision of the valley of dry bones coming to life metaphorically describes the reunification of Judah and the other tribes of Israel during the messianic kingdom. Amillennialists also interpret Ezekiel's vision as metaphorical. But the believing Jews, God's people, are promised a real resurrection, and God stakes his reputation on its literal fulfillment: "Thus says the Lord GOD: Behold, I will open your graves and raise you from your graves, O my people. And I will bring you into the land of Israel. And you shall know that I am the LORD, when I open your graves, and raise you from your graves, O my people" (Ezek. 37:12-13).

Modern theologians are, of course, free to interpret Isaiah 26 and Ezekiel 37 in whatever manner they believe is consistent with the Scriptures. But we should read Justin and other early millennialists from a grammatical-historical context and not impose our contemporary assumptions on them. That modern theologians interpret Ezekiel's vision figuratively is irrelevant because it has no bearing on early millennialists' understanding and interpretation. Early millennialists take Isaiah's description of a literal resurrection and Ezekiel's description of a mass resurrection of natural bodies of the departed Jewish saints and offer no opinion that these visions are to be interpreted metaphorically. They believed Isaiah and Ezekiel described a resurrection of the natural bodies of the departed saints who would then inherit a real messianic kingdom.

Any direct correspondence by early millennialists between the kind of resurrection described by Ezekiel and Isaiah and the first resurrection described by John is a clear reference to a resurrection of a natural body— not the raptured body. Unlike modern theologians, they interpreted Ezekiel and Isaiah quite literally and applied their prophecies of a resurrection of natural bodies of the saints *directly* to John's vision of the first resurrection, which should erase any doubt as to how they understood the nature of the first resurrection.

Therefore, when Justin describes the first resurrection as of natural bodies "sitting each under his vine, i.e., each man possessing his own married wife," he is simply matching John's vision of resurrection to Isaiah's and Ezekiel's vision of resurrection and restoration in the messianic kingdom. Justin does not need to go into much detail about the nature of the first resurrection being of the natural body because Ezekiel has already given us a graphic picture of the resurrection of the natural body. Isaiah, particularly in chapter 65, has also already provided a graphic description of the restored Jerusalem and the renewed Edenic earth, when the saints shall build houses, plant crops, and bear healthy and abundant offspring.

Justin's views on the two resurrections can be formulated:

- First resurrection = natural bodies of departed saints as defined by Ezekiel and Isaiah ("each man possessing his own wife").
- Final resurrection = the raptured spiritual bodies of the saints, or the "eternal resurrection . . . Just as our Lord also said, 'They shall neither marry nor be given in marriage, but shall be equal to the angels, the children of the God of the resurrection.'"

Tertullian (c. AD 160–220)

Tertullian, another early millennialist often cited by modern premillennialists, also refers to Christ's millennial kingdom at his second coming. He is, however, unclear as to the nature of the first resurrection. Nonetheless, he, too, definitely places the rapture of the saints destined for heaven *after* the millennium at the end of the world:

Of the heavenly kingdom this is the process. After its thousand years are over, within which period is completed the resurrection of the saints, who rise sooner or later according to their deserts [nature not clear] there will ensue the destruction of the world [the last day] and the conflagration of all things at the judgment [Judgment Day]: we shall then be changed in a moment [in the twinkling of the eye] into the substance of angels [the rapture], even by the investiture of an incorruptible nature [the final glorified body], and so be removed to that kingdom in heaven . . .[6]

In analyzing the early chiliasts' views on the first resurrection, it is important to know that they developed an unorthodox understanding of the setting of the souls or spirits of the departed saints. Instead of going to the paradise of heaven to join the "spirits of the righteous made perfect" (Heb. 12:1–2, 23), they believed the departed spirits went to a special holding place in Hades while they waited for the first resurrection. They believed Hades had two compartments: a good section that held the spirits of the departed saints where some measure of judgment occurred; and a bad section that held the spirits of departed unbelievers where judgment continues until the general resurrection on Judgment Day, when they will be resurrected in body and soul to face the full recompense for their sinful lives. The two compartments are separated as indicated by the parable of the dead rich man who is being punished in Hades, and the dead poor man named Lazarus who is at Abraham's side (Luke 16:19).

Charles E. Hill in a book titled *Regnum Caelorum* [Kingdom of Heaven]: *Patterns of Millennial Thought in Early Christianity* makes a convincing case that these beliefs of a holding place in Hades or a subterranean world became a defining characteristic of the early chiliasts, which amillennialists of their day could easily see was unbiblical. The New Testament clearly teaches that the departed spirits of the saints are in heaven—not Hades. Hill further makes the case that this particular false teaching is one of the main reasons millennialism became discredited over time.

By way of example, consider what Tertullian had to say about Hades:

All souls [believers and unbelievers], therefore, are shut up within Hades: do you admit this? . . . Why, then, cannot you suppose that the soul undergoes punishment and consolation in Hades in the interval, while it awaits . . . in a certain anticipation either of gloom or of glory? . . . In short, inasmuch as we understand "the prison" pointed out in the Gospel to be Hades, and . . . the very smallest offence which has to be recompensed there before the resurrection ["first resurrection"].[7]

Tertullian's understanding of the saints being held in Hades may explain his strange belief in the gradual and progressive nature of the first resurrection of the departed saints. Those who lived a good life—especially those martyred—would be resurrected right away, and those who committed bad deeds during their lifetimes needed to be recompensed in Hades a little longer before they would be resurrected in the millennium. As a result, they

---

[6] Tertullian, *Against Marcion*, III.25.
[7] Tertullian, *A Treatise on the Soul*, 58.1.

rise sooner or later according to their level of righteousness. Unbelievers would remain imprisoned in Hades until Judgment Day.

To understand why these early millennialists believed it was necessary for the departed spirits of the saints to be held in a "good" section of Hades before experiencing the first resurrection of a natural human body on this earth, consider the resurrection of Lazarus who died and was then resurrected into his natural body. If his spirit or soul had gone to paradise and tasted of the perfection and glory of heaven itself for four days, then when he came back to life on this earth, he may have responded to Jesus by saying, "Lord, why did you bring me be back to this miserable world? I would have preferred to have stayed in paradise!"

To early millennialists, even the 1,000-year Edenic paradise on earth would be no comparison to the paradise of heaven, which is why they may have felt compelled to develop a holding place in Hades for the spirits of the departed saints until they return to the restored earth in resurrected natural bodies like Lazarus. Only after the millennium, at the final resurrection when we receive our perfected, transformed, glorified, incorruptible, spiritual, or raptured bodies will we be able to enter body *and* soul into the paradise of heaven and be in the very presence of God the Father. Or, as Tertullian says, "we shall then be changed in a moment into the substance of angels, even by the investiture of an incorruptible nature, and so be removed to that kingdom in heaven."

It is unfortunate they developed this teaching of a temporary abode for the departed saints, because, as Hill demonstrates, these unbiblical beliefs exposed early chiliasm to legitimate criticism, causing it to be unnecessarily rejected in its entirety. They failed to realize that a return to this regenerated Edenic earth in natural bodies would not be retrogressive because John had taught that it would be a blessing for the "holy" or perfected spirits of the saints to leave heaven and experience the first resurrection even though their disembodied spirits had spent time in the heavenly paradise:

> Then I saw heaven opened [not Hades], and behold, a white horse [Christ]! . . . And the armies of heaven [departed saints], arrayed in fine linen, white and pure [souls are already perfect and holy], were following him on white horses [leaving the paradise of heaven]. . . . Also I saw the souls of those who had been beheaded for the testimony of Jesus [who came out of heaven] . . . They came to life [on the earth in real bodies] and reigned with Christ for a thousand years. . . . This is the first resurrection. Blessed and holy is the one who shares in the first resurrection! (Rev. 19:11–20:6)

Commodianus (AD 240)

Tertullian may be unclear as to the nature of the first resurrection, but Commodianus, a North African bishop, is very clear. Only two poems remain from his writings, which are dated sometime around AD 240. He interprets John's vision of the New Jerusalem as a form of recapitulation whereby the New Jerusalem descends to this Genesis earth at the beginning of the millennium instead of descending to the new heavens and new earth. But he describes the saints of the first resurrection as experiencing a form of immortality in that they will live for the entire one thousand years, while they experience natural lives of marriage and reproduction in the earthly paradise as described by Isaiah and the prophets:

> From heaven will descend the city in the first resurrection; this is what we may tell of such a celestial fabric. We shall arise again to Him, who have been devoted to Him. And they shall be incorruptible, even already living without death. And neither will there be any grief nor any groaning in that city. They shall come also who overcame cruel martyrdom under Antichrist, and they themselves live for the whole time, and receive blessings because they have suffered evil things; and they themselves marrying, beget for a thousand years. There are prepared all the revenues of the earth, because the earth renewed without end pours forth abundantly.[8]

All the departed saints, including those killed by the Antichrist during the Tribulation, will be resurrected into natural bodies at the first resurrection and will marry and reproduce for the entire one thousand years when the "renewed" earth "pours forth abundantly" as the prophets have promised. He believes the resurrected saints in their natural bodies will have a form of immortality in that they will live for the entire one thousand years.

If we combined Commodianus's teachings on the first resurrection being of the natural body with Tertullian's teachings on the final resurrection being of the immortal body, they would be formulated as follows:

- First resurrection = natural bodies of the departed saints in the messianic kingdom, or "We shall arise again . . . marrying, beget for a thousand years."
- Final resurrection = the raptured spiritual bodies of the saints, or "we shall then be changed in a moment into the substance of angels, even by the investiture of an incorruptible nature, and so be removed to that kingdom in heaven."

Irenaeus (c. AD 120–202)

Irenaeus is another highly regarded ante-Nicene millennialist. His surviving writings on the subject are more extensive than those of other early millennialists and require a more in-depth analysis. Irenaeus's teachings on the two resurrections and the millennial kingdom are found in his

---

[8] Commodianus, *The Instructions of Commodianus in Favor of Christian Disciple. Against the Gods of the Heathen,* XLIV.

books *Against Heresies*, which can be difficult to read because their primary purpose was refuting the heretical teachings of the Gnostics of that time.

The following is a summary of the Gnostics' beliefs: The human body and the material world were created by an inferior god or angel. As a result, the human body itself is inherently evil and defective, which explains why it has so many carnal and sinful passions. One day, a superior God will annihilate this defective world and our evil physical bodies, and then the liberated human spirits will ascend to the mysterious realms of heaven where Christ has gone before us in spirit only. Christ did not experience a resurrection of his evil body; only his enlightened and advanced spirit ascended to heaven, thereby escaping his evil body and this flawed and carnal world.

Irenaeus refutes these heresies by affirming that the original Genesis earth *and* the Adamic body created by God were indeed good before the fall. Proof of their goodness is derived from the fact that the Scriptures teach that this same Creator will restore the natural Adamic body and this Genesis creation in the future millennial kingdom. If the human body and this creation are so evil, then why would God the Creator as the superior God affirm their very goodness by restoring them in the future millennial kingdom of Christ? Further proof of the inherent goodness of the body is demonstrated by God resurrecting it on the last day, which is yet another resurrection of a body even though it is transformed into an incorruptible body and is taken to the new heavens and new earth, which, according to Irenaeus, is a renovated earth.

Like Commodianus, Irenaeus describes the saints of the first resurrection as having natural bodies that have a form of immortality in that they will live for the entire one thousand years. For example, after quoting from Ezekiel's description of the valley of dry bones being resurrected into natural human beings, Irenaeus describes the resurrected saints as having a form of immortality: "As we at once perceive that the Creator is in this passage represented as vivifying our dead bodies, and promising resurrection to them, and resuscitation from their sepulchres and tombs, conferring upon them *immortality*."[9] Rather than describing the immortal spiritual bodies, he used the term "immortality" to describe resurrected natural bodies, as Ezekiel described, that will not experience another mortal death during the millennium—an "immortal" natural body.

Irenaeus even believed the resurrected natural body will be progressively disciplined during the millennium in order for it to be prepared for the final resurrection. This is not a description of the perfected raptured body that is incorruptible. He believed that the saints will be made truly imperishable

---

[9] Irenaeus, *Against Heresies*, V.15.1.

and incorruptible *after* the millennium when they are taken to be in the presence of God the Father in his eternal kingdom:

> ... that Jerusalem of the former earth in which the righteous are disciplined beforehand for incorruption and prepared for salvation. ... And as he rises actually [in the first resurrection], so also shall he be actually disciplined beforehand for incorruption, and shall go forwards and flourish in the times of the kingdom [millennial kingdom], in order that he may be capable of receiving the glory of the Father [in the future heavenly kingdom]. Then, when all things are made new, he shall truly dwell in the city of God [the New Jerusalem]. For it is said, "He that sitteth on the throne said, Behold, I make all things new (*AH* V.35.2). ... But when this [present] fashion [of things] passes away, and man has been renewed, and flourishes in an incorruptible state, so as to preclude the possibility of becoming old, [then] there shall be the new heaven and the new earth. (*AH* V.34.1)

According to Irenaeus, it is only when we are taken to the Father's eternal new heavens and new earth *after* the millennium that we receive ageless bodies that are made truly immortal, imperishable, and incorruptible because we are then going to be in the very presence of God the Father.

Irenaeus believed that when Christ returns to this earth, he will bring an entourage of angels with him: "[T]he righteous shall reign in the earth, waxing stronger by the sight of the Lord: and through Him they shall become accustomed to partake in the glory of God the Father, and shall enjoy in the kingdom intercourse and communion with the holy angels, and union with spiritual beings" (*AH* V.35.1).

Irenaeus's description of the saints in communion with angels along with Christ during this time does not indicate that Irenaeus is describing the glorified raptured saints. The shepherds at the birth of Christ spent time with angels yet remained in their natural bodies. The saints of the first resurrection are not yet in their glorified bodies during the millennium, because they are still being prepared for the future "glory of God" in the eternal kingdom.

Since Irenaeus is ambiguous as to when the saints receive immortal bodies, the best way to determine how he understood the two resurrections is to identify the Scriptures he links to these resurrections. Irenaeus links the first resurrection described by John *directly* to the resurrections described by the Old Testament prophets. His favorite expression for the first resurrection is the "resurrection of the just." Notice in the following excerpt how he creates a *direct correspondence* between the nature of the first resurrection described by John to the type of resurrection defined by Isaiah and Ezekiel:

Then, too, Isaiah himself has plainly declared that there shall be joy of this nature at the resurrection of the just, when he says: "The dead shall rise again; those, too, who are in the tombs shall arise, and those who are in the earth shall rejoice. For the dew from Thee is health to them [Isa. 26:19]." And this again Ezekiel also says: "Behold, I will open your tombs, and will bring you forth out of your graves; when I will draw my people from the sepulchres, and I will put breath in you, and ye shall live; and I will place you on your own land, and ye shall know that I am the LORD [Ezek. 37:12–13]" And again the same speaks thus: "These things saith the Lord, I will gather Israel from all nations whither they have been driven, and I shall be sanctified in them in the sight of the sons of the nations: and they shall dwell in their own land, which I gave to my servant Jacob. And they shall dwell in it in peace; and they shall build houses, and plant vineyards, and dwell in hope, when I shall cause judgment to fall among all who have dishonored them, among those who encircle them round about; and they shall know that I am the Lord their God, and the God of their fathers." [Ezek. 37:21–23] (AH V.34.1)

Unlike modern theologians, Irenaeus does not interpret Ezekiel's vision of a resurrection of natural bodies as metaphorical, and even warns *against* allegorizing Ezekiel's depiction of the resurrection of the natural bodies of the saints: "If, however, any shall endeavor to allegorize [prophecies] of this kind, they shall not be found consistent with themselves in all points, and shall be confuted by the teaching of the very expressions" (AH V.35.1). Irenaeus further states that the prophecies self-refute an allegorical interpretation because the prophets plainly describe the resurrection of human beings into Adamic bodies that will eat, drink, marry, and reproduce on the promised restored earth: "they shall be confuted by the teaching of the very expressions [in question]." Irenaeus is not only rebuking anyone who allegorizes these prophecies of the resurrection of natural bodies of the departed saints, but also anyone who does not comprehend the self-evident meaning of these prophecies.

Irenaeus describes the millennial kingdom as a combination of human survivors of the Great Tribulation and the resurrected saints. The Old Testament prophets also described a period of tribulation followed by God's vengeance, wrath, and judgment against Israel's enemies, which is then followed by a resurrection and the restoration of Israel in the messianic kingdom. Because the prophets described the messianic kingdom as a restoration of the Genesis earth, the humans who survive God's judgments as well as those resurrected will live natural Adamic lives in the messianic kingdom. Irenaeus integrates this Old Testament pattern of tribulation, judgment, and subsequent messianic kingdom with John's vision of the Tribulation, judgment, and subsequent millennial kingdom:

"For, behold," says Isaiah, "the day of the Lord cometh past remedy, full of fury and wrath, to lay waste the city of the earth, and to root sinners out of it." And again he says, "Let him be taken away, that he behold not the glory of God." And when these things are done, he says, "God will remove men far away, and those that are left shall multiply in the earth [survivors of God's judgment and the resurrected saints]." "And they shall build houses, and shall inhabit them themselves: and plant vineyards, and eat of them themselves." For all these and other words [Isaiah's and Ezekiel's prophecies concerning survivors and those resurrected] were unquestionably spoken in reference to the resurrection of the just, which takes place after the coming of Antichrist, and the destruction of all nations under his rule; in [the times of] which [resurrection] the righteous shall reign in the earth. (AH V.35.1)

Irenaeus emphatically teaches that Isaiah's and Ezekiel's visions of the resurrection of the departed saints "were unquestionably spoken in reference to the resurrection of the just" alluded to by John in Revelation. This direct correspondence established by Irenaeus between Isaiah's and Ezekiel's visions and John's reference to the resurrection of the just is the key to properly discerning his understanding of the nature of the first resurrection. If in doubt, then simply read Ezekiel's description of the resurrection of the departed Jewish saints and you will see what kind of bodies he believes the resurrected saints will have in the millennium.

Do other human survivors of the Tribulation also experience marriage in the millennium like the resurrected saints Ezekiel describes? According to Irenaeus, they would. In the above quote, Irenaeus comingles human survivors and resurrected saints such that, as Ezekiel teaches, they all experience marriage. Irenaeus also references a prophecy by Jeremiah that describes these survivors as experiencing marriage, with the caveat that the resurrected saints will rule over the human survivors of God's judgments poured out at the end of the Tribulation:

... and [with respect to] those whom the Lord shall find in the flesh, awaiting Him from heaven, and who have suffered tribulation, as well as escaped the hands of the Wicked one. For it is in reference to them that the prophet says: "And those that are left shall multiply upon the earth," And Jeremiah the prophet has pointed out, that as many believers as God has prepared for this purpose, to multiply those left upon earth, should both be under the rule of the saints to minister to this Jerusalem. (AH V.35.1)

Modern premillennialists claim that Irenaeus is now differentiating between survivors who marry and reproduce and the raptured saints who do not experience marriage. But Irenaeus never describes the resurrected saints as being in their raptured bodies. Like Ezekiel, he combines those who are resurrected with those who survive the Tribulation, such that *all* humans living in the messianic kingdom experience marriage and reproduction.

Irenaeus is merely searching for prophecies to confirm John's vision of resurrected humans who will sit on thrones with authority to judge other human survivors, attributing some element of superiority to the resurrected saints. Irenaeus is not differentiating between the raptured saints and the human survivors because Ezekiel did not describe the resurrection at the valley of dry bones as being of spiritual bodies. Ezekiel teaches that *all people* living on the earth at that time will build houses, plant crops, marry, reproduce, and enjoy the restored earth.

Irenaeus wrote that the first resurrection has to be of the natural body as defined by the prophets because it is destined for the restored creation:

> . . . of the resurrection of the just, . . . when they rise again to behold God in this [Genesis] creation which is renovated, . . . For it is just that in that very creation in which they toiled or were afflicted [in natural bodies on this earth], . . . they should receive the reward of their suffering; and that in the [Genesis] creation in which they were slain because of their love to God, in that they should be revived again [in the same Adamic body in the same Genesis creation]; . . . It is fitting, therefore, that the creation itself, being restored to its primeval condition, should without restraint be under the dominion of the righteous [restored Adamic dominion over the Edenic earth]. (*AH* V.32.1)

The saints were in their natural bodies when they toiled, suffered, and, in some cases, were slain on this earth. When the same creation is "renovated" and "restored to its primeval condition," the saints will be "revived again" at the "resurrection of the just" and come back to life in the very same kind of natural bodies they had when they suffered on the earth. We will have restored natural bodies for a restored earth and will fulfill the creation mandate by subduing the earth "under the dominion of the righteous."

To further bolster his case for a literal resurrection of the natural bodies of the departed saints in a future literal millennial kingdom, Irenaeus references other kingdom promises made by Jesus that can be found in the Gospels. At the Last Supper, Jesus made the following promise to his disciples: "I tell you I will not drink again of this fruit of the vine until that day when I drink it new with you in my Father's kingdom" (Matt. 26:29). Irenaeus interpreted this promise as having a dual form of fulfillment—two kingdoms of God accessed by two different resurrections. The first kingdom is the Son's millennial kingdom accessed by the first resurrection of the disciples' natural bodies. Because this kingdom is a restoration of the Genesis creation as described by the prophets, the disciples will drink real wine from "the fruit of the vine" in natural human bodies just as they drank real wine in natural bodies with Christ at the Last Supper when he was on this earth. The second kingdom is the Father's super-celestial kingdom of heaven accessed by the final resurrection, when the disciples will drink a different kind of wine—a spiritual wine—in resurrected bodies adapted for the Father's eternal kingdom.

Irenaeus's writings oscillate between the two kinds of resurrections using a form of recapitulation. Read the following quote carefully and slowly, and see how determined he is that we understand the critical distinctions between the two kinds of resurrections necessary to access the two kingdoms of God:

> He promised to drink of the fruit of the vine with His disciples, thus indicating both these points: the inheritance of the earth in which the new fruit of the vine is drunk, and the resurrection of His disciples in the flesh [the Son's millennial kingdom]. For the new flesh which rises again is the same which also received the new cup [both are natural Adamic bodies of flesh and blood capable of drinking real wine]. And He cannot by any means be understood as drinking of the fruit of the vine when settled down with His [disciples] above in a super-celestial place [the Father's kingdom]; nor, again, [in a recapitulation of the Son's kingdom and the first resurrection] are they who drink it devoid of flesh, for to drink of that which flows from the vine pertains to flesh, and not spirit [to drink real wine from the restored earth requires a real natural body of flesh and blood]. (*AH* V.33.1)

Irenaeus uses almost identical phrasing ("new flesh which rises again is the same") when he describes the resurrection of the natural bodies of the widow's son and Lazarus: "The widow's dead son . . . and Lazarus, who had lain four days in the tomb—in what bodies did they rise again? In those same, no doubt, in which they had also died" (*AH* V.13.1). Likewise, the Son's earthly kingdom is accessed by a resurrection of the same kind of human body the disciples had when they ate and drank with Christ at the Last Supper on this earth: "for the new flesh which rises again is the same which also received the new cup." The disciples had natural bodies when they died or were slain, and they, like Lazarus, will have the same kind of natural bodies in "the inheritance of the earth." The disciples and their followers are destined to inherit the restored Genesis creation as described by Ezekiel, the prophets, and Jesus himself.

Irenaeus identifies another of Christ's promises and links it to the first resurrection and the millennial kingdom. Matthew records a conversation between Jesus and his disciples who were willing to sacrificially follow him. As a reward for their faithfulness, Jesus promised that they would receive a hundredfold [rewards] in this age during the renewal of this earth—houses, lands, children—and then eternal life in the age to come (Matt. 19:28–29). Irenaeus understood this promise to also represent the two kingdoms of God. Through the first resurrection, the disciples and all the saints will inherit an abundantly fruitful earth during the Son's millennial kingdom—

the hundredfold reward in this age; and then, through the final resurrection, they will inherit the Father's eternal kingdom of heaven:

> And again He says, "Whosoever shall have left lands, or houses, or parents, or brethren, or children because of Me, he shall receive in this world a hundred-fold, and in that to come he shall inherit eternal life." For what are the hundred-fold [rewards] in this world . . . ? These are [to take place] in the times of the kingdom, . . . The predicted blessing therefore, belongs unquestionably to the times of the kingdom, when the righteous shall bear rule upon their rising from the dead; when also the creation, having been renovated and set free, shall fructify with an abundance of all kinds of food, from the dew of heaven, and from the fertility of the earth. (AH V.33.2, 3)

The resurrected body in the Son's kingdom must "unquestionably" be of a natural body of flesh and blood because the resurrected saints will experience an Adamic paradise characterized by the disciples having houses, land, and children with "an abundance of all kinds of food" when this Genesis "creation" is "renovated and set free."

In this same paragraph, Irenaeus expounds upon an oral tradition of other teachings of Christ's pertaining to the remarkable abundance of food and wine the resurrected saints will enjoy during the Son's earthly kingdom, tying these promises to the prophecies found in Isaiah 65:

> The predicted blessing, therefore, belongs unquestionably to the times of the kingdom, when the righteous shall bear rule upon their rising from the dead; . . . as the elders who saw John, the disciple of the Lord, related that they had heard from him how the Lord used to teach in regard to these times [the messianic kingdom], and say: The days will come, in which vines shall grow, each having ten thousand branches, and in each branch ten thousand twigs, and in each true twig ten thousand shoots, and in each one of the shoots ten thousand clusters, and on every one of the clusters ten thousand grapes, . . . In like manner [the Lord declared] that a grain of wheat would produce ten thousand ears, and that every ear should have ten thousand grains, and every grain would yield ten pounds of clear, pure, fine flour; and that all other fruit-bearing trees, and seeds and grass, would produce in similar proportions; and that all animals feeding [only] on the productions of the earth, should [in those days] become peaceful and harmonious among each other, and be in perfect subjection to man. . . . And it is right that when the creation is restored, all the animals should obey and be in subjection to man, and revert to the food originally given by God (for they had been originally subjected in obedience to Adam), that is, the productions of the earth. . . . that the lion shall [then] feed on straw. And this indicates the large size and rich quality of the fruits. For if that animal, the lion, feeds upon straw [at that period], of what a quality must the wheat itself be whose straw shall serve as suitable food for lions? (AH V.33.3, 4)

In keeping with the Old Testament prophetic vision, Irenaeus describes the millennium as a time when the restored earth will produce great quantities of wine, wheat, and fruit-bearing trees. Seeds and grasses will be so nutritious and abundant that animals will no longer feed on each other, and the earth will revert to the Garden of Eden when animals ate only plants.

Irenaeus asserts that the source of these oral traditions come directly from "the elders who saw John," who gave them firsthand interpretations of the meaning of Revelation 20. He also states that John, in turn, learned these things directly from Jesus: "the Lord used to teach in regard to these times." Irenaeus claims that these oral teachings of a literal restoration, when the saints will be resurrected into natural bodies to experience the restored Adamic creation, come directly from the apostle John and Christ.

Irenaeus also alludes to an oral tradition recorded by Papias:

> And these things are borne witness to in writing by Papias, the hearer of John, and a companion of Polycarp, in his fourth book; for there were five books compiled by him. And he says in addition, "Now these things [about the restored earth and its incredible abundance] are credible to believers." And he says that, "when the traitor Judas did not give credit to them, and put the question, 'How then can things about to bring forth so abundantly be wrought by the Lord?' the Lord declared, 'They who shall come to these [times] shall see.'" (*AH* V.33.4)

This oral history is similar to the promise of a "hundredfold" reward during the renewal of this earth. Papias's fascinating collection of oral history of Christ's teachings was able to fill a whole book. It is a tragedy that his book containing these teachings on the restoration was lost in antiquity.

Irenaeus continues to build his case for the 1,000-year messianic kingdom by linking the promises given to Abraham of the Jewish Promised Land to the prophetic vision of the messianic kingdom when the Genesis creation is restored to its Edenic condition—the ultimate Promised Land. Most important, Irenaeus links these promises made to Abraham of the messianic kingdom to the church itself, which is made up of all nations. Abraham, who was justified by faith, is the father of all Gentile believers who have also been justified by faith. As a result, the church and all Gentile believers have become true spiritual descendants of Abraham. Therefore, they have become heirs of the same promises made to Abraham regarding the future messianic Promised Land. This entitles the church—all nations—to inherit the restored Genesis earth along with Abraham and the other resurrected Jewish saints. All the departed saints—Jew and Gentile—will experience a resurrection of their natural bodies as described by Isaiah, Ezekiel, and John, and thereby inherit the earthly messianic kingdom promised to Abraham:

Thus, then, the promise of God, which He gave to Abraham, remains steadfast. . . . "I will give this land to thy seed, from the river of Egypt even unto the great river Euphrates." If, then, God promised him the inheritance of the land, yet he did not receive it during all the time of his sojourn there, it must be, that together with his seed [Gentile believers], that is, those who fear God and believe in Him, he shall receive it at the resurrection of the just [in the millennial kingdom] (AH V.32.2). . . . And this again Ezekiel also says: "Behold, I will open your tombs, and will bring you forth out of your graves; . . . Now I have shown a short time ago that the church is the seed of Abraham; and for this reason, that we may know that He who in the New Testament "raises up from the stones children unto Abraham," is He who will gather, according to the Old Testament, those that shall be saved from all the nations [the church]. (AH V.34.1)

In a remarkable display of theological reasoning, Irenaeus develops a coherent and convincing biblical theology by linking the promises of an earthly kingdom given to Abraham and all his spiritual descendants, including the church, to Ezekiel's vision of resurrection and restoration, to John's first resurrection of the saints, and then to Christ's millennial kingdom. All spiritual *and* material blessings promised to Abraham and Israel as described by Isaiah and Ezekiel are extended to all believers of all time who have been justified by faith. Therefore, the millennial kingdom as John envisioned is a fulfillment of the long-awaited Jewish messianic kingdom in the Promised Land that encompasses the whole world.

Irenaeus then links all these promises of resurrection and restoration to the promise Jesus made that the meek shall inherit the earth:

Thus, then, they who are of faith shall be blessed with faithful Abraham, and these are the children of Abraham. Now God made promise of the earth to Abraham and his seed; yet neither Abraham nor his seed, that is, those who are justified by faith, do now receive any inheritance in it; but they shall receive it at the resurrection of the just [in the future millennium]. For God is true and faithful; and on this account He said, "Blessed are the meek, for they shall inherit the earth." (AH V.32.2)

All of these promises to Abraham and his spiritual descendants are confirmed by Jesus' promise that the meek (all believers of all time) "shall inherit the earth." That is because God is "true and faithful" to *all* of his promises to his people pertaining to the messianic kingdom.

Finally, Irenaeus links the final resurrection on Judgment Day to the type of resurrection in which the transformed saints will no longer be given in marriage. The Gnostics believed only the soul exists for eternity. To refute this heresy, he references the final or general resurrection, where John describes the resurrection of unbelievers from Hades who are judged and destined for hell, as well as the final resurrection of believers destined for the eternal new heavens and new earth. Irenaeus believed that God has a predetermined number of people who will become his children, and that once this set number is reached through our reproduction, human marriage and reproduction will cease, and this Adamic creation will come to an end. He believed resurrected believers at this general resurrection on Judgment Day will no longer experience marriage and reproduction. Irenaeus also describes the resurrected bodies of unbelievers as no longer experiencing marriage and reproduction, which seems obvious since they are destined for eternal punishment in the lake of fire. But he clearly places the rapture of the saints on the last day at the final resurrection:

> And therefore, when the number [of saints] is completed, [that number] which He had predetermined in His own counsel, all those who have been enrolled for life [eternal] shall rise again [in the final resurrection], having their own bodies, and having also their own souls, and their own spirits, in which they had pleased God [body, soul, and spirit united in resurrected bodies]. Those, on the other hand, who are worthy of punishment [unbelievers], shall go away into it [the lake of fire], they too having their own souls and their own bodies [body and soul], in which they stood apart from the grace of God. Both classes [resurrected believers and unbelievers] shall then cease from any longer begetting and being begotten, from marrying and being given in marriage; so that the number of mankind, corresponding to the fore-ordination of God, being completed, may fully realize the scheme formed by the Father. (*AH* II.33.5)

Once the Father's predetermined number of saints have experienced the final resurrection on Judgment Day, they will no longer experience marriage or multiply. According to Irenaeus, the rapture of the immortal children of God no longer given in marriage will occur at the final resurrection.

Irenaeus builds his case against the Gnostic heresies around the fact that both the current human body and this current earth are inherently good as the Creator originally created them by referencing God's plan to resurrect this same kind of body when the saints inherit the restored Genesis earth in the future 1,000-year messianic kingdom. If the natural human body is such an evil containment vessel, then why would God resurrect it? Irenaeus reasoned that God's millennial restoration of the natural human bodies of his people on the restored earth is absolute proof that God the Creator considers the body itself good and not an evil vessel that he intends to save us from when we die, as asserted by the Gnostics.

God never abandons this good body he created for his people. Instead, he resurrects it twice—once as a restored natural body in the Son's messianic kingdom and then again as a new kind of incorruptible or imperishable body no longer given in marriage at the final resurrection on Judgment Day when the saints are taken to the "super-celestial place" in the very presence of the Father.

His understanding of the two resurrections can be formulated as follows:

- First resurrection = natural bodies of the departed saints in the messianic kingdom as defined by the prophets and Jesus, or "'those that are left shall multiply in the earth. And they shall build houses, and shall inhabit them themselves: and plant vineyards, and eat of them themselves.' For all these and other words were unquestionably spoken in reference to the resurrection of the just, . . ." or, "the inheritance of the earth . . . and the resurrection of His disciples in the flesh. For the new flesh which rises again is the same which also received the new cup [on the earth]. . . . for to drink of that which flows from the vine pertains to flesh, and not spirit."

- Final resurrection = the raptured spiritual bodies of the saints: "all those who have been enrolled for [eternal] life shall rise again, having their own bodies . . . shall then cease from any longer begetting and being begotten, from marrying and being given in marriage."

Early millennialists, who were "right-minded Christians," understood from the Old Testament prophets, the teachings of Jesus, the book of Revelation, as well as oral traditions from the apostle John that the first resurrection was for those who believed in Christ and was of new flesh that is the same natural body of flesh as that of the disciples when they were on this earth and ate real food and drank real wine with Christ. As Abraham's spiritual descendants, these resurrected saints will experience the inheritance of the earth for one thousand years in bodies that will once again eat and drink real wine, marry, and reproduce as foretold by Isaiah, Ezekiel, and the prophets. Even Jesus promised that the saints will receive a hundredfold in the renewal of this Genesis creation when the meek will inherit the earth.

After all the saints have experienced the resurrection of their natural bodies—as defined by Isaiah and Ezekiel—and dwelt a "thousand years in Jerusalem" and become accustomed to a righteous world, then the final resurrection will take place at the general resurrection on Judgment Day, which is the "eternal resurrection" for the children of God destined for the Father's eternal kingdom. In this final resurrection—as defined by Jesus—the sons of God will be made immortal and, like the angels, shall neither marry nor be given in marriage.

Early millennialists were not the most organized writers, and their teachings on the two resurrections can be confusing, which may explain why modern scholars have misunderstood their distinctions between the two kinds of resurrections. Because modern premillennialists strongly believe the first resurrection represents the rapture of the saints, they have a difficult time accepting that the early millennialists believed the first resurrection will be of the natural body and the final resurrection after the millennium will be of the raptured spiritual body.

Origen (c. AD 185–254)

We can also determine how Irenaeus and others of like persuasion understood the first resurrection by reading their contemporary amillennial critics. Origen was one of the early critics of a literal millennium. He was more Platonic in his view of the world than Irenaeus and was repulsed by any vision of a literal earthly paradise that celebrated the pleasures of the flesh rather than those of the mind and spirit. He also developed a hermeneutic that interpreted many of the Jewish prophecies allegorically. Although many in the early church considered Origen a heretic for his universalism—the belief that all fallen men will eventually go to heaven—he was a well-read and highly respected scholar in his day and taught at the famous School of Alexandria. As a contemporary of many of these early millennialists, he was in a much better position than we are today to understand what they taught. Here are some of his observations:

> Certain persons, then, refusing the labor of thinking, and adopting a superficial view of the letter of the law [and the prophets], and yielding rather in some measure to the indulgence of their own desires and lusts, being disciples of the letter alone [literalists], are of opinion that the fulfillment of the promises of the future [messianic kingdom] are to be looked for in bodily pleasure and luxury; and therefore they especially desire to have again, after the resurrection [the "first resurrection"], such bodily structures as may never be without the power of eating, and drinking, and performing all the functions of flesh and blood [natural human body], not following the opinion of the Apostle Paul regarding the resurrection of a spiritual body [the raptured body]. And consequently they say, that after the resurrection there will be marriages, and the begetting of children, imagining to themselves that the earthly city of Jerusalem is to be rebuilt, its foundations laid in precious stones, and its walls constructed of jasper, and its battlements of crystal; that it is to have a wall composed of many precious stones, as jasper, and sapphire, . . . Moreover, they think that the natives of other countries are to be given them as the ministers of their pleasures, whom they are to employ either as tillers of the field or builders of walls, . . . and they think that they are to receive the wealth of the nations to live on, . . . And these views they think to establish on the authority of the prophets by those promises which are written regarding Jerusalem [Isaiah, Ezekiel, Micah, etc.]; . . . And from the New Testament also they quote the saying of the Savior, in which He makes a promise to His disciples concerning the joy of wine, saying, "Henceforth I shall not drink of this cup, until I drink it with you new in My Father's kingdom." . . . they think they

are to be kings and princes, like those earthly monarchs who now exist; chiefly, as it appears, on account of that expression in the Gospel: "Have thou power over five cities." And to speak shortly, according to the manner of things in this life in all similar matters, do they desire the fulfillment of all things looked for in the promises, viz., that what now is should exist again. Such are the views of those who, while believing in Christ [true Christians], understand the divine Scriptures in a sort of Jewish sense, drawing from them nothing worthy of the divine promises.[10]

Origen understood that Irenaeus and other Christian millennialists of his day were teaching that "after the resurrection," the departed saints will have natural Adamic bodies and "there will be marriages and the begetting of children" in the restored "earthly city of Jerusalem" based on the "authority of the prophets" and the New Testament "saying of the Savior." He ridicules them because they placed the second coming in conjunction with the resurrection of the natural body instead of in conjunction with the raptured spiritual body as taught by Paul.

He did not criticize them, however, as being heretical or hedonistic, although he did criticize them for having a carnal view of Christ's kingdom: "yielding rather in some measure to the indulgence of their own desires and lusts." When he says there is some measure of carnality in their teachings, there is some truth in this criticism. For example, Irenaeus believed that Christ will miraculously create a feast of all kinds of food for them, and they "shall not be engaged in any earthly occupation; but shall have a table at hand prepared for the saints by God, supplying them with all sorts of dishes" (AH V.33.2). And then there was the oral tradition alluded to by Irenaeus, when the vineyards will produce ten-thousandfold branches, twigs, shoots, clusters, grapes, and an incredible abundance of wine (AH V.33.3, 4). For someone like Origen, who held a Neoplatonic view of life and an allegorical understanding of many of the *earthly* messianic promises, Irenaeus's sometimes hyper-literal interpretation of God's earthly kingdom leaned too far toward the "indulgence of their own desires and lusts."

In defense of Irenaeus, although guilty of "some measure" of exaggeration of the earthly pleasures of the millennium, he did envision an Edenic paradise that would celebrate a righteous life in a godly kingdom—not a carnal or hedonistic life. He believed the earth will be restored by its Creator to a pristine condition and will produce an abundance of food in a positive way, similar to God's promises to Israel that they were to inherit the Promised Land flowing with milk and honey—and, of course, an abundance of wine (cf. Joel 3:17–18). The abundance of good wine in the messianic kingdom is indicative of the goodness of this Genesis creation with mankind being given in marriage and filling the earth, which is why Christ, in his first

---

[10] Origen, *De Principiis* II.11.2.

miracle at the wedding at Cana, celebrated human marriage by creating an abundance of the very best wine (John 2:6–11).

Origen's criticism of their Jewish sense of an understanding of the Scriptures is a reference to their understanding of the Old Testament prophecies, such as Ezekiel's vision of the valley of dry bones being reconstituted as human bodies that subsequently marry and have children on the restored earth. The Jewish Old Testament did not envision the New Testament kind of resurrection of an immortal spiritual body not given in marriage for the sons of God destined for a heavenly kingdom as taught by Jesus and Paul, which is why Origen criticizes their understanding of the Scriptures as not "worthy of the divine [New Testament] promises."

Origen is also criticizing their Jewish hermeneutic for adopting what he believed was "a superficial view of the letter of the law" and the prophets, whereby the promises made to Abraham and Israel are literally extended to his seed, the church, such that there will be a literal Promised Land or messianic kingdom revolving around the "earthly city of Jerusalem."

But if there is any doubt about whether Justin, Irenaeus, and other early millennialists believed the first resurrection was of the natural body or of the raptured body, Origen's description of their beliefs confirms their belief that it was of the natural body: "And consequently they say, that after the resurrection there will be marriages, and the begetting of children."

Nonetheless, some patristic scholars assert that Origen's observations are directed, not at the millennial teachings of orthodox writers like Justin and Irenaeus, but at the carnal millennialism of the Gnostic heretics, such as the Jewish heretic Cerinthus (c. 100), when he describes millennialists as having a Jewish sense of believing in the resurrection of natural bodies that would experience the "indulgence of their own desires and lusts" and "marriage." Francis Gumerlock, an amillennial patristic scholar, states the following: "Origen was referring to the carnal millennialism of Cerinthus."[11] Was Origen referring to Irenaeus or Cerinthus?

During the ante-Nicene period, there were heretical versions of the millennium that also taught that the first resurrection was of the natural body. Cerinthus, for example, advocated a carnal or even hedonistic vision of the millennial kingdom. Cerinthus was reputed to have been John's contemporary and was believed to have been a Jew by birth or conversion. He synthesized three strains of thought of his day: legalist Judaism including the Old Testament vision of an "earthly" messianic kingdom, Greco-Roman hedonism, and Gnosticism. A very strange synthesis indeed. Hedonism was associated with the heathen celebration of carnal pleasures of the fleshly body, such as gluttony and licentious sex and orgies; hedonists believed that

---

[11] Francis Gumerlock, Professor of Historical, Biblical, and Systematic Theology, Providence Theological Seminary (e-mail message to author, January 10, 2011).

there is no afterlife in which one has to face judgment and be accountable for deeds done on this earth. Cerinthus combines these heathen pleasures with the Jewish vision of an earthly paradise resulting in a millennial cerebration of the carnal flesh. As such, the first resurrection of the natural body provides an opportunity for even more gluttony, drunkenness, and sexual pleasure. The millennium becomes a heathen paradise on earth.

Cerinthus conjoins this vision of a carnal millennial kingdom with the bizarre beliefs of the Gnostics who taught that on the last day of this earth, only the pure spirit will be resurrected into the mysterious heavenly realm—not the body. The Gnostics believed that the reason the current physical body of flesh and blood produces such carnal passions and pleasures is that the material earth and the natural body were made by an inferior god and are, therefore, inherently depraved. This is why the current world and the human body are destined for annihilation by a superior God, and why only the liberated spirit ascends to the heavenly realm.

Cerinthus may have reasoned that while we are still in this carnal, inferior world made by an inferior god or angel, we might as well fulfill the purposes of this god or angel and experience all the carnal passions and pleasure of the flesh possible, especially after the first resurrection of the natural body in the Jewish messianic kingdom. During this millennial kingdom, as envisioned by the Jewish prophets and the apostle John, our sensuous natural bodies will revel in gluttony, drunkenness, and the sensual pleasures of sex in orgies associated with marriage feasts—before this inferior world is destroyed, our spirits are liberated, and we enter into the mysterious disembodied "super-celestial realm" of heaven. These chiliastic heresies were easily recognized by the early church fathers, including Irenaeus, who identified the Gnostic heretic Cerinthus several times in his books *Against Heresies*: "Cerinthus, again, a man who was educated in the wisdom of the Egyptians, taught that the world was not made by the primary God, but by a certain Power far separated from him" (*AH* I.26.1; cf. III.2.1; III.3.3–4; III.11.1).

The church historian Eusebius (c. 263–339), an amillennialist and no friend of millennialism, also makes a definite distinction between Cerinthus's heretical form of millennialism and those of sincere Christian millennialists like Irenaeus. He quotes Irenaeus and several other notable Christians who condemn Cerinthus's carnal visions of millennialism.[12] Eusebius describes Cerinthus as envisioning an "earthly" millennium as a time of "pleasures of the body" that are "altogether sensual" in nature with marriage feasts associated with pagan festivals that include "sacrifices and the slaying of victims"—a reference to human sacrifices taking place at these hedonistic feasts. Cerinthus claims that his visions of a carnal millennial kingdom came

---

[12] Eusebius, *Church History*, III.28.1-6.

by special revelations that were shown him by angels. He is characterized by Eusebius as an enemy of the Scriptures of God and as the author of heresy, deceiving men as he falsely claims that these teachings come from the apostle John. Eusebius notes that even Irenaeus calls him "an enemy of the truth" and describes his teachings as "abominable false doctrines." Cerinthus's heretical vision of the millennial kingdom was recognized as extremely hedonistic and even pagan by early church fathers.

Unlike Eusebius, who references Cerinthus by name, Origen references "certain persons" who believed in millennialism without naming anyone, which makes the analysis of whose teachings he was referring to a little more difficult. But notice that, even though he may not have agreed with their interpretation of the "divine Scriptures" and even took issue with some of their exaggerations of the bodily pleasures of the millennium, he still describes these millennialists as sincere Christian believers: "Such are the views of those who, while believing in Christ [true Christians], understand the divine Scriptures in a sort of Jewish sense." In contrast, Origen would never have described Cerinthus as a true believer in Christ or as someone who came close to understanding the "divine Scriptures." Origen's argument was with Irenaeus and other orthodox Christian millennialists who truly believed in the Scriptures, not with Gnostic heretics such as Cerinthus.

As a highly educated contemporary of many early millennialists, Origen distinguished between the heretical views of Cerinthus and those opinions of sincere Christians like Justin and Irenaeus. There is nothing of hedonistic nature in Origen's description of his fellow Christian millennialists, and he *never* describes them as heretics as Eusebius describes Cerinthus, even though he did not agree with their vision of the millennial kingdom and even ridicules their teachings regarding a literal worldly kingdom based on the resurrection of the natural bodies of the saints.

The early orthodox Christian millennialists may have believed the first resurrection was of the natural body that would eat, drink, and experience marriage, but that does not mean they were in the same camp as the chiliastic heretics like Cerinthus who believed in the resurrection of a carnal natural body that would revel in hedonistic behavior and even violent acts of human sacrifice in the millennium. It was not belief in the resurrection of the natural body that was branded as heresy by Eusebius, Irenaeus, and many others, but their pagan and hedonistic distortions of the millennial kingdom.

Irenaeus may have believed in a resurrection of the natural body with "eating and drinking and marrying" in the 1,000-year restoration, but his vision was based on the Scriptures. God's Genesis creation is inherently "good" when functioning properly.

Since Origen's description of Irenaeus's teachings is so important and revealing, we must establish that he is referring to Christian millennialists like Irenaeus and not heretical versions of chiliasm. Reading Origen's critique, it becomes evident that he wrote his observations as if he had Irenaeus's books open on his desk and was reviewing them. The following point-by-point comparison should prove this fact.

• [Origen] Certain persons, . . . are of opinion that the fulfillment of the promises of the future [messianic kingdom] are to be looked for in bodily pleasure and luxury; and therefore they especially desire to have again, after the resurrection, such bodily structures as may never be without the power of eating, and drinking, and performing all the functions of flesh and blood [natural human body] = [Irenaeus] The predicted blessing therefore, belongs unquestionably to the times of the kingdom, when the righteous shall bear rule upon their rising from the dead; when also the creation, having been renovated and set free, shall fructify with an abundance of all kinds of food, from the dew of heaven, and from the fertility of the earth (AH V.33.1).

• [Origen] . . . that after the resurrection there will be marriages, and the begetting of children = [Irenaeus] And when these things are done, he says, "God will remove men far away, and those that are left shall multiply in the earth. And they shall build houses, and shall inhabit them themselves: and plant vineyards, and eat of them themselves." For all these and other words were unquestionably spoken in reference to the resurrection of the just [the "first resurrection"], . . . (AH V.35.1).

• [Origen] And from the New Testament also they quote the saying of the Saviour, in which He makes a promise to His disciples concerning the joy of wine, saying, "Henceforth I shall not drink of this cup, until I drink it with you new in My Father's kingdom" = [Irenaeus] ". . . But I say unto you, I will not drink henceforth of the fruit of this vine, until that day when I will drink it new with you in my Father's kingdom." Thus, then, He will Himself renew the inheritance of the earth, . . . He promised to drink of the fruit of the vine with His disciples, thus indicating both these points: the inheritance of the earth [millennium] in which the new fruit of the vine is drunk, and the resurrection of His disciples in the flesh. For the new flesh which rises again is the same which also received the new cup [natural body] . . . (AH V.33.1).

• [Origen] . . . according to the manner of things in this life in all similar matters, do they desire the fulfillment of all things looked for in the promises, viz., that what now is should exist again = [Irenaeus] For it is just that in that very creation in which they toiled or were afflicted, . . . and that in the creation in which they were slain because of their love to God, in that they should be revived again . . . (AH V.32.1).

• [Origen] . . . not following the opinion of the Apostle Paul regarding the resurrection of a spiritual body = [Irenaeus] For the new flesh which rises again is the same which also received the new cup . . . (AH V.33.1).

- [Origen] . . . imagining to themselves that the earthly city of Jerusalem is to be rebuilt, its foundations laid in precious stones, and its walls constructed of jasper, and its battlements of crystal; that it is to have a wall composed of many precious stones, as jasper, and sapphire, and chalcedony, and emerald, and sardonyx, . . . = [Irenaeus] Then again, speaking of Jerusalem, and of Him reigning there, Isaiah declares, ". . . Behold, a righteous king shall reign, and princes shall rule with judgment." And with regard to the foundation on which it shall be rebuilt, he says: "Behold, I will lay in order for thee a carbuncle stone, and sapphire for thy foundations; and I will lay thy ramparts with jasper, and thy gates with crystal, and thy wall with choice stones: . . ." (AH V.14.4).
- [Origen] Such are the views of those who, while believing in Christ, understand the divine Scriptures in a sort of Jewish sense = [Irenaeus] Thus, then, the promise of God, which He gave to Abraham, remains steadfast. . . . "I will give this land to thy seed, from the river of Egypt even unto the great river Euphrates." If, then, God promised him the inheritance of the land, yet he did not receive it during all the time of his sojourn there, it must be, that together with his seed [Gentile believers], that is, those who fear God and believe in Him, he shall receive it at the resurrection of the just [in the millennial kingdom] (AH V.32.2).
- [Origen] And these views they think to establish on the authority of the prophets by those promises . . . = [Irenaeus] Then, too, Isaiah himself has plainly declared that there shall be joy of this nature at the resurrection of the just, when he says: "The dead shall rise again; . . ." And this again Ezekiel also says: "Behold, I will open your tombs, and will bring you forth out of your graves; . . . and I will place you on your own land, and ye shall know that I am the LORD" (AH V.34.1).

The correspondence between Origen's description of "certain persons" who were millennialists in his day *and* the writings of Irenaeus and even Justin are remarkable. The above comparisons clearly demonstrate that Origen's criticisms were pointed at orthodox Christian millennialists. There is very little, if any, correspondence to chiliastic heretics like Cerinthus.

The famous patristic scholar D. H. Kromminga concurs with my assessment that Origen was referring to Christian millennialists: "Although in all this chiliasm is not mentioned by name, it is plain that he [Origen] had Christians in mind who appealed to such texts as Matt. 26:29 [drink again of the fruit of the vine]; 5:6 [meek inherit the earth]; Luke 19:17, 19 [rule over cities]—all from the New Testament."[13]

---

[13] D. H. Kromminga, *The Millennium in the Church* (Grand Rapids: Eerdmans, 1945), 105.

Origen's references to Irenaeus and other ante-Nicene millennialists as believing "that after the resurrection there will be marriages, and the begetting of children" provide solid collaborating evidence that they believed the first resurrection of the departed saints will be of the natural body—not the raptured body. The very logic of Origen's criticism of the Christian millennialists was their belief that the first resurrection in conjunction with the second coming was of the *natural body* (as described by the prophets)—instead of in conjunction with the *raptured transformed spiritual body* as taught by Paul. Origen mocks them for associating Christ's second coming with the resurrection of a natural body of flesh and blood, when Paul so clearly associates the second coming with the raptured, spiritual body:

> Because if they believe the apostle, that a body which arises in glory, and power, and incorruptibility, has already become spiritual, it appears absurd and contrary to his meaning to say that it can again be entangled with the passions of flesh and blood, seeing the apostle manifestly declares that "flesh and blood shall not inherit the kingdom of God, nor shall corruption inherit incorruption." But how do they understand the declaration of the apostle, "We shall all be changed"? (*Princ.* II.10.3)

Origen is right. Justin, Commodianus, and Irenaeus do a very poor job of explaining how Christ's second coming can be associated with the resurrection of the natural body instead of the immortal spiritual body as taught by Paul. They ignore this inconsistency and do not wrestle with Paul's description of the raptured body at Christ's second coming.

Victorinus (c. AD 240–320)

Victorinus, bishop of Pettau, is the first recorded ante-Nicene millennialist to respond to Origen's pointed criticism. Historians believe he wrote the first complete commentary on the book of Revelation sometime around AD 258. Writing after Irenaeus, he drew heavily from his teachings. His commentary was highly respected by later church fathers, even by those who were amillennialists. Unfortunately, his commentary on Revelation 20 and 21 was subsequently altered by Jerome (c. 347–420), an ardent post-Nicene amillennialist, to remove all chiliastic vestiges.

For example, Jerome changed Victorinus's commentary on the first resurrection in Revelation 20 from a description of a literal resurrection of the bodies of the departed saints to one of only the souls of the saints: "The first resurrection is that of the souls through faith. This resurrection occurs in the present."[14] Jerome was part of a conspiracy to stamp out chiliasm by

---

[14] Victorinus of Pettau, *Commentarius in Apocalypsin* (*The Ancient Christian Texts*, Downers Grove: InterVarsity Press, 2011), 20.2.

destroying chiliastic writings. It would not be a surprise to discover he played a part in the disappearance of Papias's books.

When analyzing Victorinus's views on Revelation, I will be quoting from a recent translation that uses the original unaltered transcript rediscovered in 1916. Victorinus generally follows the outline in Revelation with the millennium followed by the final resurrection and the eternal new heavens and new earth. But when it comes to the description of the New Jerusalem coming down out of heaven (Rev. 21–22), he uses a form of recapitulation and asserts that the New Jerusalem comes down to the Genesis earth at the beginning of the millennium instead of coming down to the new heavens and new earth in the eternal kingdom:

> At the time of the kingdom and of the first resurrection, the holy city will appear, which, it says, will come down from heaven. It will be foursquare and decorated with jewels of different value, color and kind, and it will be like pure gold, that is, clear and transparent. It says that its street is paved with crystal and that the river of life flows through the middle, as do fountains of the waters of life. (CA 20.1)

Most important, he addresses the problem mentioned by Origen of having Christ's second coming coincide with the first resurrection of the natural bodies of the departed saints at the beginning of the millennium instead of with the final resurrection of the immortal spiritual bodies as taught by Paul. He attempts to solve this contradiction by differentiating between two kinds of trumpet blasts associated with two resurrections as referenced by Paul. The first trumpet blast mentioned by Paul is associated with the first resurrection of the natural bodies when Christ returns to this earth; then, Paul mentions a last trumpet associated with the final resurrection of the transformed "spiritual body" that takes us to the eternal new heavens and new earth.

Let's first look at Paul's teachings on the raptured body and then look at how Victorinus applies these Scriptures to Revelation 20. In the following verse Paul does not technically describe the resurrected saints as being "immortal" or "transformed" during this particular trumpet call:

> For the Lord himself will descend from heaven with a cry of command, with the voice of an archangel, and *with the sound of the trumpet of God.* And the dead in Christ will rise first. Then we who are alive, who are left, will be caught up together with them in the clouds to meet the Lord in the air, and so we will always be with the Lord. (1 Thess. 4:16–17)

Today this is often presented as a description of the rapture of the saints. But that is not how Victorinus interpreted this trumpet call. Because Paul did not specifically reference the immortal or transformed body, Victorinus believed Paul was not describing the resurrection of the glorified spiritual body when Christ returns to this earth.

According to Victorinus, Paul only describes the transformed spiritual body in his letter to the Corinthians when he writes about the *last trumpet* and the corresponding final resurrection on the last day. In this resurrection of the spiritual body, Paul does not specifically connect the second coming of Christ with this last trumpet call of God:

> Behold! I tell you a mystery. We shall not all sleep, but we shall be changed, in a moment, in the twinkling of an eye, *at the last trumpet*. For the trumpet will sound, and the dead will be raised imperishable, and we shall be changed. For this perishable body must put on the imperishable, and this mortal body must put on immortality. (1 Cor. 15:51–53)

With this last trumpet, Victorinus believes Paul is describing the final resurrection of all humans, with believers being raised into immortal spiritual bodies that will inherit heaven *and* unbelievers being raised into immortal bodies destined for eternal damnation. Victorinus is struggling to reconcile Christ's return to this earth with the first resurrection of the natural body, which obviously requires some creative interpretation of Paul's teachings. If you read Victorinus's commentary carefully, you will understand his thesis concerning the two trumpet calls representing the two resurrections:

> At the time of this first resurrection will also be that future, beautiful city [New Jerusalem on this earth] that this writing has described. Also Paul spoke in this manner to the church in Macedonia concerning this first resurrection: "For this we declare to you," he says, "by the word of God, that at the trumpet of God the Lord himself will descend from heaven to arouse [the dead from sleep]. And the dead in Christ will rise first; then we who are alive shall be caught up together with them in the clouds to meet the Lord in the air, and so we shall always be with the Lord." We have heard that he speaks of a trumpet [the first trumpet and the second coming described in 1 Thess. 4:16–17]. We observe that in another place the apostle mentions another [different] trumpet. He says to the Corinthians, "At the last trumpet the dead will rise"—they become immortal—"and we shall be changed" [the last trumpet associated with the spiritual body described by Paul in 1 Cor. 15:51–53]. He says that the dead will rise immortal in order to suffer their punishments [unbelievers at the general resurrection destined for the lake of fire]; however, it is clear that we [believers] will be changed and clothed in glory [the immortal, glorified, spiritual body]. When, therefore, we hear that there is a "last trumpet," we must understand that there has also been a first trumpet. Now these are the two resurrections. (*CA* 20.2)

Victorinus believes there are two resurrections—the first resurrection represented by the trumpet identified in Paul's letter to the Thessalonians, and the final and general resurrection represented by the last trumpet on Judgment Day when unbelievers will be raised into immortal bodies to suffer eternal punishment and believers will be raised into immortal bodies in glory, when we, as Paul says, "shall be changed" into eternal spiritual bodies that are made imperishable (1 Cor. 15). Thus, unlike modern premillennialists, Victorinus believed the resurrection of the glorified "spiritual body," as defined by Paul in 1 Corinthians 15, occurs *after* the millennium at the final resurrection when the saints are taken to the new heavens and new earth.

Victorinus defines the first resurrection of the first trumpet in the 1,000-year messianic kingdom in almost the same manner as Irenaeus. Here are some parallels with Irenaeus's teachings:

> The Scripture shows extensively that the kings of [every] region and nation, who are its servants, will bring their wealth into [the city]. . . . But here "city" refers to every region of the eastern provinces that were promised to the patriarch Abraham. It says, "Look into the heaven from the place in which you are now standing"—that is, "from the great river Euphrates to the river of Egypt"—"all the land which you see I will give to you and to your seed" (*CA* 21.2) = see Irenaeus: *AH* V.32.2; V.33.2; V.34.1.

> In this kingdom [Christ] promised to his servants, "Whoever shall have left father or mother or brother or sister for my name's sake, he will receive as a reward a hundredfold now, and in the future he will possess eternal life" (*CA* 21.5) = see Irenaeus: *AH* V.18.2-3.

> In this kingdom those who have been defrauded of their goods for the name of the Lord, also the many who have been killed by every kind of crime and imprisonment—for before the coming of the Lord, the holy prophets were stoned, killed, and cut in half—will receive their consolation, that is, their crowns and celestial rewards . . . (*CA* 21.5) = see Irenaeus: *AH* V.32.1.

> In this kingdom the whole of creation will be preserved and reestablished and will, by the command of God, bring forth good things within it. . . . In this kingdom "they will drink wine and be anointed with oil and be given over to joy" (*CA* 21.5) = see Irenaeus: *AH* V.32.1; V.33.1-4.

> Before his passion, the Lord made mention of this kingdom when he said to the apostles: "I shall not drink again of the fruit of this vine, until I shall drink it new with you in the future kingdom." This is the "hundredfold," which is ten thousand more or less (*CA* 21.6) = see Irenaeus: *AH* V.33.1.

Victorinus's descriptions of the first resurrection and the messianic kingdom as described by the prophets are strikingly similar to those found in Irenaeus's writings. He makes the same connection with the promises made to Abraham, which is a central tenant of Irenaeus's biblical theology. We have already examined Irenaeus's position that the first resurrection was of the natural body. Thus, even though Victorinus does not directly define the nature of the first resurrection, the unmistakable parallels to Irenaeus's teachings can lead to a reasonable conclusion that his beliefs were essentially the same as Irenaeus's. This conclusion is reinforced by the fact that Victorinus clearly places the glorified spiritual body, according to 1 Corinthians 15, in conjunction with the final resurrection on Judgment Day—not with the first resurrection.

Origen was dead by the time Victorinus wrote his commentary on Revelation, but Origen most likely would have heaped scorn on Victorinus's solution of the two trumpet blasts mentioned by Paul as representing two kinds of resurrections. These major inconsistencies and obvious contradictions left their teachings open for legitimate criticism by amillennialists of their day. They had the second coming occurring at the wrong time—at the beginning of the millennium in conjunction with the resurrection of the natural body instead of at the end of the millennium in conjunction with the raptured spiritual body—which is why Victorinus was forced to be very creative in his interpretation of Paul's teachings. Victorinus at least attempted to arrive at a plausible explanation for the second coming of Christ to this earth coinciding with the first resurrection of the natural body.

Lactantius (c. AD 245–325)

Lactantius is another well-known representative of early millennialism who wrote toward the end of the ante-Nicene period. He was a famous rhetorician and contemporary of Eusebius. Eusebius was a trusted friend and advisor to Emperor Constantine at the same time that Lactantius was a tutor to the emperor's son, Crispus. Both men were highly educated and important historians of the period. Lactantius also believed the first resurrection of the departed saints was of their *natural* bodies that would experience marriage and bear godly children, and that the resurrected saints would sit on thrones and rule over the survivors of the Tribulation with Christ dwelling in the midst of all mortal human beings:

But He [Christ], when He shall have destroyed unrighteousness, and executed His great judgment [at his second coming at the end of the Tribulation], and shall have recalled to life the righteous [first resurrection], who have lived from the beginning [all the departed saints], will be engaged among men [survivors of the Tribulation] a thousand years, and will rule them with most just command. Which the Sibyl [female prophet] proclaims in another place, as she utters her inspired predictions:—"Hear me, ye mortals; an everlasting King reigns." [Christ reigns among mortals who survive the Tribulation *and* those who are resurrected.] Then they who shall be alive in their bodies shall not die [the resurrected saints will live for the entire thousand years], but during those thousand years shall produce an infinite multitude [marriage and reproduction], and their offspring shall be holy, and beloved by God; but they who shall be raised from the dead shall preside over the living as judges [sit on thrones]. But the nations shall not be entirely extinguished [during Christ's judgments at the end of the Tribulation], but some shall be left as a victory for God. . . . About the same time also the prince of the devils, who is the contriver of all evils, shall be bound with chains, and shall be imprisoned during the thousand years of the heavenly rule in which righteousness shall reign in the world, so that he may contrive no evil against the people of God. After His [Christ's] coming the righteous shall be collected from all the earth [first resurrection of saints from all nations], and the judgment being completed [at the end of the Tribulation], the sacred city shall be planted in the middle of the earth, in which God Himself the builder may dwell together with the righteous [Christ's physical return], bearing rule in it [the restored earthly Jerusalem]. . . . the earth will open its fruitfulness, and bring forth most abundant fruits of its own accord; the rocky mountains shall drip with honey; streams of wine shall run down, and rivers flow with milk: in short, the world itself shall rejoice, and all nature exult, being rescued and set free from the dominion of evil and impiety, and guilt and error [during the regeneration of this Genesis earth when Satan is bound and Christ rules the world].[15]

Lactantius describes the millennial kingdom as an Adamic paradise experienced by both mortals that survive the Tribulation as well as the saints from all ages ("who have lived from the beginning") that are "recalled to life" through the "first resurrection" and will subsequently experience marriage with an almost "infinite multitude" of holy "offspring." He believes the resurrected saints will sit on thrones and "preside over the living as judges."

After describing the millennium, Lactantius proceeds to describe Satan's final rebellion, the end of this Genesis creation, the final resurrection that includes the *rapture* of the saints, Judgment Day for unbelievers, and the eternal new heavens and new earth when the raptured saints not given in marriage will be in the very presence of God Almighty. He believed the current earth is not annihilated on the last day but is purged by fire and the eternal new heavens and new earth remain a form of the current earth renewed for God's eternal children:

But when the thousand years shall be completed, the world shall be renewed by God, and the heavens shall be folded together, and the earth shall be changed [the new heavens and new earth], and God shall transform men into the similitude of angels [the final transformation of the sons of God

---

[15] Lactantius, *The Divine Institutes*, VII.24.1-4.

into immortal bodies who, like the angels, will not be given in marriage], and they shall be white as snow; and they shall always be employed in the sight of the Almighty [very presence of God the Father], and shall make offerings to their Lord, and serve Him forever [in the eternal kingdom]. At the same time [on Judgment Day when the books are opened] shall take place that second and public resurrection of all [the general resurrection], in which the unrighteous shall be raised to everlasting punishments [in the lake of fire] (*DI* VII.26.2). . . . After these things [the final judgment and final resurrection] God will renew the world [the new heavens and new earth], and transform the righteous into the forms of angels [rapture], that, being presented with the garment of immortality, they may serve God forever; and this will be the kingdom of God, which shall have no end [an eternal kingdom]. (*DI* VII.72)

Only *after* the "thousand years shall be completed" at the final resurrection on Judgment Day will the saints receive their raptured and "transformed" immortal bodies and, like angels, no longer experience marriage in the Father's kingdom. In summary, Lactantius believed the first resurrection is of the natural body and the final resurrection is of the raptured immortal body because it is destined for the eternal new heavens and new earth.

The Eschatology of the Ante-Nicene Millennialists

Early Christian millennialists believed that Revelation 20 served as a conduit for the fulfillment of all Old Testament messianic prophecies concerning the Son's earthly kingdom. John did not need to provide us with extensive details on the millennial reign of Christ because considerable information already existed. They believed all that was needed was to link John's vision to the wealth of information already existing in the writings of the prophets, such as Isaiah, Ezekiel, Daniel, Jeremiah, and Micah. In the restoration in this age, the Old Testament prophets envisioned a future messianic kingdom where the resurrected people of God, Jew and Gentile, will marry, have children, build houses, plant vineyards, and live long lives full of peace and happiness in a restored Jerusalem in the restored land of Israel on a restored Genesis earth. In their minds, the first resurrection John described must be of the natural bodies of the departed saints, when God's people from all time from every nation will repopulate the restored Edenic earth under the reign of Christ. Origen's description of their beliefs confirms this.

If the ante-Nicene millennialists were asked when Christ returns, their answer would be at the end of the Tribulation when the millennium begins. And if they were asked when the rapture occurs, their answer would be *after* the millennium at the final resurrection on Judgment Day when the children of God have their bodies transformed and glorified and taken to the Father's eternal kingdom of heaven. The rapture would be postrestoration—or after a literal restoration of this Genesis creation and the Adamic order of being.

Apart from the misplaced second coming, it could be argued that the eschatology of the ante-Nicene millennialists is essentially postrestoration. The transformation of the saints into immortal spiritual bodies not given in marriage is *after* a literal restoration as envisioned by John and the prophets and occurs on Judgment Day at the general resurrection of believers and unbelievers.

It is remarkable that early millennialists claimed to have an oral history from direct disciples of John who reported that John taught the first resurrection was of the natural body. They also recognized that this teaching matched and confirmed Isaiah's and Ezekiel's teachings on resurrection and restoration. It is important to note, however, that when they placed Christ's return to this earth at the beginning of the millennium instead of at the end of the millennium, they never claim that this particular teaching came from an oral teaching from the apostle John or his immediate disciples, such as Polycarp or Papias. Their arrival at this conclusion appears to be an assumption on their part as they attempted to sort out the prophetic puzzle.

What probably confused them was Paul's condensed version of the prophetic future in his letter to the Thessalonians in which he associates the overthrow of the Antichrist with the second coming of Christ, skipping the restoration altogether (2 Thess. 2:1–8). They associated the second coming at the end of the Tribulation with the first resurrection of the natural bodies of the departed saints. Matching Paul's abbreviated and incomplete version of the biblical future with John's first resurrection of the natural body in Revelation 20, created a major flaw in their eschatology.

The church was young; early believers were just beginning to grapple with the complex book of Revelation and learn how to create a systematic and logical set of beliefs from what John and other Old and New Testament writers had revealed. Despite its inherent complexity as an apocalyptic form of literature, Revelation was the first book to provide a comprehensive sequential format of the prophetic future. But this outline had to be harmonized with the oral history and the vast amount of information from other complex books, such as Daniel, Ezekiel, and Isaiah, as well as the rest of the New Testament Scriptures, particularly the Olivet Discourse and Paul's epistles. This was no small task as evidenced by the fact that today, almost two thousand years later, theologians are still endeavoring to navigate through this revelation and make sense out of all relevant biblical data.

Nonetheless, associating the second advent with a resurrection of a natural body at the first resurrection was a critical flaw in their proposed solution. Other amillennial theologians of the time could easily refute their teachings by referencing Scriptures that plainly teach that the resurrection associated with Christ's second coming is of the immortal spiritual body, which occurs on Judgment Day. Their strange beliefs about Hades were also subject to criticism. These deficiencies, combined with a general reaction against a seemingly worldly and Jewish-centered kingdom of God, caused millennialism to gradually lose credibility and favor.

By the time Emperor Constantine convened the Council of Nicaea in AD 325, amillennialism had become the dominant view and was beginning to morph into postmillennialism with the rise of Christian Roman emperors. For Roman Christians like Augustine, the proposition of ante-Nicene millennialists that Christ would one day restore the kingdom to Israel at a time set by the Father (Acts 1:6–7) when the Jews repent (Acts 3:19–21) with Israel serving as the chief nation in a future millennial reign of Christ no longer seemed viable given that the nation of Israel no longer existed, the Jews continued to stubbornly reject their Messiah, and the Gentile nations were becoming Christian nations in place of Israel.

Summary: The Gospel Rediscovered

Early millennialists believed that a literal 1,000-year reign of Christ will take place when the departed saints come back to life on this regenerated earth in their natural bodies to enjoy a restored Genesis creation under the Lordship of Christ. They also understood that the transformation and rapture of the body into an immortal one occurs *after* the 1,000-year restoration at the final resurrection on Judgment Day when the saints are taken to the Father's eternal kingdom. They believed that believers enter into the millennium through a process of regeneration of the human body and of creation itself, and then, on the last day, we enter into the new heavens and new earth through a process of transformation.

Irenaeus, in particular, creates a hyperlink between the following key sections of Scriptures to make his case for the messianic kingdom:

- Revelation 20 ("first resurrection" and the millennial reign of Christ) = Ezekiel 37 (resurrection of the valley of dry bones and the restoration that follows) = Matthew 19:28–29 (hundredfold reward in this age during the regeneration of this Genesis earth when Christ will "sit on his glorious throne" to rule the world) = Matthew 5:5 (the meek shall inherit the earth).

Surprisingly, all modern commentaries on Ezekiel, Matthew, and Revelation fail to note Irenaeus's strategic connection of these important sections of Scriptures. In the few places that modern theologians and scholars do reference Irenaeus's views, they incorrectly point out that he believed the "first resurrection" is of the raptured body instead of the natural body.

The critical flaw in the early millennialists' eschatology was placing Christ's second coming before the millennium. They failed to understand that the ascended Christ remains seated at the right hand of the Father in heaven when he rules over this world for one thousand years, allowing Christ's second coming to occur *after* the millennium, when he returns on the last day to transform the saints, destroy this earth, judge the world, and take the immortal children of God to his Father's house for eternity.

In many ways the views expressed in this book are a rediscovery of the gospel as taught by early millennialists. The only major revision to their eschatology is that Christ rules this world from his throne in heaven at the Father's right hand without returning to this earth to establish his rule.

It is unfortunate that early millennialists misunderstood this critical piece of the puzzle. Had they understood that Christ can bind Satan and rule this world from his throne in heaven, then postrestorationalism might have become the dominant and even orthodox view of the church for the last two thousand years.

Instead, eschatology remains a perplexing subject with many competing and contradictory views. Amillennialists leave out the important millennial reign of Christ, and premillennialists associate the first resurrection with the raptured body instead of the natural body. Theologians continue to debate three very different eschatological views: premillennialism, amillennialism, and postmillennialism—none of which can be legitimized by the Scriptures in combination with oral history emanating from the apostle John.

Contemporary theologians fail to take into account two salient facts as they develop their eschatology. One, Isaiah and Ezekiel clearly describe a resurrection of the Adamic natural bodies of the departed saints at the beginning of the future messianic kingdom. Two, the ante-Nicene millennialists claimed they had oral confirmation from known disciples of John that the first resurrection mentioned by John was of a *literal* resurrection of the natural bodies of the departed saints, which harmonizes with the teachings of the prophets.

If these facts are correct literally and historically, then the primary methodology that God will use for *all* his meek followers to inherit the promised regenerated earth during Christ's reign is a massive resurrection of his departed saints into their natural bodies. Presently neither facts are recognized by modern theologians and taken into consideration when formulating their various systems of eschatology. As N. T. Wright admits, "Ezekiel 37 is perhaps the most famous of all 'resurrection' passages in the Old Testament."[16] Yet, surprisingly, none of the prevailing eschatological views consider the possibility that Ezekiel's vision is to be taken literally.

---

[16] N. T. Wright, *The Resurrection of the Son of God.* Vol. 3 of *Christian Origins and the Question of God* (Minneapolis: Fortress Press, 2003), 119.

Postrestorationalism, however, takes these two facts into consideration and integrates them into a comprehensive biblical theology. And this modified millennialism is the closest to that of early millennialists *and* the prophets. As such, this modified framework for understanding the prophetic future warrants serious consideration and vetting by theologians. Postrestorationalism could be a rediscovery of the truth that the prophets, Jesus, and the apostles were attempting to convey to us both orally and in the written Scriptures.

13

Church and State
Before Christ's Reign

During the first few hundred years of the church, the Christian faith continued to grow tremendously, gaining more and more credibility among all strata of Roman society despite periodic persecution from the Roman Empire. By the beginning of the 300s, the majority of Romans remained pagan, but a significant number had become Christians. Out of an estimated imperial population of sixty million, some scholars estimate that by AD 312 there were approximately nine million Christians, which represents about 15 percent of the population.[1]

In 312, before a major battle, Emperor Constantine had a vision of Christ; after winning the battle, he converted to Christianity. After this life-changing experience, Constantine set out to establish Christianity as the official religion of his army, hoping to ensure future victories. He did not make Christianity the official religion of the state, but he laid the ground-work for succeeding emperors to do so. During the reign of the Emperor Theodosius, in 380, Christianity became the official state religion.

The actions of Emperors Constantine and Theodosius caught the church completely off guard, thrusting it into a situation for which it was ill-prepared theologically. In the church's formative years, the debate between millennialists and amillennialists over a future reign of Christ over this world remained a mostly academic discussion. Theologians had given little consideration to the issues of church and state, because no one considered the possibility that Christianity, which had been criminalized, would ever be in a position to become the dominant religion of the Roman Empire.

---

[1] Rodney Stark, *Discovering God* (New York: HarperCollins, 2007), 313.

The early Christians had been such a small, persecuted sect within the Roman Empire that questions of church and state did not really concern them. They had never considered the implications of being in a position of authority to rule with the civil state over the spiritual affairs of the empire.

Most important, the Roman Emperors Constantine and Theodosius became Christians at a time when millennialism had lost favor and amillennialism had become the predominant view. As a result, it was now up to the prevailing amillennial theologians and church leaders to respond to these emperors' initiatives and determine how these dramatic turn of events related to Christ's reign over this world and determine what the relationship of church and state should be. It was one thing for amillennial theologians to assert that the first resurrection represents a believer's spiritual rebirth in a metaphorical one thousand years while they waited for heaven, but now they had to consider the implications of having an emperor who fancied himself a Davidic king over the new house of "Roman Israel" right here on earth. Emperor Theodosius thought the reign of Christ had, in effect, begun and wanted to set up a Christian theocracy similar to Israel's. This was a critical turning point in Western history, and its fate rested with amillennialists.

Many thought that perhaps AD 70 was the Great Tribulation Christ predicted, and the church and state were now entering into a quasi-literal millennium with Christ ruling as King of Christian kings and Lord of Roman lords. Amillennialism, which initially assumed there was no Jewish earthly kingdom before the heavenly kingdom, was beginning to respond to the dramatic change in circumstances by morphing into a form of Gentile postmillennialism, in which the Christianized Roman world was becoming Christ's kingdom on earth. Perhaps the 1,000-year messianic kingdom had actually begun!

New Testament Emphasis on Separation of Church and State

Before examining the teachings of postmillennialists, let's examine Christ's relationship to the civil state. Luke includes an account of a time when Jesus was asked to settle a small civil dispute between two brothers: "Someone in the crowd said to him, 'Teacher, tell my brother to divide the inheritance with me.' But he said to him, 'Man, who made me a judge or arbitrator over you?'" (Luke 12:13–14). This same Jesus, who refused to act as a judge and settle a simple civil dispute between two brothers concerning an inheritance, will in the future restoration decide major geopolitical disputes between nations when he exercises his messianic reign: "For out of Zion shall go forth the law, and the word of the LORD from Jerusalem. He shall judge between many peoples, and shall decide for strong nations afar off; and they shall beat their swords into plowshares" (Mic. 4:2–3).

The Pharisees, scribes, and chief priests made a determined effort to entrap Jesus in a civil dispute, so they could find grounds to accuse him before the Roman authorities, have him arrested, and put an end to his public ministry (Luke 20:19–20). Jesus had the ability to turn these schemes of entrapment into opportunities to teach important spiritual lessons. In the process, Christ made an important distinction between the civil authorities and God's kingdom.

For example, when the Jewish teachers of the law asked Jesus whether or not it was right to pay taxes to Caesar, they were trying to entrap him. If he said it was okay to pay Roman taxes, they could then accuse him of not being the Messiah, who was supposed to restore the nation to Israel and establish justice. If he said no, they could accuse him before the Roman authorities of leading an insurrection. His answer surprised and silenced them: "'Show me a denarius. Whose likeness and inscription does it have?' They said, 'Caesar's.' He said to them, 'Then render to Caesar the things that are Caesar's, and to God the things that are God's'" (Luke 20:24–25).

Christ's millennial kingdom is going to be an earthly and theocratic kingdom in which he will finally establish a comprehensive rule over spiritual and civil matters—from the smallest details of an inheritance dispute to the disputes between nations. But, as the disciples would learn, much to their disappointment, it was not time for Christ to overthrow the Roman authorities and establish his earthly reign. The church was to operate primarily in the spiritual realm with the mission of bringing to God those who belonged to him—that is, his children. Believers become citizens in the kingdom of God, which will someday manifest itself on this earth and then in heaven. But the church will have to wait until Satan is bound and removed from this world before Christ's reign over this world begins.

The disciples followed Jesus' example and did not attempt to establish his earthly kingdom after his ascension. The disciples did not go out and make disciples of all nations by attempting to establish Christian nations or theocracies by the sword. While believers wait for the restoration, the people of God function as a church, a spiritual assembly of believers with no civil covenant with God as Israel had. The church is not a theocratic nation, nor does it wield the sword while it waits for the restoration. The church functions best in a secular state with no state-established religion, where there is religious liberty and a free marketplace of ideas, beliefs, and religious establishments.

Most Western democracies today are secular states with no established state religion as Israel had. The church in America enjoys religious liberty and functions autonomously and freely as a spiritual assembly of God's people who can meet, build their own facilities, and worship freely. In American history, the U.S. Constitution was set up to be a type of covenant between the people and the civil state. The very first amendment to the

Constitution—part of the Bill of Rights—was a non-establishment clause: "Congress shall make no law respecting an establishment of religion, or prohibiting the free exercise thereof; or abridging the freedom of speech, or of the press; or the right of the people peaceably to assemble, and to petition the Government for a redress of grievances." There would be no established national religion in this covenant with the people.

In stark contrast, the Old Testament nation of Israel was not a secular state with an autonomous religious establishment. Through Moses, God had established a spiritual-civil covenant with the Jewish people that made Israel a religious state, or theocracy. When God made a covenant with the people of Israel, which became their constitution, the first part of the Ten Commandments was indeed an establishment clause: "You shall have no other gods before me. You shall not make for yourself a carved image, or any likeness of anything that is in heaven above, or that is on the earth beneath, or that is in the water under the earth. You shall not bow down to them or serve them . . ." (Deut. 5:7–9). Judaism and the worship of Yahweh was the established religion in this spiritual-civil covenant between Yahweh and the people of Israel.

There was no religious liberty in Israel. God commanded Israel to destroy the pagan deities—their images, altars, and objects of worship— when they came to possess the land of promise. Under this spiritual-civil covenant, if a false teacher or false prophet should arise among the people, they were to kill him: "But that prophet or that dreamer of dreams shall be put to death . . . So you shall purge the evil from your midst" (Deut. 13:5).

The remainder of Deuteronomy contains a great deal of statutory law to ensure that Judaism was the only practiced religion. Extensive rules and regulations were established to control not only how this worship was to be practiced but also how false prophets, false teachers, and those who worshiped pagan gods would be dealt with. Israel was to be a theocratic nation, not a pluralistic secular state with religion autonomous from the state. It was not to be a free marketplace of pagan ideas and religions—only Judaism was allowed. When God made this type of covenant with the Jewish people, he made himself clear:

> These are the statutes and rules that you shall be careful to do in the land that the LORD, the God of your fathers, has given you to possess, all the days that you live on the earth. You shall surely destroy all the places where the nations whom you shall dispossess served their gods, on the high mountains and on the hills and under every green tree. You shall tear down their altars and dash in pieces their pillars and burn their Asherim with fire. You shall chop down the carved images of their gods and destroy their name out of that place. You shall not worship the LORD your God in that way. (Deut. 12:1–4)

The kings of Israel in conjunction with the religious authorities—the Levitical priesthood and prophets—were to uphold the Mosaic law and the spiritual-civil covenant:

> And when he [the king anointed by God] sits on the throne of his kingdom, he shall write for himself in a book a copy of this law [the Mosaic law], approved by the Levitical priests. And it shall be with him, and he shall read in it all the days of his life, that he may learn to fear the LORD his God by keeping all the words of this law and these statutes, and doing them. (Deut. 17:18–19)

The Jewish civil king and the religious authorities were to work together to maintain the spiritual purity of the religious state of Israel.

As a theocratic nation, Israel had a special mission, unlike any other nation. If Israel had been a pluralistic society with an amalgam of pagan religious practices and ideas, then the unique concept of Christ as the sacrificial Lamb of God as the Savior of the world would not have been possible. The Messiah had to come into this world through a specific nation with a distinct religious ideology and set of religious practices. The Jewish concept of a Messiah necessitated at least one nation to be used by God to bring the light of the world into this dark, sinful world.

In contrast, there is no evidence in the New Testament indicating that God made a similar spiritual-civil covenant with the church as he did with Israel. Paul regularly encountered pagan temples and worshipers, false teachers, and false prophets with false dreams in the early church. To rid the church of these false teachers, he would first expose their false teaching; if they refused to repent, he would have the local church simply eject them from the church, ending any association with them. Paul did not call for their execution in accordance with Jewish law. Again, the church did not operate like Israel and use the sword of the state to maintain religious purity. The New Testament defines the role of the church to be very different from the role of Israel and its kings, priests, and prophets.

The church is an assembly of believers that transcends race and nations. The church has a spiritual covenant with God, not a spiritual-civil covenant as did Israel. If someone breaks the spiritual covenant by teaching a false doctrine, he is to be rebuked by the church leaders; if he is unrepentant, he should ultimately be expelled from the fellowship of the church. No civil authorities would be involved as they would have been in Israel. And the false teaching would not be a criminal matter for the state to resolve through force, fines, imprisonments, or execution.

The apostles did not expect the emperor to carry a copy of the New Testament and enforce the teachings of the church. Christ can build his church without the use of the sword and without the assistance of a civil king. Ideally, the civil authorities should simply allow the church to have the freedom to grow and peacefully exist without fear of persecution, allowing Christianity to compete in a free marketplace of ideas for the hearts and minds of their neighbors.

When Paul and the early church began to make inroads among the various pagan Roman communities and cities, many citizens and local political rulers felt their religious foundation threatened. They began to strike back in defense of their gods and state. Paul urged the churches to pray for freedom from this persecution by the Roman authorities. In effect, he was instructing the church to pray for religious liberty: "First of all, then, I urge that supplications, prayers, intercessions, and thanksgivings be made for all people, for kings and all who are in high positions, *that we may lead a peaceful and quiet life*, godly and dignified in every way" (1 Tim. 2:1–2).

Paul was urging the church to pray for the ability to gather and worship Christ peacefully without interference and harassment from their pagan neighbors and the pagan religious state. Paul thought religious liberty was the most effective way for the knowledge of the gospel to be spread, for he goes on to say: "This is good, and it is pleasing in the sight of God our Savior, who desires all people to be saved and *to come to the knowledge of the truth*" (1 Tim. 2:3-4). Persecution by those who practiced state-established pagan religions greatly hindered the ability of missionaries like Paul to spread the knowledge of the truth.

Most important, there is no evidence that Jesus, Paul, or any of the apostles exhorted the church to pray for the state authorities to establish Christianity as the official state religion of Rome. Christ taught his followers to pray for the Father's will to be done on earth, but he also told them to wait on the Father to establish the Son's kingdom in his own time. During this interim period of waiting on the Father, Christ and his apostles did not teach the church to pray for Rome to become a Christian nation patterned after the state of Israel.

Christ came into this world as the rightful ruler of not only Israel but of the whole world. The Creator has a right to rule over his creation. Yet, when Christ was on this earth, he refused to exercise his rightful reign or use his supernatural powers and the powers of the state to establish his kingdom. The disciples wanted him to reign as Messiah and were expecting him to do so. They often jockeyed for power in what they thought was his impending messianic kingdom. But the mature disciples followed Christ's example and did not attempt to exercise his reign over the nations for him in his absence. They, too, waited for the Father to restore the kingdoms of the world, including Israel, to his Son in the future restoration.

From a biblical perspective, only God the Creator has the right to rule this world on a civil and spiritual level. Since Christ—who was God, the Son—refused to do so, his disciples followed his example and did not attempt to establish his reign in his absence. And, as his disciples, we, too, should advocate the creation of secular states with religious freedom and liberty while we wait for the future restoration. If we are his disciples, then we should not impose Christ's reign on this world even if one of our Christian rulers desires to do so. We, along with his other disciples, are commanded by Christ to wait for the Father to set the time in the future when Christ's enemies will be made a footstool for his feet.

Paul also made it clear that he and the church did not use the weapons of the civil realm to collect what belonged to God, but rather the power of persuasion of the truth and the conviction of the Holy Spirit:

> For though we walk in the flesh, we are not waging war according to the flesh. For the weapons of our warfare are not of the flesh but have divine power to destroy strongholds. We destroy arguments and every lofty opinion raised against the knowledge of God, and take every thought captive to obey Christ. (2 Cor. 10:3–5)

Paul did not use the sword, but the power of the Holy Spirit combined with the power of verbal and written persuasion, to destroy the spiritual and mental obstacles that hindered people from coming to Christ to join his kingdom. Because the early church did not set out to establish a theocracy through the use of the sword, the disciples and the early church were no real threat to the Roman civil authorities; their only weapons were the Holy Spirit, preaching the truth, and rational discourse to persuade converts to join them in peaceful assembly.

The Roman Empire As a Religious State

The Jews regarded Yahweh, the God of Abraham, as the God of their state. States in the ancient world were almost always religious states. The Romans had established pagan deities for the empire as a whole as well as numerous local deities with their respective temples in the Roman cities. It is important to remember that the Roman Empire at the time of the early church was not a Western-style republic in which the secular state and religious institutions were separate entities. Rome was a pagan religious state that often persecuted the church because the saints refused to worship the Roman pagan deities and the deified Roman emperors. Caesar was considered to be the son of god, and in the East he was considered god incarnate. The Roman Empire was a thoroughly pagan culture with established state and city-state deities. Roman taxes were used to support pagan priests and temple establishments. A Roman citizen's identity was wrapped up in this alliance of civil authority with pagan deities and worship. Roman citizens and subjects were required by law to honor, respect, and worship the established pagan gods of the empire.

Because Rome had conquered so many nations with differing cultures and religions, they had to allow some measure of religious pluralism to keep civil affairs peaceful. This did not, however, make Rome a secular state with religious freedom in the modern sense. Rome allowed a measure of freedom and pluralism for practical reasons, not for ideological reasons. The modern Western idea of a true secular state without an established state religion in which all religious groups are free to operate would have been a foreign concept in the ancient world—not only in the Roman Empire, but in Israel as well. The idea of the people of God worshiping as a church or peaceful assembly in a non-civil capacity without support and endorsement from the state was a novel concept in the ancient world.

The Amillennial View of Church and State

It was into this historical setting that the predominantly amillennial church fathers were thrust when several key Roman emperors became Christians and set out to establish Christianity as the official religion of the state, similar to the way Judaism had been the official religion of Israel. Amillennialism does not necessarily lead to the concept of a Christian theocracy, and most amillennialists today would certainly reject the concept. But it is easy to see how amillennial church theologians at this crucial period of history could develop a form of postmillennialism in response to the Christianization of the empire.

The amillennialists of that day reasoned that since the theocratic state of Israel had rejected its Messiah, and God had demonstrated his rejection of Israel in AD 70 by destroying their temple, then there would be no future, literal 1,000-year Jewish-led restoration. But with Emperors Constantine and Theodosius beginning to establish Christianity as the official religion of the Roman Empire, they surmised that since God rejected Israel, he intended the church, combined with the now Christian Roman state, to become the people of God on earth. Perhaps Israel's prior spiritual-civil covenant with God now transferred over to the Christian Roman Empire as Christ's messianic kingdom on earth.

Maybe Christ's 1,000-year reign had begun—not only spiritually with our rebirth, but also with Rome becoming a "holy nation." Perhaps Christ did want the disciples to make Christian states out of all nations, even if that involved the use of the sword. As long as the sword was used to advance the righteous reign of Christ, there would be no problem with the church and state working together to ensure the true worship of Christ. Maybe the Old Testament messianic prophecies were to be applied to the Gentile church and the new Christian state. Perhaps the thrones that were to reign with Christ, described by John in Revelation 20, were to be occupied by the Christian civil rulers and/or church rulers of the Christian Roman Empire.

Perhaps the church in combination with Christian Rome really was "the Israel of God."

With the approval of amillennial Christian theologians and church leaders of the time, Emperor Constantine laid the foundation for the Christian faith and church to become the official state religion of Rome. Emperor Theodosius made this official a few decades later. The Christian religion was now a department of the state, just as the military was a department of the state. The Roman government now ruled over the bishops and ecclesiastical authorities, settling theological disputes and disciplining heretics. As a result, the Roman emperors, particularly under Theodosius, began to act like the godly kings of Israel by punishing heretics and false prophets within the church. They even condoned, and often encouraged, the destruction of pagan temples by Christian zealots. For three hundred years Christianity had been criminalized. Now the pagan religions were being criminalized and replaced with state-sponsored churches.

In the theocratic kingdom of Israel, the kings of Israel were commanded to kill false prophets and destroy the pagan temples. There was no religious freedom in Israel, for God had made a spiritual-civil covenant with the nation. The Israelites were to worship only the God of Moses, or they would lose their nation and their land. Now that the emperors were Christians, the amillennialist church leaders and theologians reasoned that just as Moses established the Jewish faith for the nation of Israel, so, too, the Gentile Christian emperors were supposed to establish the Christian faith as the official and true religion of the Roman nation. In effect, the long-awaited messianic reign of Christ had begun. But instead of being a "Jewish-led" kingdom on earth, it was a Gentile-led kingdom.

Some of the most important doctrinal statements of our faith were officially formulated by councils called by Roman emperors who claimed the right to rule over spiritual matters of the church. The early ecumenical councils were, in effect, imperial councils. The Emperor Constantine called the First Council of Nicaea to deal with the Arian heresy and the doctrinal issue of the nature of Christ as eternal God.

Nicaea was the location of Constantine's country villa. He convened the council, meeting in the central hall of the imperial palace, by calling all—or most—of the bishops in the empire to Nicaea and presided over the proceedings in a manner similar to leading the Roman Senate. Constantine let the bishops do most of the arguing. When they reached an impasse, he interjected his ideas to help them reach a consensus. He then ratified the council decision, closed the council, and proceeded to make the rulings the official law of the Christian church. Bishops who disagreed with the rulings of these imperial councils or continued to teach "heresy" were warned, punished, driven out of office, and sent into exile. It was the job of the king to keep the church pure in Christ's kingdom on earth.

The Critical Role of Augustine

Augustine (AD 354–430) was born at this critical time when the Roman emperors were attempting to establish a Christian state in fulfillment of the messianic promises. He was twenty-six when Emperor Theodosius made Christianity the official religion of the Roman Empire. Augustine was not a Christian at the time, but after becoming a believer and a leading theologian, he, too, grappled with Revelation and the relationship of church and state. Augustine was the first Christian to systematically write about many Christian concepts, including the relationship of church and state. He was so influential that his teachings remained the cornerstone for Christian belief and practice for centuries, even through the Reformation in the 1500s.

Augustine eventually dismissed the idea of a *future* Jewish-centered 1,000-year restoration and concluded that the church and state were already in a quasi-literal 1,000-year period of Christ's reign, now that the empire had become Christian and was ruled by Christian emperors. Christ was already reigning—not only over the church, but over *the nations*, as well. Augustine thought the restoration had already begun. Christ's return would be after the current reign of Christ—postmillennialism.

But his view of this earthly kingdom as explained in his book *The City of God* was not utopian, for he had a good understanding of the depravity of man. His vision of Christ's reign over this world did not entail swords being beaten into plowshares. Satan was only partially bound and was still operational. Augustine believed that no Christian nation would be a true restoration of God's will on earth until the eternal kingdom begins.

Just as Israel had struggled against false prophets, pagan worship, and idolatry, so, too, would the new Christian nations. The eternal kingdom of God was to be established only at Christ's second coming. Until that time, there would be tares among the wheat in this world. There are two kingdoms operating concurrently in the world—Christ's kingdom of believers (the City of God) and Satan's kingdom of unbelievers. There is no earthly paradise before heaven. Only on the last day when God destroys Satan and purges all evil tares out of his kingdom will the City of God finally triumph as a purely holy city on earth.

Despite his overall pessimism—or realism—Augustine still believed that the reign of Christ described by John had actually begun, and he applied many Old Testament messianic psalms to the current state of Rome, now that it had become a Christian empire. His view of messianic prophecy was greatly watered down, but he believed it was literally being fulfilled through the church-state of the Christian Roman Empire. These messianic prophecies spoke of a future time when the Jewish Messiah would rule over the nations. Israel rejected him, but the Gentile nations had not. So, these messianic prophecies must transfer over to the Christian Gentile nations.

Some Christians opposed Augustine and argued that the church had no civil covenant with God. They reasoned that the apostles had not taught that the church should have the state use the sword on its behalf. They believed the church should remain an autonomous spiritual assembly, which should favor religious liberty. Augustine vehemently opposed this position. He contended that though the church itself should not use the sword, it was perfectly acceptable for the church to have the civil authorities, which were established by God, use the sword on the church's behalf. Augustine maintained that the civil authorities should punish heresy in the church during this current earthly reign of Christ. The evil, in this case, was not criminal activity but doctrinal heresy (Donatism), and the emperors had an obligation to use the wrath of the sword against those found guilty of the crime of false teachings in the church:

> But these emperors [civil authorities], whatever the occasion of their becoming acquainted with the crime of your schism [heresy] might be, frame against you such decrees as their zeal and their office demand. For they bear not the sword in vain; they are ministers of God to execute wrath upon those that do evil. (*Letters* 87.1.7–9)[2]

According to Augustine, the apostles did not advocate the use of the sword to advance the kingdom of Christ in their day because the messianic prophecies had not yet been fulfilled. But now that Rome had become a Christian empire, the messianic prophecies had come true, and Christ was now ruling over the nations. The church and state should work together in this messianic reign of Christ.

The following excerpt from Augustine's writings is extraordinary in what it reveals about Augustine's thinking. These teachings would have a major impact on the Western world for centuries to come. Read the following closely to discern the implications of what Augustine is teaching. Quoting from the messianic Psalm 2, Augustine argues:

> But as to the argument of those men who are unwilling that their impious deeds should be checked by the enactment of righteous laws, when they say that the apostles never sought such measures from the kings of the earth, they do not consider the different character of that age, and that everything comes in its own season. For what emperor had as yet believed in Christ, so as to serve Him in the cause of piety by enacting laws against impiety, when as yet the declaration of the prophet was only in the course of its fulfillment, "Why do the heathen rage, and the people counsel together, against the Lord, and against His Anointed;" and there was as yet no sign of that which is spoken a little later in the same psalm; "Be wise now, therefore, O ye

---

[2] Henry Paolucci, *The Political Writings of St. Augustine* (Chicago: Henry Regnery Company, 1962), 192.

kings; be instructed, ye judges of the earth. Serve the Lord with fear, and rejoice with trembling." How then are kings to serve the Lord with fear, except by preventing and chastising with religious severity all those acts which are done in opposition to the commandments of the Lord? . . . he serves Him by enforcing with suitable rigour such laws as ordain what is righteous, and punishment is the reverse. Even as Hezekiah served Him, by destroying the groves and the temples of the idols, and the high places which had been built in violation of the commandments of God, or even as Josiah served Him, by doing the same things in his turn. (*Letters* 185.19–36)[3]

Christ was now King of kings and Lord of lords in fulfillment of Old Testament messianic prophecies. His reign had begun. And the kings under Christ's reign should serve the Lord with fear and trembling as they enact laws and use the sword to establish true worship and righteousness in the earthly messianic kingdom of God. Just as Judaism was the established religion of the theocratic state of Israel, so, too, Christianity should be the established religion of the theocratic state of Christian Rome.

The Roman king under Christ's messianic reign should act in the same manner as the Jewish kings Hezekiah and Josiah by destroying the pagan temples and false teachings in the kingdom of Christ. There should be no religious freedom in the messianic kingdom, just as there was none in Israel.

Augustine's eschatology should be labeled as a type of postmillennialism, for as the following excerpt from *The City of God* suggests, Augustine believed that the 1,000-year reign described in Revelation 20 had actually begun in his day:

But while the devil is bound, the saints reign with Christ during the same thousand years . . . in the words, "And I saw seats and them that sat upon them, and judgment was given." It is not to be supposed that this refers to the last judgment, but to the seats of the rulers and to the rulers themselves by whom the Church is now governed [the reign has begun]. And no better interpretation of judgment being given can be produced than that which we have in the words, "What ye bind on earth shall be bound in heaven; and what ye loose on earth shall be loosed in heaven."[4]

The Roman rulers (civil and ecclesiastical) were those seated on the thrones described by John and had the authority to reign with Christ over the state and the church in Christ's earthly kingdom. According to Augustine, this is what the Old Testament prophets and the apostle John, in Revelation 20, had foreseen all along. They had predicted the day when Christ would rule the world through Christian Rome.

---

[3] Ibid., 211-212.
[4] Augustine, *The City of God*, trans. Marcus Dods (New York: Random House, 1950), 20.9.

Augustine applied another messianic prophecy, Psalm 72, to the Roman emperors now reigning with Christ. This psalm describes Christ's reign in the restoration when he will rule the whole world: "May he have dominion from sea to sea, and from the River to the ends of the earth! . . . Blessed be his glorious name forever; may the whole earth be filled with his glory! Amen and Amen!" (72:8–19). Quoting from this psalm, Augustine then writes, "Christ from the kingdom bought with His blood, which extends from sea to sea, and from the river to the ends of the earth. Nay verily; *let the kings of the earth serve Christ by making laws for Him and for His cause*" (*Letters* 93.16–19).[5] Augustine believed the reign of Christ had begun since Constantine and the other emperors had turned the Roman Empire into a Christian nation. These Christian kings were to serve Christ by "making laws for Him and his cause." They would rule with Christ over his earthly kingdom, extending from sea to sea and to the ends of the earth.

In the Old Testament, Israel was to have one religion: Judaism. Israel was not to have a multitude of pagan temples representing a pluralistic religious culture and society. The Jewish kings were supposed to maintain a single, true, Judean religion by preventing heresy and pagan forms of worship from corrupting the nation. Similarly, Augustine believed in only one Catholic Church for the Christian Roman Empire. And he had no qualms about calling on the emperor or other Christian civil authorities to punish any who were divisive or heretical within the church. The state was responsible for the purity of the church or nation. The Gentile Christian kings and the church authorities, together, were the "thrones" set up to reign with Christ and were responsible for maintaining the one holy Catholic Church in the Christian empire, just as the Jewish kings and Levitical priests were responsible for maintaining the purity of Judaism in the Jewish state.

Augustine did not support the use of capital punishment—usually burning at the stake—for a brother who strayed, but he did approve of other means of punishment including fines, torture, and imprisonment to bring the wayward brother to his senses: "But yet, before the good sons can say they have 'a desire to depart, and to be with Christ,' many must first be recalled to their Lord *by the stripes of temporal scourging*, like evil slaves, and in some degree like good-for-nothing fugitives."[6] For the next one thousand years and beyond, the Catholic Church concurred with Augustine that the use of force was a necessary form of punishment for wayward Christians who engaged in the criminal activity of promoting heresy. The Catholic Church, however, did not share his aversion to capital punishment, and heretics were often burned at the stake.

---

[5] Paolucci, 206.

[6] Ibid., 216.

Augustine's brilliance and the sheer breadth of his writings carried the day. The rest, as they say, is history. His theories on Revelation 20 and of church and state became the paradigm for the remaining Roman Empire and, subsequently, Medieval Europe, when Christ's kingdom became known as Christendom. The Catholic Church, in conjunction with the civil authorities, would reign with Christ over this world from the thrones described in Revelation throughout Catholic Christendom.

Resolution as to whether those seated on these thrones "to whom the authority to judge was committed" (Rev. 20:4) was referring to civil or ecclesiastical authorities would plague both parties for centuries. Who was actually sovereign—the church rulers or the state rulers—and who had the right to appoint key church officials such as bishops were constant battles. At times, the state had the authority to appoint key church officials. At other times, the Catholic Church was responsible for appointing these key church officials. The pope could even excommunicate the civil king if he strayed too far from the faith.

The Catholic Church, as well as the Eastern Church that split off in Constantinople, would function with this comingling of church and state for centuries. The Eastern Church, however, did not have to contend with sovereignty issues because the state/emperor became the dominant throne, with the church submissive to the emperor.

As the Catholic Church's doctrine developed over the centuries, John's reference to those seated on the thrones to reign with Christ, to whom authority was committed to judge the world (Rev. 20:4), was interpreted to mean the pope and the Catholic hierarchy more so than the civil authorities. Christ's reign had begun, and he used the pope and the church hierarchy to reign over his kingdom.

Catholic theologians combined this interpretation of the thrones found in Revelation 20 with the belief that Peter and his successors were the rock on which Christ would build his church. The popes succeeded Peter by ruling with Christ on these thrones and were given the ultimate authority to judge over the affairs of the church and state. They were the fulfillment of the prophecy of Revelation 20. Because the popes were sitting on the thrones, whatever they bound on earth was the rule of law in all matters of church and doctrine. As successors of Peter, they, too, could bind things on earth as in heaven (Matt. 16:19). The combination of these two interpretations, the succession of Peter's authority to rule and the thrones of Revelation 20, formed the foundation of the papal claim that the Roman Church is the supreme ruler over the church *and* state during Christ's reign. The pope's "throne" and *reign with Christ* became so powerful that the Church's teachings were considered to have the same authority as the Scriptures.

Augustine's incorrect application of the Old Testament messianic prophecies to the Christian state and his false interpretation of Revelation 20 resulted in a seriously flawed view of the functions of church and state for the simple reason that the millennium has not yet begun. No one is reigning with Christ, because Christ has not yet begun to exercise his messianic reign. He is still waiting on the Father to say it is time to bind Satan and then exercise his reign over this world. During this interim period, Christ is building his church by gathering lost souls out of Satan's kingdom and transferring them into his kingdom; it is obvious that he is not exercising his reign over this world. Nonetheless, Augustine's biblical ideology and eschatology would continue to be the foundation for Western civilization for another fourteen hundred years. Any Christian nation that emerged during this time was modeled after Augustine's vision and teachings.

The study of eschatology is often dismissed as inconsequential in the lives of people today. But it would be difficult to dispute that Augustine's faulty eschatology had enormous ramifications for the Western world. His postmillennial eschatology not only affected the Catholic Church and nations, but also Protestant nations that emerged out of the Reformation. The Reformers may have rejected the papal claim that the pope and Catholic hierarchy were those seated on the thrones of Revelation 20 established by God to rule over the church and state, but they did not reject the Catholic Church's understanding of Revelation 20. Those seated on the thrones to rule over Christ's messianic kingdom became Protestant church and civil rulers instead of Catholic church officials and kings or princes. Because both were operating with the use of the sword in Christ's name, it required war to make the transition from the Roman Catholic kingdom of Christ to the Protestant kingdom of Christ.

Christ's Protestant Messianic Reign

The Reformers, for the most part, did not challenge Augustine and the Catholic Church's notion of a Christian nation; they only wanted to *reform* the corrupt Catholic Church—its leadership and many of its doctrines and practices—and, subsequently, the Christian nations they represented. They still believed in one universal church and one kingdom of Christ and were willing to fight the Catholic hierarchy for the reins of power. The Reformers remained postmillennial and Augustinian in their rejection of a literal, future millennium. And they continued to believe that the now "Protestant" Christian nations were already reigning with Christ in this quasi-literal 1,000-year period.

John Calvin (1509–1564) followed Augustine's lead and believed the messianic reign of Christ had begun. He, like Augustine, rejected a future millennium based on a literal interpretation of Revelation 20, calling that interpretation so childish as to not warrant a rebuttal.[7] His opinions of church and state and the reign of Christ were virtually identical to Augustine's. In his book *Institutes of the Christian Religion*, Calvin teaches that civil government is responsible for man's spiritual well-being just as the Old Testament kings were responsible for the religious purity of the Jewish state. Calvin was obviously familiar with Augustine's writings because his logic and even the psalms he quotes are almost identical to Augustine's. Calvin, like Augustine, draws heavily from the Old Testament model when explaining the theocratic relationship of church and state. The state is responsible for both the material and the spiritual well-being of its citizens. As such, the state should prevent false teachings by the force of law. In the section of the *Institutes* titled "The Chief Tasks and Burdens of Civil Government," he explains their role:

> For it [civil government] does not merely see to it, as all these serve to do, that men breathe, eat, drink, and are kept warm, even though it surely embraces all these activities when it provides for their living together. It does not, I repeat, look to this only, but also prevents idolatry, sacrilege against God's name, blasphemies against his truth, and other public offenses against religion from arising and spreading among the people. . . . Let no man be disturbed that I now commit to civil government the duty of rightly establishing religion. (*Inst.* IV.20.3)

The very function of a Christian state under Christ's reign is to use the force of law to establish a righteous and pure kingdom on this earth. To only assign to the state the responsibility of the material well-being of the citizens is to not understand Christ's current reign.

Calvin further notes that the Scriptures sometimes describe civil rulers as "gods," or rulers on God's behalf. Note that everything in parentheses, including Old Testament biblical citations, is found in the original text of Calvin's writings. My comments are always bracketed. Calvin writes:

> What is this, except that God has entrusted to them [civil authorities] the business of serving him in their office, and (as Moses and Jehoshaphat said to the judges whom they appointed in every city of Judah) of exercising judgment not for man but for God (Deut. 1:16-17; 2 Chron. 19:6)? (*Inst.* IV.20.4)

Calvin draws directly from Old Testament law (Deut. 1:16–17; 2 Chron. 19:6) to prove that the civil authorities of his day had a duty to serve Christ by appointing judges to rule over spiritual matters.

---

[7] John Calvin, *Institutes of the Christian Religion*, ed. John T. McNeill, trans. Ford Lewis Battles (Philadelphia: The Westminster Press, 1967), Book III.25.5.

Calvin, like Augustine, also applies messianic psalms to his world, believing that the church and state were already experiencing the messianic reign of Christ. Here is a portion of a psalm of David that Calvin applied to his day:

> I will tell of the decree: The LORD said to me, "You are my Son; today I have begotten you. Ask of me, and *I will make the nations your heritage, and the ends of the earth your possession. . . .*" Now therefore, *O kings, be wise; be warned, O rulers of the earth. Serve the* LORD *with fear,* and rejoice with trembling. Kiss the Son, lest he be angry, and you perish in the way, for his wrath is quickly kindled. Blessed are all who take refuge in him. (Ps. 2:7–12)

In my opinion, this is clearly a messianic psalm describing the future restoration. But, in Calvin's opinion, Christ's reign had already begun; therefore, kings and rulers should submit to him and enforce Christianity in their kingdoms. Calvin applies this psalm to the civil authorities of his day:

> For where David urges all kings and rulers to kiss the Son of God (Ps. 2:12), he does not bid them lay aside their authority and retire to private life, but submit to Christ the power with which they have been invested, that he alone may tower over all. (*Inst.* IV.20.5)

Now that Christ is ruling the world, the kings and rulers of the world should serve him by establishing his messianic kingdom on this earth.

In Calvin's day, there were those who were disturbed by Calvin's use of the civil government in establishing religion. They argued for the right of religious freedom, even for heretics, and believed the state should only concern itself with civil affairs—not religious affairs. Calvin thought this teaching was folly and would lead to anarchy and to evil in the nations. He looked to the Jewish kings in the theocratic nation of Israel as the model for how the Messiah should rule this world through holy kings or thrones:

> Also, holy kings are greatly praised in Scripture because they restored the worship of God when it was corrupted or destroyed, or took care of religion that under them it might flourish pure and unblemished. But on the contrary, the Sacred History places anarchies among things evil: because there was no king in Israel, each man did as he pleased (Judg. 21:25). This proves the folly of those who would neglect the concern for God and would give attention only to rendering justice among men. As if God appointed rulers in his name to decide earthly controversies but overlooked what was of far greater importance—that he himself should be purely worshiped according to the prescription of his law. (*Inst.* IV.20.9)

Calvin considered it foolish to think that civil rulers under Christ's reign should only attend to secular affairs of men and not attend to the more important spiritual affairs of the people to ensure God was properly worshiped. Religious freedom should not be tolerated, for it would spawn heretical beliefs, resulting in anarchy and evil in the kingdom of Christ.

Augustine and Calvin struggled to find New Testament justification or support for their church-state ideology, which is why they spent so much time referencing Old Testament law and prophets. One section of the New Testament, however, that both Augustine and Calvin keyed in on was a teaching in Paul's letter to the Romans in which Paul admonishes fellow believers to obey the civil authorities:

> Let every person be subject to the governing authorities. For there is no authority except from God, and those that exist have been instituted by God. Therefore whoever resists the authorities resists what God has appointed, and those who resist will incur judgment. For rulers are not a terror to good conduct, but to bad. Would you have no fear of the one who is in authority? Then do what is good, and you will receive his approval, for he is God's servant for your good. But if you do wrong, be afraid, for he does not bear the sword in vain. For he is the servant of God, an avenger who carries out God's wrath on the wrongdoer. (Rom. 13:1–4)

Augustine extends this sword-bearing civil authority described by Paul to the realm of the spiritual affairs of the church: "The civil powers defend their conduct in persecuting schismatics [false teachers and heretics] by the rule which the apostle laid down" (*Letters* 87.1.7–9).[8] He also implies that, in Romans 13, Paul taught that it was a God-given duty of the civil authorities to rule over spiritual matters and to use the sword, if necessary. The civil authorities, as servants of God, were God's means of avenging the heretic and carrying out God's wrath on wrongdoers in the church.

In Calvin's interpretation and application of Romans 13, he, too, extends the right to govern the spiritual affairs of people and the church to the civil authorities. Calvin advocates that the civil authorities should exercise their authority over both spiritual and doctrinal matters as did the Old Testament rulers:

> But Paul speaks much more clearly when he undertakes a just discussion of this matter. For he states both that power [with the sword] is an ordinance of God (Rom. 13:2), and that there are no powers except those ordained by God (Rom. 13:1). Further, that princes are ministers of God, for those doing good unto praise; for those doing evil, avengers unto wrath (Rom. 13:3-4). To this may be added the examples of holy men, of whom some possessed kingdoms, as David, Josiah, and Hezekiah; others, lordships, as Joseph and Daniel; others, civil rule among a free people, as Moses, Joshua, and the judges. (*Inst.* IV.20.4)

---

[8] Paolucci, 190.

The "Christian" rulers are ministers of God as were Moses and David. According to Calvin, the theocratic kingdom has passed from the rejected nation of Israel to the Christian nations in the current reign of Christ.

Paul writes his letter to the Romans in a grammatical-historical context, and later theologians such as Augustine and Calvin interpret his teachings within their own contemporary context to come up with a different meaning than Paul intended. It seems absurd for Augustine and Calvin to think that Paul wanted the pagan Roman authorities of his day to use the sword as an instrument of God's wrath within the church and to govern the teachings and affairs of the church. On numerous occasions, Paul and others had suffered greatly from the unjust use of the Roman sword against the church. The last thing he would have advocated is that Roman authorities police the doctrines of the church. He was merely instructing the Roman Christians to be law-abiding citizens, not criminals and definitely not insurrectionists.

In Romans 13, Paul is talking about how government should *ideally* function. Note his careful choice of words: "For rulers are not a terror to good conduct, but to bad." Paul is describing how the authorities *should* function. Paul and the early church knew that the Roman government could be a real terror, even to good Christian citizens who did nothing more than worship and follow Christ.

The church was experiencing significant unjust persecution from Roman authorities. Paul knew that young Christians might be tempted to lash out against the civil government for the abuse they were experiencing. To prevent such retaliation, Paul admonished them: "Bless those who persecute you; bless and do not curse them. . . . Repay no one evil for evil, . . . Beloved, never avenge yourselves, but leave it to the wrath of God, . . . Do not be overcome by evil, but overcome evil with good" (Rom. 12:14–21).

Christ did not lead an insurrection despite his unjust treatment. Paul did not want the church to initiate one either; he wanted believers to continue being good law-abiding citizens despite the abuse they were experiencing from these civil authorities. He advised them to wait and let Christ punish their persecutors on Judgment Day.

Paul was also worried that, out of anger for the unjust abuse they were receiving, they would refuse to pay taxes as a form of protest. He told them: "Pay to all what is owed to them: taxes to whom taxes are owed, revenue to whom revenue is owed, respect to whom respect is owed, honor to whom honor is owed" (Rom. 13:7). Paul knew that not paying taxes would, no doubt, provide the Romans with yet another excuse to persecute them even more. From Paul's perspective, the early church already faced tremendous obstacles by abandoning pagan temple worship and emperor worship. Again, Paul admonished these Roman believers to be good law-abiding citizens despite their ill treatment by the civil authorities.

Augustine and Calvin distort Paul's teachings when they claim this text justifies their assertion that the civil authorities of their time should operate in the same manner as did the authorities in the theocratic state of Israel—by ruling over the spiritual matters of the church. Nothing in this text, or in the rest of the New Testament, supports this interpretation.

The reason it made sense to Augustine and Calvin was that they believed the messianic reign had already begun with Christ ruling from sea to sea with a rod of iron; as a result, the Christian rulers should emulate the Old Testament kings of Israel. As Augustine says, the time had come: "Kings shall fall down before him; all nations shall serve Him." As a result of their faulty eschatology—assuming the messianic reign of Christ had already begun—they misinterpreted Paul's letter to the Romans in a way that would have horrified him.

The City-State of Geneva

In the mid-1500s, Calvin had an opportunity to test his beliefs and established the city-state of Geneva as a type of Christian theocracy. If heretics arose and they did not respond to reason and the discipline of the church, Calvin had the civil authorities arrest them and put them on trial as criminals in a civil court of law. They were brought before the civil magistrate to be prosecuted for a crime against the Christian state as if they had burglarized or tried to burn down a church building. In Calvin's opinion, the crime of heresy was worse. Heresy was a disease of the soul that could spread like an epidemic.

Calvin himself would testify. If a person was found guilty of a serious heresy and was unrepentant, Calvin would admonish the civil authorities to burn the heretic at the stake. This seemed consistent with the Jewish rulers of old who killed false prophets to keep their false teachings from corrupting the nation.

Today, can you imagine a Presbyterian minister requesting a local district attorney to file criminal charges against an area Baptist minister because he preaches heresies? Can you envision the district judge then finding the minister guilty, sentencing him to death, and closing the church? It is mind-boggling, but that is essentially what took place in Calvin's Geneva. During the Reformation, when a group of Christians such as the Anabaptists advocated what Calvinists considered a heretical concept, such as rebaptism, as well as religious liberty, they were branded as heretics, persecuted, and eventually driven from their homeland.

Augustine and Calvin were correct about many biblical doctrines and made many positive contributions to the church and the world for which we should be thankful. But regarding their flawed understanding of Revelation

20 and the way in which they applied their postmillennial beliefs to the function of church and state, they made a colossal blunder.

The irony is that Augustine and Calvin were so intent on finding New Testament justification for the use of civil authorities to stamp out false teachings that they developed a false teaching themselves based on their misinterpretation of Romans 13. And this false teaching was not without its consequences as Europe eventually plunged into religious wars between Catholic and Protestant forces in the battle for control over the cities and states in Europe—all during the supposed reign of Christ in which peace on this earth would be so extensive that swords would be beaten into plowshares!

I am sure Calvin and like-minded others considered these wars normal, for even Israel consistently endured external wars against pagan nations and internal battles over the hearts and minds of the Jewish nation. What Calvin and other reformers failed to understand was that the very wars they were experiencing were convincing evidence and proof that the messianic reign of Christ had not yet begun; the prophets clearly teach that during Christ's reign all wars will cease, and his kingdom will be a time of absolute peace.

Moreover, the false teachings they were encountering should have caused them to realize that Satan was not bound and removed from this world as John prophesied and to reexamine their own teachings about Christ's millennial kingdom on this earth.

Martin Luther (1483–1546) had a more nuanced understanding of Christ's current reign and did not advocate a Christian theocracy, per se. But he did get caught up in the religious wars of his day and never escaped the Augustinian paradigm.

The Puritan Ideology

The Puritans continued to adhere to this postmillennial view of church and state and Christ's reign. Although sincere Christians who left a great legacy, they, too, made the same mistake as the Catholic Church and many of the Protestant Reformers by attempting to establish Christian nations during the assumed current reign of Christ. Being dissatisfied with the purity of the Anglican Church of England, they sought to establish a purer Protestant nation under Christ using the powers of the civil state to establish true doctrines in Christ's kingdom on this earth—hence the name Puritans.

The Puritans in England created the famous *Westminster Confession of Faith*, which was commissioned by an act of the English Parliament in 1647, when they gained control of the government. Puritans controlling Parliament appointed a committee of *church* scholars to draft the document. Although never officially approved by Parliament and the Church of England, it became the de facto official statement of faith for the churches in

Scotland. Religious liberty was not to be allowed, and the state had a major role in maintaining the purity of the church:

> And because the powers which God hath ordained, and the liberty which Christ hath purchased, are not intended by God to destroy, but mutually to uphold and preserve one another; they who, upon pretense of Christian liberty, shall oppose any lawful power, or the lawful exercise of it, whether it be civil or ecclesiastical, resist the ordinance of God. And, for their publishing of such opinions, or maintaining of such practices, as are contrary to the light of nature, or to the known principles of Christianity, whether concerning faith, worship, or conversation; or, to the power of godliness; or, such erroneous opinions or practices, as either in their own nature, or in the manner of publishing or maintaining them, are destructive to the external peace and order which Christ hath established in the Church, they may lawfully be called to account, and proceeded against, by the censures of the Church, and by the power of the civil magistrate.[9]

In the footnotes to this section of the *Confession*, the authors refer to Paul's instructions in Romans 13 to obey the civil authorities, extending to them the authority to rule over spiritual matters of the people and the church—just as Augustine and Calvin did. The church and the civil authorities had a God-given duty to ensure that erroneous beliefs and practices would be prosecuted by the censures of the church and the civil magistrates. The idea of expounding false beliefs "upon the pretense of Christian liberty" was, in reality, a false teaching and a form of resistance against God, and was not to be tolerated by the church or the state.

The civil authorities are not the church and cannot administer holy communion, but they do have the authority and power to regulate the church, call for special councils to establish orthodox matters of faith, and to prevent heresies with the sword:

> The civil magistrate may not assume to himself the administration of the Word and sacraments, or the power of the keys of the kingdom of heaven: *yet he hath authority, and it is his duty*, to take order, that unity and peace be preserved in the Church, that the truth of God be kept pure and entire; *that all blasphemies and heresies be suppressed*; all corruptions and abuses in worship and discipline prevented or reformed; and all the ordinances of God duly settled, administered, and observed. For the better effecting whereof, he hath power to call synods, to be present at them, and to provide that whatsoever is transacted in them be according to the mind of God.[10]

---

[9] *The Westminster Confession of Faith*, 1646 (Glasgow: Free Presbyterian Publications, reprinted, 2003), Chapter 20, "Of Christian Liberty, and Liberty of Conscience," para. 4, pp. 87-88.

[10] Ibid., Chapter 23, "Of the Civil Magistrate," para. 3, pp. 100-101.

This paragraph of the confession has footnotes with Scripture quotes to support these teachings. These footnotes refer to Ezra 7, Deuteronomy 13, 2 Kings 16 and 23, 2 Chronicles 15 and 19, and several other Old Testament guidelines for the theocratic nation of Israel in which the Jewish kings, magistrates, and judges were to enforce the Mosaic law with the sword. Violators were to have their goods confiscated, and they would be banished or even put to death. Even blasphemers were to be put to death. These verses also call for removing the high places, breaking the pagan images, and tearing down the pagan places of worship.

The Emperor Constantine used his civil authority when he called for the Council of Nicaea to deal with the Arian heresy. Thirteen hundred years later, the Puritans were still operating under the same paradigm and understanding of the kingdom of Christ on this earth.

The Puritans believed that, since Israel had rejected its Messiah, the church had replaced Israel as the people of God and should operate as Christ's kingdom on this earth, which is why they drew so heavily on the Mosaic law as a model for their Christian theocracy. They, like Augustine and Calvin, believed the reign of Christ had in some sense already begun. Christ was ruling the world through the human thrones or civil authorities that he set up to rule with him. The spiritual-civil covenant established with Israel was, therefore, extended to the Gentile Christian nations since they had inherited the messianic kingdom.

The above sections of the *Westminster Confession of Faith* were modified after the American Revolution by the American Presbyterian Assembly of 1789 for the purpose of removing much of the language concerning the authority of the civil magistrate to rule over the spiritual affairs of the people. My excerpts and footnotes refer to the original English version and not the amended American version.

To grasp what the original version advocated, try to imagine a current or past president of the United States asking Congress to appoint a select group of Christian theologians to write a comprehensive confession of the Christian faith. This group of theologians could be conservative or liberal depending on the disposition of the president and the Congress at the time. Subsequently, Congress would incorporate this document into a bill and then pass the bill, making it the law of the land that would set the standard for Christian doctrine for all Christian churches within the nation. Using this statement of faith as the basis of law, the civil authorities would then be responsible for keeping the church pure and free of false teaching and corruption. Violators would be prosecuted in federal, state, or district courts; they would be fined, imprisoned, and have their property seized. If the offense was serious, the dissidents would be put to death. Today it is difficult to imagine this scenario, but, in essence, that is what took place in Puritan England, Scotland and, to some extent, Puritan New England.

Whether or not a particular person or group of people was persecuted in England, Scotland, or Europe depended on whether the ruling monarch was Catholic, Anglican, Puritan, Presbyterian, or some combination thereof. Often, the only reason the parties out of power clamored for religious liberty was so that once they regained the power of the sword, they could then impose their orthodox beliefs on the country. It was not a true call for religious liberty.

Some Puritans really did believe in religious liberty and were known as Separatists; they did not want anything to do with the established Church of England or any other state-established religion. But most were determined to purify the state and church and reclaim it for Christ's reign.

The Puritans faced many setbacks as they rose and fell from power in England and Scotland. One Catholic Monarch, Queen Mary I of England, who reigned from 1553 to 1558, came into power and persecuted the Protestant Puritans. Her nickname Bloody Mary was well deserved. But even when in power, many Puritans were frustrated by the lack of progress in establishing Christ's godly kingdom in England.

The American Puritans

Some of the most devout Puritans, under the leadership of John Winthrop (1587-1649), saw the young American colonies as an opportunity to demonstrate to England and the world what a Christian nation properly run should look like. Winthrop led a group of English Puritans to the New World in 1630 and founded the Massachusetts Bay Colony, in conjunction with the Massachusetts Bay Company, to be this example to the world. They did not consider the Christian nation of England a pure enough example of Christ's kingdom on this earth. In America, they would serve as the light on a hill—a pure and godly representation of a Christian theocracy that would convict the Old World of its backsliding. Their model colony could then be emulated back in England, and elsewhere. This group of devout Puritans came to the New World to establish what they referred to as the "new Israel." The Puritan colony of Massachusetts was set up as a Calvinistic theocracy, modeled after the nation of Israel. Members of the colony were required by force of law to attend and pay taxes to the one established church—Congregationalist. And, of course, religious freedom was not allowed; with religious freedom, heresies could easily spread and corrupt the church and colony.

Separatists such as Roger Williams (1603–1684), an active member of the colony, rebelled against this idea that the Gentile church and nations were the new Israel. He argued that the church was solely a spiritual body or assembly of believers that did not have a civil covenant with God, as did Israel. Just as Christ refused to establish a civil reign while he was on this earth, so, too, his followers should not attempt to do so in his place. God did not establish a spiritual-civil covenant with the church as he did with the nation of Israel. The church was not Israel with a state-established religion. The church should be separate from the state and govern its own affairs without any interference from the state.

In 1636, the Puritans grew tired of Williams's constant criticism and his stubborn refusal to repent and kicked him out of the colony in the middle of a brutal winter. He survived the perilously cold travels and made it to Rhode Island, where he bought a parcel of land from the Indians and soon established the first American colony that separated the civil state from the affairs of the spiritual church. This colony was a true secular state, and people were free to determine spiritual truth and form whatever religious affiliation they so desired. Williams even had the audacity to claim that the magistrate may not punish citizens for breaking the Ten Commandments or for engaging in such activities as idolatry, false worship, blasphemy, and Sabbath-breaking. As a result, there was true religious freedom in Rhode Island as Baptists, Quakers, and even Catholics and Jews were allowed to live and worship freely. Imagine that. Atheists, too, could even live in the colony and have fundamental human rights as citizens of the colony.

Rhode Island might be the first true secular state with religious liberty in the world's history. Most important, Williams was not a secular humanist or a product of the Enlightenment. He derived his views concerning church and state from a new theological interpretation of the Scriptures. Since Christ and the disciples refused to establish a theocratic kingdom, as evidenced in the New Testament, Williams concluded that until Christ does establish his reign, it would be best to set up a secular state with no established religion, one in which people would be free to explore and find spiritual truth on their own. He understood that no person or civil authority is able to truly control a person's conscience, so why not let freedom of conscience be translated into freedom of religion.

Williams was not a biblical theologian and many of his later views dealing with personal spirituality and the church were strained, even bizarre. Nor did he have a well-developed eschatology. Yet he knew that something was dreadfully wrong with the Calvinist and Puritan understanding of the millennial reign of Christ. Despite his shortcomings, his contribution to the concept of a secular state—with the separation of church and state—is remarkable.

The American Revolution

During the American Revolution (1775–1783), the Separatists, in the tradition of Roger Williams, formed an alliance with the humanists of the Enlightenment movement who had become fed up with the centuries of religious tyranny within a state, the many religious civil wars, and the religious wars between states. The humanists agreed with the Separatists that the church was solely a spiritual assembly and the state, solely a civil body. They wanted to separate the politicians, who had their own agendas, from the theologians, who also had their own agendas. Together, they were instrumental in the formation of a federal secular state with the church and other spiritual affairs being autonomous from the state—a truly novel concept.

This unusual alliance of two groups of people from very different ideological backgrounds birthed the notion of America as a secular state that incorporated civil functions and responsibilities into its federal government, but not religious functions and responsibilities. The state was responsible for the material well-being of its citizens, while the churches were responsible for the spiritual well-being of their members. And each church or group could compete for new members in a free marketplace of ideas.

The United States Constitution, adopted in 1787, calls for a secular federal government with no established national church. Congress did not have the power or authority to form a committee to write a Confession of Faith or enact legislation to make it the law of the land. Nor did the president have the authority to appoint an archbishop or bishop. Nor did a pope have the authority to anoint the president or impeach him from office.

If a group of influential theologians began teaching a strange doctrine, the president could not convene councils of religious leaders to define major church doctrines and require them to adhere to the established doctrine of the state. The government was no longer responsible for policing the affairs of the church and punishing heretics. The state and the church were considered separate entities with different functions. They were not hostile to one another; they merely operated in different realms—one in the civil realm and the other in the religious realm.

The state had a civil covenant with the people, not a spiritual one. The people were responsible for their spiritual well-being and forming their own spiritual alliances and assemblies. They could make spiritual covenants with whatever god they chose to worship and recruit followers in a free market-place of religious ideas and practices whereby they would have to compete for the hearts and minds of their fellow man. They would have to follow Paul's example and use the Holy Spirit, the presentation of the truth, and rational persuasion to convince people to join God's kingdom. As a result of this non-establishment clause and the constitutional guarantees of civil liberties, the United States has never been plagued by religious wars as was Europe.

Neo-Puritanism

Today most postmillennialists do not make the mistake that Augustine, the Reformers, and the Puritans made in regard to the merging of church and state into a messianic kingdom on this earth. They enjoy religious liberty like the rest of us. A fringe group within the Reformed tradition, however, still believes in the establishment of Christian theocracies. Their "theonomic" position has been popularized by theologians such as R. J. Rushdoony. They maintain that in obeying the Great Commission to make disciples of all nations, we should literally create Christian nations that even follow Mosaic law.

But the Puritan idea of a Christian nation dies hard; it remains with us today in the form of neo-Puritans who insist that because America was founded as a Christian nation, it should return to its roots and once again become a Christian nation. Their concept of a Christian nation, however, has weakened a great deal; they do not advocate a theocracy in the Puritan sense. They believe in religious liberty, but they believe that in some way Christianity was and should continue to be the established religion in this country.

Modern postmillennialists continue to believe that through effective evangelism the country and the world can be Christianized, and Christ and Christianity will ascend to power over the nations—thereby establishing Christ's long-awaited messianic kingdom. Centuries of failure and religious tyranny have not dissuaded them in this quest. They fail to realize that by giving kings, princes, lords, and politicians authority over the affairs of the church, it gives Satan a strategic advantage in preventing true spiritual growth of God's kingdom. All Satan has to do to hinder Christ's kingdom is corrupt the Christian leadership, which can effectively corrupt the order of churches under the state's control. With fragmented churches autonomous from the state, he has to attempt to influence each individual denomination and church in order to corrupt the church as a whole and destroy its witness. But wise Christians can easily leave a corrupt church and start a new assembly and witness to God's love and truth. As such, Satan hates religious liberty. He would rather deal with an Augustinian framework.

The disciples were not tasked with Christian-nation building but with evangelizing individuals from every nation and group in the world. If Christ refused to establish his reign while he was on the earth, then what right do we as his disciples have to establish his reign for him? Christ will establish Christian nations by his own authority in due time after Satan is bound.

Books by neo-Puritan authors continue to appear in Christian bookstores attempting to prove that early America was indeed a Christian nation and that we should return to those glory days. There is plenty of evidence from the early Puritans to support this erroneous belief. The following quote in the book *The Separation Illusion*, by John Whitehead, is a good example of this contemporary neo-Puritan thought. As the title suggests, the author is of the opinion that there was no separation of church and state in early America, and, consequently, there should not be one today:

> It is also evident that the biblical concept of the covenant as interpreted by John Calvin is implicit in the preamble of the Constitution. "We the people of the United States" harks back to the Mayflower Compact (drafted by Calvinistic Puritans), which began, "We whose names are underwritten." The Pilgrim covenant can be traced through Calvin to God's agreement with Israel; "If ye will obey my voice . . . and keep my covenant, then ye shall be a peculiar treasure unto me" (Exodus 19:5). . . . The concept of a secular state was nonexistent in 1776 as well as 1787, and no less so in 1791 when the Bill of Rights was adopted. Rousas John Rushdoony is on target when he comments: "To read the Constitution as a charter for a secular state is to misread history, and to misread it radically. The Constitution was designed to perpetuate a Christian order." . . . the United States was once a Christian nation. At the time of the signing of the Declaration of Independence, nine of the thirteen colonies had established churches. The state governments were financially supporting the Christian religion. In most states one had to be a Christian to hold office. . . . the idea of "the Christian subculture" was abhorred by the Puritans. These Christians crossed the Atlantic Ocean to reach what they called "the Promised Land." In less than a century it was the greatest Christian nation on the earth.[11]

According to Whitehead, the Puritan version of the United States in the lineage of John Calvin was "the greatest Christian nation on the earth." In all fairness to Whitehead, I understand he has moderated his views since this book was published in 1977. Since that time, Whitehead, as a lawyer, has done some fine work on behalf of Christians and others through the Rutherford Institute, defending their civil rights against secular humanists who do not correctly understand how a secular state should function. Nonetheless, his writings are typical of the neo-Puritan ideas that flood our Christian media outlets. Rushdoony did not moderate his views before his death in 2001.

It is books and statements like these, often associated with the Christian Right, that cause the current political climate of hostility toward evangelicals in general. Many non-Christians believe that evangelicals are determined to return America to its Puritan roots. This perception can understandably be a frightening prospect to many non-Christians—especially those familiar with Western history where for centuries, civil liberties were denied ordinary

---

[11] John W. Whitehead, *The Separation Illusion* (Milford, MI: Mott Media, 1977), 23-24, 35-37.

people, and citizens were persecuted if they did not adhere to the established religion of their particular region or state.

Whitehead's analysis of the formation of the American experiment is, however, only partially true. Many Christians do not know that after the U.S. Constitution was drafted, it was initially rejected by the original thirteen colonies or states. Those states demanded that it be amended to contain a series of civil rights, commonly known as the Bill of Rights, as a condition for approval. Congress complied, and the first of these amendments says, "Congress shall make no law respecting an establishment of religion, or prohibiting the free exercise thereof; or abridging the freedom of speech, or of the press; or the right of the people peaceably to assemble, and to petition the Government for a redress of grievances." It is important to note that this only applied to the federal government—not to the thirteen states.

There were two different reasons the states wanted to restrict the new federal government from establishing a national state church. Some colonies, like Puritan Massachusetts and Episcopal South Carolina, still had state-established religions as Whitehead points out. They did not want Congress to establish a national religion that would interfere with and threaten their already-established religious state. They wanted to maintain their state theocracy and clearly saw the potential threat of the creation of a national church not based on their religious theology. Ironically, the state of Massachusetts wanted the freedom to maintain a single established church—Congregationalist—for the state, one that did not allow religious liberty and the freedom of other faiths to establish churches in their state. Baptists, Episcopalians, Catholics, Quakers, and Jews were not allowed to establish churches or synagogues in the colony.

Conversely, colonies such as Rhode Island and Pennsylvania had an opposing reason why they did not want the federal government to establish a national church. These colonies had already established secular states with true religious freedom, and they wanted constitutional assurances that the establishment of a national church would never jeopardize this liberty. They were afraid the federal government might someday want to adopt a national religion, such as the Anglican Church of England, and then attempt to impose that religion on their colony. As a condition to their adopting the Constitution and joining the United States, they wanted constitutional guarantees that this would never happen. That is, they did not want the United States to become a Christian state as described by Whitehead, which would threaten the religious liberty within their own states. Humanists, such as James Madison and Thomas Jefferson, agreed with these Separatists and formed an alliance with them. James Madison was later tasked with the responsibility of drafting these amendments or Bill of Rights, having them passed by the first Congress, and approved by the states. And the Supreme Court has been trying to safeguard these civil liberties ever since.

Over time, each of the six states that had an established state religion would realize the merits and logic of religious liberty—not just on the national level, but on the state level as well. These six religious states eventually amended their constitutions and became secular states with no established religion, modeled on the federal Constitution. But it was not until 1833 that Massachusetts finally disestablished the Puritan religion and eliminated its tax for the state-established religion. Each state had finally established its own secular government that allowed religious liberty. Neither Congress *nor* the state legislators could establish a religious state. Religious liberty had finally triumphed in the United States.

With this mixed history, neo-Puritans today can easily find historical material to support their assertion that America was originally a Christian nation. Much of this evidence is in the form of sermons, state laws, and even state constitutions from the Puritan and Anglican colonies. That does not mean, however, that the attempt by these colonies to establish a theocratic state was biblically correct—any more than the Emperor Theodosius's attempts in the Roman Empire, the Catholic popes' attempts in Europe, or Calvin's attempts in Geneva. From a biblical perspective, they all were wrong, and they all failed.

The irony of this call today by many Christian leaders for America to return to its golden days as a Christian nation is that the vast majority of neo-Puritans are from denominations that would have been prohibited from establishing churches in the original Puritan colony of Massachusetts. Only the state-established Congregational denomination was permitted at that time. They would not have been allowed to organize and build a Baptist, Presbyterian, or Pentecostal church. If they had attempted to establish a church plant, they would have been imprisoned or driven out of the colony, as was Roger Williams. The neo-Puritans of today would have been jailed, fined, whipped, and expelled from many of the original colonies—so much for the so-called golden days! Yet their call today for America to return to its roots as a Christian nation continues to fill Christian airwaves, shelves of Christian bookstores, and online Christian media.

Today the majority of neo-Puritans use the phrase "Christian nation" loosely; they do not mean that this country should actually return to a Christian theocracy. When contemporary culture does not reflect Christian values, they hearken back to the days when Christianity was the dominant influence of the culture. Other times, when religious liberty is being denied in a secular setting, they will clamor for a return to the Rhode Island version of a state that celebrated religious liberty and not the Puritan Massachusetts version. But this is a highly confusing use of the term "Christian nation," for it comingles the idea of a Christian *theocracy* with its *cultural values* with true *religious liberty,* an idea that came from Christian Separatists who were adamantly opposed to a theocracy. Rhode Island was not a Christian state; it was a secular state with religious liberty. If you want religious liberty, you want to return to the secular state of Rhode Island where Paul's prayer for religious liberty came true: "First of all, then, I urge that supplications, prayers, intercessions, and thanksgivings be made for all people, for kings and all who are in high positions, that we may lead a peaceful and quiet life, godly and dignified in every way" (1 Tim. 2:1–2).

If you want a Christian theocratic nation, then you want to return to Puritan Massachusetts, Calvin's Geneva, or Augustine's Catholic Church—counterfeit versions of Christ's future messianic kingdom. According to Augustine, Calvin, the Puritans, and the neo-Puritans of today, we are presently experiencing the messianic reign of Christ. But if that were the case, then we would expect the New Testament to be full of information dealing with how the disciples went about setting up Christ's kingdom on this earth and how this messianic nation should be governed. After all, the Old Testament provides detailed information about how the Jewish nation was to be governed. We would expect to find Paul traveling to Antioch, Ephesus, and Thessalonica to establish Christian city-states like Calvin's Geneva to begin the reign of the Messiah, furnishing them with detailed instructions on governance in Christ's earthly reign.

These would be legitimate expectations if indeed the 1,000-year reign of Christ has begun, as Augustine and others asserted. But the New Testament does not contain this type of information. And, sadly, much of Western history revolves around the struggle to answer these types of questions. Amillennial theologians prevalent in the church at the time the Roman emperors set out to establish Christianity as the official religion of the empire fell into the trap of believing that the millennial reign of Christ had begun. As a result, practical questions on governance in Christ's kingdom had to be addressed. Would an emperor like Constantine convene a council of Christian bishops in Nicaea to define church doctrine, or would a parliament call for the formation of a Westminster Confession of Faith? And because King David ruled over a monarchical Jewish theocracy, monarchical forms of government had too much staying power in Christendom or Europe. Operating from within an Old Testament paradigm, it took more than a thousand years for representative forms of government to emerge in the Western world.

The Separatists Were Right

The Separatists' biblical interpretation and logic prevailed, becoming the pattern for the federal government and, eventually, for all the states. The fact that humanists, such as Madison and Jefferson, and intellectuals, such as John Locke in England, agreed with the Separatist ideology of church and state and formed an alliance with them should not impugn the theology of these Christian Separatists. Besides, historians give too much credit to the Enlightenment philosophers for the origin of the concept of a secular state with religious liberty.

The idea originated with a new understanding of the biblical ideology going all the way back to groups like the Anabaptists during the Reformation who began clamoring for religious liberty. Roger Williams predated John Locke, considered to be a central figure of the Enlightenment and a leading proponent of religious tolerance. Williams (1603–1683) wrote about and implemented concepts that Locke (1632–1704) then wrote about several decades later. Locke was only four years old when Williams founded Rhode Island in 1636. Rhode Island was possibly the first secular state with religious liberty in history. And this was the result of a revised theological understanding of the Scriptures by Williams, not the result of humanist or Enlightenment philosophy.

Williams's tracts and writings were well publicized, and one would assume that Locke read Williams's writings, observed the colony of Rhode Island, and incorporated Williams's ideas into his own seminal essay titled "A Letter Concerning Toleration," written in 1689, or fifty-three years after Rhode Island was formed.[12] This essay proved to be one of the most important documents in Western history regarding religious tolerance and, ultimately, representative democracy. Locke was a prominent intellectual, and his teachings about religious tolerance and the function of the state had a profound effect on America's founding fathers. Madison and Jefferson took Locke's ideas on religious toleration a step further and established true religious liberty, even allowing atheists full rights as citizens of the state of Virginia, as well as of the United States.

But the origin of this ideology was not Jefferson or the humanists of the Enlightenment period. The concept of a separation of church and state with civil liberties originated with Christian Separatists, such as Williams, who derived their theories from a rereading of the Scriptures, enabling them to escape the errors of Augustine and Calvin. Religious liberty was a theological construct by believers that the humanists of the Enlightenment later absorbed into their philosophical and political ideologies.

The Origin of Civil Liberties

The First Amendment to the U.S. Constitution not only guarantees religious liberty, but also the freedom of speech, the freedom of the press, and the freedom of assembly. Religious liberty is the first liberty that is stated and is the single most important one, because all other civil and political liberties are a derivative of this seminal freedom.

---

[12] John Locke, *A Letter on Toleration*, ed. Raymond Klibansky, trans. J.W. Gough (Oxford: Oxford University Press, 1968).

When religious liberty is guaranteed through the establishment of a secular state, the remaining freedoms logically follow. Here is how it works. To experience religious liberty and freely practice your religion, whether it is Judaism, Hinduism, Buddhism, or some form of Christianity, you must have the right to *assemble* as a congregation. A freely assembled congregation, in turn, must have the right for its ministers or leaders to preach and teach, which means they require *freedom of speech*. The congregation must also be able to freely record and publish its sermons and beliefs in written form, which translates into *freedom of the press*.

Once people realized that religious liberty required the freedoms of assembly, speech, and press, then liberty for all individuals and nonreligious groups followed. One could freely form a political party that, like a religious congregation, would be free to assemble, speak, and print what it believed. Until the Western world conceived of the idea of a secular state with religious liberty, Western civilizations did not enjoy civil and political liberties any more than they did religious liberty.

Admittedly, this is a very brief overview of Western intellectual history, but it helps describe what took place during the centuries when eschatology had become distorted and brilliant men, such as Augustine and Calvin, made major mistakes in interpreting the biblical data on the future 1,000-year messianic kingdom as portrayed in Revelation 20. As a result, the comingling of church and state became terribly confused and plagued the Western world for fourteen hundred years with the resultant loss of religious liberty. This loss of religious freedom within countries reputed to be Christianized can be traced back to the Roman emperors' attempts to turn the pagan Roman Empire into a Christian Roman Empire during a time when amillennial eschatology was the prevailing view.

The amillennial church leaders at the time were ill-prepared for this unexpected turn of events, and, because of their misunderstanding of the millennial kingdom described in Revelation 20, they were vulnerable to misinterpreting the New Testament teachings on the role of the church and state. Their spiritualized interpretation of the first resurrection, combined with their belief that the 1,000-year reign of Christ had already begun, created a trap into which they fell. They falsely concluded that once the Gentile kings of the earth had become Christians, then the millennium was being realized on this earth through Christian nations ruled by Christ. Since Israel had rejected its Messiah, they reasoned that the Christian Gentile nations must be fulfilling the Old Testament messianic prophecies. The result of this misunderstanding of the messianic kingdom was a gross misunderstanding of the New Testament view of church and state, which resulted in the loss of religious liberty—as well as centuries of unnecessary persecution and tyranny.

Impact on the Islamic World

Getting eschatology wrong has had serious consequences not only in the Western world, but in the Islamic world as well. Mohammad (c. 570–632) rejected the pagan religions around him in the Saudi Arabian peninsula. He was illiterate, not able to read and analyze the Old and New Testaments himself. He listened intently to the oral teachings of both the Jewish and Christian communities in the city of Mecca, in Arabia, where he was born and lived most of his life. He absorbed their worldviews, including their views on church and state.

The Jewish community in Mecca was still anticipating a Messiah and a restored Jewish theocracy. The Jews in Mecca at that time were especially enlivened with messianic expectations. Mohammad was also exposed to the ideology associated with the Christian Roman Empire and the Catholic Church. This Christian worldview was Augustinian. The church and state were merged into a type of theocracy modeled after Israel and based on the reign of Christ that supposedly began with the Christian Roman emperors.

Christianity during Mohammad's day was an empire—a Roman Empire in the West and a Byzantine Empire in the East. The Christian Roman Empire had made an attempt in Mohammad's day to conquer neighboring Persia, modern-day Iran, with the sword in order to expand Christ's kingdom, but was repelled. Mohammad's nation in the Saudi peninsula was a pagan state typical of the ancient world.

Mohammad's strange visions led him to believe he was a prophet in the tradition of the Jewish and even Christian prophets. Mohammad's ideas are an eclectic blend of the Jewish and Augustinian Christian ideologies that he absorbed from the world around him. As a result, his vision of a spiritual kingdom on earth was one of a religious or theocratic state. He was never exposed to the concept of a secular state with religious liberty. This concept simply did not exist at that time in history.

Mohammad envisioned a kingdom that would use the sword to expand and enforce his true doctrines—just as the Christian Roman Empire had done. He and his followers set out to create an Islamic Empire, just as the Roman Christians had set out to establish a Christian Empire.

Not all Islamic states today are theocracies, however, and there is great variation in governments within the Islamic world. Modern-day Turkey is the only modern Islamic state that has experimented with the creation of a secular state. And this is the result of one man, Mustafa Kemal Atatürk (1881–1938), who tried to force it upon an Islamic society—not the result of a new interpretation of Mohammad's teachings. He was only marginally successful.

Moderate and liberal Muslims may develop a concept of a secular state modeled after Western states, but, in doing so, they are being unfaithful to

Mohammad's teachings. The more Islamic a nation is, the less religious freedom it has. Becoming a Christian in the conservative Islamic country of Saudi Arabia is a capital offense. As Islamic fundamentalists—those whose teachings are truer to the teachings of Mohammad—become more powerful in Islamic countries, such as Iran, it becomes more dangerous for Christian groups, or any other religious group, to operate.

Christians can find support in the New Testament for the separation of church and state. But in the Koran, Muslims cannot find comparable teachings that lead to the separation of church and state. All Mohammad's teachings are modeled after a Jewish theocracy or an Augustinian understanding of church and state. A reformation in the Islamic world means a return to the theocracy of Mohammad and Islamic fundamentalism.

As such, there are no equivalent Islamic separatists who, as *conservative* theologians, can reinterpret the Koran and come up with a justification for a secular state with religious liberty. The Puritans may have made serious mistakes in interpreting the Bible, but conservative theologians can go to the Scriptures and reinterpret the New Testament teachings and correct these mistakes. A conservative evangelical can build a strong case for the concept of a secular state with religious liberty from the teachings of Christ and the apostles. In contrast, the Koran offers no vision of a secular state with religious liberty. A conservative Muslim is locked into the teachings of a theocracy. The only way a Muslim can support the idea of a secular state with religious liberty is to be a *liberal* Muslim, one who is unfaithful to the true teachings of Mohammad.

Through the combined efforts of the Christian Separatists and the humanists of the Enlightenment, such as Thomas Jefferson, the Western world escaped Augustine's flawed understanding of Revelation 20. But this only occurred after centuries of religious wars and civil strife. Augustine's unbiblical interpretation of Revelation continues to haunt the world today, as most of the Islamic world remains trapped in the ideology of a religious state similar to the Augustinian view of church and state.

The faulty eschatology of amillennialism at the time of Constantine has had serious and long-lasting consequences, not only in the Western world, but in the Islamic world as well. That is why in the twenty-first century we still have to deal with Islamic states like Iran. Misinterpreting Revelation 20 had the unintended consequences of producing a faulty biblical ideology of church and state that had major historical ramifications.

What If Postrestorationalism Had Been the Prevailing View?

I have often wondered how history would have unfolded if postrestorationalism and its corresponding view of church and state had been the prevailing eschatological view at the time when Emperor

Constantine became a Christian. Church leaders and theologians would have likely advised these Roman emperors not to attempt to create a Christian nation at that time. They would have understood that the only time Christianity could be a state religion would be at an unknown future date *after* the Tribulation when Satan is removed and Christ begins his reign over this world from his throne in heaven. They would have probably advised the emperors to wait and let Christ create the Christian nations of the world when the Father said it was time.

They would have likely advised the Roman Emperors Constantine and Theodosius to first decriminalize Christianity and then systematically disestablish the pagan religions in the Roman Empire as well as in individual cities. Next, they would have encouraged them to create a state unaffiliated with any religion, that is, a secular state allowing the pagan religions, as well as Christianity, to compete for the hearts and minds of the people in a free marketplace of ideas. Favoritism would not be shown toward any particular religion, nor would state taxes be used to support one religion over the other. Most important, the sword would not be used to advance one religion over the next.

Over time, the pagan gods with their pagan priests and temples would be abandoned, becoming archeological sites, as they would be no match for Christianity. When people visit the Pantheon in Rome or the Parthenon in Athens, they no longer visit the sites to worship the Roman god Neptune or the Greek goddess Athena. They see fascinating buildings but vanquished religions. The pagan religions of Roman times could not compete with the Creator of the heavens and the earth, also a loving and personal being who could be known intimately now and for eternity. None of the pagan Roman or Greek gods were depicted as all-powerful and holy, yet loving and personal. Most were devious, selfish, unloving, and unpredictable.

The Christian idea of becoming a child of a loving God and calling him "Abba, Father," with the promise of immortality in heaven, was a radically new concept to the Romans. This is one reason Christianity, despite persecution, grew significantly in the pagan Roman world during the first three hundred years of its existence, reaching as much as 15 percent of the population—without the help of its emperors.

Neither postrestorationalism nor premillennialism was the prevailing view at the time, so none of the Christian Roman emperors were advised that establishing a secular state with religious liberty would be the best form of interim governance until Christ established his millennial kingdom. Even if the emperors had been familiar with postrestorationalism, there is no guarantee they would have heeded this counsel. The idea of a state not having an official religion was unheard of in the ancient world. A secular government would have been a difficult concept for them to grasp, much less follow. If they had, it would have been a revolutionary concept that changed the course of world history.

It seems a tragedy that amillennialism was the prevailing view at the time of Constantine's unexpected conversion. If postrestorationalism had prevailed, the church theologians would have had the emperor's ear and presented their perspective of a secular state with religious liberty as the best form of governance until Christ began his reign. Instead, the emperors were counseled by theologians who rejected the idea of a literal future 1,000-year restoration and were directed to chart a course that led to a Christian empire that dominated the Western world for more than fourteen hundred years.

The church suddenly became the recipient of the vast financial resources of the imperial regime. Rodney Stark describes the consequences in his book *Discovering God*:

> A faith that had been meeting in homes and humble structures was suddenly housed in magnificent public buildings . . . A Clergy recruited from the people and modestly sustained by member contributions suddenly gained immense power, status, and wealth as part of the imperial civil service. Bishops "now became grandees on par with the wealthiest senators." Consequently, in the words of Richard Fletcher, the "privileges and exemptions granted the Christian clergy precipitated a stampede into the priesthood." As Christian offices became another form of imperial preferment, they were soon filled by the sons of the aristocracy. . . . There was no obligation that one be morally qualified, let alone that one be "called."[13]

Many historians now recognize that medieval Europeans were even less religious than they are today. Stark points out that modern Europe is still not operating as a secular state with true religious liberty. Vestiges of state-established religions remain, making it difficult for independent evangelical churches to obtain building permits or licenses to hold public religious meetings in existing structures. Stark points out that it is still very difficult to build an evangelical church facility in Belgium and Spain. This helps to explain why modern Europe has become a spiritual wasteland and is in desperate need of religious liberty *and* evangelism.

In contrast, evangelical Christianity is flourishing in the United States where there are no federal or state-established religions and there is a free marketplace among competing churches and religions. A new church or church plant can use the facilities of a public school to become established and, as they grow, buy land and build a church building if they so desire.

---

[13] Rodney Stark, *Discovering God* (New York: HarperCollins, 2007), 328.

Creating Secular States

The most important public policy issue that Christians can advance is the creation of secular states with religious liberty, in this country and around the world. The best method for Christians to spread their beliefs is to operate within secular nations that have religious freedom. Christians should be the greatest advocates of this ideology, particularly in parts of the world where religious liberty is highly restricted, such as in Communist and Islamic nations. Freedom of religion includes the right of every person to determine his or her own eternal destiny.

I believe there will be religious liberty in the millennium, even though nations will be required to go to Jerusalem for various religious festivals of celebration. Not everyone will be a believer in the restoration. People will have the liberty to believe or not believe in Christ without fear of the sword. With Satan bound during the millennium, however, it is unlikely there will be false prophets or major forms of religious deception. Demons will no longer be active in the world to inspire false teachings, heresies, pagan deities, or atheistic forms of humanism or communism.

Secular Humanism

Many Christians mistakenly think of the ideology of secular humanism when they hear the words "secular state." As a result, they often recoil at the mention of the word *secular* in reference to the state. I have tested this on several occasions in Christian gatherings. I said something to the effect that "Christ invented the secular state." On each occasion, my fellow Christians became quite upset. Surely Christ would have advocated a Christian nation, not a secular one.

It is evident from their negative reactions that they have a fundamental misunderstanding of what a secular state is and how it should function. If a civil state is attempting to enforce humanism or naturalism—a form of religion—then it is not acting in the manner of a true secular state. In fact, secular humanism is America's greatest threat to liberty—not neo-Puritans clamoring for America to return to being a Christian nation. When secular humanism as a religion controls the state, the state becomes hostile to other religions, including Christianity.

For example, Christians and their organizations are often discriminated against and even persecuted in public schools and universities because they challenge Darwinian evolution and believe in the Genesis creation or intelligent design. This discrimination is evidence that the state is no longer operating as a secular state; it is advancing and protecting an established humanistic and naturalistic philosophy.

The concept of "secular state" should not be synonymous with "secular humanism." The secular realm should be a free marketplace of ideas that includes naturalism *and* supernaturalism as an explanation of origins and reality. But naturalists have hijacked the secular sphere. Under the pretext of separation of church and state, naturalists want to ban public school students from writing essays that discuss students' faith in the supernatural, ban Bible studies from public school grounds, and ban parachurch organizations such as Campus Crusade for Christ and InterVarsity Christian Fellowship from facilities at public universities because their bylaws require their leaders to be practicing Christians.

Naturalists also want to ban discussions of the Genesis creation in science courses and criticism of Darwinian evolution, etc. And this ban on the search for truth is coming from a supposedly liberal tradition that claims to want to explore all sources of truth in a free and open arena. America is not a secular state in the truest sense of the word, but rather a neo-pagan state with Darwinian evolution as the doctrinal foundation. In this religious state, the law excludes ideologies with a spiritual point of view from public or secular schools. Christians are free to discuss their "unscientific and irrational" ideology on their own turf, but not in a secular arena, because secular means an exclusively naturalistic realm.

This distorted secular worldview maintains that only the natural world is real and scientifically verifiable. Since God and the spiritual world are not, they are not to be discussed in the public realm. As a result, public school and university biology teachers can only teach the philosophy of Darwinian evolution. Any discussion concerning the Genesis account of creation, or even intelligent design, is considered an unconstitutional establishment of religion. One cannot challenge the doctrine of evolution, much less offer an alternative view of origins. The secular state is no longer operating as a true secular state because it advances a naturalistic philosophy at the exclusion of any ideology that is spiritual in nature.

Secular humanists have a fundamentally flawed understanding of how a secular state should function. A true secular state is one in which the discussion and consideration of the natural—as well as the supernatural—can take place in a free marketplace of ideas. There is nothing inherently wrong with studying and discussing the supernatural in secular public schools. Secular should not mean that only naturalism is to be discussed and supernaturalism excluded. The secular arena should not advocate the indoctrination of only one view. Rather, it should be a neutral forum that teaches critical thinking and supports the liberty of thought and ideas.

It is considered appalling that in countries such as Iran, Saudi Arabia, and China, entire ideologies are excluded from the marketplace of ideas. Religious police or party members within those countries regulate a closed intellectual society. Yet in this country, the leaders of our free and open public domain within public schools and universities act in the same way as those religious police and will not allow the teaching of "religious" ideology in relation to creation.

For a secular arena to properly function, it should be a free marketplace for all ideologies of origins—religious as well as humanistic or supernatural as well as natural philosophies. Young men and women should be exposed to a variety of ideologies and be taught to think critically. Let them decide for themselves what truth is. That is what liberty is all about, and how a secular forum should function. The public domain should be a free marketplace of ideas where people can explore the truth and ultimately determine their own eternal destinies. Religious liberty is the preeminent human right. A decision concerning eternal destiny is the most important decision in this life that any person can make, and no government should ever interfere with this most basic human right.

Neo-Puritan Christians also need to stop clamoring for symbols of a Christian nation in the public square. Neo-Puritans want the Pledge of Allegiance to acknowledge God in every classroom, public school athletic teams to acknowledge God in prayer, courtroom art to acknowledge God, town halls to display nativity scenes on their grounds, etc. But we do not need town hall to display a nativity scene when our church down the street can easily display one and have Christians on hand to explain the meaning of the virgin birth and God incarnate.

Has anyone ever become a Christian because of reciting the Pledge of Allegiance? Demons acknowledge God, and what good does that do them? God does not want to be paid lip service; he wants to be worshiped. And to properly worship God, a person must have a good understanding of the gospel of Jesus Christ. The Pledge of Allegiance is not the gospel. Nor is it the responsibility of the secular state to propagate the gospel. The Great Commission is the responsibility of the church.

The demands made and lawsuits filed by Christians on these issues are counterproductive and give secular humanists and naturalists another excuse to keep discussions of biblical ideology out of the public domain. We are losing the battle for the hearts and minds of people in this country because we are fighting the wrong battles with the wrong objectives. We should be fighting for a true secular public domain with true religious liberty, where free speech and free press can operate. And we need to understand the baggage that comes from hundreds of years when Christianity was the established religion of the state or colony, and how much this scares non-Christians and distracts from the gospel message and the true witness of the church. Christ wants us to use the church as our message to the world, not some pseudo-Christian nation run by politicians who may or may not be Christians. Neo-Puritanism also destroys our credibility when we encourage Islamic nations to become secular states with religious liberty.

Summary

Amillennial eschatology as it evolved into postmillennialism set the stage for the concept of a Christian nation, set in motion with Constantine's conversion and Theodosius's establishment of Christianity as the official religion of the Roman Empire. The new Christian Gentile nations and kings were considered a fulfillment of the messianic reign of Christ as King of kings and Lord of lords that was prophesied in the Old Testament and described by John in the book of Revelation.

This view of church and state not only deprived people of the Western world of religious liberty, but of all other civil liberties as well. As a result, untold numbers of Christians and other innocent people were oppressed, imprisoned, tortured, and killed during the succeeding centuries. The Spanish Inquisition (active from the late 1400s to the early 1800s), which acted as the church court of Spain enforcing the Catholic traditions, was particularly brutal. And the mistreatment of Jews throughout Europe under Christendom was especially shameful.[14] As is readily apparent, the consequences of misinterpreting Revelation 20 have been enormous.

No one knows just how much the Roman emperors and early church postmillennialists, such as Augustine, slowed progress in the Western world. The Puritan Separatists, with their revised understanding of the New Testament ideology of church and state, were able to change things. But sadly, the so-called Christian world had its eschatology wrong for more than fourteen hundred years, leaving a trail of tyranny, persecution, bloodshed, and tears—much of which could have been avoided had Revelation 20 been properly understood.

It is unfortunate that amillennialism was the prevailing view when the Roman emperors set out to establish Christ's messianic kingdom on this earth. As it morphed into postmillennialism, it provided Satan the perfect opportunity to delude sinful men into thinking they had the right to rule this world in the name of Christ. The misinterpretation of Revelation 20 resulted in the loss of religious liberty for centuries.

From an accurate reading of the New Testament, we know that Jesus, the messianic king, was crucified. And, after he was resurrected, he left this earth and ascended to heaven—without beginning his reign. Immediately before he left, the disciples asked if he was now going to establish his earthly messianic kingdom. Christ told them that only the Father knows when his reign will begin, and they should wait. He then commanded them to go out and make disciples of all nations by convincing them that he was indeed the promised Messiah, despite the fact that he is not currently exercising his

---

[14] For a heartbreaking history of the mistreatment of Jews as a result of this faulty eschatology, see Barry E. Horner, *Future Israel: Why Christian Anti-Judaism Must Be Challenged* (Nashville: B&H Academic, 2004).

reign over this world. He directed them to first approach the Jews with this gospel and then deliver it to the Gentile world. But instead of attempting to establish a messianic nation based on the Old Testament prophecies, his disciples preached almost exclusively about the kingdom of heaven.

Most important, the disciples *never tell those they disciple* to go out and establish the messianic kingdom—which is why the New Testament, unlike the Old Testament, contains no information concerning civil rules of governance. Neither the church nor the state has a spiritual-civil covenant with God as did Israel.

Will Christ ever rule over the nations? He most definitely will. In the future restoration, Christ will indeed establish his messianic kingdom when he rules over the nations from heaven. But this only happens when the Father says it is time for Christ to exercise his reign and Satan is completely removed from influencing the world. Only God the Father has the right to decide when Christ is going to rule this world—a world that was created through his Son, by his Son, and for his Son. And it only occurs after the Great Tribulation and after Satan is bound. At that time, Christ will resurrect all the departed saints into natural Adamic bodies to experience his earthly kingdom. Some of these saints will be given thrones in order to rule with him over his kingdom. But Christ and his saints will rule with absolute justice, and the entire world will experience peace. Christ will not allow any form of tyranny from human rulers. The form of governance that will be in place during the restoration will be revealed at that time.

When Christ was on this earth, he refused to get involved in the civil affairs of man because it was not time for him to reign as Messiah. It was difficult for even the disciples to wait for his reign. Not all the disciples' motives were wrong; they hated the tyranny, injustice, and evil around them and desired for God's will to be done on earth as it is in heaven. They hated the false religions around them as well, and sincerely wanted people to worship the true God.

Today many Christians have the same impatience as that of the disciples. We have an innate desire for Christ to rule the world and for God's will to be done on earth. We desire justice, and we naturally react against false teachings that bring spiritual harm. Unfortunately, we often let this desire control our thinking when we press forward in our timing by attempting to establish Christian nations instead of waiting on the Father's timing.

In the meantime, Christ wants us to use the church, a spiritual assembly of believers, to spread his message to the world—and not use the state for that purpose. Then one day, after the Great Tribulation, he will truly form Christian nations and rule as King of kings and Lord of lords, establishing true righteousness, justice, peace, and prosperity on this earth during the restoration. But only God as the Creator of this Genesis creation has the right to rule this world—when he decides to do so.

14

Israel and the Church

Origen accused the millennialists of his day of "understanding the divine Scriptures in a sort of Jewish sense" when it came to their belief in a literal messianic kingdom on this earth centered in Jerusalem. There is a great deal of truth in this accusation. Some years ago, I witnessed to a Jewish couple about my faith in Jesus Christ. As the conversation progressed, it became obvious that they considered Christianity a Gentile religion distinctly different from Judaism, assuming that its origins were from the Greeks, Romans, or some other pagan religion.

At that point, I changed the tone of the conversation and said, in effect:

Wait a minute. Jesus of Nazareth was a Jew. All his original disciples, including the apostle Paul, were Jewish evangelists who believed he was the Jewish Messiah. *Christ* is simply Greek for the Hebrew word *Messiah*. The early church in Jerusalem was essentially Jewish. Christianity is a Jewish religion despite the fact that it was spread to the Roman world by Jewish evangelists and the vast majority of its adherents has been, and continues to be, non-Jews. *Christianity* means "Christ followers" including Jews and Gentiles. As a Gentile, I am a follower of a Jewish Messiah—not a Gentile Messiah.

This historical lesson caught them by surprise. Christians get so used to viewing the church as a Gentile community with a few Jews scattered in our midst that we sometimes forget Christianity had its origins in Judaism, brought to us by Jewish evangelists. After all, as Jesus informed the Samaritan woman, "salvation is from the Jews" (John 4:22).

I made these points so forcefully that as I left the conversation, I began to ponder, *Does following the Jewish Messiah make me a Jew?* One of the greatest challenges the Jewish disciples faced as the gospel began to spread from the Jews in Jerusalem to the Gentile nations was whether or not

Gentiles, like me, who became believers were in effect converting to Judaism and, as a result, needed to follow Jewish customs such as circumcision and Jewish dietary law.

It was natural for Peter, James, and the other apostles to ask how the Gentiles would be incorporated into the Messiah's kingdom. When Gentiles were saved, were they supposed to convert to Judaism and become part of the nation of Israel? Should they be circumcised as a sign of their joining true Judaism? Or did God reject the nation of Israel for a period of time because it rejected its Messiah by having him crucified, and temporarily replace it with the interim institution of the church, a universal community of any and all of God's people who believe in Christ—circumcised and uncircumcised?

As the book of Acts and the Epistles attest, the answer to these questions consumed a great deal of the apostles' time. Remember, Paul was a Jewish apostle and evangelist specially devoted to the Gentiles and, as such, was a lightning rod in the early church regarding some of these issues. In one instance, he sharply confronted Peter over this issue of how Gentiles should be incorporated into the Jewish messianic kingdom (Gal. 2:11–14). Paul also had to contend with certain Jewish believers, some who were converted Pharisees like himself, who were going to the churches he had started throughout the Roman Empire and insisting that the Gentile believers in those churches become circumcised and follow Jewish religious customs and rituals (Phil. 3:2–3).

Paul believed these Judaizers were distorting the gospel (Gal. 1:6–7). He became so angry with them that he wished they would castrate themselves, in addition to being circumcised (Gal. 5:12). To ask a full-grown Gentile man to undergo circumcision following conversion was a wholly different matter than being circumcised as an eight-day-old infant. Paul knew that circumcision would be a major barrier for Gentile men who desired to follow Christ. As a rite of passage into the kingdom, baptism, on the other hand, was inoffensive.

The issue of Gentile circumcision became so contentious that Paul went to the Jewish elders of the church in Jerusalem in an attempt to reach a definitive church policy on the issue so that he could implement it throughout the churches he had planted in key Roman cities. The council in Jerusalem debated the issue, and even Peter acknowledged that following Mosaic law, including circumcision, had been difficult even for the Jews: "Now, therefore, why are you putting God to the test by placing a yoke on the neck of the disciples that neither our fathers nor we have been able to bear?" (Acts 15:10).

Having to submit to Jewish dietary law would have been another major barrier for Gentiles who wanted to follow the Jewish Messiah and join his kingdom. For example, imagine a modern-day Jewish evangelist preaching to unbelievers in the state of Louisiana that to become followers of Christ, they must follow Jewish law in regard to their diet. To become Christians, they would no longer be able to eat shrimp, crabs, oysters, crawfish, catfish, roasted pork, jambalaya, seafood gumbo, red beans and rice with pork sausage, and many other favorite foods. This would present an almost insurmountable barrier to evangelism. I was one of those heathens born and raised in Louisiana who grew up enjoying this cuisine. The fact that I could become a believer and follower of Jesus, the Jewish Messiah, without having to give up my native culture and cuisine was very important.

Obviously, the issue of whether a Gentile had to become a Jew upon becoming a believer was an enormous concern of the early church. If Gentiles do not need to be circumcised or follow Jewish dietary law when they become believers, then what about the Jews who believed? Is the Mosaic law abolished for them as well? Do they remain Jews? Is the church now the only relevant assembly of believers, or does Israel still have a future?

These questions are not easy to answer as evidenced by the early church's intense struggles with these issues. The fact that Paul and Peter had a major altercation over them reveals how difficult it was for the apostles themselves to come to terms with these concerns as Christianity rapidly spread from Jerusalem throughout the Roman world. How were Peter and James going to handle all the Jews in Jerusalem who became believers but remained zealous for the law? And how was a Jewish evangelist like Paul to handle these pagan Gentiles coming to believe in the Jewish Messiah?

These questions remain relevant today as theologians continue to sift through the Gospels and the apostles' teachings and actions and struggle to come up with a biblical understanding of the nature of Israel and the church. Answers to these questions have major eschatological implications as well. If you are not familiar with the debate between dispensational premillennialists and amillennialists on the subject of Israel and the church, you would be amazed at the number of books and articles that have been written on this subject, particularly as it relates to eschatology. This topic is vigorously debated. A great deal of eschatology rides on how these issues are resolved.

For example, amillennialists contend that there is no future for a restored nation of Israel under the rule of Christ during the millennium because the Jews rejected their Messiah and Christ rejected the nation of Israel. Therefore, there will be no messianic kingdom on this earth that revolves around a restored Israel. A believing Jew is like a believing Gentile in that he accepts Christ, joins the church, and becomes a part of the body of Christ in the new creation. Jews, like everyone else, are welcome to believe in Christ, but that only means they are part of the body of Christ that is going to heaven, like the rest of the church.

Many amillennialists interpret Peter's following statement to mean that the church is now the new "Israel" and, in effect, replaces the nation of Israel: "But you are a chosen race, a royal priesthood, a holy nation, a people for his own possession, . . . Once you were not a people, but now you are God's people . . ." (1 Peter 2:9–10). Believing Jews and Gentiles, as members of the church, are now part of a holy nation that is essentially not of this world, and the only future nation or kingdom is the heavenly kingdom. There is no future, restored, earthly kingdom of Israel. The church is all there is until the kingdom of heaven.

There are many problems with this interpretation, the main one being that nowhere in the New Testament is the church directly equated to Israel. Most likely, Peter is making an analogy between the chosen nation of Israel as "God's people" when they were faithful and the church—composed of believing Jews and Gentiles—as God's chosen people when they, too, are faithful and become the people of God. When Peter calls believers, or the church, a chosen race or a holy nation, he is not designating them as a literal race or civil nation like Israel, for the church is clearly made up of people from all races and nations and does not have a civil covenant with God that involves an ethnic group and nation with geographic boundaries.

The New Testament authors metaphorically compare the church to many things, such as the nation of Israel, the temple, a house—even a human body. Amillennialists are often accused of not taking the Scriptures literally. However, in this case, they are guilty of taking Peter's description of the believers as a holy nation far too literally. The idea that the church replaces the nation of Israel is not a valid deduction from this verse.

Some early amillennialists went so far as believing that the church did become the new Israel, a new type of theocratic Christian nation. And, historically, from the time of the Christian Roman Empire continuing through the Reformation, the Christian Gentile nations believed that they were, in fact, the new Israel—literally, a Christian nation with civil and spiritual responsibilities.

Their reasoning entrapped them to act as if they were a theocratic kingdom. After all, they were the messianic kingdom on earth until the second coming takes place on the last day. There was no future for Israel, so all the Old Testament messianic prophecies were loosely applied to the church and the corresponding theocratic Christian nations. As we saw in the previous chapter, this proved disastrous for religious liberty and for the church itself. Augustine and John Calvin, operating under this paradigm, had no problem asking the civil authorities to use the sword of the Christian state to enforce doctrinal purity and punish heretics, much like the Old Testament Jewish kings were supposed to punish and even kill false prophets. Israel was a theocracy, and only the religion of Judaism was to be practiced. Pagan religions were not to be tolerated. Likewise, in the Christian theocracy,

Christianity would be the only religion of the state; heretics would not be tolerated in Christ's kingdom on this earth.

In the Western world today with the existence of democratic secular states and religious liberty for autonomous churches, amillennialists do not make this same mistake. But they still see no future for Israel as a nation of God, for there is no future millennial kingdom centered on a restored Israel. They look at the modern nation of Israel, created in 1948, as a curiosity and nothing more.

Amillennialists believe that in Christ, as children of God, there is no distinction between Jew and Gentile. They fail to understand, however, that as long as God has plans for a restoration of the Adamic order of being, the distinctions between Jew and Gentile remain. One day Israel will play a strategic role in the reign of Christ over the nations of this world with the disciples acting as judges over a restored Israel.

On the other hand, many dispensational premillennialists have made too much of a distinction between Israel and the church in order to preserve the Bible's teaching on a literal messianic kingdom on this earth. Progressive dispensationalists have corrected many of these extreme distinctions between Israel and the church.

In this battle between the various camps of eschatology, much of the artillery fire results from the differing interpretations of the New Testament teachings on Israel and the church. All uses of the words *Jew, Gentile, church, Israel,* and *nation* in the New Testament are highly scrutinized and interpreted in a way to fit the various systems of eschatology. Amillennialists latch onto verses that teach there is no distinction in Christ between Jew and Gentile, and premillennialists look for verses that maintain a clear distinction between them.

If amillennialists can prove there is no future for Israel now that the church has been instituted, then it substantiates their position of no future 1,000-year restoration centered around the restored nation of Israel. Conversely, if premillennialists can prove Israel and believing Jews, distinct from believing Gentles, do have a future, then it supports their position that someday the "nation will be restored to Israel" as Jesus promised before he ascended to heaven (Acts 1:6–7).

Volumes have been written on the subject. But understanding these issues is critical to developing a coherent biblical eschatology. With the postrestorational framework and the organizing principle of the two orders of being, the distinction between the church and Israel is much simpler.

Israel and the Church from a Postrestorational Perspective

Much of the discord and confusion over this issue stems from a failure to understand and maintain a distinction between the Adamic order of being and the new order of being as children of God. Christ may be the Jewish Messiah, but, much to the surprise of the disciples, he also turned out to be God incarnate, the Son of God, and the second person of the Trinity through whom the whole world was created. And anyone, Jew or Gentile, who believes in him and his Father who sent him is born of God and becomes a new creation that is neither Jew nor Gentile.

Any person, circumcised or uncircumcised, who believes in Christ can become a child of God. In this new order of being, there is no distinction between Jew and Gentile, just as there is no distinction between male and female: "for in Christ Jesus you are all sons of God, through faith. For as many of you as were baptized into Christ have put on Christ. There is neither Jew nor Greek, there is neither slave nor free, there is neither male nor female, for you are all one in Christ Jesus" (Gal. 3:26–28). Therefore, a Gentile does not have to be circumcised or convert to Judaism in order to become a son of God and a member of the kingdom of God.

At the transformation, the Adamic distinction of being Jewish will end, for in heaven the Jewish believer will simply be a child of God. The future heavenly kingdom is not a Jewish kingdom, just as it is not an Adamic kingdom. In heaven we will not say, "There is a female child of God," nor will we say, "There is a Jewish child of God." Instead, we will simply say, "There is a child of God in the image of Christ."

As long as we are on this earth operating in the Adamic order of being, however, the distinctions between Jew and Gentile remain, just as they do between male and female. Believers live two orders of being concurrently until the last day. Then, when the new order of being is consummated, all class distinctions, racial distinctions, as well as sexual distinctions will end. Until that day, we continue to live out both orders of being simultaneously. The new order of being does not erase or terminate the Adamic order of being while we remain on this earth. Just as believers remain male and female human beings, so, too, we remain Jew and Gentile.

A believing Jew is a physical descendant of Abraham in the Adamic order of being as well as a child of God in the new order of being. But as long as this earth exists, the Jews and Israel will continue to function as an Adamic people and as a nation through which God will carry out his plan of redemption and restoration of this Adamic order of being.

In the 1,000-year restoration through the first resurrection, the remnant of believing Jews will be part of the restored nation of Israel, and the believing Gentiles from all ages will be part of their corresponding restored nation. From his throne in heaven, Christ will rule over Israel and the whole world. All members of the body of Christ get to experience the restoration as restored mortal beings, Jew and Gentile.

When God made a covenant with Abraham, it was a two-tiered promise based on the two orders of being. First, there was the spiritual promise of becoming a child of God in the new order of being, which is why, as the writer of Hebrews points out, Abraham and other Old Testament believers looked forward to the heavenly Jerusalem in the eternal kingdom of God (Heb. 11:10, 16). Also, any person—Jew or Gentile—who believes in Christ is a spiritual descendant of Abraham as a child of God, looking forward to the kingdom of heaven: "There is neither Jew nor Greek, there is neither slave nor free, there is neither male nor female, for you are all one in Christ Jesus. And if you are Christ's, then you are Abraham's offspring, heirs [of heaven] according to promise" (Gal. 3:28–29).

Entrance into the kingdom of heaven and the New Jerusalem is not based on class, race, or sex. Rather, it is based on becoming a child of God. All believers—from Abel to Abraham to Moses to every Jewish and Gentile saint until the last day—become connected to Christ at the cross and become a part of the body of Christ, his bride, and will inherit the kingdom of heaven as children of God. This is what it means to be the spiritual heirs of Abraham.

The second tier of God's promise to Abraham concerned the Adamic order of being, which includes the earthly kingdom of Israel and, ultimately, the restoration of the Genesis creation in which Israel plays a key role. God chose the physical descendants of Abraham, the Jews, to establish a spiritual-civil covenant in the specific theocratic nation of Israel to bring the Jewish-born Messiah into the world.

Sometime in the future, God will use the resurrected believing Jews and the believing nation of Israel as the vehicle to create the worldwide restoration, which completes the mission of establishing the messianic kingdom on this earth. In the restoration, *believing* Jews—past, present, and future—will experience the messianic kingdom in the physical land of Israel through the first resurrection.

If a Gentile believes in Christ, he, too, will experience the first resurrection and the restoration through his respective nation. In the restoration, there will be a hierarchy of nations in which Israel will be the central nation through which Christ will exercise his reign over all restored Gentile nations. Jesus, as the Messiah *and* as the Son of God, will then rule the whole world because it was created for him. God used Israel to bring the Messiah into the world, and he will once again use Israel to establish the messianic kingdom.

The Function of the Church in This Interim Period

With Christ sitting at the right hand of God waiting for the Father to say it is time for his earthly reign to begin, all believers are in an unusual situation. Because the worldwide theocratic kingdom has not yet begun, God institutes a way for his people, both Jewish and Gentile, to gather into a community or assembly, the church, which does not have a civil covenant with him as did Israel. The church does not function as a civil nation with ethnic identity, borders, or the civil authority of the sword. Rather, it is a fellowship of believers that transcends borders and all ethnic groups.

During this interim era of the church, God's spiritual-civil covenant with the nation of Israel as God's faithful people is temporarily suspended. After telling the Jews the parable of the unfaithful tenants, Christ rebuked the unbelieving Jewish nation: "Therefore I tell you, the kingdom of God will be taken away from you and given to a people producing its fruits" (Matt. 21:43). Christ may have been referring to other believing Jews who will produce fruit, but history has shown that the Gentiles were the ones that have largely borne the fruit of faith.

Christ also prophesied that the Jewish temple would be destroyed, which occurred in AD 70. Since 1948, Israel has operated as a civil nation, and Jews still exist as an ethnic group around the world, but as a whole, they continue to reject their Messiah. They remain hostile to Christ and are not in fellowship with God the Father. The Jewish fig tree is still not producing fruit (Matt. 21:19). In the meantime, the church, primarily made up of believing Gentiles with a remnant of believing Jews, operates as a fellowship of God's people. During this interim period, the church operates best as a non-civil institution in a secular setting with religious liberty where it is free to gather, worship, preach, teach, publish, and evangelize while it waits for the restoration. The church is not a Jewish or a Gentile institution per se, but an assembly of God's people in a non-civil covenantal relationship. The church is like a holy nation in that it is a group of the people of God from all ethnic backgrounds, but it is not a nation in the technical sense, having specific borders and using the sword of civil authorities. When a large group of people become Christians in a particular nation, that does not mean they become a Christian nation. Someday, however, these Christians will be resurrected in the restoration and will truly form the Christian nations of the world. Until that time, the church functions as an interim non-civil institution established by God for all believers, Jew and Gentile.

Because the church is not a Jewish nation, it does not have to abide by the Mosaic civil code of conduct and, therefore, does not incorporate ceremonial functions such as circumcision, Jewish dietary law, and the Jewish system of temple sacrifice into its mode of operation. Paul was quite emphatic that Gentile believers did not have to become Jews, nor be circumcised, nor follow Jewish law in order to join the church as followers of the Jewish Messiah. A Gentile does not have to become a Jew to become a child of God and experience the restoration and then the transformation.

Likewise, a Jew can become a believer and join the church without becoming a Gentile. Paul taught Jews in the church to remain Jewish and to continue to be circumcised, and he taught Gentiles in the church to remain uncircumcised Gentiles (1 Cor. 7:18). Paul's letters focus so intently on correcting those legalistic Jews who wanted the Gentiles to convert to Judaism that we often overlook the fact that he still believed Jewish believers should remain Jews. He never advocates that they relinquish their identity as Jewish believers. And he never lets us forget that he is a Jewish believer.

God has used the Old Testament nation of Israel as the vehicle to bring about his entire system of redemption. Through Israel came Jesus the Passover lamb, the Messiah. Jesus was very clear when speaking to the Samaritan woman: "salvation is from the Jews" (John 4:22). Yet, currently, the Jewish nation is laid aside because the Jews, as a whole, rejected and continue to reject their Messiah. Today the spiritual-civil covenant with Israel is in a period of temporary suspension because the vast majority of Jews continue to violate their spiritual covenant with God.

The church, which is an assembly of believers without a civil Mosaic covenant, plays an interim role for the people of God to continue to know and worship God until the restoration. As a non-civil institution, the church fills the void during this time until Satan is bound and the earthly messianic reign begins. Israel still has a future, because someday the Jews will indeed be grafted back in so that the restoration can begin. At that time, the believing nation of Israel will again be used by God to accomplish his will on this earth when all the nations of the world, including Israel, become Christian nations. This is a short overview of the distinction between Israel and the church from a postrestorational perspective. But because this is such an important topic as it relates to God's kingdom on earth and in heaven, let us explore some of the New Testament teachings on Jew and Gentile, and Israel and the church from this framework.

Romans

Several sections of the New Testament are flashpoints in the debate over Israel and the church, but none is as important as this section of Paul's letter to the Romans:

> Lest you be wise in your own conceits, I want you to understand this mystery, brothers: a partial hardening has come upon Israel, until the fullness of the Gentiles has come in. And in this way all Israel will be saved, as it is written, "The Deliverer will come from Zion, he will banish ungodliness from Jacob; and this will be my covenant with them when I take away their sins." (11:25–27)

What does Paul mean by "all Israel will be saved" and "the Deliverer will come from Zion"? Because the interpretation of this verse has become so contentious, it is important first to analyze the context of these phrases.

Throughout the book of Romans, Paul distinguishes between two groups of people and a subgroup within each group: one group is the ethnic

Jews, believers and unbelievers, and the other group is Gentiles, believers and unbelievers. The Jewish and Gentile believers are the people of God destined for heaven, and the Jewish and Gentile unbelievers are not God's people and are destined for condemnation.

The main theme of the book of Romans is that the methodology of becoming a believer and being justified before God is the same for both Jews and Gentiles. No one is justified by birthright or by works of the Jewish law, for all are sinners and are justified and reconciled to God through repentance and faith in Jesus Christ, which comes to all individuals and groups by the grace of God:

> For I am not ashamed of the gospel, for it is the power of God for salvation to everyone who believes, to the Jew first and also to the Greek. For in it the righteousness of God is revealed from faith for faith, as it is written, "The righteous shall live by faith." (1:16–17)

Both Jews and Gentiles can become God's people if they are repentant and justified by faith in Jesus Christ. But the critical point to notice in Romans is that even though Paul says all people—Jew and Gentile—are in the same boat when it comes to being justified by faith, he continues to maintain a very clear distinction between Jews and Gentiles as fellow passengers in that boat. The boat of salvation still contains two types of passengers—believing Jews and believing Gentiles. Paul is consistent in this regard. Just because Jews and Gentiles are both justified by faith, it does not mean Jews cease to exist as a distinctive group with a specific eschatological future. Paul, a believing Jew, repeats these distinctions of Jew and Gentile as he builds his case around the fact that all people (Jew and Gentile) are sinners, all people (Jew and Gentile) are justified by faith, and all people (Jew and Gentile) receive this gift of faith by God's sovereign grace.

Let us take a look in Romans at some of the many instances where Paul maintains a clear distinction between Jew and Gentile and, at the same time, says they are all the same regarding salvation:

> There will be tribulation and distress for every human being who does evil, the Jew first and also the Greek, but glory and honor and peace for everyone who does good, the Jew first and also the Greek. For God shows no partiality. For all who have sinned without the law will also perish without the law, and all who have sinned under the law will be judged by the law. (2:9–12)

> What then? Are we Jews any better off? No, not at all. For we have already charged that all, both Jews and Greeks, are under sin, as it is written: "None is righteous, no, not one; no one understands; no one seeks for God." (3:9–11)

. . . the righteousness of God through faith in Jesus Christ for all who believe. For there is no distinction: for all [Jew and Gentile] have sinned and fall short of the glory of God, and are justified by his grace as a gift, through the redemption that is in Christ Jesus, whom God put forward as a propitiation by his blood, to be received by faith. (3:22–25)

For we hold that one is justified by faith apart from works of the law. Or is God the God of Jews only? Is he not the God of Gentiles also? Yes, of Gentiles also, since God is one. He will justify the circumcised by faith and the uncircumcised through faith. (3:28–30)

He [Abraham] received the sign of circumcision as a seal of the righteousness that he had by faith while he was still uncircumcised. The purpose was to make him the father of all who believe without being circumcised [believing Gentiles], so that righteousness would be counted to them as well, and to make him the father of the circumcised [believing Jews] who are not merely circumcised but who also walk in the footsteps of the faith that our father Abraham had before he was circumcised. (4:11–12)

For the promise to Abraham and his offspring [Jew and Gentile nations] that he would be heir of the world did not come through the law but through the righteousness of faith. . . . That is why it depends on faith, in order that the promise may rest on grace and be guaranteed to all his offspring—not only to the adherent of the law [believing Jews] but also to the one who shares the faith of Abraham [believing Gentiles], who is the father of us all [Jew and Gentile]. (4:13, 16)

Therefore, since we [believing Jews and Gentiles] have been justified by faith, we have peace with God through our Lord Jesus Christ. Through him we have also obtained access by faith into this grace in which we stand, and we rejoice in hope of the glory of God. . . . Since, therefore, we have now been justified by his blood, much more shall we be saved by him from the wrath of God. (5:1–2, 9)

Paul clearly distinguishes between unbelieving Jews and Gentiles and believing Jews and Gentiles. But throughout the whole process of explaining justification by faith for all mankind, he maintains a definite distinction between Jews and Gentiles.

In the American legal system, the two most common types of financial bankruptcy are Chapter 7 and Chapter 11. In Chapter 11, a company still has some merit and, if given relief by the judge from creditors, can work itself out of bankruptcy. In Chapter 7, however, the company is in a totally hopeless condition—the judge shuts it down and any remaining assets are liquidated. Paul is teaching that all humans are in a state of total spiritual bankruptcy and are saved strictly by faith in Christ, which comes to all believers, Jew and Gentile, by the grace of God. The Jews may have been given more assets than the pagan Gentiles, but they are just as spiritually bankrupt if they do not have faith in Christ.

One way to understand the historical differences between the Protestant understanding of justification by faith and the Catholic understanding is that the Reformed tradition sees humanity as being in Chapter 7 bankruptcy and the Catholic tradition sees man as being in Chapter 11 whereby human merit along with God's grace leads to justification. Paul, however, clearly teaches that all humans are in Chapter 7 spiritual bankruptcy.

Now that Paul has established the fact that all sinners—Jew and Gentile— are justified by faith though Jesus Christ and his work on the cross, he proceeds in chapters 6, 7, and 8 of Romans to teach his readers that all believers—Jew and Gentile—who have been justified are now capable of living righteously and should start doing so. This righteous living does not justify them, but their justification in Christ makes it possible for them to start living righteously as the people of God.

People who are saved have the Holy Spirit within them and a new nature that allows them to begin living a life of righteousness. Paul was serious about this and believed that Jews and Gentiles who have become God's children can live righteous lives in this fallen world. Paul believed that God does not justify people for the sake of saving them from the wrath to come and the second death so that they may continue living a wretched life. God is a righteous and holy being. He wants not only to save sinners from condemnation on the last day, but also to save them from a fallen way of life and to restore them to living righteously while on this earth as human beings. Paul expects this process to begin now while we are still in this fallen world.

> Do you not know that all of us [Jew and Gentile] who have been baptized into Christ Jesus were baptized into his death? We were buried therefore with him by baptism into death, in order that, just as Christ was raised from the dead by the glory of the Father, we too might walk in newness of life. For if we have been united with him in a death like his, we shall certainly be united with him in a resurrection like his. We know that our old self was crucified with him in order that the body of sin might be brought to nothing, so that we would no longer be enslaved to sin. (6:3–6)

> Let not sin therefore reign in your mortal bodies, to make you obey their passions. Do not present your members to sin as instruments for unrighteousness, but present yourselves to God as those who have been brought from death to life, and your members to God as instruments for righteousness. For sin will have no dominion over you, since you are not under law but under grace. (6:12–14)

The process of sanctification is the same for believing Jews as it is for believing Gentiles. By faith all believers are called by God to be justified, sanctified, and glorified. We are destined to live for eternity with a holy God, so we should begin to live holy and righteous lives while we are on this earth.

Why Don't the Jews Believe in Their Own Messiah?

After discussing justification by faith as well as the natural progression of sanctification that follows, Paul then transitions to a related subject in order to address an issue that was undoubtedly on the minds of many Roman Gentile believers. If the Jewish people were called by God as the chosen nation to bring the Messiah into the world, then why have not the majority of Jews believed in their own Messiah and been justified by faith?

Here was Paul, a Jewish missionary, preaching to Gentiles that Jesus of Nazareth was the Jewish Messiah. Yet most of the Jews in Israel and those scattered throughout the Roman Empire did not believe in their own Messiah! Many of these unbelieving Jews persecuted Paul and the other Jewish evangelists, not only in Jerusalem, but wherever they traveled throughout the Roman world. Only a relative few believed and responded to the gospel of salvation by faith in Jesus Christ. How could Jesus be the Messiah if the Jews themselves did not receive him *en masse* as their Messiah?

Paul addressed this question by saying that he experienced great sorrow and unceasing anguish over the fact that the majority of his own kinsmen did not believe in Jesus as the Christ (Rom. 9:1–3). He then informed them that being a Jew, or a physical descendant of Abraham, did not automatically make a person a true spiritual descendant of Abraham (9:6–8).

Paul explained that there are two types of Jews. In fact, there have always been two types of Jews throughout the history of the nation, going all the way back to Abraham: believing Jews (justified by faith), who are referred to as "children of promise" (9:8), and unbelieving Jews. Unbelieving Jews either did not care about being right with a holy God or fell into the trap of believing they could achieve righteousness by works rather than by faith (9:30–32).

Although there had been a large number of Jews in Israel's past, only a remnant had been believers (9:27; 11:4–5). Those who did believe did so because of God's sovereign grace (11:5–7). God's purpose of election was operating throughout Israel's history, just as it was now operating among Gentile believers.

The readers of Paul's letter were probably wondering why God chose some and not others. Anticipating the question, Paul said the answer is beyond human comprehension (11:33–35). God is sovereign. It is his prerogative to do what he wants. He can have compassion and show mercy to those whom he chooses (9:15–16). Not all will be saved, because not all receive his sovereign grace.

After this long and somewhat complex explanation, Paul returns to the issue at hand: why is it that the Roman Gentiles are experiencing faith in the Jewish Messiah, but the Jews, who are the natural olive tree, do not accept him—their own Messiah? The Gentiles are, in effect, like a branch of a wild olive tree that is grafted into the natural olive tree, enabling them to produce the olive fruit of God. But why is the natural olive tree not producing fruit?

Paul's answer is that God's sovereign election is still operating as it has all along. With regard to the current situation of significant Jewish unbelief, Paul teaches that the Jews have only experienced a *temporary* hardening of the heart, which is why the natural olive tree is not producing fruit as it should at this time.

Paul gives a variety of reasons for this lapse in Jewish fruitfulness. One reason was to allow Gentiles to come to Christ by faith and to join in his kingdom. They have been grafted into this messianic salvation. But they should not become too conceited about this current state of affairs, because it is only temporary (11:25). Someday, the unbelieving Jews will join them as believers when they, too, are called to return to the natural olive tree.

God has a specific number of elect Gentiles that he wants to come to believe in the Jewish Messiah before large numbers of Jews start believing. When the full number of Gentiles that he has chosen is reached, then we should expect the natural heirs of the Jewish Messiah to respond *en masse* (11:25–27). Paul is certain of this, despite his great sorrow and anguish at the Jews' current hardness of heart:

> I ask, then, has God rejected his people? By no means! (11:1). . . . For if their rejection means the reconciliation of the world, what will their acceptance mean but life from the dead? (11:15). . . . For the gifts and the calling of God are irrevocable. Just as you were at one time disobedient to God but now have received mercy because of their disobedience, so they too have now been disobedient in order that by the mercy shown to you they also may now receive mercy. (11:29–31)

The day is coming when the ethnic descendants of Abraham—the natural recipients of the Messiah—will also receive God's mercy by repenting of their sins as they are justified by faith in the blood of Jesus Christ. This eventual "calling of God" to the Jews is irrevocable. It will happen no matter how disobedient the majority of Jews are currently toward God.

Paul wrote: "So I ask, did they stumble in order that they might fall? By no means! Rather through their trespass salvation has come to the Gentiles, so as to make Israel jealous. Now if their trespass means riches for the world, and if their failure means riches for the Gentiles, how much more will their full inclusion mean!" (11:11–12). They may have temporarily fallen from God's grace and the benefits of the messianic kingdom, but someday grace will indeed be shown to them as it has been shown to the Gentiles.

One phrase Paul uses to describe this future time of grace toward the Jews is "all Israel will be saved" (11:26). This term "all Israel" has puzzled many scholars. Does this mean that when God does show them mercy, every single Jew living at that time will repent? By examining the entirety of Paul's teaching in Romans, he probably did not mean every Jew. Not all Gentiles were being saved. Paul never teaches universal salvation. The word *all* does not mean every single Jew. The most likely explanation is that it means a great number, perhaps even a majority. In this reversal of fortune, after the number of Gentiles that God has predetermined come into his kingdom, then "as a whole" the Jewish people will repent and receive Jesus of Nazareth as their Messiah.

The expression "all Israel" could also have another meaning. It could refer to all "true Jews" through all time including the large number that will repent in the future. This would include the Old Testament remnant of believers who have not yet received the promises that they would inherit the earth, as well as Peter and the other Jewish disciples who have not yet experienced a hundredfold in this age, as well as the future Jews who repent *en masse*. "All Israel" may be a reference to the large number of repentant Jews combined with all past Jewish believers who, together, as children of promise will constitute all Israel—all true Jews—who will get to experience the future restoration when "the Deliverer will come from Zion."

Because the Messiah came into this world and then left, returning to his Father in heaven without establishing the Jewish messianic reign, there remains a future time when the true nation of *believing* Israel will once again play a major role in God's plans—when Christ finally exercises his reign from this throne in heaven, ruling over his resurrected mortal saints in the 1,000-year restoration.

The Messiah has always come from the Jews or Zion. But what does he deliver us from? At first, he delivers repentant Gentiles and a small number of repentant Jews from Satan's dominion of darkness and we become members of Christ's kingdom. But we remain in this fallen world with Satan as the god of this world. We, and the world, have yet to be completely "delivered" from Satan's tyranny of evil on this earth. But when the Jews finally repent en masse, this leads to the time in history when the Messiah from Zion completely delivers us from Satan's regime, and we enter into the long-promised messianic kingdom on this earth. Paul's statements "the Deliverer will come from Zion" and "he will banish ungodliness from Jacob" are probably a reference to Isaiah, which contains numerous prophecies of the coming messianic kingdom when the Jews repent. Isaiah says, "'And a Redeemer will come to Zion, to those in Jacob who turn from transgression,' declares the LORD" (Isa. 59:20). This entire section of Isaiah (chapters 59–66) contains numerous references to the future Jewish messianic kingdom on this earth that is established after a period of repentance.

Paul's phrase "the Deliverer will come from Zion" serves as a subtle hyperlink to Isaiah's messianic prophecies. Paul does not need to elaborate on what happens when the Jews finally repent, for we can simply refer back to Isaiah. Paul intends this phrase to be a window into Isaiah's vision of the Son's messianic kingdom on this earth. The following are a few examples of what we find in Isaiah when we link Paul's statement, "the Deliverer will come from Zion" to Isaiah's statement, "and a Redeemer will come to Zion":

> And nations shall come to your light, and kings to the brightness of your rising (60:3). . . . Your gates shall be open continually; day and night they shall not be shut, that people may bring to you the wealth of the nations, with their kings led in procession (60:11). . . . they shall call you the City of the LORD, the Zion of the Holy One of Israel (60:14). . . . Your people shall all be righteous; they shall possess the land forever (60:21), . . . The wolf and the lamb shall graze together; the lion shall eat straw like the ox, and dust shall be the serpent's food. They shall not hurt or destroy in all my holy mountain. (65:25)

This is just a small sampling of messianic prophecies found in Isaiah. Paul did not need to expound upon what the quote "the Deliverer will come from Zion" means. All we have to do is hyperlink to Isaiah to realize that this is the code phrase for what occurs when the Jews finally repent and are grafted back in. After the period of mass repentance when the Jews are grafted back in as believers, the messianic kingdom on this earth will unfold as prophesied by Isaiah.

Another strong connection to the Jews responding to the gospel and the resulting messianic kingdom can be found in Romans where Paul quotes from Isaiah concerning the preaching of the "good news" about the Christ: "And how are they to preach unless they are sent? As it is written, 'How beautiful are the feet of those who preach the good news!'" (10:15). This matches Isaiah 52:7–10:

> How beautiful upon the mountains are the feet of him who brings good news, who publishes peace [on earth], who brings good news of happiness, who publishes salvation, who says to Zion, "Your God reigns." The voice of your watchmen—they lift up their voice; together they sing for joy; for eye to eye they see the return of the LORD to Zion. . . . The LORD has bared his holy arm before the eyes of all the nations, and all the ends of the earth shall see the salvation of our God [the messianic kingdom realized].

Paul leaves it to his reader to carefully study Isaiah and combine it with his teachings to fill in the blanks as to what happens when the Jews finally repent and believe.

Paul quotes Isaiah so extensively throughout his letter to the Romans that it seems as if he is writing an exposition on Isaiah. Here are a few other striking similarities between Romans and Isaiah:

Paul says the following about God's sovereign election: "Oh, the depth of the riches and wisdom and knowledge of God! How unsearchable are his judgments and how inscrutable his ways!" (Rom. 11:33). *Isaiah says,* "For as the heavens are higher than the earth, so are my ways higher than your ways and my thoughts than your thoughts" (Isa. 55:9).

Paul says the following about how God has temporally abandoned the Jews: "Lest you be wise in your own conceits, I want you to understand this mystery, brothers: a partial hardening has come upon Israel, until the fullness of the Gentiles has come in" (Rom. 11:25). *Isaiah says,* "'For a brief moment I deserted you, but with great compassion I will gather you. In overflowing anger for a moment I hid my face from you, but with everlasting love I will have compassion on you,' says the LORD, your Redeemer" (Isa. 54:7–8).

Paul says the following about how God's election of the Jews is irrevocable: "I ask, then, has God rejected his people? By no means! . . . God has not rejected his people whom he foreknew. . . ." (Rom. 11:1–2). *Isaiah says,* "'For the mountains may depart and the hills be removed, but my steadfast love shall not depart from you, and my covenant of peace shall not be removed,' says the LORD, who has compassion on you" (Isa. 54:10).

Some amillennialists and postmillennialists now accept the interpretation that Paul prophesies there will come a time in the future when a major revival among the Jews will take place. A straightforward reading of Romans necessitates this interpretation. They still insist, however, that the expression "the Deliverer will come from Zion" does *not* refer to a future restoration of the nation of Israel during a millennial kingdom after a period of mass repentance by the Jews.

Paul remains obscure about what happens on this earth after the Jews finally repent. The earthly kingdom of Christ is not the major theme of any of Paul's letters, including Romans. Paul's letters focus almost exclusively on the kingdom of heaven. Believers were not the only people who read Paul's letters. An elaborate explanation of what happens when the Jews repent *en masse* would only alert the Roman authorities to a potential insurgency and make life more difficult for a young church in an already hostile Roman environment. Even if the Roman authorities made the connection to Isaiah, the prophecies in Isaiah are ambiguous enough to prevent them from making sense out of the phrase.

Romans 11:25–27 is an important piece of the puzzle, but it is not the definitive statement on the restoration. Only by connecting other passages from Isaiah and prophecies such as the following one found in Micah, do we understand how the restoration comes into focus when the Jews are no longer abandoned or hardened and are grafted back in as believers:

> Therefore he shall give them up [hardened and given over to disobedience] until the time when she who is in labor has given birth; then the rest of his brothers shall return to the people of Israel [the full number of Gentiles come in]. And he [Christ] shall stand [exercises his reign from his throne in heaven] and shepherd his flock in the strength of the LORD, in the majesty of the name of the LORD his God [the Father who puts all of Christ's enemies under his feet]. And they [Israel and the kingdoms of the world] shall dwell secure, for now he shall be great to the ends of the earth [world-wide dominion of the Messiah]. (Mic. 5:3–4)

Israel is in a state of pregnancy until the full number of Gentiles comes in. Then, she will go into labor and produce the "birth" of the believing Jews. According to Micah, this leads to the restoration when Christ shall stand and exercise his reign.

We do not know whether this revival among repenting Jews, their "inclusion," will last for twenty years, fifty years, or one hundred years before the events leading up to the Great Tribulation and then the restoration begin to unfold. We do know, however, that the gears will be set in motion when the Jews are grafted back in as believers of the Jewish Messiah from Nazareth.

There should be no doubt that God will bring about this future time when the Jews repent and believe in their own Messiah, thus, ushering in the messianic kingdom on this earth. The following prophecy by Isaiah is powerful and quite moving as it predicts with absolute certainty that God will one day bring to birth the Jewish people and the Jewish nation in the restoration:

> "Before she was in labor she gave birth; before her pain came upon her she delivered a son. Who has heard such a thing? Who has seen such things? Shall a land be born in one day? Shall a nation be brought forth in one moment? For as soon as Zion was in labor she brought forth her children. Shall I bring to the point of birth and not cause to bring forth?" says the LORD; "shall I, who cause to bring forth, shut the womb?" says your God. "Rejoice with Jerusalem, and be glad for her, all you who love her; rejoice with her in joy, all you who mourn over her; that you may nurse and be satisfied from her consoling breast; that you may drink deeply with delight from her glorious abundance [in the restoration]." For thus says the LORD: "Behold, I will extend peace to her like a river, and the glory of the nations like an overflowing stream." (Isa. 66:7–12)

But how can "a land be born in one day" and "a nation be brought forth in one moment"? The answer can be found in Revelation 20—with the first resurrection. At the end of the Tribulation when Satan is bound, Christ, when he sits on his throne at the right hand of the Father, will in *a single day* regenerate the deceased Jewish saints, and the nation of Israel will be reconstituted along with the regenerated Gentile saints and nations during the 1,000-year restoration. All the ransomed people of God, including the Jewish saints, will experience the regenerated Genesis creation when it is restored to its Creator. Literally, in one day, believing Israel from all time will come to life as a nation in the 1,000-year messianic kingdom!

Galatians

Another verse that has caused considerable debate among biblical scholars is the following one found in Paul's letter to the Galatians: "For neither circumcision counts for anything, nor uncircumcision, but a new creation. And as for all who walk by this rule, peace and mercy be upon them, and upon *the Israel of God*" (6:15–16). Did Paul use the phrase "Israel of God" to refer to circumcised Jewish believers from the nation of Israel who understand justification by faith, or is Paul describing the new creation of the church as the new Israel of God? Most amillennialists have interpreted this verse, and similar ones, to mean that the church has become the new Israel of God, and, therefore, there is no future restoration of the kingdom to Israel. But this seems an odd interpretation, for nowhere does the New Testament teach that the church is the new Israel. The terms may be analogous because they both are made up of the people of God, but Paul, in particular, is careful in all his letters to make a distinction between Jewish and Gentile believers and Israel and the church.

To understand the historical setting in which Paul wrote to the Galatians, it is important to remember the unique relationship the Jews had with the Romans. Unlike other pagan cultures the Romans had conquered and were easily assimilated into the pagan Roman culture, the conquered Jews remained fiercely devoted to a monotheistic God and would riot if forced to worship the emperors or the Roman gods. As a result, the Romans wisely gave the Jewish people in Israel and those dispersed throughout the empire a pass—they were not forced to worship the emperor and the empire's pagan gods. The Jews were given a very important cloak of immunity—as long as they could identify themselves as circumcised Jews.

Now enters Paul, converting the Gentiles to believe in the Jewish Messiah from Galilee and not requiring them to be circumcised. They do not have to become Jews to join the Messiah's kingdom. This, obviously, leaves them outside this cloak of immunity and subject to great persecution when they refuse to worship the emperor and the empire's pagan gods. His letters are full of descriptions of the hardships uncircumcised Gentile converts subsequently faced, as well as the hardships Paul faced for advocating such a doctrine.

The Judaizers, or the "circumcision party" as Paul refers to them (2:12), had infiltrated the church in Jerusalem and were then traveling around to the churches Paul had established attempting to persuade the converts to be circumcised. They offered a very tempting proposition. If the Gentile converts would be circumcised, then they, too, would fall under the Jewish cloak of immunity. In effect, they would be Jews in the eyes of the Romans and could prove their immunity by their circumcision, and they would no longer be persecuted for failing to worship the emperor and the Roman gods.

This would let the Jewish evangelists off the hook as well, for they would no longer be instigators of Gentile insubordination against the Roman gods. The newly circumcised Gentiles as well as the Jewish evangelists would both fall under the cloak of immunity given to the Jews throughout the Roman Empire. If the Jewish evangelists converted Gentiles without circumcision, they would be subject to the Romans' wrath for persuading Gentiles not to worship the pagan gods. The "circumcision party" offered a compelling opportunity: be circumcised and everyone would be spared persecution by the Romans.

But Paul resisted this temptation and insisted that the Gentiles not be circumcised even if this meant severe persecution by the Romans:

> You were running well. Who hindered you from obeying the truth? . . . But if I, brothers, still preach circumcision, why am I still being persecuted? In that case the offense of the cross has been removed (5:7–11). . . . It is those who want to make a good showing in the flesh who would force you to be circumcised, and only in order that they may not be persecuted for the cross of Christ. (6:12)

If the converted Gentiles were circumcised, then neither the Jewish evangelists nor their converts would be persecuted.

Paul recognized that once they began following Jewish law regarding circumcision, they would be more likely to follow other Jewish laws and customs: "You observe days and months and seasons and years!" (4:10). And once they started to operate under Mosaic law, they would be obligated to follow the whole law:

> For freedom Christ has set us free; stand firm therefore, and do not submit again to a yoke of slavery [to the law]. Look: I, Paul, say to you that if you accept circumcision, Christ will be of no advantage to you. I testify again to every man who accepts circumcision that he is obligated to keep the whole law. (5:1–3)

Certain Jewish leaders coming out of Jerusalem were insisting that the Gentiles in Galatia, who were coming to believe in the Jewish Messiah, should be circumcised in order to become a part of the Jewish messianic nation. Paul opposed this teaching and told them they could become members of Christ's kingdom without joining the nation of Israel and following its rules and regulations, particularly circumcision.

Paul even made a special trip to Jerusalem to meet with the influential leaders and elders, including Peter, in which the issue was settled by the Jewish leaders that the Gentiles he was leading to Christ did not need to be circumcised when they accepted the gospel (2:1–10). He reported a subsequent public rebuke of Peter in Antioch when he, and even Barnabas, became intimidated by the "circumcision party" and slipped back into legalism (2:11–14).

The centerpiece of Paul's teaching is the "new creation" or the new order of being as children of God, attained not by birthright as a Jew or even by conversion of a Gentile to Judaism. It is attained by simple faith in Jesus Christ, both for the circumcised Jew and for the uncircumcised Gentile. Paul reminds the Galatians:

> We ourselves are Jews by birth and not Gentile sinners; yet we [Jewish believers] know that a person is not justified by works of the law but through faith in Jesus Christ, so we [Jewish believers] also have believed in Christ Jesus, in order to be justified by faith in Christ and not by works of the law, because by works of the law no one will be justified. (2:15–16)

The key to understanding Paul's concluding remarks in his letter to the Galatians when he uses the phrase "Israel of God" is to remember this definition of true Jewish believers. Paul is wishing peace and mercy on both the uncircumcised Gentile believers who have accepted his gospel without being compelled to convert to Judaism *and* circumcised Jewish believers— "Israel of God"—who also understand that they are justified by faith, not as a result of their being born Jews, being circumcised, and obeying the law. Understanding this, let's reread these verses consecutively to grasp the meaning of Paul's use of the phrase the "Israel of God":

> We ourselves are Jews by birth and not Gentile sinners; yet we [Jewish believers] know that a person is not justified by works of the law but through faith in Jesus Christ, so we [Jewish believers] also have believed in Christ Jesus, in order to be justified by faith in Christ and not by works of the law, because by works of the law no one will be justified. . . . "For neither circumcision counts for anything, nor uncircumcision, but a new creation. And as for all who walk by this rule, peace and mercy be upon them [believing Gentiles], and upon the Israel of God [believing Jews]." (2:15–16; 6:15–16)

Therefore, the phrase "Israel of God" refers to circumcised believers or Jews by birth like Paul, Peter, James, Barnabas, and many other Jewish believers who "know that a person is not justified by works of the law but through faith in Jesus Christ." In contrast to the true Israel of God are the Judaizers or the "circumcision party" (2:12) who "distort the gospel of Christ" (1:7), who are "accursed" (1:9) and are "false brothers" (2:4). Paul is so angry at how they are distorting the gospel of justification by faith for the Gentiles that he wishes they "would emasculate [castrate] themselves" (5:12). Clearly, "Israel of God" refers to Jewish believers like Paul who know that it is circumcision of the heart that justifies a person. When theologians claim that Paul is describing the church as the new "Israel of God" that replaces Israel, they are completely missing the meaning of Paul's teachings. If Paul had intended his readers to understand that the church had replaced Israel, it would have been easy for him to say so.

In his letters, Paul never abolishes the distinction between Jew and Gentile, even though both groups are justified by faith and are part of the new creation. Paul never forsakes his heritage as a Jewish believer, and he repeatedly says that he is a believing Jew who has been justified by the grace of God and thus a part of the true "Israel of God." Although he has become a new creation as a child of God in the new order of being, he remains Jewish in the Adamic order of being. Just as we remain male and female, we also remain Jew and Gentile, with a great deal of prophetic truth built around these remaining distinctions. In fact, the complete deliverance of this world from Satan is tied to the period when the Jews ultimately repent and believe in their Messiah.

Ephesians

Another flashpoint in this debate over the nature of Israel and the church is in Paul's letter to the Ephesians. Paul says that the Mosaic commandments and ordinances have been abolished and that the church, as the body of Christ, has now become the "holy temple in the Lord." This important passage contains language that, when misunderstood, probably got Paul into a great deal of trouble with fellow Jewish believers in his day:

> Therefore remember that at one time you Gentiles in the flesh, called "the uncircumcision" . . . remember that you were at that time separated from Christ, alienated from the commonwealth of Israel and strangers to the covenants of promise, having no hope and without God in the world. But now in Christ Jesus you who once were far off have been brought near by the blood of Christ. For he himself is our peace, who has made us both one and has broken down in his flesh the dividing wall of hostility by *abolishing the law of commandments and ordinances*, that he might create in himself one new man in place of the two, so making peace, and might reconcile us both to God in one body through the cross, thereby killing the hostility. And he came and preached peace to you who were far off [uncircumcised Gentiles] and peace to those who were near [the "Israel of God"]. For

through him we both [believing Gentiles and believing Jews] have access in one Spirit to the Father. So then you are no longer strangers and aliens, but you are fellow citizens with the saints and members of the household of God, built on the foundation of the apostles and prophets, Christ Jesus himself being the cornerstone, in whom the whole structure, being joined together, grows into a holy temple in the Lord. In him you also are being built together into a dwelling place for God by the Spirit. (Eph. 2:11–22)

Paul uses so many metaphors for the church—citizens, house, temple of the Holy Spirit, and Christ's body—that the reader wonders what is left of the Jewish commonwealth of Israel. Paul is not saying that the Gentiles are joining the commonwealth of Israel, but, rather, that a new entity—the church as the body of Christ—has been formed for both Jewish and Gentile believers. Paul says that believing Jews and Gentiles are fellow citizens of this new household of God, growing into a holy temple of the Lord, a dwelling place for God by the Spirit.

What further need is there for a Jewish nation or a Jewish temple, for that matter? The church seems to have completely replaced the nation of Israel as the new household of God.

The key to understanding Ephesians is the same as with all Paul's letters. Paul's message centers on the new creation, the new order of being in which any person, circumcised and uncircumcised, can become a child of God through faith in Jesus Christ and is, therefore, destined for the kingdom of heaven at the transformation. Paul does not even mention the restoration in this epistle. Nowhere in Ephesians is there a link to the messianic vision, such as in Romans 11:26. This silence does not mean, however, that the Jewish and Gentile Christians will not experience the future restoration.

In fact, the entire letter of Ephesians is heaven-centric as it focuses on the new order of being. Paul wrote that in heaven there will be no temple, no nation of Israel, no distinction of Jew or Gentile, and no male or female given in marriage. Paul taught that God the Father has blessed all believers "with every spiritual blessing in the *heavenly places*" (1:3). In Christ all believers "have obtained an inheritance [in heaven]" (1:11). The presence of the Holy Spirit in believers' hearts is a "guarantee of our inheritance until we acquire possession of it [on the last day]" (1:14). Paul prayed that they fully understand "the hope to which he has called you, what are the riches of his glorious inheritance in the saints [in heaven]" (1:15–18). The entire letter is focused on the children of God inheriting heaven.

He reminded the Gentiles that before they heard the gospel and were saved, they were dead in their sins and hopelessly lost and were destined for wrath on the last day, just like the rest of mankind (2:1–3). But now they have been saved by the great love of God who has "raised us up with him and seated us with him in the *heavenly places* in Christ Jesus, so that in the coming ages [in heaven] he might show the immeasurable riches of his grace in kindness toward us in Christ Jesus" (2:6–7). Gentiles gain citizenship in this heavenly kingdom by faith in Jesus Christ as a result of the grace of God—the same theme as found in Paul's letter to the Romans. It was not the result of their becoming Jews and following the Jewish laws and ordinances.

Under the old covenant, to become a citizen of the commonwealth of Israel and a part of the people of God, a Gentile converted to Judaism by being circumcised and would then have to follow Mosaic law. Citizenship in Israel was accomplished through the law.

Some Jews believed that because they were circumcised, they were automatically citizens of God's kingdom (Phil. 3:3). Christ also addressed this in his conversations with the Pharisees who thought that because they were circumcised and descendants of Abraham, they were God's people by right (John 8:31–59). According to Jesus, as well as Paul, without circumcision of the heart and faith in Christ, a Jew was destined for hell, just like any human being. Citizenship in Israel does not guarantee citizenship in heaven.

What Paul is teaching is that adherence to the Jewish law of commandments and ordinances has been abolished as a means of citizenship into God's kingdom. Now a Gentile can become a citizen, not of Israel, but of heaven itself! Citizenship in heaven is determined solely on faith in Jesus Christ. A Gentile does not have to become a Jew and follow Jewish law to become a member of Christ's body, which is destined for heaven.

The *modus operandi* for the church will no longer be the Mosaic law. This is not to say that many of the universal moral imperatives of the law are not applicable. For example, Christ and the apostles admonished the church to follow the Ten Commandments, which revolve around loving God and loving our neighbor. Jewish and Gentile believers alike are not to worship idols; they are only to worship and love God. All Christians should love their neighbors and should not murder, steal, covet, commit adultery, etc.

Most important, the readers of Ephesians could easily understand that when Paul was referring to the Jewish law being abolished in relation to how the church functioned, he was not talking about the moral laws to love God and neighbor. The church should obey these moral laws. Ephesians contains numerous admonitions on how Christians are to live "in a manner worthy of the calling to which you have been called" (4:1). Or, "But sexual immorality and all impurity or covetousness must not even be named among you, as is proper among saints" (5:3). Paul never taught that one must obey these moral laws in order to be saved, but he was adamant that those who are saved should act like it by following these moral imperatives.

The commandments and ordinances that were abolished for the church were those that distinctly defined the nation of Israel and the Jewish identity, such as circumcision, Jewish dietary laws, and Jewish religious ceremonies and practices, particularly those related to the temple. These ordinances were intended to set the Jews apart, both as a nation and as a specific ethnic group of people through whom God would work to accomplish his purposes. The church does not have to function on the basis of Jewish national laws. The church has its own rules and regulations.

Gentile believers did not have to follow Jewish commandments and ordinances to be faithful Christians. But should a believing Jew, who has been justified by faith and is a new creation destined for heaven, still operate under Jewish ordinances? Was Paul teaching that the Jewish law is completely abolished, so that even a Jew should not follow Jewish dietary practices? Do the Jews no longer have to worship and offer sacrifices at the temple when they are in Jerusalem? Can a Jew live like a Gentile and eat pork? The problem in answering these questions is that Paul devoted so much of his writings to reassuring Gentile members of the church that they did not need to follow Jewish customs to be members of Christ's body and go to heaven that he says very little about exactly how Jewish believers should operate with regard to the Jewish law. Nowhere in the New Testament, for example, does it say that a Jewish believer has to follow Jewish law.

Perhaps the best way to answer these questions is by trying to imagine what Paul may have preached in a Jewish synagogue when he entered a Roman city for the first time. I imagine he would first attempt to prove that Jesus of Nazareth is the true Jewish Messiah and the Son of God. Christ was crucified for their sins, was resurrected, and ascended to heaven. All they needed to do to be saved and reconciled to God, in order to go to heaven, was to have faith in him.

I cannot imagine, however, Paul then telling these Jewish listeners that once they were saved, they would no longer have to follow the Jewish law. No longer would they or their children have to be circumcised, or follow Jewish dietary laws, or recognize Jewish holidays, or even worship in the temple, for all these commandments and ordinances have been abolished. There are many reasons to believe Paul never said these things when speaking in a synagogue, nor did he mean them in his letter to the Ephesians. For one, they probably would have stoned him. Two, there is no indication that Paul ever told Jewish believers to cease being Jewish. For example, in the case with Timothy, who had a Greek father and a Jewish mother, Paul followed Jewish custom:

> Paul came also to Derbe and to Lystra. A disciple was there, named Timothy, the son of a Jewish woman who was a believer, but his father was a Greek. He was well spoken of by the brothers at Lystra and Iconium. Paul wanted Timothy to accompany him, and he took him and circumcised him because of the Jews who were in those places, for they all knew that his father was a Greek. (Acts 16:1-3)

If Paul taught that all Jewish law was abolished for Jews as well, then he would not have gone out of his way to have Timothy circumcised.

I know Jewish believers who do not follow Jewish dietary law, nor worship or offer sacrifices at the temple, because there is no temple. But what is the proper thing for them to do? Should they follow Jewish dietary law and worship at the temple if there were a rebuilt temple? I suppose a Jewish believer is free to follow whatever Jewish practice and ceremonial holidays they wish. If they want to eat pork, fine; if not, that is acceptable too. If a Jew elects to follow Jewish law, they would not be considered legalistic. It is the believing Jew's prerogative to follow whatever parts of the law they choose and to observe whatever Jewish holidays they wish. On the other hand, if a Gentile insists on following Jewish dietary law, they would be accused of being legalistic.

In his first letter to the Corinthians, Paul explains this freedom for a Jewish believer like himself regarding the law:

> To the Jews I became as a Jew, in order to win Jews. To those under the law I became as one under the law (though not being myself under the law) that I might win those under the law. To those outside the law I became as one outside the law (not being outside the law of God but under the law of Christ) that I might win those outside the law. (1 Cor. 9:20–21)

Paul's adherence to the Jewish law was more for pragmatic reasons, so that he might be an effective evangelist in both worlds. He claimed that he did not have to follow the law, "though not being myself under the law," but realized that to be an effective evangelist among Jewish people, he needed to follow Jewish customs. Paul probably ate Gentile foods when he was among an exclusively Gentile group of people. But when he was among a group of Jews he was trying to convert, he would follow the Jewish dietary law.

The difference was that a Jewish believer like Paul could indeed follow the Jewish law without being considered legalistic, whereas a Gentile believer who felt compelled to follow these same laws, in order to be a part of Christ's kingdom, would be regarded as legalistic.

There were many Jewish believers in the early church who chose to remain zealous for the law. That was fine as long as they did not impose Jewish law and practices on the Gentiles who were coming to faith in Christ. As we shall see in the next section of this chapter, Paul's teachings in his letters to the Ephesians and the Corinthians could easily be misconstrued by Jewish believers and unbelievers alike to mean that Jews should no longer follow Jewish customs. This brings us to another important question: What part did the Jewish temple play in the early church, and will there actually be another Jewish temple in the restoration?

The New Temple in the Restoration

Another major disagreement and debate among biblical scholars is over Ezekiel's prophetic vision of another Jewish temple in the restoration that involves a renewed system of high priests and the offering of sacrifices. Ezekiel chapters 40–48 provide a detailed description of this rebuilt temple. This prophecy has caused much consternation among those who study eschatology.

It is one of the greatest stumbling blocks preventing both amillennialists and postmillennialists from viewing messianic prophecy literally. Even some premillennialists, who interpret prophecies literally, admit struggling with the concept of a rebuilt temple. This struggle stems from the teachings in Hebrews, which was written primarily to Jewish believers. Christ is described as the ultimate high priest who has entered into heaven on our behalf. His sacrifice on the cross was the ultimate sacrifice that takes away all our sins and makes us perfect forever: "Where there is forgiveness of these [sins], there is no longer any offering for sin" (Heb. 10:18). So why, then, does Ezekiel teach that Israel will need another temple in the restoration with another priesthood—and one that involves sacrifices, no less? This does seem baffling, but a careful reading of Hebrews, which was probably written in AD 68—before the destruction of the temple in AD 70—reveals information that should help eliminate this confusion.

Before Christ came to this earth, God's people operated under the old covenant; the only way they could approach God was through the high priest and the temple system of sacrifices. The temple contained the Holy of Holies where the Spirit of God resided among his people. Those who broke God's laws needed to take part in the priestly system of purification, year after year. The high priest performed elaborate rituals on behalf of the people. On one level, these rituals demonstrated that the Holy God could not yet be approached because man was sinful and continued to sin.

The Old Testament saints could be "filled" with the Spirit, but, in some sense, they were not indwelt with the Holy Spirit as the New Testament saints have been since Pentecost. The Old Testament vision is one of a holy God who could not indwell the hearts of sinful people. He could only dwell in the holy places of the temple. Before Pentecost, the Holy Spirit could not permanently dwell in the human heart, because Christ had not yet made the perfect sacrifice for mankind's sins.

But Christ's sacrifice changed everything:

But when Christ appeared as a high priest of the good things that have come, then through the greater and more perfect tent (not made with hands, that is, not of this creation) he entered once for all into the holy places, not by means of the blood of goats and calves but by means of his own blood, thus securing an eternal redemption. . . . Therefore he is the mediator of a new covenant, . . . For Christ has entered, not into holy places made with hands, which are copies of the true things, but into heaven itself, now to appear in the presence of God on our behalf. Nor was it to offer himself repeatedly, as the high priest enters the holy places every year with blood not his own, for then he would have had to suffer repeatedly since the foundation of the world. But as it is, he has appeared once for all at the end of the ages to put away sin by the sacrifice of himself. . . . For since the law has but a shadow of the good things to come instead of the true form of these realities, it can never, by the same sacrifices that are continually offered every year, make perfect those who draw near. . . . For by a single offering he has perfected for all time those who are being sanctified. (Heb. 9:11—10:14)

Under the new covenant based on Christ's sacrifice on the cross, the Holy Spirit can now dwell in the human heart, just as he previously dwelled in the temple, because the Christian has been made holy by Christ's sacrifice. God can actually dwell in the human heart, making a Christian the temple of God! And because of Christ's sacrifice, Christians will be able to enter into the very presence of God himself on the last day.

This is truly extraordinary. In the old covenant, saints and prophets would be filled by the Holy Spirit, but God could not technically indwell them because Christ had not yet made the perfect sacrifice on their behalf. Only after the cross and the believer's justification by faith, which declares him or her perfectly holy, can the Holy Spirit indwell a person such that he or she would be considered a temple of God: "Do you not know that you are God's temple and that God's Spirit dwells in you?" (1 Cor. 3:16). This concept was unheard of in the old covenant, before Christ. It was unthinkable that God could take up permanent residence in the sinful human heart. This was only made possible in the new covenant, after the cross.

With this understanding as a background, how can we make sense of Hebrews as it relates to Ezekiel's prophecy that predicts yet another temple and high-priestly system to be established in the restoration? The first observation is that the temple and the priestly system of sacrifices were still taking place when Hebrews was written.

With this in mind, notice that despite Christ's ultimate sacrifice for our sins, Hebrews nowhere makes the suggestion that temple worship should cease. The author even describes Christ as the ultimate high priest and the ultimate sacrifice—with the backdrop of the Levitical priesthood still functioning:

Now the point in what we are saying is this: we have such a high priest [Christ], one who is seated at the right hand of the throne of the Majesty in heaven, a minister in the holy places, in the true tent that the Lord set up, not man. For every high priest is appointed to offer gifts and sacrifices; thus it is necessary for this priest also to have something to offer. Now if he were on earth, he would not be a priest at all, since there are priests who offer gifts according to the law [the earthly priestly system still operates]. They serve a copy and shadow of the heavenly things. For when Moses was about to erect the tent, he was instructed by God, saying, "See that you make everything according to the pattern that was shown you on the mountain." (Heb. 8:1–5)

Several observations can be made. First, some priests were still offering "gifts according to the law" during the time Hebrews was written. Second, Christ is no longer on the earth but is in heaven where he serves as our heavenly high priest. Therefore, Christ is functioning as the high priest of heaven at the same time human high priests are functioning on this earth "who offer gifts according to the law." At the time Hebrews was written, the sacrificial gifts of the priests on this earth at the temple continued to serve as "a copy and shadow of the heavenly things"—Christ functioning as the high priest in heaven. Thus, both forms of priesthood—the heavenly one and the earthly one—were operating simultaneously when Hebrews was being written. Nowhere does the author teach that this is wrong and should be discontinued. He assumes that the earthly priesthood would continue even though Christ made the ultimate sacrifice and is our heavenly high priest.

Hebrews goes on to describe the new covenant with God whereby his laws are now written on people's hearts. He says, "In speaking of a new covenant, he makes the first one obsolete. And what is becoming obsolete and growing old is ready to vanish away" (Heb. 8:13). The old covenant "had regulations for worship and an earthly place of holiness" (9:1).

One could conclude that by describing something as obsolete, it would immediately cease operating altogether. However, the statement "what is *becoming* obsolete and *growing old* is ready to vanish away" would lead one to conclude that although something may be functionally obsolete, not functioning as it was originally intended, it will continue to operate in some role until it actually vanishes. It may be "growing old," but it has not yet died and vanished. We are reminded that the earth itself is, in a sense, obsolete, getting old, and will also soon vanish away:

See that you do not refuse him who is speaking. For if they did not escape when they refused him who warned them on earth, much less will we escape if we reject him who warns from heaven. At that time his voice shook the earth, but now he has promised, "Yet once more I will shake not only the earth but also the heavens." This phrase, "Yet once more," indicates *the removal of things that are shaken—that is, things that have been made—in* order that the things that cannot be shaken may remain. Therefore let us be grateful for receiving a kingdom [a heavenly one] that cannot be shaken, and thus let us offer to God acceptable worship, with reverence and awe, for our God is a consuming fire. (Heb. 12:25–29)

Hebrews has a heavenly focus. Abraham and the Old Testament saints are described as looking forward to the end of the world and the New Jerusalem in heaven—not to the messianic kingdom. God has warned us of the earth's impending destruction, and we should be glad that we are receiving the indestructible heavenly kingdom to replace it. But, of course, the world still exists. It has not been consumed by fire quite yet. We still have not received an eternal kingdom in heaven.

Likewise, the Levitical sacrificial system practiced within the temple is "becoming obsolete and growing old" and "is ready to vanish away," along with the whole earth. Both are destined to vanish and be replaced with a heavenly kingdom in which Christ will be our high priest forever, according to the order of Melchizedek (Heb. 7:15–22). From a heavenly perspective, the old covenant and the earthly high-priestly system, and even the earth itself, are ready to vanish.

This leads to a simple but critical observation. The world's destruction is still pending. Therefore, neither the earthly high-priestly system nor the sacrificial system has completely vanished. As long as the earth exists, the "priests who offer gifts according to the law" will continue to "serve as a copy and shadow of the heavenly things" until they, too, vanish when the whole world vanishes. In the meantime, Hebrews assumes that the Jews who remain on the earth would continue to go to the temple and offer sacrifices. That is, as long as the temple still stood—until it was destroyed by the Romans in AD 70.

By reading Hebrews, the Jewish believers gained a new understanding of what Christ had accomplished for them. The temple and the priestly gifts served as a picture of what Christ, the high priest of heaven, has accomplished and will continue to accomplish in heaven on their behalf. Again, nowhere in Hebrews is the abolishment of the temple or the high-priestly system advocated. Hebrews says that they continue as a pattern of heavenly things until such time as the earth itself vanishes.

By all indications, Peter, James, and the early Jewish believers in Jerusalem continued to participate in some aspects of temple worship as long as the temple existed. Believing Jews still practiced circumcision and followed their Jewish customs. We have become so accustomed to Paul's teaching that the Gentiles do not have to follow Jewish law to become members of the church and the body of Christ that we sometimes overlook the fact that Peter, along with the Jerusalem church, continued to follow the Jewish rituals at the temple. Peter's ministry to the Jewish believers revolved around the temple where they met regularly.

Let us examine a few of the instances recorded in Acts in which the temple played a prominent role in the lives of the early Jewish church:

And day by day, attending the temple together and breaking bread in their homes, they received their food with glad and generous hearts (2:46) . . . But during the night an angel of the Lord opened the prison doors and brought them out, and said, "Go and stand in the temple and speak to the people all the words of this Life." And when they heard this, they entered the temple at daybreak and began to teach. (5:19–21)

It is interesting to note that of all people, the apostle Paul—who had harshly scolded those who tried to impose Jewish rituals upon the Gentiles—continued to respect the Jewish temple as a Jewish believer himself. Many people in Paul's day had misinterpreted his teachings that Gentile believers did not need to be circumcised or follow Jewish ordinances to mean that Jewish believers also no longer needed to be circumcised or follow Jewish customs because these rituals were abolished even for the Jews.

This misunderstanding of Paul's teachings greatly upset many in the Jewish community. And when Paul returned to Jerusalem after many years in the Gentile mission field, it caused great concern among even Jewish believers. And it caused a firestorm among unbelieving Jews. Luke describes Paul's meeting with the elders of the Jerusalem church:

When we had come to Jerusalem, the brothers received us gladly. On the following day Paul went in with us to James, and all the elders were present. After greeting them, he related one by one the things that God had done among the Gentiles through his ministry. And when they heard it, they glorified God. And they said to him, "You see, brother, how many thousands there are among the Jews of those who have believed. *They are all zealous for the law*, and they have been told about you *that you teach all the Jews who are among the Gentiles to forsake Moses, telling them not to circumcise their children or walk according to our customs.*" (Acts 21:17–21)

Two critical observations can be made here. One, despite what Hebrews and Ephesians seem to imply, Luke, a Gentile writer, reports that the many thousands of Jewish believers in Jerusalem remained "zealous for the law." Two, Paul was being falsely accused of teaching Jewish believers *not* to follow Jewish customs. When Paul taught the church at Ephesus that the law of commandments and ordinances was abolished and unnecessary for justification, he did not mean that Jewish believers no longer should follow Jewish customs and religious practices. So Paul, James, and the Jerusalem church elders devised a plan for Paul to demonstrate his faithfulness to the vanishing temple worship by going into the temple and performing several Jewish rites:

"What then is to be done? They will certainly hear that you have come. Do therefore what we tell you. We have four men who are under a vow; *take these men and purify yourself along with them and pay their expenses*, so that they may shave their heads. Thus all will know that there is nothing in what they have been told about you, *but that you yourself also live in observance of the law*. But as for the Gentiles who have believed, we have sent a letter with our judgment that they should abstain from what has been sacrificed to idols, and from blood, and from what has been strangled, and from sexual immorality." Then Paul took the men, and *the next day he purified himself along with them and went into the temple*, giving notice when the days of purification would be fulfilled and the offering presented for each one of them. When the seven days were almost completed, the Jews from Asia, seeing him in the temple, stirred up the whole crowd and laid hands on him, crying out, "Men of Israel, help! This is the man who is teaching everyone everywhere against the people and the law and this place. Moreover, he even brought Greeks into the temple and has defiled this holy place." For they had previously seen Trophimus the Ephesian [a Gentile] with him in the city, and they supposed that Paul had brought him into the temple. (Acts 21:22–29)

Luke reports that Paul goes to the temple to perform the act of purification in order to prove that the false reports are indeed false and that Paul, as a Jew, does indeed live in observance of the law.

With this act of devotion at the temple, the leaders of the Jerusalem church could reassure fellow believing Jews that Paul was not advocating abolishing the commandments and ordinances for Jewish believers. But once Paul came up against unbelieving Jews, it was not so easily explained. They said, "This is the man who is teaching everyone everywhere against the people and the law and this place [the temple]." All Jerusalem was in an uproar. Paul was falsely accused and arrested.

He describes this event when he later testifies before Governor Felix: "Now after several years I came to bring alms to my nation and *to present offerings*. While I was doing this, *they found me purified in the temple*, without any crowd or tumult" (Acts 24:17–18). Governor Felix was succeeded by Governor Festus, and Paul was required to testify once more: "Neither against the law of the Jews, nor against the temple, nor against Caesar have I committed any offense" (Acts 25:8). Paul, like Peter and the other Jewish believers, did not oppose temple worship. What Hebrews says will soon vanish, has not yet vanished.

To a believing Jew in the first century, the sacrifice of an unblemished lamb by the high priest, as well as the many other symbolic rituals of thanksgiving and peace offerings, would be rich with meaning. The Jewish believer understood that Christ was the perfect sacrifice and Passover lamb; yet, sacrificial rituals continued, for they were a powerful reminder of the broken body and shed blood of Christ. These temple rituals continue to serve as patterns of the heavenly realities for the believing Jew—at least until the temple and this earth ultimately vanish on the last day.

If Peter, James, the early Jewish church, and even Paul chose to continue to worship in the Jewish temple and follow Jewish customs, though they understood all that Hebrews said to be true, then one has to conclude that these forms of worship will not vanish until the world itself vanishes. The only reason that the early Jewish church in Jerusalem ceased to participate in the Jewish temple and the high-priestly services was because the Romans destroyed the temple itself in AD 70. They did not cease, however, because of the theological reasons taught in Hebrews.

Therefore, it is quite conceivable that the temple can be rebuilt in the restoration, as prophesied by Ezekiel, without violating the teachings of Hebrews. If Peter, James, Paul, and other Jewish believers could worship in the temple in the first century without being considered legalistic or in violation of the new covenant, then there is no reason they cannot worship in the Ezekiel temple of the restoration when they come back to mortal life in the first resurrection during the millennial reign of Christ.

The restored Jewish temple described by Ezekiel would be highly problematic if Christ, the high priest of heaven, returned to this earth as premillennialists claim. Ezekiel's vision of earthly high priests offering sacrifices is virtually impossible to reconcile with Christ being on the earth. But Christ does not come back to this earth to establish the restoration. He remains in heaven as the high priest of heaven in the very presence of God the Father: "After making purification for sins, he sat down at the right hand of the Majesty on high" (Heb. 1:3).

Therefore, an earthly high priest and temple worship can continue to operate in the restoration as a shadow of the high priest in heaven, just as they operated at the time that Hebrews was written when the Jerusalem church worshiped at the temple, remaining zealous for the law. There will come a day when Christ returns to destroy this earth—it vanishes—and take us to heaven. But until that day, the temple sacrifices made on this earth during the restoration can be viewed as a ceremonial reminder, "a copy and shadow," of all that Christ accomplished as the heavenly high priest and perfect sacrifice, much like the communion service of believers is a remembrance of Christ until he comes again and takes us to the holiest place there is—heaven itself—to be in the very presence of God the Father and the glorified Christ. Only then will there no longer be a need for a temple: "And I saw no temple in the city, for its temple is the Lord God the Almighty and the Lamb" (Rev. 21:22).

The postrestorational position maintains that Christ remains in heaven at the right hand of God as he rules this world during his millennial reign; thus, the presence of a renewed temple in the restoration does not present a problem. Christ is not needed on this earth to serve as high priest; an earthly high priest already exists. Christ is needed in heaven, so that he can appear before God on our behalf—now and for eternity (Heb. 7:24–25).

Even though Christ is the perfect sacrifice for our sins and the old covenant is, in effect, obsolete as it applies to providing a way for us to enter the holy presence of God, the temple and the earthly priests' sacrifices continue to serve as a mirror of what Christ has accomplished. These vestiges of the old covenant remain as a reminder of what Christ has done until he comes again.

It should be noted that many of the offerings at the temple are not necessarily associated with the idea of propitiation for the sins of the people; rather, they are peace offerings or expressions of thanksgiving and devotion. For example, the peace offering was not to overcome hostility between God and sinners, but to express the fact that the worshiper was already at peace with God. A man can give flowers to his wife to make up for a previous altercation, but he can also give flowers to his spouse as an expression of love and gratitude for a loving and peaceful relationship.

Many of these offerings at the temple were given in the context of a communal meal, signifying an expression of joy and communion between God and his people. This would be similar to our church fellowship dinners, but a great deal more worship oriented. Likewise, the grain offering was not given for the propitiation for sin, but as a gift to God of the fruit of one's labor as a way to show gratitude to God as the source of blessings in this life.

Amillennialists do not embrace the idea of a functioning temple in a future messianic kingdom. But the existence of a rebuilt temple during the restoration essentially re-creates the same situation and conditions that existed during the time of the early church in Jerusalem. If amillennialists continue to insist that a temple and high-priestly system cannot possibly operate on this earth during the restoration when Christ reigns from heaven, then they are saying, in effect, that Peter, Paul, and the early Jewish church in Jerusalem were wrong and sinful when they remained zealous for the law and continued to participate in the temple worship after Christ ascended into heaven.

Amillennialists cannot refute the validity of the Ezekiel temple without saying that the teachings and actions of the Jewish founders of our faith were incorrect. In effect, they are saying that the Jewish apostles and elders of the Jerusalem church were hypocrites for believing in the new covenant while practicing old covenant customs at the same time. Even Paul taught one thing and practiced another. Yet, Luke plainly says that Paul, as a Jewish believer, lived in observance of the law when he was in Jerusalem and proved it by going into the temple and performing acts of temple worship.

Paul did not observe the Jewish law in order to be justified, for he knew that his justification came through his faith in Christ, who paid the ultimate sacrifice. He knew that the old covenant was no longer a viable means of cleansing a sinner. But for Jewish believers like Paul, it continued to serve as a reminder of what Christ had accomplished for them on the cross. The earthly high priest would remind them of what Christ is doing for them as their eternal high priest in heaven. By continuing to worship in the first-century temple, the Jewish apostles and the Jerusalem church were not being legalistic, nor were they attempting to reestablish the old covenant. Paul and the other apostles demonstrated the utmost respect for the temple as long as it remained standing.

The Ezekiel temple with its priestly functions in the restoration in no way reestablishes the legalistic old covenant. These same Jewish believers will one day return to this earth in the first resurrection and be thrilled to worship again in the rebuilt temple while they wait for Christ to come again when the earth and the temple finally vanish and we are all taken to the eternal kingdom of heaven to join Christ, our heavenly high priest.

The temple will play many positive roles in the restoration. For example, the Ezekiel temple will be a center of learning and judicial activity:

> They [the priests] shall teach my people the difference between the holy and the common, and show them how to distinguish between the unclean and the clean. In a dispute, they shall act as judges, and they shall judge it according to my judgments. They shall keep my laws and my statutes in all my appointed feasts, and they shall keep my Sabbaths holy." (Ezek. 44: 23–24)

Moreover, Jerusalem and the rebuilt temple will function as a judicial center of worship and truth that will extend to the whole world:

> It shall come to pass in the latter days that the mountain of the house of the LORD shall be established as the highest of the mountains, and it shall be lifted up above the hills; and peoples shall flow to it, and many nations shall come, and say: "Come, let us go up to the mountain of the LORD, to the house of the God of Jacob [the temple], *that he may teach us his ways and that we may walk in his paths.*" For out of Zion shall go forth the law, and the word of the LORD from Jerusalem. *He shall judge between many peoples, and shall decide for strong nations afar off;* and they shall beat their swords into plowshares, and their spears into pruning hooks; nation shall not lift up sword against nation, neither shall they learn war anymore. (Mic. 4:1–3)

During the restoration, the Gentile nations will also celebrate some of the Jewish festivals: "And the LORD will be king over all the earth. On that day the LORD will be one and his name one. . . . Then everyone who survives of all the nations that have come against Jerusalem shall go up year after year to worship the King, the LORD of hosts, and *to keep the Feast of Booths*" (Zech. 14:9, 16). Jerusalem and the Jewish temple of the restoration will play a major role in the messianic kingdom, and the temple will once again be a house of prayer for all nations.

In short, the temple envisioned by Ezekiel and the prophets will be all of the following:

- a center for worship and prayer
- a center for learning and dissemination of truth
- a judicial center for Israel and the world

Finally, Jesus demonstrated a deep respect for the temple and was overcome with anger when he found it turned into a marketplace for commerce and profit. He taught that the temple was a house of prayer for all nations: "And he was teaching them and saying to them, 'Is it not written, "My house shall be called a house of prayer for all the nations"? But you have made it a den of robbers'" (Mark 11:17).

Whenever Jesus was in Jerusalem, the temple was the center for his preaching ministry. He never advocated any cause against the temple nor said that its function as a house of prayer was obsolete. The fact that he predicted it would be destroyed in the future in no way suggests that he meant it would never be rebuilt according to Ezekiel's prophecy. Jesus never teaches that the destruction of the temple is a permanent condition.

Isaiah and other prophets predicted similar times of destruction for the Solomon temple when the Jews were disobedient and sent into captivity by the Babylonians. But there were many other prophecies that it would be rebuilt. Jesus knew from the prophecies of Ezekiel and Daniel that the temple he predicted would be destroyed would also be rebuilt someday. A temple would have to be rebuilt in place of the one that was destroyed in AD 70 in order for the abomination of desolation to enter and make himself out to be God, which Jesus prophesied would take place at the beginning of the Great Tribulation.

Old Testament Saints Under the Mosaic Law

Another subject we need to address is how an Old Testament Jew, who lived *before the time of Christ* under the Mosaic law, or the old covenant, could become a believer and, therefore, a true spiritual descendant of Abraham, or a "true" Jew. How could a Jew in the Old Testament become a righteous, true Jew and be a part of the remnant that lived by faith?

Sincere Jews attempted to obey the law because they had great respect for it. But because of their sinful nature, they could not consistently obey it. They recognized their disobedience and felt guilty for their sins. As sinners, they recognized that they fell short of the glory of God by violating his commandments. Then they would be remorseful and repentant. Through the prescribed Mosaic sacrificial system, they then approached God's throne of grace, seeking mercy and forgiveness. The sacrificial system itself had to be approached with the proper attitude and motive. The Old Testament is replete with accounts of those who intentionally lived wretchedly and who thought that by performing some legalistic sacrifice, they would escape God's wrath. The sacrificial system had to be approached with an attitude of true repentance.

Even then, these Old Testament saints realized that they were still sinners who continued to sin, requiring them to go to the temple over and over again to have sacrifices performed for their sins. As a result, they knew these sacrifices could not ultimately save them. By faith, they had to trust in God's character that someday he would provide a means to fully forgive them. Their faith was in God who would justify the sincerely repentant sinner. If they knew and understood God's character, they would know that he would ultimately find a way to forgive them.

This aspect of God's character is referenced in the Law of Moses and the Prophets. Moses records, "The LORD passed before him and proclaimed, 'The LORD, the LORD, a God *merciful* and gracious, slow to anger, and abounding in steadfast *love* and faithfulness, keeping steadfast love for thousands, *forgiving* iniquity and transgression and sin'" (Exod. 34:6–7). The prophet Micah also understood this aspect of God's character:

> Who is a God like you, pardoning iniquity and passing over transgression for the remnant of his inheritance? He does not retain his anger forever, because he delights in steadfast love. He will again have compassion on us; he will tread our iniquities under foot. You will cast all our sins into the depths of the sea. You will show faithfulness to Jacob and steadfast love to Abraham, as you have sworn to our fathers from the days of old. (7:18–20)

Repentant Jews who knew God's character would be the true spiritual descendants of Abraham. They knew that these sacrifices could not ultimately save them, for they would not completely appease God's anger. But if they approached this sacrificial system, which foreshadowed Christ's ultimate sacrifice, with the right attitude, they would be looking forward to the Christ crucified, as we look back to the Christ crucified. As Hebrews says, Abraham and his spiritual descendants looked forward with us to the sacrifice of Christ: "And all these, though commended through their faith, did not receive what was promised, since God had provided something better for us, that apart from us they should not be made perfect" (Heb. 11:39–40). Or, as Peter observed, "Concerning this salvation, the prophets who prophesied about the grace that was to be yours searched and inquired carefully, inquiring what person or time the Spirit of Christ in them was indicating when he predicted the sufferings of Christ and the subsequent glories" (1 Peter 1:10–11).

If the Old Testament believers had this hope and trust in God's character, it would have been well placed because through Christ their sins were eventually fully forgiven. Before Christ, God had to forbear the sins of his

Old Testament saints. He could not totally forgive them until the cross: "Christ Jesus, whom God put forward as propitiation by his blood, to be received by faith. This was to show God's righteousness, because in his divine *forbearance* he had passed over former sins" (Rom. 3:24–25). God may be loving, merciful, and forgiving, but because he is holy, he could not just simply forgive sins. As a result, the Old Testament means of sacrifice was unable to perfectly cleanse the repentant sinner. There had to be a future system of justice whereby these sins could be punished and, at the same time, forgiven. God had to forbear the sins of the past until the sacrifice of his Son. We tend to think of the cross as a system of mercy. But this form of mercy is actually a process of justice, because a righteous God cannot just forgive and forget. There had to be propitiation by the blood of the perfect Christ in order to satisfy God's justice. Only then could he fully forgive former sins and all future sins of his people who repent.

Some Jews in the Old Testament, and in Christ's day, cared about the law but made the mistake of thinking they could succeed in obeying it and could, therefore, achieve a state of righteousness. In their pride, they became self-righteous and were not true believers. They stumbled over the law, thinking it was the means for achieving righteousness when it was actually the means of revealing their incurable sinfulness! As sinners we are simply not capable of fully obeying the moral law.

Many of the Pharisees were self-righteous, as Christ showed:

> He also told this parable to some who trusted in themselves that they were righteous, and treated others with contempt: "Two men went up into the temple to pray, one a Pharisee and the other a tax collector. The Pharisee, standing by himself, prayed thus: 'God, I thank you that I am not like other men, extortioners, unjust, adulterers, or even like this tax collector. I fast twice a week; I give tithes of all that I get.' But the tax collector, standing far off, would not even lift up his eyes to heaven, but beat his breast, saying, 'God, be merciful to me, a sinner!' I tell you, this man went down to his house justified, rather than the other. For everyone who exalts himself will be humbled, but the one who humbles himself will be exalted." (Luke 18: 9–14)

The Pharisee in this parable falsely thought he had succeeded in obeying the law, thereby achieving righteousness.

Trying to achieve righteousness by works of the law is like trying to swim across the Atlantic Ocean instead of taking a boat. Those who try are missing the "boat," containing those who are justified by faith, that can take them safely across the ocean. Both Old and New Testament saints lived by faith in a holy and loving God who will justify the unrighteous by his grace. The Old Testament saints had the same faith as we do. The only difference is that they looked forward to God's loving sacrifice of his Son, and we look back to it.

When Jesus said, "Do not think that I have come to abolish the Law or the Prophets; I have not come to abolish them but to fulfill them" (Matt. 5:17), he meant exactly what he said. The law demanded perfect righteousness on the part of God's people, but it also demanded a sacrifice involving the shedding of blood as a propitiation for the sins of imperfect sinners. Because Christ was perfect, his crucifixion and shedding of blood fulfilled the law by providing the perfect sacrifice for our sins, fulfilling the law for us so that we can be declared perfect before a holy God, and we can be fully reconciled to the Father and even be indwelt by the Holy Spirit.

Plus, Christ fulfills the Law *and* the Prophets by coming into this world as the son of David, the promised Messiah. And he will fulfill *all* the messianic promises when he exercises his reign from heaven. Let there be no doubt about this, for Christ further says, "For truly, I say to you, until heaven and earth pass away, not an iota, not a dot, will pass from the Law until *all* is accomplished" (Matt. 5:18). This includes his succeeding sacrifice *and* his future messianic kingdom on this earth.

Summary

It is important to recognize the New Testament writers' ongoing distinction between Israel and the church. There are several instances where Israel is compared to the church, as the people of God, and both are referred to as a holy nation (1 Peter 2:9). These comparisons, however, are only analogies between the church, a non-civil institution, and Israel, a civil institution. The church, made up of circumcised and uncircumcised believers, does not become or replace the nation of Israel. Nowhere does Paul teach that the church replaces the nation of Israel, nor does he eliminate the distinctions between ethnic Jews and Gentiles.

Paul consistently makes a distinction between the two groups of people and a subgroup within each group. He recognizes ethnic Jews, believers and unbelievers, and Gentiles, believers and unbelievers. Paul carefully and purposefully maintains these distinctions not only throughout his letter to the Romans, but throughout all his letters that address these issues. The Jews are the ethnic descendants of Abraham, and the Gentiles are not. The Jews are circumcised, and the Gentiles are not. The Jews were entrusted with the law and the temple and with bringing the Jewish Messiah into the world, and the Gentiles were not. Jesus, as the Jewish sacrificial lamb, was not the product of a pagan religion or sacrificial system. Rather, he was the fulfillment of the Jewish religious system. Jesus is the fulfillment of the law. He is *the* seed of Abraham.

Jews and Gentiles alike are sinners and are all justified by faith in the blood of Jesus Christ by the grace of God through his sovereign election. Justification by faith is the only way for human beings (Jew and Gentile)—past, present, and future—to be reconciled to God the Father.

Paul and the disciples concluded that the Gentiles did not need to become Jews in order to belong to Christ and become members of his kingdom; they did not need to be circumcised or follow Jewish customs. In the new creation, there is no distinction between Jew and Gentile, so there is no need for Gentiles to follow the Jewish ordinances in order to be born again and join Christ's kingdom.

Even during the restoration, the distinction between Jewish and Gentile believers will remain. The disciples, Jewish believers, will rule over the twelve tribes of Israel. Likewise, thrones of Gentile believers will be raised to rule over their respective nations. Christ will reign as King of kings and Lord of lords of all nations.

As long as the Adamic order of being exists, God intends to use the true nation of Israel, made up of ethnic Jews justified by faith, as a part of his plan to create his messianic kingdom on this earth. God used Israel to bring the Messiah into the world, and he will use the regenerated Jewish people and their nation again when he establishes his messianic kingdom. Only after the restoration at the transformation will the distinctions between Jew and Gentile come to an end, just as the distinctions between male and female will end. Until then, the distinctions remain and are highly relevant to the prophetic future and the messianic kingdom on this earth.

15

God's Plan of Redemption

Nature communicates two messages. One, there is enough residual beauty, joy, and life to hear the echo of the Garden of Eden and know there must be a Creator of the immense complexity and beauty of man and nature. Two, there is something fundamentally wrong with man and nature for there to be so much misery and death and for our lives to fall so short of our human aspirations. The loving Creator of this remarkable creation must have directed his wrath toward man and nature.

I am always surprised how angry some people, including Christians, become with God when personal tragedy or natural disaster strikes them or their neighbors. Why would a loving God allow this to happen? The tragedies and disasters we experience are evidence that our loving God is not being kind and loving, but is, instead, angry with Adam and his descendants. God altered nature to cause death and destruction. The tragic things that happen to us are a reminder, or a wakeup call, that something is dreadfully wrong with the relationship between God and man.

Since the original Genesis creation was created as good, we could say that it is *unnatural* for man and nature to be in such a fallen or cursed state and for our deep aspirations to be so unfulfilled. Instead of getting angry with God when life is cruel, it would be much wiser to examine why God is angry and put a curse on man and nature.

Our physical bodies have mechanisms that alert us of illness or injury. The central nervous system uses pain to communicate to our brain that something is wrong and needs our attention. If we cut our foot, the pain signals us to stop walking and tend to the injury. With the pain and misery in this world, God is trying to send us a message. Hurricanes, tornados, earthquakes, injuries, disease, and death are part of the world's sensory message system, alerting us that something is wrong with this creation.

There is tremendous beauty in nature, but nature is also sick and screaming at us in pain—just visit a nursing home, a hospital, a war zone, or an area of poverty in the world.

I sometimes think that the ancient pagan worshipers, with their attempts to appease the gods to avert natural disasters and crop failures, had a better grip on reality than many modern scientists with their advanced degrees and sophisticated research laboratories. They may have been ignorant about the natural causes of crop failures, totally confused about why the gods were angry, and equally confused about how to appease them, but at least they recognized that the gods must be angry.

The ancient pagans understood that something was fundamentally wrong with man and nature and that the cause must be an angry spiritual being(s). Their spiritual sensory system alerted them that it was unnatural for nature to be so cruel. They recognized the discrepancy between their human aspirations for an abundant and fulfilling life and the reality of this unstable, and ultimately tragic, world.

For some, technology and materialism have taken the edge off our short existence. Some of us can live a little longer in a more comfortable and entertaining world. But every year, there is a new reminder—in the form of natural and manmade disasters—that nature and life fall far short of our aspirations and expectations. And this discrepancy between our aspirations and the reality of nature, our fragile bodies, and our dysfunctional societies should lead us to search for the cause and solution to this discrepancy.

Human aspirations come from the fact that man was originally created to live in an Edenic paradise without death and destruction. The death of a close friend or family member due to disease or human negligence never comes naturally to us. We are always struck with a deep and profound grief. Death is not natural. Something went terribly wrong.

The cause of pain and death in this world is a result of the revolt by Adam and Eve, which brought God's curse on this creation. By eating of the tree of the knowledge of good and evil, they demonstrated that they did not want to remain submissive to God. They believed that gaining the knowledge of good and evil would allow them to be self-sufficient, independent, and autonomous from God. With this knowledge, they could define for themselves what was the right and wrong way to function. They could be their own gods, no longer subject to the one, true God.

We have inherited the insubordinate nature of Adam and Eve. We refuse to accept God's definition of good and evil and sin; we define right and wrong for ourselves. We refuse to submit to God's will and are hostile toward him. That is because we have a godself that is inherently hostile to God. But God has a plan to redeem fallen man. He sent his Son into this world as a human being. And, whereas the first Adam did not pass the test of obedience and was insubordinate, bringing the curse and destruction into this world, Christ, although fully tempted and tested as a human being, passed the test and did not sin. He remained fully submissive to his Father.

Satan's temptations directed at Christ in the desert were an attempt to cause Christ to be insubordinate to the Father—as Adam and Eve were insubordinate. After Jesus was baptized, the Holy Spirit descended upon him. The Father was well pleased with his beloved Son who had become a man, but then wanted him to be tested: "Then Jesus was *led up by the Spirit* into the wilderness to be tempted by the devil" (Matt. 4:1).

Jesus' testing was far more rigorous and difficult than that of Adam and Eve who lived in a state of paradise when tested. They were living a fulfilled life in a lush garden with everything they needed. They surely did not need the fruit of the knowledge of good and evil to prosper. Jesus, on the other hand, was in a state of deprivation in an inhospitable desert—he had fasted for forty days and was hungry and in need of nourishment.

The key to understanding this temptation episode is to recognize that through the Holy Spirit, the Father commanded Christ to go into the wilderness to fast. Since it was the Father who told Christ to fast, then the Father would be the one to determine when the fast would end. Satan's first temptation was to tempt him to end the fast before the Father had said that it was time: "If you are the Son of God, command these stones to become loaves of bread" (Matt. 4:3). Christ, as the Son of God, definitely had the power to end the fast by making bread out of stones. But if he had used his divine power, he would have been insubordinate to the Father because, as a human being, God had commanded him to fast. He chose to wait on the Father to say when it was time for the fast to end: "But he answered, 'It is written, "Man shall not live by bread alone, but by every word that comes from the mouth of God"'" (4:4). In this situation, the word that had come from God the Father was to continue to fast until he said it was time to end the fast. Obedience to God and his word produces true spiritual life. Then God will take care of our material needs.

Satan's second temptation was to lure Christ to jump off the pinnacle of the temple to force the Father to save him. Succumbing to this temptation would also have been an act of insubordination, for he would not be asking the Father to perform a miracle to save him, but would, in effect, be telling the Father that he had to perform a miracle to save him from certain death. Jesus answered, "Again it is written, 'You shall not put the Lord your God to the test'" (4:7). God can tell or command us what to do, but human beings do not tell God, who is our superior, what to do; we should only ask.

Satan's third temptation was to offer Christ the kingdoms of the world if he would worship him (Satan). Proud and pompous as the god of this world, Satan even had the audacity and arrogance to think he had the right to offer the kingdoms of the world to Christ. But the kingdoms of the world rightfully belonged to Christ as the true God of this world. Christ declined the offer, because he knew that his reign over this world would only begin when the Father *decided* that it was the times or seasons for it to begin (Acts 1:7). Even now, Christ sits at the Father's right hand, waiting until the Father determines that it is time for Christ's enemies to be made his footstool. Seizing this opportunity to reign over this world as the Messiah before the Father had said that it was time would have been an act of insubordination. And, of course, to worship Satan in the process would have been the ultimate form of insubordination, for the Father had commanded, "You shall worship the Lord your God and *him only shall you serve*" (Matt. 4:10).

Unlike Adam and Eve and their descendants who are insubordinate and sinful, Christ, as the second Adam, passed the test and lived a sinless life. He was always submissive to the Father during his life on this earth. He did not deserve to be under the curse of death, but he was cursed on the cross by the Father for our insubordination and sins so those who accept him can be declared righteous and reconciled to a holy God. Once reconciled, we are destined for resurrection and eternal life, totally free from the curse of death. The process of resurrection is the key element in God's plan of redemption to solving fallen man's predicament of alienation, death, and destruction.

Death and Resurrection

According to the Scriptures, the origin of death is God, who put a curse on the Adamic order of being when Adam and Eve were disobedient and ate from the tree of the knowledge of good and evil. As fallen human beings descended from Adam, we will experience three forms of death. Because sinful man is inherently hostile to and alienated from God who is Spirit and Life, natural man experiences a form of spiritual death even during his lifetime on this earth. The second form of death is mortal death, when the natural body dies and the spirit of an unrepentant person is sent to and held in Hades. The third form of death is referred to in the Scriptures as the "second death" and occurs on Judgment Day when unbelievers are resurrected from Hades and sent to the lake of fire in body and spirit. This final form of death and God's wrath is much worse than the mortal death of the body, for it is irreversible, permanent, and eternal. Jesus said, "And do not fear those who kill the body but cannot kill the soul. Rather fear him who can destroy both soul and body in hell" (Matt. 10:28).

God's plan of redemption for those who repent and receive his Son is structured around saving us from these three forms death and is achieved through four forms of resurrection—two of the spirit and two of the body. The first form of resurrection is of the spirit of a person and takes place when he or she receives Christ. Born of Adam and Eve as sinners, we are all dead spiritually because we are alienated from the living God. But when we repent and believe in Christ, we are born again and experience regeneration.

At the moment of conversion, we are mysteriously joined with Christ in his crucifixion *and* his resurrection. Thus, our fallen spirits are raised from spiritual death and we become alive again: "Do you not know that all of us who have been baptized into Christ Jesus were baptized into his death? We were buried therefore with him by baptism into death, in order that, just as Christ was raised from the dead by the glory of the Father, we too might walk in newness of life" (Rom. 6:3–4).

Through the regenerative process of conversion, we are literally raised from the dead and experience the renewal of spiritual life as we fellowship with the living God through Jesus Christ. We are justified by faith, which allows us to be reconciled to a holy God and become living beings again, restored to a proper relationship with our Creator. As Christians, we are saved from a human nature that is inherently insubordinate and hostile to God. We become men and women of God and capable of being submissive to our Creator. We also become children of God and temporarily live a dual order of existence.

The second kind of resurrection of the spirit of a person takes place when the natural body dies or "falls asleep" and the regenerated spirit is raised up to be with the Lord in heaven. In Jesus' famous encounter with the Sadducees, he referenced Abraham, Isaac, and Jacob as examples of the spirits of the saints who had departed this world but were still living because their spirits had been raised to heaven. But they have not yet received new bodies. Only their spirits had been raised to life in heaven: "And as for the resurrection of the dead, have you not read what was said to you by God: 'I am the God of Abraham, and the God of Isaac, and the God of Jacob'? He is not God of the dead, but of the living" (Matt. 22:31–32). Hebrews refers to the living spirits of the departed saints as "a cloud of witnesses" in heaven and as "the spirits of the righteous made perfect" (Heb. 12:1, 23). Their risen spirits are alive and observing this world from heaven.

The third form of resurrection in God's plan of redemption that overcomes God's curse of death is the first to involve the human body and is referred to by John as the "first resurrection" (Rev. 20:6). This occurs at the beginning of the 1,000-year restoration when the spirits of the departed saints come down from heaven to reenter regenerated natural Adamic bodies and live again on the restored earth during the millennium. The body that is raised at the beginning of the millennium is a natural Adamic body because it is destined for a regenerated Genesis earth where the resurrected saints can marry and have children. This resurrection will be similar to the resurrection of Lazarus, except, this time, Satan will be bound and Christ will be exercising his rightful reign from heaven over the regenerated earth, which will be restored to an Edenic condition.

The fourth and final resurrection is a transformation that occurs on the last day after the millennium at Christ's second coming when the saints' mortal bodies are resurrected if asleep or raptured and then transformed into spiritual bodies that are made immortal and imperishable and taken to begin their citizenship in heaven. The natural body of the Adamic order of being ends, and the spiritual body of the new order of being as children of God begins in the new heavens and new earth:

> Behold! I tell you a mystery. We shall not all sleep, but we shall be changed, in a moment, in the twinkling of an eye, at the last trumpet. For the trumpet will sound, and the dead will be raised imperishable, and we shall be changed. For this perishable body must put on the imperishable, and this mortal body must put on immortality. (1 Cor. 15:51–53)

It was this type of resurrection of the new order of being as sons of God that Christ was referring to when he responded to the Sadducees, who did not even believe in a resurrection of the departed saints:

> The sons of this age marry and are given in marriage [the Adamic order of being], but those who are considered worthy to attain to that age and to the resurrection from the dead [God's people] neither marry nor are given in marriage, for they cannot die anymore [are immortal], because they are equal to angels and are sons of God [a new creation or new order of being], being sons of the resurrection [a resurrection like Christ's]. (Luke 20:34–36)

These four forms of resurrection are the basic framework of God's plan of redemption to save us from the three forms of death:

1. Through the first resurrection of the spirit, we are born again and become living men and women of God as well as the living children of God.
2. Through the second resurrection of the spirit, when the mortal body dies, our individual spirits are raised up to join Christ in heaven while our bodies sleep on the earth.
3. Through the first resurrection of the natural body, at the beginning of the millennium, the spirits of the departed saints enter regenerated Adamic bodies in order to experience the 1,000-year restoration of this Genesis creation as restored human beings. Christ removes and binds Satan and exercises his reign over this Adamic world from his throne in heaven.
4. Through the final resurrection, when Christ returns on the last day of this creation, our natural Adamic bodies are transformed into a new kind of immortal spiritual bodies, and we are taken to the new heavens and new earth as sons of God for eternity.

As a result of these four resurrections—two of the spirit and two of the body—a believer "shall never die" (John 11:26). That is good news about our present life of fellowship with the living God as well as about our future glorious inheritance in God's kingdom on earth and in heaven.

When his disciples asked about his second coming and the "close of the age," the Adamic age, Christ told them that "the one who endures to the end [of this age] will be saved" and brought into the eternal kingdom (Matt. 24:13). It is because of these four forms of resurrection that we will be able to endure until the end of this Genesis age and then be taken to the eternal kingdom. From the moment of the first resurrection of the spirit when we are regenerated, justified, and made holy, we can rest assured that we will never die—that is, we will endure to the end of this Genesis creation and be brought into the eternal age to come. We know by faith that as the eternal children of God, our living spirits will always be alive and that no matter what happens to our bodies, they can be—and will be—resurrected both as natural bodies and ultimately as eternal bodies at the end of this age.

As Jesus taught Martha, through the power of resurrection whoever believes in him will never die and will therefore endure to the end:

> Jesus said to her, "Your brother will rise again." Martha said to him, "I know that he will rise again in the resurrection on the last day [at the end of the age]." Jesus said to her, "I am the resurrection and the life. Whoever believes in me, though he die, yet shall he live, and *everyone who lives and believes in me shall never die.* Do you believe this?" She said to him, "Yes, Lord; I believe that you are the Christ, the Son of God, who is coming into the world." (John 11:23–27)

The divine power of resurrection is the key to God's plan of redemption for those who believe in Christ. Through resurrection, we are given life today and for eternity. As a result, believers will never die. Because of the power of resurrection of the spirit and of the body, nothing can separate us from the life and love of the living God with whom we have been reconciled through Jesus Christ. Believers, like Lazarus, will live forever.

Christ's Divine Right to Rule This World

But before the human experience ends at the close of this Genesis age and Christ comes again to take God's children to the new heavens and new earth through the final resurrection on the last day, God has an important mission for his saints to complete in this world. He wants to demonstrate to mankind and the heavenly witnesses what this Genesis creation would have been like if Adam and Eve had not sinned and been allowed to multiply and fill the earth—righteous humanity as he had originally planned when he created the Garden of Eden. God wants to redeem this creation and the

Adamic order of being and restore us to true biblical manhood and woman-hood—without the influence or presence of Satan.

When Adam and Eve succumbed to Satan's temptation, this evil, alien being entered into our world with motives to steal, kill, and destroy God's good creation. We now live in a fallen world under the dominion of Satan and under God's curse. And the current human experience is far too short and full of misery for all of us.

As Christians we aspire to know a deeply fulfilling human experience before we go to heaven. In the restoration, when Satan is bound, our human aspirations will be fulfilled, for we will get to experience the regenerated Genesis creation in all its glory. We will experience an abundant life on this earth as Christ, the Good Shepherd and rightful God of this world, restores this creation and rules the world. Satan, who is aptly called a thief, will no longer be able to rob us of the joys of this redeemed creation. God himself wants to delight in his regenerated Genesis creation once more, as he did in the beginning when he celebrated his creation as good. He wants to fellowship with righteous humanity, created in his own image, as we resume the task of subduing the earth. God intends to restore this creation to its original glory so that he can enjoy his handiwork for one thousand years.

And within the Trinity, this creation was specifically created for God the Son. This creation was created through him, by him, and, most important, for him. As a result, the restoration is for his pleasure and delight as well as for those repentant human beings who are "worthy" to be resurrected into their Adamic bodies to take part in this restored Edenic paradise.

Jesus Christ was more than a Jewish king. The Jewish Messiah was none other than the Son of God, the second person of the Trinity, who was present with the Father and the Holy Spirit as God when the world was created. Jesus Christ is the rightful ruler of not only Israel but of the whole world, because this world was made for him. The Son of God has a divine right to rule this world. After the Great Tribulation when Satan is bound, Jesus Christ will rule the world from the right hand of God the Father, and, through the power of the Holy Spirit, he will ensure that the Father's will is done on earth as it is in heaven.

The Scriptures teach that after Christ completes his 1,000-year reign over this restored earth from his throne in heaven, he will come again to conquer the last enemy, death, by transforming our mortal bodies to be like his immortal, glorified body and taking us to be with him in heaven in his Father's house for eternity. Paul tells us: "Then comes the end, when he delivers the kingdom to God the Father after destroying every rule and every authority and power" (1 Cor. 15:24). We will escape the second death or the wrath of God on Judgment Day and enter into the new heavens and new earth as children of God and as the bride of Christ, and we will experience a completely new order of being even more glorious than the first.

That is an incredible gospel! This is the gospel that evangelicals should be bringing to the world. If a person believes in Jesus Christ, he or she becomes a living being reconciled to God and destined to become a restored human being. At the same time, that person becomes a child of God for he or she is born of God. Christians will get to experience the restoration of the Genesis creation in this age through the resurrection of the natural body; then, through the resurrection of the immortal body at Christ's second coming, we will experience eternal life as children of God in the Father's heavenly kingdom in the age to come.

God's Children Come from a Preexisting Order of Being

In the Genesis account, Adam and Eve were created from "scratch." They did not originate from a previous order of existence. God began a completely new creation when he made Adam from the dust of the earth and breathed life into his newly created body of flesh and blood. God could have created the children of God in the new order of being from "scratch" in heaven. Instead, he has chosen to take preexisting fallen mankind and, through a process of rebirth and regeneration, create children of God from Adamic creatures. As a result, we are presently living two orders of being concurrently. But our final destiny is the kingdom of heaven as a single order of being as the Father's children and as the bride of Christ.

I believe the angels are so intrigued by what they are participating in and witnessing that they, too, are eager to see the day the children of God inherit the kingdom of heaven:

> Concerning this salvation, the prophets, who spoke of the grace that was to come to you, searched intently and with the greatest care, trying to find out the time and circumstances to which the Spirit of Christ in them was pointing when he predicted the sufferings of Christ and the glories that would follow. It was revealed to them that they were not serving themselves but you, when they spoke of the things that have now been told you by those who have preached the gospel to you by the Holy Spirit sent from heaven. Even angels long to look into these things. (1 Peter 1:10–12 NIV)

The angels watched as God created the heavens and the earth and Adam and then Eve. They witnessed Christ coming into this world through the virgin birth. They watched Christ dying on the cross. They were there when he was resurrected and when he ascended to heaven. They will be actively involved in the Tribulation and the restoration. Christ will send angels to gather the saints from around the world on the last day. Finally, the angels will witness the transformation of God's children when we are caught up into the clouds and taken to the new heavens and new earth. What an incredible series of events for them to behold! It is no wonder they "long to look into these things."

In heaven, we, along with the angels, will remember that we were originally fallen Adamic creatures destined for destruction. We will be forever grateful that we were able to experience a restored Genesis creation as righteous human beings for one thousand years before we were transformed into Christ's image and taken to heaven. Most important, we will remember that God in his mercy instituted a means of salvation for us whereby we would be saved from his final wrath and brought into his eternal kingdom as his beloved children.

Once we are in heaven, I can imagine angels asking, "Weren't you part of that fallen race of Adam upon whom God showed mercy? Now look at you; you are his dearly beloved, glorified children!" There is a biblical basis for this:

> But God, being rich in mercy, because of the great love with which he loved us, even when we were dead in our trespasses, made us alive together with Christ—by grace you have been saved—and raised us up with him and seated us with him in the heavenly places in Christ Jesus, *so that in the coming ages* he might show the immeasurable riches of his grace in kindness toward us in Christ Jesus. (Eph. 2:4–7)

In a remarkable revelation, Paul teaches that we will "in the coming ages" serve as an unforgettable and eternal witness in heaven of God's love and immeasurable grace and kindness toward those he redeemed from the fallen Adamic creatures. God's plan of redemption will reveal something about his character for all eternity. After witnessing Judgment Day when unbelievers experience the second death and the lake of fire, we will realize what would have happened to us had we not been saved by the grace and love of God.

Understanding the Two Orders of Being

Much of the confusion that surrounds eschatology, the kingdom of God, and our future inheritance can be attributed to the failure of theologians to understand and differentiate between the two orders of being described in the Scriptures—the Adamic order of being, mortal man as male and female and given in marriage, and the new order of being as children of God, a new creation that is neither male nor female and in heaven will be immortal and not be given in marriage. It is critical to recognize when Scriptures are referring to a future earthly kingdom that involves the restoration of the Adamic order of being in this age and when they are referring to the heavenly kingdom in the age to come that involves the new order of being as the eternal sons of God.

In the Son's messianic kingdom, nature itself is restored, the departed saints are restored to natural Adamic human beings through the first resurrection, and Christ is restored as the rightful God of this Genesis creation. The messianic kingdom in this age is characterized by the Old Testament prophets as a restored Adamic order of being with marriage and reproduction in a restored Genesis creation.

The Father's heavenly kingdom, on the other hand, is for the transformed children of God in the new heavens and new earth. When Christ refers to "the age to come," he is referring to the eternal dwelling place for the children of God after this Adamic age has come to an end. Jesus described the heavenly kingdom as a place for the sons of God who, after experiencing a resurrection like his, will "neither marry nor . . . [be] given in marriage" and will become immortal beings "for they cannot die anymore."

What kind of bodies we will have when we are transformed at the second coming of Christ and taken to heaven remains a mystery. Like pecans germinate into pecan trees and not into more pecans, our bodies will be transformed into a new kind of body adapted for the new heavens and new earth. The continuity between this current Adamic human body and the Genesis earth and the future glorified body and the new heavens and new earth also remains a mystery. But we can trust God to demonstrate his incredible creativity again when he creates a new paradise for his children beyond anything we could ever imagine.

Postrestorationalism is the correct biblical architecture because it is the only eschatology that consistently maintains the distinctions between the two orders of being and correctly identifies the kingdoms of God associated with each. Biblical data logically fits within this eschatological framework.

Premillennialists claim to believe in the fulfillment of all the messianic prophecies before the eternal heavenly kingdom is realized. But the Old Testament prophets describe the messianic kingdom as an Adamic paradise with the resurrected saints being given in marriage, having children, and seeing their children's children (Ezek. 37). Ezekiel's prophecy of the valley of dry bones coming to life as Adamic human beings in natural bodies is a graphic depiction of this future resurrection of the departed saints in the messianic kingdom. How can the disciples and their followers experience a hundredfold rewards in this age with houses, lands, brothers, sisters, father, mother, and children unless they come back to life through the first resurrection as restored human beings in their natural Adamic bodies? Jesus is describing settings and relationships that are part of the human experience. The messianic kingdom as envisioned by the Old Testament prophets and the New Testament is a restoration of the Adamic order of being. Premillennialists place the wrong kind of resurrected body, the raptured body, in the wrong kingdom.

The ante-Nicene millennialists understood that the meek inherit the restored earth through a resurrection of the natural body and inherit the kingdom of heaven at the general resurrection through the resurrection of the immortal body. They may have mistakenly put Christ's second coming in conjunction with the resurrection of the natural body, but that is easily corrected by recognizing that Christ can simply rule this earth from his throne in heaven when Satan is bound. This, in turn, allows for his second coming to occur after the millennium in conjunction with the rapture of the saints who are destined for the kingdom of heaven. This rediscovery of their postrestorational views as presented in this book, with a few corrections, seems to be the closest to their teachings, which lends credibility to the claim that this was indeed the view of the disciples. Premillennialists have everything to gain and nothing to lose by adopting postrestorationalism.

Amillennialists are right about the second coming and the rapture occurring on the last day, but they boldly claim there is no 1,000-year messianic kingdom on this earth before the eternal kingdom of heaven even though this Genesis creation was created for Christ. If amillennialists are correct, then Satan will have robbed Christ of his right to delight in his own Genesis creation. Christ will never be restored as the true God of this restored Adamic creation—his very own creation! To have this tragic, fallen creation end without this restoration would be the ultimate tragedy—not only for the saints but, most important, for the Son of God.

Everyone who lives in this fallen world with varying degrees of misery and unhappiness recognizes our short lives on this earth as a profound disappointment. The suffering brought on by human sin, demons, and the curse is heartbreaking. But the same can be said for our Creator. He, too, has been cheated out of the joy and delight of his creation. Because Satan and sin entered the world through the rebellion of mankind, with its resulting curse by God, the human experience on this earth has fallen far short of the glory of God. Glory can be defined as a way for God to delight in his wonderful creation, and that delight has yet to be truly restored.

But the Son of God has the divine right, power, and authority to restore this Genesis creation to himself in its original glory and rule over this world as King of kings and Lord of lords before he destroys this Adamic creation and takes his people to the Father's kingdom. And the Father has promised his Son that one day he will restore this Genesis creation to its rightful Lord: "The Lord [God the Father] said to my Lord [Christ], Sit at my right hand, until I [the Father] put your enemies under your feet" (Matt. 22:44). Someday the Father will restore this Genesis creation to his Son who is its rightful Lord. And no man can deny Christ this divine right.

In Revelation, John can hear the music announcing the future messianic reign of Christ over this world:

And they sang a new song, saying, "Worthy are you to take the scroll and to open its seals, for you were slain, and by your blood you ransomed people for God from every tribe and language and people and nation, and you have made them a kingdom and priests to our God, and they shall reign on the earth. . . . Then the seventh angel blew his trumpet, and there were loud voices in heaven, saying, "The kingdom of the world has become the kingdom of our Lord and of his Christ, and he shall reign forever and ever." And the twenty-four elders who sit on their thrones before God fell on their faces and worshiped God, saying, "We give thanks to you, Lord God Almighty, who is and who was, for you have taken your great power and begun to reign [over this earth]." (Rev. 5:9–10; 11:15–17)

John hears a new song and angelic trumpets foretelling the coming messianic kingdom on this earth. For some reason, amillennialists cannot hear this music. Amillennialism denies the Son this divine right, joy, and glory of delighting in his restored creation. The Messiah is cheated of his messianic kingdom. With the many inherent flaws of premillennialism, amillennialists had an excuse to reject millennialism. But with postrestorationalism and its affirmation of the second coming on the last day, they no longer have an excuse for rejecting a literal millennium.

Jesus himself insists that we understand God's word and promises: "Then he said to them, 'These are my words that I spoke to you while I was still with you, that everything written about me in the Law of Moses and the Prophets and the Psalms must be fulfilled.' Then he opened their minds to understand the Scriptures" (Luke 24:44–45). All the prophetic Scriptures about Christ and his messianic kingdom must be fulfilled. Yet, for centuries amillennialists have been denying the existence of a literal millennial reign of Christ before the eternal kingdom of heaven.

Postmillennialists also do not believe everything written about Christ and his messianic kingdom. They recognize that Christ can rule this world from his throne in heaven, but they believe the earth is never restored to its Edenic condition as predicted by the prophets. They believe only those saints fortunate enough to be living when this supposed golden era arrives get to experience the messianic kingdom. All other deceased saints, including the disciples, only get to inherit the kingdom of heaven.

But Jesus taught the disciples that in the regeneration of this world when he sits on his throne to rule this world from heaven, they would indeed receive a hundredfold reward as restored human beings. Without a real first resurrection of the disciples into their natural bodies, there is no way for this promise to come true. After this reward, through a resurrection of an eternal imperishable body, they will inherit eternal life, which will fulfill the second part of his promise to his disciples (Matt. 19:28–29). These two resurrections are the only way Christ can fulfill these promises.

And, contrary to what postmillennialists assert, Satan is not currently bound but is very much operational in this world. Today, except for the children of God, "the whole world is under the control of the evil one" (1 John 5:19 NIV). John foresees a day after the Great Tribulation when Satan will be completely bound and no longer in contact with this world. Until that time, this dark and evil world remains his dominion. Christ, as King of the world, might have the power and authority to rule this world, but he does not exercise it until the Father says it is time (Acts 1:6–7 and Matt. 22:44). The Father binds Satan as we do the work of evangelism, and the Holy Spirit gathers out of Satan's dominion of darkness those the Father has chosen to come into his kingdom. But only God can completely remove Satan from this world. In the meantime, Christ is building his church in Satan's hostile territory, which is why Christ continues to suffer when his body of believers is persecuted.

Taking the Gospel to the Jews

Perhaps the time is approaching for the Jews to be grafted back in. As we take the gospel to the Jews and pass the baton to them, it is important that we at least pass on a correct understanding of the messianic kingdom. A proponent of postrestorationalism might say the following to a Jew searching for the truth:

> Look, you are not the only one who was a little confused about Jesus of Nazareth. Even his early disciples could not figure out why he did not overthrow the tyrannical Romans and usher in his messianic kingdom during their lifetimes. That may have been one of the contributing reasons that many of the Jews rejected him, for he failed to fulfill the nationalist vision of Israel as the leading nation that would bring peace, justice, and extraordinary prosperity to the world. But what his followers did discover about Jesus of Nazareth was that he proved to be more than just a Jewish king with the potential for great power and authority. He turned out to be the Son of God himself who has the right to rule over not only Israel, but the whole world—for the whole world was created for him.
>
> As the Son of God, he was crucified for our sins, was resurrected, and has returned to his Father in heaven where he does indeed sit on the throne of David. Because he is the Son of God, his messianic throne is located at the right hand of his Father in heaven instead of on this earth. Someday Christ will rule over his messianic kingdom from this throne in heaven by resurrecting all his followers, Jew and Gentile, into natural bodies so that they will experience an earthly paradise in fulfillment of Old Testament prophecies. Even Ezekiel speaks of a day when the departed Jewish saints will come back to life and live again in an Edenic paradise where God's people will marry, be fruitful and multiply, and experience an abundant harvest on a restored earth.

Jesus attempted to explain this to the first-century Jews when he quoted from one of King David's psalms: "The Lord [God the Father] said to my Lord [Christ], Sit at my right hand, *until I* [the Father] put your [Christ's] enemies under your feet" (Matt. 22:44). When God the Father says it is time for his Son to reign, the saints of Israel will form a nation that Christ will use as the chief nation to establish peace and justice throughout the entire world as the prophets predicted. Jerusalem will become a magnificent city as the nations of the world shower it with gifts of appreciation for the earthly paradise the Jewish Messiah will bring to the world.

Then, when Christ comes again at the end of the world, he will destroy this Genesis creation and take all his followers who have become his children to a new creation and paradise in his Father's heavenly kingdom where they will receive immortal bodies adapted for heaven. Those who accept Jesus Christ get to experience both the messianic kingdom on this earth (as so beautifully foretold by Isaiah and the prophets) as well as eternal life as God's children in a heavenly kingdom.

That is very good news about the kingdom of God—especially for a Jew.

What Will Jesus Do?

The study of the gospel as it relates to the kingdom of God is a serious matter, because if our eschatology is wrong, we are either omitting or confusing what the Scriptures have said Christ *will do* in the future. Therefore, it is imperative that we correctly understand the truth about what Jesus will do according to the Scriptures. Now that Christ came to this earth, was crucified for our sins, was resurrected, and ascended to the right hand of the Father, I propose that the biblical data supports the proposition that he will do the following to establish God's kingdom on earth and then in heaven:

- Christ will continue to build his church through the Holy Spirit by gathering those whom the Father has given to him.
- Christ (or God the Father) will someday remove Michael, the archangel who restrains Satan, and the Great Tribulation will begin.
- Christ will destroy the Antichrist and the false prophet at the battle of Armageddon, at the end of the Great Tribulation.
- Christ will bind Satan at the beginning of the millennium.
- Christ will sit on his throne in heaven and establish the promised restoration through a process of regeneration at a time set by the Father, and he will rule over this earth for one thousand years by reigning from heaven at the right hand of the Father.
- Christ will resurrect all deceased saints into natural bodies to live again and reign with him in the messianic kingdom.
- Christ will destroy Satan after his final release after the millennium by sending him to the lake of fire for eternity.

- Christ will come again as promised after his millennial reign on the last day.
- Christ will gather all believers, whether asleep or alive, and transform their bodies to be like his resurrected and glorified body—immortal and imperishable.
- Christ will then take all the transformed saints to the Father's house in heaven for eternity.
- Christ will then destroy the current heavens and earth with fire.
- Christ will sit on his throne and judge every human being at the Great White Throne judgment, sending unbelievers into the lake of fire and rewarding the glorified saints with the new heavens and new earth.
- Christ will consummate the marriage with the church, his bride, in the New Jerusalem.
- Christ will then say, "It is finished." He will have completed the work of redemption that the Father has given him and will turn his kingdom over to the Father and be subject to the Father.

Conclusion

There are two basic tenets of postrestorational eschatology that allow us to understand our glorious inheritance in the kingdom of God. One, the first resurrection described by John is a resurrection of the natural Adamic body in the manner of Lazarus. In this resurrection, the departed saints will inhabit restored human bodies in a regenerated, or renewed, Genesis creation. This is not only the vision of the Old Testament prophets, but also the understanding of many of the early church fathers, especially those with an oral tradition of those close to the apostle John. Two, Christ can easily establish his 1,000-year messianic kingdom from his throne in heaven when Satan is bound. He does not need to come back to this earth to reign as King of kings and Lord of lords.

As the New Testament teaches, Christ will come again after his 1,000-year messianic kingdom on the last day of this Genesis creation to rapture the saints and take us to our inheritance in heaven. The destiny of the raptured saints is the kingdom of heaven, not the earthly messianic kingdom. As the transformed children of God, we will be the eternal bride of Christ and the eternal children of God the Father.

Distinguishing and understanding the three forms of Christ sitting on his throne is the key to discerning how the future unfolds. After ascending to heaven, Christ currently sits at the Father's right hand *waiting* until the Father says it is time for his reign to begin. But Christ is not idle; he is gathering those into his kingdom that his Father has chosen.

When Satan is bound, Christ will sit on his throne in heaven and will regenerate the earth and then govern the world. This is the form of sitting that Christ describes in his response to his disciples when they wanted to know what their reward would be for sacrificially following of him:

Jesus said to them, "Truly, I say to you, in the new world [the regeneration], when the Son of Man will sit on his glorious throne [in heaven], you who have followed me will also sit on twelve thrones [on earth through the resurrection of their natural bodies], judging the twelve tribes of Israel. And everyone who has left houses or brothers or sisters or father or mother or children or lands, for my name's sake, will receive a hundredfold [during the restoration in this age] *and* [in addition] will inherit eternal life [in the heavenly kingdom in the age to come]." (Matt. 19:28–29)

The final form of Christ sitting will be when he comes again on Judgment Day to sit on his Great White Throne to judge the world:

When the Son of Man comes in his glory, and all the angels with him [the second coming], then he will sit on his glorious throne [Great White Throne]. Before him will be gathered all the nations [the general resurrection], and he will separate people one from another as a shepherd separates the sheep from the goats. . . . Then the King will say to those on his right, "Come, you who are blessed by my Father, inherit the kingdom prepared for you from the foundation of the world." . . . Then he will say to those on his left, "Depart from me, you cursed, into the eternal fire prepared for the devil and his angels [the lake of fire]." . . . And these will go away into eternal punishment [the second death], but the righteous into eternal life [in the Father's kingdom]. (Matt. 25:31–46)

Using the postrestorational framework, we recognize that the Lord's Prayer covers a great deal of the eschatological future including the Father's kingdom of heaven, the Son's kingdom on this earth, and even the Great Tribulation. Jesus taught:

Pray then like this:
    "Our Father in heaven, hallowed be your name [as children of God, we can call him Father, and, as a first priority, we worship him].
    Your kingdom come [the Father's heavenly kingdom in the eternal age to come], your will be done, on earth as it is in heaven [on the restored earth in the Son's millennial kingdom when he establishes his reign of righteousness].
    Give us this day our daily bread, and forgive us our debts, as we also have forgiven our debtors [how we should live today].
    And lead us not into temptation, but deliver us from evil [deliver us today, as well as possibly from the coming Great Tribulation]."
(Matt. 6:9–13)

Christ taught us to worship the Father, to model lives of love, and to understand and anticipate the major eschatological events, particularly God's kingdom on earth and in heaven. The Scriptures provide us with numerous representations of the future Tribulation, the Son's messianic kingdom on earth, and the Father's eternal kingdom of heaven. Believing in these prophecies requires faith in a God whom we can trust to keep his word about what he will do to establish his kingdom on earth and in heaven.

Theologian and author Donald E. Hartley paraphrased Hebrews 11:1–6:

> So what is faith? Faith is really the heart-felt confidence of coming to pass all that is rightfully hoped for, the deep seated certitude that untranspired but promised events will eventually take place. And without this type of faith, it is impossible to please God. Why? Because when approaching God, only this faith treats him as absolutely trustworthy to keep his promises and he must therefore be a rewarder to those who earnestly seek him.[1]

If we are to please God by having faith in him and his promises, then, as a first priority, we need to understand what he has promised he will do. Christians should not consider the subject of eschatology or the kingdom of God an elective. It is the study of the very gospel itself, for it gets to the heart of what God as the Father, Son, and Holy Spirit has done, is doing, and will do. It also answers the question of what the glorious inheritance of the saints is. The meek will inherit the earth for one thousand years during the Son's kingdom and then, on the last day, inherit the Father's kingdom of heaven when Christ comes again to take us to join him in his Father's kingdom.

As long as Satan is the ruler of this world, the children of God will experience hardship in this fallen Genesis creation. That is because "the world is under the control of the evil one" (1 John 5:19 NIV). This will be particularly true in the Great Tribulation when Satan is unrestrained. But after the Tribulation, when the Father says it is time, by faith we can know that Satan will be bound, and Christ will finally use his divine power to exercise his reign over this creation from his throne in heaven. Through a process of regeneration of our human bodies and the Genesis earth, we will then experience the 1,000-year restoration in this present age.

After Christ's millennial kingdom, by faith we can know that on the last day when he comes again, we will experience a process of transformation, which allows us to enter into the new heavens and new earth in his Father's eternal heavenly kingdom as children of God and the bride of Christ in the age to come. God is absolutely trustworthy to keep his promises; the events that he promised will occur will indeed take place in the future—on earth and in heaven.

---

[1] Donald E. Hartley, "Heb. 11:6 – A Reassessment of the Translation 'God Exists,'" *Trinity Journal* 27.2 (Fall 2006): 307.

APPENDIX

Being Prepared
for the Tribulation

If postrestorationalism is the correct interpretation of the Scriptures, then the next major eschatological event facing the church is the Great Tribulation. The church today, unfortunately, is woefully unprepared because many theologians believe that the Tribulation either already took place in AD 70 (most amillennialists) or that the church will escape the Tribulation through the rapture (most premillennialists).

Premillennialists believe in a future literal Tribulation, but the vast majority are pretribulationalists or midtribulationalists who think that the church will be raptured before the persecution phase of the Tribulation begins. A relatively small number of historic premillennialists are posttribulationalists who believe that the rapture of the church will take place after the Tribulation, and, thus, the church will have to endure this period of Satan's unrestrained reign of terror.

As a result, the church is currently in a precarious position because the majority of Christians are being shepherded into the future not expecting to experience the Tribulation. If the postrestorational view as presented in this book is correct, then the church is going to be caught completely off guard when the Tribulation comes upon it and will not be spiritually, mentally, or physically prepared. This is deeply disturbing.

How much time remains before the Tribulation, no one knows. But God has revealed specific circumstances and signs that foreshadow it, allowing us time to make serious preparations for the impending perilous time.

The Jews Grafted Back In

The first major event that will precipitate the Tribulation and then the restoration is a large number of Jews grafted back in as believers in Jesus of Nazareth as their Messiah. The apostle Paul was deeply distressed by the fact that the majority of his people rejected their Messiah. But Paul also taught that the hardness of their hearts was a temporary condition and that, someday, the Jews would be as responsive to the gospel message as the repenting pagan Gentiles were (Rom. 11:25–27). When the Jews become responsive to the gospel, it will mark the time when the full number of Gentiles that the Father knew would become believers is complete.

Like the wind, the Holy Spirit moves where he desires. But when the Holy Spirit moves in the hearts and minds of the Jews, it will be a monumental event that will be evident to the world. This will be an emotional and exciting period in church history. It will be one of the greatest, if not *the* greatest, revivals in history.

The temple must also exist before the Tribulation can begin because the Antichrist will enter it as the "abomination of desolation" claiming to be God. Therefore, after the temple is rebuilt in Israel in place of the current mosque, and a leader emerges that enacts a covenant of peace between Israel and her many enemies, then the church should know that the Tribulation is at hand. An observant church will recognize the unfolding of these events and should not be surprised by the following period of persecution. The church should be comforted, however, knowing that soon after this period of intense suffering and martyrdom, the joyful restoration will follow.

The books of Revelation and Daniel describe a complex political scene between nations leading up to and during the Tribulation. Many contemporary writers have attempted to interpret some of these end-time prophecies, such as asserting that the European Common Market is the ten-nation confederacy that John mentions in Revelation, which conspires to give power to the Antichrist. But the European Union, as it is now called, has grown from an initial six nations at its inception in 1957 to twenty-eight member nations as of the date this book was published.

It is virtually impossible to determine in advance how some of these prophecies dealing with political alliances and events are to be fulfilled. Yet God has provided the church with prophetic literature for a purpose. These predictions will help the generation that does go through the Tribulation recognize the unfolding of these events and the impending persecution.

Being Spiritually Prepared for the Tribulation

Because the early church experienced so much persecution, there are many New Testament teachings that can instruct us on how to cope with suffering during the Great Tribulation. For example, the following passage in Hebrews reveals how Christ endured the tribulation of the cross:

> Therefore, since we are surrounded by so great a cloud of witnesses, let us also lay aside every weight, and sin which clings so closely, and let us run with endurance the race that is set before us, looking to Jesus, the founder and perfecter of our faith, *who for the joy that was set before him endured the cross, despising the shame,* and is seated at the right hand of the throne of God. (12:1–2)

Christ endured the cross because he looked ahead to the joy that lay before him—redeeming the church, his bride, and receiving the kingdom in his Father's glory. The key to enduring persecution during the Tribulation will be to look beyond the suffering to the joyous restoration and then to heaven itself at the transformation. Revelation 20:4 assures those who are tortured and killed during this time that they will experience the first resurrection to live again during the glorious 1,000-year reign of Christ.

As the Tribulation unfolds and the pleasures of this world are taken away because we refuse to worship a false Christ and the human experience becomes a living nightmare on earth, we should look forward to the joy set before us—the joy of being resurrected so that we might experience the earthly paradise of the Son's kingdom. Best of all, after the restoration, we will experience the transformation and get to live eternally in heaven as children of God.

The Holy Spirit will undoubtedly play a crucial role in helping faithful believers look beyond their horrific circumstances. Enduring Satan's reign of terror will require supernatural power. Christians will need to be mature in their faith. This places an enormous burden upon pastors and teachers, for they must prepare their flocks mentally, emotionally, and spiritually for the greatest period of persecution the church will ever experience.

Being Physically Prepared for the Tribulation

The second way we should plan for the Tribulation is by making physical preparations. Christ said that when we see the Antichrist enter the temple, we should head for the hills (Matt. 24:15–21). So hide as best you can. The uninhabited wilderness areas of mountains have always been good places to hide. We are warned, however, that these times will be difficult and that few will actually succeed in remaining hidden. For three-and-one-half years, the Antichrist and the rest of the world will relentlessly search for the saints, using all the advanced technology available.

Christians will receive help from no one, other than fellow Christians who will also be in hiding. Everyone with the mark of the beast will be hunting for Christians, and without that mark Christians will be easy to identify. Christians will also need sufficient supplies to remain in absolute seclusion for three-and-one-half years. Being able to successfully hide and survive for that length of time will be extremely difficult. Yet Christ teaches that we should at least attempt to hide.

What should churches do to prepare for flight when it becomes obvious that the Great Tribulation is imminent? And how will unbelievers perceive these preparations? The situation will be similar to that which Noah faced. How can individual congregations plan ahead to secure hiding places in remote wilderness areas that will be able to sustain them for such a long time without appearing foolish to the rest of the world? Ultimately, like Noah, we will be ridiculed. While the rest of the world experiences euphoria over the peace covenant between Israel and her surrounding enemies, Christians will be desperately looking for places to hide.

Some Christians will form paramilitary forces to fight force with force. In my opinion, Christians should never prepare to go to war with the Antichrist; our resistance should always be nonviolent. These efforts will be futile anyway. Time would be better spent searching for and equipping remote hiding places.

At some point in the future, a generation of Christians will face the crescendo of signs and events that signal the Tribulation is near and will look like fools preparing for it. Nonetheless, it is vital that the church begin preparations, especially when the mosque on the temple mount is destroyed and construction of the new temple begins.

If the church does nothing and waits until the Antichrist enters into a covenant of peace with Israel, then only three-and-one-half years will remain to prepare a hiding place. Finding and equipping places in wilderness areas for a sizable congregation will require extensive logistical planning. Considerable time will be required to prepare—probably more than three-and-one-half years.

Form Organizations with Dual Purposes

To help mitigate some of the aspects of this preparation, I propose the formation of an organization that would serve the primary purpose of working out the logistics of locating suitable hiding places for large numbers of believers in secluded wilderness areas and also gathering supplies to ensure survival in those locations for the three-and-one-half-year period. At the same time, this organization could function as a wilderness survival organization, similar to Outward Bound and other groups that help people learn more about themselves, teamwork, and the world around them as they learn to survive in the wilderness. Thus, even if the Tribulation does not take place in their lifetimes, they will benefit from experiencing the natural beauty of wilderness areas.

Some of the inherent problems are obvious. One cannot simply visit remote areas of the world and ask unbelievers for the location of hidden caves, for these same unbelievers would be eager to disclose these hiding places as they become caught up in the great deception of the Tribulation. Another hurdle will be blazing trails to these hideout locations. Transporting supplies and large numbers of people would create an obvious trail. A central organization will be necessary to work out the complicated logistics involved in this mission.

In the Olivet Discourse, Christ was practical when he told believers to head for the mountains when the first-century temple was about to be destroyed. Because the early church heeded his advice, they were able to get out of Jerusalem before the Romans surrounded the city and cut off their food supply. Those Jewish believers who heeded Christ's advice by going to wilderness areas outside Jerusalem escaped the horrors that followed.

The horrors of the Great Tribulation will be much worse, for they will take place worldwide. And the chances of survival will be slim, even if a person does head to the mountains to hide. Modern surveillance technology, combined with a concerted effort by deluded unbelievers to rid the world of all Christians, will make it extremely difficult to remain successfully hidden.

Christ warns of these poor odds: "Pray that your flight may not be in winter or on a Sabbath. For then there will be great tribulation, such as has not been from the beginning of the world until now, no, and never will be. And if those days had not been cut short, no human being would be saved. But for the sake of the elect those days will be cut short" (Matt. 24:20–22). It seems that few, if any, Christians will succeed in escaping from the Antichrist. Despite these odds, Christ indicates that we should be physically prepared to escape and even admonishes us to pray in advance for our flight.

If the disciples faced Class V rapids as they navigated the hostile world of the first century, then those who endure the Great Tribulation will face Class VI rapids.

Class V – Extremely difficult. Long and violent rapids that follow each other almost without interruption. River filled with obstructions. Big drops and violent currents. Extremely steep gradient. Even reconnoitering may be difficult. Rescue preparations mandatory. Can be run only by top experts in specially equipped whitewater canoes, decked craft, and kayaks.

Class VI – Extraordinarily difficult. Paddlers face constant threat of death because of extreme danger. Navigable only when water levels and conditions are favorable. This violent whitewater should be left to paddlers of Olympic ability. Every safety precaution must be taken.[1]

---

[1] "Classification of Rapids, Water Level, and Canoeists," I. Herbert Gordon, Paddling.net, accessed November 1, 2013, http://www.paddling.net/guidelines/showArticle.html?67.

510 GOD'S KINGDOM ON EARTH AND IN HEAVEN

As Christians, we know that torture and death are not the end, for when we die, our spirits will be taken to heaven to be with Christ. And we will take part in the first resurrection and live in the joyful restoration with Christ ruling the world. For the few years of hardship and possible martyrdom we may have to endure, we will be richly rewarded with one thousand years of earthly paradise. And after the restoration, we receive our ultimate reward: our inheritance in the eternal kingdom of heaven.

Christ endured the cross because he set his heart and mind on the joy set before him. So must we endure the Tribulation by looking forward to God's kingdom on earth and in heaven.

SCRIPTURE INDEX

CPSIA information can be obtained at www.ICGtesting.com
Printed in the USA
BVOW08s1314081113

335812BV00001B/1/P